STUDIES IN EVANGELICAL HISTORY AND THOUGHT

The Dispensational-Covenantal Rift

The Fissuring of American Evangelical Theology from 1936 to 1944

STUDIES IN EVANGELICAL HISTORY AND THOUGHT

A complete listing of all titles in this series
will be found at the close of this book.

STUDIES IN EVANGELICAL HISTORY AND THOUGHT

The Dispensational-Covenantal Rift

The Fissuring of American Evangelical Theology from 1936 to 1944

R. Todd Mangum

Foreword by J. Lanier Burns

PUBLISHERS
Eugene, Oregon

Wipf and Stock Publishers
199 W 8th Ave, Suite 3
Eugene, OR 97401

The Dispensational-Covenantal Rift
The Fissuring of American Evangelical Theology from 1936 to 1944
By Mangum, R. Todd
Copyright©2007 Paternoster
ISBN 13: 978-1-55635-482-3
ISBN 10: 1-55635-482-7
Publication date 5/15/2007
Previously published by Paternoster, 2007

This Edition Published by Wipf and Stock Publishers
by arrangement with Paternoster

Paternoster
9 Holdom Avenue
Bletchley
Milton Keyes, MK1 1QR
Great Britain

STUDIES IN EVANGELICAL HISTORY AND THOUGHT

Series Preface

The Evangelical movement has been marked by its union of four emphases: on the Bible, on the cross of Christ, on conversion as the entry to the Christian life and on the responsibility of the believer to be active. The present series is designed to publish scholarly studies of any aspect of this movement in Britain or overseas. Its volumes include social analysis as well as exploration of Evangelical ideas. The books in the series consider aspects of the movement shaped by the Evangelical Revival of the eighteenth century, when the impetus to mission began to turn the popular Protestantism of the British Isles and North America into a global phenomenon. The series aims to reap some of the rich harvest of academic research about those who, over the centuries, have believed that they had a gospel to tell to the nations.

Series Editors

David Bebbington, Professor of History, University of Stirling, Stirling, Scotland, UK

John H.Y. Briggs, Senior Research Fellow in Ecclesiastical History and Director of the Centre for Baptist History and Heritage, Regent's Park College, Oxford, UK

Timothy Larsen, Professor of Theology, Wheaton College, Illinois, USA

Mark A. Noll, McAnaney Professor of History, University of Notre Dame, Notre Dame, Indiana, USA

Ian M. Randall, Senior Research Fellow, International Baptist Theological Seminary, Prague, Czech Republic

To my wife, Linda P. Mangum, whose understanding, supportiveness, and consistent encouragement enabled me not only to complete this project, but actually to enjoy working on it. Thank you, Linda, for making me miss home when I am not there, and for making me sometimes even wish I were not in my study when I am home.

I also dedicate this work to my three sons, Caleb, Seth, and Jesse. Caleb was four when I began this project; he is now a college student. Seth and Jesse have never known their father to not have this project to work on. For sacrifices they have made, knowingly and unknowingly, I owe them much. Whatever may be gained by this work, I will never be as proud of it as I am my three boys.

Contents

Foreword by J. Lanier Burns		xi
Preface		xiii
List of Abbreviations		xv

Chapter 1
Mapping Fault Lines in Twentieth-Century Evangelicalism — 1
1.1 The Need for this Study — 2
1.2 The Thesis and Approach of this Study — 19

Chapter 2
The Fracturing of the Fundamentalist Coalition — 25
2.1 Two "Fundamentalisms" Emerge from the Modernist-Fundamentalist Controversies — 26
2.2 The Rift Over Premillennialism in the Orthodox Presbyterian Church — 32
2.2.1 *After-shocks from the Modernist-Fundamentalist Earthquake: The Collision of Two Conservative Agendas* — 43
2.2.2 *Hairline Fractures in the Premillennialist Coalition* — 63

Chapter 3
A Seismogram of Late-1930s American Evangelicalism — 65
3.1 Conflicting Understandings of Orthodoxy — 65
3.2 Conflicting Understandings of Premillennialism and Dispensationalism — 72
3.3 The Significance of J. Oliver Buswell's Analysis of the Controversy over Dispensational Premillennialism — 82

Chapter 4
The Tremors Travel Southward (Part 1): The Context of the Controversy Over Dispensationalism in the PCUS — 95
4.1 Dispensationalism in the Crossfire of Southern Presbyterian "Conservatism" and "Liberalism" — 97
4.2 The Inquiry from the Presbytery of North Alabama — 117

Chapter 5
The Tremors Travel Southward (Part 2): The Investigation of Dispensationalism by the PCUS Ad Interim Committee on Changes in the Confession of Faith and Catechisms — 125
5.1 The Ad Interim Committee on Changes in the Confession of Faith and Catechisms — 125
5.2 The Committee's Initial Report on Dispensationalism and Its Consignment to a Reconstituted Committee — 128

5.3	The Unanimous Findings of the Committee's Final Report and Its Adoption by the General Assembly	156
5.4	Significant Implications of the PCUS Decision Against Dispensationalism	165

Chapter 6
A Concluding Analysis of the Controversies Over Dispensationalism and Covenant Theology in the 1930s-1940s — 175

6.1	The Points at Issue	175
6.2	Significant Misunderstandings and Mistakes	176
6.2.1	*By Dispensationalists*	176
6.2.2	*By Covenant Theologians*	197
6.3	Conclusion: Is It Safe Today to Build on the Old Fault Lines?	210

Appendix 1: The Data Regarding the Denominational Affiliation of Students at Dallas Theological Seminary (1924-1995) — 213

Appendix 2: The Data Regarding the Denominational Affiliation of Faculty at Dallas Theological Seminary (1924-1995) — 217

Appendix 3: Copy of Eugene W. McLaurin, *A Suggested Report of the Ad Interim Committee on Changes in the Confession of Faith and Catechisms with Regard to the "Question as to Whether the Type of Bible Interpretation Known as 'Dispensationalism' is in Harmony with the Confession of Faith"* **(Austin, TX: Austin Presbyterian Theological Seminary, 1942)** — 219

Appendix 4: Copy of the Original Report of the 1943 PCUS Ad Interim Committee on Changes in the Confession of Faith and Catechisms as to Whether the Type of Bible Interpretation Known as "Dispensationalism" is in Harmony with the Confession of Faith — 233

Appendix 5: Copy of the Original Report of the 1944 PCUS Ad Interim Committee on Changes in the Confession of Faith and Catechisms as to Whether the Type of Bible Interpretation Known as "Dispensationalism" is in Harmony with the Confession of Faith — 241

Appendix 6: The Members of the 1943 and 1944 Ad Interim Committees on Changes in the Confession of Faith and Catechisms — 246

Bibliography — 247
Index — 307

Foreword

I met Todd Mangum about fifteen years ago, when he was thinking about places to pursue doctoral study. I was Chairman of Dallas Seminary's Theology Department and its doctoral studies at the time. We had a mutual interest in the Covenantal and Dispensational theological debates during the past century, and our friendship blossomed in our discussions of people and issues in those debates. I discovered that many of the people who are cited in his footnotes were personal friends of mine. We met many times during his studies in Dallas to talk about the topic of this book. I can only say that I am privileged that Todd has asked me to write this introduction to his book. He has been a special friend for many years!

I come from a distinguished Presbyterian heritage (then "Southern-US" and now "USA") with many professors and ministers in my family. I have the dubious distinction of being the only minister who "departed from the faith," and I still bear scars from that separation. I attended a Presbyterian boarding school, McCallie School, and Davidson College, an institution which recently disclaimed its Presbyterian heritage. I was under the care of Knoxville Presbytery until my third year at seminary (1970). I graduated from Dallas Theological Seminary, finished doctoral degrees in the humanities, chaired its theology department for more than twenty years, and presently serve as a research professor. Thus, Todd and I have arrived at common "middle" ground from opposite ends of the theological spectrum, he from a "conservative" orientation and me from a "liberal" background.

As I read Todd's work, I am intrigued by his focus on "Northern" splits from Princeton and Westminster in the name of "orthodoxy," realizing that issues in the South were distinctive yet equally hostile. These emphases seem rather quaint now, but they loomed large in former days. His study involves a century in American history that is characterized by conflict, both in terms of cultural wars and theological divisions. I remember that my ministerial choice was like trying to identify with a bubble in a boiling pot of water. You could identify with one of the options, only to discover that it was full of heat, disclaimers, and change. We must remember when we read a work like this that the American "way" is controversy in an open society. Otherwise, we will be disoriented by "disagreements" about "disagreements" that major on minor issues like J. Oliver Buswell's "commonly-called Dispensationalism" that is not "his Dispensationalism" with its premillennial equivalents.

Todd's subject involves one aspect of theological division in the past century, specifically the break between Covenant and Dispensational theologies between 1936 through 1944. In his "Introduction," he alludes to the importance of this schism with an observation that these theologies were perceived to be the only Bible-believing options. Of course, they were not, but their battles drew large numbers of constituents into their wake. His correct argument is that the "lines" between these options were drawn in those decades. His stated objective in this book is to discover exactly how and why these lines of demarcation were formed. He analyzes "original issues" between dispensationalists and covenant theologians in the only controversy in their history that has even the appearance of an authoritative verdict on the points in question. Drawing on the work of Sandeen, as modified by Marsden, Mangum argues that the break-up of the so-called "dispensationalist-Princetonian alliance" should be viewed as the culmination of a latent, long-standing rift in Reformed constituencies that was not fully manifested until the late-1940s. His metaphor for the schism is that seismic tremors along an eschatological fault-line resulted in a significant division of the theological "plates." It was a sizeable wave in an otherwise turbulent sea. He describes the break as a "falling out" between family members that developed from Chafer's acceptance of "Dispensationalism" as a label (1936) to official Reformed judgments that Scofieldianism failed to meet theological standards according to the Westminster Confession of Faith.

Mangum's detailed analysis of crucial issues covers important players like Buswell and the PCUS Ad Interim Committee on Changes in the Confession of Faith and Catechisms. Many people who served on the Committee were personal acquaintances of mine. Frankly, I find their "official" findings to be rather strange in light of my conversations with them. I am delighted that Todd offers glimpses into the broader implications of the split; issues involving ownership of property (and related economic concerns), politics (as related to consensus and control of denominations), and sociology (as related to different priorities between the northern and southern churches). A "feel" for these kinds of issues is vital for understanding the differences between denominations in general and within Presbyterianism in particular. Other tensions surface as well. An important question that is rarely asked is "why did many scholars in Chafer's generation explore alternative positions, if the Scriptures were expounded and honored in churches?" Was there not a void that needed to be filled in churches and seminaries?

The author hopes that a clear understanding of definitive differences can result in an irenic climate that can heal the harshness of past divisions. Even in his dissertation, Todd's winsome personality brightens the dryness of academic research. I commend his work to you and wish his book well, since I have labored for the same goal for a generation. The printed page cannot capture the intensity or complexity of personal struggles and ruptured relationships. He acknowledges that a "lack of clarity" characterizes these conflicts, confusions both between the covenantalists and dispensationalists as well as within the respective positions. Though the fountain may still be "muddy," we trust that Todd Mangum's work will advance our ability to accurately perceive the extent of believers' mutual, unifying commitments.

J. Lanier Burns
Dallas, 2006

Preface

One does not complete a project like this one without accumulating a lot of debts, both literally and figuratively! A page or two of acknowledgments is hardly adequate for the multitude of kindnesses shown to me since I began work on this project over ten years ago, but I do want to express my gratitude here to at least a few of the people who have helped me greatly along the way.

First of all, I thank my dissertation readers, each of whom contributed significantly to the quality of this work. My initial interest in the topic was fostered by the fine dissertation written by John David Hannah, my adviser ("The Social and Intellectual History of the Origins of the Evangelical Theological College," Ph.D. diss., University of Texas at Dallas, 1988). His expertise proved helpful over the course of this project, and his suggestions consistently proved fruitful; he also helped sharpen my thesis considerably.

Stephen R. Spencer, my second reader, stepped in willingly during Dr. Hannah's sabbatical absence. Besides thoroughly reading and marking initial drafts, Dr. Spencer also repeatedly offered me moral support and encouragement, often just when I felt I was "at the end of my rope." He was willing to guide, direct, and correct, but always with a "soft touch." In Dr. Spencer, one finds a rare combination of impressive erudition, keen intellect, rigorous scholarship, a pastor's heart, and a brother's compassion.

Dr. Darryl Hart's credentials are well known; his books and articles have gained national recognition. I was pleased at his willingness to serve as my third reader. His insights both challenged and stimulated my thinking and I have appreciated his careful and penetrating reading and analysis of my work.

I owe many thanks to several librarians whose cooperation and help greatly assisted me in my research. Robert Ibach of Dallas Seminary deserves special mention. Without his competent direction of the Turpin and Mosher libraries, this project would not have been possible. I am also thankful for his willingness to mail and fax significant articles to me in Philadelphia. Joanna Hause of Biblical Seminary, where I am presently employed, was quite helpful in tracking down articles and books for me during the later stages of my research. Diana Ruby Sanderson, Special Collections Archivist at the Presbyterian Historical Society in Montreat, NC, was especially helpful during my research stay there. Jim Walker, library clerk at Montreat, willingly devoted himself to bringing up unaccessioned files from the Montreat stacks; his remarkable servant's spirit has left a lasting impression. I am grateful to Kenneth J. Ross, Reference Librarian at the Department of History of the Presbyterian Church (U.S.A.) in Philadelphia, for his willingness to personally direct me toward what turned out to be very profitable research tacks for turning up sources I needed for this project. I thank John Booth Trotti for giving me unmitigated access to the archives at Union Seminary, Richmond, where I was able to find numerous "gems."

I would like to express special thanks as well to those who were willing to sacrifice their time and "go on record" by allowing me to interview them: Allan A. MacRae, John F. Walvoord, S. Lewis Johnson, John Witmer, J. Dwight Pentecost, and Donald K. Campbell. Each of these men was generous not only with his time, but with the "inside knowledge" they were each willing to share. I learned a lot from every one of them about not only what happened, but also about how people felt and what motivated them to do what they did. I regret that Dr. MacRae did not live to see this project completed; likewise, since the completion of my dissertation, Drs. Walvoord, Johnson and Witmer have also gone to be with the Lord. In this regard, I also am saddened that David Edwards, director of records at Dallas Seminary, succumbed to a heart attack before the dissertation was completed. On two occasions, he dropped everything, amidst his numerous demanding tasks in the Academic Office, to help me compile the statistics used to make the charts concerning the denominational affiliations of Dallas Seminary students and faculty. The "human story" is what makes history so interesting – and history writing so much fun. I was given rare opportunities on this score, because of the generosity of all these persons.

I also wish to thank my teaching assistants, Mike Konscics and David Peters, for help they provided in proofreading, copying, and filing sources for this dissertation. Mr. Peters, in particular, had the misfortune of being my teaching assistant during the final year of writing. It was he that did much of the legwork in correcting bibliographic entries, and even switching the word processing format of the entire work from WordPerfect to Microsoft Word – those familiar with computer software complications can appreciate the yeoman's service he provided! I also thank research assistants Ann Snyder and Ken and Michelle Burcham for their help in compiling the index.

My colleague in Old Testament at Biblical Seminary, Frederic Clarke Putnam, edited early drafts, copiously, skillfully, and *gratis*. I am grateful for this practical expression of friendship. Glyn D. Mangum and Austin H. Potts, my father and father-in-law respectively, dutifully proofread several early drafts. I thank them both for this service of love. My father-in-law passed away from complications of a stroke last year; though he did not live to fulfill his wish of seeing this work published, I am sure that its being published now is bringing a smile to his face where he is, just the same.

To all my friends, family, co-workers and students who prayed for me, encouraged me, and supported me during the arduous process of writing this book, I thank you from the bottom of my heart.

List of Abbreviations

ADTS	Archives of Dallas Theological Seminary
AIC	Ad Interim Committee on Changes in the Confession of Faith and Catechisms of the Presbyterian Church, U.S.
AUTS	Archives of Union Theological Seminary (Richmond, VA)
BibSac	*Bibliotheca Sacra*
CBeac	*Christian Beacon*
CH	*Church History*
CSRev	*Christian Scholar's Review*
CT	*Christianity Today*
EvQ	*Evangelical Quarterly*
GA	General Assembly of the PCUS
GTJ	*Grace Theological Journal*
JETS	*Journal of the Evangelical Theological Society*
OPC	Orthodox Presbyterian Church (formerly [from 1937 to 1939] the Presbyterian Church of America – not to be confused with today's Presbyterian Church in America)
PCUS	Presbyterian Church in the United States (i.e., Southern Presbyterian Church)
PCUSA	Presbyterian Church in the United States of America (i.e., Northern Presbyterian Church)
PrGuard	*Presbyterian Guardian*
PrOut	*Presbyterian Outlook* (until April 1944, *The Presbyterian of the South*)
PrQ	*Presbyterian Quarterly*
PrSouth	*Presbyterian of the South* (became the *Presbyterian Outlook* in April 1944)
PrStand	*Presbyterian Standard*
PThRev	*Princeton Theological Review*
SPresJ	*Southern Presbyterian Journal*
SSTimes	*Sunday School Times*
TSF Bulletin	*Tyndale Student Fellowship Bulletin*
UnSemRev	*Union Seminary Review*
WTJ	*Westminster Theological Journal*

Chapter 1

Mapping Fault Lines in Twentieth-Century Evangelicalism

On a clear spring day in the mountains of the northwest region of the United States, most campers were just finishing breakfast. It looked like another good day for hiking. Birds were singing. The air was cool and crisp. The scenic beauty all around was just breathtaking. 8:30 AM, May 18, 1980.

Suddenly and without warning, the mountain just exploded! Rocks, trees and chunks of ice were blasted to speeds of over 650 miles per hour, triggering the largest landslide in recorded history. Molten lava and ash spewed over an area of 75 square miles. In a single catastrophic day, Mount Saint Helens went from 9th to 30th in the ranking of highest peaks in Washington State. 57 people lost their lives, as did thousands of elk and millions of trees. The landscape of Johnston Ridge, Hoffstadt Bluffs and Spirit Lake will never be the same. Such is what happens when seismic shifts burst forth onto the surface, releasing pressures that have built up for years along fault lines formed deep underground.

Sociology bears similarities to geology in this respect. Sociological "fault lines" likewise generate "seismic activity" that can reconfigure whole historical movements. Sometimes pressures building deep underground can erupt suddenly onto the surface after years of dormancy.

What is taken up in this book is a study of one such fault line. The sociological rift between dispensationalists and covenant theologians in the mid-1940s resulted from tensions that had been building for decades. As sometimes happens in seismology, the dispensational-covenantal rift seems actually to have resulted from sub-tremors of a larger quake: the modernist-fundamentalist controversies of the late-nineteenth – early-twentieth-century. Once fundamentalists had separated from the modernist "liberalism" of the main body of Protestantism, frictions and fractures began to become evident among themselves, as well. The rift between dispensationalism and covenant theology is among the most significant of these. The dispensational-covenantal eruptions of the 1930s-1940s changed the entire landscape of American evangelicalism; its effects are evident still today.

Potential implications of this study could be considerable. It provides a fresh opportunity for contemporary dispensationalists and covenant theologians to re-examine the causes of conflict between them and to clarify misunderstandings. In some quarters, implications from this study could even bring traditional hostilities to an end.

1.1 The Need for this Study

Today, more than ever before, evangelical Christians are trying to reckon responsibly with their past.[1] Some of this newfound interest is doubtless due to the rise of postmodernism, which has raised awareness of how much one's own "situatedness," historical context and tradition affect the acquisition of knowledge (in general)[2] and doctrinal convictions (in particular).[3] Perhaps evangelicals' well-known concern for doctrinal orthodoxy[4] provides added

---

[1] Regarding the significant increase of evangelical historians and in historical research on evangelicalism since 1982, see the introduction by D.G. Hart in *Reckoning with the Past: Historical Essays on American Evangelicalism from the Institute for the Study of American Evangelicals* (Grand Rapids: Baker, 1995), 13-20. This post-1982 increase is accounted for in no small part by the founding of the Institute for the Study of Evangelicals that same year. The evangelical contribution to current historiography has now become so pronounced as to draw the attention of the wider scholarly community; e.g., Maxie B. Burch, *The Evangelical Historians: The Historiography of George Marsden, Nathan Hatch, and Mark Noll* (New York: University Press of America, 1996).

[2] For a cogent summary of the issues among contemporary epistemologists and hermeneuticians, see Georgia Warnke, *Gadamer: Hermeneutics, Tradition, and Reason* (Stanford: Stanford University Press, 1987). For appropriations of certain post-modern epistemological insights into evangelical hermeneutics, see Anthony C. Thiselton, *The Two Horizons: New Testament Hermeneutics and Philosophical Description* (Grand Rapids: Eerdmans, 1980); Vern Sheridan Poythress, *Symphonic Theology: The Validity of Multiple Perspectives in Theology* (Grand Rapids: Zondervan, 1987); Brian J. Walsh and Richard Middleton, *Truth is Stranger Than it Used to Be: Biblical Faith in a Postmodern Age* (Downers Grove, IL: IVP, 1995); Stanley Hauerwas, Nancey Murphy and Mark Nation (eds.), *Theology Without Foundations: Religious Practice and the Future of Theological Truth* (Nashville: Abingdon, 1994); Robert E. Webber, *Ancient-Future Faith: Rethinking Evangelicalism for a Postmodern World* (Grand Rapids: Baker, 1999); and Stanley J. Grenz and John R. Franke, *Beyond Foundationalism: Shaping Theology in a Postmodern Context* (Louisville, KY: WJK, 2001).

[3] For an interesting discussion between a post-liberal theologian and an evangelical theologian concerning what is the significance of history and tradition and what is their proper role in the formulation of doctrine, see George A. Lindbeck, *The Nature of Doctrine: Religion and Theology in a Postliberal Age* (Philadelphia: Westminster, 1984) and Alister E. McGrath, *The Genesis of Doctrine* (Cambridge, MA: Basil Blackwell, 1990).

[4] In fact, many of the initial attempts to *define* historic, American "evangelicalism" focused on the adherence to certain doctrinal tenets; e.g., Kenneth S. Kantzer and Carl F. H. Henry (eds.), *Evangelical Affirmations* (Grand Rapids: Zondervan, 1990); John Jefferson Davis, *Foundations of Evangelical Theology* (Grand Rapids: Baker, 1984); Donald Bloesch, *Essentials of Evangelical Theology*, 2 vols. (San Francisco: Harper & Row, 1978). It has been difficult for

motivation to place socio-historical influences under special scrutiny.⁵ In any case, the enormity of these influences is undeniable. One seeking to understand the phenomenon of "evangelicalism" is confronted with a complex morass of historical, sociological, and theological factors, such that evangelicalism itself is today an "essentially contested concept."⁶ That is, evangelicalism's very definition and parameters are in dispute even among its adherents.⁷

Some of the consternation about what constitutes the "essence" of American evangelicalism stems from its chaotic beginnings. A child of fundamentalism, birthed in conflict with modernist unbelievers, raised amidst tensions with fellow

---

evangelicals to reach consensus on which particular doctrinal tenets should be considered non-negotiably crucial; a consensus is developing, however, around the idea that evangelicalism is a broad, diverse coalition of "generally conservative" believers. Today's more conspicuously militant defenders of distinctive doctrinal tenets typically are regarded as a sub-set of evangelicalism, called "fundamentalists," leading George Marsden to suggest wryly, "A fundamentalist is an evangelical who is angry about something," *Understanding Fundamentalism and Evangelicalism* (Grand Rapids: Eerdmans, 1991), 1.

⁵ E.g., see Donald A. Carson, *The Gagging of God: Christianity Confronts Pluralism* (Grand Rapids: Zondervan, 1996); Michael Horton (ed.), *Confessing Theology for Postmodern Times* (Wheaton, IL: Crossway, 2000); and David F. Wells, *No Place for Truth, or Whatever Happened to Evangelical Theology?* (Grand Rapids: Eerdmans, 1993). Cf. also David S. Dockery, ed., *The Challenge of Postmodernism: An Evangelical Engagement* (Grand Rapids: Baker, 1995); James Wm. McClendon, Jr., *Convictions: Defusing Religious Relativism* (Valley Forge: Trinity Press International, 1994); and T.F. Torrance, *Reality and Evangelical Theology: The Realism of Christian Revelation* (Downers Grove, IL: IVP, 1999).

⁶ William J. Abraham, *The Coming Great Revival* (San Francisco: Harper & Row, 1984), 71-79.

⁷ Cf. also Nancey Murphy, *Beyond Liberalism and Fundamentalism: How Modern and Postmodern Philosophy Set the Theological Agenda* (Valley Forge: Trinity Press International, 1996); Richard G. Hutcheson, Jr. and Peggy Shriver, *The Divided Church: Moving Liberals and Conservatives from Diatribe to Dialogue* (Downers Grove, IL: IVP, 1999); and Elmer M. Colyer (ed.), *Evangelical Theology in Transition: Theologians in Dialogue with Donald Bloesch* (Downers Grove, IL: IVP, 1999). That there is far more diversity in the evangelical movement than was perceived even thirty years ago is a point affirmed, virtually unanimously, by more recent analysts of evangelicalism. See David F. Wells and John D. Woodbridge (eds.), *The Evangelicals: What They Believe, Who They Are, Where They Are Changing* (Nashville: Abingdon, 1975); Robert E. Webber, *Evangelicals on the Canterbury Trail: Why Evangelicals are Attracted to the Liturgical Church* (Harrisburg, PA: Morehouse, 1985); Ronald H. Nash (ed.), *Evangelical Renewal in the Mainline Churches* (Westchester, IL: Crossway, 1987); Mark Ellingsen, *The Evangelical Movement: Growth, Impact, Controversy, Dialog* (Minneapolis: Augsburg, 1988); Donald Bloesch, *The Future of Evangelical Christianity: A Call for Unity Amid Diversity* (Colorado Springs, CO: Helmers & Howard, 1988); Donald W. Dayton and Robert K. Johnston (eds.), *The Variety of American Evangelicalism* (Downers Grove, IL: IVP, 1991); Garth M. Rosell (ed.), *The Evangelical Landscape: Essays on the American Evangelical Tradition* (Grand Rapids: Baker, 1996); Jon R. Stone, *On the Boundaries of American Evangelicalism: The Postwar Evangelical Coalition* (New York: St. Martin's Press, 1999); Roger Steer, *Guarding the Holy Fire: The Evangelicalism of John R. W. Stott, J. I. Packer, and Alister McGrath* (Grand Rapids: Baker, 1999); and Mark A. Noll and Ronald F. Thiemann (eds.), *Where Shall My Wond'ring Soul Begin?: The Landscape of Evangelical Piety and Thought* (Grand Rapids: Eerdmans 2000).

believers,[8] today's evangelical movement is in search of its identity and its place in the world.[9] This study has potential to assist this search.

Numerous ideological and sociological factors, notorious to evangelical historians, come to bear in the controversies of this study. Perspectival differences between North and South, conflicting views of subscriptionism and confessionalism, differing nuances of Reformed theology and Presbyterian polity, dispensational premillennialism's impact on the popular imagination, modernist-fundamentalist battles: all are contributing factors to the 1930s-1940s controversies analyzed by this study. In assessing this volatile period, we gain an excellent lens for discerning how significant features of the current evangelical landscape came about.

Just as the identity crisis within evangelicalism has persisted to the present day, so have many misunderstandings initiated by dispensational-covenantal disputes. Perhaps these two sources of confusion are related. Thus, we are wise to revisit the points at issue between dispensationalists and covenant theologians, especially as these points were first raised and given their definition.

Several previous studies have explored the roots of American fundamentalism, its relationship to dispensationalism, and its impact on later evangelicalism.[10] A few studies have examined individuals involved in the

---

[8] See Marsden, "From Fundamentalism to Evangelicalism: A Historical Analysis," in *The Evangelicals*, 122-42; and *idem*, "Fundamentalists, Evangelicals, and New Evangelicals," in *Reforming Fundamentalism: Fuller Seminary and the New Evangelicalism* (Grand Rapids: Eerdmans, 1987), 1-11.

[9] A friend once suggested to me that (neo-)evangelicalism is something of the adolescent son of fundamentalism: though a bit embarrassed by its parents, it shares remarkable family traits with them; cf. also Darrell Bock's remark that today's "evangelical movement is like a teenager coming of age in which [he] is now facing major decisions about adulthood," in "Scandal?: A Forum on the Evangelical Mind [with Mark Noll, Alister McGrath, Richard Mouw, and Darrell Bock]," *CT* 39 (14 August 1995): 2. See also John G. Stackhouse, "Perpetual Adolescence: The Emerging Culture of North American Evangelicalism," *Crux* 29 (September 1993): 32-37. Perhaps it would not be taking this imagery too far to suggest that, with the recent upsurge in evangelical scholarship (see Mark Noll, *Between Faith and Criticism: Evangelicals, Scholarship, and the Bible in America* [Grand Rapids: Baker, 1986], especially 122-220), this adolescent son has "gone off to college" and is now trying to make his way in the world.

[10] For historical treatises that explore the inter-relationship of the Bible and Prophecy Conference movements, dispensationalism, fundamentalism, and evangelicalism see Stewart G. Cole, *The History of Fundamentalism* (New York: Richard R. Smith, 1931); Norman F. Furniss, *The Fundamentalist Controversy: 1918-1931* (New Haven, CT: Yale University, 1954); Ernest R. Sandeen, *The Roots of Fundamentalism: British and American Millenarianism, 1800-1930* (Chicago: University of Chicago, 1970); and George M. Marsden, *Fundamentalism and American Culture: The Shaping of Twentieth-Century Evangelicalism: 1870-1925* (New York: Oxford University Press, 1980). Marsden has argued convincingly that fundamentalism has always consisted of a diverse coalition of co-belligerents against modernism and that Sandeen has overstated the significance of millennialism in the fundamentalist movement (see George Marsden, "Defining Fundamentalism," *CSRev* 1 [winter, 1971]: 141-51; and Ernest Sandeen, "Defining Fundamentalism: A Reply to Prof. Marsden," *CSRev* 1 (Spring, 1971): 227-32; cf. a

1930s-1940s controversies.[11] Two studies have investigated the establishment of Dallas Theological Seminary;[12] likewise, several studies have investigated the origin and early history of the OPC, Westminster Theological Seminary, the Bible Presbyterian Church, and the controversies surrounding the establishment of each of these.[13] However, this is the first study to take up a sociological and historical-theological analysis of the debate between dispensationalism and covenant theology as it unfolded from the late-1930s to the early-1940s. Likewise, this is the only study to give in-depth attention to the 1941-1944 investigation of dispensationalism by the Ad Interim Committee on Changes in

---

similar criticism of Sandeen by LeRoy Moore, Jr., "Another Look at Fundamentalism: A Response to Ernest R. Sandeen," *CH* 37 [June 1968]: 195-202). Nevertheless, all agree that dispensationalism consistently has been a prominent strand in the fundamentalist-evangelical fabric. See also Larry Dean Pettegrew, "The Historical and Theological Contributions of the Niagara Bible Conference to American Fundamentalism" (Th.D. diss., Dallas Theological Seminary, 1976); Robert Elwood Wenger, "Social Thought in American Fundamentalism, 1918-1933" (Ph.D. diss., University of Nebraska, Lincoln, 1974); William R. Glass, "The Development of Northern Patterns of Fundamentalism in the South, 1900-1950" (Ph.D. diss., Emory University, 1991). For historical treatises on dispensationalism and its eschatological themes, see Clarence Bass, *Backgrounds to Dispensationalism, Its Historical Genesis and Ecclesiastical Implications* (Grand Rapids: Eerdmans, 1960); C. Norman Kraus, *Dispensationalism in America; Its Rise and Development* (Richmond, VA: John Knox, 1958); Timothy Weber, *Living in the Shadow of the Second Coming: American Premillennialism, 1875-1925* (New York: Oxford University Press, 1979; Douglas W. Frank, *Less Than Conquerors: How Evangelicals Entered the Twentieth Century* (Grand Rapids: Eerdmans, 1986); and Paul Boyer, *When Time Shall Be No More: Prophecy Belief in Modern American Culture* (Cambridge, MA: Harvard University Press, 1992).

[11] Ned Stonehouse, *J. Gresham Machen: A Biographical Memoir* (Grand Rapids: Eerdmans, 1954); D.G. Hart, *Defending the Faith: J. Gresham Machen and the Crisis of Conservative Protestantism in Modern America* (Baltimore, MD: Johns Hopkins University Press, 1994); Iain H. Murray, *The Life of John Murray* (Edinburgh: Banner of Truth Trust, 1982); Joe R. Boles, "The Theology of Lewis Sperry Chafer in the Light of His Theological Method," (Th.D. diss., Southwestern Baptist Theological Seminary, 1963); Jeffrey Jon Richards, "The Eschatology of Lewis Sperry Chafer: His Contribution to a Systematization of Dispensational Premillennialism" (Ph.D. diss., Drew University, 1985).

[12] Rudolf A. Renfer, "A History of Dallas Theological Seminary" (Ph.D. diss., University of Texas at Austin, 1959); John David Hannah, "The Social and Intellectual History of the Origins of the Evangelical Theological College" (Ph.D. diss., University of Texas at Dallas, 1988).

[13] D.G. Hart and John Muether, *Fighting the Good Fight: A Brief History of the Orthodox Presbyterian Church* (Philadelphia: The Committee on Christian Education and the Committee for the Historian of the Orthodox Presbyterian Church, 1995); Bradley J. Longfield, *The Presbyterian Controversy: Fundamentalists, Modernists, & Moderates* (New York: Oxford University Press, 1991); Robert K. Churchill, *Lest We Forget: A Personal Reflection on the Formation of the Orthodox Presbyterian Church* (Philadelphia: Committee for the Historian of the Orthodox Presbyterian Church, 1986); Edwin H. Rian, *The Presbyterian Conflict* (Grand Rapids: Eerdmans, 1940); and George P. Hutchinson, *The History Behind the Reformed Presbyterian Church Evangelical Synod* (Cherry Hill, NJ: Mack, 1974).

the Confession of Faith and Catechisms of the Presbyterian Church, U.S.[14] The committee's investigation is perhaps even more significant in historical hindsight than it was at the time, given that its findings came to be treated by both sides of the debate as an official ruling of Reformed-Covenant theology against dispensationalism.

The *terminus a quo* for this study is 1936, the first time that dispensationalists actually accepted the label "dispensationalist" for themselves. It appears that "dispensationalists" accepted the label only reluctantly, and largely in response to articles written against them by Northern Presbyterians.[15] As this controversy moved southward eventually into Lewis Sperry Chafer's own Southern Presbyterian denomination, the debate was enjoined along specifically dispensational-covenantal lines, again, for the first time; one searches in vain for a juxtaposition of the terms "dispensationalism" and "covenant theology" as theological opposites of the other, before the late 1930s.[16]

In fact, before the 1930s, one can find numerous instances of evangelicals conjoining theological tenets that later evangelicals would consider mutually exclusive; or at least distinctive of competing theological systems. One striking

---

[14] Henceforth, referred to as AIC.

[15] Lewis Sperry Chafer, "Dispensationalism," *BibSac* 93 (October-December 1936): 390-449. Chafer wrote this article in response to articles written by Oswald T. Allis ("Modern Dispensationalism and the Doctrine of the Unity of the Scriptures," *EvQ* 8 [January 1936]: 22-35; "Modern Dispensationalism and the Law of God," *EvQ* 8 [April 1936]: 272-89) and John Murray ("The Reformed Faith and Modern Substitutes, Part VI: Modern Dispensationalism," *PrGuard* 2 [18 May 1936]: 77-79; "The Reformed Faith and Modern Substitutes, Part VII – Modern Dispensationalism: The 'Kingdom of Heaven' and the 'Kingdom of God,'" *PrGuard* 2 [17 August 1936]: 210-12). Allis and Murray wrote these articles against "dispensationalism," they said, out of concern that the newly formed OPC be set on a solidly Reformed doctrinal foundation, uncompromised by the defective doctrines too commonly found in the broader fundamentalist-evangelical movement.

[16] Philip Mauro seems to have been the first one to employ the derogatory term, "dispensationalism," in his book, *The Gospel of the Kingdom with an Examination of Modern Dispensationalism* (Boston, MA: Hamilton Brothers, 1928). Allis and Murray (see previous note) appear to have been following Mauro's lead in using this terminology. The phrase "covenant theology" has its etymological roots in the phrase "federalist theology" (cf. the Latin term, foedus, "covenant"), which usage goes back to the sixteenth century. I am not suggesting that this was the first time the terms were used, but, rather, that this was the first time the terms were used in juxtaposition. The term, "dispensationalism," like so many theological labels, appears to have been coined by its opponents. At first, "dispensationalists" objected to the phrase "modern dispensationalism" entirely, especially to the adjective, "modern"; see Rollin Thomas Chafer, "'Modern' Dispensationalism," *BibSac* 93 (January-March 1936): 129-30; cf. *idem*, "Dispensationally-Colored Premillennialism," *BibSac* 95 (April-June 1938): 257-58. That Lewis Chafer would come to refer to the position opposing him by the awkward label, "covenantism" ("Dispensational Distinctions Challenged," *BibSac* 100 [July-September 1943]: 338), may indicate that this is the first time the positions are consciously polarizing. Both terms seem clearly designed to label in an unflattering manner, as often takes place when ideological lines of demarcation are first being defined.

example of such a combination is the work of Southern Baptist James Robinson Graves. His defense of premillennialist eschatology appeared in an 1883 book, entitled, *The Work of Christ in the Covenant of Redemption Consummated in Seven Dispensations*. It is exactly as it sounds: a seamless combination of the covenantal system (with its covenant of redemption, covenant of works, and covenant of grace[17]) and dispensational premillennialism (with its seven distinct dispensations[18] and its exhortation to employ consistently "literal interpretation"[19]).

Of course, Graves, the father of "Landmarkism," is known for his having generated a fair share of ideological eccentricities. Nonetheless, he should not simply be dismissed. He is generally acknowledged as the one who "helped introduce dispensational premillennialism into Southern Baptist life."[20] It is noteworthy that such a popularizer of early dispensationalism was also a covenant theologian[21] (and a "5-point Calvinist"[22]). It is also of interest that

---

[17] James Robinson Graves, *The Work of Christ in the Covenant of Redemption Consummated in Seven Dispensations* (Memphis, TN: Baptist Book House, 1883), 63-65, 66-78, 79-94; cf. *The Westminster Confession of Faith*, chapter 7: *Of God's Covenant with Man* (which affirms the covenant of works and the covenant of grace) and Chapter 8: *Of Christ the Mediator* (which, implicitly, affirms the covenant of redemption; see especially article 6), in *The Westminster Standards: The Westminster Confession of Faith, The Larger Catechism, The Shorter Catechism*, 1647-48, reprint (Philadelphia: Great Commission Publications, n.d.), 10-12.

[18] Graves' last dispensation is eternity future (the "consummation"); otherwise, his dispensational scheme is very similar to C.I. Scofield's. Graves' dispensations are: Adamic, Antediluvian, Patriarchal, Legal-Jewish, Gospel-Gentile, millennium, and the consummation; Scofield's dispensations are: innocence, conscience, government, promise, law, grace, and kingdom (*The Scofield Reference Bible: 1917 Edition*, [New York: Oxford University Press, 1917], 5, n. 5. Cf. also Charles Ryrie's comparison of dispensational schemes in *Dispensationalism Today* (Chicago, IL: Moody Press, 1965), 84; and the more recent comparison of dispensationalist schemes in David J. MacLeod, "Walter Scott, A Link in Dispensationalism Between Darby and Scofield?" *BibSac* 153 (April-June 1996): 175-78.

[19] Graves, "Appendix A: Principles of Interpretation," in *Covenant of Redemption*, 556; cf. Ryrie, *Dispensationalism Today*, 21: "If plain or normal interpretation is the only valid hermeneutical principle, and if it is consistently applied, it will cause one to be a dispensationalist. As basic as one believes normal interpretation to be, to that extent he will of necessity become a dispensationalist." Ryrie makes this point at least five other times (see pp. 45, 86-98, 158, 187-89).

[20] H. L. McBeth, *Dictionary of Baptists in America*, ed. Bill J. Leonard (Downers Grove, IL: IVP, 1994), s.v. "Landmark Baptists," 167. See also Danny E. Howe, "An Analysis of Dispensationalism and its Implications for the Theologies of James Robinson Graves, John Franklyn Norris, and Wallie Amos Criswell" (Ph.D. diss., Southwestern Baptist Theological Seminary, 1988). Cf. also David Dockery's summation: "J.R. Graves was the first premillennialist I know of in Southern Baptist life. . . . Dr. Graves was the first dispensationalist for sure in Southern Baptist life" ("Forum: Eschatology," *SBC Life* 2 (June/July 1994): 6.

[21] Graves' covenant theology even passes Stephen R. Spencer's criteria for deciding whether a theological system is genuinely covenant theology ("Reformed Theology, Covenant Theology, and Dispensationalism," in *Integrity of Heart, Skillfulness of Hands: Biblical and Leadership Studies in Honor of Donald K. Campbell*, ed. Charles H. Dyer and Roy B. Zuck [Grand Rapids:

Southern Baptists, to this day, have not so segregated dispensationalism and covenant theology as their Presbyterian and Independent Bible brethren have.[23]

Furthermore, Graves is not completely alone at the time in his willingness to embrace what many, later on, would consider strange combinations. Consider the following: James Hall Brookes (whom C.I. Scofield called his "first and best teacher in the oracles of God"[24]) merged Southern Presbyterian ecclesiology, including James Henley Thornwell's "spiritual nature of the Church,"[25] with

---

Baker, 1994], 245). I.e., unlike most Baptists, Graves not only affirms all three theological covenants – redemption, works, and grace – but he also is willing to apply the covenant of grace to believers (like Abraham) and their (spiritual) seed (see Graves, *Covenant of Redemption*, 76). With only slight differences in nuance, Graves' position is virtually identical to that of covenantalist stalwart, Louis Berkhof (*Systematic Theology* [Grand Rapids: Eerdmans, 1939], 273). Berkhof even clarifies that such variations of nuance are variations *within* Reformed/Covenant/Federalist theology.

[22] Graves, *Covenant of Redemption*, 95-108.

[23] See the interesting discussion of this point by Paige Patterson, David Dockery, and Millard Erickson in "Forum: Eschatology," 6-10. A recent example of a Southern Baptist eclectically fusing aspects of covenantal and dispensational thought is Russell Moore, *The Kingdom of Christ: The New Evangelical Perspective* (Wheaton, IL: Crossway, 2004).

Though it was within the Presbyterian churches that dispensationalism surfaced most notably as a point of controversy, the fundamentalist-modernist controversies were often most pronounced, especially in the South, in Baptist churches (which denominations in the U.S. are also larger). Consequently, historians have often used Baptist expressions of the fundamentalist-modernist controversies as their prototypes to define and characterize the ideologies that clashed therein. For observations and examples of this point, see Glass, "The Development of Northern Patterns of Fundamentalism in the South," 281-346; Edward L. Queen, II, *In the South the Baptists are the Center of Gravity: Southern Baptists and Social Change, 1930-1980* (Brooklyn, NY: Carlson Publishing), 55-74; Furniss, *The Fundamentalist Controversy*, 103-26; and even the unabashedly partisan fundamentalist work by George W. Dollar, *A History of Fundamentalism in America* (Greenville, SC: Bob Jones University Press, 1973), 7-172.

[24] C.I. Scofield, "In Memoriam. James Brookes," *Truth* 23 (June 1897): 312. Scofield met Brookes as an original organizer and early President of the Niagara Bible Conference, and may, in fact, have gotten the distinction between Israel (as an "earthly people") and the Church (as a "spiritual, heavenly people") from him; cf. James Brookes, *Israel and the Church*, reprint (Chicago: The Bible Institute Colportage Ass'n, 1900), 12; and C.I. Scofield, *Scofield Reference Bible: 1917 Edition*, 1204, n. 2. Chafer adopted Scofield's distinction between Israel and the Church, and greatly elaborated it: see Chafer, *Grace* (Wheaton, IL: Van Kampen Press, 1922), 238-39; and "Dispensationalism," 406, 448. In expanding the distinction between Israel and the Church, Chafer's dispensationalism seems more Darbyite than Brookesian (see below, and Floyd Elmore, "A Critical Examination of the Doctrine of the Two Peoples of God in John Nelson Darby," [Th.D. diss., Dallas Theological Seminary, 1990]).

[25] Carl Sanders defends Brookes' inclusion as a faithful Presbyterian by demonstrating that Brookes was not deserting Southern Presbyterianism in his development of the Israel/Church distinction. Rather, he was merely trying to elaborate the "spiritual nature of the Church," a tenet originally set forth by Robert Dabney and, especially, James Henley Thornwell. It is only in historical hindsight that we find Brookes' Israel/Church, earthly people/heavenly people distinction being articulated by Scofieldian-Chaferian dispensationalists in a way that clashed

certain features of Darbyite-Plymouth Brethrenism and American premillennialism.[26] W.H. Griffith Thomas, an Oxford scholar who helped found Dallas Theological Seminary,[27] combined Darbyite dispensationalism[28] and a "victorious life" (Keswickian) view of sanctification[29] with an otherwise Reformed soteriology[30] and with a sacramentalist (Anglican) view of the Lord's Supper.[31] Clarence Larkin, best known perhaps for his dispensational charts, articulated a position very close to traditional Reformed theology in his handling of the

---

with Southern Presbyterian doctrine; see Carl E. Sanders II, especially chapter 4, "If this be Presbyterianism . . . ," in "The Premillennial Faith of James Brookes" (Ph.D. diss., Dallas Theological Seminary, 1995), 97-152. Sanders trenchantly and meticulously defends his thesis over against the charge set forth by Joseph H. Hall ("James Hall Brookes – New School, Old School, or No School," *Presbyterion: Covenant Seminary Review* 14 [January 1988]: 35-54), who would deny Brookes any legitimate claim to Presbyterianism.

[26] Cf. Larry V. Crutchfield, *The Origins of Dispensationalism: The Darby Factor* (Lanham, MD: University Press of America, 1995), see especially 13-14; and Sanders, "James Brookes." Sanders gives the best nuanced summary overall: "As for the Brethren movement in general, there is some evidence of contact with Brookes, but the evidence for influence, especially early on, is far less extensive than the weight often given to it. When the role of American premillennialism [as opposed to British Plymouth Brethrenism] is considered, especially as dispensational ideas began to affect it, questions about the extent of the Brethren influence on Brookes and how direct it was remain significant obstacles to assigning it a significant role. The theory that Brookes was the conduit for bringing Brethren ideas to America . . . seems untenable. The origins of Brookes' premillennialism and the influences on it are much broader than this simplistic analysis. The web of relationships and influences affecting his thought is both murky and complex" (54).

[27] See Hannah, "History of the Evangelical Theological College," 154-70; and Renfer, "A History of Dallas Theological Seminary," 63-82.

[28] Thomas' adoption of Darbyite theology was more overt than Brookes' or Graves'; see Richard A. Lum, "W.H. Griffith Thomas and Emergent American Fundamentalism" (Ph.D. diss., Dallas Theological Seminary, 1994), 137-38.

[29] It was Griffith Thomas, in fact, who responded to B.B. Warfield's critique of Lewis Chafer on this point; cf. B.B. Warfield, "Systematical Theology: [Review of] *He That is Spiritual* by Lewis Sperry Chafer," *PThRev* 17 (April 1919): 322; and W.H. Griffith Thomas, "The Victorious Life. Parts I, II." *BibSac* 76 (July-September and October-December 1919): 267-88; 455-67. For a more recent, and superbly nuanced comparison of Chafer's and Warfield's views, see Randall Gleason, "B.B. Warfield and Lewis S. Chafer on Sanctification," *JETS* 40 (June 1997): 241-56. A helpful summary is also provided by Thomas H. Cragoe, "W.H. Griffith Thomas," in *Handbook of Evangelical Theologians*, ed. Walter A. Elwell (Grand Rapids: Baker, 1993), 67-81 (regarding Griffith Thomas' Keswickian view of sanctification, see 80-81).

[30] For a helpful discussion of Thomas' Reformed soteriology, see Lum's section entitled, "Evangelical and Reformed Theologian," in "W.H. Griffith Thomas," 120-31. Lum argues convincingly that Thomas was no less committed to Reformed theology (in its Anglican form) than Warfield.

[31] This "sacrament" is like the Passover, he suggests, in that it, too, represents "a covenant or federal rite between God and man. The Eucharist was associated with the New Covenant" (W.H. Griffith Thomas, "Of the Lord's Supper," in *The Principles of Theology: An Introduction to the Thirty-Nine Articles* [London: Longmans, Green and Co., 1930], 391). See also, Cragoe, "W.H. Griffith Thomas," 81.

Mosaic Law and its relationship to the New Testament believer.[32] When we look beyond these prominent figures (Graves, Griffith Thomas, Brookes, Larkin) to lesser-known figures, we find even more startling combinations.[33]

Simply put, before the 1930s, it is hard to find any clear line of demarcation between dispensationalism and covenant theology. More to the point, no one seemed even to be attempting to draw such. This study seeks to discover exactly how and why these lines of demarcation were formed.

While some of the individual issues of the 1930s-1940s disputes had been raised previously,[34] the controversies from 1936 to 1944 are distinctive for the *way* in which they are disputed. In the 1936-1944 controversies, the issues are no longer argued in *à la carte* fashion. For the first time, individual points of controversy coalesce into what both sides argue are irreconcilable *systemic* differences between them. A brief survey of the writings of this period bears out this point.

In his initial response to Allis and Murray in 1936, Chafer seems taken aback by the accusation that his theological positions were in conflict with the "covenant theology" of the Westminster Confession.[35] Though he chides Allis and Murray for using a man-made confession, rather than Scripture alone, as a theological authority, Chafer seems clearly reticent to oppose directly a creedal statement to which he himself, as an ordained Presbyterian clergyman, had professed subscription. He insists that he is being faithful to his ordination vows

---

[32] Clarence Larkin, *Rightly Dividing the Word of Truth* (Philadelphia: Fox Chase, 1921), 293; cf. the *Westminster Larger Catechism*, Qs. 115-21.

[33] One particularly striking example is that of Henry Dana Ward, an Episcopalian cleric in Philadelphia who was commonly thought to have been influenced by Millerite (i.e., Seventh Day Adventist) ideas. Writing under the pseudonym, Senior Harvard, his mid-nineteenth-century work separates sharply the "earthly people" from the "heavenly people," and the "earthly kingdom" from the "heavenly kingdom"; *The Gospel of the Kingdom; A Kingdom Not of this World: Not in this World; but to Come in the Heavenly Country, of the Resurrection from the Dead, and of the Restitution of All Things* (Philadelphia: Claxton, Remsen & Haffelfinger, 1870). Despite the unusual backdrop for his work and Ward's own theological eccentricities notwithstanding, he ends up with a dispensational scheme that looks a great deal like the Scofieldian system that would come some forty years later!

[34] E.g., Willis W. Mead, *The Modern Outcry Against the Law* (London: Samuel E. Roberts, 1914); Mauro, *The Gospel of the Kingdom* (1928); and Albertus Pieters, *A Candid Examination of the Scofield Bible* (Swengel, PA: Bible Truth Depot, 1938).

[35] Again, Allis and Murray were not the first ones to make this accusation, but their articles were the first to do so in a published forum. In his survey of the growing Presbyterian opposition to the dispensational theology of early Dallas Theological Seminary, Hannah traces the earliest objection to dispensationalism on Confessional grounds to E.C. Gould, a Southern Presbyterian cleric and former missionary. Presaging the 1940s' controversy remarkably, Gould wrote a series of letters to Chafer in 1916 in response to Chafer's recently published book, *The Kingdom in History and Prophecy*. "Gould's response to Chafer was that the rigid distinctions made by dispensationalists were unwarranted, that Chafer explicitly taught two means of salvation (e.g., that the Old Testament was in conflict with the Epistles), and that dispensationalism was in conflict with the Church's standards" (Hannah, "Social and Intellectual History of the Evangelical Theological College," 349).

in accepting the Bible as "the *only* infallible rule of faith and practice," that he is in "general agreement" with the Westminster Confession (all that the Confession demands, he declares), and that the dispensationalist tenets Allis and Murray find unacceptable by creedal standards are simply "outside the range of those creeds."[36]

In 1936, Chafer is willing to affirm the potential legitimacy of the covenant of grace/covenant of works/covenant of redemption rubric,[37] though he remains adamant that the Mosaic period should not be considered as within the covenant of grace.[38] Chafer consistently insisted that a sharp contrast had to be maintained between the Old Testament and New Testament;[39] his view on this would also be a constant point of controversy.

This sore point in the discussion with Allis and Murray would fester into an open wound by the time Chafer's views were investigated by the AIC in the early 1940s. Chafer's apparent advocacy of two ways of salvation, one in the Old Testament, another in the New Testament,[40] would repeatedly come under critique by Reformed theologians, who insisted that such a "dispensationalist" construction violated the one "covenant of grace."

By 1943, Chafer's views do not seem to have changed much, but, by then, his tone toward covenant theology had become considerably more antagonistic. Chafer no longer toys with the possibility that, if nuanced in a certain direction, covenantalist phrases and concepts might be acceptable. Rather, after describing "Covenantism" (his terminology) as "that form of theological speculation which attempts to unify God's entire program from Genesis to Revelation under one supposed Covenant of Grace," he dismisses its formulation as completely untenable. "That no such covenant is either named or exhibited in the Bible and that the covenants which are set forth in the Bible are so varied and diverse that

---

[36] Chafer, "Dispensationalism," 396, n. 1.

[37] Specifically, Chafer says that such a structure is "conceivable" ("Dispensationalism," 439). Both John F. Walvoord and Donald K. Campbell independently related to this writer that they had heard Chafer say either in class or in personal conversation that he had held to the covenantal theory at one time but, as a result of the 1930s-1940s controversies, came to believe it was in error; John F. Walvoord, interview by author, Dallas, Texas, 11 April 1995; and Donald K. Campbell, interview by author, Dallas, Texas, 2 May 1995. In several of Chafer's early writings, he speaks of New Testament salvation in terms of the believer entering into "God's unconditional covenant made in His (Christ's) blood"; e.g., Lewis Sperry Chafer, *True Evangelism* (Grand Rapids: Kregel Publications, 1911); *idem, Salvation* (Dallas, TX: Lewis Sperry Chafer, 1917), 91-92; *idem, Grace*, 76-79. Craig Blaising also observes, "When Chafer published his *Systematic Theology* in 1947-48, he included several harsh comments reflecting the controversies of the preceding years. Critical comments were made about the covenant of grace, although in the first volume he affirmed a traditional three-covenant structure [cf. Chafer, *Systematic Theology*, 1:42; 4:156]" ("Lewis Sperry Chafer," in *Handbook of Evangelical Theologians*, 95).

[38] Chafer, "Dispensationalism," 438-39.

[39] Ibid., 441-42.

[40] E.g., ibid., 439.

they preclude a one-covenant idea, evidently does not deter many sincere men from adherence to the one-covenant theory."[41]

One senses a growing partisanship also in the details of Chafer's comparison between "covenantism" and "dispensationalism." Biblical teaching supports "dispensationalism," he says, in that "dispensations are an integral feature of the Bible."[42] "Covenantism," on the other hand, represents a distortive "idealism"; the covenant of grace in particular, he says, must be "superimposed on the Sacred Text."[43]

What has caused such a change in posture from 1936 to 1943? Chafer himself discloses the reason in his introductory remarks: the AIC investigation of his views (i.e., "dispensationalism") has prohibited a more amicable framing of issues and has brought premillennialists and non-premillennialists to a lamentable crossroads in their relationship. "Up to the present time, premillennialists have been content to go on in fellowship with sound men who may have disagreed with them as to interpretation."[44]

Remarkably, these are almost the exact words used, just three years earlier, by covenant amillennialist James Bear, in his assessment of the situation. In his view, too, premillennialists and non-premillennialists had lamentably come to a crossroads. Only, in his view, it was the premillennialists who were to blame.

> It has been said in the past that if Christians could agree on other fundamental doctrines, they could agree to disagree on eschatology, and could still work together in harmony. However since the rise of Dispensationalism and Russellism and Adventism such harmonious cooperation does not seem possible, for those who hold these views have their whole Biblical and religious viewpoint colored by their view of eschatology and they are intolerant towards all those who do not agree with them.[45]

For both dispensationalists and covenant theologians, it seems that the circumstances leading up to and culminating in the AIC investigation represented their parting of ways. Significantly, Bear was on the committee that put dispensationalism under investigation; and Chafer's writings were a primary source used by the AIC to determine what represented dispensationalist teaching.

The year 1944, in which the AIC submitted its unanimous report to the GA. declaring "dispensationalism" out of harmony with the Westminster Confession of Faith, thus serves appropriately as the *terminus ad quem* for this study. Not

---

[41] Chafer, "Dispensational Distinctions Challenged," 338.
[42] Ibid.
[43] Ibid.
[44] Ibid., 337.
[45] James Bear, "Shall We Revise the Standards?" *PrSouth* 115 (12 June 1940): 3. The following year, as the AIC was undergoing its investigation of the compatibility of dispensationalism with the Westminster Standards, Bear wrote a seven-part series of articles entitled, "The Presbyterian Standards vs. The Scofield Bible," *PrSouth* 116 (19 March - 30 April 1941).

only did the 1944 AIC report represent back then the culmination of hostilities that had been building for decades, it remains to this day as close to an official denunciation of dispensationalism by a Reformed-Covenantalist body as has ever been produced.

It is appropriate at this point for us to clarify the nature of the AIC and its significance, both theological and ecclesiastical. The AIC was an advisory committee to the PCUS General Assembly,[46] not an arm of ecclesio-political power *per se*. The committee could take no official action, nor could it render any official sanction or censure; these could be carried out only by the full GA, or, more likely in the Southern Presbyterian Church, by individual presbyteries working under guidelines provided by the GA.[47]

However, as Chafer observed, the AIC investigation was "of more moment than its own import would indicate."[48] The AIC was significant not so much for what it officially *mandated*, as for what ideological, ecclesiastical, and socio-political dynamics it *manifested* (or even *aroused*). Even before the AIC reached its unanimous decision, Chafer realized that whatever verdict it rendered could carry great weight, not just in the PCUS, but in other denominations, as well. As Chafer suspected, the AIC decision could impact disagreements between dispensationalists and covenant theologians wherever they might be found.[49]

Furthermore, though the AIC was merely an advisory committee, its findings against dispensationalism were publicized as an official judgment of officers of the church, both in church papers and in a separate pamphlet published and distributed by the Executive Committee of Religious Education and Publication of the PCUS. Though technically not a *de jure* mandate for its constituents, the decision of the AIC was nevertheless treated as such *de facto*. Ernest Trice Thompson's summarization is well-nuanced.

> The Assembly did not recommend that any steps be taken against the teaching of dispensationalism, but some sessions, armed with the Assembly's statement, barred such teaching from their church schools, and one presbytery, at least, indicated that it would receive no more graduates from the Evangelical Theological College of Dallas [i.e., Dallas Theological Seminary] into its membership.

---

[46] Henceforth, referred to as GA.

[47] As might be expected, the Southern Presbyterian Church, a defender of "States' rights," was more reluctant than her Northern counterpart to issue mandates to her presbyteries from one central ecclesiastical authority. The Southern Church preferred to carry out its policies through individual presbytery initiatives. See *The Distinctive Principles of the Presbyterian Church in the United States, commonly called the Southern Presbyterian Church* (Richmond, VA: Presbyterian Committee of Publication, 1871); *The Book of Church Order of the Presbyterian Church in the United States* (Richmond, VA: Presbyterian Committee of Publication, 1938), especially "Form of Government," 1-94, and "The Rules of Discipline," 97-151.

[48] Chafer, "Dispensational Distinctions Challenged," 337.

[49] Ibid., 337-38.

> Within a few years dispensationalism had ceased to be a disturbing factor in the church.[50]

For our study, the AIC report also provides valuable insight into how the theological issues between dispensationalists and covenant theologians were framed and understood at this crucial moment in their debate. Its credibility is further confirmed when we see that its criticisms of dispensationalism have been maintained by covenant theologians ever since.[51]

The dispensationalists scrutinized by the AIC report, especially C.I. Scofield and Lewis Sperry Chafer, are still today well-recognized as patriarchs of dispensational theology. Though Chafer claimed to the end that his views were misconstrued and that the AIC report was a libelous attack[52] (a charge we will investigate later on), the AIC motivation does not seem to have been personal. Rather, the AIC focused attention on Chafer's views because it recognized him as a viable representative of the dispensationalist position.[53] While it will be important for us to determine whether or not the AIC succeeded in discerning Chafer's views correctly, the AIC's choice of Chafer as a dispensational prototype (alongside Scofield) does seem sound.

The covenant theologians who served on the AIC may be less familiar than Scofield or Chafer to us today, but we should not fail to recognize their prominence at the time. To a man, the nine members who served on the AIC were truly august figures in the Southern Presbyterian Church: four were past or future Moderators of the General Assembly of the PCUS;[54] three were past or future moderators of state synods;[55] two were sitting presidents of PCUS

---

[50] Ernest Trice Thompson, *Presbyterians in the South, Volume Three: 1890-1972* (Richmond, VA: John Knox, 1973), 488.

[51] Cf., for example, William E. Cox, *An Examination of Dispensationalism* (Phillipsburg, NJ: P & R, 1963); Jon Zens, *Dispensationalism: A Reformed Inquiry into its Leading Figures & Features* (Phillipsburg, NJ: P & R, 1980); Curtis I. Crenshaw and Grover Gunn, *Dispensationalism Today, Yesterday, and Tomorrow* (Memphis, TN: Footstool Publications, 1985); Vern Sheridan Poythress, *Understanding Dispensationalists* (Grand Rapids: Zondervan, 1987); John H. Gerstner, *Wrongly Dividing the Word of Truth: A Critique of Dispensationalism* (Brentwood, TN: Wolgemuth & Hyatt, 1991); Keith A. Mathison, *Dispensationalism: Rightly Dividing the People of God?* (Phillipsburg, NJ: P & R, 1995); and Michael D. Williams, *This World is Not My Home: The origins and development of dispensationalism* (Geanies House, Fearn, Ross-shire, Scotland: Mentor Press, 2003).

[52] Lewis Sperry Chafer, "Inventing Heretics Through Misunderstanding," *BibSac* 102 (January-March 1945): 1-5.

[53] This point will be taken up in chapter 4 (below).

[54] They were, in chronological order of their election, Samuel Sibley (1934), James Green (1946), Benjamin Lacy (1950), and Frank Caldwell (1966).

[55] They were, in chronological order of their election, Benjamin Lacy (Moderator of the Synod of North Carolina, 1934), Frank Caldwell (Moderator of the Synod of Kentucky, 1948), and Eugene McLaurin (Moderator of the Synod of Texas, 1949).

seminaries;[56] another was founder and headmaster of one of the most prestigious all-male prep schools in the South;[57] three were seminary professors, each at a different PCUS school.[58]

The illustriousness of these committee members was no accident. This committee originally was appointed to revise the Church's doctrinal standards. Especially in light of the then-very-recent fundamentalist-modernist controversies, a more sensitive theological task can hardly be imagined. Southern Presbyterians would have regarded the work of this committee as holding the essence of their Church in its hands. Its decision regarding the (in)compatibility of Chafer's views with the Presbyterian Church Standards could not help but be of decisive, historic importance.

Significantly, the AIC declared "dispensationalism" an aberrant theological system, not because of its premillennialist eschatology, but because of its deviation from the covenant theology of the Westminster Standards. In fact, the AIC took pains to clarify that premillennialism *per se* was not a problem. Though Chafer never accepted the distinction between dispensationalism and premillennialism, he did accept the distinction between dispensationalism and covenant theology. Once this distinction between "dispensationalism" and "covenant theology" was firmly drawn by both sides, the gulf between the two theological systems was fixed.

From the beginning, however, the two sides used the same terminology in different ways, they attached differing levels of importance to specific doctrinal points, and they each contradicted what correlations and implications the other side derived from points on which they disagreed. One objective of this study is to sort all this out, and discern how the dialogue between dispensationalists and covenant theologians has been impacted by misrepresentation and confusion.

One other clarification deserves special mention before we begin a more detailed analysis. Though the AIC was justified in using Scofield and Chafer as representatives of dispensationalism as we have mentioned, we today are at sufficient historical distance to see that the Scofield-Chafer version of dispensationalism represented only one strand of dispensationalism's constituency, and only one stage of dispensationalism's theological development. Craig Blaising and Darrell Bock, in their historical analysis of the dispensationalist movement, have suggested "Four discernable phases of the dispensational tradition can be identified, each one accenting certain features . . . and adding its

---

[56] Benjamin Lacy was President of Union Theological Seminary in Richmond, VA; Frank Caldwell was President of Louisville Presbyterian Seminary in Louisville, KY.

[57] James P. McCallie directed the McCallie School for Boys in Chattanooga, TN.

[58] James Bear was Professor of the Literature and Interpretation of the New Testament at Union Theological Seminary in Richmond, VA; Eugene McLaurin was Professor of New Testament Language and Exegesis at Austin Theological Seminary in Austin, TX; James Green was Professor of Doctrinal Theology at Columbia Seminary in Columbia, SC (then Decatur, GA, where it is today). A Chair in Green's honor was established in 1946 (which Green also filled until he retired).

own characteristic emphases: (1) Niagara premillennialism (pre-Scofieldian dispensationalism), (2) Scofieldism, (3) essentialist dispensationalism, and (4) post-essentialist, or progressive, dispensationalism."[59]

It is intriguing to find that some of the changes in dispensationalism from Scofieldism[60] to essentialist dispensationalism[61] concern the very points at issue in the 1940s AIC controversy. In fact, the tenets of Scofieldian dispensationalism that came under the strongest indictment by the AIC were the very tenets that dispensationalists quietly retracted in the essentialist dispensational era. This is further evidence that the AIC controversy was a potent factor in dispensationalism's development as a theological system.

One might think that these modifications in dispensational theology would have brought the two systems closer together in the essentialist dispensationalist era, but such was not the case. This was in part because essentialist dispensationalists, rather than working to bridge the gulf between the two sides, instead submitted new charges against covenant theology and suggested new points of difference between the dispensational and covenantal systems.[62] This further suggests that the sociological polarization between the two sides may be as substantial as their actual theological differences.

Stephen R. Spencer has observed that the polarization of dispensationalism and covenant theology so dominated evangelical theologizing of the late-twentieth century that evangelicals came to commonly assume that they were the only Bible-believing systematic theological options. Consequently, many have assumed that to refute covenant theology is to establish dispensationalism or vice versa.[63] This assumption, which was "more commonly found in dispensational writings, but it occurs in covenant works as well,"[64] Spencer rightly identifies as an *error*. Nevertheless, the prevalence of this assumption may help account for why rapprochement has not been sought sooner, and why polarization intensified between dispensationalists and covenant theologians even when their theological positions, in reality, were growing closer. While we will surface this point later in more detail, it deserves fuller examination beyond what we will be able to undertake in this study.

---

[59] Craig A. Blaising and Darrell L. Bock, *Dispensationalism, Israel and the Church: The Search for Definition* (Grand Rapids: Zondervan, 1992), 379.

[60] "Scofieldism," the dispensationalism of the *Scofield Reference Bible* of 1909 and 1917 (especially as elaborated by Lewis Sperry Chafer), is what was under investigation by the AIC.

[61] "Essentialist dispensationalism" is that strand of dispensationalism found, e.g., in Charles Ryrie's *Dispensationalism Today* or the *New Scofield Reference Bible* of 1967.

[62] Compare, for example, the objections that Lewis Chafer submitted against covenant theology in his *Systematic Theology* (1948), 4:156-251, 311-13; and 7:96-99, 122-76; to those submitted by Charles Ryrie in *Dispensationalism Today* (1965), 86-109, 177-91.

[63] Spencer, "Reformed Theology, Covenant Theology, and Dispensationalism," 238-39.

[64] Ibid., 239.

Accordingly, though others before have claimed to have defined and elucidated the issues once and for all,[65] the points at issue today between dispensationalists and covenant theologians remain as unclear as ever.[66] In some quarters of evangelicalism, an irenic spirit prevails between dispensationalists and covenant theologians, which emphasizes points of (newfound) agreement and areas of (potential) rapprochement.[67] In other quarters, old battles lines are

---

[65] The *sine qua non* of Charles Ryrie's 1965 book, *Dispensationalism Today*, seems to have been submitted with the intention of clarifying definitively what constitutes dispensationalism *qua* dispensationalism (over against covenant theology). While some essentialist dispensationalists did accept Ryrie's work as the definitive treatise, for many others, Ryrie's *sine qua non* served more as a *starting point* for dispensationalist self-examination, rather than the closing of the question Ryrie sought. Consequently, in 1979, Earl Radmacher could observe "a growing rapprochement that has been taking place between covenant theologians and dispensational theologians of orthodox persuasion over the last decade. . . ." ("The Current Status of Dispensationalism in Its Eschatology," in *Perspectives on Evangelical Theology*, ed. Kenneth S. Kantzer and Stanley N. Gundry [Grand Rapids: Baker, 1979], 163). In 1982, this "growing rapprochement" was manifest in the presidential address to the Evangelical Theological Society by prominent dispensationalist Kenneth Barker ("False Dichotomies Between the Testaments," *JETS* 25 [January 1982]: 3-16). A landmark treatise, which openly conceded that some traditional dispensationalist tenets had ascribed too great a disparity between the Old and New Testaments, Barker's address seemed clearly designed to highlight mistakes in his own tradition in an effort to bring the two sides closer together, both in theological and in sociological position.

[66] E.g., see "Free Space for Dialogue Outside of Our Circles, Interview with Darrell L. Bock: Does the New Testament Reshape Our Understanding of the Old Testament?" *Modern Reformation* 9 (July/August 2000): 48-50. When asked, "What do you see as the key differences between Covenant and Dispensational theologies?" (48), Bock mentions three points. One point, however, he says "normally gets raised but I don't think applies," viz., the point that "concerns law and Grace. It is often said that Covenant theology and Dispensational theology differ on this theme. But I don't think this is correct" (49). The second point concerns the (future) role of national Israel, which Bock views as key. Yet, even on this point, Bock provides significant qualification. "I don't necessarily mean the future of the Jews per se, ethnically, as some in the reformed camp see the possibility of a significant number of Jews coming to Christ in the end. I am speaking specifically of a role for national Israel. The issue is whether national Israel as an administrative structure is still in the plan of God. Dispensationalists answer this question 'yes' and Covenant theologians tend to answer 'no'" (48-49). Regarding the hermeneutical approaches of dispensationalism and covenant theology, i.e., what essentialist dispensationalists argued was the fundamental difference between them, Bock says, "Hermeneutically, there is a difference between the two approaches. Although I think the distance is lessening significantly as a result of more recent discussion. There is room for a better conversation between the two camps today" (48).

[67] The irenic spirit of Barker's 1982 article ("False Dichotomies Between the Testaments") continued in a series of dialogues between dispensationalists and covenant theologians; among them: *Continuity and Discontinuity: Perspectives on the Relationship Between the Old and New Testaments; Essays in Honor of S. Lewis Johnson, Jr.*, ed. John S. Feinberg (Westchester, IL: Crossway, 1988); and the dialogue conducted between Elliot E. Johnson and Tremper Longman at the Dispensational Study Group of the Evangelical Theological Society in 1986, published as, Elliot E. Johnson, "What I Mean by Historical-Grammatical Interpretation and How that

being redrawn with renewed vigor.[68] Thus, there is today a general lack of consensus or clarity as to what constitutes dispensationalism *qua*

Differs from Spiritual Interpretation," *GTJ* 11, 2 (1990): 157-69; and Tremper Longman, III, "What I Mean By Historical-Grammatical Exegesis – Why I Am Not a Literalist," *GTJ* 11, 2 (1990): 137-55. Though never reaching complete agreement, both Johnson and Longman came to acknowledge that they both had misunderstood and underestimated the hermeneutical cogency of the other side.

As early as 1984, Robert Saucy concluded that "The subsequent development of dispensational theology as well as non-dispensational covenant theology has led to a convergence on the issue of law and grace with regard to salvation. . . ." ("Contemporary Dispensational Thought," *TSF Bulletin* 7 [March-April 1984]: 10); and, in 1986, "With a clearer statement by dispensationalists of a single divine method of salvation by grace through faith for all time and the modifying of the previous sharp antithesis between the dispensations of law and grace during the Mosaic economy, the law-grace issue concerning salvation among dispensationalists and non-dispensationalists has been rendered passé" (*idem*, "The Crucial Issue Between Dispensational and Nondispensational Systems," *Criswell Theological Review* 1 [fall, 1986]: 151). Likewise, in 1987, after surveying a number of watershed issues between the two systems, covenant amillennialist Vern Poythress suggested, "[S]ome modified dispensationalists agree with the points made in the whole of this chapter. So, provided we are able to treat the question of Israel's distinctiveness in the Millennium as a minor problem, no substantial areas of disagreement remain" (*Understanding Dispensationalists*, 51).

Presaged by the 1988 article by Craig Blaising ("Development of Dispensationalism by Contemporary Dispensationalists," *BibSac* 145 [July-September 1988]: 254-80), the 1990s ushered in the development of "progressive dispensationalism"; e.g., Craig Blaising and Darrell Bock, eds., *Dispensationalism, Israel and the Church*; *idem*, *Progressive Dispensationalism: An Up-to-Date Handbook of Contemporary Dispensational Thought* (Wheaton, IL: Bridgepoint Books, 1993); and Robert Saucy, *The Case for Progressive Dispensationalism: The Interface Between Dispensational & Non-Dispensational Theology* (Grand Rapids: Zondervan, 1993). The recently published study by Russell Moore (*The Kingdom of Christ*) represents an even further rapprochement between the two sides. Without undue hyperbole, he claims (and establishes convincingly) that evangelicals on both the covenantal and the dispensational sides have now come to a "new consensus" in regard to the kingdom; building on the combined efforts and theological reflections of what he calls "modified covenant theologians" and "progressive dispensationalists," Moore asserts that evangelicals today have to come generally to agree that the kingdom was inaugurated at Christ's first coming and that the New Testament age represents an "already-not yet" progressively transitional period that culminates in the eschaton upon Jesus' return.

[68] Several works, representing a more traditional dispensationalist stance (or "normative dispensationalism," if one accepts their own terminology), critique progressive dispensationalism for its alleged concessions and insist that traditional dispensationalist opposition to covenant theology must be reaffirmed; e.g., Wesley R. Willis and John R. Master, eds., *Issues in Dispensationalism* (Chicago, IL: Moody Press, 1994); and Charles Ryrie, *Dispensationalism* (Chicago, IL: Moody Press, 1995). There are some covenant theologians, also, who continue to suggest that the old lines of demarcation between dispensationalism and covenant theology were useful and should be preserved; most notably, Gerstner, *Wrongly Dividing the Word of Truth*; Mathison, *Dispensationalism: Rightly Dividing the People of God?*, and Williams, *This World is Not My Home*.

dispensationalism[69] and what core issues separate dispensationalism and covenant theology.

The study taken up here analyzes what was *originally* at issue between dispensationalists and covenant theologians in the only controversy in their history that has even the appearance of an authoritative verdict on the points in question. By comparing how those points were argued then with how they have been handled since then, we may further clarify the issues between dispensationalism and covenant theology and correct key misunderstandings in their historical dialogue. Simultaneously, we increase our understanding of underlying causes of tensions within the evangelical movement generally, which also persist.

While full reconciliation between the two sides may be an overly optimistic goal, we have good reason to believe that this study could put discussion between dispensationalists and covenant theologians generally on a better plane. The clarifications provided should enable all concerned to put peripheral points aside, thereby minimizing distractions that too often have drained evangelical energies. By dispelling misrepresentations that have frustrated advocates of both positions from the beginning, the efforts of those who would advance dialogue between the two sides may be directed toward matters of genuine concern and importance. Our hope is that whatever attention is henceforward captured by the dispensational-covenantal controversy may be focused on points that are really at issue, or, at the very least, on points that are worth the effort put into understanding them.

1.2 The Thesis and Approach of this Study

I propose that the years 1936-1944 represent the crucial time period for framing the issues between dispensationalism and covenant theology, and that the controversies of this time period produced the formation of these two ideologies as distinct "camps" within American evangelicalism. My thesis suggests (*inter alia*) that some adjustment is needed in what has become a standard characterization of "dispensationalist" and "Princetonian" parties in the early "fundamentalist alliance," viz, that "dispensationalists" and "Princetonians," though affirming incompatible theological systems, temporarily allied themselves in order to combat their common enemy, modernism.

---

[69] The disagreement on this fundamental point among dispensationalists themselves has coaxed some anti-dispensationalists to cheer what they predict is the inevitable collapse of the dispensational theological system; the most overt and shrill of these is Greg L. Bahnsen and Kenneth L. Gentry, Jr., *House Divided: The Break-Up of Dispensational Theology* (Tyler, TX: Institute for Christian Economics, 1989). Dispensationalism is clearly in something of an identity crisis, but this is not the first time dispensationalism has gone through such a crisis, and survived.

First suggested by Ernest R. Sandeen,[70] this assessment was modified some by George Marsden. Marsden alleviated some of Sandeen's reductionism by identifying more parties in the fundamentalist coalition, adding revivalism, anti-intellectualism, pietism, et al., as parties in the coalition of fundamentalist co-belligerents. Nevertheless, Marsden (and others after him) agreed with Sandeen's specific assessment of the nature of the coalition between "dispensationalists" and "Princetonians."[71]

In contrast to this, my thesis suggests that the relationship between the "dispensationalist" and "Princetonian" parties was not an "alliance" of disparate ideological groups which temporarily joined together in a common fight against modernism. Though there were such alliances formed during this period (e.g., between Baptists and Presbyterians), the "dispensationalist/Princetonian alliance," specifically, was different on just this point. That is, they did not begin as separate entities so as to join together in an awkward *marriage de convenance* (that unsurprisingly ended in divorce). Rather, the "dispensationalists" and "Princetonians" started out in the same sociological group, in the same ideological group (and, indeed, even in the same *denominational* groups).

In this instance, it was not the (temporary) merger (and then re-separation) of two disparate groups that changed the sociological complexion of American Christianity. Rather, it was the separation into two distinguishable entities from what was before an amalgam, impervious to such sharp distinguishability. My thesis is that the ideological constitution of evangelicalism significantly evolved in the 1930s-1940s in such a way that theologians, historians, and sociologists are now able to identify (only *a posteriori*) two distinct groups.[72]

---

[70] Ernest R. Sandeen, "Toward a Historical Interpretation of the Origins of Fundamentalism," *CH* 36 (March 1967): 66-83.

[71] Marsden, "Defining Fundamentalism"; and *idem*, *Fundamentalism and American Culture*, 93-118, 200-01. Also see Joe L. Coker, "Exploring the Roots of the Dispensationalist/Princetonian 'Alliance': Charles Hodge and John Nelson Darby on Eschatology and Interpretation of Scripture," *Fides et Historia* 30, 1 (winter-spring 1998): 41-56. Coker adds nuance to Marsden's and Sandeen's assessment, and responds to "the consensus among those who have criticized Sandeen" (e.g., Paul Kemeny, "Princeton and the Premillennialists: The Roots of the *marriage de convenance*," *American Presbyterians* 71, 1 [1993]: 17; and William R. Hutchinson, *The Modernist Impulse in American Protestantism* [Durham, NC: Duke University Press, 1992], 198), that Sandeen's "use of the term 'alliance' is an overstatement while his phrase 'not wholly compatible' is an understatement" (Coker, "Exploring the Roots of the Dispensationalist/Princetonian 'Alliance,'" 41).

[72] On a side note, I am not entirely satisfied with the classification of the parties as "dispensationalist" and "Princetonian." While not an altogether erroneous framing, it suggests some unnecessarily misleading connotations. For instance, this framing disguises the fact that Allan MacRae was no less a "Princetonian" than John Murray, while it simultaneously exaggerates the extent of their opposition throughout the time that they worked together, in which time they actually got along quite well. Westminster colleagues like MacRae and Murray began, as best they knew, each with an equal commitment to a united vision. True, they would come to be affiliated later on with factions that opposed one another vigorously, but these

I am arguing that the break-up of the so-called "dispensationalist-Princetonian alliance" should more properly be viewed in the context of a larger ideological rift forming between dispensationalism and covenant theology, which rift was not fully established until the late-1940s. By recognizing that ideological blocs are form*ing* (not already form*ed*) in earlier stages of the controversy, we avoid anachronism and more clearly see how confusions and ambiguities in the later dispensationalist-covenant theological division originated (rather than peaked) in the largely unspecified frictions that distressed the so-called "dispensationalist/Princetonian alliance." The perspective I am suggesting also allows for more insightful (and less patronizing) explanations for why repressed disagreements escalated into open conflict between fellow "fundamentalists" in the 1930s-1940s, and for why such conflict did not erupt earlier.

My explanation is that the early fundamentalist-evangelical movement was, ideologically and sociologically, an "organic complex."[73] Not all the specific tenets and values of an organic complex are expressly articulated, nor are they always consciously, cognizantly embraced. Rather, some of even the most significant tenets and values are intuitively sensed and subliminally assumed as one is assimilated into the community and its worldview.[74] In the organic

---

factions were in a mere seminal stage of development until well after both of them had departed Princeton.

I think this example is indicative of the kind of anachronism to which the "dispensationalist-Princetonian" framing is generally prone; it inclines one all along to project later polarizations onto earlier stages of evangelical-fundamentalist history, and exaggerates the force of hostilities during periods when these hostilities were yet latent. Since part of my thesis is that the lines of demarcation are just forming during the 1930s-1940s, I recognize that no terminology will be completely satisfactory, as such categorizing often can be introduced only *a posteriori*. Considering this, I suggest that framing the issues in terms of "dispensationalism" vis-à-vis "covenant theology" provides the most satisfactory classification overall. This framing has the advantage of some historical precedence of usage, and does sufficient justice to sociological and theological considerations, too.

An even more precise framing would be "classical dispensational premillennialism" vis-à-vis "Dutch Reformed covenant amillennialism." This classification more precisely identifies not only the theological issues in dispute, but also the contrasts of *ethos* that more subtly contributed to the sociological clash. Unfortunately, the precision is gained through virtually neologistic terminology that would require too burdensome a level of defense, explication, and qualification for me to insist upon it. My strategy, therefore, will be to achieve the desired nuance through analysis, while we content ourselves throughout this study with the nomenclature of "dispensationalism" vis-à-vis "covenant theology."

[73] I am here deliberately employing the descriptive terminology and concepts first suggested by Max Kadushin in another, very different, context; Max Kadushin, *Organic Thinking* (New York: Bloch Publishing Co., 1938), 2-16, 183-211; *idem*, *The Rabbinic Mind* (New York: Bloch Publishing Co., 1952), 24-31. I am indebted to E.P. Sanders (*Paul and Palestinian Judaism* [Philadelphia: Fortress Press, 1977], 72-75) for introducing me to this line of thinking suggested by Kadushin.

[74] Cf. the helpful description of the nature of "worldviews" by N.T. Wright: "Worldviews ... are like the foundations of a house: vital, but invisible. They are that *through* which, not *at* which, a

complex of the early fundamentalist-evangelical community, individual doctrinal tenets and practical theological values were emphasized differently among the various members of the movement. These differences were initially accommodated, ignored, or perhaps even unnoticed, because the basic beliefs and aims of the movement were as yet inchoate, and had not yet been connected in an entirely logical way.

This does not necessarily suggest any glaring incoherence in the ideology. It does suggest that a more subconscious awareness of shared values was what really provided the movement's initial cohesion, rather than their doctrinal declarations, even though these doctrinal declarations functioned, at times, as effective "social and/or cultural boundary markers."[75] While we can see, in retrospect, that the one common element that "fundamentalists" of various kinds consistently shared was their opposition to modernism, they may well have believed themselves to be pursuing more positive agendas (as their publication of numerous doctrinal manifestos may indicate).

Their separate agendas, which various strands of the movement came to advocate, did turn out sometimes to be incompatible; that, in historical hindsight, is indisputable. Nevertheless, what I am arguing is that these disparate agendas *developed* – and, in their development, *grew* more incompatible as time went on. This is why the parties involved came to "recognize" their incompatibility only in time, and is also why we see the incompatibilities so much more clearly now – but, again, only in historical hindsight. Specifically, I will argue that the fundamentalist value of "biblical truth" raised a corresponding concern for

---

society or an individual normally looks; they form the grid according to which humans organize reality, not bits of reality that offer themselves for organization. They are not usually called up to consciousness or discussion unless they are challenged or flouted fairly explicitly, and when this happens it is usually felt to be an event of worryingly large significance" (*The New Testament and the People of God* [Minneapolis: Fortress Press, 1992], 125). To be consistent with Wright's terminology, the debate between dispensationalists and covenant theologians should be described as a debate over "basic beliefs and aims" (ibid., 126), which form a sub-set of worldview, not the worldview, *per se*. (E.g., a "worldview conflict" would perhaps describe the larger issues at stake in the modernist-fundamentalist controversy; whereas both dispensationalists and covenant theologians shared the basic conservative, evangelical worldview, they came to oppose one another at the level of basic beliefs and aims). The point of significance to notice, nonetheless, is the largely subconscious nature of both, and the fact that, in regard to either worldview or basic beliefs and aims, specific tenets may not be fully raised to consciousness, or fully formed in anyone's mind, until they are *challenged*. As Wright has observed in another context, "history does not seem to have moved . . . in neat unilinear patterns" (ibid., 108). Likewise, Wright has suggested some historiographical corrective measures for New Testament scholarship (e.g., to recognize the *development* – rather than merely the *presence* – of the diversity of ideologies in the pre-Christian to early-Christian eras; see ibid., 167-214), which are strikingly similar in kind to those I am recommending to historians of the fundamentalist-evangelical movement.

[75] Again, I am deliberately using the terminology employed by Wright, *The New Testament and the People of God*, 124.

"doctrinal purity." This heightened concern for doctrinal purity, in turn, surfaced latent disagreements and accentuated doctrinal differences between members of the fundamentalist movement. Once this happened, rifts developed between the fundamentalist constituents, among them, the rift between dispensationalism and covenant theology.

The break-up of the fundamentalist-evangelical "organic complex," therefore, was not just a return to disparate parties which only momentarily had allied themselves. Rather, this break-up represented the formation of new lines of demarcation between conservative, Bible-believing Christians. This is especially true of the rift between ideologues of dispensationalism and covenant theology. Rather than representing some sort of return to the way things were before, their rift represented more a "falling out" between former friends.

Accordingly, just as when individuals have a "falling out," grievances are magnified and often projected onto what was "always true" in the relationship ("Well, you know, I always hated that about her!"), so likewise, such phenomena can be detected in sociological polarizations of greater proportions. These phenomena increase and intensify when the new institutions and organizations created by such sociological divisions must compete for constituents and resources.[76]

All this can be observed in the dispensational-covenantal rift alongside and in conjunction with their theological disagreements. My approach in this study, therefore, will incorporate both socio-historical and systematic-theological considerations in its analysis.

Chapter 2 examines the aftermath of the modernist-fundamentalist controversies and explains how intra-conservative tensions, largely unrecognized and repressed at first, gradually materialized into two competing conservative agendas. This chapter explores how these competing agendas raised and then intensified traditional eschatological disagreements and caused a rift between conservative, Northern Presbyterian premillennialists and amillennialists in the late-1930s. This historical analysis provides an initial explanation for how these events prepared the way for a more trenchant separation of dispensationalism and covenant theology shortly thereafter.

Chapter 3 scrutinizes the various sociological and theological elements that contributed to this late-1930s split between amillennialists and premillennialists in the fledgling conservative Presbyterian churches in the North. Sharply contested points in their dispute are analyzed. Some implications are drawn, as well, from points that seem confused or ambiguous at this early stage in the debate (1936-1938), especially those that later on grew substantially in their

---

[76] For insightful explication of these sociological phenomena, see Robert Wuthnow, *Meaning and Moral Order: Explorations in Cultural Analysis* (Los Angeles, CA: University of California Press, 1987), 154-214; also *idem*, *Rediscovering the Sacred: Perspectives on Religion in Contemporary Society* (Grand Rapids: Eerdmans, 1992); and Mary Douglas, *Purity and Danger* (Boston, MA: Routledge & Kegan Paul, 1966).

perceived significance. A fuller explanation is then provided for how elements in this Northern controversy catalyzed the explosive dispute between dispensationalists and covenant theologians in the South within the next few years.

Chapters 4 and 5 examine the Southern Presbyterian Church's investigation of dispensationalism, which finally determined that dispensationalism and covenant theology were irreconcilable theological systems. Chapter 4 investigates how dispensationalism came into the crossfire of conservative-liberal battles already taking place within Southern Presbyterianism. Chapter 5 explores the methodology and reasoning of the AIC in its determination that dispensationalism was out of harmony with the Westminster Standards. Sociological factors, along with the doctrinal points of dispute, are observed and analyzed. Significant historical implications of the AIC investigation and reports are also explored.

Chapter 6 offers a closing summary and analysis of the key points of the dispensationalist-covenantalist debate as it unfolded from 1936 to 1944. I seek to determine the impact of the 1930s-1940s dispensationalist-covenant theological debate on later evangelicalism by surveying significant distinctives and anomalies of the 1930s-1940s debate, as compared with the debate's later manifestations.

The conclusion reflects on the implications of the 1930s-1940s debate for contemporary evangelicalism, particularly where the findings of this study could contribute to current dialogues between dispensationalists and covenant theologians. I suggest a strategy for clearing up persistent misunderstandings and for pursuing potential areas of rapprochement. I also suggest that hard questions remain for both sides. Some closing thoughts offer a brief cost-benefit analysis of the dispensationalist-covenantalist debate for past, present, and future evangelicalism.

CHAPTER 2

The Fracturing of the Fundamentalist Coalition

The early twentieth-century modernist-fundamentalist controversies unleashed tremendous sociological forces on American Christianity.[1] Both sides in the struggle expended vast resources and energies, but losses suffered by the fundamentalist side were most severe. Nowhere were these losses more dramatic than in the PCUSA battles.[2] When fundamentalists left (or were expelled from) this mainline body, they sacrificed vast organizational funds, institutional resources, and even church property that they, in truth, had paid for.[3]

---

[1] For observations of specifics concerning this point, see James Davison Hunter, *American Evangelicalism: Conservative Religion and the Quandary of Modernity* (New Brunswick, NJ: Rutgers University Press, 1983), 27-48; Joel A. Carpenter, *Revive Us Again: The Reawakening of American Fundamentalism* (New York: Oxford University Press, 1997), xi-xiv, 3-123; David Harrington Watt, *A Transforming Faith: Explorations of Twentieth-Century American Evangelicalism* (New Brunswick, NJ: Rutgers University Press, 1991), 33-48; and, also, various essays in *Reforming the Center: American Protestantism, 1900 to the Present*, ed. Douglas Jacobsen and William Vance Trollinger, Jr. (Grand Rapids: Eerdmans, 1998). The significance of the early 20th-century controversies is also demonstrated in Martin Marty's classic history, *Modern American Religion*, 2 vols. (Chicago: University of Chicago Press, 1986). For other sources that examine the modernist-fundamentalist controversies and the history of American fundamentalism and evangelicalism, see chapter 1 (above), nn. 6-10.

[2] See Edwin H. Rian, *The Presbyterian Conflict* (Grand Rapids: Eerdmans, 1940), 248-57; As Robert Wuthnow has observed, "In the twentieth century, Presbyterians' involvement in the conflict between fundamentalists and modernists again sets their history apart from that of many other denominations. The conflict was particularly intense among Presbyterians because it revolved around a number of hotly contested issues . . . . Only among Northern Baptists were the battles waged by the fundamentalists as intense" ("Restructuring of American Presbyterianism," in *The Presbyterian Predicament: Six Perspectives*, ed. Milton J. Coalter, John M. Mulder, and Louis B. Weeks (Louisville, KY: WJK, 1990), 28-29.

[3] See Rian, *The Presbyterian Conflict*, 248-57; Robert K. Churchill, *Lest We Forget: A Personal Reflection on the Formation of the Orthodox Presbyterian Church* (Philadelphia: Committee for the Historian of the Orthodox Presbyterian Church, 1986); and George P. Hutchinson, *The History Behind the Reformed Presbyterian Church Evangelical Synod* (Cherry Hill, NJ: Mack, 1974). For the most detailed account, see articles from 1935-38 in both the *Christian Beacon* and the *Presbyterian Guardian*, two publications from the conservative side of the argument, which chronicled these events in detail.

Even where material losses were not so substantial, fundamentalists commonly were deemed the clear losers. American evangelical Christianity has never fully recovered from the wounds suffered during this time period. Nevertheless, historians and sociologists today are discovering that earlier predictions of conservative Christianity's demise[4] were greatly exaggerated.

From our vantage point, it would appear that, rather than being destroyed, evangelicalism was merely driven underground. Its retreat from public confrontations and showdowns with modernist liberalism may actually have been strategic. Rather than surrendering, American evangelicalism seems instead to have been retooling and regrouping, and has since re-emerged as a significant force in American thought, culture, and life.[5]

Our study takes us into the evangelical subculture as it was just beginning this retooling process in the 1930s-1940s. The mentality we find there is very different from the defeatist, wistful anti-intellectualism that earlier histories of the fundamentalist movement might have led us to expect. Rather, we find people who have sacrificed much for their cause, but who still remain confident that they can counter the subversive forces threatening their culture, if only they remain faithful to their divine calling. In the 1930s-1940s, conflicts erupt between them as they seek to discern exactly what that calling is.

2.1 Two "Fundamentalisms" Emerge from the Modernist-Fundamentalist Controversies

Once Princeton Seminary had been reorganized in 1929, the school's administration was put firmly in the hands of anti-fundamentalists.[6] Consequently, J. Gresham

---

[4] E.g., Stewart G. Cole, *The History of Fundamentalism* (New York: Richard B. Smith, 1931), 321-35; Frederick Lewis Allan, *Only Yesterday: An Informal History of the 1920s* (New York: Harper & Bros., 1931), 155-87; cf. also Norman F. Furniss, *The Fundamentalist Controversy, 1918-1931* (New Haven, CT: Yale University Press, 1954); Richard Hofstadter, *Anti-Intellectualism in American Life* (New York: Alfred A. Knopf, 1963); Wilbur J. Cash, *The Mind of the South* (New York: Alfred A. Knopf, 1941, reprint, New York: Doubleday & Co., 1956); and Blanche McCrary Boyd, *The Redneck Way of Knowledge: Down-Home Tales* (New York: Alfred A. Knopf, 1982).

[5] See Christian Smith, *American Evangelicalism: Embattled and Thriving* (Chicago: University of Chicago Press, 1998); Carpenter, *Revive Us Again*; George M. Marsden, ed., *Evangelicalism and Modern America* (Grand Rapids: Eerdmans, 1984); Nancy Tatom Ammerman, *Bible Believers: Fundamentalists in the Modern World* (New Brunswick, NJ: Rutgers University Press, 1987); Randall Balmer, *Mine Eyes Have Seen the Glory: A Journey into the Evangelical Subculture* (New York: Oxford University Press, 1989); and Robert Wuthnow, *The Restructuring of American Religion: Society and Faith Since World War II* (Princeton, NJ: Princeton University Press, 1988). Cf. also Gabriel Fackre, *Restoring the Center: Essays Evangelical & Ecumenical* (Downers Grove, IL: IVP, 1998); and Thomas C. Oden, *Requiem: A Lament in Three Movements* (Nashville: Abingdon, 1995).

[6] Rian, *The Presbyterian Conflict*, 60-87; D.G. Hart, *Defending the Faith: J. Gresham Machen and the Crisis of Conservative Protestantism in Modern America* (Baltimore, MD: Johns Hopkins University Press, 1994), 108-32. I recognize that "anti-fundamentalists" is a cumbersome term, but it is the most accurate term to characterize those in view. Not all were modernists, but all

Machen and several of his colleagues left to establish Westminster Theological Seminary.[7] In 1936, disciplinary measures were taken against them for their "rebellious" activities (establishing a new seminary, and, especially, establishing an Independent Board for Presbyterian Foreign Missions). At this, Machen and his colleagues left the PCUSA altogether, and founded the Orthodox Presbyterian Church.[8]

These ventures were part of a wider pattern. In establishing their own churches, papers, schools, and other institutions, conservatives (lumped together by their enemies as "fundamentalists"[9]) were expanding their vision beyond a mere defensive opposition to modernism to pursue a farther reaching, more constructive vision.[10] This expansion of vision brought new problems, however. Especially

---

those put in control of Princeton in 1929 did agree that "fundamentalist" positions and tactics were culpably schismatic.

[7] Ibid., 88-108; Bradley J. Longfield, *The Presbyterian Controversy: Fundamentalists, Modernists, & Moderates* (New York: Oxford University Press, 1991), 162-80; and Hart, *Defending the Faith*, 127-28.

[8] The Orthodox Presbyterian Church originally was called the Presbyterian Church of America, but, because of a lawsuit filed in 1939 by the PCUSA, was forced to change its name; see D.G. Hart and John Muether, *Fighting the Good Fight: A Brief History of the Orthodox Presbyterian Church* (Philadelphia: The Committee on Christian Education and the Committee for the Historian of the Orthodox Presbyterian Church, 1995), 15-54. For treatments of the formation and early history of the OPC, see also Longfield, *The Presbyterian Controversy*; Churchill, *Lest We Forget*; and Rian, *The Presbyterian Conflict*, 127-248. For sake of consistency, I have replaced references to "The Presbyterian Church of America" in all quotations from 1936-39 with "[OPC]" throughout.

[9] Harry Emerson Fosdick, "Shall the Fundamentalists Win?", in *American Protestant Thought in the Liberal Era*, ed. William R. Hutchison (Lanham, MD: University Press of America, 1968), 171-72. Clarence Edward Macartney was first to respond to Fosdick's sermon with a pair of articles, entitled, "Shall Unbelief Win?: An Answer to Dr. Fosdick [Parts 1 and 2]," *Presbyterian* 102 (13 and 20 July 1922): 8-10, 26, and 8-10, respectively. Reflecting on Fosdick's sermon later, he remarked, "It was the first time I had ever seen or heard the word Fundamentalist used in a religious significance" (Clarence E. Macartney, *The Making of a Minister* [Great Neck, NY: Channel Press, 1961], 184). Cf. Longfield, *The Presbyterian Controversy*, 3-127; Furniss, *Fundamentalist Controversy*, 112-86; George W. Dollar, *A History of Fundamentalism in America* (Greenville, SC: Bob Jones University Press, 1973), 150-76; and George M. Marsden, *Fundamentalism and American Culture: The Shaping of Twentieth-Century Evangelicalism: 1870-1925* (New York: Oxford University Press, 1980), 164-75.

[10] For accounts of fundamentalist efforts to take on a more aggressive agenda, see Dollar, *History of Fundamentalism in America*, 150-76; Furniss, *Fundamentalist Controversy*, 112-86; and Marsden, *Fundamentalism and American Culture*, 164-75. The World's Christian Fundamentals Association, organized by William Bell Riley in 1919, perhaps most clearly depicts the fundamentalist vision of winning the world to the fundamentalist cause. After 1922 (i.e., after Fosdick's use of the label), several fundamentalist leaders adjusted the titles of their works apparently to encourage (or take advantage of) the perception that "fundamentalism" was a well-orchestrated, national, or world-wide movement. E.g., in 1927, Riley changed the name of his paper from *The Christian Fundamentals in School and Church* to *The Christian Fundamentalist*. A year later, J. Frank Norris changed the name of his paper from *The Searchlight* (formerly *The Fence Rail*) to *The Fundamentalist*.

where the fundamentalist vision was intermingled with a renewed emphasis on traditional Reformed objectives, intra-conservative strife ensued. Two issues, both of which were central in the PCUSA fundamentalist-modernist controversies,[11] came into play also in breaking up the fundamentalist coalition (especially the Presbyterian bloc of this coalition), viz.: (1) the issue of doctrinal litmus tests; and (2) the issue of confessional subscription.

First, note the two sets of "fundamentals" asserted by conservatives during the course of the fundamentalist-modernist controversies. The first set was affirmed by premillennialist leaders at the Niagara Bible Conference of 1895;[12] the second set was affirmed by the 1910 General Assembly of the PCUSA.[13] Set side-by-side, they appear as follows:

---

[11] Cole, *History of Fundamentalism*, 102-03; Marsden, *Fundamentalism and American Culture*, 176-84; cf. also J. Gresham Machen, *Christianity and Liberalism* (New York: Macmillan, 1923). See also the arguments exchanged in the turmoil concerning the "Auburn Affirmation" of 1924; e.g., "AN AFFIRMATION: Designed to safeguard the unity and liberty of the Presbyterian Church in the United States of America," included as Appendix B in Charles E. Quirk, "The Auburn *Affirmation*: A Critical Narrative of the Document Designed to Safeguard the Unity and Liberty of the Presbyterian Church in the United States of America in 1924," (Ph.D. diss., University of Iowa, 1967), 397-99; see also 116-35, 261-79, 498-516; Carl McIntire, "'Auburn Affirmation,'" *CBeac* 1 (20 August 1936): 1-2, 7-8; Gordon H. Clark, "The Auburn Heresy," *CBeac* 1 (20 August 1936): 3; *idem*, "The Auburn Heresy," *SPresJ* 5 (15 July 1946): 7-9; Murray Forst Thompson, "The Auburn Betrayal: Parts I-V," *PrGuard* 10 (10 November 1941): 113-14, 125-27; (25 November 1941): 133-34; (10 December 1941): 154-55; (25 December 1941): 165-67; and 11 (25 January 1942): 24-25; and L. Nelson Bell, "The Auburn Affirmation Is Actually Not an Affirmation of Faith But a . . . [*sic*] Dissent From Evangelical Truth," *SPresJ* 10 (10 October 1951): 3-4.

[12] Cf. Cole, *History of Fundamentalism*, 34; and Larry Dean Pettegrew, "The Historical and Theological Contributions of the Niagara Bible Conference to American Fundamentalism," (Th.D. diss., Dallas Theological Seminary, 1976), 139-61. Pettegrew demonstrates that the Niagara Bible Conference doctrinal statement was likely authored by James Brookes, an early dispensationalist who had significant influence on C.I. Scofield. For discussion of the relationship of the Niagara Bible Conference to early dispensationalism, see also Craig A. Blaising, "Debut at Niagara," in *Dispensationalism, Israel and the Church: The Search for Definition* (Grand Rapids: Zondervan, 1992), 16-20; and Marsden, *Fundamentalism and American Culture*, 43-71. For discussion of the organic relationship of the Niagara Bible Conference to Dallas Theological Seminary, see John David Hannah, "The Social and Intellectual History of the Origins of the Evangelical Theological College" (Ph.D. diss., University of Texas at Dallas, 1988), 193-200.

[13] Cole, *The History of Fundamentalism*, 98-99; Marsden, *Fundamentalism and American Culture*, 117.

Niagara Fundamentalism	Presbyterian Fundamentalism
(1) the inerrancy of Scripture	(1) the inerrancy of Scripture
(2) the Deity of Christ	(2) the virgin birth of Christ
(3) the virgin birth of Christ	(3) the substitutionary atonement of Christ
(4) the substitutionary atonement of Christ	(4) the bodily resurrection of Christ
(5) the physical resurrection of Christ and His coming bodily return to earth	(5) the authenticity of Christ's miracles.

The two sets of "fundamentals" are similar, yet not identical; not wholly incompatible to be sure, but yet not the same either. Heuristically, we can distinguish the two lists as "Niagara Fundamentalism" and "Presbyterian Fundamentalism," so long as we recognize that fundamentalists themselves, at the time, did not draw such a distinction. Indeed, the distinction has escaped the notice of many historians since then.[14]

As Marsden suggests, "The classic five points . . . appear to have been formulated by liberals, while fundamentalists' own lists varied in number and content."[15] This may supply additional evidence for my contention that the early fundamentalist movement was an organic complex whose concerns overlapped and intermingled, but whose beliefs and aims were not yet clearly articulated or fully established.

In any case, the opponents of fundamentalism believed they could identify the "fundamentalists" by a thumbnail sketch of doctrines they thought all "fundamentalists" insisted upon. We, on the other hand, can identify early signs of intra-fundamentalist volatility by comparing and contrasting the different sets of doctrines insisted upon by different constituents in the early fundamentalist coalition.

---

[14] For instance, Cole mistakenly assumes that it was the *same* five points that were affirmed by both the Niagara Bible Conference of 1895 and the General Assembly of the PCUSA in 1910 (*History of Fundamentalism*, 34, 98-99). Likewise, Churchill's treatise is a history of the OPC, but his listing of the "five fundamentals" (probably following Cole, directly or indirectly) is that of the Niagara Bible Conference, rather than of the 1910 PCUSA General Assembly (*Lest We Forget*, 30). Cole's mistake was first detected by Ernest R. Sandeen, *The Roots of Fundamentalism: British and American Millenarianism: 1800-1930* (Chicago: University of Chicago Press, 1970), xiv-xv. Marsden suggests, "The 'five points of fundamentalism,' in the classic form they were given in Stewart Cole's history . . . seem to appear first in the *Christian Century* XL (August 16, 1923), p. 1040" (Marsden, *Fundamentalism and American Culture*, 278, n. 3). The *Christian Century* editorial likely was following Harry Emerson Fosdick's list in "Shall the Fundamentalists Win?" (*Christian Work* 112 [10 June 1922], reprinted in *American Protestant Thought: The Liberal Era*, ed. William R. Hutchison [New York: Harper & Row, 1968], 173.)

[15] Marsden, *Fundamentalism and American Culture*, 278, n. 3.

Might the two sets of "fundamentals" affirmed by "Niagara fundamentalists" and "Presbyterian fundamentalists" actually have come into competition with one another as early twentieth-century fundamentalism advanced?[16] Pursuing this question begins to explain how seemingly innocuous eschatological disagreements could escalate into a rancorous intra-conservative dispute.

Sorting for similarities and differences between the two sets of "fundamentals," the following chart results:

Niagara Fundamentalism	Same or Different?	Presbyterian Fundamentalism
(1) the inerrancy of Scripture	Same	(1) the inerrancy of Scripture
(2) the Deity of Christ [implying authenticity of His miracles], His virgin birth, His substitutionary atonement, and physical resurrection	Same	(2) the authenticity of Christ's miracles [which demonstrated His Deity], His virgin birth, His substitutionary atonement, and bodily resurrection
(3) Christ's coming bodily [premillennial] return to earth	**Different**	[(3) other major tenets of the Westminster Standards]

Marsden observes, "During the 1920s, 'the five points of fundamentalism' sometimes referred to the Presbyterian points and sometimes to the Presbyterian points with the premillennial return of Christ substituted for the miracles as point no. 5."[17] This occasional "substitution" of premillennialism for one of the other Presbyterian "fundamentals" surfaces a difference in certain impulses within the early fundamentalist movement.

To a "Niagara fundamentalist," the "coming bodily return of Christ" commonly implied "the coming premillennial return"; for such a fundamentalist, premillennialism was a doctrine clearly taught in the Bible. Such a person might well feel a closer affinity to those who saw this eschatological point as clearly as they, even if such kindred eschatological spirits were found more often in denominations outside the Presbyterian or Reformed ones.[18] To a "Presbyterian fundamentalist," on the other hand, Calvinistic themes and confessional distinctives would be most crucial. Such a person would be alarmed at any intrusion of

---

[16] Such a suggestion is hinted at, but undeveloped, by Douglas Edward Herman, "Flooding the Kingdom: The Intellectual Development of Fundamentalism, 1930-1941" (Ph.D. diss., Ohio University, 1980), 118-45.

[17] Marsden, *Fundamentalism an American Culture*, 262, n. 30.

[18] E.g., Merril T. MacPherson, "Why I Am Pastor of an Independent Church," *CBeac* 2 (12 August 1937): 3-4; and "Premillenarian Request of Duryea," *CBeac* 1 (20 August 1936): 2, 8. Cf. also Churchill's frustration at premillennialist Presbyterians who seemed more at home with other premillennialists than with the "truly Reformed" (*Lest We Forget*, 29-40, 91, 126-35).

Arminian or other un-Reformed proclivities, though this same person would likely see debates over eschatology as an interesting, but inconsequential, curiosity.[19]

What is particularly interesting for us is that both impulses can be found intermingled, often indistinguishable and sometimes utterly confused, among Presbyterian conservatives involved in the fundamentalist-modernist controversies.[20] The modernist-fundamentalist controversies threw the Presbyterian Church into an identity crisis. What we can now see is that, even after "fundamentalists" in the PCUSA withdrew, the identity crisis remained. The eschatological debate, and the dispensational-covenantalist debate that followed it, were products as well as causes of the identity crisis that persisted.

I suggest that this is the key to understanding why the covenantal-dispensational debate, a debate between two Bible-believing, "fundamentalist" camps within *conservative* Presbyterianism, would eventually manifest the same intensity as the fundamentalist-modernist debate that preceded it. It is because both disputes were a fight for identity; first, a fight for the essence of the Presbyterian Church, then a fight over what Presbyterian distinctives should be stressed and what Presbyterian distinctives should be downplayed in order to implement the most effective strategy for combating modernism and for advancing a proper Reformed, evangelical agenda.

Likewise, this explains why these conservative groups became less and less tolerant of doctrinal differences, even as their level of doctrinal agreement actually increased (albeit within a smaller community of faith). Notice that *both* types of "fundamentalist" had to compromise their concerns, at least insofar as tolerating others' dissent from them, in order to survive in the larger Presbyterian body before 1936.[21] It was only after they together departed from the old church that the "fundamentalists" became unwilling to compromise with one another.[22]

---

[19] E.g., Ned B. Stonehouse, "The Creed of Our Fathers," *PrGuard* 4 (10 April 1937): 1-2; R.B. Kuiper, "Two Features of the Reformed Faith," *PrGuard* 4 (October 1937): 161-63; *idem, As To Being Reformed* (Grand Rapids: Eerdmans, 1926). As Alan E. Lewis points out, Reformed theology has consistently been most concerned with God's redemption and restoration of this Creation, rather than with its future end or annihilation; Reformed theologians occasionally have explored the consummation of God's ends, which are revealed in Scripture and adumbrations of which can be presently discerned, but, as a rule, Reformed theology has displayed little interest in chronologically ordering future events ("Eschatology," in *Encyclopedia of the Reformed Faith*, ed. Donald K. McKim [Louisville, KY: WJK, 1992], 122-24).

[20] E.g., Charles R. Erdman was the one who wrote the defense of premillennialism in *The Fundamentals*, remarking, "The return of Christ is a *fundamental doctrine* of the Christian faith" (*The Fundamentals: A Testimony to the Truth*, ed. Amzi C. Dixon, Louis Meyer, and Reuben A. Torrey [Chicago: Testimony Press, 1910-1915], 4:301) Yet Erdman was the very one who, as moderator of the 1925 PCUSA General Assembly, appointed the commission that investigated Machen, eventually leading to Princeton being reorganized, and fundamentalist ministers being deposed; see Longfield, *The Presbyterian Controversy*, 128-80; and Hart, *Defending the Faith*, 117-28.

[21] This point is presented most clearly by J. Gresham Machen, "What Fundamentalism Stands for Now," *New York Times* (21 June 1925), reprinted in *"What is Christianity?" and Other Addresses*, ed. Ned B. Stonehouse (Grand Rapids: Eerdmans, 1951), 253; and *idem*, Statement submitted to the committee of investigation of Princeton Theological Seminary, 23 November

Everyone in the new church agreed that the Achilles' heel of the old church was its unwillingness to take hard stands on what naïve persons considered obscure doctrinal points. The conservatives withdrew in order to take those necessary, hard doctrinal stands. As Hart and Muether explain:

> One cannot understand the OPC's emphasis on doctrine without an appreciation of the doctrinal crisis out of which the OPC arose. For Machen and his supporters, irreconcilable differences in belief lay at the heart of the controversy. The theological views of modernists and Christian orthodoxy were mutually exclusive. For the sake of the purity of the church, separation was necessary. And the struggles in which Machen engaged go far in explaining the character of the church.[23]

"Niagara fundamentalists" and "Presbyterian fundamentalists" clashed when it came to determining which doctrines had to be upheld without latitude and which did not. They all wanted to set the new church on the most solid doctrinal ground. They all wanted to further the church's testimony, and to take advantage of what cooperation could legitimately be garnered among like-minded evangelicals.[24] The devil, one might say, was in the details.

2.2 The Rift Over Premillennialism in the Orthodox Presbyterian Church

It was shortly after the OPC had been formed, in 1936, that a dispute over "dispensational premillennialism" erupted. It all began with the publication of three sets of articles, all written by Westminster Seminary professors, all from the perspective of traditionalist Presbyterianism. All three argued that establishing a true Presbyterian Church meant repudiating any intrusion of "anti-Reformed" teachings, specifically Arminian and "dispensationalist" teachings, which were too commonly found in the general evangelical-fundamentalist movement. Taking up a different aspect of this one central thesis, each article sought one common objective: to

---

1926, quoted in Ned B. Stonehouse, *J. Gresham Machen: A Biographical Memoir* (Grand Rapids: Eerdmans, 1955), 337-38.

[22] Even archconservative Carl McIntire commended the "eschatological liberty" afforded to pre-, post-, and a-millennialists in the PCUSA. He chastened his amillennialist brethren for threatening this freedom in their attacks on dispensationalism ("Premillennialism," *CBeac* 1 [1 October 1936]: 4). Cf. the response of R.B. Kuiper, who rebuked McIntire for his commendation of such "freedom"; it was such freedom, Kuiper claimed, that had (inadvertently) permitted the increase of "naturalistic postmillenarians" in the old denomination ("Has the Presbyterian Guardian Attacked Premillennialism?: The Reply of Dr. Kuiper," *PrGuard* 3 [14 November 1936]: 54-55).

[23] Hart and Muether, *Fighting the Good Fight*, 38-39.

[24] Sloat's 1950 arguments reflect the history of this discussion in the OPC, and provide further confirmation of my point here; see Leslie W. Sloat, "Should Conservatives Cooperate?" *PrGuard* 19 (February 1950): 23; and *idem*, "Calvinists Can and Do Cooperate!" *PrGuard* 19 (March 1950): 43.

establish a "truly Reformed," "true Presbyterian" identity over against a less vigilant one.[25]

The last of these articles (Kuiper's) was not intended to criticize anyone really, but rather to encourage members of the newly formed OPC in the kind of genuine, pure Presbyterian Church they had created. Amidst his praise, Kuiper made the following, brief digression:

> The General Assembly had the privilege of examining several graduates of Westminster Seminary for licensure and ordination. It would have warmed the cockles of the heart of any Christian Reformed minister to hear how closely they were questioned about the two errors which are so extremely prevalent among American fundamentalists, Arminianism and the Dispensationalism of the Scofield Bible. The Assembly wanted to make sure that these prospective ministers were not tainted with such anti-reformed heresies.
>
> All of which goes to show that synod used no vain words when it spoke of "the tie that binds us in the propagation and defense of our common Reformed faith."
>
> The [OPC] is not just another fundamentalist church. Its basis is strictly Reformed.[26]

Of the three sets of articles, Kuiper's made the briefest mention of dispensationalism and had the most innocuous intent. Yet, ironically, these remarks drew the most fire from premillennialists in the OPC. Apparently, for them, it served as the proverbial "last straw."

Carl McIntire wrote an editorial in the *Christian Beacon* voicing the umbrage of premillennialists. After taking issue with Kuiper's recounting of facts,[27] McIntire

---

[25] The first set was by Old Testament professor Oswald T. Allis ("Modern Dispensationalism and the Doctrine of the Unity of Scripture," *EvQ* 8 [January 1936]: 22-35; and "Modern Dispensationalism and the Law of God," *EvQ* 8 [July 1936]: 272-89). The second set was by Systematic Theology professor John Murray; his articles had actually begun in late-1935 as an unremarkable defense of Presbyterian orthodoxy over against modernism. Once the church had split, however, Murray apparently decided to raise his sights and shoot for a more ambitious form of "orthodoxy"; his later articles argued against Arminianism, then against "modern dispensationalism" ("The Reformed Faith and Modern Substitutes, Part 1," *PrGuard* 1 [16 December 1935]: 87-89; *idem*, "The Reformed Faith and Modern Substitutes, Part II," *PrGuard* 2 [3 February 1936]: 142-43; *idem*, "The Reformed Faith and Modern Substitutes, Part III," *PrGuard* 2 [17 February 1936]: 163-64; *idem*, "The Reformed Faith and Modern Substitutes, Part IV: Limited Atonement," *PrGuard* 2 [16 March 1936]: 200-01, 211; *idem*, "The Reformed Faith and Modern Substitutes, Part V," *PrGuard* 2 [20 April 1936]: 27-29; *idem*, "The Reformed Faith and Modern Substitutes, Part VI: Modern Dispensationalism," *PrGuard* 2 [18 May 1936]: 77-79; and *idem*, "The Reformed Faith and Modern Substitutes, Part VII – Modern Dispensationalism: The 'Kingdom of Heaven' and the 'Kingdom of God,'" *PrGuard* 2 [17 August 1936]: 210-12; this last article was continued as "The 'Kingdom of Heaven' and the 'Kingdom of God,'" *PrGuard* 3 [9 January 1937]: 139-41). The third and final article was written by practical theology professor R.B. Kuiper ("Why Separation Was Necessary," *PrGuard* 2 [12 September 1936]: 225-27).

[26] Kuiper, "Why Separation Was Necessary," 227.

forwarded his central complaint. "Furthermore, the even more significant matter at this point is that, without any effort to distinguish the good from the bad, Dr. Kuiper calls the 'Dispensationalism of the Scofield Bible' an 'anti-reformed heresy.' Heresy is not a pleasant word. The remark in regard to the 'Dispensationalism of the Scofield Bible' is an attack upon the premillennialists, as heretics."[28]

OPC amillennialists consistently denied this last charge, claiming that it was only un-Reformed ("dispensationalist") premillennialism they found unacceptable.[29] As tempers flared, and the OPC was threatened with a split just as it was getting started, J. Gresham Machen sought to intervene with several articles that tried to clarify this point.[30] He, too, insisted that a distinction must be made between acceptable, Reformed varieties of premillennialism and the unacceptable, un-Reformed Dispensationalism of the Scofield Bible.

> There are surely many persons who, though they hold to the Premillennial view of the return of the Lord, reject the Dispensationalism of the Scofield Bible. We agree with these Premillennialists and we agree with Professor Kuiper in such rejection. The Dispensationalism of the Scofield Bible seems to us to be quite contrary to the system of doctrine taught in the Westminster Standards.[31]

Machen even went so far as to try to explain how some premillennialist Presbyterians, though themselves acceptably Reformed, might still be fond of using the Scofield Bible, despite its gross errors: "It is quite possible that many persons know and love the Scofield Reference Bible without really agreeing with the false teaching that is in it. By salutary misunderstanding or ignoring of Dr. Scofield's notes they may be prevented from taking into their souls the errors that those notes

---

[27] "In the first place we are quite sure that there has been some serious mistake made by Dr. Kuiper in regard to the facts related by him concerning the licensure of the two Westminster men. We were present, and we have also consulted others who were present at the time, and in the examination of the students relative to their views of eschatology no reference was made to the 'Scofield Bible.' There was a question asked concerning an alleged and little known form of so-called dispensationalism which violated the covenant of grace. The Rev. H. McAllister Griffiths, a premillennialist, editor at that time of The Presbyterian Guardian, immediately arose and said that question needed to be stated thus, 'Do you believe that the Bible teaches only one way of salvation and that by the blood?' Mr. Griffiths said that if they answered this question in the affirmative it would satisfy him, and ought to be enough for anybody else. This was answered in the affirmative, and the question concerning dispensationalism was dropped. Therefore, we are at a loss to understand why Dr. Kuiper can assert that these two men condemned the 'Dispensationalism of the Scofield Bible,' which was not even under discussion" (Carl McIntire, "Premillennialism," 4).

[28] Ibid.

[29] This point was made emphatically in Kuiper's response to McIntire's editorial ("The Reply of Professor Kuiper," 54-55).

[30] J. Gresham Machen, "Premillennialism," *PrGuard* 3 (24 October 1936): 21; *idem*, "The Root of the Trouble," *PrGuard* 3 (14 November 1936): 41-42; *idem*, "The Dispensationalism of the Scofield Bible," *PrGuard* 3 (14 November 1936): 42-43; and *idem*, "The Millennial Question," *PrGuard* 3 (14 November 1936): 43-44.

[31] Machen, "The Dispensationalism of the Scofield Bible," 42.

contain."[32] Machen acknowledged that not everything in the Scofield notes were erroneous; indeed, in Machen's view, "some of the worst things in the notes are actually contradicted by other passages that the notes themselves contain. By a happy inconsistency Dr. Scofield is prevented from drawing fully the disastrous consequences of his theory as to the history of God's dealings with men."[33] Machen's final verdict, though, was the same as Allis', Murray's, and Kuiper's. "But we do mean very definitely that if a man really does accept all the teaching of those notes, according to their real meaning, he is seriously out of accord with the Reformed Faith and has no right to be a minister or elder or deacon in The [OPC].[34]

Premillennialists were nonplussed by such distinctions. McIntire chided critics of the Scofield notes to "cease their veiled and continued attacks upon the premillennialist position concerning 'dispensationalism' . . . ."[35] Said McIntire:

> We are unable to see in our own thinking how the a-millennialists can say they grant liberty to the premillennialists and then turn in such a manner as this and condemn them as heretics. We firmly believe that by far the majority of the people in the [OPC] are premillenarians, and the Church committed to the Westminster Confession of Faith is not committed to the particular view held by any individual.[36]

Again, Machen tried to explain, "[A] great many people think that 'Premillennialism' and the 'Dispensationalism of the Scofield Bible' are the same thing, so that when Professor Kuiper declared that the 'Dispensationalism of the Scofield Bible' is an anti-Reformed heresy he was also declaring that Premillennialism is an anti-Reformed heresy."[37] Machen remained convinced that the key to resolving the conflict lay in the ability to distinguish between premillennialism and dispensationalism.

> In view of that fact, one of the pressing needs of the hour is the sharp separation between these things that are so sadly confused. The Premillennial view of the time of the Lord's return is not an anti-Reformed heresy. A man may hold to it and be a minister in a truly Reformed or Presbyterian Church. But the Dispensationalism of the Scofield Bible is, we are convinced, just as Professor Kuiper says it is, an anti-Reformed heresy indeed. It is quite out of accord with the system of doctrine contained in the Westminster Confession of Faith and Catechisms.[38]

---

[32] Ibid.
[33] Ibid.
[34] Ibid.
[35] McIntire, "Premillennialism," 4.
[36] Ibid.
[37] J. Gresham Machen, "The Presbytery of California and the 'Christian Beacon,'" *PrGuard* 3 (28 November 1936): 71.
[38] Ibid.

Because premillennialists never fully accepted this distinction between dispensationalism and premillennialism, suspicions and animosities continued to escalate. Premillennialists would eventually leave the OPC before any further action was taken against them. OPC amillennialists always insisted that no further action was ever pending, but premillennialists never fully trusted these reassurances. Close scrutiny uncovers a variety of reasons for this distrust.

First, though the three Westminster critics of dispensationalism probably had not intended to produce their articles at the same time, their appearing in rapid succession gave the appearance of a well-coordinated attack.[39] This fostered a perception among premillennialists that the amillennialists were trying to drive them out of the new denomination.

Secondly, though all the non-premillennialists offered assurance that premillennialism *per se* was acceptable, the combination of rationales they offered as to why the premillennialist view could be acceptable within the OPC was awkward, even incoherent. One premillennialist, Allan A. MacRae, had heard theology professor John Murray say in private conversation that he found the premillennial view tolerable only because he believed it was within the parameters of the Confession of Faith. When pressed as to what he would want done if ever he were convinced premillennialism was outside confessional parameters, Murray said that he honestly did not know.[40] Compare that to the view of J. Gresham Machen:

> It is true, the Westminster Confession of Faith and Catechisms teach not the Premillennial view but a view that is opposed to the Premillennial view. That is particularly plain in the Larger Catechism (Q. 87 and 88). But subscription to the Westminster Standards in The [OPC] is not to every word in those Standards, but only to the *system* of doctrine which the Standards contain.[41]

The two rationales presented by Murray and Machen seem directly at odds. In view of such incongruities, we perhaps cannot blame the premillennialists for being nervous, despite repeated amillennialist reassurances.

Thirdly, OPC leaders refused to put any guarantee in writing that church-wide toleration of premillennialism would be perpetuated, despite repeated premillennialist requests to do so.[42] In truth, these requests were denied more out of concern to preserve the OPC's confessional integrity than out of desire to malign the premillennial view. In fact, one of the most vocal opponents of these resolutions was J. Oliver Buswell, himself a premillennialist and moderator of the Assembly that

---

[39] This point is made explicitly by Charles Trumbull in his editorial responding to the controversy: Charles G. Trumbull, "Notes on Open Letters: Dispensationalism and the Scofield Reference Bible – Are They Heresies?" *SSTimes* 79 (20 February 1937): 130, 132-33.

[40] Allan A. MacRae, interview by author, Quarryville, PA, 3 August 1993.

[41] Machen, "Premillennialism," 21.

[42] See "Premillenarian Request of Duryea," 2; "Actions by the Presbytery of California: The Overture," *PrGuard* 3 (14 November 1936): 55; and J. Gresham Machen, "Congregations and the Millennial Question," *PrGuard* 3 (14 November 1936): 45.

considered most of them.[43] Even still, many premillennialists felt put out by these denials.

Fourthly, though OPC amillennialists continually assured premillennialists that a "truly Reformed, truly Presbyterian" premillennial eschatology was possible, premillennialists had a hard time providing a version that actually met with their approval. The rough handling that J. Oliver Buswell's premillennial view received provides a case in point.

OPC premillennialism could hardly be better represented than by J. Oliver Buswell, moderator of the second OPC General Assembly,[44] president of Wheaton College, and a well-known outspoken advocate of OPC doctrinal purity and Reformed distinctives. By January of 1937, Buswell had offered both an article[45] and a book[46] defending the kind of premillennialism that he hoped would be found acceptable by those attacking "the dispensationalism of the Scofield Bible."[47] No sooner had these works been published, however, than a scathing rejoinder once again appeared in the *Presbyterian Guardian* by John Murray.

Whatever faint praise Murray gave to "Dr. Buswell's premillennialism" was invariably accompanied with criticism – criticism so caustic, at times, it bordered on spite.

> Dr. Buswell's eschatological position is much saner and therefore more defensible than that of many premillenarians. We are sorry to

---

[43] J. Oliver Buswell "left the chair in parliamentary fashion," in order to argue "from the floor" against the adoption of these resolutions. "Dr. Martin Luther Thomas, another staunch premillenarian," then voiced his agreement with Buswell. In their opinion, within a truly Reformed church such as theirs, such a resolution could prove to be *dis*advantageous, as it could suggest that the premillennial position needed special creedal accommodation to be preserved. They also felt that the resolution invariably would provoke more, not less, controversy, and would serve only to distract the Church from more important business ("The Second General Assembly of the [OPC]," *PrGuard* 3 [28 November 1936]): 70, 83). J. Gresham Machen then added his yet another powerful voice of dissent to these resolutions (ibid). Thus, the resolutions were defeated. We observe that the coming year would prove Machen's remarks on the issue to be prescient: "We said above that we are opposed to 'counting noses' on this question [premillennialist vs. amillennialist] among individuals. We are still more opposed to 'counting noses' among congregations. If we are going to have congregations of our church divided into two rival camps – the Premillennial congregations on the one side and the Amillennial congregations on the other – then we think we ought to be divided into two entirely separate churches at the start. That would certainly be far more conducive to brotherly feeling than any hardening of opinions on this matter practically into the fixity of dogma by the labeling of congregations one way or the other within the limits of what purports to be the same Church" (Machen, "Congregations and the Millennial Question," 45).

[44] Buswell had been nominated for moderator by Cornelius Van Til, which nomination was seconded by Carl McIntire. Van Til and McIntire together escorted Buswell to the platform at the 1937 General Assembly. See Edward A. Steele, III, "Buswell, The Man," in the "J. Oliver Buswell Commemorative Issue," *Presbyterion: Covenant Seminary Review* 2 (Spring-Fall 1976): 9-10; also "Dr. Buswell Chosen Moderator," *PrGuard* 3 (28 November 1936): 78-79.

[45] J. Oliver Buswell, Jr. "A Premillennialist's View," *PrGuard* 3 (14 November 1936): 46-47.

[46] J. Oliver Buswell, Jr., *Unfulfilled Prophecies* (Grand Rapids: Zondervan, 1937).

[47] See Buswell, "A Premillennialist's View," 46-47; cf. *idem, Unfulfilled Prophecies*, 32-33.

say, however, that the little book by which he has set it forth is exceedingly disappointing. It is characterized by gross unfairness and misrepresentation, and his exegetical argumentation is frequently very inconsequential. Looseness and carelessness are, we fear, the rule rather than the exception.[48]

Even Murray's infrequent compliments seemed back-handed, as though they were really thinly veiled critiques of more widely recognized forms of premillennialism (e.g., "Many of the fantasies frequently associated with presentations of premillennialism are conspicuous by their absence"[49]). Throughout the review, there was not a single point of substance from Buswell's treatise that Murray received positively. As though it would help ease the sting of his critique, Murray clarified, "We do not accuse Dr. Buswell of deliberate distortion. He has, however, shown himself seriously incompetent . . ."[50] Murray concluded, "We should have hoped that we might be able to recommend [Dr. Buswell's work] as a fair and reasonably scholarly presentation of the premillennial view. We do not have the happiness to be able to do so."[51]

In short, Buswell's premillennialism seemed to fare no better under Murray's investigation than had "modern dispensationalism."[52] In fact, Murray's review gave the distinct impression that *no* premillennial view could ever hope, really, to be defended competently. "Dr. Buswell's polemic is for premillennialism; ours must be against it,"[53] seemed to premillennialists to represent more and more the underlying attitude of the OPC, in general.

Thus, Charles Trumbull voiced the complaint of many premillennialists when he described the OPC as having "an attitude of mere toleration . . . toward the great multitude of true Christians who rejoice in what they count the Scriptural truth of the premillenial coming of Christ."[54] Trumbull observed that there were an exceptional

---

[48] John Murray, "Dr. Buswell's Premillennialism: A Review by John Murray," *PrGuard* 3 (27 February 1937): 209.

[49] Ibid., 206.

[50] Ibid.

[51] Ibid., 209.

[52] In the introduction to his book, Buswell had been willing to suggest that he had placed himself "on dangerous ground" in attempting "to disagree with such distinguished scholars as Warfield and Vos . . .". With exaggerated modesty, perhaps, Buswell even said, "I have not the slightest doubt that a hundred mistakes will be discovered by my friends as they read this work." (*Unfulfilled Prophecies*, 3). Nonetheless, premillennialists were none too keen on Murray's attempting to meticulously highlight each and every one of these mistakes in a review that went on for three and a half pages, but still lamented, at one point, "We wish we had space in which to quote the whole page in order to show the complete falsity of [Buswell's] allegation" (Murray, "Dr. Buswell's Premillennialism," 206). As for the reaction of Buswell himself to Murray's caustic review, apparently his written response bordered on acrimony; the editors of the *Presbyterian Guardian* informed their readers, "we are unwilling to publish [one section of Buswell's response] since, in our opinion, the section impugns the motives of the reviewer and is misleading in certain respects" ("Two Communications from Dr. Buswell," *PrGuard* 4 [10 April 1937]: 12).

[53] Ibid.

[54] Trumbull, "Dispensationalism and the Scofield Bible," 132. Cf. "S. S. Times Speaks on 'Pre-

few, "staunch Presbyterians" within the OPC who "regret" this attitude – regret shared also by those, perhaps like himself, "who [otherwise] would naturally be inclined to unite with this new denomination"[55] – but his impression was that the general attitude of OPC leaders toward premillennialism was unfortunately one of contempt. Trumbull objected, particularly, to the "vigorous teaching at Westminster Theological Seminary, Philadelphia, of what is known as amillennialism,"[56] and to the repeated attacks on "dispensationalism and premillennialism . . . in *The Presbyterian Guardian* of Philadelphia, which, while not an official organ, has been the unofficial voice of certain leaders in the new denomination."[57]

This pretty much summarized the feeling of premillennialists within the OPC. Even if their view continued to be tolerated *de jure*, they were becoming convinced that it would be deliberately and methodically marginalized *de facto*, both in the OPC and at Westminster Theological Seminary.[58]

Fifthly, mounting tensions were increased by a couple of other controversies brewing around this same time, in which the protagonists fell along much the same lines even though the specific issues involved were different. One of these controversies concerned the Independent Board for Presbyterian Foreign Missions. Specifically, it concerned those on this board who had been removed from the old church (PCUSA), but who, instead of joining the new Presbyterian Church (OPC), had simply remained "independent." A controversy ensued over whether the explicitly Presbyterian OPC should continue using such an "independent" board as its missions agency.[59]

All of the "independents" in question were premillennialists who had been Presbyterians previously, but who, having been "burned" by one denomination, did not feel compelled to join another one. The two most prominent were Harold S. Laird and Merril T. MacPherson. Dr. Laird, after having been defrocked from the First and Central Presbyterian Church of Wilmington, Delaware, established the First Independent Church (also in Wilmington); though officially independent, the church's doctrinal standards were the Westminster Confession of Faith and Catechisms.[60] Merril T. MacPherson became head of the Philadelphia Fundamentalists and pastored the Church of the Open Door. This church was composed mainly of those faithful to MacPherson after the PCUSA forcibly removed him in January

---

Mil.' Question," *CBeac* 2 (25 February 1937): 2, 4-5.

[55] Ibid.

[56] Ibid., 130.

[57] Ibid. A *Presbyterian Guardian* editorial once again emphatically denied Trumbull's characterizations (Ned B. Stonehouse, "Amillennialism and Westminster Seminary," *PrGuard* 3 [13 March 1937]: 219-20). Nevertheless, premillennialists perhaps cannot be blamed for thinking they had gotten this impression honestly, that this message had in fact been delivered to them unmistakably.

[58] Allan A. MacRae, interview by author, Quarryville, PA, 22 July and 3 August 1993.

[59] See Hutchinson, *The History Behind the Reformed Presbyterian Church Evangelical Synod*, 233-37; and Hart, *Defending the Faith*, 163-64.

[60] See "Rev. Harold S. Laird Leaves Westminster: Secretary to the Board of Trustees Since Organization," *CBeac* 2 (29 April 1937): 1-2;

1936, literally locking him out of his church building, the Central-North Presbyterian Church in Philadelphia.[61]

Defenders of the Independent Board for Presbyterian Foreign Missions argued that, despite the so-called "independency" of some of its members, all its members were clearly regarded as firm allies by everyone before the formation of the new church. Cutting off ties with them now would be a bitterly ironic display of ingratitude. Indeed, they argued, did not the old church accuse all the Orthodox Presbyterians, even they themselves, of "Independency," when they had formed the Independent Board for Presbyterian Foreign Missions in the first place?[62]

This argument recalled the original, controversial rationale for establishing the Independent Board, which was that it might be a trustworthy alternative to the Mission Board of the PCUSA. Creating a rival mission board had made clear that Presbyterian "fundamentalists" suspected PCUSA missionaries of being tainted with liberalist heresy; it was the single most offensive act to PCUSA leaders in the entire modernist-fundamentalist controversy and was also the single most common reason given for "fundamentalist" ministers being defrocked.[63]

The board was the brainchild of J. Gresham Machen,[64] who had been its president since its founding in 1933. In November of 1936, after a heated discussion, the membership voted to install MacPherson as vice-president, and Laird as president (despite Machen's earnest pleas to remain in this position). This move was thought by several of Machen's supporters to be an undermining of genuine "Presbyterianism," and, more pointedly, a betrayal of their most capable leader.[65]

Simultaneously, and entangled with these controversies, another set of disagreements arose over the proper Christian stance toward a number of personal lifestyle issues, including use of "intoxicating liquors," smoking, attending movies,

---

[61] See MacPherson, "Why I Am Pastor of an Independent Church," 3-4, 7; cf. "Philadelphia Fundamentalists Express Sympathy to Mr. MacPherson," *PrGuard* 2 (17 February 1936): 172; and "Church of Open Door Observes Anniversary," *CBeac* 2 (17 June 1937): 1.

[62] See "Presbyterians Fill Vacancies on Board for Foreign Missions: Small Group Resigns, and Declares Board Would Not Adopt Resolution Approving its Charter and Denouncing Independency," *CBeac* 2 (3 June 1937): 1-2, 4; and Carl McIntire, "Independency," *CBeac* 2 (3 June 1937): 4.

[63] See Rian, *The Presbyterian Conflict*, 97-257; Longfield, *The Presbyterian Controversy*, 181-235.

[64] Even some conservatives believed that Machen had gone too far in creating a rival mission board. E.g., Clarence E. Macartney issued a public statement condemning the board; Samuel D. Craig revealed, in a *Christianity Today* article, that he and twelve others had resigned as trustees of Westminster Seminary because of their disagreement with Machen over the Independent Board (*CT* 6 [February 1936]: 195); and Oswald T. Allis, who had left Princeton with Machen, resigned from the faculty of Westminster in 1936, because he could not support the Independent Board; Rian, *The Presbyterian Conflict*, 97-100; Longfield, *The Presbyterian Controversy*, 210-12; Hutchinson, *The History Behind the Reformed Presbyterian Church Evangelical Synod*, 208-10; Hart and Muether, *Fighting the Good Fight*, 32; and Allan A. MacRae, interview by author, Quarryville, PA, 3 August 1993.

[65] See Hutchinson, *The History Behind the Reformed Presbyterian Church Evangelical Synod*, 233-37; and Hart, *Defending the Faith*, 163-64.

dancing, and card playing.[66] Of these, the issue that generated the most discussion concerned the use of alcoholic beverages.

Within the OPC, advocates of total abstinence typically conceded that use of alcohol was not inherently sinful (e.g., they recognized that Jesus turned water into wine, an alcoholic beverage[67]). However, they believed that "expediency or advisability" argued against even a moderate use of alcohol, given the "speed-machine world" in which we live, "where there are no well-established social inhibitions."[68] Defenders of the moderate use of alcohol, typically of European background,[69] had trouble understanding why a temperate use of alcohol would stir such vigorous, emotional opposition. It seems these emotions could be understood only in light of the distinctive history of the issue in the U.S., where, among Christians, alcohol use was commonly regarded as an appalling vice, responsible for ravaging homes, destroying families, and threatening to undermine the peace and order of the entire society.

In the U.S., Christians had fought hard to gain passage of the Prohibition amendment (1919), only to see that legislation grow unpopular, then ineffective, until, finally, it was repealed (1933).[70] For many American fundamentalists, opposition to alcohol use had become instinctive, as had resentment toward those who advocated for its use. Meanwhile, the (mostly European) OPC Christians who advocated for alcohol's moderate use also saw the issue in straightforward terms; though they came to just the opposite view. They saw the issue as being one in which latitude toward individual judgment clearly should prevail, "on the principle that Christians should be free to follow the dictates of their own consciences in 'matters where the Bible has not pronounced judgment.'"[71] Some abstinence

---

[66] See Hutchinson, *The History Behind the Reformed Presbyterian Church Evangelical Synod*, 229-37; Hart and Muether, *Fighting the Good Fight*, 46-50.

[67] E.g., see R. Laird Harris, "Sunday School Lesson," *PrGuard* 3 (24 October 1936): 33; J. Oliver Buswell, Jr., *The Christian Life* (Grand Rapids: Zondervan, 1937), 86. Interestingly, biblical convictions against the use of alcohol seemed to grow stronger with time among the advocates of complete abstinence, as the controversies over alcohol intensified; see Hutchinson, *The History Behind the Reformed Presbyterian Church Evangelical Synod*, 229-31.

[68] Buswell, *The Christian Life*, 86-87 (the development of Buswell's entire point is contained in pp. 58-95).

[69] Machen was the outstanding exception to this; though an American, he also opposed Prohibition and he conscientiously refused to insist on complete abstinence as a principle of contemporary Christian conduct.

[70] See Marsden, *Fundamentalism and American Culture*, 13; and Mark Noll, *A History of Christianity in the United States and Canada* (Grand Rapids: Eerdmans, 1992), 295-99; Marsden and Noll both make mention also of conservative (evangelical) Christian involvement in the founding of the Temperance Party in 1869, the Women's Christian Temperance Union in 1874, and the American Anti-Saloon League in 1895. By 1897, abstinence from alcohol was a staple of American conservative Christian ideology, as reflected in the bestseller by Charles Sheldon, *In His Steps*, 1897, reprint (Waco, TX: Word Books, 1988), 60, 85-96, and *passim*. For a summary of the differences of opinion on the alcohol question in the OPC, see Hutchinson, *The History Behind the Reformed Presbyterian Church Evangelical Synod*, 225-30; Hart and Muether, *Fighting the Good Fight*, 49-51; and Hart, *Defending the Faith*, 164.

[71] Hart and Muether, *Fighting the Good Fight*, 50.

advocates found such defense of alcohol use by Christians nearly scandalous. Buswell warned Machen that the disagreement over alcohol was "'far more likely' to divide the church than 'any question of eschatology.'"[72]

To add to it all, Machen's premature and wholly unforeseen death on 1 January 1937 intensified the bitterness of all these controversies. In their grief, some of those who had sided with Machen in these last intra-conservative squabbles, publicly blamed the independent, premillenarian "fundamentalists" for his death.[73] To say the least, polarizations that had begun before Machen's death grew only more acute afterward.

And so, having failed to advance the premillennial view in the OPC and feeling more and more disenfranchised, premillennialists grew restless and ever more vigilant to gain official recognition for premillennialism in other organizations where they enjoyed prominence. In February of 1937, the Philadelphia Fundamentalists, whose membership included such well-known figures as E. Schuyler English and Merril T. MacPherson, adopted premillennialism constitutionally as their official doctrinal stance.[74] According to published reports,[75] they adopted this resolution partly in the hope of securing stronger ties with the "World Christian Fundamentalists Association," a larger, nationally known, and explicitly premillennial organization.[76]

---

[72] Hart, *Defending the Faith*, 164, quoting a letter from Buswell to Machen, 4 December 1936.

[73] Hart numbers even Machen's sister-in-law, Helen Woods Machen, among those who claimed that the November 1936 Independent Board meeting episode substantially weakened Machen's physical condition and stamina, setting him up for his fatal illness a month later (*Defending the Faith*, 163-64). Allan A. MacRae, who was at this Independent Board meeting, claimed that the entire episode was a tragic misunderstanding, provoked in no small part by well-meaning disciples of Machen who encouraged him to take personally the innocuous and perceptive suggestion by James Bennett, a lawyer from New York, that one man (Machen) should not be the head of every affiliate organization of the OPC. Machen did get very upset at the meeting, but, MacRae insisted, in a short time he gained a proper perspective on this whole thing and calmed down (Hart confirms this; *Defending the Faith*, 164). The sharp change in climate from Philadelphia to North Dakota (where he contracted pneumonia and died), his rigorous schedule, which he actually expanded before his northwest trip with a draining mountain climbing expedition, all might be considered more obvious factors in hastening Machen's death, rather than this tiff at the end of a life well acquainted with more substantive battles. As MacRae observed, none were more grieved by his death than those who happened to have opposed him at this meeting in November. As for the suggestion that this November episode might have contributed to his weakened physical condition? "Preposterous," responded MacRae (interview by author, Quarryville, PA, 2 June 1996).

[74] See "Fundamentalists Adopt Pre-Mil. View: Philadelphia Adopts Resolution with Little Opposition," *CBeac* 2 (11 February 1937): 1-2; cf. "Premillennialism Adopted Constitutionally by Philadelphia Fundamentalist Group: Several Premillennialist Members Raise Protests," *PrGuard* 3 (27 September 1937): 214.

[75] Ibid.

[76] Ironically, Glass lists "including premillennialism in it[s] doctrinal statement" among the factors that "hampered" the WCFA, which "never reached its goal of uniting Protestant conservatives under its fundamentalist banner" ("The Development of Northern Patterns of Fundamentalism in the South," 54-55).

This move only heightened animosities between OPC amillennialists and premillennialists and strengthened the impression that the premillennialist brand of "fundamentalism" was inherently at cross purposes with the "truly Reformed" agenda of the OPC. Finally, in June of 1937 several of the Presbyterian premillennialists split from the OPC altogether to form the explicitly premillenarian Bible Presbyterian Church.[77]

2.2.1 After-shocks from the Modernist-Fundamentalist Earthquake: The Collision of Two Conservative Agendas

> Briefly, [fundamentalism] was militantly anti-modernist Protestant evangelicalism. Fundamentalists were evangelical Christians, close to the traditions of the dominant American revivalist establishment of the nineteenth century, who in the twentieth century militantly opposed both modernism in theology and the cultural changes that modernism endorsed. Militant opposition to modernism was what most clearly set off fundamentalism from a number of closely related traditions, such as evangelicalism, revivalism, pietism, the holiness movements, millenarianism, Reformed confessionalism, Baptist traditionalism, and other denominational orthodoxies. Fundamentalism was a 'movement' in the sense of a tendency or development in Christian thought that gradually took on its own identity as a patchwork coalition of representatives of other movements. Although it developed a distinct life, identity, and eventually a sub-culture of its own, it never existed wholly independently of the older movements from which it grew. Fundamentalism was a loose, diverse, and changing federation of co-belligerents united by their fierce opposition to modernist attempts to bring Christianity into line with modern thought.[78]

In scrutinizing the circumstances that led to the break-up of the early OPC, we come to understand more clearly the tensions created by fundamentalism's diverse constituents and may add nuance to Marsden's classic appraisal. As Marsden suggests, "Reformed confessionalism" and "denominational orthodoxy" were strands of the fundamentalist "patchwork." How these strands would be woven into,

---

[77] See "Bible Presbyterian Fellowship Formed," *CBeac* 2 (10 June 1937): 1, 8; "'Bible Presbyterian Synod' Organized by Members Withdrawing from [OPC]: New Organization Joined by Fourteen Members and Three Elders," *PrGuard* 4 (26 June 1937): 99-100; "Bible Pres. Church Form of Government," *CBeac* 3 (18 August 1938): 1-2, 4-5; "Bible Presbyterian Synod Constituted a Church of the Lord Jesus Christ," *CBeac* 3 (8 September 1938): 1-2; "Bible Synod Adopts Historic Westminster Confession; Form of Government Determined" *CBeac* 3 (15 September 1938): 1-2, 5, 7. See also Rian, *The Presbyterian Conflict*, 227-44; Churchill, *Lest We Forget*, 123-35; Hart and Muether, *Fighting the Good Fight*, 41-57, 105-19; and Hutchinson, *The History Behind the Reformed Presbyterian Church Evangelical Synod*, 237-96.

[78] Marsden, *Fundamentalism and American Culture*, 4.

or deliberately pulled out away from, the other strands of the fundamentalist coalition seems to be the driving question of the late-1930s OPC controversies.

My contention is that, just as the ideology of the conservative Presbyterian "organic complex" was challenged – and thereby clarified – by the modernist-fundamentalist controversies of the 1920s, so likewise the 1936-38 controversies raised to consciousness what exactly were conservative Presbyterians' "basic beliefs and aims."[79] It turns out that, though their basic beliefs were similar, their aims proved to be quite dissimilar. As these aims developed, differences became pronounced enough to eventuate in two conservative agendas, which parted ways and pursued their own courses.

The circumstances that led to the separation of these two agendas were unique, distinctive to the array of convictions, commitments, and personalities linked together at that exceptional point in time. I, therefore, reject (as overly reductionist) explanations that characterize this rift as essentially a regression to some earlier controversy.

Among these, I reject the suggestion of Marsden himself that the issues that sparked the 1937 division were essentially the same as those that split "Old School" and "New School" Presbyterians a hundred years earlier.[80] Since this suggestion has garnered the support of historians on different sides of the controversy,[81] let me elaborate in more detail my objections to this suggestion. In so doing, my own thesis will be further clarified and reinforced.

---

[79] Again, I am employing for my thesis the terminology originally set forth by Max Kadushin (*Organic Thinking* [New York: Bloch Publishing Co., 1938], 2-16, 183-211; *idem*, *The Rabbinic Mind* [New York: Bloch Publishing Co., 1952], 24-31); E.P. Sanders (*Paul and Palestinian Judaism* [Philadelphia: Fortress Press, 1977], 72-75); and N.T. Wright (*The New Testament and the People of God* [Minneapolis, MN: Fortress Press, 1992], 125-26). Within an "organic complex," the worldview and fundamental convictions are more intuitively sensed and more subconsciously passed on by a given community. "Basic beliefs and aims" represent the ideological understandings and sociological aspirations that are more consciously affirmed and thus are more openly discussed and debated by that community.

[80] George Marsden, "Perspective on the Division of 1937," in *Pressing Toward the Mark: Essays Commemorating Fifty Years of the Orthodox Presbyterian Church*, ed. Charles G. Dennison and Richard C. Gamble (Philadelphia: The Committee for the Historian of the Orthodox Presbyterian Church, 1986), 296. Cf. also, in the same collection, *idem*, "The New School Heritage and Presbyterian Fundamentalism," 169-82. Cf. also Elwyn A. Smith's summarization: "A historian is tempted to generalize this history by seeing long-term swings between Old Side-Old School and New Side-New School trends. . . . For example, fundamentalism did not take form until the twentieth century, and when it did, it sustained the New Side emphasis on conversionism at the side of a nominal orthodoxy well to the right of Old School Calvinism" ("Presbyterianism in America" in *Encyclopedia of the Reformed Faith*, ed. Donald K. McKim [Louisville, KY: WJK, 1992], 298)..

[81] E.g., Hutchinson affirms the correlation between Old School and New School Presbyterianism as helpfully setting the 1936-38 controversies "against the background of the larger history of the old Church"; he adds, "This thesis is ably propounded by G. M. Marsden . . ." (*The History Behind the Reformed Presbyterian Church Evangelical Synod*, 242-43). Likewise, Hart cites, and builds upon, Marsden's thesis in his assessment of these events (*Defending the Faith*, 165-70, 207, nn. 8, 12, 16).

We first consider Marsden's framing of the 1936-38 division in terms of "strict," "objective," "authoritarian" subscriptionism (Old School) vs. "subjective," conversion-oriented, confessional latitudinarianism (New School).[82] In this framing, Machen and the Dutch Reformed at Westminster would represent the Old School *redivivus*, and Buswell, MacRae, et al., the New School.

When we look closely, however, we find that this description does not match the division of parties in 1936. Machen, remember, believed premillennialism violated a strict interpretation of the Westminster Standards; yet, he affirmed a "New School" type of rationale for accepting premillennialists within the OPC anyway. Recall that, in his view, "subscription to the Westminster Standards in The [OPC] is not to every word in those Standards, but only to the *system* of doctrine which the Standards contain."[83] J. Oliver Buswell, on the other hand, argued in very "Old School" fashion that strict subscriptionism was what provided the strongest rationale for accepting premillennialism within confessional parameters. In his view, the Westminster Divines, some of whom were premillennialists themselves, had deliberately left open the question of eschatological chronology so as to allow for a spectrum of views that implicitly included the premillennial view (in much the same way that, through a decided ambiguity of language, the question of supralapsarianism or infralapsarianism had been deliberately left open in the Confession).[84]

Examples such as this could be multiplied, in which the parties on each side are insufficiently accounted for, or actually defy the role assigned them, by the "Old School/New School redivivus" framing. Likewise, depiction of the 1930s controversies as a contest between a "New School" party content with a truncated list of basic, fundamentalist doctrinal affirmations and another party wanting a full-orbed Presbyterianism[85] is similarly unsatisfactory. In 1936, McIntire, no less than Machen, celebrated the founding of the OPC as the founding of a "true Presbyterian church." McIntire provided twice as many specifics than Machen for what this vision of doctrinal purity should entail, and he publicly articulated this vision two weeks sooner than Machen.[86] Even after leaving the OPC, the Bible Presbyterians cannot be characterized as more doctrinally lenient than the OPC. Though the Bible

---

[82] Marsden, "Perspective on the Division of 1937," 297, 323.

[83] Machen, "Premillennialism," 21.

[84] J. Oliver Buswell, Jr., "Premillennialism and the Reformed Faith: Has the 'Pre' a good standing?" *SSTimes* 76 (5 May 1934): 289-91; also "The Second General Assembly of the [OPC]," 70, 82-83; and "Dr. Buswell Speaks on Millennial Issue," *CBeac* 1 (17 December 1936): 7. Ironically, Buswell and Kuiper were closer on this point than either were to Machen (cf. R.B. Kuiper, "What's Right with the Orthodox Presbyterian Church?, Part One: Narrow in the Good Sense," *PrGuard* 15 [25 November 1946]: 323-24, 333; and *idem*, "What's Right with the Orthodox Presbyterian Church?, Part Two: Broad in the Good Sense," *PrGuard* 15 [10 December 1946]: 314-43). Cf. also John Frame, "Infralapsarianism" and William Klempa, "Supralapsarianism," in *Encyclopedia of the Reformed Faith*, 193-94, and 360-61.

[85] Marsden, "The New School Heritage and Presbyterian Fundamentalism," 169-81; also, Churchill, *Lest We Forget*, 29-31.

[86] Cf. Carl McIntire, "The True Presbyterian Church: Sermon Delivered Sunday Evening, June 7, 1936," *CBeac* 1 (11 June 1936): 2-3; J. Gresham Machen, "A True Presbyterian Church at Last," *PrGuard* 2 (22 June 1936): 110.

Presbyterian Synod added premillennial clarifications to the Westminster Standards, it deleted nothing save one (virtually inconsequential) phrase – it even preserved the OPC's elimination of the 1903 (PCUSA) amendments.[87]

Besides, the issues in contention in 1837 and 1937 were very different. What commissioner to the 1937 OPC Assembly would have been "at home"[88] with the Old School Presbyterian defense of slave labor?[89] Who among the 1937 commissioners would have been "at home" with the "New Theology" of New School Presbyterianism?[90]

I suggest that it is more helpful to recognize that *both* sides in the 1937 division had already established themselves as more "Old School" than "New School" when they broke with Princeton because of its alleged doctrinal compromises.[91] Perhaps it is somewhat useful to hearken back to the Old School-New School division in assessing that break; but similarities with the Old School-New School controversy pretty much end there.[92] One can understand the temptation to see "history repeat itself in [a] one-hundred-year cycle,"[93] but, as with most temptations, one is better

---

[87] "Proposed Changes to Confession of Faith," *CBeac* 3 (18 August 1938): 2. Deleted were the words "increased until it shall cover the earth" from the Confession of Faith, Chap. XXXIV, Sec. IV. Cf. also "Bible Synod Adopts Historic Westminster Confession; Form of Government Determined," *CBeac* 3 (15 September 1938): 1-2, 5, 7. "It is noteworthy that the [Bible Presbyterian] Synod of 1938 . . . rejected the 1903 revisions of the Confession of Faith" (Hutchinson, *The History Behind the Reformed Presbyterian Church Evangelical Synod*, 249); cf. also Hutchinson's account of McIntire's insistence, when the Bible Presbyterian Church was formed (4 June 1937), that it "would be 'a Presbyterian Church in every sense of the word'" over against, e.g., the view of Milo Jamison, who "wanted a 'Bible Church'" (247).

[88] This is Marsden's language ("Perspective on the Division of 1937," 296).

[89] See Jack P. Maddex, Jr., "Old School/New School," in *Encyclopedia of Religion in the South*, ed. Samuel S. Hill (Macon, GA: Mercer University Press, 1984), 570-72; and Ernest Trice Thompson, "The South and Sectionalism," *PrOut* 131 (17 January 1949): 5-6. Thompson's coverage of Southern Old School views of slavery (and other issues pertaining to relations between black and white races) is developed extensively in his *Presbyterians in the South, Volume One: 1607-1861* (Richmond, VA: John Knox Press, 1963); and *Presbyterians in the South, Volume Two: 1861-1890* (Richmond, VA: John Knox Press, 1973). It should be clearly understood that, because it regarded slavery as a socio-political issue, i.e., an area into which the Church should not intrude, Old School Presbyterianism opposed abolitionism, not just "extreme abolitionists," *pace* Hart and Muether (*Fighting the Good Fight*, 169, in an example of the influence of Marsden's thesis). The inadvertent strain for a "clarifying" adjective (viz., "extreme") I think is telling, serving as but one illustration of how strained really is the attempted correlation between the 1830s and the 1930s disputes overall.

[90] E.g., the members of the OPC, whether premillennial or non-premillennial, would likely have assessed and objected to the "New School" theology as vigorously as Lewis Cheeseman (*Differences Between Old and New School Presbyterians* [Rochester, NY: Erastus Darrow, 1848]).

[91] This is a point made by two authors representing opposite sides of the 1920s controversies; Rian, *The Presbyterian Conflict*, 13-28, 60-108; and Lefferts A. Loetscher *The Broadening Church* (Philadelphia: University of Pennsylvania Press, 1967), 9-18, 90-156.

[92] This, in fact, is exactly the place where Loetscher (*The Broadening Church*, 1-77, 136-56); Rian (*The Presbyterian Conflict*, 13-18); and Longfield (*The Presbyterian Controversy*, 32-180) all wisely end their drawing of this correlation.

[93] So Marsden, "Perspective on the Division of 1937," 296.

off not indulging it for very long. Marsden is right to clarify that "it is only partially true to say that there is a continuity between the New School and modernism,"[94] but, unfortunately, he then goes on to propose an even more significant continuity between the New School and fundamentalism; in doing so, he seems to screen out the gnat only to swallow the proverbial camel, historiographically speaking. "The situation was confused enough at the time, and may only become more so by the partial application of social theories based on other times and places."[95]

This flaw in Marsden's analysis does not, of course, mar significantly his otherwise masterful historiographical work. And, to be fair, simplification and generalization are normally useful tools for the historian, especially when use of such allows detection of broad overall patterns; it would be pedantic to object to their use as heuristic helps. What I am suggesting, nonetheless, is that the factors involved in the 1937 split in the OPC are especially subtle and complex, so that we must be more wary than usual.[96]

Likewise, prolepsis is another useful tool, normally, for presenting historical developments, but, in this case, prolepsis can all too easily develop into distortive, unhelpful anachronism. So, I am also suspicious of accounts of this controversy that speak in terms of what was "always clear" or what was "never in doubt" in the mind of Machen or McIntire or whoever else be deemed the keenest visionary of the OPC founders.[97]

My take on these events from 1936 to 1938 suggests that nothing was simple or clear, not even in the minds of the participants. All along it seems they were caught in a complex web of competing objectives, ambivalences, and the difficult task of prioritizing what they often agreed were all worthy goals.

---

[94] Marsden, "Perspective on the Division of 1937," 297.

[95] I am here borrowing the words of N. T. Wright, used originally, of course, in a very different context (*Jesus and the Victory of God* [Minneapolis, MN: Fortress Press, 1996], 159).

[96] Though Marsden notes the cautions of other historians against "any over-simplified attempt to extend the Old School-New School line of cleavage into the new Biblical questions," (quoting Loetscher, *The Broadening Church*, 27, in Marsden, "The New School Heritage and Presbyterian Fundamentalism," 169), Marsden succumbs, in my judgment, to just such oversimplification.

[97] This terminology is found commonly within works written, in part, to justify stances taken by one or the other side of the controversy. E.g., Churchill, *Lest We Forget*; Hart and Muether, *Fighting the Good Fight*; Marsden, "The New School Heritage and Presbyterian Fundamentalism," and "Perspective on the Division of 1937," are all published by The Committee for the Historian of the Orthodox Presbyterian Church. On the other side is Hutchinson, *The History Behind the Reformed Presbyterian Church Evangelical Synod*, published by the (now defunct) Mack Publishing Co., the unofficial publication arm of the Bible Presbyterian Church/Reformed Presbyterian Church Evangelical Synod. Cf. also Carl McIntire, "The Independent Board Challenged the Great Apostasy of the 20th Century and Drew the Line Between Belief and Unbelief in Christian Ministries and Made Church History," *Biblical Missions* (August 1993): 5-7; Carl McIntire, "Dr. Machen," *CBeac* 1 (7 January 1937): 4, 6; "Ind. Board Object of New Attack: Westminster Men Lead Attack and Move to Form New Board," *CBeac* 2 (10 June 1937): 1, 4-5, 7; "Independency," *CBeac* 2 (3 June 1937): 4; "The Independent Board Carries On Despite New Attacks," *CBeac* 2 (24 June 1937): 2, 4, 7.

It is not that the context is impossible to understand. Anyone who has ever served on a committee or board in which some issue becomes hotly disputed can relate to the dynamics of these circumstances. One does not normally stomp off in a huff the moment some disagreement arises. Whether or not one's own view wins the day in the end, somewhere along the way one goes through a process of weighing priorities. The person perhaps asks himself, "Is this 'a hill worth dying on'?" or "Is this something I can live with?" Rarely will a single issue divide members of a tight-knit group irreconcilably, and the chances of such division decrease if everyone has agreed, from the start, to a detailed doctrinal or vision statement. Usually, it takes a cluster of issues, some consolidation of various factors over time – each on their own inconsequential perhaps, but, cumulatively, attaining a power greater than the sum of the parts – to achieve, in their combined force, that critical mass where a person or bloc of persons feels pushed to win at whatever cost, or leave.

This is the sort of accumulation of factors that we see taking place in the 1936-38 OPC controversies. This in mind, we begin to understand the dynamics of polarization that were at work. Even the sorts of dynamics that battlefield analysts commonly observe seem to have come into play in the 1936-38 controversies; for instance, what might be called the "no turning back now" phenomenon, or the "raising the ante" phenomenon.[98] These phenomena refer to a relatively straightforward principle: the determination to achieve an objective grows in proportion to the costs sustained. If the costs sustained are excessive, then the level of commitment to achieving that objective likewise will be exceptionally high ("no turning back now"). If there are unanticipated costs, or if costs accumulate over time to an unexpectedly high level ("raising the ante"), then the likelihood increases that further objectives, likewise unanticipated (or at least previously unannounced), will get added to the original agenda ("no turning back now") so as to retroactively justify those original costs.

We can see these phenomena progressively taking effect in 1936-38 in three stages (conveniently demarcated by the OPC General Assembly Meetings one, two, and three). In stage one, there is a relatively minor squabble over whether the 1903 PCUSA amendments to the Westminster Confession should be deleted in the OPC's confession. Not a word had been mentioned about revising the Confession before the OPC had been formed. Yet once the costs of being expelled from the PCUSA had been sustained, the "ante was raised." In the arguments for deleting these 1903 amendments, one can detect a clear theme of "no turning back now"; having come so far and sacrificed so much to gain a "true, pure Presbyterian church," so the arguments go, the OPC should not be content now with any half measures or compromises (despite the willingness to endure such compromises before).[99]

---

[98] An eloquent example of such analysis of battlefield exploits is provided by Ernest Hemingway, "Introduction," in *Men at War: The Best War Stories of All Time*, ed. Ernest Hemingway (New York: Bramhall House, 1942), xi-xxvii.

[99] See Ned B. Stonehouse, "What Was Back of the Revision of 1903?" *PrGuard* 2 (26 September 1936): 247-49; John Murray, "Shall We Include the Revision of 1903 in Our Creed?" *PrGuard* 2 (12 September 1936): 249-51; and J. Gresham Machen, "A Step to Avoid," *PrGuard* 3 (10 October 1936): 1-2. See also Marsden, "Perspective on the Division of 1937," 302.

At this point, no party lines of dispute are clearly drawn.

> [T]he issue of the exclusion of the 1903 amendments from the constitution was not ultimately one of the major factors in the division of the denomination. . . . Whatever notes of discord there were at that First General Assembly seem to have been swallowed up by the dominant theme of harmony and of hope. "There were sometimes vigorous exchanges of opinion," commented the Guardian. "But always there was the unity of the spirit in the bond of peace." [H. McAllister Griffiths, "Editorial: Looking Backward and Ahead," PrGuard 2 (22 June 1936): 111]. When the First General Assembly adjourned there were only intimations of anything [sic] but concord among its members.[100]

"We desire to say again that we think it to be a matter of central importance that the 1903 Amendments to the doctrinal standards of the Presbyterian Church in the U.S.A. should be omitted from our Standards," Machen urged just before the next Assembly. He then noted, gratefully, "We are glad to observe that the Presbytery of California, though severely critical of us on another matter [viz., premillennialism], is with us in this matter."[101]

However, those caught by surprise by this "raising of the ante" – deleting the 1903 amendments was a factor in costing some of them their church properties[102] – now had an even higher stake in winning the next round of any fight that should occur. Stage two brought that next fight: over premillennialism.

This issue was more central to the core concerns of all sides. They all had separated from the PCUSA in large part because of their concern for purity of doctrine. A good portion of the premillennialists among them felt that premillennialism was an aspect of that "doctrinal purity" for which they had sacrificed so much. For them, the premillennial view was not just a view to be allowed, but was rather a key plank in a thoroughly conservative treatment of Scripture.[103] On the other hand, non-premillennialists had up to then been willing to overlook the premillennial aberration, but many deemed it not thoroughly consistent with the confessionally sustained Reformed faith for which they, too, had fought hard.[104]

---

[100] Marsden, "Perspective on the Division of 1937," 302.

[101] J. Gresham Machen, "The 1903 Amendments," *PrGuard* 3 (14 November 1936): 45. Thus, Marsden's statement, which he makes just after the previous quotation, is not quite accurate. "But by the time the Second General Assembly met, five months later, the lines of division between the two parties in the church had already been sharply drawn" ("Perspective on the Division of 1937," 302).

[102] Rian, *The Presbyterian Conflict*, 234-35; Hutchinson, *The History Behind the Reformed Presbyterian Church Evangelical Synod*, 224; and Hart and Muether, *Fighting the Good Fight*, 47.

[103] E.g., McIntire, "Premillennialism," 4; Allan A. MacRae, "The Millennial Kingdom of Christ," *CBeac* 2 (16 March 1937): 3-4, 7; MacPherson, "Why I Am Pastor of an Independent Church," 3.

[104] E.g., Murray, "Dr. Buswell's Premillennialism," 206, 209; *idem*, "What Is Amillennialism?" *PrGuard* 3 (27 March 1937): 242-44; Kuiper, "Why Separation Was Necessary," 226-27; *idem*, "The Reply of Dr. Kuiper," 54-55; *idem*, *As To Being Reformed* (Grand Rapids: Eerdmans, 1926),

At this time, though, in 1936, there were not sufficient representatives of either position that felt strongly enough to make a division of "sides" clear-cut. At that time, at least some of the premillennialists did not want an added constitutional confirmation of premillennialism any more than they wanted premillennialism outlawed.[105] Likewise, non-premillennialists were careful to make clear that the unity of the church was far more important to them than espousal of any particular eschatological view.[106] One can find threats of a split in some quarters,[107] but the critical mass for division has not yet been reached. Yet the forces of division have now begun to accumulate enough to make an inchoate formation of sides visible. Political maneuvering for position and vying for power begins to take hold. This seems mostly to be what the fracas over "independency" is about (i.e., concerning the "independency" of the Independent Board for Presbyterian Foreign Missions, and the controversial election of Laird over Machen as its president).

Finally, stage three: open warfare breaks out. Yet another major issue comes into play, viz., the use of alcoholic beverages. It so happened that some of the very premillennialists who did not feel strongly enough about premillennialism to favor a split did feel so strongly about the abstinence issue (or, at least, about abstinence and premillennialism together).[108] Swirling around the ideological and tactical points of disagreement, meanwhile, are numerous other, less tangible factors that added momentum to the forces of division.

There were severe personality conflicts. And, the personalities involved were strong; these persons had already proven themselves resolute enough to leave the PCUSA, and to lead their churches and other people under their influence to leave with them, at great cost. A certain panache, a streak of stubbornness, is required to take these kinds of actions – character traits which, of course, have an underside.

Perhaps the picture can be brought into sharper focus by considering a contrasting example of what did *not* come into controversy, but could have, had the unique circumstances been different. Consider: why did John Murray's views on the Decalogue, particularly his sabbatarian views, not come into play in the controversy? It was not because Murray was so complacent that he would not contend for his convictions strongly; he was willing to forego ordination in his own beloved Free Presbyterian Church of Scotland because of his views on these

---

123-31; Ned B. Stonehouse, "The Creed of Our Fathers," 253-54.

[105] We recall the arguments of premillennialists Buswell and Martin Luther Thomas against the addition of premillenarian adjustments to the OPC doctrinal standards; "The Second General Assembly of the [OPC]," 70, 83.

[106] Kuiper, "The Reply of Professor Kuiper"; Machen, "Premillennialism"; *idem*, "The Root of the Trouble"; and *idem*, "The Millennial Question."

[107] Hart and Muether, *Fighting the Good Fight*, 47.

[108] This is particularly true in the case of Buswell; see the sections, "Strong Drink," and "Christian Liberties," in Buswell, *The Christian Life*, 85-91. See also Allan A. MacRae, "Dr. Allan A. MacRae Resigns Seminary: Founder of Westminster Opposes Its Present Stand," *CBeac* 2 (29 April 1937): 2; also Carl McIntire, "Abstinence," *CBeac* 2 (17 June 1937): 4 (though McIntire apparently would have been willing to split earlier, over premillennialism alone). Cf. also Hart, *Defending the Faith*, 164-66; Marsden, "Perspective on the Division of 1937," 320; and Hutchinson, *The History Behind the Reformed Presbyterian Church Evangelical Synod*, 236-37.

points.[109] He would one day write a book in which he defended these views in no uncertain terms.[110] Nor was it that these issues were inherently benign; such issues had been a factor in several splits within the Scottish Presbyterian church over the past 250 years.[111] OPC constituents certainly were not united on these issues. So, why did these issues not become part of the 1936-38 controversies when other, similar issues did?

The reasons are telling. Murray was the lone Scottish Presbyterian at Westminster. Thus, even when his views seemed strident, his isolated, minority status precluded his ever being perceived as a threat. Imagine, though, if Machen had brought with him more than one "true blue Scot" from Princeton?[112] What if half of the faculty members of Westminster had been of such stock? In such a scenario, Murray's distinctly Scottish views might have posed quite a problem. We can begin to understand, then, why the Dutch-Reformed emphasis, which was in fact represented by three of the eight original faculty members of Westminster,[113] could be perceived by some as having an ominous influence on Machen and as carrying undue weight in forming the vision for the new American Presbyterian denomination.

Additionally, Murray had a soft spoken quality that endeared him even to those who might occasionally disagree with him strongly; his mild demeanor also permitted his more strident views to be tolerated as quaint – quixotic at times, perhaps, but overall quite harmless.[114] On the other hand, views defended by

---

[109] Iain H. Murray, *The Life of John Murray* (Edinburgh: The Banner of Truth Trust, 1982), 35-36.

[110] John Murray, *Principles of Conduct: Aspects of Biblical Ethics* (Grand Rapids: Eerdmans, 1957), 82-106, 181-201, 202-28, 263-65.

[111] See Ian Hamilton, *The Erosion of Calvinist Orthodoxy: Seceders and Subscription in Scottish Presbyterianism* (Edinburgh: Rutherford House Books, 1990), 126; David Lachman, *The Marrow Controversy, 1718-1723: An Historical and Theological Analysis* (Edinburgh: Rutherford House Books, 1988), 395-401; also N.R. Needham, "Sabbatarianism," in *Dictionary of Scottish Church History and Theology*, ed. Nigel M. de S. Cameron, David F. Wright, David C. Lachman, and Donald E. Meek (Downers Grove, IL: IVP, 1993), 737-38.

[112] This is R.B. Kuiper's description of Murray ("What's Right with The Orthodox Presbyterian Church, Part Two," 341).

[113] Viz., Cornelius Van Til, R.B. Kuiper, and Ned Stonehouse.

[114] Allan MacRae related to me several examples of Murray's peculiar sabbatarian views manifesting themselves in charming, sometimes humorous, ways. Murray visited MacRae while he was studying in Germany. Knowing that it was Murray's first time in that country, MacRae took Murray on a tour of sites in downtown Berlin after church one Sunday. Murray sat quietly as they rode around, MacRae garrulously remarking on various buildings, streets, shops, etc. Finally, MacRae asked Murray how some of the structures compared to the architecture in Scotland, to which Murray replied, "I do not like to think on such things on the Sabbath." For a few years, Murray and MacRae were the only bachelors on the faculty at Westminster, and so were often invited together to parishioners' homes as Sunday dinner guests. More than once, MacRae heard Murray give an answer similar to what he had given MacRae in Germany, should their hosts query Murray about sports or politics "on the Sabbath." Apparently, Murray had strict scruples regarding the ninth commandment, too. On one occasion, several Westminster faculty were at a social event playing a parlor game called, "I doubt it." The game required players to deceive those on the other team concerning such things as how many of a certain card one was holding, etc. John Murray was glad to play, but was soon discovered to be

Cornelius Van Til or others of "the Dutch" seemed consistently to strike others as abrasive, and sometimes downright pugnacious.[115] Not only did the Dutch variety of Reformed theology seem to have a hard-line, hyper-Calvinist quality to it that made many of the American Presbyterians uneasy,[116] those representing it at Westminster seemed to defend it with an air of condescension that struck those already uncomfortable as all the more disagreeable.

We get a glimpse of these dynamics in published reports of early assembly meetings. For instance, in late 1936, Carl McIntire was embroiled in a vicious court battle involving his church property, valued, at that time, at $200,000.00 (i.e., well over $2,000,000.00 in today's dollars).[117] In considering the question of the new church's doctrinal standards at the second General Assembly, McIntire acknowledged that the PCUSA amendments of 1903 were "weak"; he was not himself thrilled with their theological nuance. However, given that most all the commissioners to that OPC Assembly had earlier been willing to subscribe to them, McIntire argued that continuing under the same creed as before seemed "the normal thing to do."[118]

> Mr. McIntire went on to say that the adoption of those standards would be of immense help in the retention of church property, since we could then say that we still had exactly the same creed as before. To this Dr. Cornelius Van Til promptly replied by saying, "Shall we be Arminians before the courts this year, with the full expectation of

---

dreadful at the game – his scruples would not allow him to "bear false witness" even in such a frivolous context! (Allan and Grace MacRae, interview by author, Quarryville, PA, 3 August 1993).

[115] John Frame, an admirer and biographer of Van Til, mentions Van Til's penchant for satire, and for intimidating questioners with sardonic erudition; he could endure those who disagreed with him, adds Frame, but "he often took on a kind of preaching mode, in which every intellectual issue became a matter of loyalty to the Scriptures and the Reformed standards, and any deviation became a concession to non-Christian thought" (*Cornelius Van Til: An Analysis of His Thought* [Phillipsburg, NJ: P & R, 1995], 30). According to Frame, Van Til's preferred style of engagement was "one of confrontation, not at all one of dialogue. . . . He also regularly said harshly negative things about Roman Catholic theology, Arminianism, and even 'less consistent Calvinism.' He often spoke about the 'isolation' of the Reformed faith over against the rest of the theological world. . . . Whether he was right or wrong in this, the result was more isolation. He was not in dialogue with these other types of theology; he confronted them. It was not a relationship in which the parties could learn from one another; rather, it was a fight to the finish" (35-36).

[116] "Some Dutch-American groups" are specified by Peter Toon, along with only two other groups (viz., Strict and Particular Baptists), as affirming "hyper-Calvinism" ("Hyper-Calvinism," in *Encyclopedia of the Reformed Faith*, 190). I understand, of course, that defining "hyper-Calvinism" (and what makes it "hyper") historically has proven to be notoriously difficult. My point here is that Dutch-Reformed theology, in general, has had a reputation for being a particularly strong variety of Reformed theology, even among advocates of Reformed theology.

[117] Rian refers to the McIntire case as "the most outstanding case [in the modernist-fundamentalist controversies] involving church property" (*Presbyterian Conflict*, 249).

[118] Carl McIntire, as quoted by Thomas R. Birch, "The Second General Assembly of the [OPC]," *PrGuard* 3 (28 November 1936): 82.

being Calvinists next year?" Debate was cut off by the moving of the previous question, and the New Jersey overture was, to the gratification of many, lost."[119]

We get a feel, then, for the sort of personality and socio-political dynamics at work in the 1936-38 controversies. The original faculty of Westminster consisted of Machen, MacRae, Robert Dick Wilson, O.T. Allis, Paul Woolley, Van Til, Kuiper, and Stonehouse. In 1930, systematic theologian John Murray joined the Westminster faculty; that same year, Wilson, MacRae's mentor, died. Allis would leave Westminster in 1935 over disagreements with Machen concerning the Independent Board.

This meant that, by 1936, MacRae, Woolley, and Stonehouse were the only faculty members at Westminster who had served in the PCUSA with Machen and who had left that American Presbyterian Church to start the OPC. Van Til left the Christian Reformed Church (a Dutch-Reformed body) to start the OPC in 1936; Kuiper did not leave the Christian Reformed Church and Murray did not leave the Free Church of Scotland to join the OPC until after Machen's death.[120] Stonehouse was also of Dutch-Reformed background; his views were very much in line with Van Til's and Kuiper's. Woolley, though a premillennialist like MacRae, was nevertheless vigorously loyal to Machen; he could be counted on to follow whatever course Machen deemed best – to convince Machen was to convince Woolley.[121]

Some causes of the growing division are thus put in perspective. In 1930, the "old Princeton" evidentialist voice of Robert Dick Wilson[122] was lost, while throughout the 1930s the very vocal, Dutch-Reformed "presuppositionalist" voice of Cornelius Van Til just got stronger. Some of the most strident of John Murray's Scottish-Reformed sympathies fell much in line with the Dutch-Reformed.[123] Furthermore, the Dutch seemed to have a growing influence on Machen, patriarch of them all; with Machen went Woolley (and a host of others). In other words, the early changeover of personnel at Westminster represented, to some degree, a trade of Princeton-style American Presbyterianism for a narrower, European brand of

---

[119] Ibid.

[120] See R.B. Kuiper, "What's Right with The Orthodox Presbyterian Church, Part Two: Broad in the Good Sense," 341; and Murray, "Life of John Murray," 69.

[121] Woolley himself says as much in *The Significance of J. Gresham Machen Today* (Nutley, NJ: P & R, 1977), 38-48. This was certainly the impression Woolley gave to others at the time; see "Woolley Protests Seminary Story," *CBeac* 2 (1 July 1937): 2; "Premillennialism Adopted Constitutionally By Philadelphia Fundamentalist Group: Several Premillennialist Members Raise Protests," *PrGuard* 3 (27 September 1937): 214; also Allan A. MacRae, interview by author, Quarryville, PA, 2 June 1996.

[122] See D.G. Hart, "Robert Dick Wilson," in *Dictionary of the Presbyterian & Reformed Tradition in America*, ed. D.G. Hart and Mark A. Noll (Downers Grove, IL: IVP, 1999), 278.

[123] Cf. the following essays in *The Practice of Confessional Subscription*, ed. David W. Hall (Lanham, MD: University Press of America, 1995): W. Robert Godfrey, "Subscription in the Dutch Reformed Tradition," 67-75; J. Ligon Duncan, III, "Owning the Confession: Subscription in the Scottish Presbyterian Tradition," 77-91; John Murray, "Creedal Subscription in the Presbyterian Church in the U.S.A.," 247-62; and John R. Muether, "Confidence in Our Brethren: Creedal Subscription in the Orthodox Presbyterian Church," 301-10.

Reformed theology, which was not what MacRae, Buswell, McIntire, et al. had in mind when they sacrificed their church properties, ordinations, and denominational standing – sacrifices that none of these Europeans had made – to found a new American Presbyterian denomination.[124]

This helps explain why it was not until R.B. Kuiper, one of "the Dutch," took an off-handed swipe at the Scofield Bible, that OPC premillennialists became agitated enough to respond. They had initially let the articles against "modern dispensationalism" by Murray pass.[125] Nonetheless, from these premillennialists' perspective, these were persons who were not even members of their church, who had made none of the sacrifices they had made, setting themselves up as arbiters of what was or was not "Reformed" enough for their church. It was not that OPC premillennialists were just "thick" and failed to grasp the distinctions that Kuiper and Murray suggested between "acceptably Reformed" premillennialism and unacceptable, "un-Reformed" premillennialism. Rather, OPC premillennialists objected to these people being the ones who decide the terms of acceptability in the first place.

That Machen seemed willing to go along with their terms only made matters worse for OPC premillennialists. They began to feel like a persecuted minority; in other words, just like they had felt in the old PCUSA, which they had sacrificed much to escape. It was not long before these premillennialists began complaining that the same "machine" mentality of the old church had overtaken the new one.[126]

---

[124] Though it simmers beneath the surface throughout most of the conflict, Carl McIntire voiced this objection explicitly in his response to criticisms of the "independency" of the Independent Board for Presbyterian Foreign Missions. "Certainly their charges that the Board is not Presbyterian fall to the ground with their own weight. Every member of the Board has fought for the great truths of the Presbyterian faith and polity. . . . The issue certainly could not be one of the [OPC] because even after the departure of the Westminster element the [OPC] had a majority of actual members on the Independent Board. . . . Only three men were objected to – Mr. Laird, Mr. MacPherson, and Dr. Brumbaugh. These three men have sacrificed their churches and their ecclesiastical life for the great fundamentals of the Scripture and the testimony of the Independent Board. These men were asked to leave the Board. Think of it! They who asked it have paid no price – they are not pastors!" ("Independency," 4). Cf. R.B. Kuiper, "Presbyterianism versus Independentism," *PrGuard* 6 (April 1939): 63-64.

[125] "[T]he editor of the *Guardian*, McAllister Griffiths, himself a premillennialist, tried to make emphatically clear that [Murray's] articles were not to be interpreted as an effort to read premillennialists out of the church, for Presbyterians believe in 'eschatological freedom' to hold various views about the second coming of Christ" (Hutchinson, *The History Behind the Reformed Presbyterian Church Evangelical Synod*, 222; quoting from Griffiths' introduction to Murray's articles, *PrGuard* 2 [4 May 1936]: 44, 52). Griffiths served as editor of the *Presbyterian Guardian* until September 1936; see J. Gresham Machen, "A Man for the Hour," *PrGuard* 2 (12 September 1936): 221-22.

[126] H. McAllister Griffiths, "Since the Syracuse General Assembly: Machine Politics in the [OPC]." *CBeac* 2 (September 1937): 1-2. See also Hutchinson, *The History Behind the Reformed Presbyterian Church Evangelical Synod*, 224-25. References to a political "machine" recalled the complaint Machen submitted originally against the PCUSA. "The first act of the Assembly is to elect a Moderator. One of you ought to nominate a moderator who is opposed to the present Modernist and indifferentist machine, and all of you ought to vote for him. There is not the slightest chance that any such Moderator will be elected, but that does not affect your

Look closely, and one finds that the real complaint is against the Dutch exerting undue influence.

> Eight years ago three ministers of the Presbyterian Church in the U.S.A. associated with themselves one other Presbyterian minister (myself) and four members of other communions, in establishing an institution to train men to carry on the spiritual succession of the old Princeton Seminary. Today, in the providence of God, two of the three founders have died and the other has left the Seminary. Control of the Faculty and direction of its policies has passed into the hands of a small alien group without American Presbyterian background... The alien group to which I have referred considers no one to be truly Presbyterian unless he agrees with them in everything which they choose to call essential to being "Reformed" – much of which is derived from their own non-Presbyterian background.[127]

Likewise, McIntire explained, "Our own feeling about the matter is that the great issue of the day is Modernism and unbelief, and . . . we cannot walk with these men because they are trying to build a Christian Reformed Church instead of a Presbyterian Church . . .".[128]

As long as Machen was alive, the premillennialists seem to have held out hope of reversing the situation; perhaps they thought they could eventually win Machen (back) to their side. In any case, it is clear in retrospect that only Machen's views, actions, and manner held any potential for appeasing all sides. For instance, Machen himself practiced total abstinence from both alcohol and tobacco, but he opposed Prohibition on principle and he was known to supply other faculty with fine cigars.[129] No one was identical to Machen on this volatile issue, yet his views and practices put no one's nose too far out of joint, either. This is paradigmatic for understanding Machen's central role in holding the conservative Presbyterian coalition together.

Accounting for Machen's response to the controversy over "dispensationalism" is, therefore, most worthwhile. Three different explanations of Machen's "true feelings" toward dispensational premillennialism have been offered by different biographical analysts.

---

duty in the slightest" (J. Gresham Machen, "What Should True Presbyterians Do at the 1936 General Assembly [of the PCUSA]?" *PrGuard* 2 [18 May 1936]: 70).

[127] MacRae, "MacRae Resigns Seminary," 1-2.

[128] McIntire, "Give Thanks," 4. Cf. Frame's analysis, which, though terse, is nonetheless one of the few to identify this point precisely. "The controversy was over dispensationalism, 'Christian liberty' (the legitimacy of alcoholic beverages), and the vague feeling among the departing members that the new movement was becoming too Dutch, that it was losing its roots in American Presbyterianism" (*Van Til: An Analysis of His Thought*, 24).

[129] Ned B. Stonehouse, *J. Gresham Machen: A Biographical Memoir* (Grand Rapids: Eerdmans, 1954), 391-32; Woolley, *The Significance of J. Gresham Machen Today*, 19-20; Hart and Muether, *Fighting the Good Fight*, 50; Hart, *Defending the Faith*, 164; Allan A. MacRae, interview by author, Quarryville, PA, 3 August 1993.

Hart and Muether contend that Machen, from the beginning, had a clear, explicit, and exclusively Reformed-Presbyterian agenda, which would tolerate premillennialists only insofar as they were willing to affirm this agenda. Under this view, Machen always had substantial reservations about the un-Reformed proclivities of certain premillennialist ideologies, and thus consistently held a clear line in his mind, beyond which he would not cross, that demarcated how far he would go in supporting a premillennial variety of conservatism. He was never desirous of its becoming very influential in the agenda he was trying to establish.

> From its inception the OPC was faced with a choice between being Reformed and being fundamentalist. From Machen's perspective there was never any doubt about what the church should be. He had left Princeton to found Westminster in order to perpetuate the training of Old School Presbyterian ministers. And he helped to found the OPC as a church in which Westminster's graduates could minister. As it turned out, the Reformed identity of the OPC after the division of 1937 was virtually identical to Machen's original vision for the church.[130]

Churchill offers a slightly different explanation. He suggests that Machen, despite what he thought were minor disagreements, genuinely supported and wholeheartedly leagued with (dispensational) premillennialists initially. He became disillusioned with them, only later on, when he found that they adamantly supported un-Reformed doctrines and that they maneuvered contentiously to get their positions established. Under this view, Machen only gradually and reluctantly withdrew his support from these un-Reformed premillennialists, eventually feeling forced to combat directly these former allies.

> Dr. Machen and those who marched with him against apostasy had to draw their supporters from this conservative element of the church. But many in the conservative sector had been pulled away from the breadth of true presbyterian doctrine and life into a narrow fundamentalism. . . . Up until the time of the formation of The Orthodox Presbyterian Church, everyone had engaged in a common battle against modernism. Dr Machen was well aware of the tides of unbelief flowing from Germany, for he had studied there; but he was not as familiar with the undertow of dispensationalism. At any rate, his awareness of modern fundamentalism never included the notion that those who upheld dispensationalism and the "pre-mil" position would weaken either the stand against liberal unbelief or the desire

---

[130] Hart and Muether, *Fighting the Good Fight*, 52. Hart and Muether explain Machen's earlier support for Presbyterian dispensational-premillennialist, Donald Grey Barnhouse, as follows: "Machen was by no means a supporter of Barnhouse, a minister partial to dispensational premillennialism and indifferent to Westminster – but Machen was alarmed by the proceedings [against Barnhouse, conducted by liberal PCUSA officers], believing it would set an important precedent" (33). Cf. Hart's similar explanation for Machen's earlier relationship with the World's Christian Fundamentals Association and with other predominantly Baptist and dispensational-premillennialist fundamentalist groups (*Defending the Faith*, 64-65).

to maintain a truly presbyterian heritage. When this, in fact, began to take place I believe it was a surprise to him and a source of deep heartache. As he became more aware of the danger and as the conflict increased, this time behind his own lines, he met it forthrightly, urging us to "dust off our catechism," to open our Bibles and to get our priorities in order. With the same care and precision that he had displayed in the struggles against modernism, he exposed the methods and conclusions of dispensationalism as unscriptural and dangerous.[131]

MacRae offers a third explanation. In MacRae's view, Machen started out with a vision for Westminster Seminary and for the OPC which all the constituents of the conservative Presbyterian movement could affirm, one that was Reformed and Presbyterian, but that was evangelical and Christian first and foremost. Some of Machen's supporters, however, were less magnanimous, were more doctrinaire in their Calvinism, and were more fastidious in the subscriptionism they demanded. Once the new denomination was founded, Machen came more and more under the sway of these fellows, and became more and more enamored with their narrower vision of what a "truly Reformed, truly Presbyterian" church should be. Though Machen was never a premillennialist, dispensational-premillennialism was not of particular concern to him, either; it was not an ox he would have gored. But once these more "truly Reformed" colleagues did make dispensationalism an issue, Machen felt his hand was called. He did agree with their doctrinal position (i.e., he was not a premillennialist), so, put in the position of having to publicly declare himself, Machen sided with them. Unfortunately, from MacRae's perspective, this meant that the OPC unnecessarily alienated some of its strongest supporters and simultaneously narrowed its vision considerably from where it had started, to the point that only the most intolerant and dogmatic of its Reformed-Presbyterian constituents could fully support the new direction taken.[132]

Which of these explanations is correct? In truth, good evidence could be used to support any one of them. MacRae and Churchill both knew Machen personally, so we are intrigued by their agreement, *contra* Hart and Muether, that Machen wholeheartedly leagued with premillennialist supporters at first, that he willfully overlooked some of their disagreements and considered them minor in light of their greater common cause against modernism. On the other hand, Hart's and Muether's conclusions are supported by the best research, including personal letters, which provide insight into Machen's private feelings and thoughts to which neither MacRae nor Churchill ever had access.[133]

---

[131] Churchill, *Lest We Forget*, 129-31.

[132] MacRae, "Dr. Allan A. MacRae Resigns Seminary," 1-2, 8; interview by author, Quarryville, PA, 22 July and 3 August 1993.

[133] We understand that what one says in such private moments may not reflect the totality of how one "really" feels; anyone who has ever "vented their spleen" to a friend, spouse, or other close family member knows that. Nevertheless, in my judgment, Hart's use of personal letters to bring unique insight into what Machen was thinking at the time is consistently helpful; e.g., Hart, *Defending the Faith*, 64, 89, 151, 185, n. 15, 186, n. 19, 191, nn. 12-13, 192, n. 19, 204, n.

MacRae's explanation seems to fit best, *prima facie*, with my own thesis, in that his explanation explicitly confirms my contention that divergent agendas among Machen's original supporters developed over time. Some of the weaknesses in the other explanations are overcome by MacRae's explanation, and some strong points in the other explanations can be incorporated into his, as well. For example, MacRae accounts for Machen's tentativeness in explaining why dispensational premillennialism was not a focus of concern before 1936, and why Machen's feelings against it grew so pronounced only after the OPC was formed.[134] Churchill accurately recounts the adversarial relationship between those holding the "pre mil position" and those most outspoken about their "desire to maintain a truly presbyterian heritage,"[135] but Churchill overlooks that this adversarial relationship started with attacks on premillennialist sentiments from two persons who were not, at the time, even members of the OPC. MacRae's explanation, on the other hand, accounts for why some of the most vocal premillennialists (e.g., McIntire, MacRae, Buswell) would have begun the "truly presbyterian" OPC with Machen, while some of the most hard-line Reformed-Presbyterians (e.g., Kuiper, Murray) did not join the OPC until after Machen's death. For these and similar reasons, I find MacRae's explanation to be quite satisfactory, at least as satisfactory as the other two.[136]

For the sake of argument, though, let us imagine that the explanation that differs most from MacRae's (viz., Hart's and Muether's) is correct. In that case, Machen would always have regarded the premillennialists with a certain ambivalence. Knowing that their position was not strictly within confessional parameters, and knowing that his vision was for a confessionally pure church, Machen also would have known all along that the premillennial position would one day probably need to be marginalized; and he well might have suspected that premillennialists would not be happy about that. It is true, as Hart and Muether correctly observe, that Machen's celebrity status as the hero of conservative, biblical faith did sometimes blind other conservatives to points at which Machen disagreed with them.[137] Thus, it is possible

---

41, 206-07, nn. 7, 9, 10.

[134] Hart and Muether acknowledge this tentativeness, but do not explain it; see *Fighting the Good Fight*, 46.

[135] Churchill, *Lest We Forget*, 131.

[136] This explanation has gained a recent advocate also in John Frame, "Machen's Warrior Children," in *Alister E. McGrath and Evangelical Theology: A Dynamic Engagement*, ed. Sung Wook Chung (Carlistle, Cumbria, England: Paternoster Press, 2003), 113-17.

[137] Hart and Muether, *Fighting the Good Fight*, 45-51; Hart, *Defending the Faith*, 64-65, 105-07. Another striking example of this phenomenon is noted by John Hannah, who cites a letter from Machen to Lewis Sperry Chafer, in which Machen states, unmistakably, "I do not hold the premillennial view and that view is not in accordance with the main tradition of Princeton Seminary which we are endeavoring to preserve" (letter, J. Gresham Machen to Lewis Sperry Chafer, 1 August 1929, J. Gresham Machen Papers, Archives, Westminster Theological Seminary, Philadelphia, Pennsylvania). Hannah observes: "In spite of Machen's clear statement, Chafer wrote a month later, 12 September 1929, to a board member, H.R. Todd, that he felt Machen was a premillenarian at heart. 'I think this [premillennialism] is clearly taught in John 16:12, though one hesitates to imply that good men of the character of Dr. Machen are not spirit taught. In his case, however, I am satisfied that he is and that he really holds the premillennial position in his heart' (Lewis Sperry Chafer Papers, ADTS). Perhaps the best that can be said at

that premillennialists simply did not "hear" Machen clearly when he articulated his original vision for the OPC.

Even if this depiction of the situation be completely accurate, however, what implications should be drawn from that is still not clear. Machen was, indisputably, a central figure in the early history of the conservative Presbyterian resistance movement. However, Machen's original vision was multifaceted, and, as everyone acknowledges in one way or another, the perception of that vision as it was caught by means of his public persona was potentially broader still. Therefore, we should recognize that "the original vision" for Westminster, the OPC, and its affiliates was likewise potentially bigger than Machen's alone.

Machen himself seemed aware of this in the way he responded to the controversies. Even when the fight over premillennialism was most contentious, Machen's critiques of "un-Reformed" varieties of premillennialism consistently carried a softer tone than his colleagues', and were careful always to clarify that Reformed varieties of premillennialism were allowable. In critiquing even the "heresy" contained in the Scofield notes, Machen alone was willing to suggest that acceptable, Reformed premillennialism might be affirmed even among those fond of *using* the Scofield Bible![138]

Some OPC premillennialists did regret some of Machen's later stances, but, even then, they still maintained that *they* were the ones who actually were being most faithful to Machen's *original* vision.[139] In their mind, Machen's regrettable stances resulted from his being overly influenced by others.[140]

Thus, even if Hart and Muether are right that the narrower, more sharply-focused vision of the OPC resulted simply from Machen's own vision becoming more clearly manifest and more fully enacted, the perspective of Machen's supporters who did not agree with this narrower focus still should be taken into account. For whatever reason, rightly or wrongly, they did not become aware of this more sharply-focused agenda, so as to initiate a competing one, until after they had joined the original group, which they thought, rightly or wrongly, promoted a different agenda and which they thought was everyone's original aim. Because Machen consistently displayed a willingness to compromise with them, much more than did the more hard-line of his followers,[141] they may even have felt that Machen himself confirmed their impression as to what was the original vision.

---

this point is that Chafer confused noncombativeness with belief; the worst to be said is that he was blinded by false assumptions" ("The Social and Intellectual History of the Evangelical Theological College," Ph.D. diss., University of Texas at Dallas, 1988, 355, n. 347).

[138] Machen, "Premillennialism," 21; *idem*, "The Root of the Trouble," 41-42; *idem*, "The Dispensationalism of the Scofield Bible," 42-43; and *idem*, "The Millennial Question," 43-44.

[139] "[I]n fairness to both [sides], it would seem that neither party saw itself as splitting an existing church but as maintaining the 'true spiritual succession' of the old [PCUSA]" (Hutchinson, *The History Behind the Reformed Presbyterian Church Evangelical Synod*, 242).

[140] Buswell even suggested this to Machen directly, a suggestion that Machen did not receive well; see John W. Sanderson, Jr., "Buswell as Churchman," *Presbyterion: Covenant Seminary Review* 2 (Spring-Fall 1976): 118-19, and 129, n. 11.

[141] Hart and Muether also acknowledge this point (*Fighting the Good Fight*, 51-52).

We can understand, then, why Machen's death, right at the crucial moment of arbitration between the growing concerns and conflicts, was such a crushing blow to whatever chances remained of reconciling the parties. Machen represented not only the undisputed leader of the Presbyterian fundamentalist coalition, but he was also the one person in whom all the various pieces of the coalition fit. Not only were his mediation skills lost, Machen himself represented the very fabric of their unity. Without his presence, the strands unraveled. Grief contributed to this unraveling, in that expressions of grief sometimes took on ecclesio-political dimensions. Anger, which for some evolved into outright blame, became easily focused on those who disagreed with the stances Machen last took. Fear and denial became manifest in political defensiveness and desperation.[142]

Further, the power vacuum created by Machen's death threw the parties into more determined quests to advance their aims, or at least to retain their former balance of power. This balance became increasingly difficult to maintain, as advocates of the strictest aspects of Machen's leanings became ever more vigilant to see those strictures carried through, and as those desiring to revive the spirit of Machen's earlier, more tolerant, coalition-building character also became more desperate. This vigilant desperation on both sides finally consolidated all the components of their varied controversies into that critical mass of division. Once Machen died, and the Dutch with their allies gained even more power, the premillennialists ceded.

No one knew in the beginning how this was all going to turn out. Clarence Macartney did not know in the 1920s that his zealous support for Machen's conservative stands would encourage Machen to create (in his words) a "schism" of "seceders."[143] Machen did not know that his vigorous defense of biblical orthodoxy would bring not only Niagara fundamentalists into his cause, but, with them, a zeal for premillennialism as vigorous as his own zeal for the full Reformed faith. Presbyterian premillennialists did not know how influential Dutch Reformed theology would become in the new denomination they were helping to build, nor did they suspect that their support of a young, promising leader, named Carl McIntire, would one day result in a megalomaniacal political "machine" far more controlling than anything they had seen in either the PCUSA or the OPC.[144] In short, people

---

[142] One can detect these elements particularly in Carl McIntire's reporting of events that transpired shortly after Machen's death ("Give Thanks," *CBeac* 2 [10 June 1937]: 4). McIntire reported the Independent Board meeting at which the resignations from several of those whom McIntire called "the Westminster group" were received. That already tense meeting was disrupted, at one point, by a woman who "turned to the majority of the Board and declared, 'the death of Dr. Machen is on your hands.' The Westminster group and other women nodded assent" ("Presbyterians Fill Vacancies on Board," 5).

[143] Longfield, *The Presbyterian Controversy*, 104-27, 174-80; Churchill, *Lest We Forget*, 125.

[144] See the comparison drawn by Buswell, et al., between the political "machine" said to exist in the early OPC and that which had existed previously in the PCUSA, and that controlled by McIntire in the Bible Presbyterian Church in the 1950s; Hutchinson, *The History Behind the Reformed Presbyterian Church Evangelical Synod*, 224-25; also 237-42. Hutchinson observes that "McIntire was a fervent, indeed imitative, admirer of J. Gresham Machen" and suggests, "Perhaps he saw himself as Machen's successor in the leadership of the movement even before

were embedded in the events of history, not always firmly in control of even what role they themselves were playing in them.

Such was how the character and agenda of the OPC developed throughout the late-1930s. Whatever particular explanation one prefers to account for the development of the competing agendas, my central thesis stands: it was not until after the positions polarized – their numerous attempts to achieve a compromise having failed – that two competing agendas actually were set.

How best to combat modernist unbelief was the core issue of concern. Closely behind this core concern was the concern to establish a full-orbed biblical and Reformed orthodoxy in the new church. It was passion for this objective that provoked the battles over eschatology. These were the central issues that gave rise to two competing agendas in the early OPC. The "two sides" that formed around these competing agendas may now be profiled with clarity.

On one side were premillennialists who not only believed premillennialism was a clear biblical doctrine, but who also believed that conservative Presbyterianism should (continue to) league itself with other conservatives who may not have been as strictly Reformed as they. This was a time when roughly twenty percent of Westminster Seminary students were Methodists;[145] in their minds, forging alliances with (or, at the very least, avoiding needless alienation of) such fellow conservative Christians, was the soundest strategy for the greater cause: defending biblical Christianity against the intrusion of modernist unbelief in the wider Church.

On the other side were Reformed purists who believed that compromising with Arminianism or with un-Reformed varieties of dispensational-premillennialism was tantamount to compromising with unbelief, more subtle, but no less pernicious than that form of unbelief found in modernism.[146]

Machen's premature death. At any rate, from that point onward McIntire felt providentially appointed to succeed Machen as the recognized leader, not only of the Presbyterian Separatist Movement, but of the whole fundamentalist separatist movement as well" (265). Hutchinson insightfully clarifies, "At the same time, to make [McIntire] the primary factor in the development of events would be a gross oversimplification of the facts. In the first place, it makes the mistake of taking for granted that the McIntire of 1937 is precisely the McIntire of later years, although it cannot be denied that indications of his later outlook were evident back then. Secondly, it overlooks the fact that many able and learned men, who have long since repudiated the objectionable elements in McIntire's position, associated themselves with the Bible Presbyterian movement" (238).

[145] Hart, *Defending the Faith*, 162.

[146] E.g., John Murray, "The Reformed Faith and Modern Substitutes, Parts I-VII" which set Arminianism and modern dispensationalism right alongside modernism as heterodox forms of doctrine, all totally unacceptable within a truly Reformed, truly Bible-believing church. Likewise, R.B. Kuiper defended this latter viewpoint in "A Plea for Peace," the last article written before the final turn of events which split the OPC. Kuiper confirms some of our suspicions about subtle factors contributing to the division, when he says, "For instance, to play up in our midst the differences between East and West, charter-members and later arrivals, Scotch and Dutch, is not only uncalled for, but is sure to prove divisive, because un-Christian" ("A Plea for Peace," *PrGuard* 4 [24 April 1937]: 20). I am intrigued by Kuiper's mention of a division between "Scotch and Dutch." I have discovered no such contention between these two parties; the suggestion of such may be merely a foil, designed to "mention without really mentioning" the

From here, Marsden's conclusions are similar to my own.[147]

> [T]he division represented a conflict of the two major traditions in American Presbyterianism. This . . . explanation was intimated at the time of the division in the claims of each side that the other had departed from "historic Presbyterianism." On the one side this division was sometimes represented as a conflict between "historic Presbyterianism" and "fundamentalism"; while on the other side it was termed "Historic American Presbyterianism" *versus* a non-American (Dutch and Scottish) Reformed tradition. Neither of these representations is totally accurate; but they do support the contention of the present study that the division reflected a conflict of two traditions within conservative Presbyterianism in America . . . The two traditions do not represent two incompatible theological traditions. Rather, they represent two approaches to the same tradition. . . . Each of these traditions has always included many of the traits more strongly characteristic of the other. . . . One observer characterized this difference as being similar to the difference between the sales and the research departments of a modern industry. The sales department is anxious to get the product on the market even if the product is not yet in its most perfect state; while the research department insists that caution should be taken not to present a shoddy product. Often one side has a difficult time understanding the emphasis of the other, even though each one has a legitimate function.[148]

Where my thesis agrees and disagrees with Marsden's can also now be made fully clear. In my judgment, Marsden is correct to look for a polarizing force of "two traditions within conservative Presbyterianism in America," but he looks for that polarizing force in the wrong place. It was not the Old School-New School division of a century past that was impelling the polarization,[149] but more contemporary and more subtle differences between "Niagara fundamentalism" and "Presbyterian fundamentalism."

---

real source of contention, viz., between Dutch-Scotch Reformed and American Presbyterianism. Perhaps referring too directly to the real point of contention would have hit too close to home?

[147] Compare Marsden, "Perspective on the Division of 1937," 321-22 to my analysis, above.

[148] Marsden, "Perspective on the Division of 1937," 322-23; in the latter part of this analysis, Marsden is quoting the observation of George S. Christian, "Let's Not Talk about a Split in the Bible Presbyterian Church," (a paper presented by the author, 1955), 1.

[149] The Old School-New School breach had been mended after all, in 1869, meaning not only that the two sides had agreed to tolerate one another, but also that both sides, over time, were "moderated" by each other. American Presbyterian theology, less pristine in its Reformed theology than some of its European counterparts anyway, became even more of a hodgepodge. Cf. Loetscher, *The Broadening Church*, 1-18, 155-56. Loetscher makes it clear that he approves of these "moderating" influences. Some conservatives would be less sanguine about this leavening influence on each other's doctrinal stances, which the reunion of Old School and New School represented; in any case, that such mutual influence did take place, Loetscher nevertheless amply demonstrates.

Therefore, I find it much more helpful to follow through on Marsden's other suggestion, that modernist unbelief provoked a counter-movement called "fundamentalism," which was a "patchwork coalition" of conservative impulses. These conservative impulses included evangelicalism, revivalism, premillennialism, Reformed confessionalism, and the conservative versions of individual denominational orthodoxies.[150] In the type of fundamentalism found in Northern Presbyterianism, one finds a breed of conservatism concerned with finer points of doctrine in a tradition already known for priding itself in doctrinal erudition. Doctrinal convictions among members of this group were espoused and defended with especial vigor. It is not surprising that theological differences within this group could escalate into major conflicts.

We should also recognize that division, itself, is a centrifugal force; once a split over a certain issue occurs, other conflicts that come behind it tend to be more pronounced and more strident. Personality conflicts and socio-political factors also must be taken into account in order to explain adequately all the forces at work.

Those considerations notwithstanding, the root conflict was a clash of two conservative agendas: the agenda that wanted to focus on the preservation of individual, denominational orthodoxy (i.e., pure Reformed Presbyterianism); and the agenda that wanted to pursue wider cooperation between conservative Bible-believers for the sake of defeating modernistic unbelief in the wider Christian church. This is the separation of aims that accompanied the subtle separation of beliefs in the two circles of fundamentalism, "Presbyterian Fundamentalism" and "Niagara Fundamentalism."[151]

2.2.2 Hairline Fractures in the Premillennialist Coalition

We have observed that amillennialist critics of the Scofield Bible consistently insisted upon a distinction between (un-Reformed) dispensationalism and (Reformed) premillennialism, often with reassurances to their premillennialist respondents in the OPC that *their* variety of premillennialism was "OK." However,

---

[150] Marsden, *Fundamentalism and American Culture*, 4.

[151] It is intriguing that only the latter would retain the less-than-coveted label, "fundamentalist." It seems that J. Gresham Machen had a part in establishing this distinction; shortly before his death, he had written to J. Oliver Buswell that the Independent Board was "at the parting of the ways between a mere fundamentalism, on the one hand, and Presbyterianism on the other"; quoted in Hart, *Defending the Faith*, 164. Nevertheless, these so-called "fundamentalists" in the Northern Presbyterian churches claimed, both before and after Machen's death, to be the ones truly maintaining Machen's original heritage. In a front page article entitled, "JESUS CHRIST DETHRONED: Fundamentalists Ousted – Church to Split," the *Christian Beacon* of 4 June 1936 mentioned nine Presbyterian ministers who had been defrocked for their involvement in the Independent Board for Presbyterian Foreign Missions; the three pictured are Carl McIntire, J. Gresham Machen, and Merril T. MacPherson; cf. "Dr. Machen is Taken, Pneumonia Fatal: Prominent Fundamentalist Stricken on Preaching Tour," *CBeac* 1 (7 January 1937): 1, 4; and McIntire, "Dr. Machen," 4-5.

Allan A. MacRae, an OPC premillennialist, responded, "Never have I met a man who said that he held the un-Biblical views which are attacked."[152]

Premillennialist Presbyterians might well have wondered why their amillennialist brethren were attacking this allegedly ignoble strand of premillennialism that, as far as they knew, did not even exist. Several concluded that the attacks must have really been intended for *them* (for premillennialists generally)[153] and that the views described in these attacks were just building a straw man.[154] Northern Presbyterian premillennialists agreed that the views described and attacked were indeed "un-Biblical."[155] But here is the wrinkle: these so-called straw-men views actually did have some real, non-straw, proponents. . . about 1500 miles southwestward.

In Dallas, Texas, in the latter part of 1936, Lewis Sperry Chafer responded to the articles by Allis, Murray and Kuiper with an article entitled "Dispensationalism"[156]; only, unlike his Northern premillennial counterparts, he did not concede that the Scofield notes under criticism were unorthodox errors. Instead, he defended each and every one of these so-called "anti-Reformed heresies." To say the least, Chafer's response put Northern Presbyterian premillennialists in an awkward position (though only Buswell ever publicly voiced his disagreements with Chafer[157]).

In the late 1930s, one must look closely to see the hairline fractures in the premillennialist coalition. These hairline fractures would grow, however, and would eventually merge with lines of division already formed between premillennialists and non-premillennialists. It was these lines of division that would become the fault line between "dispensationalism" and "covenant theology." It is worth our while to analyze further these lines of division as they were being formed, in 1936-38.

---

[152] Allan A. MacRae, "Dr. Allan A. MacRae Resigns Seminary," 2.

[153] This was Allan A. MacRae's exact conclusion (ibid.); cf. also Carl McIntire, "Premillennialism." J. Oliver Buswell was one of the few premillennialists at the time who understood and accepted the distinction amillennialists were making between premillennialism and dispensationalism; see Buswell, "A Premillennialist's View," 46. He tried to clarify the points at issue for both sides, which attempt we will investigate in the next chapter.

[154] MacRae, "MacRae Resigns from Seminary," 2.

[155] Ibid.; cf. Buswell, "A Premillennialist's View."

[156] Lewis Sperry Chafer, "Dispensationalism," *BibSac* 93 (October-December 1936): 390-449.

[157] Buswell, "A Premillennialist's View."

CHAPTER 3

A Seismogram of Late-1930s American Evangelicalism

After a major earthquake, the job of seismologists becomes easier in a sense, yet at the same time more exacting and more crucial. Having been alerted to the general location of a major fault line, the job of predicting when and where other tremors might occur is more straightforward. At the same time, because aftershocks can often pose as great a danger as the original quake, the need for accurate assessment is made all the more acute.

The historian of twentieth-century American Christianity is placed in a similar position. It is not difficult to detect the major fault line of division between 1920s modernists and fundamentalists. With this fault line exposed, we are well on our way to discovering derivative lines of division within American evangelicalism thereafter. Discerning when, where, and how exactly these lines were being formed through the 1930s-1940s is a more exacting task, yet crucial to determining how subtle divisions might affect dialogues between evangelicals in the present day.

As we have just begun to see, within conservative, Northern Presbyterianism, 1936-38 was a period of great volatility. During this brief time period, a conflagration erupted between eschatological views, subscriptionist views, different types of Reformed theological views, and varying "dispensationalist" views, which, properly understood, take us far in explaining intra-evangelical conflicts that have persisted to the present day.

In the last chapter, we examined sociological factors that helped shape the historical unfolding of these controversies. In this chapter, we put the theological and ideological aspects of these controversies under investigation. What results is something like an ideological seismogram, a measurement of patterns of developing theological ideas, which are coming into conflict with one another and forming lines of division. In fact, I will argue that this "ideological seismogram" actually detects the rupture of "dispensationalism" and "covenant theology."

3.1 Conflicting Understandings of Orthodoxy

We now can unpack the ideological implications of two different types of fundamentalism ("Presbyterian fundamentalism" and "Niagara fundamentalism") contending against one another in the early OPC. As we have observed, Presbyterian fundamentalism's subscriptionist emphases commonly generated suspicions toward Arminian tendencies and toward "modern dispensationalism," which were both found in the larger evangelical movement.

Though only "Niagara fundamentalists" would retain the label, "fundamentalist," it was not because their brand of "fundamentalism" was the more doctrinaire. As OPC historian, Robert Churchill, explains:

> Historically, the term *fundamentalist* refers to those people who, in contrast to the theological liberals (or modernists) upheld what came to be known as the Five Fundamentals of the faith. [He then lists the five Niagara "fundamentals."] These are beliefs essential to historic Christianity. Therefore every true Christian who upholds these truths is a fundamentalist. Since every Calvinist or Reformed believer also upholds these essential doctrines of the Christian faith, they may consider themselves fundamentalists in the truest sense of the term. However, adherents to the Reformed faith would argue that there are more doctrines essential to the Christian faith than merely the five mentioned above. In other words, they believe in more fundamentals than the fundamentalists do.[1]

In the controversies of the 1920s and 1930s, the meaning of the term "fundamentalism" was evolving. Apparently, before 1930, any anti-modernist conservative could be included under the broad "fundamentalist" umbrella. In the 1930s, however, the term came to refer almost exclusively to premillennialists. (So, Churchill's delineation between "old fundamentalists" and "new fundamentalists,"[2] though awkward and never really catching on, is quite accurate in this regard.) It is the tension between Niagara Fundamentalism and Presbyterian Fundamentalism that is central to understanding this development.

"Presbyterian fundamentalism" was concerned with doctrinal orthodoxy, and diagnosed one's orthodoxy through confessional, subscriptionist measures. "Niagara fundamentalism," too, was concerned for doctrinal orthodoxy, but it posed a different set of litmus tests for discerning it. Abstinence from alcohol (and similar sorts of personal conduct issues) seemed to serve as a line of sociological demarcation.[3] Doctrinally, premillennialism seemed to be for them a key litmus test, serving in much the same capacity as strict confessional subscription for Presbyterian fundamentalists.

Apparently, some Niagara fundamentalists even suspected those who rejected premillennialism of also rejecting belief in the Second Coming altogether – an

---

[1] Robert K. Churchill, *Lest We Forget: A Personal Reflection on the Formation of the Orthodox Presbyterian Church* (Philadelphia: Committee for the History of the Orthodox Presbyterian Church, 1986), 30.

[2] Ibid., 31, and *passim*.

[3] E.g., see J. Oliver Buswell, Jr., *The Christian Life* (Grand Rapids: Zondervan, 1937), 81-95.

unfortunate misunderstanding.⁴ While there was no explicit statement of eschatological chronology in the Presbyterian "fundamentals,"⁵ conservatives of any eschatological variety (premillennialist, postmillennialist, or amillennialist) agreed that Christ would return *personally* and *bodily*. It was the affirmation of Christ's *personal, bodily* return (rather than belief in His *premillennial* return) that distinguished conservatives from liberals; thus, Niagara fundamentalists who used premillennialism to distinguish theological conservatism from liberalism were actually drawing the line at the wrong place.

Hermeneutical and exegetical differences contributed to this and similar such misunderstandings. Within modernism, an anti-supernaturalist hermeneutic reduced the cataclysmic aspects of biblical prophecy to metaphors or allegories that depicted humankind's ethical advance under the moral teachings of Christ.⁶ Even before the turn of the century, conservatives sounded the alarm against this sort of "spiritualizing hermeneutic," warning people to hold fast to a "literal hermeneutic" which alone preserved the Bible's rightful authority.⁷ All conservatives rejected the modernist type of "spiritualization."

This was also one of the points J. Gresham Machen tried to clarify in 1936.

> Many Christian people, believing in the full truthfulness of the Bible, hold th[e] Premillennial view. Other Christian people, believing with equal firmness in the truthfulness of the Bible, reject the

---

⁴ Churchill recounts one such instance where this misunderstanding surfaced dramatically. In the late 1930s, he wrote a letter to the elders of the Tacoma Independent Bible Church, inviting them to join the Orthodox Presbyterian Church (the church had been a Presbyterian Church before the 1920s-30s controversies). "Back came a letter, signed by four elders, saying that they could never think of becoming part of a church that did not believe in the second coming of Christ – a totally false accusation and one which revealed how far those in Tacoma had drifted from their presbyterian and Reformed moorings"; Churchill, *Lest We Forget*, 133.

⁵ I.e., as affirmed by the 1910 PCUSA General Assembly.

⁶ See Gerald Bray, *Biblical Interpretation Past and Present* (Downers Grove, IL: IVP, 1996), 255-375. Also, in *Historical Handbook of Major Biblical Interpreters*, ed. Donald K. McKim (Downers Grove, IL: IVP, 1998), see, especially, Scott J. Hafemann, "F.C. Bauer," 285-89; Colin Brown, "Hermann Samuel Reimarus," 346-49; Dawn DeVries, "Friedrich Daniel Ernst Schleiermacher," 350-55; Robert C. Morgan, "David Friedrich Strauss," 364-68; Hans Rollman, "William Wrede," 394-98; Donald A. Hagner, "C.H. Dodd," 476-81; H. Martin Rumscheidt, "Adolf von Harnack," 491-95; and Calvin R. Mercer, "Albert Schweitzer," 523-26.

⁷ E.g., see James Robinson Graves, *The Work of Christ in the Covenant of Redemption Consummated in Seven Dispensations* (Memphis, TN: Baptist Book House, 1883), "Appendix A: Principles of Interpretation," 556-58. Cf. Charles Hodge, *Systematic Theology* (New York: Scribner, Armstrong and Co., 1874), 1:160; and John Nelson Darby, *The Collected Writings of John Nelson Darby*, 1860-82, reprint, ed. William Kelly (Kingston-Thames: Stow Hill Bible and Tract Depot, 1962), 31:142. A helpful analysis of this point is given by Joe L. Coker, "Exploring the Roots of the Dispensationalist/Princetonian 'Alliance': Charles Hodge and John Nelson Darby on Eschatology and Interpretation of Scripture," *Fides et Historia* 30 (winter-spring 1998): 41-56. See also George M. Marsden, *Fundamentalism and American Culture* (New York: Oxford University Press, 1980), 16-71, 85-195.

Premillennial view and hold that our Lord's return will be followed immediately by the last judgment. Both these groups of Christian people accept with equal clearness and firmness the great doctrine of the personal and bodily return of Christ and reject with equal abhorrence the Modernist "spiritualizing" or explaining away of that doctrine.[8]

Nonetheless, premillennialists continually found it difficult to distinguish the "spiritualizing" hermeneutic of modernism from the "deeper," "mystical," "typical" or "theological" sense emphasized by Reformed (especially Dutch-Reformed) non-premillennialists in their exegeses of Old Testament narratives, Divine promises, and prophetic literature throughout the Bible.[9] Premillennialists therefore accused non-premillennialists of employing a liberal hermeneutical method (albeit, thankfully, only inconsistently, they often added).

So, in response to Oswald T. Allis' suggestion that "Dispensationalism shares with higher criticism its fundamental error,"[10] Lewis Sperry Chafer retorted that non-premillennialist hermeneutics "shares the fundamental error" of liberal hermeneutics.

> Each of the two major passages on the virgin birth of Christ – one in the Old Testament (Isa. 7:14 with 9:6, 7) and one in the New Testament (Lk. 1:31-33) – record the prediction, in addition to the virgin birth, that Christ will occupy the Davidic throne forever. Concerning this revelation, it should be observed that the liberal theologian spiritualizes both the virgin birth and the Davidic throne; the partial dispensationalist "shares the fundamental error" of the liberal theologian to the extent of spiritualizing the Davidic throne; while the dispensationalist, believing that no justification can be advanced for so violent a change of method of interpretation within the bounds of an utterance confined almost to one sentence, spiritualizes neither the birth nor the throne. And is it not probable that many theological graduates who in their training were encouraged to spiritualize the Davidic throne have thereby counted

---

[8] J. Gresham Machen, "Premillennialism," *PrGuard* 3 (24 October 1936): 21.

[9] E.g., see Louis Berkhof, *Systematic Theology* (Grand Rapids: Eerdmans, 1939), 610-15; *idem*, *Principles of Biblical Interpretation (Sacred Hermeneutics)* (Grand Rapids: Baker, 1950), 40-66, 133-66. Berkhof thoroughly denounces the "allegorizing" method of Philo, Clement of Alexandria, and Origen (*Principles of Biblical Interpretation*, 14-24); he even critiques the "excessive typology" of Cocceius (29-30). He also insists upon consistent "grammatical-historical interpretation," which he sometimes also calls the "literal" (25, 85, 152), "simple" (27, 60-61), "plain" (74-75), or "true scientific" (21) method, which leads to the discernment of Scripture's "real sense" (59) or "real explanation" (113). Yet, Berkhof also insists that the purely "literal," "grammatical" or "historical" sense of Scripture does not itself alone always provide Scripture's *only* "real" meaning (40-66, 133-66).

[10] Oswald T. Allis, "Modern Dispensationalism and the Doctrine of the Unity of Scripture," *EvQ* 8 (January 1936): 24.

themselves justified in spiritualizing the virgin birth or any other feature of divine revelation?[11]

Within the OPC, Allan MacRae expressed a similar concern.

DESTRUCTIVE METHODS OF INTERPRETATION

The truth of the matter is that both postmillennialism and amillennialism reject precious teachings which are plainly taught in Scripture. In doing so they introduce a method of interpretation which is utterly destructive. Some apply this method only in a few chapters of the New Testament. Others apply it widely in both Old and New Testaments. It is not a matter of merely taking figurative language as figurative. Most language contains figurative expressions. It is a matter of taking an entire framework of a passage figuratively, and passing beyond the bounds of any sane use of figures whatever. A pinch of salt in a dish of soup is good. If one pours a bucket of salt into a quart of soup, the result is disagreeable and dangerous to health. This is the so-called spiritualization. If a man rejects premillennialism, let me plead with him to be utterly inconsistent, and to restrict his spiritualization to a few passages. For if he applies it widely, he must give up many other precious truths of God's Word.[12]

For Reformed, amillennialist interpreters, the teaching of the Bible itself as it unfolded from Old Testament to New Testament was what yielded recognition of the "typical" character of the Old Testament. Far from imposing a "liberal hermeneutic," they claimed they were merely recognizing and employing the Bible's own method for interpreting itself.[13] Berkhof even suggested that anyone who fails to recognize the "typical" character of the Old Testament is guilty of the same "too carnal conception of Israel and its religious institutions" found among those who "regard the Old Testament simply as the fruit of historical development"; the hermeneutic of the "millenarians," he suggested, was like that of the "Rationalists."[14]

Thus, just beneath a relatively minor difference in eschatological chronology, was the perception, on both sides, of a significant hermeneutical divide in the way each side handled Scripture. Both sides were trying to fortify their defenses against modernism, and each side saw the other as compromising those defenses, and as imbibing subtle but dangerous elements of the liberal ideology that had poisoned their old church.

Moreover, Presbyterian fundamentalists and Niagara fundamentalists disagreed in how they defined orthodoxy. Presbyterian fundamentalists defined orthodoxy

---

[11] Lewis Sperry Chafer, "Dispensationalism," *BibSac* 93 (October-December 1936): 400.
[12] Allan A. MacRae, "The Millennial Kingdom of Christ," *CBeac* 2 (18 March 1937): 7.
[13] Cf. Vern Sheridan Poythress, *Understanding Dispensationalists* (Grand Rapids: Zondervan, 1987), 78-129.
[14] Berkhof, *Principles of Biblical Interpretation*, 75.

confessionally, and their subscriptionist emphasis drove them away from the more general fundamentalist-evangelical movement and towards a more isolated denominationalism. The Niagara fundamentalist definition of orthodoxy allowed cross-denominational agreement on a more widely shared set of basic doctrinal tenets. This propelled them towards fuller cooperation with the larger fundamentalist-evangelical movement.[15] When premillennialism came under attack (at least as was their perception at the time), premillennialists' shared defense of a now beleaguered doctrine served to further diminish other lines of denominational division between them, some of which had separated Bible-believing Christians for centuries.

Though self-described "dispensationalists" denied being anti-denominational, their emphasis clearly was never on denominational distinctives. For instance, Dallas Seminary, a non-denominational, dispensationalist institution, faced the charge of anti-denominationalism from the earliest days of its founding. In 1931, Rollin Chafer, Lewis' brother and registrar of Dallas Seminary, took issue with an article that had "treat[ed] 'dispensationalism' and 'undenominationalism' as synonymous."[16] He responded that, while "undenominationalism" was characteristic of *some* dispensationalists (namely of the Darbyite, Plymouth Brethren variety), such was not characteristic of the *majority* of them.

> Those who follow Mr. Darby not only in his teaching concerning the dispensational divisions of Scripture but also his adverse views on church organization and an ordained ministry, constitute a comparatively small company of earnest Christians who have been spoken of as an "undenominational denomination." On the other hand, the great majority of well-known men who hold, teach and preach the doctrines of Christianity in the light of the dispensational divisions found in the Scriptures are affiliated with the various Christian denominations.[17]

He then reported the results of a recent survey of graduates, which revealed that fifty percent were Presbyterians, and another forty percent were ministering within other denominations.[18]

Even in the midst of this response, however, Rollin Chafer conceded that, for dispensationalists, denominational loyalties were of only secondary concern. Those involved with Dallas Seminary, he said, "recognize that the sheep of God are scattered amongst many fellowships and that one of the great needs of the hour is

---

[15] With slight differences in emphasis, my analysis here is virtually identical to that of D.G. Hart (*Defending the Faith: J. Gresham Machen and the Crisis of Conservative Protestantism in Modern America* [Baltimore, MD: Johns Hopkins University Press, 1994], 160-70).

[16] Rollin Thomas Chafer, "Confusion of Ideas," *Evangelical Theological College Bulletin* 7 (June 1931): 5.

[17] Ibid.

[18] Ibid.

that these should be ministered unto through the organizations and agencies which, in spite of their imperfections, God uses to open doors for testimony."[19]

This manifests a pattern here among dispensational premillennialists, even among those who, like Lewis and Rollin Chafer, belonged to and were officially ordained in formal denominations. Though they did not necessarily stand apart from their denominations, it seems that their primary loyalties were to their inter-denominational or non-denominational affiliations.[20]

This is significant in view of how crucial was confessional subscription to conservative Presbyterians. Lewis Chafer defied confessional tenets more baldly than any Presbyterian premillennialist before him, which perhaps explains why the actions taken against his views would be more severe. Nevertheless, Chafer's diatribes against "fixation on creeds" do recall some of the reasons given by Northern Presbyterian premillennialists for why they left Westminster Seminary and the OPC. These people also resented the attacks on "modern dispensationalism," which they, too, said resulted from an overly narrow creedal focus. One complained of his being continually confronted among his amillennialist colleagues with "an inflexible determination to enforce their own peculiar notions [of what is "essential to being 'Reformed'"] by crushing the broad evangelical point of view."[21] Another complained that

> [while] from 1929 to 1933 the main interest and topic of conversation [at Westminster Seminary] was Modernism. From 1933 to 1934 on, the main subject of discussion seemed to be premillennialism and "modern dispensationalism." I can testify to sufficient effort expended upon me (unsuccessfully) by amillennial faculty members to know that they regarded premillennialism as being a deadly error little short of heretical, and as involving principles of Biblical interpretation which were, as they believed, "unreformed."[22]

---

[19] Ibid.

[20] This pattern is observed also by Marsden (*Fundamentalism and American Culture*, 46-195, *passim*); and John David Hannah ("The Social and Intellectual History of the Origins of the Evangelical Theological College" [Ph.D. diss., The University of Texas at Dallas, 1988], 367-72).

[21] Allan A. MacRae, "Dr. Allan A. MacRae Resigns Seminary: Founder of Westminster Opposes Its Present Stand," *CBeac* 2 (29 April 1937): 2.

[22] H. McAllister Griffiths, "The Character and Leadership of Dr. Machen," *CBeac* 2 (2 September 1937): 2. Cf. the debate among Northern Presbyterian conservatives over "creedalism vs. independentism": Ned B. Stonehouse, "The Creed of Our Fathers," *PrGuard* 4 (10 April 1937): 1-2; "[Wilbur] Smith Leaves Independent Board: Revelation Announces Move; Mandate of Assembly Obeyed," *CBeac* 2 (22 April 1937): 1-2; R.B. Kuiper, "A Plea for Peace," *PrGuard* 4 (24 April 1937): 21-24; Ned B. Stonehouse, "Westminster Seminary Today," *PrGuard* 4 (15 May 1937): 37-40; "Presbyterians Fill Vacancies on Board for Foreign Missions: Small Group Resigns, and Declares Board Would Not Adopt Resolution Approving Its Charter and Denouncing Independency," *CBeac* 2 (3 June 1937): 1-2, 4; Carl McIntire, "Independency," *CBeac* 2 (3 June 1937): 4; "'Bible Presbyterian Synod' Organized by Members Withdrawing

The pattern of these conflicts reflects the underlying influence of the modernist-fundamentalist controversy heightening tensions between fellow conservatives in its wake. Presbyterian conservatives were trying to repel modernist intrusion by demanding more punctilious subscription to the church's doctrinal standards. Unbeknown to them, however, conservatives actually disagreed among themselves as to just how fastidious the required confessional subscription should be.[23] Once conservatives tried to construct their own institutions and tried to implement their own vision(s) for these institutions, the problem became acute. Concerns for punctilious confessional subscription ended up colliding with concerns to preserve the traditional latitude afforded to competing eschatological viewpoints.

Thus, cracks of division widened between premillennialist and non-premillennialist conservative Presbyterians, as a larger pattern of differences between Niagara fundamentalism and Presbyterian fundamentalism began to emerge more and more clearly. The strain of these fractures likewise began to take its toll on the entire fundamentalist-evangelical movement. We draw our attention now to the smaller cracks found on the premillennialist side of the divide.

3.2 Conflicting Understandings of Premillennialism and Dispensationalism

We have mentioned already how OPC premillennialists initially were baffled by critiques of "dispensationalist" positions that they did not even know existed. These critiques centered mostly on notes contained in the *Scofield Reference Bible*, though writings of other so-called "modern dispensationalists" were commonly quoted to confirm that an entire "school of thought" was in view.[24]

---

from Presbyterian Church of America," *PrGuard* 4 (26 June 1937): 99-100; Merril T. MacPherson, "Why I Am Pastor of an Independent Church," *CBeac* 2 (12 August 1937): 3-4, 7; R.B. Kuiper, "Two Features of the Reformed Faith," *PrGuard* 4 (October 1937): 161-63; "Bible Presbyterian Synod Adopts Historic Westminster Confession," *CBeac* 3 (15 September 1938): 1-2, 5, 7; R.B. Kuiper, "Presbyterianism versus Independentism," *PrGuard* 6 (April 1939): 63-64; Leslie W. Sloat, "Should Conservatives Co-operate?" *PrGuard* 19 (February 1950): 23; *idem*, "Calvinists Can and Do Cooperate!" *PrGuard* 19 (March 1950): 43; *idem*, "Taking Documents Seriously," *PrGuard* 20 (15 May 1951): 84.

[23] This is a discussion that has continued in American Presbyterian churches to the present day; see *The Practice of Confessional Subscription*, ed. David W. Hall (Lanham, MD: University Press of America, 1995).

[24] E.g., John Murray quoted from four dispensationalist sources in his series of articles against dispensationalism ("The Reformed Faith and Modern Substitutes: Modern Dispensationalism" *PrGuard* 2 [18 May - 17 August 1936]: 77-79, 210-12); viz., the *Scofield Reference Bible* (New York: Oxford University Press, 1911); Lewis Sperry Chafer, *The Kingdom in History and Prophecy* (Findlay, OH: Dunham Publishing Co., 1915); Arno C. Gaebelein, *The Jewish Question* (New York: Our Hope Publishers, 1925); and Charles Lee Feinberg, *Premillennialism or Amillennialism?* (Grand Rapids: Zondervan, 1936). Murray also pointed out that Scofield had written the "commendatory introduction" to Chafer's book, as had Chafer for Feinberg's book; the impression of an inbreeding of ideas is clear. Of these four works, Feinberg's and Gaebelein's were quoted but once briefly, while Scofield's and Chafer's works were given

In the North, premillennialists typically dismissed these critiques as attacking views they did not share, and took umbrage at the insinuation that the views under attack were views they espoused. In late 1936, however, this response became harder to sustain. In an article entitled, "Dispensationalism," Lewis Sperry Chafer reluctantly not only accepted the label "dispensationalist," but he confirmed that views described by its critics were, in fact, views that he (and his mentor, C.I. Scofield) affirmed. He then defended each of these so-called "anti-Reformed heresies," including the following:

> (1) the Bible contains two, mutually exclusive religions (Judaism and Christianity);[25]
> (2) the Mosaic Law has been abrogated *in toto*, till its revival in a future Kingdom Dispensation;[26]
> (3) the gospels posit a sharp distinction between the Kingdom of Heaven and the Kingdom of God, the former applying only to the Jewish nation as the earthly people, and the latter applying only to the Church as the heavenly people;[27]
> (4) the New Testament posits a sharp distinction between the "gospel of the kingdom" and the "gospel of the grace of God";[28]
> (5) the Lord's Prayer was not intended for use by New Testament believers, and the Sermon on the Mount was not intended for application in our contemporary context;[29] and
> (6) redemptive history cannot be said to reveal the unfolding of one Divine covenant of grace, because such a model fails to do justice to the variety of covenants which the Bible records, including at least one (the Mosaic) that is wholly conditional.[30]

The variety of understandings in 1936-37 as to what constitutes the theological system called "dispensationalism" is intriguing. At this stage of the controversy, Northern Presbyterian premillennialists sometimes conceded to the label "dispensationalist" (and generally believed, in any case, that they were the ones being identified by the label), even though they explicitly disavowed the points most bothersome in so-called "dispensationalism" to its non-premillennialist critics.

This fact is demonstrated remarkably by a 1937 *Christian Beacon* article entitled, "The Faith of a Dispensationalist," by Arthur J. Dieffenbacher. This

---

extended attention, a pattern that would continue in later critiques of dispensationalism.

[25] Chafer "Dispensationalism," 411-12.
[26] Ibid., 413-18.
[27] Ibid., 425.
[28] Ibid., 436-37. He also says: "To such a degree as the soteriology of Judaism and the soteriology of Christianity differ, to the same degree do their eschatologies differ. The problems which beset the soteriology of Judaism are largely due to confusion which arises when the elements which are peculiar to the soteriology of Christianity are imposed upon Judaism" (421n). Though Chafer would later deny in the strongest terms that he taught "two ways of salvation," one can see that such statements lend themselves to the charge.
[29] Ibid., 443-48.
[30] Ibid., 438-44.

"dispensationalist" is a 5-point Calvinist, affirms the unity of the Covenant of Grace, and declares that, even though the *penalties* of the Mosaic Law for the Christian have been abrogated, "its essential moral principles" continue into the present age.[31] In the "Questions and Answers" section of the *Christian Beacon* of 8 April 1937, the editors actually *correct* a questioner who suggests, "While all salvation is of Jesus Christ, yet there are two salvations: Jewish, or General, administered by Messiah and the saints during Judgment-Millennium-Resurrection. The salvation of the Church is unto spirit-being and heavenly."[32] The editors reply:

> The letter is somewhat confusing as to what the questioner means. However, we can be sure of one thing: men of all ages whether Jew or Gentile, of the age past, present, or future, are saved only by faith in the shed blood of the Lord Jesus Christ. Men in the Old Testament were saved by their faith in the coming Messiah, as described in the fifty-third chapter of Isaiah, and men in the New Testament age are saved by their faith in the Messiah who has come, and who has been crucified in our stead.[33]

These "dispensationalists," in other words, were putting forth the exact opposite conclusions as Chafer and Scofield on the very points of concern raised against the "anti-Reformed" tendencies of dispensational theology.

It seems that the debate between dispensationalists and covenant theologians was intermingled from the beginning with the debate between premillennialists and non-premillennialists, in a way that has generated much confusion then and now. A good measure of this confusion has been due to a subtle phenomenon: from the beginning, "dispensationalists" (i.e., those actually accepting the label, those taking up the defense of "dispensationalist" tenets) consistently defined "dispensationalism" more broadly, and in a way that linked the "dispensationalist" system more closely and more directly to premillennialism, than did those who used the label "dispensationalist" to identify a set of errors.

> I never yet have read or heard an exact definition of "modern dispensationalism." It is an inclusive term which, like "modern art" or "modern politics," might cover a host of diverse and even contradictory things. . . . We were told that not everything called "modern dispensationalism" was under fire, but only those forms of dispensationalism "which denied the unity of the covenant of grace." . . . In other words, "modern dispensationalism" was deemed inferentially of teaching that in different dispensations men were saved in different ways. And it was further charged that even if the "modern dispensationalist" concerned did not admit that this teaching involved some other ground of salvation in different dispensations, yet if this view could by a logical extension be shown to be

---

[31] Arthur J. Dieffenbacher, "The Faith of a Dispensationalist," *CBeac* 2 (9 September 1937): 1, 8.
[32] "Questions and Answers," *CBeac* 2 (8 April 1937): 4.
[33] Ibid. Cf. also Griffiths, "The Character and Leadership of Dr. Machen," 1-2, 6-7.

inescapably involved in his system, he had violated the "unity" of the covenant of grace, and was therefore not merely "unreformed," but positively heterodox. With this as a piece of pure logic, there can be no quarrel. . . . But to intimate that Dr. Scofield's notes deny the unity of the Covenant of Grace is preposterous, and can only be made plausible by the drawing of many gratuitous conclusions from them which are not implied in them at all, and which are utterly foreign to their spirit. But behind all this misdirected zeal . . . I think, there lies a half seen realization upon the part of post- and amillennialists that there is a great difference between them both on the one hand, and premillennialists on the other, when they view unfolding human history as revealed in the Bible.[34]

Recognizing the difference between the way dispensationalists themselves defined "dispensationalism" and the way anti-dispensationalists defined it will prevent the common mistake of simply accepting the anti-dispensationalist framing of terms and issues, and then assuming that all those defending themselves against anti-dispensationalist denunciations must be doing so because they affirm the views under attack.[35] The reason this is such a seductive trap is because the anti-dispensationalist framing of issues does potentially provide a clear delineation of what is "acceptably Reformed" premillennialism *vis-a-vis* unacceptable, "dispensational" premillennialism. The clarity of their delineation, and the fact that at least *some* "dispensationalists" clearly defended the views being denounced makes it easy to overlook the fact that dispensationalists from the beginning consistently rejected their delineation of terms and issues, however clear. The fight was, in part, over these delineations of terms and issues, and, especially, over whom had final say in determining these.

This, I suggest, is what is behind MacRae's objection to what he called the "building of a straw man" in critiques of "dispensationalism."[36] MacRae's precise objection is not valid, because the views described by Murray, Kuiper, Allis, Stonehouse, and Machen did have some live, flesh-and-blood exponents. Nevertheless, there is a broader point underlying MacRae's objection that should not be missed. In the mind of many OPC premillennialists, the points that OPC amillennialists were attacking in what they called "dispensationalism" (1) had few (if any) exponents; and (2) were minor mistakes hardly worthy of the protracted sort of attack to which amillennialist insisted upon subjecting them.[37]

---

[34] Griffiths, "The Character and Leadership of Dr. Machen," 2, 6.

[35] E.g., this is the very mistake made repeatedly by John Gerstner, *Wrongly Dividing the Word of Truth: A Critique of Dispensationalism* (Brentwood, TN: Wolgemuth & Hyatt, 1991), 31-72, 103-272. Gerstner's work is but a more pronounced example of what has been a common mistake throughout the twentieth-century dispensationalist-covenant theology battles. We will address this point more fully in chapters 5-6, below.

[36] MacRae, "MacRae Resigns from Seminary," 2.

[37] Allan A. MacRae, interview by author, 22 July and 3 August 1993, Quarryville, PA. Cf. Carl McIntire, "Premillennialism," *CBeac* 1 (1 October 1936): 4.

Thus, the line of demarcation between unacceptable "dispensationalism" and acceptable (Reformed) premillennialism was not nearly so clear in the minds of OPC premillennialists as it was in the minds of OPC non-premillennialists. As Marsden observes, even those premillennialists deemed "acceptably Reformed" in the OPC "were convinced that their premillennialism involved a form of dispensationalism."[38]

H. McAllister Griffiths, for example, a premillennialist, was the editor of the *Presbyterian Guardian* that originally published, introduced, and defended Murray's articles denouncing "modern dispensationalism." Griffiths' original view was that, though Murray denounced an aberrant form of premillennialism strongly, Murray did not in these articles violate the "historically regarded. . . area of permitted [eschatological] liberty" between pre-, post-, and a-millennialists.[39] Griffiths became disenchanted, however, as the debate between dispensational premillennialists and covenant amillennialists became more pointed.

> I believe that things have gone very wrong in the [OPC], and in Westminster Seminary. I have been forced with extreme reluctance to the conclusion that both these movements have been deflected from the original and sound principles upon which they were founded. . . . But while premillennialism was thus being quietly raked with dialectical machine gun fire, the first open attack came, not frontally, but from the flank. It came as an attack upon "modern dispensationalism" and centered upon the volume popularly known as the "Scofield Bible." . . . It is true that there is a bare form of premillennialism in which it is possible to think of the coming of Christ as being prior to the millennium, and to hold that view unrelated to the bulk of the prophecies of the Bible. But I do not know one premillennialist in a hundred who holds such a restricted view. The real premillennialist views the events revealed of the end-time in proportion and perspective, as part of a great, unified unfolding of the various dispensations of God's providence to man. . . . To him there could be no distinction between a bare belief that

---

[38] George M. Marsden, "Perspective on the Division of 1937," in *Pressing Toward the Mark: Essays Commemorating Fifty Years of the Orthodox Presbyterian Church*, ed. Charles G. Dennison and Richard C. Gamble (Philadelphia: Committee for the Historian of the Orthodox Presbyterian Church, 1986), 306.

[39] H. McAllister Griffiths, "Eschatological Freedom," *PrGuard* 2 (4 May 1936): 44, 52. "The series of articles by Mr. John Murray appearing in the GUARDIAN is emphatically not to be interpreted as an effort to read pre-millenarians out of the communion of the church. Pre-millenarians are found on the Board and faculty of Westminster Theological Seminary, on the Board and in the staff of The Independent Board for Presbyterian Foreign Missions, and in the membership and staff of The Presbyterian Constitutional Covenant Union. These persons believe that there is no incongruity between the Reformed Faith and belief in the pre-millennial return of our Lord. As we understand it, the dispensationalism against which Mr. Murray will write is of a kind that denies the fundamental unity of the Covenant of Grace, which is an essential doctrine of the Reformed Faith" (52).

Christ will return before the millennium and those other great doctrines which God has revealed in consonance and in harmony with it. To him the attack on "modern dispensationalism" was simply a flank attack upon the whole premillennial way of looking at the Bible and its prophecies. In this I think that the premillennialist was exactly right, and I think that, in their hearts, those making the attack know it, too.[40]

Subtle dynamics surrounding the Scofield Reference Bible contributed to premillennialists' growing disillusionment. Premillennialists seemed keenly aware that certain critiques of the Scofield Bible, even if not directly aimed at premillennialism, were nonetheless critiques that only non-premillennialists would make.[41]

The sociological dynamic at work in this is something like that at work in the Jordanian protests against U.S. actions in the early-1990s Gulf War. Privately, the Jordanians were willing to list their own grievances against Saddam Hussein, but they resented U.S. involvement in the situation nonetheless. To them, the U.S. represented a non-Palestinian, imperialist "bully," hardly the nation to vindicate them against a fellow Palestinian, who had been a hero in past days, even if U.S. actions could rectify some of their own grievances against him.[42]

Similarly, some premillennialists in the late-1930s were willing to concede that significant errors occasionally appeared in the Scofield notes, but, in a context of growing resentment towards what they perceived as scorn, premillennialists were wholly unappreciative of *amillennialists'* efforts to point these out.[43] For many premillennialists, the Scofield Reference Bible, whatever its flaws, represented the most effective instrument to date for popularizing their eschatological view. If the Scofield Reference Bible was not to them a "sacred cow," it was at least esteemed enough that premillennialists knew not to criticize it in an unqualified manner. Only non-premillennialists would do that[44] – and that is the sociological rub.

---

[40] Griffiths, "The Character and Leadership of Dr. Machen," 1, 2, 6; cf. also *idem*, "Since the Syracuse General Assembly: Machine Politics in the [OPC]," *CBeac* 2 (9 September 1937): 1-2.

[41] Ibid.

[42] See Dean Fischer and James Wilde, "Facing a No-Win Scenario: An Interview with King Hussein of Jordan," *TIME*, 5 November 1990, 41-42; Bruce W. Nelan, "They Don't Need to Fight," *TIME*, 12 November 1990, 34; Lisa Beyer, "The Gulf War: What Kind of Peace?" *TIME*, 28 January 1991, 38-40; and Lance Morrow, "Saddam and the Arabs: The Devil in the Hero," *TIME*, 28 January 1991, 64-66.

[43] My coming to recognize these dynamics was greatly assisted by Allan A. MacRae, interview by author, 3 August 1993, Quarryville, PA. In MacRae's mind, the best solution to the occasional flaws in the Scofield Bible was not to denounce it wholesale, but to correct the errors so as to make the already good work it represented even better. This MacRae did, by joining the revision committee of the New Scofield Reference Bible in the mid-1960s. See also E. Schuyler English, "The New Scofield Reference Bible," *BibSac* 124 (April-June 1967): 125-32.

[44] Wilbur Smith seems to represent the common attitude among premillennialists throughout the 1930s-1940s controversies. "Throughout [*Prophecy and the Church* (Phillipsburg, NJ: P & R, 1945)], Dr. Allis particularly attacks the teachings of the Scofield Reference Bible. Now,

Consequently, the Scofield Reference Bible became the lightening rod upon which premillennialist-amillennialist conflagrations repeatedly alighted.

Lewis Sperry Chafer's unqualified enthusiasm for the Scofield Bible may have been unusual, too, in that he was willing to defend the Scofield notes *in toto*, no matter if certain of them seemed to have antinomian implications or violated the "one covenant of grace" idea. Still, he agreed with premillennialists in the North (whether or not they endorsed the Scofield notes as unequivocally as he) that premillennialism and dispensationalism amounted to the same thing. In fact, he initially suggested that, technically speaking, "dispensationalism" denoted an even broader classification than that.

> What men, then, . . . should be classed as dispensationalists? The answer to this question might be stated in a variety of ways. Three of these may suffice: (1) Any person is a dispensationalist who trusts the blood of Christ rather than bringing an animal sacrifice. (2) Any person is a dispensationalist who disclaims any right or title to the land which God covenanted to Israel for an everlasting inheritance. And (3), any person is a dispensationalist who observes the first day of the week rather than the seventh. To all this it will be replied that every Christian does these things, which is obviously true; and it is equally true that, to a very considerable degree, all Christians are dispensationalists. However, not all Christians, though sincere, are as well instructed in the spiritual content of the Scriptures as others, nor have they seen the necessity of recognizing other and deeper distinctions which do confront the careful student of the Word of God.[45]

We see, then, that the period from 1936 to 1937 was a confusing, turbulent period for premillennialists, though the turbulence was mostly under the surface. At first (in early-mid 1936), it looked as though OPC premillennialists would unite with OPC non-premillennialists in defending the unity of the covenant of grace against those who did not. Then, abruptly, premillennialists of all varieties came to unite in common opposition to non-premillennialism. This sort of vacillation is probably due to the fact that, up until June 1937, OPC premillennialists had a foot firmly planted in both the Presbyterian fundamentalist and Niagara fundamentalist camps.

---

because we thoroughly disagree with the major conclusions of this volume, and because we believe that the Scofield Reference Bible, as against Dr. Allis, is right more times than it is wrong, we would confess at once that our learned author has pointed out some regrettable statements in this famous reference Bible. . . . Granting all this, we must now say that there are statements, however, in Dr. Allis's volume that are unfair, others that are inadequate, some that are unsupported by evidence, and many that are definitely wrong" ("Israel and the Church in Prophecy," *SSTimes* 87 [24 November 1945]: 927, 940). Cf. Buswell's defense also of "the general 'system of doctrine' underlying the dispensationalism of the Scofield Reference Edition of the Bible" ("A Premillennialist's View," *PrGuard* 3 [14 November 1936]: 47).

[45] Chafer, "Dispensationalism," 391-92.

Among 1930s premillennialists, if there were two poles of thought, they were represented by Lewis Sperry Chafer and J. Oliver Buswell.[46] Buswell, moderator of the second OPC General Assembly and advocate of strict subscriptionism, represented the type of premillennialism most at home within Presbyterian fundamentalism. Chafer, president of an independent, fundamentalist school, which he founded to carry on the tradition and *ethos* of the Bible conference movement,[47] was outspokenly anti-subscriptionist except as concerned basic doctrines affirmed by all fundamentalists;[48] he was the epitome of Niagara fundamentalism.

Initially, these two types of premillennialism had seemed to be joined together within a wholly amicable relationship. In 1926-27, Wheaton College, of which Buswell was president, invited Chafer to be its commencement speaker and, at that commencement, conferred upon him an honorary Doctor of Divinity degree. In 1927, Dallas Seminary, where Chafer was president, "reciprocated the compliment and had Dr. Buswell as the commencement speaker and presented him with the D.D. degree."[49]

The 1930s controversies, however, strained their relationship to the breaking point. In early 1937, Buswell wrote a letter to Charles Trumbull, editor of the *Sunday School Times*, about problems he saw in Chafer's views, saying, "I do feel that Dr. Chafer's closest friends ought to endeavor to open his eyes to the implications of the weak points of his teaching."[50] Already in 1934, Buswell had written an article in the *Sunday School Times*, which hinted that there were some varieties of premillennialist views that were not wholly consistent with the Reformed faith. He mentioned no names, nor even specific viewpoints, only that "some have carried the dispensationalism to great extremes, and have insisted upon views that others cannot conscientiously accept as Scriptural."[51] At that time,

---

[46] Cf. Buswell, *The Christian Life*; idem, *Unfulfilled Prophecies* (Grand Rapids: Zondervan, 1937); and Lewis Sperry Chafer, *Grace* (Wheaton, IL: Van Kampen Press, 1922); idem, *The Kingdom in History and Prophecy* (Findlay, OH: Dunham Publishing Co., 1915). Though Buswell and Chafer took a similar approach to prophecy, their positions on the relationship of Law and Grace, and of the proper application of Old Testament and New Testament to the Christian life, were diametrically opposed.

[47] Hannah, "Social and Intellectual History of the Evangelical Theological College," vii-viii, 145-230, 368-79.

[48] See Chafer, "Dispensational Distinctions Challenged," 337-45; idem, "Dispensational Distinctions Denounced," 257-60.

[49] Edward A. Steele, III, "Buswell, the Man," *Presbyterion: Covenant Seminary Review* 2 (spring-fall 1976): 9.

[50] Quoted in letter, Lewis Sperry Chafer to J. Oliver Buswell, Jr., 8 May 1937, Lewis Sperry Chafer papers, ADTS. Robert C. McQuilkin, president of Columbia Bible College, also wrote Trumbull, with similar concerns (letters, Robert C. McQuilkin to Charles G. Trumbull, 20 February 1937, 6 May 1938, and 3 August 1938, in "Dispensationalism" file, Robert C. McQuilkin Papers, Columbia Bible College, Columbia, SC; all cited by William R. Glass, "The Development of Northern Patterns of Fundamentalism in the South, 1900-1950," [Ph.D. diss., Emory University, 1991], 238-39, n. 35).

[51] J. Oliver Buswell, Jr., "Premillennialism and the Reformed Faith: Has the 'Pre' a Good Standing?," *SSTimes* 76 (5 May 1934): 291.

Buswell suggested, "In this there must be latitude for individual freedom."[52] When Allis's and Murray's articles came out in 1936, however, Buswell felt compelled to distinguish more clearly the kinds of premillennialism that did not deserve such repudiation as that which Murray and Allis had attacked.[53]

This proved greatly offensive to Chafer. Besides writing to Trumbull to clarify himself to his old friend,[54] Chafer also wrote to Buswell.

> Back of [your criticisms] is an apparent assumption on your part that you, yourself, have all these problems perfectly adjusted and what is lacking on my part is to be instructed. Doubtless these "weak points" are those on which I disagree with you. So far as I know there is little disagreement as to my position among Bible teachers generally. . . . I cannot understand why I should be singled out as the person who is responsible for clear distinctions between Christianity and Judaism. These distinctions have been recognized and accepted by a multitude of worthy men in this and past generations. In fact, by all well-trained premillennialists.[55]

Chafer was irked that Buswell would depart from what up to then had been a "gentleman's agreement" among premillennialists, that what differences of opinion existed between them would be considered inconsequential, not publicly marked out. Chafer expressed both disapproval and perplexity at this departure in the article giving his own response to Murray's and Allis' attacks.

> A new claim has been recently made by some, namely, "I am a Premillennialist, but not a Dispensationalist." This statement evidently supposes that Premillennialism is a belief in an event which is isolated from all that precedes and all that follows it. The term *Premillennial* conveys the thought that Christ comes *before* the Millennium. . . . As well might it be argued that though the sun rises in the morning it will neither be preceded by darkness nor accompanied by light as to contend that Christ will come to the earth again, as the Scriptures relate that coming to all that precedes it and all that follows, without causing the most stupendous dispensational changes.[56]

---

[52] Ibid.
[53] Buswell, "A Premillennialist's View," 46; *idem*, "Two Communications from Dr. Buswell," *PrGuard* 4 (10 April 1937): 12-16.
[54] Letter, Lewis Sperry Chafer to Charles G. Trumbull, 30 March 1937, Lewis Sperry Chafer Papers, ADTS.
[55] Letter, Lewis Sperry Chafer to J. Oliver Buswell, Jr., 8 May 1937, Lewis Sperry Chafer papers, ADTS.
[56] Chafer, "Dispensationalism," 393-94. Chafer would maintain this same position (including even the same illustration about differences brought by the sunrise) when a distinction between confessionally consistent premillennialism and "dispensationalism" was drawn also by the AIC in 1944 (Chafer, "Dispensational Distinctions Denounced," 257).

Privately, Chafer wrote to Buswell, "There is evidently a difference of opinion [between us] as to what the human terms [for salvation] may have been in past ages, but this is certainly a very minor issue and does not justify statements which create the impression that I am heretical if, after forty years of careful research, I have come to certain Biblical conclusions on these matters."[57]

Buswell apparently felt he had been placed in an impossible situation. In his reply to Chafer's letter, his frustration is evident.

> Man, can't you see it! Re-read Murray's article and Allis' also. I do not remember whether Allis mentioned you by name, but Murray did repeatedly. Now I am a premillennialist, and you are a premillennialist. I stand for the fundamentals of the Christian faith as set forth in the system of doctrine contained in the Westminster Confession and Catechisms. Mr. Murray stands for that same system of doctrine. My name is closely associated with yours and has in the past been closely associated with Mr. Murray's. Now Mr. Murray attacks my premillennial view in the classroom and does not distinguish it from your dispensational view which he attacks in a series of articles. I am responsible for my influence on our Wheaton graduates. I do not see how I could conscientiously have kept silent. I prayed and studied much to make my reference as kindly as possible. I do not see how I could have spoken in any kindlier way. The premillennial view is not identical with your view of the dispensation of law. I defend the premillennial view. You are under attack from the enemies of premillennialism for points of doctrine which I personally do not accept. I regard you as an honored brother in the Lord, but under the circumstances I found it my duty to write the article in the Guardian, distinguishing between premillennialism and your interpretation of the dispensation of law. The Scofield Bible was under attack in what seemed to me a very unfair way. Although I do not regard the notes as inerrant, my article in the Guardian defended the Scofield Bible to such an extent that the editors felt it necessary to preface my article with the statement that they did not agree with me.[58]

At this point, Buswell was clearly hoping to preserve premillennialism's good standing in the OPC. Within a month, however, other issues (surveyed in the last chapter) contributed to splitting the church anyway, making Buswell's endeavor moot. Those premillennialists who were formerly members of the OPC from that point on became decidedly more inclined towards Niagara fundamentalism than Presbyterian fundamentalism.[59] After all, Buswell's premillennialism had fared little

---

[57] Letter, Lewis Sperry Chafer to J. Oliver Buswell, Jr., 8 May 1937, Lewis Sperry Chafer papers, ADTS.

[58] Letter, J. Oliver Buswell, Jr. to Lewis Sperry Chafer, 24 May 1937, Lewis Sperry Chafer papers, ADTS.

[59] We should be careful not to overstate this inclination. When the Bible Presbyterian Church was

better with OPC non-premillennialists than had Chafer's premillennialism anyway.[60] Thus, disagreements among premillennialists, for the time being, were set aside. Nevertheless, for our purposes, Buswell's 1936 delineation of differences between premillennialists – including his delineation of varieties of *dispensational* premillennialism – proves most significant, and is worth a closer look.

3.3 The Significance of J. Oliver Buswell's Analysis of the Controversy over Dispensational Premillennialism

In November 1936, clarifying (for the last time, it turns out) why his version of premillennialism should be considered "acceptably Reformed" within the OPC, J. Oliver Buswell stated emphatically, "Whereas I am ardently a premillennialist, my own personal views are quite extremely opposed to what is commonly called dispensationalism."[61] I suggest that Buswell is being very careful in his wording here; he does not actually say that he is not a dispensationalist (despite the obvious effect of his words). What he says, precisely, is that he is opposed to "what is *commonly called* dispensationalism." In context, all he may be saying is that he, too, strenuously opposes the positions that Murray and Allis, in their articles, have dubbed "dispensationalism."

This is not the final classification of choices that Buswell offers, however. In fact, he describes the label "Dispensationalism" as a "dangerous term," whose usage is in need of "limitation" given the variety of meanings assigned to it by different people. Buswell wonders aloud how helpful this choice of term really is, given that "dispensations" have consistently been observed in Scripture and considered significant by faithful representatives of the Reformed faith (including the Westminster Confession itself).[62]

To sharpen and clarify the meaning(s) of the term "dispensationalist," Buswell offers the following additional categorizations to specify "among those who call themselves premillennialists" what is held by the "many who also call themselves

---

formed, there was a case made for the formerly-OPC premillennialists' forming simply a "Bible Church," which proposal was rejected (see George P. Hutchinson, *The History Behind the Reformed Presbyterian Church Evangelical Synod* [Cherry Hill, NJ: Mack, 1974], 246-53). The Bible Presbyterian movement is described most accurately as a group that self-consciously tried to merge (or, perhaps, to compromise between) Niagara fundamentalism and Presbyterian fundamentalism. Even the name "Bible Presbyterian" is indicative of this; the name was suggested as something of a compromise between the desire for the type of church found in the "Independent Bible" movement (i.e., Niagara fundamentalism) and the "truly Reformed, true Presbyterian church in every sense of the word" (ibid., 247). In fact, they believed that they were the ones preserving the original vision for the conservative movement which had originally been in view when they broke with the PCUSA (Griffiths, "The Character and Leadership of Dr. Machen," 6-8.

[60] See chapter 2, above, pp. 35-39.
[61] Buswell, "A Premillennialist's view," 46.
[62] Ibid., 46-47.

dispensationalists."⁶³ (1) "[A]mong this premillennialist-dispensationalist group there has come to be a very strong reaction against the form of dispensational teaching which denies the unity of the covenant of grace";⁶⁴ (2) "Bullingerism and hyper-dispensationalism are in thorough disrepute among the great majority of so-called dispensationalist-premillennialists . . . There being this reaction against wrongfully dismembering the Word of truth, many premillennial-dispensationalists have also reacted against certain notes in the Scofield Reference Edition of the Bible."⁶⁵ (3) "I must not claim, however, that all those who reject Bullingerism are awake to the danger of these particular Scofield notes";⁶⁶ Buswell refers to those in this group as "the moderate form of dispensationalism which holds that law and grace are supplementary, but which regards the Mosaic system not as a means of grace but as a legalistic economy."⁶⁷ (4) Most dispensationalists, Buswell insists, recognize that "the general 'system of doctrine' underlying the dispensationalism of the Scofield Reference Edition of the Bible does not deny the unity of the covenant of grace."⁶⁸ Thus, "The quotations [by Murray] from a leading dispensationalist [i.e., Lewis Sperry Chafer] . . . do not fairly represent the system of doctrine taught in the notes of the Scofield Reference Edition of the Bible."⁶⁹ Buswell nevertheless is willing to concede that a small strand of dispensationalism is represented by the view "expressed by my good friend, quoted by Professor Murray, [which] is extreme, and inconsistent with the unity of the covenant of grace."⁷⁰

If we put all of these categorizations together on a chart, plot them in order (left to right) from those positions that affirm the most drastic discontinuities to those that affirm the least discontinuities between Old and New Testament dispensations, and supply names of exponents for each, we get something like the chart on the next page.

---

⁶³ Ibid.
⁶⁴ Ibid.
⁶⁵ Ibid.
⁶⁶ Ibid.
⁶⁷ Ibid., 47. Buswell refers to those holding this view as holding a "moderate form of dispensationalism," with which he does also disagree. He begins his disagreement, however, by noting that this view, which suggests "the Mosaic system [is] not a means of grace but [is] a legalistic economy," . . . is manifest in many of the arguments of our amillennial friends" (ibid). Buswell is, frankly, right about this, e.g., as is demonstrated copiously by David Lachman, *The Marrow Controversy, 1718-1723: An Historical and Theological Analysis* (Edinburgh: Rutherford House, 1988), 36-73, 389-408, 450-61.
⁶⁸ Ibid., 47.
⁶⁹ Ibid.
⁷⁰ Ibid.

A Diagram of "Dispensationalist-Premillennialist" Positions as They Existed in 1936 According to J. Oliver Buswell ("A Premillennialist's View")

Position/Category	"Premillennialists who call themselves dispensationalists" (Buswell's first category; includes all the positions below)			
	"Bullingerism," "Hyper-Dispensationalism"	"Extreme Dispensationalism"	"Moderate Dispensationalism"	"Dispensationalists who affirm the unity of the covenant of grace"
Major Tenets	1) Thoroughly, explicitly, and self-consciously denies the unity of the covenant of grace; 2) Peculiar in how late and how little is the scriptural revelation intended for the present-day people of God.	1) Rejects Bullingerism; 2) but maintains an inconsistent, self-contradictory position concerning the law and the covenant of grace; 3) believes the covenant of grace was temporarily suspended at Sinai	1) Rejects Bullingerism; 2) but "not awake to the danger of certain Scofield notes" (46).	1) Grudgingly willing (?) to accept the label "dispensationalist," but nevertheless affirm the unity of one covenant of grace; 2) Disagree sharply both with Bullingerism and with certain Scofield notes
Representative Exponents	Ethelburt W. Bullinger, "Hyper-Dispensationalists"	Lewis Sperry Chafer, certain isolated notes of the Scofield Bible	Unclear. Perhaps average lay-people who find the Scofield Bible useful? Probably those whom Buswell refers to as the "ordinary pastor, evangelist, or Bible teacher who calls himself a 'Scofield Bible-premillennialist-dispensationalist'" (47).	Buswell lists no specific examples, but we might infer the following: Allan A. MacRae, John F. Walvoord, Others who served on the revision committee of the New Scofield Reference Bible (1967), Buswell himself?
How Widespread Is Its Espousal (according to Buswell)	Very Few. "Bullingerism and hyper-dispensationalism are in thorough disrepute among the great majority of so-called dispensationalist-premillennialists" (46).	Virtually unique. "Ask almost any ordinary pastor, evangelist, or Bible teacher who calls himself a 'Scofield Bible-premillennialist-dispensationalist' and he will say emphatically that the opinion expressed by my good friend … is extreme" (47).	Ambiguous. Buswell seems to believe that the majority of dispensationalists fit in this category; could suggest that he sees problems in "dispensationalism" being from ignorance or carelessness, rather than from actual doctrinal aberration.	Many. "Among this premillennialist-dispensationalist group there has come to be a very strong reaction against the form of dispensational teaching which denies the unity of the covenant of grace" (46).

I am not suggesting that everything in Buswell's categorizations should be accepted as gospel; the precise accuracy of a couple of his suggestions is open to question. For example, Buswell suggests that the Scofield notes under critique are isolated aberrations from its overall "system of doctrine." But is this true? Though Buswell characterizes Chafer's theological inferences as being out of harmony with the overall system of theology presented by the Scofield Bible, would not Chafer, Scofield's long-time disciple, who traveled with him for years on his itinerate teaching and preaching ministry, likely be the more reliable interpreter of Scofield? It would stand to reason that Chafer's and Scofield's views were probably very similar, rather than widely divergent. And, if Chafer's interpretation of Scofield essentially represented what the Scofield notes were really intending, then what Buswell calls "extreme dispensationalism" was probably not so unique or rare at the time as Buswell suggests.[71] And besides, however rare were Chafer's views in 1936, they almost certainly became more prevalent after this controversy and after Chafer's influence had been extended for a number of decades through his well-known dispensationalist institution and writings.

Likewise, Buswell portrays "the great majority of those who call themselves dispensationalist-premillennialists" as being in the categories furthest to the right on the chart; that is, as either "moderate" (merely needing to be "awakened to the danger in certain Scofield notes"), or, like himself, in firm disagreement with the notes under critique, but nevertheless in agreement with the Scofieldian theology overall. I suspect that Buswell may "tilt the scale to the right" in this portrayal, that he may be overstating (probably unintentionally) how many are the "dispensationalists" who hold the more confessionally acceptable forms of "dispensationalism."

In truth, though, the numbers suggested by most everyone at the time seem suspiciously large, suspiciously small, or just plain fuzzy. One can readily find among different writers contradictory uses of terms like "few," "many," "vast number," "most," and "the great majority" among conflicting assessments of how great or how small is the true representation of a certain viewpoint being recommended or repudiated.[72] As best I can tell, though, no actual surveys were ever taken, so people presumably are merely reflecting the impressions taken from their own experiences. We should take any quantitative suggestions as to how widespread is a given view, therefore, with a grain of salt, recognizing that no one has derived their numbers from a methodical, documented accounting.

---

[71] Buswell's impression was clearly shared by others, nonetheless. Griffiths, too, says, "If there is a 'lunatic fringe' (as there may be in *any* world-wide movement) which teaches that men were differently saved at different times, the average modern premillennialist has no interest in it" ("The Character and Leadership of Dr. Machen," 6).

[72] Cf. the discrepancies in descriptions of how many people affirm a given viewpoint between Buswell, "A Premillennialist's View"; Chafer, "Dispensationalism"; and James E. Bear, "Dispensationalism and the Covenant of Grace," *UnSemRev* 49 (July 1938): 285-307; *idem*, "Historic Premillennialism," *UnSemRev* 55 (May 1944): 193-222.

We do not need precision, however, to see Buswell's categorizations as highly significant. If the categories he suggests existed at all in 1936, this in itself is noteworthy. Of particular interest is the remarkable similarity between Buswell's 1936 categories and the categories suggested by Blaising and Bock in their description of dispensationalism in our day.[73] Blaising and Bock's "classical-Scofieldian dispensationalism" seems similar to Buswell's "extreme dispensationalism"; what they describe as "essentialist-revised dispensationalism" seems similar to Buswell's "moderate dispensationalism"; and, finally, what they describe as "progressive dispensationalism," at least in its more Reformed versions, seems to have significant overlap (at least potentially) with Buswell's last category. This last category is Buswell's most ambiguous, though it is within this category that Buswell includes "the great majority of so-called dispensationalist-premillennialists"[74] that he had encountered in his (largely Presbyterian) acquaintance. These "dispensationalists" are those who affirm a confessionally compatible form of premillennialism, who disagree with the isolated, aberrant notes in the Scofield Bible, but who nevertheless embrace a Scofieldian "system of doctrine" overall.[75]

Of course, if the correlation I am making is correct, it would place even some self-described "normative dispensationalists" (most notably, John Walvoord) within the group on Buswell's chart that has the most significant overlap with progressive dispensationalism. This requires some explanation, given how outspoken have been some of these "normative dispensationalists" in their critiques of progressive dispensationalism.[76]

When one looks carefully at some of the most common normative dispensationalist objections to progressive dispensationalism, one discovers details that must be fit into a larger picture. Walvoord, for instance, sees progressive dispensationalism as "an attempt to redefine dispensationalism to make it less offensive to those of other beliefs, such as amillennialists and even nondispensational premillennialists. One of the tendencies has been to soften and to somewhat blur the distinction between the various dispensations."[77] The rest of Walvoord's argument is against such "blurring of distinctions" which would make such "softening" possible.

I think it is worth asking why Walvoord would object to such progressive dispensationalist "softening" when he himself publicly affirmed the unity of the covenant of grace, and when he himself expressed confidence that this central tenet of Reformed-Covenant theology may be safely incorporated into a

---

[73] Craig A. Blaising and Darrell L. Bock, *Dispensationalism, Israel and the Church: The Search for Definition* (Grand Rapids: Zondervan, 1992), 379.
[74] Buswell, "A Premillennialist's View," 46-47.
[75] Ibid.
[76] E.g., John Walvoord, "Biblical Kingdoms Compared and Contrasted," in *Issues in Dispensationalism*, ed. Wesley Willis, John Master, and Charles Ryrie (Chicago: Moody, 1994), 75-91.
[77] Ibid., 88.

thoroughly dispensationalist theology[78] (views that are themselves in direct opposition to those of fellow "normative dispensationalist," Charles Ryrie[79]).

Of course, Walvoord's embrace of this central tenet of "covenant theology" also requires some explanation, given how vigorous were his own critiques of "covenant theology" at one time.[80] A combination of elements provides that explanation. First, even amidst his critique of covenant theology, Walvoord (again, unlike Ryrie[81]) was careful to qualify, "Covenant theology is [an] illustration of overstatement of that which is true in its right perspective. All

---

[78] John F. Walvoord, "The New Covenant," in *Integrity of Heart, Skillfulness of Hands: Biblical and Leadership Studies in Honor of Donald K. Campbell*, ed. Charles H. Dyer and Roy B. Zuck (Grand Rapids: Baker, 1994), 187-88, 197-99; idem, *Major Bible Prophecies* (Grand Rapids: Zondervan, 1991), 189; idem, *The Prophecy Knowledge Handbook* (Wheaton, IL: Victor Books, 1990), 140. Stephen Spencer correctly observes that some of Walvoord's earlier critiques of "covenant theology" "overlook[ed] the variations within the covenant tradition" ("Reformed Theology, Covenant Theology, and Dispensationalism," also in *Integrity of Heart, Skillfulness of Hands*, 251). Cf. also Spencer's observation that Walvoord's dispensationalism makes "the distinction between covenant theology and dispensationalism a matter of emphasis . . . rather than a matter of separate and exclusive assertions" (251). Apparently, Walvoord has held reservations about Scofield's and Chafer's denial of one covenant of grace for at least forty-five years. "In a letter written in 1956, the President of Dallas Seminary, Dr. John F. Walvoord, said, 'I feel that our statement on dispensations is much nearer the norm among contemporary dispensationalists than some of Dr. Chafer's explanations.' Walvoord felt that 'in many places he [Dr. Chafer] does seem to overemphasize the legal character of the Mosaic dispensation as well as the millennial kingdom and to put a similar stress on grace in the present age.' Declaring himself to be in general harmony with Chafer's teachings, Walvoord said he believed 'it is fair to state that Dr. Chafer should be regarded somewhat in the role of a creative thinker who, like all other creative thinkers, states things somewhat differently than others and sometimes over-states distinctions in an effort to make his point'" (Daniel Fuller, *Gospel and Law: Contrast or Continuum?* [Grand Rapids: Eerdmans, 1980], 37; quoting from a letter, John F. Walvoord to Daniel P. Fuller, 23 November 1956). Walvoord's remarks in this letter to Fuller are consistent with remarks he also made to me in my interviews, Dallas, TX, 11 and 18 April, 2 May 1995. Cf. also similar remarks by E. Schuyler English and Wilbur Smith in "Is Evangelical Theology Changing?" *Christian Life* 17 (March 1956): 16-19.

[79] Ryrie insists that, whatever "developments" may have taken place in the history of dispensational theology, "basic differences remain" between dispensationalism and covenant theology; in fact, for a view to be recognized legitimately as dispensationalist, it must, *qua* dispensationalism, be in conflict with covenant theology at certain key points ("Update on Dispensationalism," in *Issues in Dispensationalism*, 24). To illustrate and substantiate this claim, Ryrie offers a series of rhetorical questions: "Can the reformed covenant of grace ever be satisfactorily assimilated into any dispensational system? Can the Millennium ever be deliteralized enough or placed far enough in the background to make the premillennial system tolerable to amillennialists (which almost all covenant people are)? Can the discontinuities in dispensationalism be overshadowed enough to bring acceptability, or will the discontinuities (i.e., distinctives) fade into near oblivion?" (24). Ryrie seems unaware that, especially by the first of these rhetorical questions, he has actually singled out fellow "normative dispensationalist" stalwart, John Walvoord!

[80] John F. Walvoord, *The Millennial Kingdom* (Findlay, OH: Dunham Publishing Co., 1959), 92-93.

[81] Charles Ryrie, *Dispensationalism Today* (Chicago: Moody, 1965), 43-47, 98-105, 177-91.

Reformed theologians would agree that God has a complete and comprehensive purpose as stated in the theological doctrine of the decree of God. Under this concept, all events of every classification have been determined by God from eternity past. . . . All the events of the created world are designed to manifest the glory of God."[82] Secondly, Walvoord says he never intended to critique covenant theology *per se* in a wholesale manner, only *certain varieties* of covenant theology (viz., *amillennial* varieties).[83] And finally, by his own accounting, Walvoord's understanding of covenant amillennialism in 1956 was greatly influenced by C. Fred Lincoln's assessment of covenant theology,[84] which understanding Walvoord would later modify, even conceding that his own critique of what he termed "covenant theology" in 1956 stood in need of better nuance. Despite the fact that he publicized his (partial) agreement with covenant theology only very late in life, he maintained to the end of his life that he had held these same views since before his ordination in the Presbyterian denomination in 1934; what he always opposed was any form of covenant amillennialism.[85]

With all this in mind, we can discern something significant in Walvoord's position as a whole. Throughout the 1980s and 1990s, Walvoord insisted adamantly on a relatively subtle distinction to set his position apart from progressive dispensationalism: viz., though the Bible's unfolding plan of redemption may legitimately be characterized as the unfolding of one covenant of grace, "harder" distinctions between the individual dispensational manifestations of this one covenant grace must be maintained than what progressive dispensationalism is willing to embrace.[86] Meanwhile, Walvoord diminished as insignificant the even greater difference his position had with other prominent "normative dispensationalist" positions, which insist that proper dispensationalism inherently opposes the very idea of one covenant of grace. I suggest that this striking disproportion of alliances itself points to some of the significant sociological consequences of the falling out between dispensationalism and covenant theology through the 1930s-1960s.

Walvoord took over the presidency of Dallas Seminary in 1952, just after the death of his beloved mentor, Lewis Sperry Chafer, and just as the animosities between dispensationalists and covenant theologians had reached their zenith. We can only speculate as to what would have happened had the polarization been diffused, rather than intensified, fifteen years earlier with the publication of

---

[82] Ibid., 92.
[83] John F. Walvoord, interview by the author, Dallas, TX, 11 April 1995. "Amillennial soteriology" is indeed the title of the chapter in which his critique of "covenant theology" is forwarded (ibid., 84-93).
[84] See C. Fred Lincoln, "The Covenants" (Th.D. diss., Dallas Theological Seminary, 1942); *idem*, "The Development of the Covenant Theory," *BibSac* 100 (January-March 1943): 134-63; and *idem*, "The Biblical Covenants, Parts 1-3" *BibSac* 100 (April-December 1943): 309-23, 442-49, 565-73.
[85] John F. Walvoord, interview by the author, Dallas, TX, 11 April 1995.
[86] Walvoord, "Biblical Kingdoms Compared and Contrasted, 88-91.

Buswell's 1936 article. It is possible that Walvoord, despite his affirmation of one covenant of grace, still would have come to insist just as adamantly on sharp distinctions between the church age and the millennial kingdom (e.g., as over against the suggestions of today's "progressive dispensationalists"),[87] but I, frankly, doubt it. I find his disparagement of suggested motives of progressive dispensationalists noteworthy. Without the polarization of the 1930s-1940s, would Walvoord have reason to oppose so vigorously attempts to mediate between "other views"; that is, if he did not regard those "other views" with such contempt?

Of course, ultimately, we cannot know for sure. We do know, however, that Walvoord and other like-minded dispensationalists were able to work in remarkable harmony with Presbyterian, Reformed-Covenant premillennialists (like Allan A. MacRae) to revise the very notes in the Scofield Reference Bible that proved so bothersome to covenant theologians of the 1930s-1940s.[88] I also find MacRae's impression of this committee to be of some significance (which impression Walvoord shared[89]): "We as a committee were in overall agreement, our disagreements were very slight – our disagreements grew a lot wider among our students."[90]

It appears to me that the polarizations which came in the years after Buswell's article pushed "dispensationalism," as a whole, further toward the "anti-covenantalist" elements of its ideological and sociological makeup. Whereas, in November 1936, dispensational premillennialists were trying to demonstrate their compliance with covenantalist, confessional standards, sociological momentum moved in the exact opposite direction once this was deemed futile.

This would account for how "classical dispensationalism" (i.e., Scofieldian-Chaferian dispensationalism) would come to be deemed as the "classical" form of dispensational ideology. Outside of "hyper-dispensationalism," which apparently was always a marginal view, "classical dispensationalism" stands in sharpest contrast to covenant theology; it rose to prominence in the debate with covenant theology in the 1930s-1940s, which formed the context for dispensationalism's very identity.

This hypothesis also accounts for how the myth would arise that a "normative" form of dispensationalism has always been affirmed by "true dispensationalists," which "normative" form provides a clear list of tenets to be affirmed or denied by anyone wishing to discern whether a theological view or system is truly "dispensationalist."[91] If dispensationalism be defined in terms of its conflict with covenant theology, then "essentialist dispensationalism" could

---

[87] Walvoord, "Biblical Kingdoms Compared and Contrasted," 88-91.
[88] I will take up this point in more detail in chapters 5 and 6, below.
[89] John F. Walvoord, interview by the author, Dallas, TX, 2 May 1995.
[90] Allan A. MacRae, interview by the author, Quarryville, PA, 3 August 1993.
[91] Carl Sanders II, "The Myth of Normative Dispensationalism," unpublished paper delivered at the Annual Meeting of the Evangelical Theological Society, Danvers, MA, 17 November 1999.

perhaps be held up as the standard. It has the strongest track record of establishing itself over against covenant theology, it has garnered the widest consensus among self-described dispensationalists as remaining true to the "central core" of dispensationalist tenets, and it is also quite successful in relieving many of the inconsistencies and problems of other, more "extreme" versions of dispensationalism. It even makes sense, in such an accounting, why essentialist dispensationalists would prefer to call their view "classic dispensationalism,"[92] so as to stress the perceived connection with Scofield and Chafer.

Even still, it simply is not true that essentialist dispensationalism represents a set of tenets to which all dispensationalists everywhere through all time have believed.[93] In truth, there has always been a fairly wide variegation of positions included under the label "dispensationalism," ever since the term was first coined. Ironically, as we have just observed, one can detect evidence of this variegation even among self-described "normative dispensationalists" attempting to present a united front against "progressive dispensationalism" today!

Despite the claim of some essentialist dispensationalists that progressive dispensationalist ideas have been suggested only recently (at least within *dispensationalism*),[94] we find a vague (though more thoroughly covenantalist) prototype of "progressive dispensationalism" in Buswell's 1936 categorizations. One might ask why the resemblance is so vague; and also why today even some progressive dispensationalists are making so pronounced an effort to distinguish their "progressive" version of dispensationalism from covenant theology.[95]

---

[92] E.g., Ryrie, *Dispensationalism*, 11; Gary Gromacki, "Progressive Dispensationalism," *Journal of Ministry and Theology* 3 (fall, 1999): 97-100.

[93] Sanders, "The Myth of Normative Dispensationalism."

[94] E.g., Walvoord, "Biblical Kingdoms Compared and Contrasted," 88-91; Ryrie, *Dispensationalism*, 161-81.

[95] E.g., Robert Saucy, "The Crucial Issue Between Dispensational and Non-Dispensational Systems," *Criswell Theological Review* 1 (January 1986): 155-65; Darrell Bock, "Why I Am a Dispensationalist with a Small 'd'," *JETS* 41 (July 1998): 386-88, especially n. 5; *idem*, "Charting Dispensationalism," *CT* 38 (12 September 1994): 26-29; *idem*, "Free Space for Dialogue Outside of Our Circles, Interview with Darrell L. Bock: Does the New Testament Reshape Our Understanding of the Old Testament?" *Modern Reformation* 9 (July/August 2000): 48-50; and *idem*, "Hermeneutics of Progressive Dispensationalism," and "Covenants in Progressive Dispensationalism," in *Three Central Issues in Contemporary Dispensationalism: A Comparison of Traditional and Progressive Views*, ed. Herbert W. Bateman IV (Grand Rapids: Kregel Publications, 1999), 90-94, 172-73. Each of these treatises declares that progressive dispensationalism demonstrates itself to be genuinely *dispensationalist* just because it is *not* compatible with covenant theology on certain key issues (mainly concerning the relationship between Israel and the Church). Within the same volume in which Bock makes this point several times (*Three Central Issues in Contemporary Dispensationalism*), however, J. Lanier Burns provides a more circumspect accounting of the relationship between "progressive dispensationalism" and "covenant theology" ("Israel and the Church of a Progressive Dispensationalist," 263-91). While acknowledging that evangelical theologians of various persuasions, including his fellow progressive dispensationalist colleague, Darrell Bock, have traditionally regarded the distinctive eschatological role for national Israel as a "determinative issue" between the two camps (264), he never goes so far as Bock does in claiming this

Might it not be, again, because the polarizations brought on by the 1930s-1940s covenant-dispensationalist conflicts caused both sides to retreat from middle ground and to reinforce positions which distinguished each side from the other?

Here, again, my thesis comes into play. I suggest that what one confronts repeatedly in the history of the debate between dispensationalism and covenant theology is the sociological function of doctrinal formation and affirmation, and the powerful influence of this sociological force on doctrinal development.[96] The controversies of the 1930s-1940s, with its doctrinal and sociological polarizations, formed the context that established for many the very identity of "Reformed" (covenant theological) communities over against "dispensationalist" ones, and vice versa. Buswell's article allows us practically to pinpoint when exactly these lines of division were being drawn.

Had Buswell's categorizations been accepted by premillennialists and non-premillennialists alike in the OPC, then the Chafer-Scofield version of premillennialism likely would have been isolated, and a hard-and-fast distinction between Reformed-covenantalism and non-Reformed dispensationalism (an aberrant from of premillennialism) might have been set forever. But this did not happen. Instead, Buswell's mediating position was firmly rejected by OPC non-premillennialists. Thus, because the categorizations that Buswell had observed then served no one very well, sociologically speaking, they were thereafter largely ignored by all sides. These lines of division, for all practical purposes, eventually vanished from view, but not because Buswell's categorizations were invalid or non-existent at the time. Indeed, the reappearance of similar categories today may be indication that they never actually disappeared altogether. Rather, they were only concealed from view, as the differences that still existed among "dispensationalists" from the time of the 1937 split were minimized or ignored. The outstanding exception to this felicitous minimization of differences was the breach between Buswell and Chafer, which apparently was never fully repaired.[97]

"distinctiveness" for his own view. Rather, he encourages his dispensationalist brethren to further dialogue with covenant theologians on this issue, because, he says, the questions thereby raised "about the text expose preunderstandings of dispensationalists that might otherwise be glossed" (272). In concluding his essay, Burns suggests that many issues could not be addressed that are of importance to the historical dispensationalist-covenantalist debate. Nevertheless, in clarifying the place of his own essay in this debate, Burns explicitly declares that he has been pressed by his exegetical and theological study to take a "middle ground" (290).

[96] Cf. George Lindbeck, *The Nature of Doctrine* (Philadelphia: Westminster Press, 1984); and Alister E. McGrath, *The Genesis of Doctrine: A Study in the Foundations of Doctrinal Criticism* (Cambridge, MA: Blackwell Publishers, 1990). While McGrath argues that Lindbeck overstates the sociological nature of doctrine, they are agreed that doctrine does serve significant sociological functions, viz., 1) to provide a social identity (i.e., grounds for "fellowship," to use the terminology of evangelicalism); 2) to interpret history, including one's own; 3) to interpret one's experience; and 4) to assert truth claims.

[97] Apparently, Chafer shared publicly what he had told Buswell in a private letter in 1937, regarding the untenable, theological "inconsistency" in Buswell's covenant premillennialist construction (letter, Lewis Sperry Chafer to J. Oliver Buswell, 8 May 1937, Lewis Sperry

Had a period of stillness followed the 1937 OPC split, the variety of (dispensational) premillennial views may have been allowed to recover and regroup. Then perhaps the fissures between premillennial views might never have widened and the previous amalgam of premillennialist views might have permanently re-solidified. But this did not happen either.

Some ties between disparate premillennialist viewpoints were rejoined (at least for a time) once premillennialists separated from the OPC; for a while, the similarities between premillennialists, rather than differences, received the greater emphasis.[98] But, alas, a clean break between two clearly demarcated eschatological camps, premillennialism vs. non-premillennialism, was not to be. Such a clear division of eschatological alliances was refused by events about to take place.

As the 1930s drew to a close, just as the country was recovering out of the Great Depression, so also premillennialism was beginning to mend its wounds. Little did they know, however, that, in both cases, they had suffered only the first wave of troubles; their most challenging days lay ahead. America was about to enter the Second World War, which, for many, would make their previous

---

Chafer papers, ADTS). The argument that dispensationalism was merely "consistent premillennialism" over against "partial" or "inconsistent" varieties of premillennialism was picked up by Chafer's students, colleagues, and successors. See C. Fred Lincoln, "The Biblical Covenants [Part 3]," *BibSac* 100 (October-December 1943): 565-73; also *idem*, "Covenant, Dispensational, and Related Studies," unpublished course notes, Dallas Theological Seminary, ca 1950, (I am indebted to Donald K. Campbell for providing me a copy of these notes). In Lincoln's course notes is found one of the few explicit references to Buswell as being the one in view in dispensationalist critiques of "those who declare that they are 'Premillennialists' but not Dispensationalists" (10). Other critiques of "non-dispensational premillennialism" are included in John F. Walvoord, "The New Covenant with Israel," *BibSac* 103 (January-March 1946): 16-27; *idem*, "The Theological Context of Premillennialism," *BibSac* 108 (April-June 1951): 270-81; *idem*, "The Abrahamic Covenant and Premillennialism, Parts 1 and 2," *BibSac* 108 (October-December 1951) and 109 (January-March 1952): 414-22, and 37-46; Charles C. Ryrie, "The Necessity of Dispensationalism," *BibSac* 114 (April-June 1957): 243-54; Alva J. McClain, "A Premillennial Philosophy of History," 113 (January 1956): 111-16; Nickolas Kurtaneck, "Excellencies of Dispensationalism," *GTJ* 3 (January 1962): 3-11. Hannah observes, too, that Chafer's and Buswell's falling out created a rift between Dallas Theological Seminary and Wheaton College, as well ("Social and Intellectual History of the Evangelical Theological College," 358-60), rifts that have not been bridged to this day.

[98] See pp. 26-40, above. Allan A. MacRae and Carl McIntire remained at least very friendly with "dispensationalists" after the 1936-37 controversies, cooperated often with them, conducted meetings and conferences together with them, etc., a pattern that likely was repeated elsewhere, too. MacRae even contributed to the Pilgrim Bible and served on the revision committee of the New Scofield Reference Bible of 1967, making him, by definition in many minds, a "dispensationalist" (despite MacRae's never being comfortable with the label); Allan A. MacRae, interview by author, Quarryville, PA, 3 August 1993 and 23 January 1997. Cf. Leslie W. Sloat, "Pilgrim on the Wrong Road: New Bible Edition Promotes Dispensational Teachings," *PrGuard* 17 (September 1948): 220-22; *idem*, "Pilgrim on the Wrong Road (2): Ancient and Modern Errors Among Teachings of New Bible," *PrGuard* 17 (October 1948): 239-41. See also E. Schuyler English, "The New Scofield Reference Bible," 125-32, especially nn. 1-3.

financial losses seem small in comparison to the kinds of sacrifices they were about to suffer. Likewise, exponents of the Chafer-Scofield theology may have been perturbed by mid-1930s Northern Presbyterian critiques of "dispensationalism"; the premillennialist coalition may have been rattled. But they had seen nothing yet.

CHAPTER 4

The Tremors Travel Southward (Part 1): The Context of the Controversy over Dispensationalism in the PCUS

In June of 1940, the very year in which the PCUS General Assembly took up the question of dispensationalism's orthodoxy, Union Seminary professor James Bear, the man who would prove most influential on the investigating committee, published an article in the *Presbyterian of the South*, titled, "Shall We Revise the Standards?". This article not only exhibits the analysis that would soon be embodied in the AIC report, but also voices the umbrage felt by Southern Presbyterians at certain recent activities of Northern Presbyterian premillennialists.

> [The Bible Presbyterian Church is] attempting a degree of proselyting in the Southern Presbyterian Church which, as far as I know, is without parallel. . . . [F]or some time now, some in **The Bible Presbyterian Church** have been seeking adherents in their group from our church by sending our ministers and others in positions of leadership free copies of the publication, the **Christian Beacon**. This is no inexpensive undertaking for a small and financially weak church, and some one is furnishing the money for a purpose, and undoubtedly that purpose is either to win over the Southern Presbyterian Church to their point of view or to divide it, carrying off what they can of the membership. Signs of the dividing process are already evident in our church, as all who read the **Christian Beacon** know, for it joyfully features the churches which have already been split, telling how the pastor has carried off a part of his flock to form in our Southland a **Bible Presbyterian Church**. It is reported among us that other churches are getting into a serious condition because of the propaganda of those who agree with

the teaching of the **Bible Presbyterian Church** and are also in danger of being divided.[1]

According to Bear, the "teaching of the Bible Presbyterian Church" that was creating such a stir was premillennialism – a virulent brand of premillennialism unwilling to accept any potential marginalization doctrinally or ecclesiastically.[2] This brings us very close to the question of how dispensational premillennialism became an issue in the PCUS.[3]

The impression of virulence was created by the unique situation in the Northern Presbyterian context at the time. Premillennialists in the Northern Presbyterian Church had always contended that their eschatological view was within the doctrinal parameters laid out by the Westminster Standards. However, once the premillennialists had formed their own church, they decided to ensure perpetuation of their view by making a few, key adjustments in the Confession of Faith. These adjustments Bear noted with clear disapproval.

> Till the **Bible Presbyterian Church** revised the Westminster Standards, they had no **creedal** justification for their viewpoint. No early creed of the church teaches their viewpoint. The creeds of the modern church date from the Reformation period, and not one of them teaches or even suggests a Millennial Kingdom. . . .
>
> It has been said in the past that if Christians would agree on other fundamental doctrines, they could agree to disagree on eschatology, and could still work together in harmony. However since the rise of Dispensationalism and Russellism and Adventism such harmonious cooperation does not seem possible, for those who hold these views have their whole Biblical and religious viewpoint colored by their view of eschatology and they are intolerant towards all those who do not agree with them.
>
> The changes which the **Bible Presbyterian Church** has made in the Westminster Standards not only frankly teach Premillennialism but also give a creedal basis for all who wish to justify themselves in developing the whole field of Dispensational teaching. The fact that they have had to make these changes shows that they themselves acknowledge that their position was not taught in the Westminster Standards.[4]

---

[1] James E. Bear, "Shall We Revise the Standards?," *PrSouth* 115 (12 June 1940): 3 (bold text original).

[2] Ibid.

[3] The words are chosen very carefully here; *premillennialism* had a part in how *dispensationalism* became an issue in the PCUS. We must always remember that there were three premillennialists on the committee that found dispensationalism out of accord with the Westminster Standards. Premillennialism *per se* was not the deciding issue in the AIC's final report. We will address the point more fully later, but the belief that premillennialism was the central issue in question, despite explicit clarifications to the contrary, was a misunderstanding that has persisted.

[4] Bear, "Shall We Revise the Standards?," 3.

Three premillennialists would sit on the committee when it handed down its decision three years later. Nevertheless, the AIC would come to much the same conclusion about *dispensational* premillennialism that Bear articulated in this article.

How exactly did dispensational premillennialism get into such a predicament, especially given what Bear refers to as the customary Presbyterian willingness "to agree to disagree on eschatology, and . . . still work together in harmony"?[5] The answer to that question lies, once again, in how the debate flowed from North to South.[6]

4.1 Dispensationalism in the Crossfire of Southern Presbyterian "Conservatism" and "Liberalism"

The PCUS was generally more conservative all around than her Northern counterpart. The Southern Presbyterian Church was more thoroughly "Old School" than even conservative segments of the Northern Presbyterian Church.[7] Plus, the Southern Church just held her traditions in higher esteem and with greater reverence than did the North. Southern culture's *conservatism* is understood as a virtual truism among students of the South.[8] Southern Presbyterian historian Ernest Trice

---

[5] This customary latitude had been afforded in both Northern and Southern Presbyterian churches; cf. J. Gresham Machen, "Eschatological Freedom," *PrGuard* 2 (4 May 1936): 44, 52.

[6] "Despite its past associations and its present notoriety as the element of southern religion that leads to the characterization of the region as the Bible belt, fundamentalism was not native to the South. It was primarily northern and urban in origin and was a movement with a distinctive theology and marked by a militant opposition to liberalism. This concern for theology led to particular patterns of denominational controversy in the North as fundamentalists tried [to] reverse the growing influence of liberals within their churches. The appearance of this system of beliefs in the South in the early twentieth century resulted from the enlistment of some southern Protestants with the consequence leading to disputes within southern churches similar to those that had developed in the north" (William Robert Glass, "The Development of Northern Patterns of Fundamentalism in the South, 1900-1950" [Ph.D. diss., Emory University, 1991], 2-3).

[7] Jack P. Maddex, Jr., "Old School/New School," in *Encyclopedia of Religion in the South*, ed. Samuel S. Hill (Macon, GA: Mercer University Press, 1984), 570-72.

[8] Probably the most famous analyst – and most ardent defender – of Southern conservatism is the late Richard Malcolm Weaver of the University of Chicago (e.g., see his *The Southern Tradition at Bay: A History of Postbellum Thought* [New Rochelle, NY: Arlington House, 1968]). For less flattering evaluations of the conservatism prominent in Southern culture, see Wilbur J. Cash, *The Mind of the South* (New York: Doubleday, 1941); or Blanche McCrary Boyd, *The Redneck Way of Knowledge: Down-Home Tales* (New York: Alfred A. Knopf, 1982). University of North Carolina professor, John Shelton Reed and his wife, Dale Reed, have put together a popular level anthology of Southern culture entitled, *1001 Things Everyone Should Know About the South* (New York: Doubleday, 1996); the South's conservatism is highlighted both humorously and seriously at key points. Regarding southerners' theological conservatism, see Norman F. Furniss, *The Fundamentalist Controversy: 1918-1931* (New Haven, CT: Yale University Press, 1954), 119, 147.

Thompson states matter-of-factly, "Among Southern Presbyterians generally the five 'fundamentals,' endorsed by the General Assembly of the Presbyterian Church in the U.S.A., were accepted without question."[9]

While the demeanor of Southern culture and ideology has been universally recognized as conservative, closer scrutiny reveals that "Southern conservatism" is multi-layered.[10] In the Southern Presbyterian Church, especially, we need to peel away and study these layers if we are to understand the dynamics at work in the 1940s controversy. Three kinds of "conservatism" form the dominant strands of Southern Presbyterian conservative thought in the 1940s: 1) theological conservatism; 2) Confessional conservatism; and 3) socio-political (Confederate) conservatism.

Theological conservatism affirmed the inerrancy of Scripture, the Deity and Virgin Birth of Christ, and other "fundamentals" of the faith. It was a theological battle between theological conservatives and liberals that was at the heart of the modernist-fundamentalist controversy in the North, as we have seen. In the South, though, theological conservatism was *not* really at issue.

Even self-described "liberals" in the Southern Presbyterian Church were careful to clarify that they were *theologically* conservative, at least where it counted.[11] This is true even in the writings of the most outspoken and perhaps most well known Southern Presbyterian "liberal" of the time: John A. MacLean, pastor of the prestigious Ginter Park Presbyterian Church in the heart of the Southern Presbyterian ecclesiastical center in Richmond, Virginia.[12] In a series of articles,[13]

---

[9] Ernest Trice Thompson, *Presbyterians in the South, Volume Three: 1890-1972* (Richmond: John Knox Press, 1973), 324. Glass concurs: "[S]outherners did not go to the barricades with their northern brethren in the denominational controversies of [the] 1920s despite the efforts of northerners to create a southern wing of their movement. For one reason, southern Protestants did not see their denominations succumbing to theological liberalism; for the most part, their denominations still affirmed and defended orthodoxy. . . . The disease was in the northern denominations, and the absence of institutional ties insulated and protected southern churches" ("The Development of Northern Patterns of Fundamentalism in the South," 65).

[10] For a recent essay that argues this point, see Donald G. Matthews, "'We have left undone those things which we ought to have done': Southern Religious History in Retrospect and Prospect," *CH* 67 (July 1998): 305-25.

[11] This point is clearly expressed by John M. Alexander in his two-part article, "Must a Theological Conservative Be a Social Conservative?" *PrSouth* 118 (3 and 10 November 1943): 6-7 and 5-6.

[12] See "Southern Presbyterian Notables: John Allan MacLean," *PrOut* 129 (20 January 1947): 8-9. The phrase "ecclesiastical center" is MacLean's own description of the city of Richmond (John Allan MacLean, "Liberalism in the Southern Presbyterian Church," *PrOut* 127 [13 August 1945]: 4). It is an apt description. Within a three block section just off Chamberlayne Avenue is located Ginter Park Presbyterian Church, Union Theological Seminary, and the Assembly's Training School (which later became the Presbyterian School of Christian Education). These three institutions, though officially unaffiliated, historically enjoyed significant cooperation and even occasional sharing of facilities and faculty. Additionally, both the *Union Seminary Review* and the *Presbyterian Outlook*, two publishing staples of the Southern Presbyterian Church, were published out of Richmond; again, though officially unaffiliated, the two publications shared

MacLean explained and defended the Southern Presbyterian liberalism that was fast gaining ground.

MacLean clarified that the "mild liberalism" of the Southern church should be distinguished from the more radical, more dangerous, and more unacceptable types of "liberalism" in the Northern church,[14] a point all the more significant given the "relative" nature of such terms as "conservative" and "liberal" anyway. MacLean was even willing to place himself on the "spectrum" for his readers, so as to clarify the import of his point.

> At home in the South, this writer has always thought of himself as moderately liberal, but as a student in Edinburgh, Scotland, he was classed as a dyed-in-the-wool conservative. As a matter of fact, so far as the big things of our faith are concerned, the differences between the two groups of Christians in our denomination are more seeming than real. As the word "liberal" is used in the North and in Europe, it could hardly be applied to our church, and instead of employing the term, it would probably be more accurate to classify our members as "progressive conservative" and "ultra-conservative" or "progressive" and "fundamentalist." Though, of course, all of us believe ourselves to be fundamental, so far as the real Christian truth is concerned.[15]

Historical-theological hindsight largely vindicates MacLean's point here. MacLean affirmed the full Deity of Christ,[16] the substitutionary atonement (though he clarified that Southern Presbyterian liberals also find enough value in "the moral influence" theory to incorporate it into their understanding of the overall "big idea" of what the atonement accomplished[17]), and the bodily return of Christ.[18] He did not

---

significant overlap in administrative personnel and editorial staff. Not surprisingly, Ginter Park Presbyterian Church, which MacLean pastored, served (and does so still today) as the parish home of virtually all the faculty and most of the student body of Union Theological Seminary, the flagship seminary of the Southern Presbyterian Church. See "John Allan MacLean Fellowship Established by Ginter Park Church," *PrOut* 130 (2 February 1948): 11-12. The press release announcing the construction of Schauffler Hall, a facility shared by both the school and the church, indicates how far back the warm relationship between Ginter Park Presbyterian Church and Union Theological Seminary went: "Schauffler Hall," *PrStand* 60 (6 August 1919): 5.

[13] John Allan MacLean, "Liberalism in the Southern Presbyterian Church: First of Three Articles Seeking to Building [sic] a Bridge of Understanding Between Men of the Same Loyalties, but of Different Temperaments," *Presbyterian Outlook* [the same journal as the *Presbyterian of the South*; the journal changed its name, as indication of its "broader" perspective, in April, 1944] 127 (13 August 1945): 4-6; "What Southern Presbyterian Liberals Believe," *PrOut* 127 (20 August 1945): 5-7; and "What Southern Presbyterian Liberals Are Driving At," *PrOut* 127 (27 August 1945): 6-7.

[14] MacLean, "Liberalism in the Southern Presbyterian Church," 5.

[15] Ibid.

[16] MacLean, "What Southern Presbyterian Liberals Believe," 6.

[17] Ibid.

[18] Ibid.

affirm the inerrancy of Scripture, but he did affirm the overall *authority* of Scripture, pointing out that Southern Presbyterian "'liberals' would hardly go so far as either Calvin or Luther" in disparaging the book of James (Luther), or in suggesting that Luke knowingly passed on "mistakes" in his historical accounts (Calvin).[19]

Thus, as far as "liberals" go, MacLean, who represents the left-most pole of the Southern Presbyterian Church, is not all that liberal. He is, at most, neo-orthodox; his use of Luther and Calvin as historical precedents sounds very much like Barth[20] and Brunner[21] on the same point. Compared to the liberalism of, say, Paul Tillich, who suggested that theological language (including that of the Bible) is merely one way humans express ineffable, existential issues of "ultimate concern,"[22] MacLean looks almost like a fundamentalist; or, compared to even the milder liberalism of Walter Rauschenbusch, who discarded the substitutionary atonement entirely in favor of the moral influence view,[23] MacLean is downright right-wing.[24] Today, MacLean's positions might be considered within the "progressive wing" of evangelicalism,[25] rather than "liberal."[26] Even using Kenneth Cauthen's older framing, MacLean could be considered "liberal" only as he fits within "evangelical liberalism," a much more conservative type of liberalism which Cauthen sharply distinguishes, as a class, from "modernistic liberalism."[27]

---

[19] Ibid.

[20] Karl Barth, *Doctrine of the Word of God*, vol. 1, part 1 of *Church Dogmatics*, ed. and trans. G. W. Bromiley and T. F. Torrance (Edinburgh: T. & T. Clarke, 1936), 126-28.

[21] Emil Brunner, *The Christian Doctrine of God* (Philadelphia: Westminster Press, 1950), 107-11.

[22] Paul Tillich, *Systematic Theology*, vol. 1 (Chicago, IL: University of Chicago Press, 1951), 14-15.

[23] See Walter Rauschenbusch, *A Theology for the Social Gospel* (New York: MacMillan, 1917), 154-55.

[24] My choices of Tillich and Rauschenbusch for comparison are, admittedly, arbitrary, but they do make the point as to where MacLean is on the "spectrum" of liberalism. For fuller treatments of how liberalism consists of a spectrum of viewpoints, see Kenneth Cauthen, *The Impact of American Religious Liberalism* (New York, NY: Harper & Row, 1962); and Lloyd J. Averill, *American Theology in the Liberal Tradition* (Philadelphia, PA: Westminster Press, 1967). For essays typifying or analyzing theological liberalism as an ideology, see William R. Hutchison, ed., *American Protestant Thought: The Liberal Era* (New York, NY: Harper & Row, 1968); and Robert S. Michaelsen and Wade Clark Roof, eds., *Liberal Protestantism: Realities & Possibilities* (New York, NY: Pilgrim Press, 1986).

[25] His positions on the inspiration and authority of Scripture, for instance, seem very similar to those of Jack B. Rogers and Donald K. McKim of Fuller Seminary (*The Authority and Interpretation of the Bible: An Historical Approach* [New York: Harper & Row, 1979]); William Abraham of Southern Methodist University's Perkins School of Theology (*The Divine Inspiration of Holy Scripture* [New York: Oxford University Press, 1981]); or Donald G. Bloesch of Dubuque Theological Seminary (*Holy Scripture: Revelation, Inspiration & Interpretation* [Downers Grove, IL: IVP, 1994]).

[26] E.g., see Gordon Kaufman, *Systematic Theology* (New York, NY: Charles Scribner's Sons, 1968), 69.

[27] Cauthen, "Types of American Liberalism," in *The Impact of American Religious Liberalism*, 26-37. Glass's observation is also helpful: "Historians have labeled the two liberal parties as

By this point, the labels are just clearly inadequate, if not misleading, which itself raises a significant question. What purpose did the labels "conservative" and "liberal" serve, if they did not sufficiently delineate the theological differences between the two sides? And, given how conservative MacLean was theologically, *why* would he *label himself* a "liberal?"

Whatever theological differences existed between "liberals" and "conservatives" in the Southern Presbyterian Church served mainly as a springboard for debate over the real issues of difference between them. Theological differences were the focus of dispute in the North, but not in the South. In fact, in the South, misplaced emphasis on relatively minor theological differences could serve merely to distract from the more substantive points at issue, which takes us directly to the other components of Southern Presbyterian "conservatism."

Confessional conservatism upheld the Church's Confession of Faith as the binding authority for the Church. Most confessional conservatives were theological conservatives who held tightly to the authority of the *Westminster Confession* just because they believed it reflected the teaching of *Scripture*, the inerrant, final authority. Ecclesiastically, the Confession often served as the whip with which to drive from the Church those who threatened to undermine the Church's scriptural authority or who might compromise the Church's foundational theological stances.[28]

Confessional conservatives typically were staunch Calvinists, who believed that the Calvinist, Reformed elements of their Church's confession were key components of its *raison d'être*. A common theme of their writings was to suspect those who would modify "unpopular" Calvinist elements in the *Westminster Confession* of wanting to compromise other fundamental doctrines, as well. Conservatives consistently argued that any such compromises would gravely undermine the doctrinal purity and ecclesiastical testimony of the Church.[29]

While other theological disagreements were alluded to covertly and were argued through innuendo and insinuation, the "liberal-conservative" clash over the Calvinist nature of the creed was direct and overt. In March of 1944, MacLean's controversial article, "Needed – An Evangelistic Creed," appeared in the *Presbyterian of the South*.[30] Quoting several passages from chapter 3 of the *Westminster Confession* regarding God's decree, by which "some men and angels are predestined unto everlasting life, and others are fore-ordained to everlasting

---

scientific modernists and evangelical liberals, . . . but most fundamentalists did not distinguish between the two, using the terms liberal or modernist almost interchangeably" ("The Development of Northern Patterns of Fundamentalism in the South," 27).

[28] This strategy is explained and defended explicitly by William Childs Robinson ("The Authority of the Lord Jesus Christ as Exercised in the PCUS," *SPresJ* 1 [November 1942]: 11-14).

[29] E.g., see Henry B. Dendy, "The Calvinistic Creed of Presbyterians," *SPresJ* 3 (May 1944): 3; John R. Richardson, "Our Distinctive Presbyterian Emphasis," *SPresJ* 4 (August 1944): 13; Robert F. Gribble, "Calvinistic Complexion," *SPresJ* 4 (August 1944): 15-17; and J.E. Flow, "Some Doctrines of the Southern Presbyterian Church," *SPresJ* 7 (2 August 1948): 16.

[30] John Allan MacLean, "Needed – An Evangelistic Creed: Can We Overcome the Calvinistic Complex?" *PrSouth* 118 (29 March 1944): 5-7.

death," MacLean asked: "DOES ANYONE BELIEVE THIS TODAY?" and "ARE WE 'HERALDS OF A PASSION OR CUSTODIANS OF AN HEIRLOOM?'"[31]

Such a direct assault on the Church's confession is startling, even from our historical distance. Yet the response to this article among Southern Presbyterian readers was by no means entirely negative. Of course, some were alarmed; some even proposed that MacLean should resign from his Presbyterian ministerial status if he could no longer uphold the Church's *Confession of Faith*. But a good many others praised the article, commending MacLean for boldly voicing what they, too, had felt for a long time.[32]

Donald W. Richardson, moderator of the General Assembly at the time (1944), wrote an editorial the next week entitled, "The Presbyterian Church and Evangelism," which cited the lack of Southern Presbyterian Church growth as evidence that the Church indeed was not evangelistic enough.[33] Though not mentioning MacLean or his recent article by name, the editorial seems clearly intended as a show of support for MacLean's sentiments.[34] It seems the idea was growing among all but the confessional conservatives that the Church's traditional Calvinism was at fault for dampening its evangelistic zeal.[35]

A closer look reveals that this discussion over the *Confession*'s Calvinistic emphases was just the tip of the iceberg. In 1903, the Northern Church had adjusted its Confession, in part to facilitate a rapprochement with the less Calvinistic, Cumberland Presbyterians. The strategy was successful; there was a merger between those two Presbyterian bodies in 1906.

Southern Presbyterians commonly viewed the Northern recapture of the Cumberland Presbyterians, who came mostly from the border state of Kentucky, as an impressive *coup*. Many believed that the Southern Presbyterian Church would be smart to pursue reunification in like manner with the Northern Church, as well. For advocates of reunion, merger with the North represented a considerable financial and numerical boon for their church. For them, the Calvinistic elements of the confession represented a needless, arcane obstacle.

Such contemplations, of course, only heightened the tensions between confessional "conservatives" and confessional "liberals." Confessional conservatives were none too keen on merging with the Northern Church, anyway; they were not

---

[31] Ibid., 5 (the all-capital letters are original).

[32] See "Letters," *PrOut* 118 (26 April 1944): 7; and "Letters," *PrOut* 118 (17 May 1944): 10.

[33] Donald W. Richardson, "The Moderators Speak: The Presbyterian Church and Evangelism," *PrOut* 118 (24 May 1944): 5.

[34] Another article by MacLean appeared just below Richardson's editorial. With a much more homiletical emphasis, it was also much less controversial; it was entitled, "The Prayer of a Modern Pharisee, By One of Them," *PrOut* 118 (24 May 1944): 5.

[35] See James Quarles, review of *Studies in the Confession of Faith: The Five Points of Calvinism Examined*, by Rev. Robert Ware Jopling, *UnSemRev* 55 (February 1944): 139-46. Both Jopling and Quarles are Southern Presbyterians, the former a minister, the latter a judge. By the end of the review, it is clear that both have come to the same conclusion: the five points of Calvinism are less biblical than Arminian tenets and the Confession should be modified to encourage the Church toward a more evangelistic thrust.

about to compromise their own doctrinal stand to accommodate it. Besides, many confessional conservatives were also socio-political conservatives who would not have wanted to merge with the Northern Church even if a doctrinal compromise could be achieved.[36] This takes us to the third and final component of "Southern Presbyterian conservatism."

Socio-political (Confederate) conservatism was that strand of traditionalism in the Southern Presbyterian Church that sought to preserve the socio-political stances of the Old South.[37] There was a doctrinal element to this: the "spiritual nature" of the Church. The impetus of this doctrinal tenet was that the Church should not engage itself in socio-political matters because it was to be a strictly *spiritual* entity.[38]

The aversion to involving the Church in socio-political issues was most apparent (and the conflict between "conservatives" and "liberals" most acute) in regard to issues of racial inequity. For the socio-political conservative, the black person's poor plight was a matter for social charities to address, perhaps, but certainly not an issue in which the Church should become politically entangled. Under this view, the Church's sphere of responsibility included evangelism, developing one's relationship with God, and cultivating charitable relationships with one's neighbor. Any measures taken to redress economic or societal injustice that exceeded the bounds of simple benevolence overstepped those boundaries of what rightfully belonged within the Church's sphere of responsibility.[39]

---

[36] The point was put straightforwardly by J.R. Bridges and R.C. Reed: "To be perfectly frank, we can see little good that is to come out of the organic union of two bodies who can love each other better in separate organizations, where their differing views and sentiments [on issues of race and racial equity] can find free expression without creating friction or irritation" ("Editorial: The Negro a Stumbling Block to Church Union," *PrStand* 59 [3 April 1918]: 3).

[37] See Drew Gilpin Faust, *The Creation of Confederate Nationalism: Ideology and Identity in the Civil War South* (Baton Rouge, LA: Louisiana State University Press, 1988); and Charles Reagan Wilson, "The Lost Cause," in *Encyclopedia of Religion in the South*, 412-13.

[38] This point was the original Southern Presbyterian response to Northern assaults on the South's "peculiar institution" (i.e., slavery). In the words of James Henley Thornwell: "[The Church] has no right to interfere directly with the civil relations of society. Whether Slavery be perpetuated or not, whether arrangements shall be made to change or abolish it, whether it conduces to the prosperity of the State or hinders the progress of a refined civilization, – these are questions not for the Church but the State, not for Ministers but for statesmen. Christian men may discuss them as citizens and patriots, but not as members of the Church of Jesus Christ" (*The Collected Writings of James Henley Thornwell*, Vol. IV, ed. John B. Adger and John L. Girardeau [Richmond: Presbyterian Committee of Publication, 1873]: 500-01. Cf. Robert L. Dabney, "Lecture LXXIII: The Civil Magistrate," and "Lecture LXXIV: Religious Liberty," in the *Syllabus and Notes of the Course of Systematic and Polemic Theology Taught in Union Theological Seminary, Virginia* (Richmond: Presbyterian Committee of Publication, 1890), 862-87. For helpful analysis of the formation and establishment of these viewpoints in the PCUS, see Ernest Trice Thompson, *Presbyterians in the South, Volume One: 1607-1861* (Richmond: John Knox Press, 1963), 323-412, 510-71.

[39] For a clear articulation of this viewpoint, see J. Sprole Lyons, "The Problem of Relation of White and Colored Races," *PrStand* 60 (8 October 1919): 4.

Further, any means of rectifying societal injustice that held potential for integrating the races was, for these Southerners, entirely out of the question. L. Nelson Bell articulated this point in no uncertain terms.

> In reading this message from the Federal Council [the "Annual Race Relations Message"], one agrees heartily with those recommendations looking toward the elimination of unfair and unjust discriminations. But one looks in vain for any recognition of the fact that there is a line **which must not be crossed**. In fact this message states that Christians "should be unprejudiced and wise enough to bridge and cross the chasms of racial isolation and segregation."
>
> Is racial segregation un-Christian? Is one un-Christian who feels that unrestricted social relations are unwise? If the Federal Council and those who accept the leadership of the Council in this matter take this position, we can but feel that harm must inevitably result. If, on the other hand, they will make a clear statement affirming that their goal is **not** unrestricted social equality, their leadership will not be regarded with distrust.
>
> As we stated above: **there is a line which must be drawn and which must not be crossed**. This line was, we believe, established by God when He made men of different races. . . .
>
> We wish to affirm that we do not believe that segregation is un-Christian. In fact, it is a kindness to those of both races. If that one point is accepted by white and negro leaders who are working for a solution, a long step forward will have been taken.[40]

"Liberals" considered such a stance socially irresponsible, politically disreputable and personally embarrassing.[41]

Other issues besides civil rights were on the "liberal" agenda, as well. Southern Presbyterian "liberals" openly lamented the wide disparity between rich and poor within the United States and worldwide. From 1945-1952, several articles appeared in the *Presbyterian Outlook* that considered hypothetical and practical advantages of a communist economic system over a strictly capitalistic one.[42]

---

[40] L. Nelson Bell, "Race Relations – Whither?" *SPresJ* 2 (March 1944): 4-5 (bold text orginal); cf. the similar stances of William Childs Robinson, "Distinguishing Things that Differ," *SPresJ* 5 (15 January 1947): 3-4; and J.E. Flow, "Is Segregation Un-Christian?" *SPresJ* 10 (29 August 1951): 4-5.

[41] The writing of John Allan MacLean, again, gives us some indication of their feeling. See John Allan MacLean, "Progressive Presbyterianism," *PrOut* 118 (19 April 1944): 6. For similar calls for racial justice, see also William Crowe, "Our Church and the Negro in the South [Parts I and II]," *UnSemRev* 51 (April and July 1940): 248-63, 329-40; W.H. Mills, "Our Church's Duty to the Negro," *PrSouth* 116 (19 February 1941): 5-6; and J. McDowell Richards, "Brothers in Black," *PrSouth* 116 (5 November 1941): 4-6.

[42] See Ernest Trice Thompson, "The Christian and His Economic Relations," *PrOut* 127 (26 November 1945): 13-14; "Protestant, Catholic, and Jewish Leaders Unite in a Declaration of Economic Justice," *PrOut* 128 (4 November 1946): 5-6; "Editorial: Capitalism and Communism," *PrOut* 130 (13 September 1948): 8; "A More Christian Economic System,"

Once it was apparent that communistic governments seemed consistently to have rogue, totalitarian tendencies, the "liberal" Presbyterians wrote more critically of them; nevertheless, they openly lamented the economic inequalities that seemed especially prevalent in capitalist countries.[43] "Liberals" often endorsed and, in some cases, actively participated in constructing official clerical admonitions on these matters (such as the declarations on economic justice from the Federal Council of Churches).[44]

The conservative response was predictable. Some declared the suggestions of these liberals to be outright scandalous.[45] Clearly, the liberals' suggested tactics for relieving poverty did require far more cooperation between Church and State, and a far more centralized State at that, than traditional Southern Presbyterianism would tolerate.[46] Making this very point, John R. Richardson wrote, in 1944, that a "distinctive emphasis in our Standards is the separation of Church and State," and cited both James Henley Thornwell and the "Presbyterian fathers [who] had a large part in the framing of the first article of the Bill of Rights" in support of this traditional separation.[47]

It is these matters that form the true heart of division between Southern Presbyterian "liberals" and "conservatives." Even the arguments over Calvinism paled in comparison to the socio-political divide insofar as what truly energized the polarization. And if we set aside the Calvinist-Arminian disagreement, we can see that both sides could otherwise draw from the broader, "traditional" Reformed ideology to support their doctrinal views. In this ironic sense, there was not a wide *theological* disparity between them.

PrOut 130 (25 October 1948): 1. Such open flirtation with communist ideas reveals that the time is one before McCarthyism and the Cold War, during that brief period when communist Russia was, technically, an ally of the United States against Nazism and fascism.

[43] See Holmes Rolston, "Editorial: I'm Against It," *PrOut* 131 (31 January 1949): 8; John C. Bennett, "The Issues Raised by Communism for Christians," *PrOut* 134 (14 January 1952): 5-6.

[44] "Protestant, Catholic and Jewish Leaders Unite in a Declaration of Economic Justice," 5-6; "I Was An Hungered and Ye Gave Me No Meat," *PrOut* 128 (28 January 1946): 5-6; "A More Christian Economic System," *PrOut* 130 (25 October 1948): 1-5; MacLean, "What Southern Presbyterian Liberals Are Driving At," 6-7; Thompson, "The Christian and His Economic Relations," 13-14.

[45] Henry B. Dendy and John Temple Graves, "Editorial: Two Nationally Known Editors Expose Radical Teaching of Federal Council Leaders," *SPresJ* 5 (15 January 1947): 2-3.

[46] This objection from traditional Southern Presbyterians to the activities of the Federal Council of Churches was submitted as early as 1921. See J.R. Bridges and R.C. Reed, "Editorial: Given an Inch, Taking an Ell," *PrStand* 62 (22 June 1921): 3.

[47] John R. Richardson, "Our Distinctive Presbyterian Emphasis," *SPresJ* 3 (August 1944): 14. The quotation from James Henley Thornwell came from Thornwell's address to the First General Assembly of the Presbyterian Church in the Confederate States of America, the year before his death, enumerating reasons why the Southern Presbyterian Church had to separate from the Northern Church; *Minutes of the First General Assembly of the Presbyterian Church in the Confederate States of America, 1861* (Augusta, GA: Presbyterian Church in the United States), 51-60.

Rather, it was the proper *role* of theology in the *function* of the Church that was at the heart of their dispute. Conservatives believed that the primary function of the Church was to teach the truth of the Presbyterian, Calvinistic heritage. Vigilant confessionalists and thoroughgoing traditionalists, they cherished the legacy of such stalwarts as James Henley Thornwell and Robert Lewis Dabney. They revered these ancestors' teachings on the "spiritual nature of the Church" and their biblical defense of Southern Presbyterianism *jure divino*, with its well-ordered, nigh-unto-aristocratic structure. To them, the PCUS was the last stronghold of these great truths.[48]

Liberals considered such traditions quaint relics of a by-gone era; some repudiated them as dangerous obstacles to Southern Presbyterian advancement and as hindrances to biblically rectifying historically reinforced societal injustices. For them, theological positions were a means to an end, not a *raison d'être*. In their view, the Church's *raison d'être* is to spread the Gospel and advance the kingdom of God, a kingdom that is both spiritual *and* socio-political in nature.[49]

Tensions mounted when plans for merger with the PCUSA accelerated in the 1940s.[50] The conservative, provincial instincts of Southern Presbyterianism, together with its greater emphasis on the autonomy of local presbyteries and sessions, had enabled the Southern Church to postpone for twenty years a "fundamentalist-modernist" confrontation of the kind that troubled the Northern Church.[51] Even still, the Southern Church watched the events of the 1920s-30s in the Northern Church with horror. The Northern Church was her sister church, after all; they shared her basic DNA.

---

[48] Cf. Wilson, "The Lost Cause."

[49] See the following studies: E. Brooks Holifield, *The Gentleman Theologians: American Theology in Southern Culture, 1795-1860* (Durham, NC: Duke University Press, 1978); Anne C. Loveland, *Southern Evangelicals and the Social Order, 1800-1860* (Baton Rouge, LA: Louisiana State University Press, 1980); Samuel S. Hill, Jr., *Southern Churches in Crisis* (New York, NY: Holt, Rinehart and Winston, 1967); idem, ed., *Religion and the Solid South* (Nashville, TN: Abingdon Press, 1972); Charles Reagan Wilson, ed., *Religion in the South* (Jackson, MS: University of Mississippi Press, 1985); and C. Van Woodward, *Origins of the New South* (Baton Rouge, LA: Louisiana State University Press, 1951).

[50] One can perceive the tensions present in the *Presbyterian Guardian*'s reporting of the General Assembly of the PCUS in 1948: "The plan of union is to be 'held in abeyance' for five years. So the Southern General Assembly has decided unanimously. Within the Southern Church the strife has been severe between those who want to unite with the North and those who oppose union on various grounds, a chief ground being the doctrinal Modernism of the Northern Church. . . . Strategy at the Southern Assembly was somewhat devious. The unionists wanted to press for a final decision in 1949. The opponents of union wanted a decision now, in the apparent belief that enough would fear a division and vote with the conservative minority against union. The Assembly produced a compromise, which each side seems to regard as a victory . . ." (Arthur W. Kuschke, Jr., "Five Years for the South?" *PrGuard* 17 [July 1948]: 172).

[51] See Furniss, *The Fundamentalist Controversy*, 142; and Thompson, *Presbyterians in the South, Volume Three*, 274-339.

Talk of reunion with the Northern Church was not new; the suggestion was made almost as soon as the Civil War had ended.[52] A formal plan for reunion was not submitted to the PCUS General Assembly, however, until 1943.[53]

There were standard Southern Presbyterian objections to the idea, among them: (1) the Northern Church, being nearly four times the size of the Southern Church, would surely consume the Southern church if they merged. (2) Cherished distinctives of the Southern Presbyterian Church would surely be lost. (3) There were awkward questions that had to be answered to make reunion possible, regarding who was at fault and what was at issue when the two bodies split in the first place (at the beginning of the Civil War in 1861). Rejoining the Northern Church could besmirch the sacred memory of beloved ancestors, who bravely fought and died to preserve values that now were safeguarded only by the Southern Church.[54]

By the time of the 1943 Plan of Reunion, though, there was an additional, even more serious objection to reunion. The PCUSA was an apostate church, claimed

---

[52] Ernest Trice Thompson discerns in early-1880s editions of the *Christian Observer* three viewpoints in regard to Southern Presbyterian re-union with the Northern Church. "First, a minority group within the church who held that it was wise for the church to enter upon conference with the purpose of securing organic union. Second, a group, much smaller in the *Observer*'s estimation, whose feelings toward the Northern Church and the Northern people was so vehement as to make them resist any discussion or inquiry as to the duty of the church in this matter. The third group, which in the judgment of the *Christian Observer*, represented the large majority of the church, two-thirds or even three-fourths (perhaps because this was the *Observer*'s position) desired first and foremost to preserve the harmony of the church. Since some in the church were so intensely averse to any steps toward union, they were opposed to any present discussion of the issue. They desired at the same time to maintain the most cordial relations with their brethren in the Northern Church" (*Presbyterians in the South, Volume Two: 1861-1890* [Richmond: John Knox Press, 1973], 263). The earliest article Thompson cites on this point is an unsigned article in the *Southern Presbyterian Review*, entitled "The Presbyterian Reunion North and South," dated July, 1871.

[53] E.C. Scott, "History of the Plan," in *A Pamphlet Concerning the Matter of the Union of The United Presbyterian Church of North America, The Presbyterian Church in the United States of America, and The Presbyterian Church in the United States* (Richmond: Presbyterian Committee of Publication, 1954), 3.

[54] For a summary of the Southern Presbyterian Church's "distinctive principles" and perhaps the earliest written argument against reunion with the Northern Church, see *The Distinctive Principles of the Presbyterian Church in the United States, commonly called the Southern Presbyterian Church, as set forth in the formal declarations, and illustrated by extracts from proceedings of the General Assembly from 1861-70, to which is added extracts from the O[ld] S[chool] Assembly, from 1861-67; and Explanatory Remarks* (Richmond: Presbyterian Committee of Publication, 1870). The points made against reunion with the Northern Church were maintained with remarkable consistency by conservative Southern Presbyterians; even as late as 1952, these same points are recapped in an article opposing reunion by W.H. Frazer, "Why I Favor Preserving the Southern Church," *SPresJ* 11 (23 July 1952): 7-9. For a summarization of these points by a Southern Presbyterian strongly *in favor* of reunion with the Northern Church, see Ernest Trice Thompson, "The South and Sectionalism," *PrOut* 131 (17 January 1949): 5-6; idem, *Presbyterians in the South, Volume Two*, 13-264, idem, *Presbyterians in the South, Volume Three*, 13-121, 274-301, 486-584.

conservatives, that would inevitably drag the Southern Church down to its heretical level should they be undiscerning enough to unequally yoke itself with it. By the 1940s, this had become the primary objection to reunion.[55]

Some twenty-five years after the Auburn *Affirmation* was published, and some fifteen years since it had played any major role in a controversy in the North, the *Presbyterian Guardian* reported, "[The] Auburn Affirmation *Becomes* Issue in the South."[56] In 1946, the long-time president of Davidson College, Walter Lingle, a strong advocate of reunion, lamented, "In the minds of some it [the Auburn *Affirmation*] is the chief obstacle standing in the way of the re-union of the Presbyterian Church in the United States, and the Presbyterian Church in the United States of America."[57] Why was this? Because, conservatives claimed, the Auburn *Affirmation* was an affirmation of liberalism, and the fact that so many leaders of the Northern Presbyterian Church signed this document proved that the PCUSA was apostate.[58]

---

[55] Conservatives, both North and South, opposed reunion on these grounds. In the North, Edwin H. Rian (ironically, in an article written just three years before he, himself, would be "reunited" with the PCUSA) commended the *Southern Presbyterian Journal* for its strong opposition to reunion. "Why are we so interested in seeing opposition to this union?" he asked. "The answer is plain: The Presbyterian Church in the U.S.A. is under the control of those who do not adhere to the Bible as the Word of God and to the Westminster Confession of Faith. . . . On the other hand, the southern church is not entirely free of modernist tendencies. We are convinced, however, that there is much more faithfulness to the Bible in that church and we hope that the conservatives can secure control of the denomination. If any union takes place, the southern group will be swallowed up, for it is only one-fourth the size of the Presbyterian Church in the U.S.A. and Modernism will reign supreme in the united church" ("'The Southern Presbyterian Journal' and Union," *PrGuard* 13 [10 September 1944]: 251-52). A short, four-paragraph article in the *Southern Presbyterian Journal* exemplifies the position Rian commended in the Southern Church. "In all the articles that have been written and published, no one has yet given any good reason for this union; but there seems to be a great number of good reasons against it. Many of the leaders in the Northern Church are Modernists. About two years ago, the Moderator of their General Assembly said that the Virgin Birth, the Miracles of Christ, the Atonement and the Resurrection, were only theories and not facts. . . . We cannot afford to join in with them as we cannot accept the Modernist beliefs" (W.A. Cochran, "Save the Southern Presbyterian Church," *SPresJ* 5 [15 February 1947]: 4).

[56] "Auburn *Affirmation* Becomes Issue in South," *PrGuard* 20 (15 October 1951): 200 (emphasis added). The *Guardian* was a little behind in this report, perhaps, but not by much.

[57] Walter L. Lingle, "The Auburn Affirmation," *PrOut* 128 (8 April 1946): 6.

[58] Carl McIntire, "'Auburn Affirmation,'" *CBeac* 1 (20 August 1936): 1-2, 7-8; Gordon H. Clark, "The Auburn Heresy," *CBeac* 1 (20 August 1936): 3; *idem*, "The Auburn Heresy," *SPresJ* 5 (15 July 1946): 7-9; Murray Forst Thompson, "The Auburn Betrayal: Parts I-V," *PrGuard* 10 (10 November 1941): 113-14, 125-27; (25 November 1941): 133-34; (10 December 1941): 154-55; (25 December 1941): 165-67; and 11 (25 January 1942): 24-25; L. Nelson Bell, "The Auburn Affirmation Is Actually Not an Affirmation of Faith but a . . . Dissent From Evangelical Truth," *SPresJ* 10 (10 October 1951): 3-4. Cf. also Charles E. Quirk, "The Auburn *Affirmation*: A Critical Narrative of the Document Designed to Safeguard the Unity and Liberty of the Presbyterian Church in the United States of America in 1924" (Ph.D. diss., University of Iowa, 1967), 106-35, 261-79.

The fight between Southern Presbyterian "liberals" and "conservatives" provides an intriguing background for our understanding the place of Chaferian dispensationalism in the context of the volatile 1930s-40s. Sociologically and ecclesiastically, the fight between Southern Presbyterian "liberals" and "conservatives" had a very significant effect on how the dispensationalist-covenantalist debate evolved. The 1920s to 1940s was a time of high anxiety for conservatives in the Presbyterian denominations. The "forces disrupting the churches" were enemies of Christianity from *within* the church[59]; these wolves – as conservatives perceived them – were very good at disguising themselves in sheep's clothing. It is not difficult to imagine, therefore, that suspicions might run high even among fellow "sheep" (i.e., fellow theological conservatives).

Heightened tensions between Southern Presbyterian "conservatives" and "liberals" would prove detrimental to dispensationalism's reception in the PCUS also because Lewis Sperry Chafer's theology fit *neither* Southern Presbyterian conservatism nor Southern Presbyterian liberalism very well. While Chafer was theologically conservative in a broad sense, he was far from being a confessional conservative. He was not even a very good Calvinist. He advocated a "4-point Calvinism," and, in his defense of this stance, even voiced concern that the traditional Calvinist doctrine of "limited atonement" could dampen evangelistic zeal[60] – the exact concern, we may recall, of Southern Presbyterian "liberals"!

On the other hand, Chaferian dispensationalism was not at all conducive to liberal concerns for advancing the Kingdom of God on earth socio-politically, the very concerns that liberals considered most important of all. On this point, Chaferian dispensationalism was as conservative as the most ardent Southern Presbyterian conservatism, denying the Church any socio-political role at all in this age.[61] The objections dispensationalists submitted against Christian involvement in socio-political reform,[62] in fact, were identical to those submitted by Southern Presbyterian conservatives against "liberals."[63]

Thus, Chaferian dispensationalism found itself opposed to the core concerns of *both* Southern Presbyterian liberals *and* Southern Presbyterian conservatives just as the controversy between them was reaching its zenith. As these two factions within the Southern Presbyterian Church polarized, Chaferian dispensationalism found itself in a theological crossfire, vigorously opposed by both sides.

---

[59] Henry B. Dendy, "Forces Disrupting the Churches," *SPresJ* 4 (August 1944): 2-4.

[60] Lewis Sperry Chafer, "For Whom Did Christ Die?" *BibSac* 105 (January-March 1948): 7-35.

[61] See Lewis Sperry Chafer, "Dispensationalism," *BibSac* 93 (October-December 1936): 415-17, 422-25; *idem*, *Grace* (Wheaton, IL: Van Kampen Press, 1922), 80-352.

[62] E.g., see John Henry Bennetch, "Editorial: Racial Lines," *BibSac* 106 (January-March 1949): 131; *idem*, "Editorial: Capitalism," *BibSac* 106 (April-June 1949): 258; *idem*, "Editorial: Communism," *BibSac* 106 (April-June 1949): 259; and John F. Walvoord, "Book Review: *The Uneasy Conscience of Modern Fundamentalism* by Carl F. Henry," *BibSac* 104 (July-September 1947): 364.

[63] E.g., see L. Nelson Bell, "Blowing Out Sparks at a Three-Alarm Fire," *SPresJ* 3 (October 1944): 2.

The Northern Presbyterian situation served to confirm the suspicions of many Southern Presbyterians who feared the prospect of unorthodox elements creeping into the church. In a few recent instances, clergymen of more modernist persuasion had tried either to sneak into their Southern ranks by transferring in from the North or had sneaked out of a Southern Presbyterian Church into a Northern one without following the proper procedures for re-assignment.[64] Additionally, North-South rivalries for parishioners, rivalries which went back to Civil War days, were being revived in some districts, with intense acrimony.[65]

Reports from the North of the fundamentalist-modernist controversies, especially as recounted by conservative sources, only strengthened the misgivings of the Southern Presbyterian Church toward the North – and initiated some new anxieties concerning the possibility of modernist compromise within its own ranks. The experience of the Northern Church made it clear that "Christian-talking" people in positions of authority could not always be considered trustworthy. Before long, Southern Presbyterian conservatives began sounding the alarm against modernist intrusion into their *own* Church, invariably pointing to the Northern Church as the archetypical example.[66] Conservatives in the North, in turn, continually reinforced these warnings.[67]

Thus, while at first it might be surprising that some of the earliest objections to dispensationalism in the South came from very *conservative* Presbyterians, once we understand the dynamics in play at the time, this makes sense. Many dispensationalists in the South were transplanted Northerners and transfers from other denominations. Were not these the very places from which seditious, modernist doctrines were rumored to come?

The charge of B.W. Baker, a Southern Presbyterian cleric from Happy, TX, that an incipient "modernism" permeates the teaching of the Scofield Reference Bible thus makes sense, but only in light of this background.[68] While Baker's specific

---

[64] See Thompson, *Presbyterians in the South, Volume Three*, 279.

[65] Ibid., 28-121, 250-301.

[66] The conservative *Southern Presbyterian Journal*, especially, provided the forum for such arguments throughout the 1940s.

[67] "Southern Church Division Similar," *CBeac* 1 (23 July 1936): 1, 7; "[Hon. Arthur W., brother of J. Gresham] Machen Complains to Southern Church," *CBeac* 2 (22 April 1937): 1, 5; "Southern Church," *CBeac* 2 (24 June 1937): 4; John Murray, "Proposed Confessional Revision in the Presbyterian Church in the United States," *PrGuard* 4 (November 1938): 207-10; Thomas R. Birch, "The Presbyterian Guardian and the Southern Church," *PrGuard* 7 (25 March 1940): 88; "Southern Presbyterians Enjoy Visit of Dr. Young," *PrGuard* 14 (15 August 1945): 236-37; Paul Woolley, "Assemblies North and South," *PrGuard* 17 (July 1948): 178-79; Oswald T. Allis, "The New Presbyterian USA Curriculum for Sunday Schools: 'Christian Faith and Life – A Program for Church and Home'; A Critique of the New Curriculum [Parts I-III]," *SPresJ* 7 (15 November 1948): 6-9; (1 December 1948): 5-10; (15 December 1948): 12-15; "Southern Presbyterian Property," *PrGuard* 19 (July 1950): 124.

[68] In 1934, Baker posed this question in a set of articles: "Is there modernism in the teachings of C.I. Scofield?" Baker realized, "This question will startle many people. For many years, the name of Scofield has been associated with the ultra-conservatives in doctrine, and his followers have cried their fundamentalism from the house-tops" ("Is There Modernism in the Teachings

charges were somewhat rash and odd,[69] they do alert us that at least some conservative Southern Presbyterians were none too pleased with the Scofield Reference Bible. We also get some insight into how modernist-fundamentalist hostilities could fuel suspicions against dispensationalism.

Baker suggested that implications of some of Scofield's teachings demonstrated that "modernism," perhaps subconsciously through his Congregationalist upbringing, had found its way into Scofield's "heart." Baker forwarded this accusation, even though he acknowledged that Scofield's explicit statements and actions indicated a firm belief in the Bible's authority and truthfulness.[70] Few fair-minded persons can blame Scofield's protégé, Lewis Sperry Chafer, for wondering aloud,

> why a periodical of the character of the "Presbyterian of the South" should lend its pages to the publishing of such erroneous material and thus become party to the dissemination of what proves to be almost unqualified misrepresentation, and the problem is not lessened when it is remembered that Dr. Scofield was a clergyman of the Presbyterian U.S. Assembly for some years before and up to the time of his death, and that from the standpoint of world-wide recognition for worthy achievement few, if any, have arisen within that denomination who exceed him.[71]

Besides these points, there is something communicated outside the content of the articles written by Baker and Chafer that is worth raising more fully. It took more than two years for Chafer's reply to Baker's articles to appear in the *Presbyterian of the South*. This is because his reply was not given, initially, to the *Presbyterian of the South*, but to *Our Hope*, a dispensational paper, edited by the vigorously independent former Methodist, Arno C. Gaebelein.[72]

Chafer also indicated that he was not familiar, before this incident, with "the Reverend B.W. Baker, Th.D., whose name appears in the Year Book of the Presbyterian Church, U.S., as the pastor of two small churches in the Panhandle

---

of Dr. C.I. Scofield?" *PrSouth* 109 [28 February 1934]: 6).

[69] The main points of Baker's articles were: in teaching that Jesus taught a kingdom that was "at hand" and then "postponed," Scofield was denying the infallibility of Jesus' teaching; in teaching that Christ offered and then failed to deliver the kingdom, Scofield was denying the Deity of Christ; and, finally, by teaching that Christ genuinely offered the kingdom *before* dying on the cross, Scofield was denying the necessity of the Atonement; Baker, "Is There Modernism in C.I. Scofield?"; *idem*, "Is There Modernism in the Teachings of Dr. C.I. Scofield: Part II," *PrSouth* 109 (7 March 1934): 7-8; and *idem*, "Is There Modernism in the Scofield Bible? A Reply to Dr. L.S. Chafer," *PrSouth* 111 (18 March 1936): 2.

[70] Ibid.

[71] Lewis Sperry Chafer, "Was C.I. Scofield a Modernist?," *Our Hope* 41 (September 1934): 160; reprinted in *PrSouth* 111 (12 February 1936): 3.

[72] Lewis Sperry Chafer, "Was C.I. Scofield a Modernist?" *Our Hope* 41 (September 1934): 160-65; cf. the preface to "Was C.I. Scofield a Modernist?" by Lewis Sperry Chafer, *PrSouth* 111 (12 February 1936): 3.

District of Texas, and a member of the Dallas Presbytery."[73] This, too, is interesting because, in truth, Baker had been quite active in Chafer's own presbytery; in fact, his ministry in the "Panhandle District" was supported by the Church's Home Mission board.[74]

A survey of the official minutes of Dallas Presbytery meetings provides an explanation for how Chafer and Baker could have been clerics in the same presbytery, yet have so little contact with one another outside of this less-than-cordial exchange in the Church papers. Baker attended presbytery meetings faithfully. Chafer, doubtless due to his preaching and speaking schedule, frequently requested permission to "labor outside the bounds of Presbytery"; thus, he often was absent at denominational meetings. Baker worked as a minister for the denomination; Chafer was president of a school wholly unaffiliated with the denomination.

These things prove nothing as to who was correct or incorrect in their dispute, of course. The point that is significant for our purposes is that Chafer and Baker seem to have moved in different circles. More specifically, Chafer seems to fit the pattern, noted earlier, which some historians have identified as common among dispensationalists: their primary loyalty was to the broad American evangelical coalition rather than to their individual denominations.[75]

This point would be especially significant in a conservative, "Old School," Southern Presbyterian context, which is exactly the context of dispensationalism in a place like Dallas, Texas. Glass's summary is helpful.

> While in many ways fundamentalism resembled the main lines of conservative southerners's [sic] theology, there were differences. Conservative southern Protestants certainly endorsed fundamentalist insistence on the supernatural character of Christianity and on the importance of evangelism, but premillennialism, particularly of the dispensational variety, was an important stumbling block to fundamentalist recruiting efforts among southern Protestants. . . . Additionally as these doctrines came to suggest separation not just from the world but also from organizations that tolerated liberalism, southern Protestants backed away from alliances with fundamentalists because of their intense loyalty to their own denominations and

---

[73] Ibid. Chafer is clearly perturbed; the implication of bumpkinism seethes just beneath the surface, an implication that did not escape Baker. In the final installment of this indecorous exchange, Baker responded, "The attempt to belittle an opponent, which runs through all of Dr. Chafer's article, is a case of the well recognized ad hominen [sic] fallacy. Or to be more specific, it is that form of the ad hominen [sic] fallacy known as the argumentum ad vericundiam [sic]" ("A Reply to Dr. L.S. Chafer," 2).

[74] *Minutes of the One Hundred and Fourth Stated Meeting of the Presbytery of Dallas* (Austin, TX: Von Boeckmann-Jones Co., 1931), 104.

[75] See George M. Marsden, *Fundamentalism and American Culture: The Shaping of Twentieth-Century Evangelicalism, 1870-1925* (New York: Oxford University Press, 1980), 46-195, *passim*; and John David Hannah, "The Social and Intellectual History of the Evangelical Theological College" (Ph.D. diss., University of Texas at Dallas, 1988), 367-72.

> their perception that their denominations were orthodox. This fidelity also made fundamentalism suspect because of [the fundamentalist] movement's inter-denominational cooperation. Many southern Protestants felt that ties to other organizations or concerns represented disloyalty to southern denominations. These differences in theology and concerns form the main lines of distinguishing conservative southern Protestantism from fundamentalism.[76]

For conservative Southern Presbyterians, the *Westminster Confession* was crucial, not just for setting apart its own denominational distinctives, but for setting apart orthodoxy, generally, from apostasy. The significance of the *Confession* is clearly articulated in the article entitled, "The Authority of the Lord Jesus Christ as Exercised in the Presbyterian Church, U.S.," by staunch conservative, William Childs Robinson. In this article, Robinson unequivocally affirms the Word of God as the sole authority of the Church. Nonetheless, he clarifies, this fidelity to the Word of God does not in any way nullify the legitimate role of the Church's doctrinal standards; quite the contrary. Says Robinson:

> In governing the Church, our courts do not need to start *de novo* in their interpretation of Scripture. Our Book [of Church Order] states, "The Confession of Faith and the larger and Shorter Catechisms of the Westminster Assembly, together with the formularies of government, discipline and worship, are accepted by the Presbyterian Church in the U.S. as standard expositions of Scripture in relation to both faith and practice" (173). Thus, without thereby adding to the terms of ordination, the Assembly has the right to offer *in thesi* deliverances declaring certain things which are stated in the very language of these formularies to be involved in the ordination vows, as it did in 1939, justified in 1940, and maintained in the Lilly resolution of 1942.[77]

The *in thesi* resolutions to which Robinson refers were designed to insure that clerical ordination vows in the Southern Presbyterian Church constituted an *ex animo* "acceptance of the infallible truth and divine authority of the Scriptures, and of Christ as very and eternal God, who became man by being born of a virgin, who offered Himself a sacrifice to satisfy divine justice and reconcile us to God, who rose from the dead with the same body with which he suffered and who will return

---

[76] See Glass, "The Development of Northern Patterns of Fundamentalism in the South," 11-12; cf. also 40, 113-14.

[77] Robinson, "The Authority of the Lord Jesus Christ as Exercised in the Presbyterian Church U.S.," 13. This quotation is from section V, "The Authority of the Presbyterian Standards." Childs' point is that the Westminster Standards have a secondary, derivative authority, but its authority is derived from Scripture and is secondary only to Scripture itself. This represents the standard Confessional Subscription view, common among conservative Presbyterians; see the essays in *The Practice of Confessional Subscription*, ed. David W. Hall (Lanham, MD: University Press of America, 1995).

again to judge the world."⁷⁸ That is, the Southern Presbyterian Church was taking the same stand *mutatis mutandis* as the Northern Presbyterian Church of 1910, when it, too, had affirmed the "fundamentals" of the faith – only in the Southern Church, there was no Auburn *Affirmation* protest in response.

It was via *Confessional subscription* that Southern Presbyterian conservatives ensured fidelity to the evangelical faith throughout its church leadership. These *in thesi* resolutions made it clear that, by agreeing to abide by the Church's doctrinal standards at ordination, Southern Presbyterian ministers were affirming the very doctrinal tenets that had been disputed by "modernists" in the Northern Presbyterian Church. So clearly was this point made in the Southern Church, that the only real threat of a "liberal overthrow," like that in the North, was by reunion with the Northern Church, which brings our analysis full circle.

We have some idea, then, of the significance of the Westminster Standards to conservative Southern Presbyterians. When, despite the overtly conservative stand taken by the Southern Assembly, self-described "liberal" pastor, John Allan MacLean, assailed the Calvinistic doctrines of the Confession,⁷⁹ Henry B. Dendy responded, "Every statement of essential Calvinistic doctrine in our Standards the Bible substantiates by equally bold and bald statements of its own. Yet the former is the chosen object of attack. The reason is plain. In a Christian land, where the Scriptures are widely reverenced, it is cheaper and safer to assault the Presbyterian Standards than to assault the Bible."⁸⁰

And so, at a time when it was difficult to discern between wheat and tares in the church, ensuring that ministers in the church actually subscribed to the teachings of the Confession of Faith became especially important to conservatives. This added concern for punctilious subscription to the Confession was not propitious for dispensationalists within the denomination, though. Their de-emphasis of denominational creeds had the potential of making them suspect, perhaps especially among conservative *Presbyterians* (with the emphasis on the latter term).⁸¹ Chafer would eventually retort to his detractors that his views were "recognized as true by those who receive their doctrine from the Sacred Text rather than from man-made creeds."⁸² However, no truly conservative Presbyterian would drive such a wedge between the Scriptures and the *Westminster Confession*.

When the Northern controversies were viewed from the South, the primary response was concern that the "trouble" of the North not travel southward. Trouble*makers*, therefore, needed to be suppressed. In the end, it seems that the

---

⁷⁸ *A Digest of the Acts and Proceeding of the General Assembly of the Presbyterian Church in the United States, 1861-1944: Authorized by the General Assembly*, ed. E. C. Scott, Stated Clerk of the 1944 General Assembly (Richmond: Presbyterian Committee of Publication, 1945), 209-10.

⁷⁹ MacLean, "Needed – An Evangelistic Creed," 5-7.

⁸⁰ Dendy, "The Calvinistic Creed of Presbyterians," 3.

⁸¹ The *in thesi* resolutions originally were conceived as a means of detecting and expelling liberal tendencies. That dispensationalists, in 1941, had become unintended victims of these resolutions is alluded to by Robinson, "The Authority of the Lord Jesus Christ as Exercised in the PCUS," 13.

⁸² Lewis Sperry Chafer, "Inventing Heretics Through Misunderstanding," *BibSac* 102 (1945): 2.

main lesson learned by Southern Presbyterian leaders was that troublemakers, whether modernist or fundamentalist, could be identified by their attitude toward the *Confession*. Once the "fundamentalists" severed themselves from the "modernists," Southern Presbyterian leaders took note that it was the *premillennialists* who then had to separate again, and adjust the *Westminster Confession of Faith* to accommodate their view.[83] And to make matters worse, these premillennialists seemed to have a nasty habit of splitting Southern Presbyterian churches and carrying off the membership to their "independent" organizations.[84]

To a Southern Presbyterian, few actions could be considered less Christian (or less Presbyterian). As in the North (though Northern sources are almost never cited by Southern Presbyterian principals), the focus eventually narrowed from premillennialism to that peculiar, troublemaking variety of premillennialism found among adherents of the Scofield Bible: dispensationalism.[85]

---

[83] This is exactly James Bear's observation in his article, "Shall We Revise the Standards?" We recall that this was also the very impression Northern Presbyterian premillennialist, J. Oliver Buswell, wished to *avoid* – the reason he originally opposed revising the Confession ("The Second General Assembly of the Presbyterian Church of America," *PrGuard* 3 [28 November 1936]: 83; for Buswell's entire statement, see "Buswell Speaks on Millennial Issue," *CBeac* 1 [17 December 1936]: 7). Cf. also J. Oliver Buswell, Jr., "Premillennialism and the Reformed Faith," *SSTimes* 76 (5 May 1934): 289-91.

[84] This is Bear's greatest complaint. See Bear, "Shall We Revise the Standards?" The "Bible Presbyterians" were not the only ones doing this, though. As Glass recounts, Dallas Seminary graduates were fast gaining a reputation for doing much the same; first, refusing to use Presbyterian materials in churches they pastored (preferring, instead, materials of an "independent" nature), then splitting churches, carrying off large portions of the membership to form independent, premillennial (i.e., dispensationalist) congregations. See Glass, "The Development of Northern Patterns of Fundamentalism in the South," 130-280, 347-425.

[85] As early as 1921, R.C. Reed, editor of the *Presbyterian Standard*, had said this about the Scofield Bible: "We hope our Sunday School teachers are not using the Scofield Bible. If so, we repeat our advice, don't burn them, but put them away where they can do no harm" ("The Scofield Bible Again," *PrStand* 62 [6 April 1921]: 2). Walter L. Lingle, moderator of the 1920 General Assembly, president of Austin Theological Seminary from 1924-29, and then of the prestigious Davidson College from 1929-41, had also taken issue with Scofield's notes; see Lingle, "Some of Dr. Scofield's Interpretations." The first Southern Presbyterian to identify the Scofield variety of premillennialism as "dispensationalism" was James Bear ("Dispensationalism and the Covenant of Grace," *UnSemRev* 49 [July 1938]: 285-307); see also Bear's articles that would anticipate the decision of the 1944 committee on which he served: *idem*, "The Presbyterian Standards vs. the Scofield Bible," *PrSouth* 116 (19 March 1941): 6-7; *idem*, "The Presbyterian Standards vs. the Scofield Bible: II. The Doctrine of the Covenant of Grace," *PrSouth* 116 (26 March 1941): 5-6; *idem*, "The Presbyterian Standards vs. the Scofield Bible," *PrSouth* 116 (2 April 1941): 7-8; *idem*, "The Presbyterian Standards vs. the Scofield Bible: III. The Mediatorial King and His Kingdom," *PrSouth* 116 (9 April 1941): 5-6; *idem*, "The Presbyterian Standards vs. the Scofield Bible: IV. Divergent Views of God's Revelation," *PrSouth* 116 (16 April 1941): 5-6; *idem*, "The Presbyterian Standards vs. the Scofield Bible: V. The General Resurrection and the Final Judgement," *PrSouth* 116 (23 April 1941): 5-6; and *idem*, "The Presbyterian Standards vs. the Scofield Bible: VI. Concluding Statement," *PrSouth* 116 (30 April 1941): 6-7. In 1944, as the AIC was about to submit its report to the GA, Bear published two final articles on the subject; viz., "Dispensationalism: I. The Heart of this

A final catalyst brought all of these tensions to an explosive level. This final ingredient not only fomented further dissension between Southern Presbyterian conservatives and liberals, but also stimulated both groups to place "dispensationalism" under harsher scrutiny. That was the economic exigency of the late 1930s-early 1940s.[86]

As gift income shrank during the Great Depression through the end of World War II (1929-1945), the difficult sociological process began of determining which churches and charitable organizations would be funded – and survive – and which would not. Under such conditions, inter-organizational, and intra-Church tensions could not help but rise.[87]

It is astounding, in historical hindsight, that such times of general economic hardship saw several conservative organizations and schools established. We already have mentioned several: Dallas Theological Seminary (1924), Westminster Theological Seminary (1929), the Orthodox Presbyterian Church (1936), the Bible Presbyterian Church (1937), and Faith Theological Seminary (1937).[88] Economic hardships might well have shut down any of these organizations.

Times were not easy for even well-established organizations. From 1927-1940, nine different Southern Presbyterian colleges closed, or merged with other schools, because of financial strains.[89] In 1940, the PCUS conducted a thorough evaluation of the financial stability of the Church's remaining educational institutions, which study brought bad news to the Southern Presbyterian Church.

The Report of a Survey of the Colleges and Theological Seminaries of the Presbyterian Church in the U.S. concluded that the PCUS was still supporting too many schools.[90] It recommended further closings and mergers, the most startling of these being a recommended merger of Austin and Columbia Seminaries, perhaps

---

System," *PrOut* 118 (26 April 1944): 6; and "Dispensationalism: II. Dispensationalism vs. the Reformed Faith," *PrOut* (3 May 1944): 5-6.

[86] For explication of how economic stresses may serve as sociological catalysts for changes in social structures and orders, see Robert Wuthnow, *Meaning and Moral Order: Explorations in Cultural Analysis* (Los Angeles, CA: University of California Press, 1987), 154-214.

[87] See Thompson, *Presbyterians in the South, Volume Three*, 260-65, 453-60, for an analysis of how these tensions impacted the PCUS.

[88] These examples were part of a trend, as shown by Glass ("The Development of Northern Patterns of Fundamentalism in the South," 132-37). From 1924 to 1950, forty-four new "fundamentalist" schools were founded, twenty-four of them in the South. Cf. "Listing Sound Bible Institutes," *SSTimes* 66 (26 January 1924): 50; "Evangelical Schools and Colleges, 1950," *United Evangelical Action* 15 (15 June 1950): 12-16; Harold W. Boon, "The Development of the Bible College or Institute in the United States and Canada since 1880 and Its Relationship to the Field of Theological Education" (Ph.D. diss., New York University, 1950): 49; S.A. Witmer, *The Bible College Story: Education with Dimension* (Nanhasset, NY: Channel Press, 1962): 39; and Larry J. McKinney, "An Historical Analysis of the Bible College Movement during Its Formative Years" (Ed.D. diss., Temple University, 1985).

[89] See Thompson, *Presbyterians in the South, Volume Three*, 456.

[90] George A. Works, *The Report of a Survey of the Colleges and Theological Seminaries of the Presbyterian Church in the U.S.* (Louisville, KY: Board of Christian Education of the PCUS, 1942).

into a new school in Nashville, Tennessee.[91] Thompson reports in retrospect, "No colleges were closed and there were no mergers as suggested in the Works Report, but the report did serve as nothing else had done to awaken the church to its educational responsibility."[92]

The PCUS was therefore none too keen on the competition brought by the new, non-Presbyterian schools, such as Dallas Seminary. Reports that some of these "independent" institutions drew their support by lambasting their own PCUS schools as bastions of liberalism[93] did not help matters.[94]

Glass's point concerning the reaction of the mainline denominations to the emergence of such "fundamentalist" schools as Dallas Seminary in the South is noteworthy. "Fundamentalist institutions developed in the South in the twenties and thirties as they did in [the] north [sic] and were an important part of the emerging network of fundamentalist schools and organizations. . . . The appearance of these schools provoked the first sustained reaction in southern denominations against the fundamentalist presence in their region."[95] If denominational officials looked unfavorably upon non-denominational institutions like Dallas Seminary, their view of the "independent" kinds of theologizing propagated in these institutions (viz., "dispensationalism") would likely be unfavorable as well.

In summary, the historical situation of the late 1930s-early 1940s in the PCUS was something of a powder keg. Dispensationalism's perceived role of competitor to the PCUS's already struggling educational institutions was the spark.

4.2 The Inquiry from the Presbytery of North Alabama

On 17 April 1940, the Presbytery of North Alabama voted to overture the General Assembly (meeting the next month) "to survey the situation relative to our Theological Seminaries and other institutions from which applicants come seeking ordination to our Presbyteries," and to appoint a "committee [to] give particular attention to the institutions advocating the type of Bible interpretation commonly known as 'Dispensationalism', to discover whether or not this doctrine is in accord with the Confession of Faith, especially with Chapter XIX [*Of the Law of God*]."[96]

---

[91] Ibid., 12-20.

[92] Thompson, *Presbyterians in the South, Volume Three*, 457.

[93] Ernest Trice Thompson, "The Campaign Against the Colleges," *PrOut* 127 (10 September 1945): 8.

[94] In South Carolina, when the synod was asked to approve the intention of John R. Richardson to serve as board member at both Columbia Presbyterian Theological Seminary and Bob Jones University, one synod representative snapped, "You cannot serve God and Baal!" Though this remark was later dropped from the record, it was reported, nonetheless, in the *Southern Presbyterian Journal* by L. Nelson Bell ("An Unfortunate Incident," *SPresJ* 7 [15 November 1948]: 2).

[95] Glass, "The Development of Northern Patterns of Fundamentalism in the South," 12-13.

[96] *Minutes of the Presbytery of North Alabama*, 16-17 April 1940, Florence, AL, 15.

The Presbytery of North Alabama was a conservative presbytery[97] that gave enthusiastic financial support to PCUS educational institutions.[98] The GA initially relayed this overture to the Committee on Theological Seminaries, consistent with the concern that rival non-Presbyterian schools teaching "dispensationalism" may have been hurting the Church's own schools. As this concern gave way to the even greater concern that "dispensationalism" could be compromising the theological purity of the Church, the overture was passed on to the committee working on the Church's doctrinal standards.

Ironically, another communication to the GA from the North Alabama Presbytery's actually called for discharging the Ad Interim Committee on Changes in the Confession of Faith and Catechisms[99]; it was certainly not their idea to have the investigation of dispensationalism taken up by that committee. Instead, this Presbytery proposed:

> 1. That an Ad Interim committee be appointed to survey the situation relative to our Theological Seminaries and other institutions from which applicants come seeking ordination in our Presbyteries.
>
> 2. That the committee give particular attention to the institutions advocating the type of Bible interpretation commonly known as "Dispensationalism", [sic] to discover whether or not this doctrine is in accord with the Confession of Faith, especially with Chapter XIX [Of the Law of God].
>
> 3. That the attitude of our Church on this matter be clearly defined, both toward applicants for admission into its ministry and toward ministers now in our Presbyteries who are promoting the above-mentioned doctrine.[100]

---

[97] While our primary interest is in the third communication to the GA from this Presbytery (just quoted), in point of fact the first two communications provide clear demonstration of the Presbytery's conservative nature: communication 1 rejects any present plan for reunion with the Northern Church and communication 2 rejects previously proposed changes to the Confession of Faith on the grounds that these proposed changes embrace language that is "Arminian rather than Calvinistic"; *Minutes of the Presbytery of Northern Alabama*, 16-17 April 1940, 14-15.

[98] Ibid., *passim*; even a cursory scan of the *Minutes* from the 1920s-1950s reveals this Presbytery's financial support and its genuine interest in the welfare of the Church's schools, especially Louisville and Columbia Theological Seminaries.

[99] *Minutes of the Presbytery of North Alabama*, 16-17 April 1940, 15.

[100] *Minutes of the Presbytery of North Alabama, 1940*, 15-16. S. Lewis Johnson recalls that Dr. J. Rupert McGregor, pastor of the South Highland Presbyterian Church in Birmingham, Alabama (the PCUS church that Johnson attended in the early 1940s), "was not happy with Southeastern Bible College" (a dispensational school established in Birmingham in 1934) because McGregor "felt dispensationalism was out of accord with the Presbyterian Standards." Johnson had heard similar misgivings from people at First Presbyterian Church in Birmingham, as well (S. Lewis Johnson, interview by the author, 14 April 1995, Dallas, TX). While these views would have affected the Birmingham, Alabama Presbytery rather than the North Alabama Presbytery from which the 1940 overtures came, Johnson's recollection nevertheless may help establish how

While points 2 and 3 focus specifically on dispensationalism, point 1 seems deliberately ambiguous. The call for a new Ad Interim Committee to "survey the situation relative to our Theological Seminaries" is reminiscent of a call which the GA had heeded in 1936. At that time, several presbyteries had asked that the GA "investigate the curricula of all our seminaries, and to propose changes."[101] Though the GA had heeded this earlier call, it seems that two different agendas were actually at work.

Apparently, the conservative presbyteries hoped for some reassurance that their seminaries were staying true to Scripture and to their Southern Presbyterian roots. Specifically, they wanted assurances that PCUS schools were being preserved from the modernism that had ruined Northern Presbyterian seminaries.[102] Meanwhile, less conservative presbyteries were hoping simply to improve the facilities, increase the pay scale and number of faculty, and make the curricula of their seminaries more up-to-date.[103] All wanted change in the seminaries' structure and programs, but change in different ways and for different reasons.[104]

The GA and its Ad Interim Committee on Curricula of the Theological Seminaries interpreted these overtures as a call for studying how the curricula and structures of the PCUS schools could be up-dated and strengthened.[105] John R. Richardson expressed well the conservative disappointment with these reports and studies.

> It is evident that the theological education of our day needs strengthening. Many seem to feel that this should come about by Seminary consolidation. One would judge that given sufficient endowment, imposing buildings and a large faculty, we would presto have a stronger theological education. For our part we would not discourage our institutions in their endeavor to seek large

---

common was the concern about dispensationalism among Presbyterians in that region. The North Alabama Presbytery may have been more particularly concerned about the dispensational institution in its own back yard (i.e., Southeastern Bible College) when it sent its overture to the GA. Regardless, it was Chafer, and by implication the institution which Chafer headed, that would come to be more scrutinized by the GA's action.

[101] *Report of the Ad Interim Committee on Curricula of the Theological Seminaries* (Richmond: Presbyterian Committee of Publication, 1936), 3.

[102] Though representing only the extreme faction of this conservative wing, H. Waddell Pratt, stated clerk of the Synod of South Carolina, expressed this message pointedly: Some "members of the Church [i.e., the PCUS] are unwilling to . . . support the Boards of the Church . . . [because] those Boards are supporting men who are teaching doctrines which de-throne Christ from His place in the Bible as understood by historic Presbyterianism" ("History Repeats Itself," *Bulletin of the Independent Board for Presbyterian Foreign Missions* [July, 1936]; quoted in "Southern Church Division Similar," *CBeac* 1 [23 July 1936]: 7).

[103] See Thompson, *Presbyterians in the South, Volume Three*, 455-57.

[104] Ibid., 456.

[105] See *Report of the Ad Interim Committee on Curricula of the Theological Seminaries*, 3-7. This report led to the more fiscally focused study by Works, *The Report of a Survey of the Colleges and Theological Seminaries of the Presbyterian Church in the U.S.*, and to the appointment of a Standing Committee on Theological Seminaries.

endowments, erect bigger buildings or increase their faculty. We would like to point out, however, that these things alone will not strengthen theological education. If we continue to labor under this impression, great will be our disillusionment.[106]

Further, when conservative presbyteries saw that their "call for investigation" was misinterpreted by the GA, they sent additional overtures that were more pointed[107] – the Presbytery of North Alabama was one of these. The Presbytery of North Alabama even sent the following resolution to the presidents of the schools it financially supported (viz., the Assembly's Training School; Columbia Theological Seminary; Louisville Theological Seminary; and Southwestern University):

> **Resolution on Bible Teaching in Our Education Institutions.**
> The Confession and Larger Catechism, to which all our ministers and elders subscribe at their ordination, teach that "it pleased God" to commit the saving revelation "wholly unto writing" so that the Holy Scripture is "The Word of God written" and "the very Word of God" which was "immediately inspired of God and by His singular care and providence kept pure in all ages," that by the Holy Spirit "all writers were inspired to record infallibly the mind and will of God," and that by the saving faith He inspires, "a Christian believeth to be true whatever is revealed in the Word, for the authority of God Himself speaketh therein."
>
> Therefore, the Presbytery of North Alabama overtures the several educational institutions, in whose support the Presbytery has a part, to take adequate measures to insure that the teaching in these institutions maintain the genuineness and authenticity of the several Books of the Holy Scripture, and that those higher critical views which regard large segments of the Bible as "deceptive" and "fraudulent" be refuted in their instruction.[108]

---

[106] John R. Richardson, "Stronger Theological Education," *SPresJ* 3 (January 1945): 3.

[107] The Presbytery of Harmony re-issued its call for the GA "to make careful inquiry into the curricula and instruction of our Theological Seminaries," indicating its dissatisfaction with the GA's response up to then; the Presbytery of Knoxville sent an overture "requesting that the General Assembly 'appoint a fact-finding committee to determine the teaching of our four Theological Seminaries and their respective faculties as to the doctrine of the inspiration of the Scriptures'" (*Minutes of the Eighty-First General Assembly of the Presbyterian Church in the United States* [Austin, TX: Von Boeckmann-Jones Co., 1941], 47). Three Presbyteries went so far as to call for an investigation specifically of the views of Ernest Trice Thompson, professor of Church History at Union Theological Seminary. Thompson's views of the inspiration of Scripture, as expressed in his regular "Sunday School lessons" in the *Presbyterian of the South*, had raised the suspicions of conservatives (cf. Thomas R. Birch, "Glasgow vs. Thompson: Heresy Charges in the Presbyterian Church in the U.S.," *PrGuard* 9 [10 February 1941]: 35-36; Tom Glasgow, "What Does the Southern Presbyterian Church Mean by 'Inspiration of Scripture?'" *SPresJ* 5 [15 February 1947]: 5-6).

[108] *Minutes of the Stated Fall Meeting of the Presbytery of North Alabama* (Sheffield, AL: Standard Print, 1943), 17.

Union Theological Seminary in Richmond (conspicuously absent from the North Alabama Presbytery's support list) was viewed with special suspicion. For the conservatives, a thorough investigation of what its faculty was teaching, not just a broad analysis of curricular development, would have been most desirable.

Since the GA had consistently refused to undertake this kind of investigation,[109] conservative presbyteries may have been seeking ways to motivate the GA to reconsider. It is possible that the Presbytery of North Alabama was looking for a doctrinal viewpoint that both conservatives and liberals in the PCUS could agree merited investigation. If so, "dispensationalism" fit the bill.

Whatever one supposes regarding the motivation for proposing an investigation of dispensationalism, it is beyond doubt that, once that investigation had been taken up, conservatives saw a clear precedent for carrying out much-needed doctrinal investigations of other, more significant aberrations.

> [T]he Assembly of 1941 instructed its committee on revisions to examine current Dispensationalism and point out wherein that movement differs from the Standards of the Church. But while we are using this measuring rod to judge Dispensationalism, it certainly behooves us before the great searcher of hearts to examine our own teaching, the books we prescribe for credit courses, and the teachers we introduce into our conferences by these same standards. Diverse weights and diverse balances, both are an abomination to me, saith the Lord (Proverbs 20:10).[110]

---

[109] In response to the flood of overtures from presbyteries calling for further investigation of teachings (and teachers) in PCUS schools, the GA in 1941 finally ruled as a matter of ecclesiastical law that, without a lower court (e.g., a Synod) bringing a specific charge of heresy to it for a ruling, the GA had no authority to initiate such an investigation (*Minutes of the Eighty-First GA* [1941], 47-49). In this ruling, there is a pointed allusion to the fact that Ernest Trice Thompson had been cleared of charges of heresy (brought by the Synod of Appalachia, the Synod of North Carolina, and the Presbytery of Concord) by Thompson's Presbytery (East Hanover) and further investigation of the matter had been refused by the Synod of Virginia; see Birch, "Glasgow vs. Thompson."

Further, the GA report went on to quote specifically from "the Charter of Union Theological Seminary," which read, in part: "The Seminary shall be under the care of the Synods of Virginia, North Carolina, West Virginia and Appalachia by whom directors shall be appointed as hereinafter described who shall constitute an executive body, to be known as 'The Board of Directors of Union Theological Seminary in Virginia'" (*Minutes*, 48). In the view of this GA report, these (lower) authorities had already investigated the matter and resolved it; it would be inappropriate for the GA to now interfere. As unhappy as conservatives might be with this ruling (e.g., see Daniel S. Gage, "The Mistakes of the General Assembly of 1941," *SPresJ* 1 [January 1943]: 18-23), this decision could be interpreted as merely preserving the autonomy and rights traditionally recognized as belonging to individual presbyteries and synods. Even if this be the correct interpretation, however, the GA was not being entirely consistent in its exercising such "restraint"; it had persistently and vigorously taken up the cause of any overture that requested pursuance of reunion with the PCUSA, regardless of the level of resistance encountered among the presbyteries.

[110] Robinson, "The Authority of the Lord Jesus Christ as Exercised in the Presbyterian Church

The investigation of dispensationalism clearly came at a time when the viability of PCUS schools was at the forefront of concern among the leadership. The 1940 GA "set aside the church years 1941-1943 as a period in which responsibility for Christianity should be laid, by a joint campaign of publicity, upon the heart and conscience of the church."[111] The GA was unified in wanting to shore up their denominational institutions even *before* they received the dire conclusions from the George Works study in 1942[112] and before the viability of these institutions was further challenged by the shortage of funds coinciding with the nation's entrance into the War in 1941. All this took place just as the AIC was taking up its investigation of dispensationalism, a distinctive doctrine taught in non-Presbyterian institutions. From a dispensationalist standpoint, the timing of all this could not have been worse.

The North Alabama Presbytery's overture certainly got the GA's attention. In fact, the North Alabama Presbytery's overture gained more attention from the GA and its committees than any other 1940 overture. The entire overture was initially turned over to the Standing Committee on Theological Seminaries. Corresponding to the three parts of the overture, this Standing Committee issued a three-part response.

In response to the call for a general investigation of PCUS seminaries, the committee referred the North Alabama Presbytery to its responses to similar overtures. The GA's previous policy of refusing to take up such investigations was said to apply here. The committee distinguished, however, the call to investigate "*our* Theological Seminaries and ministers of our Church" from the call to investigate "other institutions." In regard to this request to investigate "other institutions from which come candidates to our presbyteries," the committee responded "in the negative, since the General Assembly has no authority of any kind over these institutions."[113]

In declaring so pointedly the lack of PCUS responsibility toward any supervision over these non-Presbyterian institutions, the committee is going beyond standard concern for restraint, which the GA commonly reiterated in other rulings. The PCUS committee seems to be warning its constituents about the special dangers of "independent" schools. If conservative presbyteries are concerned about the GA's limited authority over its *own* schools, the committee seems to say, know that it exercises *no* authority over non-Presbyterian institutions.

This warning gave conservatives pause. For instance, in his call for "stronger theological education," John R. Richardson hoped for "more emphasis placed on the study of English Bible," "more emphasis on evangelism," "more emphasis upon the

---

U.S.," 13. The editors mention in an introduction that this article was presented first as a sermon "to the Presbyterian Ministers' Association of Atlanta, Ga., and preached as the doctrinal sermon to the Fall 1942 Meeting of North Alabama Presbytery."

[111] Thompson, *Presbyterians in the South, Volume Three*, 456.
[112] Works, *The Report of a Survey of the Colleges and Theological Seminaries of the Presbyterian Church in the U.S.*
[113] *Minutes of the Eighty-First GA [1941]*, 60.

great Christian doctrines of the Bible," and "more care . . . given in the selection of theological teachers."[114] These were the areas that were highlighted by Lewis Sperry Chafer as distinctive strengths of the program of study he had helped establish at Dallas Theological Seminary.[115] Could such an independent school be an alternative – indeed, might it be the only alternative – for Southern Presbyterians dissatisfied with their own seminaries' programs?

This seems to be the question engaged by the Standing Committee on Theological Seminaries in this ruling – and their response to the North Alabama Presbytery suggests an emphatic "No!" Conservatives would stop short of so sharp a rejection of all independent institutions,[116] but as far as a *dispensational* institution like Dallas Seminary was concerned, this negative response would come to be shared by Southern Presbyterians, liberal and conservative alike.

As to the third part of the North Alabama Presbytery's overture, the Standing Committee on Theological Seminaries recommended, "That the General Assembly refer to the Ad Interim Committee on Revision of the Confession of Faith the question as to whether the type of Bible interpretation known as 'Dispensationalism' is in harmony with the Confession of Faith."[117]

We can only speculate as to how the GA might have responded had the overture asked for an investigation of whether the type of Bible interpretation known as "higher criticism" or the system of theology known as "neo-orthodoxy" is in harmony with the Confession of Faith. It is speculation that dispensationalists have brooded on ever since.[118]

---

[114] Richardson, "Stronger Theological Education," 4.

[115] Hannah, "Social and Intellectual History of the Origins of the Evangelical Theological College," 140-80; Rudolf A. Renfer, "A History of the Dallas Theological Seminary" (Ph.D. diss., University of Texas at Austin, 1959), 62-82; and John A. Witmer, "What Hath God Wrought? – Fifty Years of Dallas Theological Seminary, Part I: God's Man and His Dream," *BibSac* 130 (October 1973): 291-304.

[116] This, too, was a point of contention between liberals and conservatives. Cf. Thompson, "The Campaign Against the Colleges," 8; John R. Richardson, "Straining Out a Gnat and Swallowing a Coffin," *SPresJ* 4 (1 April 1946): 2; and L. Nelson Bell, "An Unfortunate Incident," *SPresJ* 7 (15 November 1948): 2. PCUS loyalists, especially those who dismissed concerns about PCUS schools "going liberal," simply could not understand how PCUS conservatives could in good conscience divert support away from PCUS institutions and toward non-PCUS institutions when the PCUS schools already were struggling financially, and when recent studies demonstrated that the PCUS was stretched thin just trying to maintain the institutions it already had (see Thompson, *Presbyterians in the South, Volume Three*, 456-59).

[117] *Minutes of the Eighty-First GA [1941]*, 60.

[118] Glass reports that, even at the time, premillennialist Southern Presbyterians like Robert McQuilkin of Columbia Bible College wanted "to use this situation to turn the tables of the liberals. If the Committee's seminary professors insisted 'on giving Premillennialism a black eye,' McQuilkin suggested that the laymen [on the Committee; i.e., L. Nelson Bell, J.P. McCallie, and Samuel Sibley, who were also the premillennialist representatives on the Committee] issue a minority report 'to open up the whole question honestly. Why should we not have a Committee of the Assembly investigating whether the system of interpretation called liberalism or modernism is in harmony with the Confession of Faith?'" (Glass, "Northern

In 1941, the GA approved the recommendation of the Standing Committee on Theological Seminaries to turn over the investigation of dispensationalism to the Ad Interim Committee on Changes in the Confession of Faith and Catechisms. It sent forward only the third portion of the North Alabama overture to this Ad Interim Committee, with the instruction to add to its task an investigation "as to whether . . . Dispensationalism is in harmony with the Confession of Faith."[119]

Patterns of Fundamentalism in the South," 240, quoting a letter from Robert C. McQuilkin to J.P. McCallie, 2 August 1943). The dispensationalists available for interview who were living at the time were unanimous in their judgment that the GA was egregiously inconsistent in pursuing the investigation of dispensationalism with such vigor, while it allowed "liberalism" to flourish unimpeded (John F. Walvoord, interview by the author, Dallas, Texas, 11 and 18 April 1995; J. Dwight Pentecost, interview by the author, Dallas, Texas, 31 May 1995; Allan A. MacRae, interview by the author, Quarryville, Pennsylvania, 22 July 1993; S. Lewis Johnson, Jr., interview by the author, Dallas, Texas, 7 and 14 April 1995; and Donald K. Campbell, interview by the author, Dallas, Texas, 2 May 1995).

[119] *Minutes of the Eighty-First GA [1941]*, 60.

CHAPTER 5

The Tremors Travel Southward (Part 2): The Investigation of Dispensationalism by the PCUS Ad Interim Committee on Changes in the Confession of Faith and Catechisms

5.1 The Ad Interim Committee on Changes in the Confession of Faith and Catechisms

Overtures calling for the appointment of a committee to revise the doctrinal Standards of the PCUS are recorded as early as 1902, but it took more than thirty years for such a committee to be established.[1] We detect, therefore, a movement in the Southern Presbyterian Church to revise its *Confession of Faith* at the same time that the Northern Presbyterian Church was revising its *Confession*,[2] but the more conservative Southern Presbyterians resisted this impulse for a time, refusing to revise even the sternest Calvinistic statements.

There might not have been a Confessional Revision Committee at all, had it not been for the concern to produce a more readable, "popular statement of the belief of [the] Church." This popular statement was completed within a year and accepted by the GA in 1913.[3] This statement apparently became so popular that a call for its inclusion in the official doctrinal standards of the PCUS gained wide support.[4] It was this call that prompted the formation of a Confessional Committee.

> In 1931, in answer to an overture from East Hanover Presbytery, the General Assembly took the following action: "That Overture No. 90 from East Hanover Presbytery asking that the "Brief Statement" drawn from our Standards be bound in our Confession of Faith and Catechism, be answered in the affirmative with the direction that the

---

[1] See Thomas W. Currie, "Reasons for the Revision of the Presbyterian Standards," *UnSemRev* 50 (January 1939): 124.

[2] This 1903 revision was what enabled the PCUSA to accept into their Church the (Arminian) Cumberland Presbyterian Church (see John Murray, "Shall We Include the Revision of 1903 in Our Creed? A consideration of the theological character of certain amendments to the doctrinal standards of the Presbyterian Church in the U.S.A." *PrGuard* 2 [26 September 1936]: 249-51; Ned B. Stonehouse, "What was Back of the Revision of 1903? An historical survey of the movement of 1890-1903 for revision of the Confession in the Presbyterian Church in the U.S.A." *PrGuard* 2 [26 September 1936]: 247-49).

[3] Currie, "Revision of the Presbyterian Standards," 124.

[4] Ibid.

Explanatory Note ordered by the General Assembly at the time of its adoption be published with the Statement." (See Minutes of the General Assembly, 1931, p. 64).[5]

It is impossible to ascertain the intentions behind this overture; this was the presbytery of Union Theological Seminary, Ernest Trice Thompson, and John Allan MacLean (the one who would proclaim to the Presbyterians in the South in 1944, "Needed – An Evangelistic Creed"[6]). Whatever the motivation, it was this overture that led to the formation of the Ad Interim Committee on Proposed Changes in the Confession of Faith and Shorter Catechism,[7] despite the GA's having rejected similar proposals for thirty years.

The GA in 1935 decided that it needed a committee to study the advisability and feasibility of officially incorporating the popular-level doctrinal summation into the Church's doctrinal standards. That GA also decided that this committee ought to consider other suggested changes, too.[8] The suggestion from the Presbytery of Memphis concerning membership on this Committee was also approved: "said committee [is] to consist of the professors of Systematic Theology in our own Theological Seminaries, with our present Moderator, Dr. Henry H. Sweets, who shall be the Chairman."[9]

This Committee would eventually bring some significant changes to the *Confession*. In 1942, for example, the GA approved the AIC's resolution to adopt "two proposed additional chapters to the Confession of Faith, 'Of the Holy Spirit' and 'Of the Gospel,' identical with those which had been added to the Northern Presbyterian Confession a generation earlier."[10] Such changes laid the initial groundwork for the reunion of the PCUS and the PCUSA in 1983.

In the late 1930s, however, the AIC was still viewed as generally conservative; it had proposed nothing more controversial than some relatively minor changes in wording, and a few additions. Some controversy, nevertheless, surrounded even these modest changes; e.g., adding the word "love" to the definition of God in the answer to Question 4 of the Shorter Catechism; removing the statement that the number of the elect was "so certain and definite that it cannot be either increased or diminished," and also the phrase describing the nature of fallen man as "made

---

[5] Ibid.
[6] John Allan MacLean, "Needed – An Evangelistic Creed: Can We Overcome the Calvinistic Complex?" *PrSouth* 118 (29 March 1944): 5-7.
[7] As overtures requesting changes to the Larger Catechism also were referred to this Committee, it became the "Ad Interim Committee on Changes in the Confession of Faith and Catechisms." By the 1940s, remarks recorded in the official Assembly Minutes refer to this Committee as the Ad Interim Committee on Confessional Revision (though this was never, technically, its title). No attempt has been made to discern a pattern in the choice of reference. Henceforward, the "Ad Interim Committee on Changes in the Confession of Faith and Catechisms" will be abbreviated, as "AIC."
[8] Currie, "Revision of the Presbyterian Standards," 125.
[9] Ibid.
[10] Ernest Trice Thompson, *Presbyterians in the South, Volume Three: 1890-1972* (Richmond: John Knox Press, 1973), 492.

opposite to all good" (Westminster Confession, Chapter III). There was vigorous debate over these changes between Columbia Seminary faculty members William Childs Robinson and James B. Green (who served on the AIC which had proposed these changes).[11]

The very nature of the AIC's work seems to have made PCUS conservatives nervous; they questioned the AIC's every proposal and viewed every suggested change with suspicion. In a less-than-successful effort to allay these suspicions, James B. Green wrote a five-part defense of the changes suggested at the 1938 GA; these articles were published in both the *Christian Observer* and the *Mississippi Visitor*.[12] His last article (which followed the article entitled "The Fourth and Final Statement") not only alerts us to just how heated the discussion had become, but it also allows us to see how seriously the Committee members regarded their work.

> When I sent to the papers my fourth statement on behalf of the Committee on Revision of the Standards, I called it my last. But another seems to be necessary, as an opponent of revision [i.e., Robinson] continues to criticize the committee and its work. My first thought was to ignore these criticisms. But my second thought is, if they are unanswered, some may conclude that they are unanswerable, and that would not be good for the cause of truth, which is supreme. . . . It is argued that the committee's proposals betray a tendency to liberalism, or at least abet the liberal movement. . . . Let me say for the committee that it has not the least sympathy with the said attitude toward creeds now being abandoned abroad and adopted at home. For one member of the committee, since its work was practically finished, has published a book on the Apostles' Creed, warmly commending it to the Church. Another member for years has been annually taking a class of theological students through the Confession and Catechisms, endeavoring to lead them not only into a knowledge of those documents, but also into the appreciation and use of them. No member of the committee will take second place to any opponent of revision in his estimate of the value and necessity of creeds. A proposal to change the

---

[11] Ibid., 491.

[12] Though the articles were published in both the *Christian Observer* and the *Mississippi Visitor*, the author, James B. Green, clipped the article from only one or the other for his files. I obtained the following from those files, kept at the Presbyterian Historical Society in Montreat, NC: James B. Green, "Revision of the Confession of Faith and Catechism: Statement From a Member of the Ad Interim Committee," *Christian Observer* (22 June 1938): 11; idem, "A Second Statement for Committee on Revision of Standards," *Mississippi Visitor* (July 1938): 5-6; idem, "A Third Statement on Behalf of Committee on Revision of Standards," *Christian Observer* (27 July 1938): 11; idem, "The Fourth and Final Statement on Behalf of Committee on Revision of Standards," *Mississippi Visitor* (September 1938): 6; and idem, "Further Statement on Behalf of Committee on Revision of the Standards," *Christian Observer* (15 March 1939): 10.

Standards may proceed from the love and esteem of them, from the desire to see them made more useful.[13]

Even making the relatively minor changes of the AIC's early years required the AIC to obtain several extensions from the GA (1935-1941); this was doubtless due to the sensitive nature of their task. As the work dragged on, the AIC's membership changed; nonetheless, the intent to have a committee of able representatives from the four PCUS Seminaries was preserved.

By the time the AIC received its 1941 mandate to investigate dispensationalism, James B. Green was the only member left from the original (1936) committee. The members of the 1941 AIC represented a complex mixture of interests and viewpoints, but we will see that the conservative members of the committee consistently took key roles in the investigation of dispensationalism.

5.2 The Committee's Initial Report On Dispensationalism and Its Consignment to a Reconstituted Committee

Benjamin Lacy,[14] president of Union Theological Seminary in Richmond, VA and Frank Caldwell, president of Louisville Presbyterian Theological Seminary in Louisville, KY, probably represent the "progressive wing" of the 1941-43 committee, though their theological positions are hard to pinpoint. Lacy certainly *tolerated* "progressive" views at Union, though his own writings were not very controversial.[15] Caldwell served on the controversial "Committee on Cooperation and Union" through the 1940s,[16] but, again, his writings give little indication of his ideological stance.[17]

---

[13] Ibid.

[14] Lacy was from a renowned Presbyterian family; his father, Benjamin Lacy, Sr., was treasurer of the North Carolina Synod for almost thirty years. Lacy and James Hall Brookes, whom C.I. Scofield called his "first and best teacher in the oracles of God" ("In Memoriam. James Brookes," Truth 23 [summer, 1897]: 312), had the same grandfather: Drury Lacy. Thus, in an ironic twist, Brookes' theological "grandson," classical dispensationalism, came under official investigation by his grandfather's biological grandson. I am indebted to Bill Smith, research librarian at Union Theological Seminary in Richmond, for helping me trace these biological connections.

[15] Benjamin R. Lacy, *Revivals in the Midst of the Years* (Richmond: Presbyterian Committee on Publication, 1943); idem, "Leading Men to Jesus Christ," PrOut 132 (23 October 1950): 4. These devotional exhortations typify Lacy's public presentations. Perhaps his most controversial publication was a 1948 article in which he pled for continued PCUS participation in the World Council of Churches (Benjamin R. Lacy, "American Seminaries and Protestant Reconstruction: Seminary president says withdrawal from cooperation in face of world's present needs would be 'a sin calling for great repentance,'" PrOut 130 [2 February 1948]: 6-7).

[16] "The Outlook Pulpit [Biographical Sketch]," PrOut 128 (18 February 1946): 1, 5. In 1954, Caldwell became the chairman of this controversial committee, and co-wrote the case for reunion with the PCUSA, which was published in a pamphlet (Frank H. Caldwell, Guy T. Gillespie, James A. Jones and John R. Richardson, *A Pamphlet Concerning the Matter of the Union of The United Presbyterian Church of North America, The Presbyterian Church in the*

Though Caldwell and Lacy would be heavily involved in the movement to strengthen PCUS seminaries,[18] a logical area of interest for PCUS seminary presidents, there is nothing that would suggest they were behind the attacks on dispensationalism. As chairman, Lacy delivered the Committee's report on dispensationalism in 1943,[19] but he had done little of the writing. When the 1943 GA remanded the report for revision, Lacy and Caldwell resigned, Lacy reminding the GA "that he had served on this committee for several years"[20] and "both these gentlemen stating that they had done all they could do on the committee."[21]

James B. Green, professor of Systematic Theology at Columbia Presbyterian Theological Seminary at Columbia, SC, was "known as a stalwart conservative."[22]

United States of America, and The Presbyterian Church in the United States [Richmond: Presbyterian Committee of Publication, 1954]).

[17] Caldwell published occasional homilies in the church papers (e.g., Frank H. Caldwell, "The Outlook Pulpit: 'The Christian as Lover,'" *PrOut* 128 [19 February 1946]: 5-6). He published one book, *Preaching Angles* (Nashville, TN: Abingdon Press, 1954); and edited another, *The Church Faces the Isms: [Written by The Members of the Faculty of the Louisville Presbyterian Theological Seminary, Louisville, Kentucky*, ed. Arnold Black Rhodes, Frank H. Caldwell, and L.C. Rudolph (Nashville, TN: Abingdon Press, 1958), which, interestingly, contained a chapter on "dispensationalism" (95-110, written by William D. Chamberlain); Caldwell wrote the chapter on "Denominationalism and Ecumenism" (175-91).

[18] In 1944, as Chairman of the Advisory Committee on Christian Education, Caldwell reported to the GA that much had been done in the previous two years to reverse the dire situation of the PCUS described by the Works Report (Thompson, *Presbyterians in the South, Volume Three*, 457-58).

[19] "The Assembly's Ad Interim Committee on changes in Confession of Faith and Catechisms, [was] reported through the Chairman, Dr. B. B. Lacy" (Henry B. Dendy and L. Nelson Bell, "Meeting of the General Assembly," *SPresJ* 2 [June 1943]. 9). Cf. an almost identical wording in "Saturday, May 29: 'Dispenaionalism'[sic] Report Recommitted," *PrSouth* 118 (2 June 1943): 3.

[20] "Dispensationalism' Report Recommitted," 9.

[21] "Meeting of the General Assembly," 4.

[22] Thompson, *Presbyterians in the South, Volume Three*, 491. (Thompson mistakenly lists Green as the "chairman of the ad interim committee"). Others corroborate Thompson's description of Green's reputation. See the section on "James Benjamin Green" in Morton H. Smith, *Studies in Southern Presbyterian Theology* (Phillipsburg, NJ: Presbyterian & Reformed Publishing Co., 1962). Smith concludes this survey, "As we look back over our survey of the theology taught at Columbia Seminary from its founding through the professorship of J.B. Green, we may characterize it all as orthodox, Old School, Presbyterian theology." Cf. also Green's obituary in the Minutes of the 1968 Mississippi synod; there he is described as "a man of strong conviction. He had a Biblical and reasonable faith. No one ever doubted his faith and conviction concerning the Word of God. He stood upon the great doctrines and truths and proclaimed them as Moses the Law Giver, Elijah the Prophet, Paul the Theologian, and Christ the Lord. He spoke 'with authority.' Dr. Green taught and preached with clarity. . . . His method of teaching was catechetical and clear cut," and "His teaching never left any doubt or confusion in the minds of his students as to what he believed or sought to impart to them." He is also described as "a man of loyalty. . . . During trying days when it seemed Columbia Seminary might be closed or joined with another Seminary, Dr. Green, more than anyone else, fought for the continued life of this institution even though he was a graduate of another seminary. There was no question of his allegiance to the Presbyterian Church, its boards, agencies, and institutions" ("In Memoriam: Rev. James Benjamin Green D.D.," *Minutes of the*

Yet, he served as the "point man" for the AIC, announcing and defending the AIC's more controversial suggested changes to the Confession and Catechisms throughout the late-1930s.[23] It would appear that the time and effort required by these other committee responsibilities precluded his diverting his attention to yet another issue. He signed the AIC report on dispensationalism in both 1943 and 1944. Otherwise, he appears to have played no role in drawing up the committee's findings.

Samuel Hale Sibley, Chief Judge of the U.S. Court of Appeals for the Fifth Circuit in Atlanta, Georgia,[24] and the only layman on the AIC in 1941, was perhaps the committee's most conservative member. He had been moderator of the GA in 1934, one of only a handful of laymen ever to be elected to that post. His lack of formal theological training,[25] however, became a factor as he wrestled with the investigation of dispensationalism. He "confessed that he did not realize he was a premillennialist until he read the literature sent to him by the committee and was 'surprised to learn' that premillennialists were 'theologically suspect.'"[26]

Sibley refused to sign the 1943 report condemning dispensationalism. Ambivalent about the committee's findings, Judge Sibley was apparently put off by the appearance of impropriety in the way the investigation was conducted.[27] Despite assurances from other committee members that Sibley's objection was misdirected,[28] the GA seemed moved by his concern. In response – to alleviate any appearance of impropriety – the moderator added two known premillennialists to the Committee: L. Nelson Bell and J.P. McCallie. L. Nelson Bell was the one who had most vociferously objected to non-premillennialists' casting judgment on [a

---

Synod of Mississippi of the Presbyterian Church in the U.S. [Jackson, MS: Belhaven College, 1968], 74-75).

[23] Green, "Revision of the Confession of Faith and Catechism: Statement From a Member of the Ad Interim Committee," 11; *idem*, "A Second Statement for Committee on Revision of Standards," 5-6; *idem*, "A Third Statement on Behalf of Committee on Revision of Standards," 11; *idem*, "The Fourth and Final Statement on Behalf of Committee on Revision of Standards," 6; *idem*, "Further Statement on Behalf of Committee on Revision of the Standards," 10. Cf. also *idem*, "Theology in a Changing World," *UnSemRev* 53 (November 1941): 21-22; and "The Distinctive Teachings of Presbyterianism," *UnSemRev* 47 (July 1936): 366-78.

[24] Biographical information is provided in *Proceedings of a Special Session of the Court En Banc in Memory of the Honorable Samuel H. Sibley* (Atlanta, Ga.: United States Court of Appeals for the Fifth Circuit, 1959).

[25] Sibley was classically trained as a lawyer. As he was completing his law degree, he even taught classes in Latin and Greek (ibid., 12).

[26] Letter from Samuel H. Sibley to the chairman of the AIC, 2 December 1943; quoted by William Robert Glass, "The Development of Northern Patterns of Fundamentalism in the South: 1900-1950" (Ph.D. diss., Emory University, 1991), 238.

[27] This led to an awkward moment when the report was delivered to the GA. "Explanation was made at this point regarding the failure of Judge Sibley to sign the report which was signed by Dr. Lacy, Dr. Frank H. Caldwell, Dr. J.B. Green and Dr. E.W. McLaurin, of the four seminaries. Judge Sibley's conviction was that 'if we are trying anyone he should be brought into court and not tried covertly,'" ("'Dispensationalism' Report Recommitted," 9).

[28] "Dr. Lacy explained that the other members of the committee had [t]aken the view that many of those who have taught these doctrines are not living – such as Dr. Scofield – and, therefore, could not be 'tried'" (ibid.).

form of] premillennialism.[29] Like Sibley, Bell was concerned "that the report would do a serious injustice to those who held that view [i.e., the premillennial view], but who were not dispensationalists."[30]

Adding two premillennialists to the AIC was an equitable solution to Sibley. The next year he, with the others, signed the report, making the judgment against dispensationalism unanimous. It is obvious, nonetheless, that Sibley was not a key figure in the formation of the AIC's actual report.

That task apparently fell, insofar as the 1943 report is concerned, almost exclusively to Eugene W. McLaurin. Very little information is available concerning McLaurin. He rarely published even journal articles, despite his academic credentials. When he received his doctorate (a Ph.D. in Greek from the University of Texas, 1952), the *Southern Presbyterian Journal* said, "The Ph.D. in Greek is relatively rare in any institution. Dr. McLaurin's is the second ever to be awarded by the University of Texas."[31] Perhaps the announcement of his accomplishment in this conservative paper indicates that he had friends in conservative circles. His own positions on the controversies of the day between "liberals" and "conservatives" were never published, however.

McLaurin served twenty years in the pastorate, including fourteen months as a chaplain in World War I. In 1938, he became professor of New Testament Language and Exegesis at Austin Theological Seminary.[32] Apparently, the time which might have been devoted to publishing was spent on his education,[33] and on writing his very technical dissertation, "The Influence of Hebrew and Classical, Septuagint, and Hellenistic Greek Elements in the Redemptive Terms of the Greek New Testament."

There is no indication that he had any agenda against dispensationalism. Nevertheless, when the AIC chairman asked the faculty members on the committee to research and submit a report for the committee, McLaurin took the request seriously. McLaurin seems to have relied on and been convinced by James Bear's articles, which critiqued dispensationalism as out of harmony with the Confession of Faith.[34] McLaurin's paper lists several points at variance with the PCUS

---

[29] Ibid. Bell apparently came to this conclusion independently of Sibley; he seems not to have even known that Sibley held the premillennial view – when Bell voiced his objection early in the discussion (before Sibley had made known his reason for refusing to sign the report), part of his concern was "that the committee which reported had no one of pre-millennial views on it" (ibid.).

[30] Ibid.

[31] "Dr. Eugene William McLaurin, M.A., Ph.D., D.D.," *SPresJ* 11 (2 July 1952): 13.

[32] "The Outlook Pulpit [Biographical Sketch]," *PrOut* 134 (21 April 1952): 5. He was pastor of three different PCUS churches, all in Texas: in Edna, TX (1916-20), Sweetwater, TX (1920-23), and Ballinger, TX (1923-36).

[33] As even the *Outlook*'s biographical sketch explained, "Post-graduate studies at the Universities of Chicago and Texas have claimed his attention in recent years" (ibid.).

[34] James Bear, "Dispensationalism and the Covenant of Grace," *UnSemRev* 49 (July 1938): 285-307; *idem*, "Shall We Revise the Standards?" *PrSouth* 115 (12 June 1940): 3-4; and *idem*, "The Presbyterian Standards vs. the Scofield Bible, Parts I-VI," *PrSouth* 116 (19 March - 30 April 1941). McLaurin refers the reader to these articles at the end of his treatise.

standards in the *Scofield Reference Bible*, in the writings of Lewis Sperry Chafer, Harry A. Ironside, William Bell Riley, James M. Gray, and Harrison H. Gregg.[35]

The preface of *A Suggested Report of the Ad Interim Committee on changes in the Confession of Faith and Catechisms with Regard to the "Question as to Whether the Type of Bible Interpretation Known as 'Dispensationalism' is in Harmony with the Confession of Faith*," printed by Austin Presbyterian Theological Seminary, gives the following account: "The faculty of Austin Presbyterian Theological Seminary, through Rev. E.W. McLaurin, submitted the following paper. This paper, with some additions not included below, and with some minor changes, became the report of the committee."[36]

This adds a valuable historical detail as to how the AIC's report was constructed. With this document in hand, we can see the committee's changes, adjustments, and additions; further, we can, perhaps, discern some of the logic behind their actions.

It is unfortunate that the document gives no hint about McLaurin's motivations, perspective or biases. Yet, in another sense, this may mean that McLaurin went about this task as a researcher seeking objective answers to a legitimate academic question. The original work has the look and feel of a research paper (the format was modified in the committee's final version). Despite his historical obscurity, McLaurin set the tone for the AIC's report. He had neither instigated the controversy nor placed dispensationalism under investigation. He appears to have approached his job as a scholar, competently researching the subject he was assigned.

At the Assembly meeting in 1942, a year after the AIC received its mandate to investigate dispensationalism from the GA's Standing Committee on Theological Seminaries, they reported:

> Your Committee feels that there are definite points in which certain teachings associated with Dispensationalism are out of harmony with our Standards. We found it, however, impossible to complete this report in time to be published in the Blue Book prior to the meeting of the General Assembly, and there are, furthermore, other points which we desire to clarify before this matter is brought definitely before the General Assembly.[37]

By 1943, the AIC was ready with a full report. By comparing this report with McLaurin's original draft, we can discern what aspects of the report received the most attention from the rest of the committee.

---

[35] See Appendix 3, below. Cf. *Light on Prophecy* (Philadelphia, PA: The Christian Herald, 1918).

[36] *A Suggested Report of the Ad Interim Committee on Changes in the Confession of Faith and Catechisms with Regard to the "Question as to Whether the Type of Bible Interpretation Known as 'Dispensationalism' is in Harmony with the Confession of Faith* (Austin, TX: Austin Presbyterian Theological Seminary, 1942), i.

[37] "Report of AIC," in *Minutes of the Eighty-Second GA* (Austin, TX: Von Boeckmann-Jones Co., 1942), 122.

The committee anticipated the concern expressed by Samuel H. Sibley that their investigation of dispensationalism seemed to make all premillennialists "theologically suspect."[38] The committee tried, albeit unsuccessfully, to forestall such concerns. McLaurin stated that the "point at issue . . . is not primarily a view of the millennium."[39] The committee significantly expanded this point.

> It is not at all a controversy in regard to the millennium, since our denomination has always had, and still has, room for millennialists, a-millennialists, post-millennialists, and pre-millennialists in its ranks. The main point at issue, let it be emphasized, is whether the system of Bible interpretation known as Dispensationalism is in harmony with Presbyterian doctrines as set forth in the Westminster Standards.[40]

Both McLaurin's draft and the 1943 AIC report acknowledged the difficulty of deciding what sources would most fairly depict the dispensational position. The AIC report simply said the sources used were "the writings of the generally-recognized exponents of these teachings."[41] McLaurin gives a more elaborate description of the difficulties encountered.

> [I]t is difficult to determine exactly the principles of Dispensationalism accepted by most Dispensationalists, since there is no officially formulated system of this school of Bible interpretation.[42] In this report only those beliefs held by all Dispensationalists as recorded in the writings of their leading authors, and in opposition to the teachings of our standards, are considered.[43]

The committee seems to have detected some overstatement in McLaurin's claim that views he included were "beliefs held by all dispensationalists." Not only did they eliminate this statement, but, when discussing Scofield's distinction between "law" and "grace," the AIC report clarifies (as McLaurin does not), "Some

---

[38] Letter, Samuel H. Sibley to the AIC, 2 December 1943. Lewis Sperry Chafer made the same point: "Since dispensational distinctions form an integral feature of the premillennial interpretation of the Scriptures, all premillennialists are challenged by this investigation" ("Dispensational Distinctions Challenged," *BibSac* 100 [July-September 1943]: 337).

[39] McLaurin, *A Suggested Report of the AIC*, 1.

[40] "Appendix: Report of the AIC: The Questions as to Whether the Type of Bible Interpretation Known as Dispensationalism Is in Harmony with the Confession of Faith," in *Minutes of the Eighty-Third General Assembly of the Presbyterian Church in the United States, with an Appendix* (Austin, TX: Von Boeckmann-Jones, Co., 1943), 123. (See Appendix 4, below.)

[41] Ibid.

[42] This point reiterates Bear's observation three years previously: "Is their [dispensationalists'] teaching in harmony with [the Westminster Confession]? What do they teach about God's dealings with the human race? In trying to answer these questions we immediately face a difficulty, – Whom shall we take as the authoritative spokesmen for the Dispensational group? They have formed no church and have drawn up no full and authoritative statement of belief" ("Dispensationalism and the Covenant of Grace," 289).

[43] McLaurin, *A Suggested Report of the AIC*, 1.

[dispensationalists], however, do not follow Dr. Scofield in his distinction between 'law' and 'grace,' but hold that all are saved by grace."[44]

Some of McLaurin's material was re-organized in the AIC report, but the points were largely unchanged. The quotes provided by McLaurin became the frame of reference for the committee's work; in a few places, quotations by Charles Feinberg or Arno C. Gaebelein were added. The AIC report eliminated all quotations from fundamentalist William Bell Riley, James Gray (president of Moody Bible Institute), as well as quotations from the lesser-known conference speaker, Harrison Gregg. The *points supported* by the excluded quotations were *not* eliminated, however. The quotations were *replaced* by what the committee apparently thought were *clearer* dispensational articulations of the same points. If there is a pattern in the differences between McLaurin's draft and the committee's final version, it is apparently due to McLaurin's being more concerned to demonstrate that the views described were *widely* held by dispensationalists, whereas the AIC report was more concerned to present *clearly* the views being repudiated.

This refinement was not propitious for Chafer and Scofield. In fact, one of Chafer's complaints about the report was, "Out of the eight men cited [by the AIC] as defenders of dispensational interpretation six are quoted but once briefly. The bulk of the mass of quotations are of the late Dr. C.I. Scofield and the writings of the Editor of BIBLIOTHECA SACRA [i.e., Chafer himself] (mostly as found in this journal) with the latter more quoted than the former."[45] Chafer apparently took the report as a personal attack.

Chafer had brought some of this focused attention upon himself, though, by his 1936 article responding to John Murray and Oswald T. Allis. The introduction to the AIC report quoted Chafer's own disclosure that his views diverged from those of Murray and Allis because his views diverged from the traditional Reformed articulation of the Covenant of Grace; this is a doctrine, the AIC went on to note, that is expressly contained in the Westminster Standards.[46]

Yet Chafer's comments would grow even more cavalier towards the Church's doctrinal standards as the controversy heightened. In an editorial responding to the AIC's 1943 report, Chafer remarked:

> By this challenge of the Assembly's Ad-Interim Committee, the lines are drawn between a very great company of Bible expositors who through years of unwearied study of the Sacred Text accept the doctrine of dispensations as the key to the right understanding of the Bible and the theological theorists who revert in argument not to a "Thus saith the Lord," but to man-made creeds. Herein is a phenomenon. What, indeed, underlies this inordinate exaltation of a creed to the point where in practical usage it is considered as authoritative as the Bible itself? Certainly the creed is not so

---

[44] "Report of the [1943] AIC," 123, n. 2.
[45] Chafer, "Dispensational Distinctions Challenged," 344.
[46] "Report of the [1943] AIC," 123, n. 1. The point in this section is clear; the advocates of dispensationalism themselves recognize that their view diverges from the Church's Standards.

elevated because of the notion that it is infallible, for the early portion of this very report by the Assembly's Committee, which later discredits dispensational distinctions, recommends "changes in the Confession of Faith and the Catechism."[47]

As if it were not enough to challenge the notion of confessional subscription in general, Chafer went on to postulate that biblical incompetence, together with feelings of intimidation upon being confronted with compelling dispensationalist argumentation, might be the true motivation for the AIC's findings.

> Is it not possible that there are men who, being individually conscious that for want of extended examination of the Scriptures, know themselves to be unable to face on biblical grounds the constructive teaching advanced by the dispensationalist and therefore hide behind a creed, believing that their bulwark is imperviable [sic] since the creed is dogmatic and since there are many others who like themselves seek the same shadow for protection? It is quite possible for an individual to embrace a creed who has never given even a passing consideration to the Bible itself.[48]

Chafer can hardly have thought that such inflammatory remarks would gain him a more favorable hearing from the AIC members investigating his views. We can only assume that either: 1) he was so enraged by the AIC's 1943 report that in a moment of indiscretion he vented his anger on paper, not considering the potential effect of his words; or 2) he recognized that the AIC had *correctly* concluded that his views were out of accord with the *Confession*, but he believed that such a finding should be deemed inconsequential by those "more studied" in the Bible's teaching. His remarks, in that case, would have been intended to prepare his supporters for the inevitable, and represented a strategy of going on the offensive against more subscriptionist Presbyterians.[49]

Whatever his motive, expressions of disdain for the Presbyterian doctrinal standards, and for Presbyterian leaders, could only exacerbate perceptions that dispensationalist influences mostly served to undermine the authority, efforts,

---

[47] Chafer, "Dispensational Distinctions Challenged," 338-39.

[48] Ibid.

[49] Both publicly and in private correspondence, James Bear, who joined the AIC after the 1943 report was recommitted, had suggested that Chafer's views were out of accord with the Westminster Standards. He had challenged Chafer to try to get changes made in the Standards, if Chafer genuinely believed the Standards were untrue to Scripture ("Shall We Revise the Standards?," 3). Cf. also the seven-part series of articles by Bear in the *Presbyterian of the South*, entitled, "The Presbyterian Standards vs. The Scofield Bible" 116 (19 March - 30 April 1941). For documentation of the correspondence of letters between Bear and Chafer, see John David Hannah, "The Social and Intellectual History of the Origins of the Evangelical Theological College" (Ph.D. diss., University of Texas at Dallas, 1988), 360-61. Hannah's interpretation seems warranted: "Bear was calling for a showdown; he wanted the church to make a formal judgment as to the orthodoxy of dispensationalism" (361). In 1943-44, Bear would get his wish.

leaders, organizations, and institutions of the PCUS. The 1943 AIC report made it clear that, aside from whatever doctrinal differences were present, the PCUS was not willing to tolerate such subversion.

> [W]e find that many ministers and laymen are uninformed as to the characteristic teachings and emphases of Dispensationalism. Even more serious than the apparent logical divergence of Dispensational doctrines from the teaching in our Standards are the divisive practical effects of Dispensationalism in the Church. In many congregations which have become indoctrinated with its teachings, the Sunday School materials edited and published by our own Executive Committee are depreciated and are not used, so-called inter-denominational Sunday School materials being substituted. Likewise our own Presbyterian institutions of Christian education, Young Peoples' Conferences, and other agencies of the Church are depreciated, and sometimes labeled as "modernistic" or "atheistic" because not "rightly dividing the word of truth" in accordance with Dispensationalist teachings and Dispensationalist methods of interpreting Scripture. Thus the loyalty of Presbyterians to their own agencies and institutions is undermined and funds which might otherwise be available for work carried on by our own Church are diverted to so-called "Faith Missions" and "Interdenominational Bible Institutes." In a number of instances the issue of Dispensationalism has become so acutely divisive in local congregations as to require drastic actions on the part of presbyteries, such actions usually being taken after it was too late to keep congregations from being rent asunder.[50]

The AIC had been commissioned by the GA to discern whether or not dispensationalism was out of harmony with the *Confession* and *Catechisms*. How could they find otherwise when the best-known contemporary exponent of dispensationalism, himself a Southern Presbyterian, had publicly conceded as much?[51]

---

[50] "Report of the [1943] AIC," 122.

[51] Chafer's complaint about the narrow focus of the previous report notwithstanding, the 1943-44 AIC narrowed the focus even further: "we shall limit our quotations to the writings of two outstanding exponents of Dispensationalism: Dr. C.I. Scofield (especially as found in certain notes in the *Scofield Reference Bible*) and Dr. L.S. Chafer, who has written extensively on the subject" ("Report of the AIC: The Question As To Whether the Type of Bible Interpretation Known as Dispensationalism Is in Harmony With the Confession of Faith," in *Minutes of the Eighty-Fourth GA* [Austin, TX: Von Boeckmann-Jones, Co., 1944], 124). The introduction of the 1944 report, like the 1943 report, again cites a Chafer article, but this time the editorial cited is the one quoted above ("Dispensational Distinctions Challenged"). Apparently, from the point of view of the AIC, Chafer's hubris made him, and his brand of dispensationalism, a legitimate target. Since he had conceded the case, they might as well focus their investigation on his views and avoid alienating other premillennialists who were not so presumptuous as to glibly dismiss the *Confession*'s teachings.

At the 1943 Assembly meeting, however, these questions had not yet been closed entirely. The conclusion of the 1943 AIC report, "representing the faculties of the four [PCUS] theological seminaries, was that the teachings of 'Dispensationalism' and of the Confession on the questions studied are irreconcilable."[52] But, as mentioned above, the one premillennialist on the committee had refused to sign the report and other confessionally conservative premillennialists, upon hearing the report, were also concerned that it made premillennialists, in general, theologically suspect.

> In the discussion which followed the presentation of the report, Dr. L. Nelson Bell, former medical missionary, said that the committee which reported had no one of pre-millennial views on it; that the report inadvertently would do serious injustice to those who held that view, but who were not dispensationalists.[53] He objected to the findings of the committee ... [and] made a motion to recommit this report and to include two additional members of pre-millennial views so as to bring in a report which would be acceptable to everybody.[54]

Another member even made a "substitute motion to table the report," which failed.[55]

At that point, a few persons exhorted the Assembly toward greater unity, one stating "that all controversial matters are out of order in this day and time."[56] After hearing Judge Sibley's explanation as to why he did not sign the report, "Dr. Bell's motion to recommit the matter with the addition of two premillenniarians [sic] was adopted."[57] The assembly found Bell himself to be a logical choice to take this responsibility, along with J.P. McCallie, founder and president of the McCallie School for Boys in Chattanooga, Tennessee.

This did not quite end the grumbling, however. Apparently, Frank Caldwell took offense at the suggestion that the report was inadequate. After Bell's motion passed, Caldwell "submitted his resignation saying that the report represented the 'collaboration of the four theological seminaries and even the addition of two pre-millinarians [sic] will not substantially improve it.'"[58] Taking his lead, Lacy "also submitted his resigna[t]ion, agreeing with Dr. Caldwell in the fact [t]hat the report represented the attitude of the faculties of all the seminaries."[59] "These

---

[52] "'Dispensationalism' Report Recommitted," 9.
[53] To be more precise (according to Bell himself), "it seemed that this report confused *extreme dispensationalism* and the moderate premillennial view held by many" ("One Elder Looks at the General Assembly: Dispensationalism," *SPresJ* 2 [June 1943]: 7 [emphasis added]). Cf. the point made by "J.K. Roberts, of Clinton, S.C., disclaiming any sympathy for dispensationalism, felt that 'many mild dispensationalists will be offended if the report is adopted as it stands'" ("'Dispensationalism' Report Recommitted," 9).
[54] "'Dispensationalism' Report Recommitted," 9.
[55] Ibid.
[56] Ibid.
[57] Ibid.
[58] Ibid.
[59] Ibid.

resigna[t]ions were accepted, after some debate, with the provision that these men should name their successors."[60]

No single record details the discussion that followed their resignations, or what led the GA to allow (or require?) Caldwell and Lacy to name their own successors. Collating the various records, however, gives some clues to what the interaction might have entailed. The *Presbyterian of the South* recounted Bell's motion to add two premillennialist members to the committee "so as to bring in a report which would be acceptable to everybody."[61] The account of Bell and Henry B. Dendy, which appeared in the *Southern Presbyterian Journal*, nuanced this point more precisely. "In the discussion which followed a motion was made to re-commit this report and to include two additional members of premillenial [sic] views so as to bring in a report, which, while condemning extreme dispensationalism, would be acceptable to men of various millenial [sic] views of our Church."[62]

Caldwell, though, still defended the report as it stood. Dendy and Bell give some indication why.

> The report had stated that "it is not at all a controversy in regard to the millenium, since our denomination has always had, and still has, room for millenialists, a-millenialists, post-millenialists, and pre-millenialists in its ranks. The main point at issue, let it be emphasized, is whether the system of Bible interpretation, known as dispensationalism is in harmony with Presbyterian doctrines as set forth in the Westminster Standards."[63]

The *Presbyterian of the South* mentions the concern then raised by Calvin Reid.

> Dr. J. Calvin Reid, of Columbus, Ga., inquired if the committee should be instructed as formerly, i.e., to compare the dispensational teachings with the teachings of the Confession, pointing out that much of the discussion of the morning had disregarded the Confession and its teachings. The moderator, without other instructions by the Assembly, reiterated the previous commission.[64]

Putting all this together, it seems that the debate that followed Caldwell's and Lacy's resignations centered around whether the report really needed to be recommitted for further study. Although premillennialists apparently were concerned, the report stressed that it did not condemn premillennialism *per se*, but dispensational views averse to the Confession.

Furthermore, Bell's express intention to preserve the report's condemnation of "extreme dispensationalism" might have cast even further question on the need for continued deliberation by the Committee. Caldwell's contention, that "even the

---

[60] Ibid., 9, 14.
[61] Ibid., 9.
[62] Dendy and Bell, "Meeting of the General Assembly," 4.
[63] Ibid.
[64] "'Dispensationalism' Report Recommitted," 14.

addition of two pre-millinarians [*sic*] will not substantially improve it,"[65] suggests this.

The GA, however, apparently preferred to err on the side of avoiding offense, or the very appearance of inequity, even if doing so meant continued, potentially superfluous deliberation. The report was recommitted to a revamped committee.

Asking Caldwell and Lacy to choose their own successors may have been intended as a vote of confidence. It certainly guaranteed perpetuation of their perspective on the committee. Indeed, whatever sympathy on the AIC toward the dispensational view may have been garnered by adding two premillennialists was counter-balanced by Caldwell's and Lacy's choices of successors.

Caldwell's choice of successor was Felix Bayard Gear,[66] who held impressive educational credentials[67] and whose research on dispensationalism was apparently known to Caldwell.[68] Gear was named the AIC's chairman, despite his being the committee's youngest member (at age 44), and despite his being, at this stage of his

---

[65] Ibid., 9.

[66] Gear was Associate Professor of Bible at Southwestern College at Memphis (which changed its name to Rhodes College in 1983), a PCUS Liberal Arts college. With the exchange of Gear for Caldwell, Louisville Seminary was no longer represented on the AIC. Technically, therefore, the Committee no longer had representatives from "all four of the Theological Seminaries." Nonetheless, Gear's appointment seems to have preserved the *spirit* of this intent, just the same.

[67] He received training at Union Seminary (Richmond), Princeton Seminary, Edinburgh University, and Harvard University (Felix B. Gear Biographical File, Archives of the Presbyterian Historical Society, Montreat, NC). In 1946, he would become James B. Green Professor of Theology at Columbia Theological Seminary, replacing Green himself upon his retirement. Green and Gear also served together on this Ad Interim Committee.

[68] The fruit of this research would be delivered in a series of lectures in the mid-late 1940s, entitled, "Dispensationalism: A Modern Substitute for Historical Christianity." (Even though Gear never quotes John Murray's articles, "The Reformed Faith and Modern Substitutes: Modern Dispensationalism," *PrGuard* 2 [18 May 1936]: 77-79; and [17 August 1936]: 210-12, the similarity in his choice of title is striking). The exact dates of these lectures are unknown; they are collected, without mention of dates, locations, or context of their presentation, in the Felix B. Gear papers, Presbyterian Historical Society, Montreat, NC. Internal evidence provides our only clues. The audience appears to be composed of fellow PCUS ministers (e.g., he repeatedly refers to "our church"), though it is difficult to tell whether it is a group of fellow professors, pastors, or a mixed group, including perhaps lay elders and deacons. Curiously, when Gear quotes from the AIC report, he quotes from the 1943 (rather than the 1944) report, though he had not served on the 1943 committee at all and had chaired the 1944 committee. This might indicate that these lectures were delivered before 1944, except that a couple of times he quotes from O. T. Allis' *Prophecy and the Church*, which was published in 1945. It may have been that the lectures were prompted by Gear's involvement in the 1944 AIC condemnation of dispensationalism, in which case Gear was using the 1943 report to help substantiate the claims of the 1944 report, which he oversaw and which he was defending. We cannot prove this inference, however. In any case, the bulk of Gear's sources in these lectures are either classical Reformed sources (e.g., Calvin, Edwards, the Reformed Confessions) or dispensationalist works published in the late 19th-early 20th century. This is the research being referred to as that which Caldwell might have known about in 1943.

career, more of an "up-and-comer" than an established figure. He evidently had the respect of his colleagues on the AIC.[69]

What his attitude was toward dispensationalism, there can be no doubt. Copious references in his course notes to John Calvin's *Institutes* and the theological writings of Southern Presbyterian stalwart Robert Dabney display a reverence for the Reformed tradition as embraced by the Southern Presbyterian Church.[70] On the other hand, Gear was heard to say after the AIC investigation that, in dispensationalism,

> we are confronted with a dogmatism which asserts itself in an arrogant assumption of superior knowledge on the part of really very ignorant people. . . . [I]n all the distortions they make of the scripture in their efforts to "squeeze" their system into it or out of it, they seldom ever admit the possibility that they might make a mistake. They come somehow to feel that they have more understanding than all their teachers if they know the <u>Scofield Reference Bible</u>. With this superficial system at their finger tips they cannot err.[71]

Frustrated at what he saw as a subversive force that split churches and undermined peoples' confidence in their pastors,[72] he may well have been eager to be part of the effort to rid the church of dispensationalism.

Gear seems to have been the only person on the AIC besides James Bear (see below) who had examined dispensationalism before arriving on the committee (perhaps why Caldwell chose him). Like Bear, Gear recognized a distinction between premillennialists generally, and *dispensational* premillennialists, stating, "all Dispensationalists are Premillenial [sic] in their view of the Lord's return, but not all Premillenielists [sic] are Dispensationalists."[73] Like every other Southern Presbyterian that investigated dispensationalism, Gear quoted Bear's articles;

---

[69] Apparently, Gear and Bell forged a friendship during this time period in which they worked together on the AIC. Gear was elected Moderator of the 1964 GA, a tumultuous time to be in such a position. Race relations were strained throughout the country, and in the PCUS in particular. In a controversial decision that enraged the representatives of Memphis, which was formerly Gear's own place of ministry, Gear moved the 1964 GA from Memphis, TN (the meeting place designated by the 1963 GA) to Montreat, NC, because the Memphis Presbytery refused to seat African-American delegates. Bell took a more conservative view on race relations than Gear; nevertheless he provided some helpful, friendly counsel to Gear in a series of letters (Felix B. Gear and L. Nelson Bell papers, Archives of the Presbyterian Historical Society, Montreat, NC).

[70] Gear's course notes (e.g., "Theology 302," and "Theology 303") were obtained from the Felix B. Gear papers, Presbyterian Historical Society, Montreat, NC. Gear also published two treatises on the history and biblical defense of Presbyterian doctrine: *Basic Beliefs of the Reformed Faith: A Biblical Study of Presbyterian Doctrine* (Richmond: John Knox Press, 1946) and *Can Calvinism Live Again?* (Richmond: Presbyterian Committee of Publication, 1964).

[71] Gear, "Lecture IV: Dispensationalism and Historical Christianity," 4-6.

[72] Ibid.

[73] Gear, "Lecture II: Premillenialism [sic] as Distinguished from Dispensationalism," 1.

however, Gear seems to have reached his conclusions independently. Gear offered a distinctive historical theological analysis of the dispensationalist system through Plymouth Brethrenism. This allowed him then to use the nineteenth century writings of Robert Dabney opposing the Plymouth Brethren, *mutatis mutandis*, against "the distinctive features of the movement [which] have been carried over into the modern dispensational theory."[74] Thus, Gear's addition to the Committee added a viewpoint that was not only thoroughly acquainted with dispensationalism, but was also firmly opposed to its teachings and wary of the threat it posed to the PCUS.

Lacy chose as his successor James Edwin Bear, who was Henry Young Professor of Biblical Literature and Interpretation of the New Testament at Union Theological Seminary in Richmond (where Lacy was president). Bear was easily the most widely recognized expert in the South on the relationship between dispensationalism, premillennialism, and the *Westminster Confession*. He had begun writing on the subject in 1938,[75] when he was apparently prompted to write his own article after reading the exchange between Lewis Sperry Chafer and Oswald T. Allis.[76]

Bear, like Allis and Murray,[77] affirmed amillennialism;[78] he was also quite familiar with the history of the Northern Presbyterian controversies between amillennialists and premillennialists.[79] In a sense, J. Oliver Buswell was vindicated by Bear's arguments, in that Bear's argumentation brought to pass exactly what Buswell had feared and what he had warned his fellow OPC premillennialists about explicitly.[80] Bear pointed to the changes made to the *Confession* by the Bible Presbyterian Church as evidence that "dispensational premillennialism" (his term

---

[74] Ibid.

[75] Bear, "Dispensationalism and the Covenant of Grace."

[76] For some reason, Allis's writings are often quoted by Southern Presbyterian opponents of dispensationalism, but John Murray's articles never are. One plausible explanation for this is that the *Presbyterian Guardian* may not have had the readership among Southern Presbyterians that the *Evangelical Quarterly* did. Ironically, the Bible Presbyterian publication, the *Christian Beacon*, does seem to have gotten some attention from among PCUS members. But, Bear offers an explanation for this: "[S]ome [unknown persons] in the **Bible Presbyterian Church** have been . . . sending our ministers and others in positions of leadership free copies of their publication, the **Christian Beacon**" ("Shall We Revise the Standards?," 3 [bold text orginal]).

[77] As observed in the previous footnote, Bear cites Allis, not Murray, even though Bear's delineation of even the term "amillennialism" is nearly identical to Murray's. Bear wrote: "A new term has been coined for the view which was held by the church long before 'Postmillenarianism' came into existence. This term is 'Amillenarianism'. 'A-' is the Greek negative, and the term means 'no millennium', no thousand year kingdom on earth either before or after the coming of Christ. When Christ comes again there will be both good and evil at work in the world. When He comes He will make a final separation through Judgment, and then the final order of life will begin" ("The Second Coming of Christ," *PrSouth* 115 [29 May 1940]: 5). Cf. John Murray, "What is Amillennialism?" *PrGuard* 3 (27 March 1937): 242-44.

[78] Bear, "The Second Coming of Christ," 5.

[79] Bear outlined and evaluated this history in "Premillenarians and Our Church Standards," *PrSouth* 115 (24 July 1940): 4-6.

[80] See Buswell's contention in "The Second General Assembly of the [OPC]," *PrGuard* 3 (28 November 1936): 83.

for the views affirmed by the Bible Presbyterian Church) could accommodate itself to the *Confession* only by altering it.

> Thus the real contrast in views today is between that of the Premillenarian, who believes that Christ returns to establish an earthly, millennial kingdom (it being insisted today that this will be primarily the restored Jewish monarchy), and the view of the Amillenarian, who believes that Christ comes to establish His eternal, heavenly kingdom. This latter view, that of the Amillennialist, has always been the dominant view of the church as evidenced by its creeds. It is the view taught in our own **Confession of Faith** and **Catechisms**. If any one wishes proof of that they may find it in the radical revisions that the **Bible Presbyterian Church** (that Premillennial group which has been favoring the ministers of the Southern Presbyterian Church with its publication, **The Beacon**) has made in the **Westminster Confession of Faith** and **Catechisms** so that they might have a creedal basis for their premillennial beliefs. Amillennialism is the view taught by our Standards as we have received them.[81]

Bear, nevertheless, devoted one article (and sections of several others) to the thesis that "historic premillennialism," as opposed to "dispensational premillennialism," is confessionally acceptable, given the traditional latitude understood to be provided by the parameters of the PCUS doctrinal standards.[82] Bear lit upon dispensationalism's expectation of a revival of the Jewish nation as the pivotal point at which it became an unacceptable variety of premillennialism. This distinctive, he argued, leads inexorably to more significant divergences, such as the claim that Jesus' "kingdom" is overtly Jewish in character and entirely future in its fulfillment. These "dispensationalist" teachings, he claimed, fostered negligence toward our present Christian (kingdom) responsibilities here on earth.[83] Acceptable

---

[81] Bear, "The Second Coming of Christ," 5 (bold text original).

[82] James Bear, "Historic Premillennialism," *UnSemRev* 55 (May 1944): 193-222. One gets the impression that Bear considered non-dispensational premillennialism only *barely* tolerable. At one point in his critique of dispensationalism, Bear discloses, "Certainly all modern Premillennialists have eschatological beliefs which are not those held by the Reformed Churches" ("The Presbyterian Standards vs. The Scofield Bible, Part 1," 6). In another article, after acknowledging that there is a wide variety among premillennial views, some of them more, some less, consistent with the Church's doctrinal standards, Bear observes matter-of-factly, "The Premillenarians ... have many variations among themselves to what they think the Bible teaches, and they teach many things which are certainly not in accord with the **Westminster Confession**" ("Premillenarians and Our Church Standards," 5). Like J. Gresham Machen in the North (but unlike John Murray), it seems that Bear was willing to allow a doctrinal *variance* for premillennialists who were not troublesome about the issue; that this was Bear's position is especially clear in "Premillenarians and Our Church Standards," 4-6.

[83] Bear, "Dispensationalism and the Covenant of Grace," 285-307; *idem*, "The People of God," *UnSemRev* 52 (October 1940): 33-63; *idem*, "The People of God in the Light of the Teaching of the New Testament," *UnSemRev* 52 (January 1941): 128-58; *idem*, "The People of God According to the Fathers of the Early Church," *UnSemRev* 52 (July 1941): 351-74; and *idem*,

varieties of premillennialism, he insisted, rightly recognize (with the Church's doctrinal standards) that Christ's current Kingship logically entails certain sociopolitical earthly responsibilities for His current subjects.[84]

What about Chafer's suggestion that the framing of the issue by the AIC "is not well stated. As set before the Assembly, it questions the harmony between dispensational teaching and the Confession of Faith, . . . whereas, the issue should be whether there is harmony between dispensational teaching and the Sacred Text itself"[85]? Bear was prepared for such an objection.

> In discussing Dispensationalism and the Covenant of Grace, it will *not* be our purpose . . . to *prove* the Covenant of Grace from Scripture. Such evidence is set forth in the standard works of theology produced by the great Reformed Theologians. This doctrine is also incorporated in the Standards of our Church, [cites the *Confession of Faith*, Ch. VII; *The Larger Catechism*, Questions 30-36] and we have no reason to change our opinion that our *Confession of Faith* contains "the system of doctrine taught in the Holy Scriptures" [cites the *Form of Government*, par. 115, sec. (2)].[86]

It would seem, therefore, that Chafer gravely underestimated his opponents when he simply dismissed them as those who "know themselves to be unable to face on biblical grounds the constructive teaching advanced by the dispensationalist and therefore hide behind a creed" or in thinking that a man like Bear was given "to embrace a creed who has never given even a passing consideration to the Bible itself."[87] Bear received such remarks with particular umbrage, and replied that such reproaches made a "choice demanded."

> For a long time, [dispensationalism] spread, hardly recognized. Many pastors were unacquainted with Dispensational principles and had not tried to find out what was being taught out of the Scofield Bible. Dispensationalists called themselves Premillenarians, and if any one criticised or questioned their teaching, they would quickly reply that the questioner was either ignorant of the Bible or was not loyal to it. Not to hold the Dispensational scheme of the Second

---

"Historic Premillennialism," 193-222.

[84] Ibid. Also, Bear, "The Second Coming of Christ," 5. See also *idem*, "The Kingdom of God or World Revolution, Parts I and II," *PrOut* 127 (15 and 22 October 1945): pp. 5-6 in both issues.

[85] Chafer, "Dispensational Distinctions Challenged," 337-38.

[86] Bear, "Dispensationalism and the Covenant of Grace," 287. The 1943 AIC report shared the same viewpoint, stating: "[The main point at issue between Dispensationalism and the Church's doctrinal standards] is not primarily a matter of Biblical foundations for the two systems, since both claim to be based on the Bible alone. It is not a matter of a sound exegesis of Scripture, although ultimately the question of whether Dispensationalism is in harmony with the Standards of our Church will be answered by sound exegesis"; "Report of the [1943] AIC," 123.

[87] Chafer, "Dispensational Distinctions Challenged," 338-39.

Coming was proof either of ignorance of the Bible or a rejection of the Return of Christ.[88]

Citing Chafer's comments above as a manifestation of dispensationalists' "typical attitude," Bear declared, "A quotation like this from a Southern Presbyterian who is also a leading Dispensationalist shows us how pressing is the issue."[89]

Bear's suggested ideological and exegetical distinctions between "dispensational premillennialism" and "historic premillennialism" are important to a degree; the 1943 AIC largely followed Bear's arguments on these points.[90] However, that this line of argument was *dropped* from the 1944 report (even though Bear was now on the committee)[91] makes us wonder if Bear's suggested points of distinction had successfully raised the essential points of difference, after all.

We need not wonder about how significant was the impact of the Northern Presbyterian controversies on Bear's analysis, however. Bear's challenge to Southern Presbyterian "dispensationalists," just before the AIC took up its investigation of dispensationalism (1940), makes abundantly clear how profoundly the Northern Presbyterian history had influenced Bear's perspective.

> Such is some of the historical background of the rise of the **Bible Presbyterian Church**, and certain inferences seem to be valid. One of the dominant factors in their withdrawal was their insistence on the fundamental importance of their view of Christ's coming. They could have remained with the parent body and been Premillennialists. They wished to make the Premillennial position a fundamental doctrine, and they wished liberty to accept the Dispensational teaching (as much as they personally choose), and so they did the only honest thing. They withdrew and revised the **Confession of Faith** to suit their views. We may not agree with those views, but we do not question their right to form their own church and follow the dictates of their own conscience. We do assert, however, in their insistence on the **fundamental importance** of their view of what will happen when Christ comes again, and in the scheme of Biblical interpretation which they have woven around this doctrine, they are standing out of accord with the belief and teaching of the historic Presbyterian Church. If they are not sufficiently acquainted with the Reformed interpretation of the Bible to recognize that they are out of harmony with it, they should at least realize that "by their fruits ye shall know them". If this Dispensational Premillennialism was in harmony with the historic interpretation of the church there would not be these doctrinal

---

[88] James E. Bear, "Dispensationalism," *PrOut* 118 (3 May 1944): 5.

[89] Ibid., 6. Ominously, the end of this article contained an announcement in bold type that would demonstrate just how "pressing" the PCUS did indeed consider the issue: "**Next week: Report of the General Assembly's ad-interim Committee on Dispensationalism.**"

[90] "Report of the [1943] Ad Interim Committee," 125-28.

[91] We can suppose that this was likely due to the influence of the premillennialists on the committee, for whom Bear's logic presumably was problematic.

schisms and divisions which we find wherever this teaching is introduced.[92]

Bear then submitted what would in a very short time prove to be the "bottom line" for the whole GA, recognizing that dispensational premillennialists were now interspersed among their own ordained clergy.[93]

> Can a Premillennialist be a minister or officer in the Southern Presbyterian Church? Yes, unless his own views disqualify him. If he can show a Christian tolerance and active good will towards his brethren who do not believe the Bible teaches Premillennialism, and does not question either their sincerity or their scholarship in the Bible. If his view of God's dealing with men is in accord with that held through the ages and which is popularly known as the Covenant of Grace – that God has one plan of salvation for His people who are **one** people (the Old Testament prophecies being fulfilled in the Church), and that the destiny of His people is primarily spiritual – then he is an asset to our church, and we can agree to disagree as to what God will do on Christ's return and will together labor to build up the people of God, the church, for which Christ died.[94]

Bear's baiting Chafer to try "to revise our *Confession of Faith* in accordance with the teaching of this 'Dispensational truth'"[95] was no innocuous suggestion.[96] Bear

---

[92] Bear, "Premillenarians and Our Church Standards," 6.

[93] "Today, many in the Presbyterian Church feel a new embarrassment. Within the evangelical churches Dispensational Premillenarianism has been widely spread, and our own Southern Presbyterian Church is no exception" (Bear, "The Second Coming of Christ," 3).

[94] Bear, "Premillenarians and Our Church Standards," 6.

[95] Bear, "Dispensationalism and the Covenant of Grace," 307. Bear floated this suggestion before dispensationalists at least four other times, publicly and privately ("Shall We Revise the Standards?", 4; *idem*, "The Presbyterian Standards vs. The Scofield Bible, Part VI," 6; *idem*, "Dispensationalism: II. Dispensationalism vs. The Reformed Faith," 5-6; and letter, James E. Bear to Rollin T. Chafer, 4 October 1937, James E. Bear Papers, ADTS; cited in Hannah, "The Social and Intellectual History of the Evangelical Theological College," 361, n. 367).

[96] Leaders of at least one so-called "dispensationalist" institution apparently knew better than to challenge the Church's doctrinal standards if they wanted to remain in the good graces of the PCUS. Bear had suggested that "Dispensationally-colored Premillennialism is taught in The Moody Bible Institute, The Bible Institute of Los Angeles, The Dallas (Texas) Theological Seminary and the Columbia (South Carolina) Bible College" ("Dispensationalism and the Covenant of Grace, 285). "H. Waddell Pratt, theology professor at [Columbia Bible College] and Robert McQuilkin, its president, wrote Bear that they did not teach dispensationalism and explained to their students the errors of dispensationalists. Heading a school that attracted a large number of students from Presbyterian churches and running a campground that Presbyterian ministers and laypeople patronized, McQuilkin was concerned that this support not be compromised by misleading information and asked Bear to publish a retraction" (Glass, "Northern Patterns of Fundamentalism in the South," 236, n. 29). Columbia Bible College was well-known for its premillennialist eschatology and for its Keswick view of sanctification, making it understandable why Bear would have identified it as a "dispensational" institution.

well knew what would be the likely result of such a confrontation; he certainly knew what his own response would be.

Nevertheless, in 1943, just as Bear arrived on the committee, Chafer took the bait, challenging "any theological Rip Van Winkle to awaken to the recognition of that which has developed doctrinally since a company of good men drew up the Confession of Faith."[97] Moreover, he asked,

> Have we reached the hour when maturity of understanding of the Sacred Text is to be penalized only because it finds and presents many vital truths which were not gained by worthy men of three centuries ago? Would it not be a wiser course, in view of the present accepted liberty to revise the standards of the Church, so to reconstruct its text that a latitude may be accorded to the large number of men who can accept only a dispensational theology and thus allow them to remain in the fellowship of their brethren?[98]

And so, the die was cast. In view of Chafer's direct challenge, it became possible for Bear[99] and the committee[100] to delineate Chafer's views convincingly as being opposed to the teaching of the PCUS doctrinal standards. (Whether this delineation of *Chafer's* views resulted in a more accurate understanding of *dispensationalism per se* vis-à-vis the *Confession*, or vis-à-vis covenant theology, remains an open question, however.)

Though Bear joined the Committee only in 1943, it was largely his work that provided the lines of argument used by the AIC throughout its investigation. McLaurin's draft may have served as the basis for the 1943 AIC report, but Bear's work was the reference point for both. Thus, we could accurately say that Bear, albeit proleptically before his official appointment, was the AIC's most influential member.[101]

L. Nelson Bell was one of two premillennialists added to the AIC in 1943. Had he contributed nothing but his signature to the AIC report, his name alone would have advanced the report's credibility among Southern Presbyterian conservatives

---

That McQuilkin would have objected to this characterization raises again the intriguing question as to what makes *dispensational* premillennialism distinctive. Bear did publish the requested retraction in a later edition of the *Union Seminary Review* (50 [January 1939]: 112). To my knowledge, only the president of Columbia Bible College objected to Bear's identifying his institution as "dispensational." Likewise, only the president of Dallas Theological Seminary took up Bear's challenge to try to have the Church's doctrinal Confession changed in a dispensationalist direction.

[97] Chafer, "Dispensational Distinctions Challenged," 341.
[98] Ibid., 345.
[99] See Bear, "Dispensationalism: Parts I and II."
[100] See below, "The Unanimous Findings of the Committee's Final Report and Its Adoption by the General Assembly."
[101] This fact may account for Bear's sometimes being mistakenly identified as the AIC's *chairman*: Daniel P. Fuller, *Gospel and Law: Contrast or Continuum?* (Grand Rapids: Eerdmans, 1980), 30; John Gerstner, *Wrongly Dividing the Word of Truth* (Brentwood, TN: Wolgemuth & Hyatt, 1991), 63.

more than anything *in* the report itself. Even before his son-in-law, Billy Graham, became famous (Graham married Bell's daughter, Ruth, on 13 August 1943),[102] the very face of staunch Southern Presbyterian conservatism was Lemuel Nelson Bell.

Bell established his conservative credentials early and maintained them most consistently. Born, raised, and educated in Virginia,[103] a student of medicine, not theology, he never came under the sway of the "liberalism" rumored to be in control of his home state's PCUS theological institution. Bell had left a prestigious medical practice in the United States[104] to become "Chief Surgeon of Tsingkiangup General Hospital, [the] largest (380 beds) China hospital under the PCUS Board of World Missions of that time."[105] There he served as a medical missionary for twenty-five years (1916-1941), until Japan's invasion of China and the general political turmoil of the time forced Bell to return to the United States.[106]

Bell came back to the United States sounding the conservative alarm.[107] He was at the forefront of every conservative cause in the PCUS. In 1942, one year after his return from China, Bell, with Henry B. Dendy, founded the *Southern Presbyterian Journal*, the journalistic voice of Southern Presbyterian conservatism throughout the late twentieth century.[108]

---

[102] For Graham's own personal account of his relationship with both Ruth and L. Nelson Bell, see Billy Graham, *Just As I Am: The Autobiography of Billy Graham* (Grand Rapids: Zondervan, 1997), 71-710, *passim*. Those fond of the ministry of Billy Graham cannot help but be touched at seeing in the order of service at Bell's funeral, held at Montreat Presbyterian Church, that George Beverly Shea sang, Cliff Barrows led the music, and Billy Graham delivered a message written originally by Bell himself (L. Nelson Bell Biographical File, Presbyterian Historical Society, Montreat, NC).

[103] Originally from Waynesboro, VA, Bell took his pre-medical studies at Washington and Lee University in Lexington, VA, and obtained his M.D. from the Medical College of Virginia in Richmond (L. Nelson Bell Biographical File, L. Nelson Bell Papers, Presbyterian Historical Society, Montreat, NC).

[104] He even received a grant from the Rockefeller Foundation to pursue post-graduate work in surgery (ibid.).

[105] Ibid.

[106] Harold Lindsell, "L. Nelson Bell: In Memoriam," *CT* 17 (31 August 1973): 5.

[107] For a biographical account of how Bell's experience in China helped strengthen his conservative resolve, see John Charles Pollock, *A Foreign Devil in China: The Story of Dr. L. Nelson Bell, an American Surgeon in China* (Minneapolis, MN: World Wide Publications, 1971).

[108] L. Nelson Bell, "Editorial: WHY? Why THE JOURNAL at this time?," *SPresJ* 1 (May 1942): 2. Bell also helped establish *Christianity Today* in 1956, a similar conservative journalist voice for a broader evangelical constituency. The idea for such a journal came from Billy Graham, who says, "The first man I shared my vision with was my father-in-law, Dr. Bell. His wisdom served as a compass. It amazed me to learn that a similar idea for a magazine had often occurred to him. He became a key person in developing *Christianity Today*" (*Just As I Am*, 287). Cf. the issue of *Christianity Today* that eulogized Bell just after his death; the cover contains his picture and is entitled, "L. Nelson Bell: 1894-1973," *CT* 17 (31 August 1973). This issue also announced that *Christianity Today* and the Billy Graham Evangelistic Association were together establishing the L. Nelson Bell Visiting Lectureship program for Christian seminaries.

The type of conservatism advocated by a Southern Presbyterian like Bell entailed a trouble spot for Chaferian dispensationalism, however. For PCUS conservatives, fidelity to the *Confession* was sacrosanct.[109] Enforcement of confessional subscription was the conservatives' *judicial* means of protecting their Church from seditious ideological forces. Thus, where one finds a conservative argument calling for the expulsion of unacceptable views from the church, there one also invariably finds a call for enforcement of the confessional subscription professed in clerical ordination vows.[110]

L. Nelson Bell's opposition to the Auburn *Affirmation* provides a clear example of this strategy.[111] Bell was able to defend the "five fundamentals" from the *Confession of Faith*, and then contrast these "fundamentals" with specific statements from the Auburn *Affirmation*. Consequently, Bell called for the application of proper judicial enforcement, as outlined by Robinson in one of the first editions of the *Southern Presbyterian Journal*.[112] In the PCUS, Bell and Robinson insisted, false teaching is properly detected – and expelled – by demonstrating that teaching's dissonance with the Church's doctrinal standards. This was a foundational point for Southern Presbyterian conservatives in their battle against theological liberalism.

Thus, it is hard to imagine anything that could have alienated conservatives more than Chafer's disparagement of confessional subscription as the refuge of someone seeking to hide his biblical ignorance. Indeed, Chafer seems to be in

---

[109] See L. Nelson Bell, "What Is Progress?," *SPresJ* 1 (April 1943): 21; *idem*, "Blowing Out Sparks at a Three-Alarm Fire," *SPresJ* 3 (October 1944): 2; *idem*, "A Layman Looks at Liberalism," *SPresJ* 4 (15 September 1945): 3; *idem*, "Unthinkable," *SPresJ* 7 (1 March 1949): 2-3; *idem*, "A Warning," *SPresJ* 9 (15 May 1950): 4; and *idem*, "The Auburn Affirmation Is Actually Not an Affirmation of Faith But a . . . Dissent From Evangelical Truth," *SPresJ* 10 (10 October 1951): 3-4.

[110] This is the exact argument of Hugh Martin ("My Ordination Vow Binds My Church," *SPresJ* 3 [August 1944]: 11). Martin describes the ordination vow as "a compact between me and my Church." He then pointedly asks, "Do I, then, come under obligation to the Church without the Church coming under obligation to me? Who would make an assertion so outrageous?" Martin's concluding sentence makes his case: "Our Ordination Vow taking us bound to our Confession settles that we have a Constitution, clearly enough defines it, renders us answerable to it and pledges the Church reciprocally as amenable to it also." Conservatives regularly employed this line of reasoning in their objections to liberal influences, e.g., as that present in the Federal Council of Churches, because of the tenets upheld by such organizations being "contrary . . . to the system of doctrine in our standards and . . . contrary to the Holy Scriptures" (I am quoting here, as virtually a random example of dozens that could likewise be quoted, from the overture sent to the 1942 GA by the Presbytery of West Hanover, requesting that the GA withdraw PCUS membership in the Federal Council of Churches; this example happens to be cited also by Henry B. Dendy, "Forces Disrupting the Churches," 2). This exact line of argument was employed also by conservatives in the *Northern* Presbyterian Church (Robert E. Brown, "Ordination Vows: What Do They Mean in the Presbyterian Church in the U.S.A.?" *PrGuard* 12 [25 July 1943]: 213-14).

[111] Bell, "The Auburn Affirmation," 3.

[112] William Childs Robinson, "The Authority of the Lord Jesus Christ as Exercised in the PCUS," *SPresJ* 1 (November 1942): 11-14.

agreement with the "liberals" when he dismisses the *Confession* as merely a "man-made creed" that may be adjusted without undue concern. The "liberty to revise the standards," which Chafer heralded,[113] was a liberty taken exclusively by the *liberals* in the Church. This helps explain how Chafer found his views unanimously opposed by a committee that contained even such a staunch PCUS conservative premillennialist as L. Nelson Bell.

One might otherwise have thought Bell and Chafer to be natural allies. They shared a similar eschatological view. They both were in significant positions of Christian leadership, which they had each achieved without formal theological training. They both regarded this fact with ironic pride, touting their lack of educational credentials as indication of their having taken a path that escaped the influence of liberalism and other falsehoods prevalent in the academy, and that afforded them a superior "outside-the-Beltway" perspective.[114] They also were alike in their sharing the pattern, noted earlier as common among evangelicals, of feeling such an affinity with conservatives outside their denomination as to join and start non-denominational organizations and ventures.

In the early 1940s, this affinity to non-denominational associations was more obviously true of Chafer than Bell, yet Bell, too, was sometimes criticized for being overly involved in "independent" activities.[115] Even in 1944 (i.e., before he helped found *Christianity Today* and the Billy Graham Evangelistic Association[116]), it seems Bell was sympathetic to "independent" conservative causes and organizations, perhaps even to independent schools.[117] This sympathy may have motivated Bell to insist that all statements from the 1943 report that condemned dispensationalism for its alleged "divisive practical effects" and "undermining of

---

[113] Chafer, "Dispensational Distinctions Challenged," 345.

[114] Chafer was more overt than Bell in making this claim; he claimed straightforwardly, "The very fact that I did not study a prescribed course in theology made it possible for me to approach the subject with an unprejudiced mind and to be concerned only with what the Bible actually teaches" (*Systematic Theology*, [Dallas, TX: Dallas Seminary Press, 1947], 8:5-6). Bell never went on record with a claim quite so audacious. Yet, he, too, cautioned his readers about the dangerous influence of the Academy in his book, *While Men Slept* (Garden City, NY: Doubleday, 1970). "Satan's greatest victory began when he implanted in the minds of Adam and Eve doubt as to the truthfulness of God's Word, and he continues his work today in the classroom of Dr. I. Doubtit, through the writings of Professor W. E. Knowbetter, and from the pulpit of Dr. Will Knott Believe." He also was fond of pointing out that he was a *layman*. He titled his response to MacLean's articles, "A Layman Looks at Liberalism." He published a tract entitled "A Layman Looks at the Resurrection." And, many of his articles make note of his lay status. He also regarded his lay status as an advantage in his successful run for moderatorship of the 1972 General Assembly, The pamphlet promoting his candidacy was entitled, "a layman and his faith," and his supporters wore lapel pins urging representatives to "RING THE BELL FOR A LAYMAN" (L. Nelson Bell Biographical File, Presbyterian Historical Society, Montreat, NC).

[115] The strongest criticisms of Bell in this regard would come long after the events involving the 1944 AIC. See Worth McDougald, in "Moderator Candidates Interviewed," *Presbyterian Survey* 62 (June 1972): 3, 15.

[116] See Graham, *Just As I Am*, 303, 673.

[117] Cf. John R. Richardson, "Straining Out a Gnat and Swallowing a Coffin," *SPresJ* 4 (1 April 1946): 2.

Presbyterian loyalty"[118] be eliminated. Such statements are absent from the 1944 report.[119] Are these Bell's fingerprints on the refurbished report?

The 1944 report also specified more narrowly why *dispensational* premillennialism was outside the parameters of the *Confession*, while other forms of premillennialism could be accepted as safely within those bounds. While the 1944 report narrowed the focus of the section on the "root of the difference," it also expanded the explanation of those differences, yielding four separate sections that specified and explained four distinct dispensational "divergences" from the *Confession*.

> A. The Rejection of the Unity of God's people;
> B. The Rejection of One Way of Salvation;
> C. The Rejection of One Destiny for All of God's People;
> D. The Rejection of the Bible as God's one Revelation to His One People.[120]

Conspicuously *absent* from the 1944 Report, however, is the 1943 report's sections on "The Kingdom," and "The Kingly Work of Christ."[121]

Though even the 1943 report had declared "It is not at all a controversy in regard to the millennium, since our denomination has always had, and still has, room for millennialists, a-millennialists, post-millennialists, and pre-millennialists in its ranks,"[122] the *kind* of premillennialism this report actually permitted was greatly restricted. Nor was this restrictiveness helped by the historical digression it included.

> The early Millenarians, (and others like them down through the ages), believed that the present kingdom of Christ would have a glorious *earthly* stage after His Advent, but they insisted that this earthly stage of the kingdom was to be enjoyed by the *Church*, and expressly reject the idea that the Jewish nation as such was to receive the blessings promised to God's people in the Old Testament. [cites Bear's 1941 article, "The People of God According to the Early Church Fathers."][123]

The 1944 report deleted all such implications that only a highly qualified, supersessionist version of premillennialism could be tolerated.[124] The language in the above paragraph, specifically, was softened considerably. In place of its sweeping condemnation of any eschatological expectation for the Jewish nation to be revived as God's people, the following sentence was inserted: "Whatever may be

---

[118] Cf. "Report of the [1943] AIC," 122.
[119] See "Report of the [1944] AIC."
[120] "Report of the [1944] AIC," 124-25.
[121] Cf. "Report of the [1943] AIC," 125.
[122] Ibid., 123.
[123] Ibid., 125-26.
[124] Regarding the definition, history and ideology of supersessonism (sometimes called "replacement theology" – the idea is that the predominately Gentile New Testament church replaces, supplants or supercedes ethnic Israel as the people of God), see R. Kendall Soulen, *The God of Israel and Christian Theology* (Minneapolis, MN: Fortress Press, 1996).

the national destiny of the Jewish people, according to the Confession of Faith their becoming a spiritual blessing to the world and to the Church will be contingent upon their acceptance of Jesus as the Messiah and thereby becoming a part of the Church."[125]

Furthermore, the 1944 report asserted even more strongly that it was *not* condemning premillennialism per se.

> It is the unanimous opinion of your Committee that Dispensationalism as defined and set forth above is out of accord with the system of the doctrine set forth in the Confession of Faith, not primarily or simply in the field of eschatology, but because it attacks the very heart of the Theology of our Church, which is unquestionably a Theology of one Covenant of Grace. . . .
>
> Your Committee wishes also to make the following statement of clarification: Most, if not all, adherents to the type of Dispensationalism dealt with in this report hold the Premillennial view of our Lord's return; but not all Premillennialists accept this form of Dispensationalism. Therefore, the Committee wishes to make it clear that it has endeavored solely to consider the particular type of Biblical interpretation defined above, and known as Dispensationalism and that it understood the assignment of the Assembly to limit it to this task. In view or this fact, this report should not be considered as in any sense a criticism of Premillennialism as such.[126]

There are no minutes of the AIC's discussions; thus, it is impossible to establish Bell's role in the changes between the 1943 and 1944 versions of the report. Nonetheless, we cannot help but notice two points: 1) each of these changes represents a *departure* from the line of argument used by James Bear in the journal articles from which the 1943 report had quoted extensively (even though Bear was himself now on the committee); and 2) each of the changes directly mitigates the concern Bell had expressed before he joined the committee; viz, that the 1943 report had criticized premillennialism in general, rather than a particular, unacceptable version of premillennialism. We are drawn to an obvious explanation: Bell influenced the committee so that it modified its report.

If so, then Bell's influence was significant indeed. The changes incorporated into the 1944 report effectively nullified those objections that Chafer had forwarded against the 1943 report having greatest potential to draw premillennialists generally – even conservatives generally – to Chafer's side (including such claims as the committee was composed of "liberals" looking for a pretext to drive conservative Bible believers out of the church,[127] or that it was composed of people ignorant of the Scriptures or otherwise infatuated with man-made creeds,[128] or that the

---

[125] "Report of the [1944] AIC," 124.
[126] Ibid., 126-27.
[127] Chafer, "Dispensational Distinctions Challenged," 339-40.
[128] Ibid., 337-39.

arguments of the 1943 AIC report had liberal and/or amillennialist underpinnings[129]). The wording of the 1944 report undermined such appeals to non-dispensational conservatives and PCUS premillennialists, and effectively isolated Chafer's particular dispensational views, subjecting them to full denunciation by the PCUS.

The signatures of Bell and James Park McCallie (known by his friends as "Dr. J.P."[130]) added to the impression that dispensationalism was rejected by conservative Southern Presbyterians. Though perhaps not as well-known as Bell, McCallie was no less stalwart a Southern Presbyterian conservative. Also a layman, McCallie had obtained a Ph.D. in astronomy at the University of Virginia. With this extensive scientific training, he remained convinced that evolutionary theories of the origin of the universe were untenable. Despite the infamous Scopes trial, which was held less than 100 miles from his own home, McCallie was a vigorous defender of biblical creationism to the end of his life.[131]

McCallie's strictness and personal discipline were manifest in the school he founded with his brother, Spencer Jarnigan McCallie. The McCallie School for Boys, which J.P. McCallie ran for nearly half a century, was a full military preparatory school.[132] It was one of the most prestigious boys' schools in the South; some of the wealthiest sons of the South went there.[133]

A champion of conservative causes,[134] McCallie also lobbied heavily against PCUS membership in the Federal Council of Churches, urging denominational leaders to enroll the PCUS in the National Association of Evangelicals instead.[135] His involvement in the anti-FCC movement would bring him into an intriguing controversy in 1947 with PCUS "liberals". At an "anti-Federal Council meeting held in Greenville, S.C.," McCallie, Bell, and several other conservatives alleged that scandalous ideas were being propagated by Federal Council leaders.[136] The

---

[129] Ibid., 340-44. In Chafer's mind, liberalism and amillennialism were closely linked, a misimpression we will address in the last chapter.

[130] I thank J. Lanier Burns, chairman of the department of Systematic Theology at Dallas Theological Seminary and a 1961 graduate of the McCallie school, for this and other significant details included in this section (J. Lanier Burns, interview by the author, Dallas, TX, 19 June 1996). A brief biographical sketch is also included in an article announcing McCallie's receiving the Russell Colgate distinguished service citation from the International Council of Religious Education ("J.P. McCallie to Get Colgate Citation for Outstanding Service," *PrOut* 131 [24 January 1949]: 1).

[131] See J.P. McCallie, "Earth's Golden Age," *SPresJ* 1 (December 1942): 22.

[132] It ended its military program during the Vietnam War (sometime in the late 1960s-early 1970s).

[133] J. Lanier Burns, interview with the author, Dallas, TX, 19 June 1996.

[134] Besides his firm stand against evolution, he published several articles opposing ecumenism, because he felt that it compromised the doctrinal integrity of PCUS foreign missions (J.P. McCallie, "I Went to Cleveland," *SPresJ* 1 (February 1943): 10-11; and *idem*, "Our Church and World Missions," *SPresJ* 2 (February 1944): 16-17).

[135] J.P. McCallie, "Why I Want to Co-operate With the National Association of Evangelicals Rather than with the Federal Council," *SPresJ* 5 (15 December 1947): 7-8.

[136] "Editorial: So This Is Called 'Informing the Laymen'!" *PrOut* 129 (25 August 1947): 8.

editor of the *Presbyterian Outlook* was outraged particularly at McCallie's presentation and singled him out for extensive critique. One particular point of this critique is especially interesting, in light of McCallie's participation in the AIC ruling on dispensationalism.

> When we come closer to Dr. McCallie's reasons for the "false" teachings of the Council, we are able to understand much about his personal opposition that does not appear on the surface. These policies of the Council, he says, are the result of a faulty view of the Second Coming of Christ! (Now we are getting somewhere!) Then, he declares: "It is the Council's intention to bring in the Kingdom of God on earth!" Magnificent! Evidently Dr. McCallie failed to remind his hearers of a prayer common to the Christian world which every man in his audience has prayed thousands of times. He neglected to repeat, or to lead them in praying: "Thy Kingdom come. Thy will be done on earth as it is in heaven!" He surely did not read them the Larger Catechism's explanation of those petitions (Q. 191-192). The trouble with the Council, at the lips of Dr. McCallie, is that it is too greatly concerned with seeking the triumph of Christ's Kingdom on earth. Wonderful failing!
>
> But something Dr. McCallie did not inform these interested laymen about has to do with what he calls a "faulty view" of the doctrine of the Second Coming of Christ which he says the Council holds. Dr. McCallie evidently neglected to inform the laymen that his own view of this matter is not contained in a single creed of the Christian church. It is not in the Confession of Faith; it is not in our catechisms. In fact, his view of this particular point is understood to be basically like that of the Dispensationalists, and our General Assembly has spoken in no uncertain terms on Dispensationalism.[137]

Thus, McCallie and Bell[138] had thrown in their faces the decision of the very committee on which they themselves had served and whose decision they themselves had signed. The irony is inescapable. Yet, the *Outlook* editor had a point in noticing a similarity between McCallie's view and dispensationalism.

McCallie affirmed both premillennialism and pretribulational rapturism,[139] eschatological views which could easily have made him a firm ally of Chafer's dispensationalism. So, why did he not feel such affinity? The reason is instructive and alerts us to a pattern among premillennialist (Southern) Presbyterians as the controversy heightened and, perhaps more relevantly, as Chafer's remarks became more strident.

---

[137] Ibid.

[138] "Dr. Bell's 'information' should also be seen in the light of Dr. McCallie's position, for these two laymen hold similar views in theology. As they point out, this has much to do with the positions a man takes" (ibid.). This is one of the few cases in which Bell apparently took a lower profile than McCallie; he at least got off easier in this editorial.

[139] He outlines both these eschatological positions in "Earth's Golden Age," 23.

McCallie was appointed to the AIC in 1943; a layman, "apparently feeling out of his league in the theological discussions in the committee's meetings, [he] turned to an interdenominational fundamentalist for advice."[140] That "interdenominational fundamentalist" was fellow Southern Presbyterian, Robert C. McQuilkin, president of Columbia Bible College in Columbia, SC. Glass's overview is helpful.

> McQuilkin's participation needs explanation. First he believed that dispensationalism represented a distortion of the Bible. He had played a similar role in 1937-38 in educating Charles G. Trumbull, editor of the Sunday School Times,[141] about dispensationalism while Chafer debated professors of Westminster Seminary. See R[obert] C. M[cQuilkin] to Charles G. Trumbull, 20 February 1937, 6 May 1938, and 3 August 1938, in Dispensationalism File, in RCM Papers. Furthermore, he believed that through influencing McCallie he could protect the relationships with southern Presbyterian churches he had carefully cultivated to support his college and

---

[140] Glass, "Northern Patterns of Fundamentalism in the South," 238.

[141] Some might even have considered the *Sunday School Times* a dispensationalist paper given how many and how often dispensationalist writers contributed to it. Trumbull's well-known friendship with C.I. Scofield may also have contributed to this impression (see Charles Trumbull, *The Life Story of C.I. Scofield* [New York: Oxford University Press, 1920]; cf. George M. Marsden, *Fundamentalism and American Culture: The Shaping of Twentieth-Century Evangelicalism, 1870-1925* [New York: Oxford University Press, 1980], 96-99). A Keswick view of sanctification was a conspicuous point of emphasis in both Trumbull's paper and at McQuilkin's Columbia Bible College; it was this Keswick view of sanctification that provoked some of the first Reformed criticisms of Chafer's and Scofield's ideas (see Benjamin B. Warfield, "Systematical Theology: Review of *He That Is Spiritual* by Lewis Sperry Chafer," *PThRev* 17 [April 1919]: 322-27; cf. W.H. Griffith Thomas, "The Victorious Life, Parts I and II," *BibSac* 76 [September-December 1919]: 267-88, 455-67). This Northern Presbyterian criticism had a similar Southern counterpart, too (see J.R. Bridges and R.C. Reed, "'The Victorious Life,'" *PrStand* 61 [11 February 1920]: 1; and R.A. Lapsley, "Side Tracked," *PrStand* 61 [10 March 1920]: 6; cf. Lewis Sperry Chafer, "Are Victorious Life Teachers 'Side Tracked?'" *PrStand* 61 [7 April 1920]: 4, 8). Thus, again, a distinctive view (in this case, a distinctive view of sanctification) may have become associated with "dispensationalism," adding to the confusion. Trumbull was best known for being "active in a host of fundamentalist and undenominational agencies . . . . He was vice president of the World's Christian Fundamentals Association and the American Tract Society, . . . was treasurer of the Belgian Gospel Mission, a director of the Pioneer Mission Agency, Keswick Colony of Mercy and Victorious Life Testimony" ("Charles Gallaudet Trumbull," *PrGuard* 9 [10 February 1941]: 34). Lesser known was that "he was an elder of the Presbyterian Church in the U.S.A." (ibid). One of the first meetings of the Covenant Union, a conservative planning and lobbying group in the PCUSA spearheaded by J. Gresham Machen and Charles Woodbridge before the splits, actually met at Trumbull's home ("Covenant Union Meeting At Home of Dr. Trumbull," *PrGuard* 2 [20 April 1936]: 38). That even such a close friend and early supporter of the dispensational movement as Trumbull was being influenced away from the kind of "dispensationalism" put under investigation by the PCUS is intriguing. This point gives us pause as to what *kind* of dispensationalism was being investigated and confronts us with the question, once again, of whether there were other "kinds" of dispensationalism in existence at the time that might have escaped the critiques of Presbyterian conservatives.

campground. He explained that Presbyterian leaders had criticized his endeavors as "contrary to the denominational scheme of things" and for "drawing support away from the church work. . . . Now it confuses matters greatly to link these things with the discussion of dispensationalism and the Confession of Faith."[142]

Thus the influence on McCallie (and Trumbull) away from "dispensationalism" came from one who was himself sometimes "mistaken for" a "dispensationalist"![143] What seems to have happened is that, as Chafer's views came under increasing scrutiny in the Presbyterian churches, many "dispensational" premillennialists became less and less willing to be associated with Chafer's distinctive views. This, of course, was devastating for Chafer's views in the AIC investigation. It meant that even a staunch conservative, premillennialist, pretribulational rapturist supporter of conservative independent institutions like J.P. McCallie would distance himself from Chafer's peculiar anti-confessional stances.

McCallie was on the AIC for only one year; he may have felt "out of his league" in trying to discern the theological issues involved in his assignment. He even expressed misgivings (similar to Sibley's) about the procedure, remarking to McQuilkin, "My only feeling of incompetence in this matter is that we are trying Dr. Chafer without a hearing on his part."[144] Nonetheless, his signature on the

---

[142] Glass, "Northern Patterns of Fundamentalism in the South," 238-39, n. 35.

[143] James Bear's 1938 article in the *Union Seminary Review* had made the following observation: "Dispensationally-colored Premillennialism is taught in The Moody Bible Institute, The Bible Institute of Los Angeles, The Dallas (Texas) Theological Seminary and the Columbia (South Carolina) Bible College" ("Dispensationalism and the Covenant of Grace," 285). Six months later, the following "Statement" appeared:

> "In my article on 'Dispensationalism and the Covenant of Grace,' in the July, 1938, UNION SEMINARY REVIEW, I included Columbia Bible College among the institutions that taught 'dispensationally-colored premillennialism.' Dr. Robert C. McQuilkin, president of Columbia Bible College, writes me that although they teach pre-millennialism they oppose the form of dispensational teaching discussed in the REVIEW article which leads to the logical conclusion that some men in some dispensations have been saved by works.
>
> Dr. McQuilkin writes that the teachings of the Bible College 'are not colored at any point by the dispensational doctrines you discuss. As you yourself suggest, all Christians believe in dispensations in one way or another. The crux of the matter comes in not recognizing that God's plan of salvation by grace through faith runs through all the dispensations and that the requirements of God's moral law are unchanged in all dispensations. We greatly deplore the dispensational teaching that leads to such conclusions as that the Lord's prayer is not to be used by Christians, or that the Sermon on the Mount is not primarily for Christians, or that the great commission is Jewish and not for this present age, or that God's law is not a rule of life for Christians.'"
>
> JAMES E. BEAR

("A Statement," *UnSemRev* 50 [January 1939]: 112).

[144] Letter, J.P. McCallie to Robert C. McQuilkin, 5 November 1943; cited by Glass, "Northern Patterns of Fundamentalism in the South," 244, n. 48.

decision added one more high-profile conservative vote against the orthodoxy of dispensationalism.

In 1944, the AIC submitted its findings to the GA as to "whether the type of Bible interpretation known as Dispensationalism is in harmony with our Confession of Faith." Their answer was unanimous: "It is not."

5.3 The Unanimous Findings of the Committee's Final Report and Its Adoption by the General Assembly

It took less than a year[145] for the enlarged AIC to come to its unanimous conclusion. The 1944 report, which was only three pages long, and which journal accounts summarized in a single page,[146] narrowed the focus of the investigation from that of the 1943 report. Shorter and narrower, it was no less powerful in its import.[147]

The 1943 report had tried to limit its consideration to "only important doctrines,"[148] but the 1944 report limited its focus even further to only two broad areas of doctrinal disagreement.[149] The latter of these points, "Dispensational Divergences from the Confessional Interpretation of the Work of the Exalted Christ," was presented in little more than half a page.[150] This means that the bulk of the 1944 report was devoted to establishing the first plank of confessional departure, "The Fundamental Divergence of Dispensationalism from the Covenant Theology of the Presbyterian Church."[151]

---

[145] I say "less than a year," because the editor of the *Presbyterian of the South* had gotten word already in the first week of March, 1944 (i.e., only eight months after the previous General Assembly) that "the assembly's **ad interim** committee . . . is bringing in a unanimous report" ("In Passing, A Column of News and Opinion: Unanimous Report," *PrSouth* 118 [8 March 1944]: 16).

[146] Henry B. Dendy, "Report of Meeting of the General Assembly: The Question As to Whether the Type of Bible Interpretation Known as Dispensationalism Is in Harmony With the Confession of Faith," *SPresJ* 3 (July 1944): 6; and "Reports to the General Assembly: Report on Dispensationalism," *PrOut* 118 (10 May 1944): 5.

[147] "Unanimous Report," 16. Promised the editor: "**The Presbyterian of the South**, during coming weeks will present a vital discussion of this issue, interpreting its meaning, and its error and suggesting a course to follow." This promise was fulfilled by AIC member, James Bear, in a two-part series of articles ("Dispensationalism, Parts I and II").

[148] "Report of the [1943] AIC," 123.

[149] Under each of these two broad headings were listed and explained two more specific "dispensational divergences" (which, altogether, composed the list of four mentioned above). See also Appendix 5, below, "Report of the 1944 PCUS Ad Interim Committee on Changes in the Confession of Faith and Catechisms as to Whether the Type of Bible Interpretation Known as 'Dispensationalism' Is in Harmony with the Confession of Faith."

[150] "Report of the [1944] AIC," 126.

[151] Ibid., 124-25. Though the 1944 report listed the same two broad points of dispensational divergence from the *Confession* as the 1943 Report, the point receiving the greatest *emphasis* of these two was exactly reversed. The 1943 Report, following McLaurin's and Bear's outlining of issues, had devoted three full pages to demonstrating dispensationalism's divergence from the *Confession* in regard to the nature and corresponding Christian

The 1944 report was also more direct in how it established what sources and what methods it would use to ascertain the dispensational position. The section of the 1943 report titled, "The Data for Answering the Question" was eliminated, as was the section that explained the criteria used for establishing what doctrines were "important" enough to be investigated. Also deleted were the copious footnotes citing various dispensational writers.

All this was unnecessary given the method of the 1944 report. After a brief section defining the terms "dispensation" and "dispensationalism," (using quotations from Scofield and Chafer), the 1944 report stated straightforwardly, "Such dispensational teaching is expounded by many in our day, but we shall limit our quotations to the writings of two outstanding exponents of Dispensationalism: Dr. C.I. Scofield (especially as found in certain notes in the *Scofield Reference Bible*) and Dr. L.S. Chafer, who has written extensively on this subject."[152]

And so, the 1944 report delineated divergences of "dispensationalism" from the covenant theology of the *Westminster Confession* and *Catechisms* by occasionally alluding to the *Scofield Reference Bible*, but most often by using quotations from Chafer's articles.[153] Likewise, the conclusion of the 1944 Report used Chafer's own words against him:

> As Dr. Chafer clearly recognizes, there are two schools of interpretation represented here, which he rightly designates as "Covenantism" as over against "Dispensationalism." (*Bibliotheca Sacra*, Vol. 100, No. 399, [i.e., "Dispensational Distinctions Challenged," 1943], p. 338.) In fact, the divergence of Dispensationalism from the Covenant Theology of our Church is so obvious to Dr. Chafer that he suggests a revision of the Standards of the Church so as to make room for those who no longer hold to the Reformed tradition of a Covenant Theology. (*Ibid*, p. 345).[154]

---

responsibilities of "the Kingdom" and "the Kingly work of Christ," while it had devoted less than a page to dispensationalism's divergence from the *Confession*'s "one covenant of grace." One implication: the 1943 report could more easily have been mistaken for an amillennial attack on premillennialism. The 1944 report reversed this emphasis doubtless, in part, to correct this impression.

[152] "Report of the [1944] AIC," 124. As might be expected, Chafer complained even more strenuously at this decision, protesting "this report centers almost wholly upon the Editor of BIBLIOTHECA SACRA [i.e., himself] as the supposed chief exponent of dispensational teaching" (Lewis Sperry Chafer, "Dispensational Distinctions Denounced," *BibSac* 101 [April-June 1944]: 257).

[153] Once the decision was made to limit the focus to Scofield and Chafer, it was inevitable that Chafer would be quoted most often, not least because the Scofield estate had denied permission to quote from notes of the *Scofield Reference Bible* (James Bear, "The Scofield Bible Can't Be Quoted!" *PrSouth* 115 [21 August 1940]: 4-5).

[154] "Report of the [1944] AIC," 126. Apparently the committee concluded that, since he had publicly conceded this point already, allowing Chafer to appear personally before either the AIC or the GA to defend his views would be unnecessary, unhelpful, and unwise. To Chafer's great consternation, all his requests to defend his views in person and to appeal the findings of the AIC were denied (letter, Lewis Sperry Chafer to E.C. Scott, D. D., Stated Clerk, 11 June

The points of the 1943 report that had stalled its previous acceptance had been eliminated in the 1944 version, so this version was adopted rather easily by the GA. The outgoing moderator, "Dr. [Donald W.] Richardson moved that the report be approved and adopted."[155]

Only one point needed yet to be clarified: what action, if any, would be demanded by the AIC report. The report, as it stood, contained this clarification: "It is the unanimous opinion of your Committee that Dispensationalism as defined and set forth above is out of accord with the system of the doctrine set forth in the Confession of Faith, not primarily or simply in the field of eschatology, but because it attacks the very heart of the Theology of our Church, which is unquestionably a Theology of one Covenant of Grace."[156] It also clarified the committee's understanding of what *judicial* implications might accompany its findings. Seeming particularly concerned that its report not be abused by an overly aggressive GA, the committee stated:

> Inasmuch as there is some difference of opinion concerning the status and use of such a report, your Committee desires to state that it does not understand that the Assembly instructed it to provide a statement of doctrine which shall be a substitute for, or an amendment to, any doctrinal statements contained in the Constitution of the Church or any part thereof. Nor does it understand that this report, if approved by the Assembly, is to be regarded as an amendment to ordination vows of ministers, ruling elders, or deacons. It is simply an interpretative statement which may be used by the Presbyteries as they deem wise.[157]

We should perhaps point out that the liberal wing of the Church would be happier with such a clarification than the conservative wing. Liberals had no interest in defending dispensational premillennialism, but they seemed to recognize Robinson's point that, if dispensationalism could be found by the GA out of accord

---

1945; letter, E.C. Scott to Lewis Sperry Chafer, 5 June 1945; and letter, E.C. Scott to Lewis Sperry Chafer, 23 May 1945; letter, Lewis Sperry Chafer to the General Assembly of the Presbyterian Church, U.S. c/o Rev. E.C. Scott, D.D., Clerk, 19 May 1945; all in Lewis Sperry Chafer papers, ADTS. Chafer claimed that his being so prohibited caused the AIC to misrepresent his views. "When the personnel of the Committee was changed a year ago, the writer in correspondence with a member of the Committee offered at his own expense to meet with the Committee at any time or place and to do what could be done to clarify the issues involved. No such invitation was extended to me. Likewise, it is evident to all that the mails are available and it would have been of little trouble to address a letter which would have saved the Committee from publishing so damaging an error. Any attempt to state another person's beliefs, when those beliefs are neither known nor comprehended, will usually do more harm than good" (letter, Lewis Sperry Chafer to the General Assembly of the Presbyterian Church, U.S. c/o Rev. E.C. Scott, D.D., Clerk, 19 May 1945, Lewis Sperry Chafer papers, ADTS).

[155] Dendy, "Report of the General Assembly," 6.
[156] "Report of the [1944] AIC," 127.
[157] Ibid., 127.

with the Church's doctrinal standards and, upon that basis, forcibly expelled, then so could other doctrinal views deemed unfavorable by another GA.[158]

Thus, Ernest Trice Thompson, representing the liberal response to this report, commended the committee for its "balance and restraint," and regarded the AIC's clarification of the limitations of its judicial effect as "striking a blow for freedom."

> Appointed last year for the purpose of studying the Dispensational system in its relation to our Westminster standards, the committee finds that Dispensationalism – certainly the form of it held by men like Dr. Chafer and taught in the notes of the Scofield Bible – is out of accord with our Confession at fundamental points, and that "it attacks the very heart" of our church's theology. These findings it reports to the Assembly with no mincing of language or pulling of punches. But having gone so far, the committee wisely goes no further. It makes no recommendation to the Assembly as to what ought to be done with the Dispensationalists in our church, and does so for a sound and simple reason. It knows the Assembly has no right to initiate action of any kind against the Dispensationalists, or even to say to the presbyteries what the presbyteries must do about them. For exactly as a presbytery has no right, under our church law, to tell a minister whether or not he may smoke, so an Assembly has no right under our law to tell a man or a presbytery whether he or it can be both Dispensationalist and Presbyterian at the same time. Aside from the Assembly's act of adopting this committee's report, or receiving it as information, whatever disciplinary action, if any, is taken as a result of it will – if it be legal action – have to be taken by individual presbyteries and by them alone.[159]

Why such "restraint" would be deemed so commendable by the liberal wing of the Church is revealed in Thompson's next remarks.

> Time and again, when tempted to forget this principle and to usurp the authority of the presbyteries as courts of original jurisdiction our Assemblies have wisely refused to do so. Now and then, to be sure, a particular Assembly has declared overwhelmingly that, **in its opinion**, a certain belief or doctrine (like that of evolution) is out of harmony with our standards; but to say whether a man believing in evolution, Dispensationalism, Barthianism, socialism or any other kind of "ism" is thereby unfitted for a place in the Presbyterian church – that is a decision to be arrived at by each presbytery as its own conscience and wisdom shall dictate.[160]

Lest anyone misunderstand his point, or miss the implications of it for Southern Presbyterian conservatives, Thompson went on to make clear that, in his view, this

---

[158] See Robinson, "The Authority of the Lord Jesus Christ as Exercised in the PCUS," 13-14.

[159] Ernest Trice Thompson, "A Committee Draws a Line," *PrOut* 118 (17 May 1944): 12.

[160] Ibid. (bold print original).

was the Northern Presbyterian conservatives' *mistake* in 1910 and 1923 and was the *virtue* of the 1924 Auburn *Affirmation*.

> It was in protest against a violation of this principle by a Northern Presbyterian Assembly, it might be well to recall, that the famed Auburn Affirmation came into being. Whatever else that Affirmation was – and we here leave its doctrinal merits or demerits entirely aside – it was fundamentally an act in defense of Presbyterian liberty, a rebellion against an Assembly which endeavored without warrant to bind the presbyteries concerning what it termed the "five fundamentals" of Presbyterianism.[161]

The judicial clarification in the 1944 AIC report might have assuaged the concerns of liberals in the Church, but conservative premillennialists had another concern entirely. Conservatives might well have objected to the report's suggestion (which liberals heralded) that a view deemed out of harmony with the *Confession* could still be deemed tolerable by some individual Presbytery willing to stomach its confessional disagreement.

On the other hand, *premillennial* conservatives, like the premillennial conservatives in the North before them, wanted to ensure that whatever was deemed out of accord with the doctrinal standards in *dispensational* premillennialism would not be projected onto premillennialism generally. The 1944 report had reduced and softened considerably the 1943 report's anti-premillennial sections concerning the Confession's teaching on Christ's current reign and kingship. This section was not eliminated entirely, however.[162] At least one premillennialist at the GA was made uncomfortable by the anti-premillennial implications of the report's final section.

---

[161] Ibid.

[162] Perhaps the most pointedly anti-premillennial remarks that remained in the 1944 report were those that appeared just before the "Conclusion." "Dispensationalism teaches a series of resurrections and judgments, spaced over more than a thousand years. It is the opinion of your Committee that the above statement of the Confession of Faith does not admit of a multiplicity of resurrections and judgments as taught by many Dispensationalists" (Report of the [1944] AIC, 126). One frankly has to read a lot into the qualification "as taught by many dispensationalists" to interpret this sentence as anything but a repudiation of any form of premillennialism. If *no* "multiplicity of resurrections" be allowed, how is *any* premillennial view allowed, since premillennialism, by definition, affirms a resurrection of saints before the millennium and a second resurrection of the wicked at the end of the millennium? There seems to be only a few possible explanations for how three premillennialists could sign this particular portion of the 1944 report: 1) the three premillennial laymen simply did not catch its full implications for the premillennial view; 2) they regarded the anti-premillennial implications in the statement as *possible* but not *required* (i.e., they thought the statement was sufficiently ambiguous to include, with some maneuvering perhaps, an interpretation that allowed acceptable forms of the premillennial view); or 3) they found overwhelming the evidence which McLaurin, Gear, and Bear had surfaced, which demonstrated that a non-premillennial eschatology was, technically, the teaching of the *Westminster Confession* and (especially) the *Larger Catechism* and they considered the premillennial view fortunate to get by with only this passing reference.

Bell's, McCallie's and Sibley's signatures on the report notwithstanding, "Gaston Boyle offered an amendment to the last paragraph to clarify the meaning."[163]

Doubtless wearied by the prospect of facing the same stumbling blocks to acceptance of the 1944 report that had stymied the 1943 report, the GA quickly carried the amendment,[164] which read:

> Your Committee wishes also to make the following statement of clarification: Most, if not all, adherents to the type of Dispensationalism dealt with in this report hold the Premillennial view of our Lord's return; but not all Premillennialists accept this form of Dispensationalism. Therefore, the Committee wishes to make it clear that it has endeavored solely to consider the particular type of Biblical interpretation defined above, and known as Dispensationalism and that it understood the assignment of the Assembly to limit it to this task. In view of this fact, this report should not be considered as in any sense a criticism of Premillennialism as such.[165]

Chafer began his response to the 1944 AIC report at this distinction.

> First, the Committee claims that its criticism is not directed against *Premillennialism* but is directed against *Dispensationalism*. This sets up a distinction which for want of a factual basis must be classed as fantastic. As well might it be asserted that the sun will rise in the morning but that it will not be dark before nor will it be light after the sun rises. Doubtless it is possible to give a superficial assent to the general idea that Christ's return will be before His kingdom is set up on the earth and not to have carried any of the issues which are involved to their logical and Scriptural conclusions.[166]

Today, more than fifty years later, debate continues as to who was right, Chafer or the AIC, as to whether dispensationalism and premillennialism may be legitimately distinguished. Regardless of who was right in 1944, and Chafer's strenuous objection to the distinction notwithstanding, this amendment to the AIC report enabled its ready acceptance by the GA. "The amended report was then adopted as a whole."[167] The report then went to the individual ministers and presbyteries, where the real import of this committee's judgment would take effect.

It was not all that unusual for a GA committee's report to be sent to presbyteries for advice or counsel. Less common, but not wholly unusual, was the practice of sending *decisions* of a committee to the presbyteries as information.[168] What was

---

[163] Dendy, "Report of Meeting of the General Assembly," 6.
[164] Ibid.
[165] "Report of the [1944] AIC," 127.
[166] Chafer, "Dispensational Distinctions Denounced," 257.
[167] Dendy, "Report of Meeting of the General Assembly," 6.
[168] *A Digest of the Acts and Proceedings of the Presbyterian Church in the United States, 1861-1944, Authorized by the General Assembly* (Richmond: Presbyterian Committee of Publication,

quite unusual was to send a *doctrinal* decision to the presbyteries in *pamphlet* form, giving the appearance of a decree or edict of the GA.

This is what was done in the case of the AIC report on dispensationalism. The pamphlet was entitled, *Dispensationalism and the Confession of Faith*.[169] The entire form of the document communicated that this was an official conveyance from the GA. And it was so treated, even by those who commended the AIC for its "balance and restraint" in *not* prescribing a course of action for the presbyteries.[170]

But did not even the AIC report itself describe its findings as "simply an interpretative statement which may be used by the Presbyteries as they deem wise"? Did it not emphatically *deny* that it was "a statement of doctrine which shall be a substitute for, or an amendment to, any doctrinal statements contained in the Constitution of the Church or any part thereof"?[171]

This is all true. Nevertheless, the GA was not being duplicitous in its adoption and distribution of the AIC report. Nor were those who used the report as an authoritative Church conveyance being devious in so using it. This is because of the traditional Confederate (states' rights) orientation of the Southern Presbyterian Church. The PCUS GA was far more reluctant than her Northern counterpart to prescribe a course of judicial action to its presbyteries or to insist that GA's doctrinal judgments be forcibly thrust upon the presbyteries.[172] The PCUS was generally more doctrinally conservative, but its Southern character meant that the

---

1945) and *Minutes of the GA, passim.*

[169] *Dispensationalism and the Confession of Faith: Report of the Ad Interim Committee on Changes in the Confession of Faith and Catechisms as to Whether the Type of Bible Interpretation Known as Dispensationalism is in Harmony with the Confession of Faith*, prepared and distributed by order of the 1944 General Assembly (Richmond: Executive Committee of Religious Education and Publication, 1944).

[170] Ernest Trice Thompson had said in one context, "Whether one agrees, therefore, with the findings of the ad interim Committee on Dispensationalism, or whether one disagrees, every Presbyterian eager to safeguard liberty of interpretation and the rights of individuals before our church law, will rejoice in the committee's balance and restraint. As to what the various presbyteries ought to do in regard to the Dispensationalists within their ranks, or what Dispensationalists themselves ought to do in the light of this report, it is not our purpose here to offer an opinion" ("A Committee Draws a Line," 12.) Yet, in another, later context, he states that the adoption of the AIC report by the GA had made dispensationalism an officially-recognized "heresy" ("Scofield Bible's Heresy," *PrOut* 127 [13 August 1945]: 15).

[171] "Report of the [1944] AIC," 127. Thus, Hannah is accurate in his insistence that the Committee Report was, technically, "merely advisory" (Hannah, "The Social and Intellectual History of the Evangelical Theological College," 361). Hannah points this out in his assessing the account of Fuller (*Gospel and Law*, 30-33). Yet, Fuller is not wholly inaccurate in his saying "the Southern Presbyterians had charged him [Chafer] with heresy" (33) – see previous footnote.

[172] This was a point that the Southern Presbyterians claimed from the very beginning was one that differentiated the PCUS from the PCUSA (see the section titled, "Concerning the Powers of the Several Courts of the Church. Their Relations to Each Other and to the Office-Bearers and People," in *The Distinctive Principles of the Presbyterian Church in the United States, Commonly Called the Southern Presbyterian Church, as set forth in the formal declarations and illustrated by extracts from proceedings of the General Assembly from 1861-70* [Richmond: Presbyterian Committee of Publication, 1870], 86-90).

PCUS also distinctly cherished the inviolable sovereignty and autonomy of the individual Presbyteries.

In this light, the AIC's claim that its report was "simply an interpretative statement" to be "used by the Presbyteries as they deem wise" was really no grand proclamation of restraint. To the contrary, it would have been surprising had the AIC tried to overstep such a boundary.

Instead, the AIC recommended the course of action by which the PCUS GA had consistently addressed other heresies and doctrinal anomalies. These included such confessional divergences as the "doctrines of the Christian Church"; doctrines of the "Assembly of God" churches (i.e., charismatic teachings); and teachings of the 7th Day "Adventist Church."[173] In each of these previous cases (dating from 1891 to 1932), the GA's ruling was the same.

> Because of the clarity and fullness of the presentation of Christian truth in our Confession of Faith and Catechisms, . . . the General Assembly simply reaffirms its faith in the great fundamentals of our Church as set forth in our Confession of Faith and Catechisms, and declines to make additional declarations of doctrine. . . . It is felt that this matter can best be decided by pastors and sessions in local situations.[174]

What this history seems to manifest is the Southern reticence to impose *de jure* decisions from higher, centralized authorities to lower, localized authorities. Far better, to Southern minds, was the policy of letting local authorities handle troublesome factions as best they saw fit. It was not that Southern power structures promoted anarchy; it was that they seemed more concerned to exercise their authority subtly.[175]

How the AIC report was adopted and distributed by the GA, and how it was "enforced" by local presbyteries provides a case in point of how PCUS authority was effectively exercised in general. While it is true that the AIC report was not a *de jure* pronouncement that specified a course of action to be followed by all in the church, it was nonetheless treated as a *de facto* ruling of the Church.[176]

A few presbyteries apparently disagreed with the AIC's findings and welcomed dispensationalists into their pulpits and churches anyway.[177] To do so was a right

---

[173] See the section of GA rulings concerning the Confession of Faith, in *A Digest of the Acts and Proceedings of the GA of the PCUS*, 54-55.

[174] Ibid.

[175] See Thompson's section entitled *"Jure Divino* Presbyterianism," in *Presbyterians in the South, Volume Two: 1861-1890* (Richmond: John Knox Press, 1973), 414-20; and *Presbyterians in the South, Volume Three*, 400-90.

[176] Some 45 years later, one can still find, in official Committee reports and overtures, references to this 1944 AIC report as a "judgment" of the Church and as a "statement . . . upheld by the General Assembly"; see e.g., *Minutes of the One Hundred-Seventeenth General Assembly of the Presbyterian Church in the United States* (Austin, TX: Von Boeckmann-Jones, Co., 1977), 3.

[177] The Rev. Stephen B. Williams, stated clerk of the Louisiana Presbytery and Moderator of the Synod of Louisiana, registered his disagreement with the AIC report in a pamphlet entitled,

afforded them by the PCUS traditional understanding of its authority structure. This was, however, exceptional.[178]

Dispensationalists could not expect to survive long in the PCUS relying solely on the support of this small number of churches. Where could dispensationalists fit in the PCUS after the 1944 decision? After all, liberal churches might not be vigilant about confessional subscription, but they would hardly be amicable towards dispensationalists given their disagreements on a host of other issues. Conservatives, on the other hand, might agree with dispensationalists on any number of doctrinal and socio-political stances, but they would not deem disharmony with the doctrinal standards as inconsequential. Even Stephen Williams, who wrote in defense of Chafer's views, said, "If it is true . . . that Dispensational theology is manifestly out of harmony with the Standards of our Church, then . . . those who teach that doctrine should be brought to trial in their respective Presbyteries as speedily as possible."[179]

Given that dispensationalism could hope to survive in the PCUS only in conservative circles, and given the fact that conservative Presbyterians would take the *de facto* condemnation of dispensationalism by the PCUS GA most seriously, it is not hard to explain why this "advisory" report so effectively eliminated dispensational influence from the PCUS. This result is exactly what several historians have observed. "Within a few years [of the AIC report] dispensationalism had ceased to be a disturbing factor in the church."[180] "The Assembly's action laid the foundation for purging dispensationalists. . . . Chafer believed the report was a personal attack on him that the Dallas Presbytery would use to excommunicate him. The presbytery took no action, but Chafer became a pariah at its meetings."[181] Moreover, the school Chafer headed, Dallas Theological Seminary, "was suddenly separated from its ecclesiastical moorings in the Reformed tradition."[182]

Dispensational Truth (Alexandria, LA: Good Tidings Press, 1945).

[178] In S. Lewis Johnson's recollection, for Dallas Seminary graduates to be ordained in Presbyterian churches at all after 1944, they had to be ordained in the North, in theologically conservative churches concerned more with liberalism than with dispensationalism (S. Lewis Johnson, interview by the author, Dallas, Texas, 7 April 1995).

[179] Williams, *Dispensational Truth*, 6. The point that Williams is trying to make is that it is *not* true that dispensationalism is out of harmony with the doctrinal Standards and that is why no such action is necessary (he is actually quoting James R. Viser of Greenville, SC in framing the issue just this way). Both Williams and Viser were staunch conservative Southern Presbyterian dispensationalists who disagreed with the findings of the AIC. Their rhetoric is employed to try to help Chafer, by stating how strongly they affirm the importance and necessity of confessional subscription (*contra* the liberals or other confessionally less conservative Presbyterians). While their point is that one can be a vigilantly loyal confessionalist and still affirm dispensationalist views, it is not difficult to see how their point could backfire: should fellow conservatives *agree* with them in their assessment of confessional subscription being essential, but also *agree* with the AIC's assessment of dispensationalism's being out of harmony with the *Confession*, then conservatives, just as Williams and Viser imply, would be the ones most vigilant to expel dispensationalists from the church.

[180] Thompson, *Presbyterians in the South, Volume Three*, 488.

[181] Glass, "Northern Patterns of Fundamentalism in the South," 246.

[182] Hannah, "The Social and Intellectual History of the Evangelical Theological College," 364.

5.4 Significant Implications of the PCUS Decision Against Dispensationalism

Given the relationship between the 1930s controversy in the North and this 1940s controversy in the South, the AIC report may accurately be said to culminate Reformed-Covenantalist opposition to dispensationalism and pronounce a definitive verdict against it. Many Reformed-Covenantalist critiques of dispensationalism written since 1944 have used this report as a reference point;[183] others simply preserve the argumentation from the AIC reports as the standard Reformed objections to dispensationalism.[184]

The PCUS controversy was no less significant in its effect on dispensationalism. "Suddenly separated from its moorings in the Reformed tradition,"[185] dispensationalism responded by becoming less Reformed, sometimes even anti-Reformed.

We see this point illustrated when we examine the effect of this controversy on Dallas Theological Seminary, the "capital" of dispensational theology. A survey of that institution's enrollment and placement records[186] reveals a pattern that may be paradigmatic. Specifically, these records indicate an adjustment in the school's main

---

[183] E.g., Fuller, *Gospel and Law*, 30-33; Gerstner, *Wrongly Dividing the Word of Truth*, 63-64; Jon Zens, *Dispensationalism: A Reformed Inquiry into its Leading Figures & Features* (Phillipsburg, NJ: P & R, 1980); 42-49.

[184] John Wick Bowman, "The Bible and Modern Religions: II. Dispensationalism," *Interpretation* 10 (1956): 170-187; Wes Auger, *A Critique of the Scofield Bible* (Little Rock, AR: Challenge Press, 1972); William E. Cox, *An Examination of Dispensationalism* (Phillipsburg, NJ: P & R, 1963); *idem*, *Why I Left Scofieldism* (Nutley, NJ: P & R, 1977); Curtis I. Crenshaw and Grover Gunn, *Dispensationalism Today, Yesterday, and Tomorrow* (Memphis, TN: Footstool, 1985); and Keith A. Mathison, *Dispensationalism: Rightly Dividing the People of God?* (Phillipsburg, NJ: P & R, 1995). Cf. also "RPC/ES Statement on Dispensationalism," *PrGuard* 38 (1974): 239-47.

A significant illustration of this point is also found in the work of George Eldon Ladd; see his *Crucial Questions About the Kingdom of God* (Grand Rapids: Eerdmans, 1952); and *The Blessed Hope* (Grand Rapids: Eerdmans, 1956). In these works, Ladd claims that the premillennialism to which he subscribes is acceptable in that it is a *non-dispensational* premillennialism. The Baptist Ladd never mentions the PCUS controversy, nor even the articles by James Bear, but, rather, traces the Reformed objections to dispensationalism exclusively through Oswald T. Allis. Nonetheless, that he deems his form of premillennialism as more acceptable than dispensational forms just *because* his view eschews the very tenets listed as dispensationalist mistakes by the 1943-44 AIC demonstrates my point. The controversy of the late 1930s, which culminated in the 1944 AIC ruling, defined the issues of debate between dispensationalism and covenant theology within evangelicalism.

Moreover, the exchange between Ladd and John Walvoord, who followed Chafer as president of Dallas Theological Seminary, not only continued hostilities between dispensationalists and non-dispensationalists, but took the debate between dispensationalists and covenant theologians (especially "covenant premillennialists") to the next level (John Walvoord, *The Rapture Question* [Findlay, OH: Dunham Publishing Co., 1957], 127-140); and *The Blessed Hope and the Tribulation* [Grand Rapids: Zondervan, 1976]).

[185] Hannah, "The Social and Intellectual History of the Evangelical Theological College," 364.

[186] See Appendix 1.

base of support, away from a Reformed-Presbyterian constituency[187] and toward an independent or Baptist constituency. Slight faltering of the Reformed-Presbyterian constituency can be seen in the late 1930s, but the rapid decline of this constituency in the late 1940s is most remarkable (see chart 1, below, page 168[188]). The transformation of the faculty was about five years behind that of the graduates,[189] but was no less dramatic (see chart 2, below, page 169).[190] The startling transformation of constituencies traced in these charts graphically illustrates the sociological effect of the PCUS debate on dispensationalist ideology.[191]

Glass's research concurs with my own in regard to the effect of the 1944 AIC report on dispensationalists seeking ordination in the PCUS. One case in point he mentions is that of a Dallas Seminary graduate whose presbytery rejected his application without even examining him; the presbytery listed the reasons for their rejecting his application as: "his position at an interdenominational school [he was Dean of Southeastern Bible School] as service outside the bounds of the Presbytery, his attendance at a denominationally unapproved seminary [i.e., Dallas Seminary], and his dispensationalism."[192] This case was unusual in that this presbytery did not

---

[187] When Dallas Theological Seminary was founded in 1924, and throughout its early years, Presbyterian students and faculty were predominant. Hannah, the seminary's church historian, observes: "While the [seminary] was officially non-denominational, the majority of its faculty in the 1920s, the general focus of its teaching, and many of the students were Presbyterian. Speaking of the faculty, Chafer noted in 1925 that they were 'almost wholly drawn from the Southern and Northern Presbyterian Churches.'. . . On another occasion he stated, 'The simple fact is that we are teaching the most conservative Presbyterian interpretations here and we include on our faculty now seven Southern Presbyterian ministers.' . . . Perhaps the Presbyterian nature of the institution is most clearly captured in the assertion 'it [the Seminary] stands on the great vital truths embodied in that marvelous document, The Westminster Confession of Faith' [Letter, Lewis Sperry Chafer to D.S. Kennedy, editor of the Presbyterian, Dallas, Texas, 23 October 1924, Lewis Sperry Chafer Papers, ADTS]" (Hannah, "The Social and Intellectual History of the Evangelical Theological College," 346).

[188] For a detailed accounting of numbers used to construct this chart, see Appendix 1.

[189] This is to be expected. The effect of the Presbyterian Church's negative assessment of dispensationalism could be almost immediate on graduate placement, but not immediate on Presbyterian faculty representation. Presbyterians already employed as faculty would not leave the school (or their Presbyterian churches) the instant the decision was rendered. Rather, Presbyterian representation on the faculty would be affected mostly by attrition, as the faculty of the 1940s was replaced in the 1950s and 60s. Many Presbyterian faculty members did leave their Presbyterian Churches, but, again, not immediately.

[190] For substantiation of the figures, see Appendix 2.

[191] We will take up this point, below, and in the next chapter. The two charts also illustrate the thesis of Hannah's dissertation ("The Social and Intellectual History of the Evangelical Theological College, vii-viii); viz., that Dallas Seminary was formed with the purpose, initially, of training evangelical leadership to permeate the various denominations in the U.S. However, as time went on, it came instead to supply the leadership for the growing fundamentalist-evangelical network, which was largely independent, non-denominational and oriented to parachurch ministry.

[192] Glass, "Northern Patterns of Fundamentalism in the South," 247. The student's name was James Mooney, and this incident occurred in 1945, just one year after the GA had adopted the AIC report. "Mooney described the presbytery meeting where his opponents characterized his

even bother to examine the candidate's views. Not so unusual, though, was a candidate's dispensational views, discovered during the ordination hearing and examination, being listed as a cause for the candidate's rejection.[193]

In this way, the AIC report "laid the foundation for purging dispensationalists." Glass clarifies: "Nor does it appear that presbyteries used the report against dispensationalists already in presbyterian churches. Rather presbyteries used it to prevent others from holding presbyterian pulpits."[194] This explains how Chafer himself was "grandfathered" by the PCUS decision (he died in 1952 still holding his PCUS membership[195]) and also is consistent with Thompson's description of how the AIC report was used by PCUS presbyteries.[196]

This also corresponds closely with the memory of those dispensationalists who were living at the time and were available for interview. S. Lewis Johnson graduated from Dallas Seminary in 1946 and taught New Testament and Systematic Theology there for over thirty years. He recalls that, before 1944, people in Presbyterian churches would often say with affection, "We think of Dallas Seminary as a Presbyterian school." Such affectionate remarks stopped abruptly, he recalled, after this controversy.[197]

For several years, Johnson had taught a Sunday School class at the First Presbyterian Church of Dallas, but, in 1946, he was prohibited from continuing this ministry. His affiliation with Dallas Seminary was given as the reason. This church used the 1944 AIC ruling, Johnson says, as official sanction by the PCUS to remove dispensational influences from the Southern Presbyterian churches.[198]

Others tell similar stories. When John Walvoord, who was pastor of the Rosen Heights Presbyterian Church in Ft. Worth, Texas, transferred to Dallas in 1951 to become full-time professor of theology at Dallas Seminary, he hit an unexpected snag. The acceptance of such transfers was normally routine, Walvoord recalled. In

---

'entire course of training in the Dallas Seminary as a 'mistake' and extend[ed] condolences to me for being 'misguided.' I have never experienced such an insulting, discourteous, bitter and vindictive attitude anywhere or at any time' [Letter, James S. Mooney to Lewis Sperry Chafer, 24 April 1945, in Lewis Sperry Chafer Papers, ADTS]."

[193] See Glass, "Northern Patterns of Fundamentalism in the South," 246-49.
[194] Ibid., 246-47.
[195] This is not to say that Chafer suffered no repercussions from the AIC decision. Shortly after this ruling, the PCUS ruled Chafer's clerical status as "superannuated," even though, according to John Walvoord, his physical condition had not noticeably deteriorated in the years preceding this change of status (John Walvoord, interview by the author, 19 June 1996, Dallas, TX). And, according to Glass, Chafer became "a pariah at [PCUS Presbytery] meetings" ("Northern Patterns of Fundamentalism in the South," 246). Yet, Glass also mentions that, in a letter dated 31 March 1949, to Graham Gilmer, a fellow Southern Presbyterian, Chafer "indicated [his] desire to move his [denominational] affiliation elsewhere, but he 'had not been able to take any action in that respect because of my relation to the Seminary.' This comment suggests that Chafer believed that continuing his membership in the southern Presbyterian church would benefit graduates of the seminary. In short, he still dreamed of supplying conservative pastors to the denomination to help maintain its orthodoxy" (Ibid., 246-47, n. 54).
[196] Thompson, *Presbyterians in the South, Volume Three*, 488.
[197] S. Lewis Johnson, interview by the author, Dallas, TX, 7 April, 1995.
[198] Ibid.

The Dispensational-Covenantal Rift

Denominational Affiliation of DTS Graduates (1925-1995)

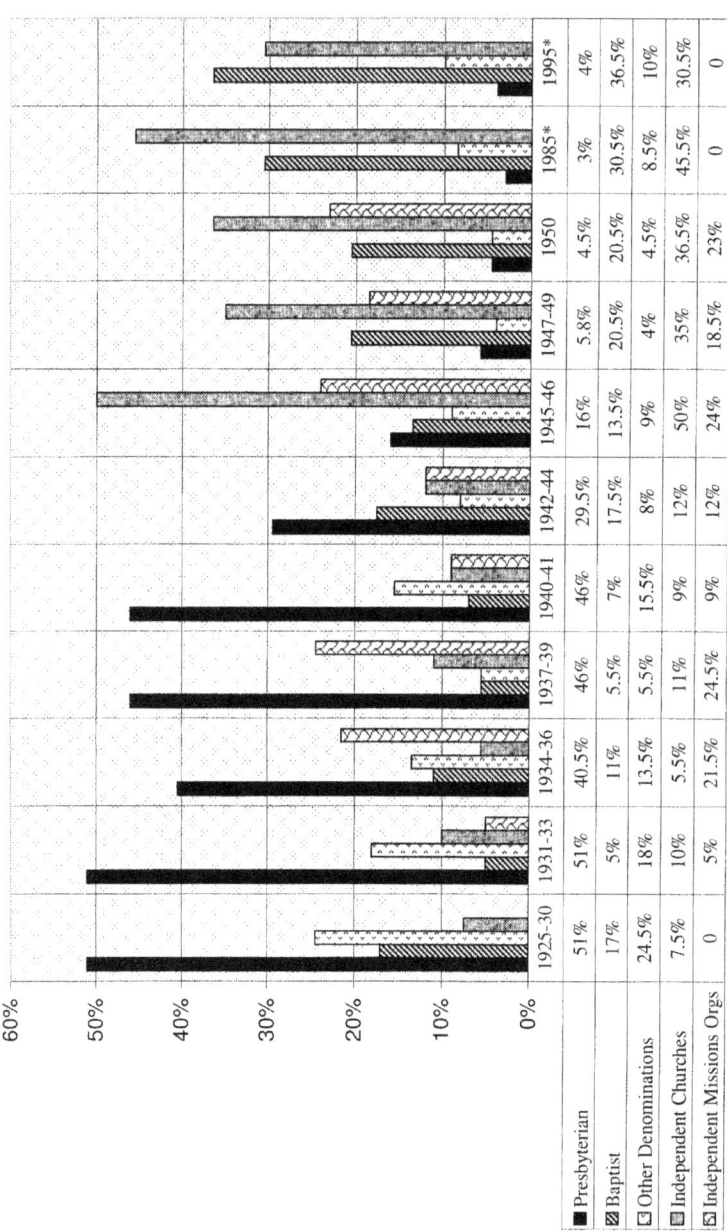

*1985 and 1995 figures are based on students enrolled, rather than graduates.

The Tremors Travel Southward (Part 2)

Denominational Affiliation of DTS Faculty (1925-1995)

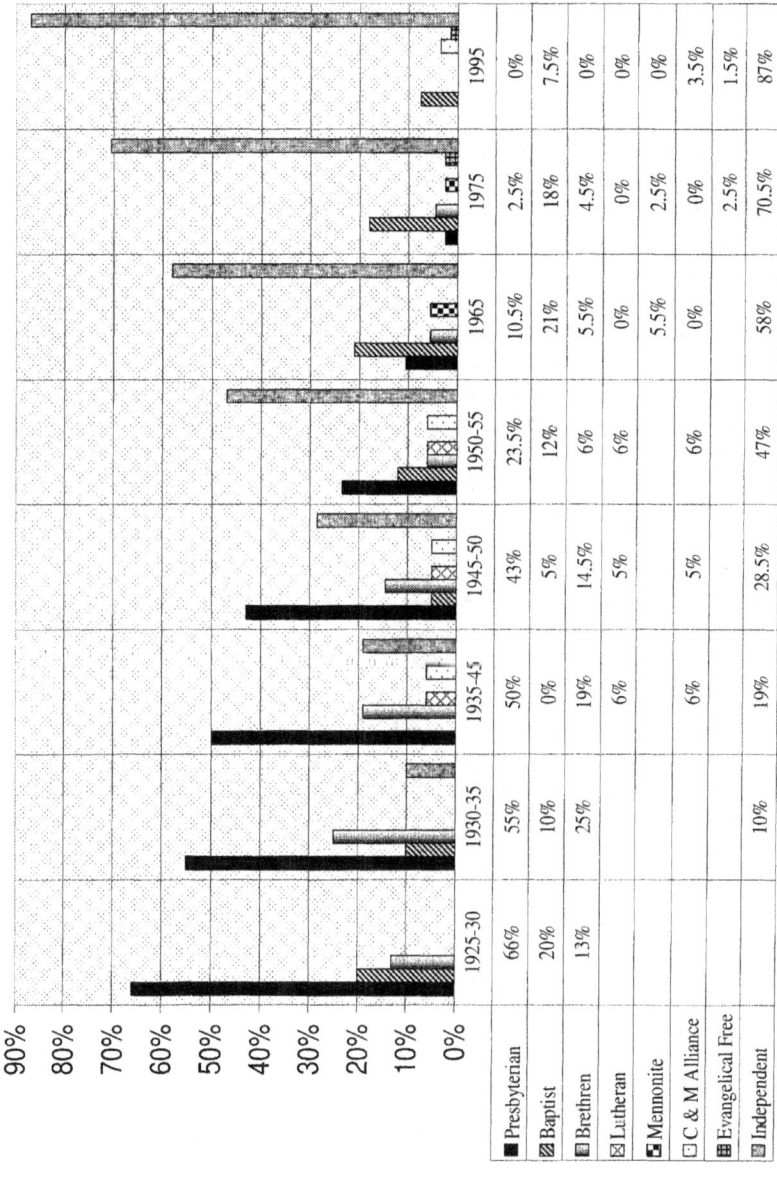

	1925-30	1930-35	1935-45	1945-50	1950-55	1965	1975	1995
Presbyterian	66%	55%	50%	43%	23.5%	10.5%	2.5%	0%
Baptist	20%	10%	0%	5%	12%	21%	18%	7.5%
Brethren	13%	25%	19%	14.5%	6%	5.5%	4.5%	0%
Lutheran			6%	5%	6%	0%	0%	0%
Mennonite						5.5%	2.5%	0%
C & M Alliance			6%	5%	6%	0%	0%	3.5%
Evangelical Free							2.5%	1.5%
Independent		10%	19%	28.5%	47%	58%	70.5%	87%

his case, though, the Dallas Presbytery refused to accept the transfer of a Dallas Seminary faculty member into their jurisdiction. As a result, Walvoord was forced to transfer into the Independent Fundamental Churches of America instead. And, though he had received a letter from the Ft. Worth Presbytery stating that he had left there in good standing, Walvoord remembers the denominational paper in Dallas reporting that he had been kicked out, as "one of those speckled birds that subscribes to the teachings of the Scofield Reference Bible."[199] Again, the 1944 GA action was cited as sanctioning his ouster.[200]

Even non-Presbyterians involved with Dallas Seminary at the time remember the AIC decision as being very significant for the school. John Witmer, who was ordained in the United Brethren Church, was not himself unhappy to see Dallas Seminary move away from the predominant Presbyterian influence. He was hired as the seminary's director of Public Relations in 1947. From his perspective, if such a potential public relations fiasco as the PCUS ruling of 1944 had to happen, "it couldn't have happened at a better time." In 1945, World War II ended and the soldiers came home. The shortage of students was over, and Dallas Seminary simply drew its new students out of this abundant supply from non-Presbyterian sources.[201] With this, the change of constituencies was complete.[202]

Even if dispensationalism was not inherently un-Reformed before that time, we could only expect that students and faculty that were drawn from Dallas Seminary's new, un-Reformed constituency after 1944 would bring their un-Reformed

---

[199] John F. Walvoord, interview by the author, Dallas, Texas, 19 June 1996. Unfortunately, regional PCUS denominational papers are no longer preserved or available. This means that many historical details, such as Walvoord provided in my interview, though valuable, are unable to be corroborated with written records.

[200] Ibid.

[201] John Witmer, interview by the author, Dallas, Texas, 18 May 1995.

[202] I have not tried to establish what direct effect the PCUS actions had on institutions other than Dallas Theological Seminary, though it may be assumed that these events probably would have had the *most direct* effect on Dallas Seminary because its founder and president was actually named, his views denounced, in the AIC report. C.I. Scofield, who founded Philadelphia College of Bible, was also mentioned in the 1944 Report, but this institution was not within the parameters of direct PCUS judicial actions. At any rate, no attempt has been made to discern what effect the 1940s PCUS actions had on that institution.

However, even if we were to assume that this PCUS decision affected *only* Dallas Theological Seminary (a highly unlikely supposition), even then, this controversy could be said to have had a dramatic effect on dispensationalist-covenantalist relations generally. The anti-covenantalist works written by dispensationalists in the 1940s, 50s, and 60s, were all written by Dallas Seminary graduates, to a man influenced either directly by Lewis Sperry Chafer, or by those who were so directly influenced. Indeed, this pattern still continues today (Renald E. Showers, *There Really is a Difference! A Comparison of Covenant and Dispensational Theology* [Bellmawr, NJ: The Friends of Israel Gospel Ministry, 1990]). Showers was a student of Charles Ryrie, who was a student of Chafer. Showers is a graduate of Dallas Seminary and former professor of Theology and Church History at Philadelphia College of Bible. The framing of the issues as they were delineated by dispensationalists in the late 1940s-early 1950s is preserved in his 1990 treatise.

viewpoints with them.[203] Thus, the sociological and ecclesiastical impact which we have just surveyed cannot be separated from the change towards covenant theology, in both tone and content, in dispensationalist works written in the 1940s and 50s.

One more element in this change should be mentioned. At the time when Chafer was receiving the most intense criticisms from Reformed-Covenantalists, C. Fred Lincoln, an independent, Scofieldian dispensationalist who had come to Dallas Seminary from the Central American mission field,[204] was writing what would become a highly influential dispensationalist treatment of covenant theology.

One year after the PCUS began its investigation of dispensationalism's orthodoxy (1942), Lincoln completed his dissertation under Chafer on "The Covenants," a historical presentation and critical evaluation of covenant theology. At the same time that Chafer was responding in *Bibliotheca Sacra* to the AIC's investigation, Lincoln published his articles on covenant theology, which were essentially excerpts of his dissertation.[205]

Lincoln's arguments seemed to influence Chafer toward a less favorable view of covenant theology; one finds Chafer referring to Lincoln's work and employing arguments from it in his own articles at the height of his controversy with his denomination.[206] Chafer, along with the train of dispensationalists who would

---

[203] I am deliberately speaking in generalizations here, but I am also consciously avoiding overgeneralization. I am assuming (not without data, of course) that a general correlation exists between Reformed-Covenant theology and Presbyterianism; I am also assuming (again, not without data) that a general correlation exists between dispensationalism as a movement and Dallas Theological Seminary. I recognize that exceptions may exist (so I do not deny that one may occasionally find an Arminian, premillennialist Presbyterian or a Reformed, amillennialist Independent Bible Church minister). Nevertheless, I do also suggest that, once the Presbyterian influence on Dallas Seminary was markedly reduced, and once a history of hostilities had made the relationship between dispensationalists (especially dispensationalists at Dallas Seminary) and covenant theologians palpably less amicable for both sides, dispensationalism, as a theological system, developed in a less Reformed direction, in a direction less amenable to covenant theology, and vice versa. Part of what I am establishing (*inter alia*) is that these changes can be detected both sociologically and historical-theologically.

[204] Lincoln served as Bible professor and Business Manager at Dallas Theological Seminary until his retirement in the 1960s (John F. Walvoord, interview by the author, Dallas, TX, 11 April 1995).

[205] C. Fred Lincoln, "The Development of the Covenant Theory," *BibSac* 100 (January-March 1943): 134-63; *idem*, "The Biblical Covenants: Parts 1-3," *BibSac* 100 (April-June 1943): 309-23, (July-September 1943): 442-49, (October-December 1943): 565-73.

[206] See Chafer, "Dispensational Distinctions Challenged," 338, 345; *idem*, "Inventing Heretics Through Misunderstanding," *BibSac* 102 (1945): 1-5. Chafer uses the term "covenantism" to describe his opponents' position for the first time in the 1943 article, "Dispensational Distinctions Challenged." He cites Lincoln for support with this comment: "For a scholarly, impartial, and complete treatment of the Covenant Theory, see an article, "The Development of the Covenant Theory," by Dr. C. Fred Lincoln, in BIBLIOTHECA SACRA , No. 397, Jan-Apr., 1943. This most illuminating treatise should be read by every person who subscribes to the Covenant Theology" (338, n. 1). It is not unreasonable to assume that Chafer had investigated covenant theology – and perhaps even enlisted Lincoln to help him do so – as a result of the 1943 AIC investigation. Baited by Bear, Chafer concludes that he *is*, in fact, in disagreement with the covenant theology of the Westminster Standards, but, accepting

follow him in their denunciation of covenant theology,[207] seems to have used Lincoln's work as a veritable guide to understanding the view that opposed their "dispensationalism."

In 1952, just before Chafer's death, Lincoln headed a committee that revised Dallas Seminary's doctrinal statement. Among the revisions was this one, which for all practical purposes, sealed dispensationalism's opposition to covenant theology officially: "We believe that the dispensations are not ways of salvation nor different methods of administering the so-called Covenant of Grace."[208]

So, prominent dispensationalists (at Dallas Seminary, at least) relied heavily on Lincoln's work to provide them guidance in framing the issues at this most crucial stage in their debate with covenant theologians. However, as Stephen R. Spencer has observed, Lincoln's "treatment of covenant theology is unfortunately inaccurate at numerous points and therefore is not a reliable guide."[209]

Lincoln's "findings," he also concludes that covenant theology is so obviously in error as to make realistic the goal of getting the PCUS to abandon this tenet. This suggested scenario would fit with Craig Blaising's observations. "When Chafer published his *Systematic Theology* in 1947-48, he included several harsh comments reflecting the controversies of the preceding years. Critical comments were made about the covenant of grace, although in the first volume he affirmed a traditional three-covenant structure. . . . In his book, *Grace*, Chafer uses the terms 'covenant of works' and 'covenant of grace' to refer to the two rules of life, law and grace, which are distinguished by dispensation. This, of course, is not the way the terms were ordinarily used by Reformed theologians. Chafer also uses the phrase 'covenant of faith' as a synonym for covenant of grace (*Grace*, 102, 106, 121, 157, 164-65, 187, 193). The incorporation of this material in volume 4 of the *Systematic Theology* leads to conflicting statements about the covenant of grace (cf. 4:156 with 4:229)" ("Lewis Sperry Chafer," in *Handbook of Evangelical Theologians*, ed. by Walter A. Elwell [Grand Rapids: Baker, 1993], 95).

[207] John F. Walvoord, *The Millennial Kingdom* (Findlay, OH: Dunham, 1959), 105-10; and Charles Ryrie, *Dispensationalism Today* (Chicago: Moody Press, 1965), 177-91. Cf. Showers, *There Really Is a Difference!*, which, though never citing Lincoln, cites Ryrie extensively.

[208] From the "Doctrinal Statement," *Annual Catalogue of the Officers and Students of Dallas Theological Seminary and Graduate School of Theology* 28 (March-April 1952): 73. The committee that made this revision was headed by Lincoln and included two other members: Charles Nash and John Walvoord. All changes to the doctrinal statement, before they were actually adopted, were cleared by Lewis Sperry Chafer, who died in August 1952 just three months after the committee finished its work (John F. Walvoord, interview by the author, Dallas, TX, 11 April 1995). Interestingly, Walvoord insists that this statement does not *demand* the interpretation that Lincoln would likely have given it; viz., a flat denial of the idea of a covenant of grace (see Lincoln, "The Biblical Covenants," 309). Walvoord does himself affirm the idea of a covenant of grace, as well as a covenant of redemption ("The New Covenant," in *Integrity of Heart, Skillfulness of Hands: Biblical and Leadership Studies in Honor of Donald K. Campbell*, ed. Charles H. Dyer and Roy B. Zuck [Grand Rapids: Baker Books, 1994], 198). He suggests that the adverb "only" could legitimately be implied in the statement; i.e., "We believe that the dispensations are not [*only*] different methods of administering the so-called Covenant of Grace."

[209] Stephen R. Spencer, "Reformed Theology, Covenant Theology, and Dispensationalism," in *Integrity of Heart, Skillfulness of Hands* (Grand Rapids: Baker, 1994): 239, n. 5. Spencer was professor of theology at Dallas Theological Seminary when he wrote this assessment.

Yet, that was the guide used by dispensationalists, nonetheless, however flawed may have been the guidance it provided. Moreover, dispensationalist responses to covenant theology (as well as the negative assessment of dispensationalism that provoked these reactions) were polemical treatises written in self-defense, when the writers felt themselves engaged in a struggle for ideological and sociological survival. Forged in the heat of battle, the issues between dispensationalism and covenant theology fused significant inaccuracies and misunderstandings together with genuine issues of contention.

Yet, this framing of the issues would be conveyed to followers of both sides thereafter. All this was part of the legacy of the 1940s dispensationalist-covenantalist conflict. We today are just beginning to sort truth from error in this legacy ingloriously bequeathed to American evangelicalism.

CHAPTER 6

A Concluding Analysis of the Controversies Over Dispensationalism and Covenant Theology in the 1930s-1940s

6.1 The Points at Issue

If anything is clear in the debate between dispensationalism and covenant theology in the 1930s-1940s, it is that the points at issue between them were *not clear* to the actual participants. To the end, Lewis Sperry Chafer refused to accept the framing of issues insisted upon by covenant theologians. In his mind, the key issue was always premillennialism. The same straightforward hermeneutical methodology that surfaced recognition of the Bible's premillennial eschatology would also inevitably force recognition of other dispensational distinctives, he contended.

Covenant theologians insisted, just as adamantly and just as consistently, that their objections to so-called "dispensationalism" had little or nothing to do with its premillennial eschatology. Rather, their concerns focused on the Scofield-Chafer soteriology, particular the apparent advocacy of "two ways of salvation," one way in the Old Testament, another in the New Testament. In their minds, "dispensationalism's" illegitimate separation of Old Testament and New Testament brought with it a host of other serious errors, including antinomianism, indolence concerning contemporary social responsibility, and denominational infidelity.

The two sides' inability to ever agree on what was actually at issue exacerbated misunderstandings. Sociological polarization is a centrifugal force, anyway; once the two "sides" were clearly demarcated by the end of the 1940s (even though the theological and ideological points which separated them were not), chances of reconciliation were decreased. This has meant that clarification of their misunderstandings was also impeded, which is why such has not taken place even to the present day.

Today, both sides have built strong constituencies around the idea that their side opposes certain alleged grave errors advocated by the other side. This means that clarifying misunderstandings today could be all the more significant, but also all the more difficult.

6.2 Significant Misunderstandings and Mistakes

6.2.1 By Dispensationalists

Premillennialists in both the North[1] and the South[2] never heard, or else never believed, covenant theologians' repeated insistence that their objection was not to dispensationalist eschatology. It is certainly true that covenant amillennialists disagree with dispensational premillennialism, and that covenant amillennialists argued against dispensational premillennialism for more than a century. It is true that some of the most adamant critics of dispensationalism, from the beginning, were covenant amillennialists. Nevertheless, when dispensationalists took covenantalists' objections to dispensationalism as purely an amillennial objection to premillennial eschatology, they were allowing themselves to believe, at best, a *half-truth*.

Most covenantalist critics of dispensationalism during the crucial period of our investigation clarified explicitly and repeatedly that their (principal) objection was *not* against dispensationalism's eschatological chronology, but against the distinctively heterodox, anti-Confessional tenets of dispensational soteriology and dispensational hermeneutics, which set the New Testament in sharp contradiction to the Old Testament (particularly the Mosaic Law). Especially in historical hindsight, how unambiguous and how numerous are these clarifications is astonishing.[3]

---

[1] E.g., Carl McIntire, "Premillennialism," *CBeac* 1 (1 October 1936): 4.

[2] E.g., Rollin Thomas Chafer, "Eschatological Liberty," *BibSac* 93 (July-September 1936): 387-88; Lewis Sperry Chafer, "Dispensationalism," *Bib Sac* 93 (October-December 1936): 393-94, 445-49; *idem*, "Dispensational Distinctions Challenged," *BibSac* 100 (July-September 1943): 337-45; *idem*, "Dispensational Distinctions Denounced," *BibSac* 101 (April-June 1944): 257-60.

[3] E.g., R.B. Kuiper, (unpublished) letter to the editor of the *Christian Beacon*, Carl McIntire, 6 October 1936, published (for the first time) as "The Reply of Professor Kuiper," *PrGuard* 3 (14 November 1936): 54; J. Gresham Machen, "The Root of the Trouble," *PrGuard* 3 (14 November 1936): 41-42; *idem*, "Premillennialism," *PrGuard* 3 (24 October 1936): 21; J. Oliver Buswell, "A Premillennialist's View," *PrGuard* 3 (14 November 1936): 46; Ned B. Stonehouse, "A Clarification of Some Issues," *PrGuard* 3 (13 March 1937): 217-18; James Bear, "Dispensationalism and the Covenant of Grace," *UnSemRev* 49 (July 1938): 286, 305; *idem*, "Premillenarians and Our Church Standards," *PrSouth* 115 (24 July 1940): 5; *idem*, "Historic Premillennialism," *UnSemRev* 55 (May 1944): 193-222; also *idem*, "Dispensationalism: Parts I and II," *Presbyterian Outlook* 118 (26 April and 3 May 1944): 6 and 5-6 (respectively); "Appendix: Report of the Ad Interim Committee on Changes in the Confession of Faith and the Catechisms, Part II: THE QUESTION AS TO WHETHER THE TYPE OF BIBLE INTERPRETATION KNOWN AS DISPENSATIONALISM IS IN HARMONY WITH THE CONFESSION OF FAITH," in *Minutes of the Eighty-Third General Assembly of the Presbyterian Church in the United States, with an Appendix* (Austin, TX: Von Boeckmann-Jones Co., 1943), 122; "Appendix: Report of the Ad Interim Committee on Changes in the Confession of Faith and Catechisms: THE QUESTION AS TO WHETHER THE TYPE OF BIBLE INTERPRETATION KNOWN AS DISPENSATIONALISM IS IN HARMONY WITH THE CONFESSION OF FAITH," in *Minutes of the Eighty-Fourth General Assembly of the Presbyterian Church in the United States, with an Appendix* (Austin, TX: Von Boeckmann-Jones Co., 1944), 126-27. Cf. also J. Oliver Buswell, Jr., "Premillennialism and the Reformed Faith: Has the 'Pre' a good standing?" *SSTimes* 76 (5 May 1934): 289-91.

Lewis Sperry Chafer, in particular, never faced squarely what was the primary objection to his theological ideas. Chafer railed against those who accused him of teaching "two ways of salvation."[4] Nevertheless, even his most poignant attempts to relieve himself of the charge seem actually to justify the accusation.

> What they [dispensationalists] teach, if at all, is that Judaism had its requirements summed up in works of the Law of Moses, which system, or religion, is not now in effect, and that Christianity has its requirements summarized in faith and is now the one and only basis of acceptance before God. Those are the clear teachings of the Scriptures, to which men do not it seems always give sincere heed....
>
> When talking to an individual and in respect to the present provision for the salvation of lost men, the Savior said to Nicodemus: "For God so loved the world, that he gave his only begotten Son, that whosoever believeth in him should not perish, but have everlasting life" (John 3:16). Likewise, when talking to an individual respecting the securing of eternal life as it was promised in the Jewish kingdom expectation, Christ held the following conversation with the lawyer (i.e., a teacher of the Mosaic system): "And, behold, a certain lawyer stood up, and tempted him, saying, Master, what shall I do to inherit eternal life? He said unto him, What is written in the law? how readest thou? And he answering said, Thou shalt love the Lord thy God with all thy heart, and with all thy soul, and with all thy strength, and with all they mind; and thy neighbour as thyself. And he said unto him, Thou hast answered right: this do, and thou shalt live" (Luke 10:25-28).
>
> There is no question to be raised about these words or their precise meaning. "This do, and thou shalt live" is far removed from the words found in John 3:16 or even Romans 6:23: "For the wages of sin is death; but the gift of God is eternal life through Jesus Christ our Lord."
>
> Are there, then, two ways to be saved today? The dispensationalist says No, because he recognizes Judaism to be in abeyance at the present time, and this text of Luke 10, which might be called the *John 3:16 of Judaism*, does not apply to believers today. But the Covenant theologian, who must include well-nigh everything in his system of teaching, is faced with both statements on the lips of Christ.[5]

And so the article ends.

Several points capture our attention. First, the addition of the word "*today*" in the question that begins the final paragraph is curious. It suggests that Chafer believes that the PCUS charge is against classical dispensationalism's advocating "various plans of salvation" *today* (a charge that Chafer easily refutes as a

---

[4] Lewis Sperry Chafer, "Inventing Heretics Through Misunderstanding," *BibSac* 102 (January-March 1945): 1-5 (emphases original).

[5] Lewis Sperry Chafer, "Are There Two Ways to Be Saved?" *BibSac* 105 (January-March 1948): 1.

misrepresentation). Yet the Committee Report had specifically clarified, "Dispensationalism, magnifying the distinction which is made between law and grace (*which dispensationalists hold to be mutually exclusive* – Chafer, *Grace*, p. 231 ff.), agrees that men are NOW saved by grace through faith, but teaches that in other dispensations men have been saved by 'legal obedience.'"[6] Chafer's argumentation concerning there being only one plan of salvation in effect *today*, therefore, amounts to *ignoratio elenchi* – he is either misrepresenting or misunderstanding the true point at issue.

What is perhaps even more striking is the impression Chafer gives that he has uncovered an example that is "clear" (his word), in which "there is no question to be raised" (his terminology) about the Bible's presenting (indeed, of *Jesus*' presenting) two different, mutually exclusive methods of salvation in the two different ages, "Mosaic" and "Christian." So confident is he that the two sets of passages he quotes are irreconcilable that he ends the article on this point – with the insinuation that covenant theology is untenable just because it demands a reconciliation of passages that are obviously impossible to reconcile. Is this an example, in Chafer's mind, of covenant theologians' espousing an untenable theology borne out of ignorance of the Bible?

While there is no shortage of terms like "clear," "without question," and "no argument can be raised" in Chafer's treatise, one can detect hints here and there that even Chafer may recognize he is on precarious ground. He qualifies his claim that "dispensationalists teach" his view with the phrase, "if at all." Perhaps most tellingly of all, he flatly refuses to concede forthrightly to the charge that he does, in fact, believe that the Bible's two testaments present two different, mutually exclusive ways of salvation, despite that being the definite implication of his argument.

Here is one instance in which the two sides seem consistently to have talked past one another in this debate. Chafer clearly in his own mind did not teach "two

---

[6] "Report of the [1944] Ad Interim Committee," 125 (emphases original). Committee member, James Bear, had also made this point in an earlier article. "Of course it might be said that since the Dispensationalists believe that all men in *this dispensation* are saved by grace through faith, no great harm will be done by their preaching. Certainly they will not mislead men as to how they may be saved *now*. It is because they are preaching salvation by grace to their living hearers that their preaching is blessed. But it is not this preaching of salvation by grace *now* that makes them Dispensationalists. All of the evangelical churches are preaching salvation by grace. But the Dispensationalists declare that their great contribution lies in the fact that 'Dispensational truth' is the key to the understanding of God's Word and His dealings with men. They alone 'rightly divide the Word of truth.' It is because they offer to give a truer insight into the Bible that they attract many. They do give a *new* insight, but much that is new is not true, especially in theology. The new insight they give in the meaning of covenants and dispensations leads to the 'truth' that those in the Mosaic dispensation were saved by 'legal obedience' in contrast to us who are saved 'by the personal acceptance of the finished work of Jesus Christ'[cites dispensationalist William Evans, *Outline Study of the Bible*, p. 34]. We are not here arguing whether this 'truth' is Scriptural or not. But we do say that their teaching is radically different from the accepted view of our Church" ("Dispensationalism and the Covenant of Grace," 301-02 [emphases original]).

A Concluding Analysis 179

ways of salvation." When he was permitted to use his own terminology and to provide his own framing of issues, the phrase "two ways of salvation" did not appear. It was a phrase he would not even approve of apparently – he vigorously objected to this and similar phrases being used to describe his view.[7]

Nonetheless, once one gets beyond the salvos of vigorous objections, one finds reason to question the denials (sometimes even in the very arguments employed in those denials). That is, there are elements in his teaching that sound exactly like the doctrines deemed anti-Confessional by the PCUS Committee, which *they* identified by the description, "The Rejection of One Way of Salvation."

Of course, this raises the question as to whether *they* should have been allowed to use terminology that the exponent of the view objected to. With this question comes a series of other hard questions. What if Chafer really did espouse the tenets described by the AIC Report, but he nevertheless was sincerely opposed to the *terminology* used to describe his views? Who has legitimate final say in determining what terminology is appropriate?

If the PCUS Committee misrepresented Chafer's view, then of course Chafer had a legitimate complaint. If, however, the PCUS Committee *accurately* represented Chafer's view, but Chafer simply disliked the unflattering *terminology* and *labels* which they attached to that (accurate) presentation, then his complaint should have been more nuanced. In that case, Chafer could object to the *terminology*; he could suggest a more felicitous set of terms to use. All this would be legitimate, so long as the objection to *terminology* is *not* mistaken for a *refutation* of the charge itself.

Close analysis of Chafer's responses to the PCUS Committee Report suggests that this was in fact one mistake he made.[8] He apparently disliked the connotations of the description "various and diverse plans of salvation for various groups," and he engaged these connotations as points of libel; viz.: 1) "various plans of salvation" made it sound, in Chafer's mind, like he denied that salvation was always by grace (i.e., including in the Old Testament);[9] 2) similarly, it made it sound like he denied

---

[7] We should point out, however, that it was not only Chafer's *detractors* that "misunderstood" his teaching so as to employ such phrases to describe the view. An *exponent* of Chaferian dispensationalism wrote in to the *Christian Beacon* in 1937, asserting, "While all salvation is of Jesus Christ, yet there are two salvations: Jewish, or General, administered by Messiah and the saints during Judgment – Millennium – Resurrection. The salvation of the Church is unto spirit-being and heavenly . . ." ("Questions and Answers," *CBeac* 2 [8 April 1937]: 4).

[8] In the nomenclature of formal and informal logic, what we are describing is the fallacy of "quibbling." See Gerald Runkle, *Good Thinking: An Introduction to Logic* (Philadelphia, PA: Holt, Rinehart and Winston, 1981), 54-55: "When a party to a discussion gives a different meaning (lexically or stipulatively) to a word that has already been used and whose meaning is clear, he is quibbling. He may by his ill-advised action produce a disagreement that is merely verbal. The parties to the dispute, if they are not alert, may as a result believe that they are in genuine disagreement (when they are not). Or they may become so confused they fail to recognize the nature of whatever genuine disagreement may be present."

[9] "Are there two ways by which one may be saved? In reply to this question it may be stated that salvation of whatever specific character is always the work of God in behalf of man and never a work of man in behalf of God. This is to assert that God never saved any one person or group

that the blood of Christ was always the efficacious means of Divine atonement (including for Old Testament saints).[10] That Chafer did *not* deny either of these tenets he makes abundantly clear.

Nevertheless, the question remains: Did the AIC charge him with denying *these* positions? Or was their critique directed toward something *else* that Chafer actually *did* teach, which was what *they* had in mind by the phrase, "various and divergent plans of salvation for various groups in different ages"?[11] This is a highly significant question.[12]

It is possible that the two parties in the discussion may have been talking about two different *kinds* of *causes* in salvation. We are helped by the distinctions in terminology provided by (Reformed) scholasticism, between the *meritorious cause* of salvation and the *instrumental cause* of salvation.[13] For example, using this nomenclature in regard to New Testament salvation: the meritorious cause is Christ's (past) blood atonement provided on the cross (which merit was confirmed by God the Father in resurrecting His Son, Jesus, from the dead); the instrumental cause – that is, the cause that God uses to actually make that merit effective for the individual – is faith.[14] Both classical dispensationalism and covenant theology agreed on these points in New Testament salvation.

---

of persons on any other ground than that righteous freedom to do so which the Cross of Christ secured. There is, therefore, but one way to be saved and that is by the power of God made possible through the sacrifice of Christ" (Chafer, "Inventing Heretics Through Misunderstanding," 1).

[10] Ibid. Also see Chafer, "Dispensational Distinctions Denounced," 258-59. "To this [i.e., the charge of teaching multiple ways of salvation in various ages] it is answered, as answered before, that the Editor has never held such views and that he yields first place to no man in contending that a holy God can deal with sin in any age on any other ground than that of the blood of Christ."

[11] "Report of the [1944] Ad Interim Committee," 124.

[12] Craig Blaising's summary is accurate: "It did not matter to his detractors that he [Chafer] viewed the death of Christ as equally foundational for both systems, law and grace, a fact which he himself believed exonerated him from the charge" ("Lewis Sperry Chafer," in *Handbook of Evangelical Theologians*, ed. Walter A. Elwell [Grand Rapids: Baker, 1993], 93). The question we want to pursue is *why* did it "not matter to his detractors"? Also, *why* did Chafer believe that this point "exonerated him from the charge" when "his detractors" did not? Likewise, Blaising's summarization is accurate when he says, "That he [Chafer] saw in the Bible two substantially different religions (Christianity and Judaism) which entailed different and opposed rules of life and different eternal destinies (heavenly vs. earthly) was sufficient in the minds of many to make stand the charge that he believed in two different kinds of salvation and thus two ways of salvation" (93-94).

[13] See Richard A. Muller, *Dictionary of Latin and Greek Theological Terms: Drawn Principally from Protestant Scholastic Theology* (Grand Rapids, MI: Baker Books, 1985), s.v. "causa instrumentalis" and "causa meritoria," 62-63.

[14] See Francis Turretin, *Institutes of Elenctic Theology*, 1696, reprint edition, translated by George Musgrave Giger, edited by James T. Dennison, Jr. (Phillipsburg, NJ: P & R, 1994), "Sixteenth Topic: Justification," 2:633-88; William Ames, *The Marrow of Theology*, 1629, reprint edition, translated and edited by John D. Eusden (Durham, NC: Labyrinth Press, 1968), 162; also Charles Hodge, *Systematic Theology*, 1873, reprint edition (Grand Rapids: Eerdmans, 1993), 3:118-212. Cf. also John Calvin, *Institutes of the Christian Religion*, 1559, reprint

Concerning the *instrumental cause* in the Mosaic age (and in the future kingdom age), however, there appears to be some significant disagreement. Covenant theologians insist that the instrumental cause (as well as the meritorious cause) is consistent: viz, salvation is always *sola fide*;[15] to a great extent, this consistency is what underlies their model's positing one covenant of grace from the Fall to the close of history.[16] For Chafer, however, the instrumental cause seems to fluctuate from dispensation to dispensation, between law-keeping (which he sometimes clarifies may be prompted by faith[17]) and faith alone.

Specifically, Chafer seems to use the phrase, "human terms of salvation," for what the scholastics had termed "instrumental cause." If this correlation be correct, Chafer's argument in his article, "Inventing Heretics Through Misunderstanding" (which was written in response to the PCUS judgment), yields an intriguing point.

> Are there two ways by which one may be saved? . . . God never saved any person or group of persons on any other ground than that righteous freedom to do so which the Cross of Christ secured. There is, therefore, but one way to be saved and that is by the power of God made possible through the sacrifice of Christ.

---

edition, Library of Christian Classics, XX, translated by Ford Lewis Battles, edited by John T. McNeil, (Philadelphia: Westminster Press, 1960), Book III, Chapter XI, pp. 725-54.

[15] See Charles Hodge, *Justification By Faith Alone*, 1841, reprint edition, ed. John W. Robbins (Hobbs, NM: Trinity Foundation, 1995); cf. *The Westminster Confession of Faith*, chapter XI, "Of Justification," especially section II: "Faith, thus receiving and resting on Christ and his righteousness, is the alone instrument of justification . . . "; and section VI: "The justification of believers under the old testament was, in all these respects, one and the same with the justification of believers under the new testament"; cf. Chapter VII, "Of God's Covenant with Man" and *The Westminster Larger Catechism*, Questions 31-36. Cf. also John Murray, *The Covenant of Grace: A Biblico-Theological Study* (Phillipsburg, NJ: P & R, 1953), 3-30.

[16] This is exactly how this point was framed against classical dispensationalism by Bear ("Dispensationalism and the Covenant of Grace," 288-305). Using Charles Hodge's explication of the Covenant of Grace as a reference point, Bear asserts what covenant theology (as affirmed by the Westminster Standards) means by one plan of salvation: "Dr. Hodge by the word 'same' emphasizes four aspects of the Covenant of Grace. (1) There is *one* plan of salvation, offered in a central covenant-promise made to the human race, a promise re-affirmed by many covenants, but still 'the same promise of deliverance.' (2) There is *one* Redeemer, our Lord Jesus Christ. (3) There is *one* condition on *man's* side for participation in the blessings of redemption. That condition is faith. [Cites Hodge, *Systematic Theology*, 2:371.] (4) There is *one* common destiny for all men who qualify by the one condition of faith" (289, emphases original). This point was reiterated by Eugene W. McLaurin, *A Suggested Report of the Ad Interim Committee on Changes in the Confession of Faith and Catechisms with Regard to the "Question as to Whether the Type of Bible Interpretation Known as 'Dispensationalism' is in Harmony with the Confession of Faith* (Austin, TX: Austin Presbyterian Theological Seminary, 1942), 8.

[17] "Faith in the Old Testament saint led to works which are to be the ground of his future acceptance or rejection. Faith in the Christian leads to the finished work of Christ and to good works in daily life after he is saved which result in a reward. The Old Testament saint will be saved by faith expressed in works; the Christian is saved by faith apart from works" (letter, Lewis Sperry Chafer to Charles G. Trumbull, 30 March 1937, Lewis Sperry Chafer Papers, ADTS).

> The far lesser question as to the precise human terms upon which men may be saved is quite a different issue. . . . The Bible indicates three different requirements as the human terms upon which man has been, or now may be, saved.
>
> First, God imputed righteousness to Abraham, which righteousness is the foremost feature of God's salvation, on the sole ground that Abraham believed or amened [*sic*, from "amen"] God. Abraham believed God respecting a son whom he would himself generate. The passage -- Genesis 15:2-6 – should be considered with worthy attention. By divine design, Abraham was the pattern of salvation by grace and the great Apostle draws his illustrations regarding grace almost exclusively from the life of this one Old Testament character.
>
> Second, God imputes righteousness to those in this age who believe, which righteousness is the foremost feature of salvation, on the one demand that they *believe*; but this belief is not centered in a son which each individual might generate, as in the case of Abraham, but in the Son whom God has given to a lost world, who died for the world and whom God has raised from the dead to be a Saviour of those who do believe. . . .
>
> Third, the salvation of Israel . . . is unique in every particular. . . . It yet remains to be seen that the salvation of the nation of Israel, though the precise character of that salvation has not been fully disclosed, extends to every individual. . . . [I]t is disclosed that the salvation of an Israelite, who lived in the Mosaic age, which age will be completed in the coming Tribulation, was guaranteed by covenant; yet the individual could, by failing to do God's revealed will as contained in the Mosaic Law, sacrifice his place in the coming Kingdom and be cut off from his people (cf. Lk. 10: 25-28; 18:18-21; Matt. 8:11, 12; 24:50, 51; 25:29, 30). Jehovah's salvation of Israel will be on the ground of Christ's death. The human terms, because of the covenant promise regarding their salvation, are not the same as that required of Abraham or of any individual in this age, whether Jew or Gentile.[18]

If the point at issue was whether the *instrumental* cause may change from dispensation to dispensation, then Chafer's adamant insistence on the singularity and consistency of the *meritorious cause* misses the point – nor does his vigorous defense of this single meritorious cause relieve his view of the charge of teaching "two ways of salvation" the way he thinks it does. On the other hand, his explicit affirmation of changes in instrumental cause from dispensation to dispensation establishes the very point of his detractors' objection.

Chafer's unfamiliarity with the sociological and ideological dynamics at work in his denomination (the PCUS) also contributed to his misunderstanding the covenantalist objections to his theology. He imagined a vast modernist-liberal

---

[18] Chafer, "Inventing Heretics Through Misunderstanding," 1-5.

conspiracy arrayed against him for his conservative biblical and theological views.[19] Chafer's passing on this perspective to his allies and successors[20] meant that the dialogue between conservative dispensationalists and conservative covenant theologians would be poisoned for most of the twentieth century.

This "poisoning" effect impacted how the "two ways of salvation" aspect of Chafer's theology would be engaged in the discussion that progressed between later dispensationalist and covenant theologians. It is truly remarkable how thoroughly Chafer's construction was abandoned by dispensationalists in the generation of dispensationalists that followed him. Even those dispensationalists who would affirm most tenaciously the impetus behind Chafer's Mosaic-age soteriology (viz., his denial of any aspect of "law" in the New Testament age of grace) still refused to defend his articulation of soteriology in the Mosaic age.

Rather, Chafer's "clarifications of himself" were used by later dispensationalists to reverse his teaching on the point entirely; dispensationalists simply conceded that, on this point, Chafer and Scofield had made a (minor) mistake.[21] One searches in

---

[19] Chafer, "Dispensational Distinctions Challenged," 339-40. As William Robert Glass demonstrates, Chafer's consistency in sharing this view of the matter both publicly and privately seems to indicate that his linking the attack against dispensationalism to theological liberalism was not merely a rhetorical insinuation; he apparently genuinely believed that the objections to his positions were due to aggressive liberal forces allied against him ("The Development of Northern Patterns of Fundamentalism in the South, 1900-1950" [Ph.D. diss, Emory University, 1991], 241-53).

[20] John F. Walvoord, interview with the author, Dallas, TX, 11 April 1995. Walvoord's recounting of Chafer's perspective was the most explicit, but all the conservative premillennialists who were alive at the time of the controversy whom I interviewed (viz., Allan A. MacRae, J. Dwight Pentecost, S. Lewis Johnson, Donald Campbell) alluded to a similar theory of what happened in this 1930s-40s clash between dispensationalists and covenant theologians; i.e., that the clash was, in large part, a clash between conservative Bible believers and liberals.

[21] E.g., see Charles Ryrie, *Dispensationalism Today* (Chicago, IL: Moody Press, 1965), 120; also H. Chester Woodring, "Grace Under the Mosaic Covenant" (Th.D. diss., Dallas Theological Seminary, 1956), especially 208-09. In personal interviews, John F. Walvoord summarized what appears to have become the standard dispensationalist recounting of this revision in dispensational theology: that arguments presented by later dispensationalists, e.g., as in Woodring's dissertation, finally articulated what dispensationalists before then had *meant*, but had failed to articulate. What earlier dispensationalists (e.g., Scofield, Chafer, Feinberg) had actually said, admittedly, were overstatements, which they did not really mean (John F. Walvoord, personal interview with the author, 11 and 18 April 1995, Dallas, TX). Walvoord's response to John Murray's (1936) critique of dispensationalism was instructive. Murray had honed in on two quotations from Charles Feinberg's book, *Premillennialism or Amillennialism* (1945): "God does not have two mutually exclusive principles as law and grace operative in one period" (126); and "The principles of law and grace are mutually destructive; it is impossible for them to exist together" (175). Walvoord observed, "Feinberg is just quoting or borrowing from Chafer there," and then said, "Well, I see Murray's point . . . but Murray really misunderstood Chafer. They [Chafer and Feinberg] said this, but they didn't really mean it." I then asked Dr. Walvoord if my supposition was correct, that dispensationalists in the generation after Chafer had reversed Chafer's position on salvation in the Old Testament; specifically, I asked, is it proper to suggest that "revised dispensationalists" changed "classical dispensationalism" on at least one of the points originally at issue with covenant theology? He

vain, after 1952 (the year of Chafer's death), for a dispensationalist affirmation of Chafer's soteriological construction of the Mosaic age, in which Israelite salvation allegedly was gained "under an unyielding meritorious basis."[22]

A particularly striking manifestation of this reversal is found in the (revised) notes of the *New Scofield Reference Bible* of 1967. Scofield's original comment on John 1:17 had been a focal point of critique in the 1944 PCUS Report; it was also a note that Chafer had defended forcefully. In other words, it was a point that clearly contrasted classical dispensationalism from covenant theology in the defining moment of their debate.

Remarkably, this note is significantly overhauled in the 1967 Scofield Bible. Furthermore, E. Schuyler English, chairman of the *New Scofield Bible* editorial committee, explained the change in this note as follows:

> Scofield's note on grace at John 1:17 needs clarification. Although nowhere else in his writings does Scofield imply such a thing,[23] this

---

replied, "I object to the word 'change.' . . . We softened the distinction between law and grace, but we really didn't disagree with them [i.e., classical dispensationalists]." Throughout, Walvoord was more candid about pointing out errors in the Scofield Bible than about discussing potential errors in Chafer's theology. (E.g., "On some points, Scofield was just flat wrong or in error. Scofield made some blunders. . . . But saying this is not saying the system is wrong. Dispensationalism is broader than Scofield and Chafer. . . . There has always been diversity in dispensationalism"). This perspective is consistent with J. Dwight Pentecost's contention, as early as 1967: "In the generations since the Scofield Reference Bible originally appeared, there have been many clarifications, expansions, and refinements of the dispensational interpretation of Scripture. They have been included in the new [1967] edition [of the *New Scofield Reference Bible*]. This present work is not so much a revision of Scofield's work, suggesting that this represents a new or changed position, as it is an expansion and refinement of his position, representing development in the system Scofield taught" ("Book Reviews: *The New Scofield Reference Bible*," *BibSac* 124 [January-March 1967]: 170). In the current context, one clash between essentialist-revised-normative dispensationalists and progressive dispensationalists is over what sort of change constitutes "development" and what sort of change constitutes "abandonment"; cf. Craig Blaising, "Development of Dispensationalism by Contemporary Dispensationalists," *BibSac* 145 (April-June 1988): 254-80; and Charles Ryrie, "Update on Dispensationalism," in *Issues in Dispensationalism*, ed. Wesley R. Willis and John R. Master (Chicago, IL: Moody Press, 1994), 15-16.

[22] Chafer, "Dispensationalism," 440.

[23] This is not really true; other notes in the Scofield Bible do seem to reinforce (rather than contradict) the implications of Scofield's note on John 1:17. One of these, which seems particularly consistent with the John 1:17 note, is Scofield's note on Ex. 19:5: "What, under law, was *condition*, is under grace, freely *given* to every believer. The 'if' of v. 5 is the essence of law as a method of divine dealing, and the fundamental reason why 'the law made nothing perfect' (Rom. 8. 3; Heb. 7. 18, 19). The Abrahamic (Gen. 15. 18, *note*) and New (Heb. 8. 8-12, *note*) covenants minister salvation and assurance because they impose but one condition, faith" (*Scofield Reference Bible: 1917 Edition* [New York, NY: Oxford University Press, 1917], 93). The *New Scofield Reference Bible* of 1967 eliminates the last sentence of this note and replaces it with a more circumspect observation of the order of requirement and blessing in the different covenants; likewise with the other notes mentioned. One finds a similar consistency in Chafer's writings, with the same implications.

In other words, English (along with other revised-essentialist-normative dispensational-

footnote says: "The point of testing [in the church age] is no longer legal obedience as the condition of salvation, but acceptance or rejection of Christ, with good works as a fruit of salvation (refs.)." This misleading statement has been corrected. As in the footnote at Genesis 1:28 . . . the fact that salvation has been and always will be, whatever the age or dispensation, by grace through faith in God's redemptive provision in Christ and His sacrificial death, has been stressed.[24]

The new note reads as follows:

> Grace, Summary: (1) Grace is "the kindness and love of God our Savior toward man . . . not by works of righteousness which we have done . . . being justified by his grace" (Ti.3:4,5,7). As a principle, therefore, grace is set in contrast with law (Rom.11:6), under which God demands righteousness from men, as, under grace, He gives righteousness to men (Rom.3:21-24; 8:3-4; Gal.2:16; Phil.3:9). Law is connected with Moses and works; grace, with Christ and faith (Jn.1:17; Rom.10:4-10). Under law blessings accompany obedience (Dt.28:1-6); grace bestows blessing as a free gift (Rom.4:3-5; Eph.2:8).
>
> (2) In its fullness, grace began with the ministry of Christ involving His death and resurrection, for He came to die for sinners (Jn.1:17; Mt.11:28-30; 16:21; 20:28; Rom.3:24-26; 4:24-25). Under the former dispensation, law was shown to be powerless to secure righteousness and life for a sinful race (Gal.3:21-22). Prior to the cross man's salvation was through faith (Gen.15:6; Rom.4:3), being grounded on Christ's atoning sacrifice, viewed anticipatively by God (Rom.3:25; see Gen.1:28, heading, *note*, par. 3); now it is clearly revealed that salvation and righteousness are received by faith in the crucified and resurrected Savior (Jn.1:12-13; 5:24; 1

---

ists) seems to have engaged in some "revisionist history" on this point. Close scrutiny of Scofield's and Chafer's writings does not support the claim that they (classical dispensationalists) made only occasional, careless, unguarded statements that sound like "two ways of salvation," but which are so inconsistent with the rest of classical dispensationalist writings as to make it "obvious" that the statements are isolated mistakes. Rather, Scofield and Chafer actually seem consistent on the point (even if, insofar as the content of the point itself, they are in the wrong).

[24] E. Schuyler English, "The New Scofield Reference Bible," *BibSac* 124 (January-March 1967): 130. Committee member John Walvoord also acknowledged that he and others on the committee were "very conscious" of criticisms that had been previously raised (e.g., by the PCUS investigation) in the process of their revising certain notes, such as this one on John 1:17. Interestingly, Walvoord also disclosed that, even though the committee varied as to their vigilance in affirming classical dispensational tenets (e.g., varying from the very mild dispensationalism of Allan A. MacRae and Wilbur Smith to the very strong, classical dispensationalism of Charles Feinberg, Alva J. McClain and Clarence Mason), revisions in the notes were all voted on and had to be approved unanimously in order to actually be included in the *New Scofield Reference Bible* (interview by the author, 2 May 1995, Dallas, TX).

Jn.5:11-13), with holiness of life and good works following as the fruit of salvation (Jn.15:16; Rom.8:2-4; Eph.2:8-10; Ti.2:11-14).

(3) There was grace before Christ came, as witnessed by the provision of sacrifice for sinners (Ex.20:24-26; Lev.5:17-18; 17:11). The difference between the former age and the present age, therefore, is not a matter of *no* grace and *some* grace, but rather that today grace reigns (Rom.5:21), in the sense that the only Being who has a right to judge sinners (Jn.5:22) is now seated upon a throne of grace (Heb.4:14-16), not imputing unto the world their trespasses (2 Cor.5:19).[25]

Is this a case in which dispensationalism has simply conceded or capitulated to covenant theology? Not exactly. The changes in the Scofield note on John 1:17 do reverse much of Scofield's original note; many of the original criticisms from covenantalists might be allayed by these changes. At the same time, distinctions between the dispensations are still emphasized even in the new note.

Similarly, some dispensationalist critiques of the earlier dispensational construction do look very much like the critiques of earlier covenant theologians.[26] Nonetheless, hostilities between the two camps during the era of "essentialist dispensationalism" remained, and ardently so. Why?

An explanation is provided in Charles Ryrie's framing of the issue in his (1965) work, *Dispensationalism Today*. Ryrie concedes that earlier dispensationalists had made several careless misstatements concerning differences in the terms of salvation between Old Testament and New Testament (which we, too, have observed). He then goes on to articulate what is the dispensationalist position "today" regarding what fluctuates and what stays the same over time in the provision of salvation. "The dispensationalists' answer to the problem is this: The *basis* of salvation in every age is the death of Christ; the *requirement* for salvation in every age is faith; the *object* of faith in every age is God; the *content* of faith changes in the various dispensations."[27]

---

[25] *New Scofield Reference Bible* (New York, NY: Oxford University Press, 1967), note on John 1:17, p. 1124.

[26] E.g., in 1982, dispensationalist Kenneth L. Barker, in his presidential address to the Evangelical Theological Society, gave a presentation that would effectively open up the discussion between dispensationalists and covenant theologians on this and other points. Among the points he listed as "False Dichotomies Between the Testaments," was this: "The third false dichotomy (actually the first major one) is that the OT is the Testament of law while the NT is the Testament of grace" ("False Dichotomies Between the Testaments," *JETS* 25 [January 1982]: 6-10). Barker's point here is indistinguishable from the exact point being made by covenantalist critics of this point in Chafer's and Scofield's theology some forty years earlier.

[27] Ryrie, *Dispensationalism Today*, 123. The seminal origins of this framing of issues may be detected in the course notes of Ryrie's teacher, C. Fred Lincoln. Lincoln was stridently opposed to even the very rubric of covenant theology; it is simply impossible to conjecture that Lincoln had any conscious inclination toward moving dispensationalism in a direction more favorable to that system. E.g., in his systematic theology course notes, in the section titled, "Covenant, Dispensational, and Related Studies," he describes the covenant theologian as one who "slyly and without foundation or reason accuses the dispensationalist of teaching more

There is no question that Ryrie's framing here represents a significant "refinement" (his term) of the classical dispensational construction. There is also no question that this refinement moved dispensationalism toward a view more compatible with covenant theology. The chart below identifies points of agreement and disagreement between 1) Ryrie's framing of issues; 2) the view of Lewis Sperry Chafer; and 3) covenant theology.

Ryrie's Position	Chafer's Position (Agree/Disagree?)	Covenant Theology's Position (Agree/Disagree?)
The *basis* of salvation in every age is the death of Christ;	Agree	Agree
the *requirement* for salvation in every age is faith;	**DISAGREE**	**AGREE**
the *object* of faith in every age is God;	Agree	Agree
the *content* of faith changes in the various dispensations.	Agree	Ambiguous (See below)

What we notice first of all is that Ryrie has moved the dispensationalist position from disagreement to agreement with covenant theology (and likewise from agreement to disagreement with Chafer's position) on what had been the exact watershed point of difference between the two theological systems as defined in the PCUS investigation of dispensationalism. The issue in that dispute, as we have

---

than one way of salvation" (p. 8). He describes the "covenant premillennial" view of "J. Oliver Buswell" as being a view that "comes from those who have lightly accepted the truth of the second coming of the Lord, but who have never realized its implications nor the fact that the second coming of the Lord is properly related to a distinctive truth as set forth in a well rounded dispensational system of interpretation"; i.e., it "attempts to reconcile the error of 'covenantism' with premillennial truth. . . . They fail to comprehend, therefore, that the Scripture shows that the systems of law and grace are completely in contrast and irreconcilable" (p. 10). Their opposition to classical dispensationalism, he says, "repeats the groundless fallacy that the dispensationalists teach that there are two or more ways of salvation" (p. 10). In Lincoln's description of the "distinctive responsibility" of the age of grace, he makes a key qualification, however, which even he himself may not perceive is a significant refinement of Chafer's position: "It must constantly be remembered that God has always been gracious and that Christ's shed blood and man's faith have been at all times the basis of man's salvation in every age" (p. 33); C. Fred Lincoln, "Covenant, Dispensational, and Related Studies," course notes, Dallas Theological Seminary, 1947; I am grateful to Donald K. Campbell, who gave me these course notes from his own files.

It is not difficult to imagine that Ryrie, Lincoln's student, put the various strands of what Lincoln says here into a more organized format. Like Lincoln, Ryrie preserved the hostility with covenant theology, even though the real point of contention with covenant theology was one they themselves largely removed.

surveyed above, was the classical dispensationalist variation in instrumental cause (or, to use Ryrie's term, "requirement for salvation") from dispensation to dispensation. Ryrie eliminates this variation, making his "essentialist dispensationalism" consistent with covenant theology on this point.

All the more curious, therefore, is what Ryrie says in the line that follows his four-fold (basis/requirement/object/content) framing: "It is this last point, of course, which distinguishes dispensationalism from covenant theology, but it is not a point to which the charge of teaching two ways of salvation can be attached."[28]

The problem with this statement is that what Ryrie singles out as being the focal point of disagreement had actually *not* been a point at issue at all up to then. Up to then, the question as to what was the "content of faith" required of Old Testament saints had not even been a question raised by covenant theologians;[29] nor was this the reason for the charge of "two ways of salvation."[30] Ryrie's point, as framed in this context, therefore, amounts to yet another instance of *ignoratio elenchi*.[31]

If Ryrie was deliberately trying to change the focus of discussion, his strategy would prove successful. In fact, this change of focus (whether deliberate or indeliberate) allowed him and other dispensationalists to explicate more fully the "content of faith" question, placing dispensationalism in its discussion with

---

[28] Ryrie, *Dispensationalism Today*, 123-24.

[29] With this in mind, the intensifier, "of course," in Ryrie's framing is especially intriguing. Why this straining for emphasis on a point, which, in actuality, covertly shifts the focus of discussion? Perhaps the firmness with which his teacher, C. Fred Lincoln, taught him the dispensational basis of contention with the "sly," "unwarranted" covenant theological position (even though he had re-framed the points of contention) misled Ryrie into a false confidence that this *must* be the "real" point of contention? (Cf. Lincoln, "Covenant, Dispensational, and Related Studies"); also see note 27, above.

[30] For instance, when James Bear originally forwarded against dispensationalism the charge of teaching two ways of salvation (1938), he quotes Hodge (and, in fact, surfaces the same quotation from Hodge that Ryrie does in *Dispensationalism Today* to prove that covenant theology denies any increase in the content of faith required from Old Testament to New Testament [122]), but he never once mentions a problem with the "content of faith." Rather, using Hodge as the reference point, he says in the section titled, "THE SAME CONDITION REQUIRED FOR PARTICIPATION [in the benefits of redemption]": "Doubtless it has already become evident from the quotations given that Dispensationalists seem to hold that there are *two ways on man's side* by which man may come into living relation to God. Of course, the Church holds that there is but one. It has declared that man is not saved by his obedience, nor by what he does. He is saved through *faith*, which is not a work of merit, but an attitude, a relationship. He is saved by his humble reliance upon the grace of the living God as it is revealed in His Word and in His Son"; Bear, "Dispensationalism and the Covenant of Grace," 299 (emphases original).

[31] The fallacy is the same as Chafer's (i.e., *ignoratio elenchi*), as noted, above (see pp. 177-83). Ryrie, like Chafer before him, goes on to argue for a difference between "man's side" and "God's side" in salvation; arguing that once this is understood, the charge of "two ways of salvation" should be removed (see Ryrie, *Dispensationalism Today*, 124-25). Ryrie also suggests that covenant theologians "confuse the tests of a dispensation with a way of salvation" (126). This appears to again add a touch of revisionist history, in behalf of the classical dispensationalists, in order to further distance the dispensational position from the charge of "two ways of salvation."

covenant theology on a much more favorable plane, while they ironed out wrinkles elsewhere in the dispensationalist system.

For instance, one of these wrinkles was the dispensational understanding of the role of animal sacrifices in the Old Testament. Safe behind the lines from their battle with covenant theology, dispensationalists refined this point in their system. The classical dispensationalist explanation of *how* the animal sacrifices provided an efficacious atonement made it seem like the blood of bulls and goats could, *ex opere operato*,[32] provide a genuine, *temporary* propitiation, the one significant shortcoming of these sacrifices being merely their lack of permanency.[33] Such a construction is possible if one is willing to affirm a purely nominalist connection of

---

[32] To the extent that classical dispensationalism maintained an *ex opere operato* efficacy for the Mosaic animal sacrifices, it was similar in its construction of Old Testament soteriology to that of Roman Catholic models; the efficacious nature of the *sacrifices* in the classical dispensationalist structure sounds virtually identical to the efficacious nature of *sacraments* in Roman Catholicism (in both cases, they are efficacious *ex opere operato*). Concerning the meaning and implications of the phrase, *ex opere operato*, see Muller, *Dictionary of Latin and Greek Theological Terms*, s.v. "ex opere operato," 108; cf. "The Canons and Decrees of the Council of Trent," *De Sacramentis in Genere*, Canons V-VIII, 1563, in Philip Schaff, *The Creeds of Christendom, Volume Two: The Greek and Latin Creeds*, 1889, reprint edition (Grand Rapids: Baker, 1983), 120-21. The theological idea denoted by the phrase, *ex opere operato*, is affirmed in these canons, though the phrase itself is not actually used there. The phrase apparently originated with Augustine, who, in battling the Donatists, used this phrase to describe his own position in opposition to their *ex opere operantis* view; for a good summary of the developments of Roman Catholic sacramental soteriology, with reference to this Augustinian origin and its development by medieval scholastics, see Jaroslav Pelikan, *The Christian Tradition, A History of the Development of Doctrine* (Chicago, IL: University of Chicago Press, 1984), especially *Volume 3: The Growth of Medieval Theology (600-1300)*, 190-214; and *Volume 4: Reformation of Church and Dogma (1300-1700)*, 291-302. Calvin, in 1559, explicitly condemned what would be officially affirmed by the Council of Trent four years later (in 1563). In his explication of the mystical benefits to which faith joins the believer in the Eucharist, Calvin says, "It is good that our readers be briefly apprized of this thing also: whatever the Sophists have dreamed up concerning the *opus operatum* is not only false but contradicts the nature of the sacraments, which God so instituted that believers, poor and deprived of all goods, should bring nothing to it but begging"; John Calvin, *Institutes of the Christian Religion*, 1559, edited by John T. McNeill, translated by Ford Lewis Battles, Library of Christian Classics, vol. XXI (Philadelphia: Westminster Press, 1960), Book IV, Chapter XIV, section 26, p. 1303. The battle lines drawn over this point in the mid-16th century between Protestants and Catholics have largely remained to the present day.

[33] See the *Scofield Reference Bible: 1917 Edition*, note on Lev. 16:6, p. 148. This distinction between the temporary "covering" of sin in the Old Testament vis-à-vis the permanent "taking away" of sin in the New Testament remained popular in dispensational treatises for many years; cf. John Feinberg, "Salvation in the Old Testament," 71-72. Cf. also Ryrie, who says, "The writer of the book of Hebrews does not say [in Heb. 10:4] that sins were not forgiven, but he says that those sacrifices were inadequate to remove absolutely and finally the spiritual guilt of a person before God" (*Dispensationalism Today*, 129). In this explanation, Ryrie seems to qualify Heb. 10:4 with the words "absolutely and finally" (i.e., "permanently"?). The reading that results, then, would be: "For it is impossible for the blood of bulls and goats to take away sins [*permanently*; implication: they *could* take away sins *temporarily*]." In this explanation, Ryrie seems to be following the classical dispensational construction.

instrumental cause(s) to Christ's meritorious provision of saving benefits (which classical dispensationalism does, in fact, seem to affirm).[34] Such a nominalist connection, likewise, would allow for a fluctuating instrumental cause, including an instrumental cause that put salvation on a legalistic, unyielding meritorious basis, as Chafer imagined the cause of salvation in the Mosaic era to be.

Seemingly unnoticed in such explanations, however, is the point that, if Old Testament sacrifices were even temporarily efficacious *ex opere operato* (or, if, to use Ryrie's words, they provided "a genuine atonement for sins . . . simply because they were offered"[35]), then the instrumental cause of salvation, in that case, would be the ceremonial law. It would not be salvation by faith (*sola fide*), but salvation by *works* of the ceremonial law. Such a construction was not consistent, however, with the revised dispensationalist demand that the requirement of salvation from dispensation to dispensation be always the same (viz., faith). Ryrie himself seems to recognize this, at least vaguely; one can detect some flinching at the prospect of

---

[34] The classical dispensationalist position, as articulated by Chafer and followed, to an extent, by Ryrie, seems to follow a nominalist logic similar to that of late medieval theologians; for further explication of medieval nominalism, see the very helpful article by Heiko Oberman, "Some Notes on the Theology of Nominalism, with Attention to its Relation to the Renaissance," *Harvard Theological Review* 53 (1960): 47-76; also Paul Vignaux, *Nominalisme au XIVe Siècle* (Paris: Librairie Armand Colin, 1948). That is, for Chafer and the classical dispensationalists, the "conditions" God attached to the reception of salvation's benefits were genuinely nominalist – they were not actually linked in a realist (i.e., genuinely ontological) cause-and-effect relationship. Because the connection between the receiver of atonement and the atonement provided was merely nominalistic anyway, the issue, for Chafer, "as to the precise human terms upon which men may be saved" was a "far lesser question" (Chafer, "Inventing Heretics Through Misunderstanding," 1). This could also be why "Chafer couldn't understand how anyone could think he taught two ways of salvation" even though he "contributed to this confusion" (John F. Walvoord, interview by the author, Dallas, Texas, 18 April 1995). This nominalist understanding of the terms of salvation seems to be what Chafer is asserting (via *ignoratio elenchi*) when he says, "The colossal error which supplies any point to the contention of those who accuse others of believing that there are two ways by which the lost may be saved is just this, that neither works nor faith of themselves can ever save anyone. It is God's undertaking and always on the ground, not of works or faith, but on the blood of Christ" (ibid).

The Westminster Standards do not explicitly address the points at issue between nominalists and realists (or those whom Heiko Oberman calls "ontologists"), but the direction of its covenant theology seems more in line with realism than with nominalism. The AIC, for its part, surfaced some of this in a footnote in the 1943 Report (see 124, n. 7), but dropped it from the 1944 Report; perhaps it was just too arcane and philosophical. Some implications of the point were surfaced by committee member, James Bear, outside the Report ("Dispensationalism and the Covenant of Grace," 298-99, 302-05; *idem*, "The Presbyterian Standards vs. The Scofield Bible, Part II," *Presbyterian of the South* 116 [26 March 1941]: 5). Likewise, committee chairman, Felix B. Gear, briefly addressed this point as well, in "The Covenants," and "Covenant Theology" in "Theology 303 Course Notes," in Felix B. Gear Papers, Presbyterian Historical Society, Montreat, NC. Gear also says, partly in reference to this point perhaps, that dispensationalism "has its own metaphysics," ("Lecture IV: Dispensationalism and Historic Christianity," transcript, 1945, Felix B. Gear papers, Presbyterian Historical Society, Montreat, NC).

[35] Ryrie, *Dispensationalism Today*, 128.

bringing his argument to its full conclusion when he says: "the offerings . . . could point a believing worshiper to a better sacrifice which would deal finally with the entire sin question. This might be called an ulterior efficacy in the sacrifices which did not belong to them as sacrifices but as prefigurations of a final dealing with sin."[36] We see the "wrinkles," apparent in such vacillations, therefore gradually being ironed out in dispensationalism, as Ryrie and other dispensational writers contemplate the implications of the requirement of salvation in every dispensation being *sola fide*.[37]

---

[36] Ibid., 129.

[37] In fact, Ryrie's own development on this point is extremely instructive. In *Dispensationalism Today*, Ryrie declares: "Unquestionably the Old Testament does ascribe efficacy to the sacrifices. Again and again the Scriptures declare that when the sacrifices were offered according to the law 'it shall be accepted for him to make an atonement for him' (Lev.1:4; 4:26-31; 16:20-22). In none of these passages is there any indication that the effectiveness of the sacrifices depended on the spiritual state of the person offering them. Neither do the Scriptures imply that the offerer had to have some glimmer of understanding of the prefigurative purpose of these sacrifices for them to be effective for him. The face value interpretation of these passages assigns a genuine atonement for sins to the sacrifices simply because they were offered" (127-28). As we have observed, Ryrie was the key figure in refining classical dispensationalism and revising its "two ways of salvation" construction. Concerning the efficacy of the OT animal sacrifices, however, vestiges of the older construction seem to remain.

Even in this explanation in *Dispensationalism Today*, development can be detected, however. Ryrie has moved some from the position he had articulated in *The Grace of God* (Chicago, IL: Moody Press, 1963), in which he had said, "Although any individual Israelite could be related to God directly, all were related theocratically. Thus the sacrifices which were brought were efficacious in restoring the offender to his forfeited position as a Jewish worshiper and in thus reconciling him to God as Head of the theocracy. . . . To sum up: the sacrificial system did have a particularized efficacy in restoring the offerer automatically [*ex opere operato?*] to his theocratic governmental privileges" (121). In *Dispensationalism Today*, Ryrie revises this explanation in two ways: first, he expands the distinction between the theocratic position of the Israelite and the *spiritual* position of the Israelite: "Under the law the individual Israelite by birth was related to God through the theocratic state. He sustained this relationship regardless of his spiritual state . . . All Israelites were related to God theocratically; some were also related spiritually. The bringing of the sacrifices restored the offender to his forfeited position as a Jewish worshiper and restored his theocratic relationship" (128). This refined position presumably would leave room for the suggestion that the sacrifices restored the offender to a right theocratic state *ex opere operato*, but to a right spiritual state only through faith. Significantly, however, Ryrie never explicitly draws this conclusion – neither in *Dispensationalism Today*, nor in the updated (1995) edition, *Dispensationalism*. His position as stated here, therefore, is as far as Ryrie ever goes. Secondly, though Ryrie *does* preserve the "simply because they were offered" language concerning what level of faith and understanding was required of the Israelite for the sacrifices to be efficacious, and though he does not explicitly deny that the efficacy of the sacrifices in restoring the *theocratic* relationship of the Israelite was "automatic," he does explicitly deny such "automatic" efficacy in regard to restoring the Israelite's *spiritual* relationship: "[T]hose sacrifices were inadequate to remove absolutely and finally the spiritual guilt of a person before God. This was done only by the death of Christ and not by Levitical offerings. The offerings themselves could not automatically effect spiritual salvation" (*Dispensationalism Today*, 129).

In the final analysis, what we observe is that Ryrie's earlier works manifest the earlier

In *Dispensationalism* (1995), as in *Dispensationalism Today* (1965), Ryrie suggests that the problem of the efficacy of Old Testament sacrifices might be solved with a distinction between eternal life and temporal life under the Law. "Therefore, it is entirely harmonious to say that the means of eternal salvation was by grace and that the means of temporal life was by law. . . . This has to be the case, contradictory as it may seem to some. The law could not save, and yet the law was the revelation of God for that time."[38] This revises Chafer, in that Chafer suggested that extended "temporal life" (on the "new earth") was all the "earthly people" (Israelites) could hope for.[39] Dispensationalists before Ryrie had suggested other refinements of Chafer's construction, which Ryrie seems to build upon; e.g., that the *sacrifices* (considered "ceremonial law" by covenant theologians) should not be considered "law" at all.[40] This made for a mediating position, albeit a somewhat unstable one perhaps, between Chaferian classical dispensationalism and covenant theology.

Thus, Chafer's construction was clearly being refined by essentialist dispensationalists, which refinements would in turn be refined by later dispensationalists.[41] In other words, in the case of at least some dispensationalists, there was throughout the twentieth century a gradual but unmistakable movement away from a sharp dispensational contrast between Mosaic-Age Law and Church-Age grace through faith, and toward a construction that, like covenant theology, acknowledged a difference in the way salvation by grace *sola fide* was administered, but that nevertheless insisted that salvation, in any age, is *sola gratia, sola fide, soli Christo*. Likewise, the number of qualifications and clarifications of

---

(i.e., classical) dispensationalist construction, while his later works demonstrate a more "revised dispensationalist" understanding. The revisions in his own works would actually make his own position more consistent with the soteriological framing he himself had articulated (i.e., the basis of salvation, requirement of salvation, object of faith, content of faith framing).

[38] Ryrie, *Dispensationalism*, 117.

[39] See Chafer, *Grace*, 152-243.

[40] E.g., see Alva J. McClain's explanation: "1. Hypothetically, the law could give life if men kept it. . . . 2. But this keeping of the law had to be perfect. . . . Furthermore, this perfection of obedience included the inward attitude as well as the outward act, the thought as well as the deed (Matt. 5:28). The question has been raised: Did not the law provide for failure to keep it? The answer is: Yes, in a certain sense, through the ritual of animal sacrifice. But here we must be careful to remember two things: First, the smallest failure meant that the law was broken. Second, the blood of animal sacrifices could never take away sins. The sacrifice prescribed by the law did indeed bear witness to a way of salvation, but that way was wholly outside and apart from all law (Rom. 3:21). 3. Certainly no man (Christ excepted) ever kept the law in a complete sense. . . . 4. Actually, then, the law can save no sinner" (*Law and Grace* [Winona Lake, IN: BMH Books, 1954], 17-18).

[41] E.g., Allen P. Ross, "The Biblical Method of Salvation: A Case for Discontinuity," in *Continuity and Discontinuity: Perspectives on the Relationship Between the Old and New Testaments: Essays in Honor of S. Lewis Johnson, Jr.*, ed. John S. Feinberg (Westchester, IL: Crossway Books, 1988), 161-78. Ross agrees with Ryrie that the content of faith increases from dispensation to dispensation, but Ross also insists that salvation (temporal or eternal) is ultimately always grounded in faith alone. Similarly, see Ken Barker, "False Dichotomies Between the Testaments," 6-10.

this point by these dispensationalists seemed over time to decrease – gradually, circumspectly perhaps, but no less unremittingly.

The classical dispensational view of the temporary, *ex opere operato* efficacy of animal sacrifices eventually gave way, in the revised dispensationalist era, to a construction that made offering animal sacrifices an expression of the individual Israelite's faith in God's mercy, which faith, so expressed, was the actual instrumental cause of salvation.[42] This revision did not make the dispensational soteriological construction of the Mosaic-age identical with the traditional covenantalist construction, perhaps, but it certainly made the two views much more compatible. Meanwhile, by focusing attention on the "content of faith" question, Ryrie and the essentialist dispensationalists focused the point of discussion on an aspect of covenant theology that was ambiguous.

Some covenant theologians had, it seems, been loathe to admit any distinction in the degree of understanding required for saving faith to be effective for the one being saved in Old Testament times.[43] Some covenant theologians would even "take the bait" Ryrie offered in his framing of issues in *Dispensationalism Today*, and engage dispensationalism at this point, as though willingness or unwillingness to acknowledge an increase in understanding within saving faith was, indeed, the foundational point of difference between them.[44]

In truth, however, there had never been unanimity demanded by covenant theologians on this point.[45] In any case, before Ryrie focused the discussion here, covenant theologians had not forwarded *this* point against dispensationalism as the foundational area of disagreement between the two theological systems.

Significant implications of this point may be readily observed in the dialogical work that was the *Festschrift* for S. Lewis Johnson: *Continuity and Discontinuity: Perspectives on the Relationship Between the Old and New Testaments*.[46] This was

---

[42] The first clear dispensationalist affirmation of this construction seems to have been set forth by Hobart E. Freeman, "The Problem of the Efficacy of the Old Testament Sacrifices," *GTJ* 4 (January 1963): 21-28.

[43] E.g., Charles Hodge: "It was not mere faith or trust in God, or simple piety, which was required, but faith in the promised Redeemer, or faith in the promise of redemption through the Messiah" (*Systematic Theology, Volume II* [London: Nelson, 1872], 368.)

[44] E.g., John Gerstner, *Wrongly Dividing the Word of Truth* (Brentwood, TN: Wolgemuth & Hyatt, 1991), 161-64; Curt Daniel, *The History and Theology of Calvinism* (Dallas, TX: Scholarly Reprints, 1993), 63-64.

[45] E.g., J. Barton Payne states, "That, to satisfy God, God must die, that men might inherit God, to be with God, was incomprehensible under the Old Testament seminal knowledge of the Trinity, the incarnation, and the crucifixion followed by the resurrection" (*An Outline of Hebrew History* [Grand Rapids: Baker, 1954], 222). Ryrie quotes Payne as demonstrating an "obvious fallacy" in covenant theology (*Dispensationalism Today*, 123), since Payne, as a covenant theologian, cannot possibly believe (in Ryrie's understanding of covenant theology) that the "content of faith" could increase from Old Testament to New Testament. In truth, the problem is not in Payne's nuance, but in Ryrie's portrayal of covenant theology; covenant theology does not *inherently* preclude the content of faith changing from Old Testament to New Testament, even though Ryrie is correct in his pointing out that *some* covenant theologians historically have taken that stance.

[46] Edited by John S. Feinberg (Westchester, IL: Crossway Books, 1988).

the first published forum (1988) of a discussion between dispensationalists and covenant theologians that did not have an explicitly polemical purpose. In this set of essays, writers spoke *to* one another, rather than against (and around) each other.

In his essay on the continuity of salvation from Old Testament to New Testament, covenantalist Fred H. Klooster seems genuinely puzzled by the dispensational insistence that increase in the content of faith is what distinguishes their system from his. Regarding how much understanding was required of Old Testament saints, Klooster says, "That sounds like an altered version of the now famous questions: 'What did he know? And when did he know it?' This is a difficult question to answer."[47]

Klooster recognizes that "Ryrie and [John] Feinberg ["Salvation in the Old Testament"] argue that covenant theologians overestimate Adam and Eve's personal understanding"[48] (as well as the understanding of other Old Testament saints), and that dispensationalists try to make this the crucial point of difference between dispensationalism and covenant theology. Yet, Klooster muses,

> Could they [Adam and Eve, et al.] understand the mother promise as a clear pointer to Jesus of Nazareth? Of course not, and I doubt that any covenant theologian ever meant that. Scripture is undoubtedly an inspired selection from a much fuller original revelation, but our knowledge of this early history is limited to what Scripture reveals. When God clothed our first parents with garments of skin ([Gen.] 3:21), he may have introduced animal sacrifice, but we do not really know. When at the birth of Cain Eve said, "With the help of the LORD I have brought forth a man" (4:1), she may have had God's gracious promise of Gen 3:15 in mind, but we cannot be sure. The details of their personal knowledge are not revealed to us. Unless Scripture provides specific clues, we can never know how much understanding a particular believer had. Perhaps we tend to underestimate what OT believers understood . . . On the other hand, one is shocked at how little Peter understood of his revelationally given confession of Jesus as the Christ (Matt 16:13-28).[49]

If Klooster's response is paradigmatic (as I am inclined to think it is), then Ryrie had focused attention on a point of ambiguity in covenant theology, but he had not focused on what was really the point at issue between covenant theology and dispensationalism (i.e., *ignoratio elenchi*). There was one happy outcome from this particular point of misunderstanding, though. The content of faith question turned out to be a healthy point of discussion for the two camps to consider together. As Klooster remarks:

> When I read the two Hodge quotations [which Feinberg and Ryrie had quoted] in their context, they do not appear as ambiguous to me

---

[47] Klooster, "The Biblical Method of Salvation: Continuity," 141.
[48] Ibid.
[49] Ibid., 141-42.

as they apparently do to Feinberg [and Ryrie]. In other words, I do not believe Hodge was referring to the revelation of the name of the Redeemer to Adam and Eve or to their knowledge of the identity of that Redeemer. Rather, I understand him to say that the Redeemer who from the beginning 'has been held up as the hope of the world' we now know to be Jesus of Nazareth, Jesus the Christ. Be that as it may, if Hodge thought Adam and Eve could or did know that the promised one was specifically Jesus of Nazareth, I would also disagree. However, Feinberg [and Ryrie] ha[ve] made a worthy contribution to the discussion which helps to avoid misunderstanding by sharply distinguishing what has been revealed and what could be known in each specific period of redemptive revelation.[50]

In this discussion, we may observe a pattern that seems common in the historical discussion between dispensationalists and covenant theologians. Somewhere, what is at issue gets altered and confused, so that the dialogue partners end up talking past one another in framing the issues of debate.

Especially once the sociological line of division between dispensationalists and covenant theologians was clearly drawn in 1944, Chafer's misunderstandings seemed to merge with Niagara fundamentalists' suspicions of non-premillennialism. Dispensationalist arguments against covenant theology consistently insinuated that dispensationalism resulted from straightforward reliance on biblical authority, while covenant (amillennial) theology resulted from liberal or semi-liberal allegorizing or spiritualizing. This highly partisan assessment[51] became the received standard for

---

[50] Ibid., 143-44.

[51] The low point in dispensationalist-covenantalist relations may have been the publication of C. Fred Lincoln's four articles that argued against covenant theology as a truly "ridiculous" system, which must "pass over" and "distort" Scripture's clear teaching in order to advance its own unbiblical notions; C. Fred Lincoln, "The Development of the Covenant Theory," *BibSac* 100 (January-March 1943): 134-61; and *idem*, "The Biblical Covenants, Parts I-III," *BibSac* 100 (April-December 1943): 309-23, 442-49, 565-73. These articles were based on Lincoln's dissertation, "The Covenants," (Th.D. diss., Dallas Theological Seminary, 1942). Lincoln repeats the charge of George N.H. Peters (*The Theocratic Kingdom of Our Lord Jesus, the Christ*, 1883, reprint ed., [Grand Rapids: Kregel, 1952], 1:47-101) (picked up by Chafer, as well) that covenant theology embraces "an artificial system of typology, and allegorizing interpretation," which violates "the historical principle" of interpretation, "the first fundamental to Bible study" ("Development of the Covenant Theory," 160). In general, Lincoln seems to regard covenant theology as not rising to even this high a level of sophistication in its errors; he seems to believe that covenant theology is espoused out of ignorance and carelessness more even than out of liberal hermeneutical presuppositions. Throughout his articles, Lincoln describes the covenantalist scheme as an "artificial and unsatisfactory" system (ibid), which "serves only to misconstrue, divert from, and bedim the real teaching of Scripture regarding the true Covenants" ("Biblical Covenants, Part I," 309), and which must resort to "ridiculous explanations" and "unsupportable inventions" ("Biblical Covenants, Part II, 444-45) to be defended. He concludes his series of articles with this indictment: "The covenant theorists nowhere give an adequate treatment of the teaching on the covenants which have here been noted. They pass over the revelation we have in the Bible on the various covenant relationships of God to the nation Israel. In lieu of that they have

understanding covenant theology by dispensationalists; in turn, dispensationalists in the post-Chaferian era seemed to grow progressively more strident in their claim that their theological system alone provided an effective defense against liberalism.[52] Ryrie's classic framing of the dispensationalist *sine qua non*, which claimed to set apart dispensationalism from covenant theology definitively, included not one point of covenant theologians' actual objections, which *they* claimed set apart covenant theology from dispensationalism.[53]

It took a while for dispensationalists to hone their hermeneutical stance into an alleged "consistent" point of differentiation from covenant theology. To do this meant that the "revised/essentialist dispensationalists" (of the Ryrie era) had to eliminate, and then distance themselves from, the elaborate typologizing employed by previous dispensationalists (such as Scofield and Chafer). In doing so, they argued that they were merely developing more consistently the ideals of the theological system they had inherited. The hermeneutic they advocated was certainly "flatter," and less inclined to recognize figures of speech; this "flatness" certainly distinguished the revised-essentialist hermeneutic from that of covenant

---

arbitrarily designated certain features of God's relationships with man by covenants of their own invention, the names of which nowhere appear in the Bible, whose doctrine is not set forth in the Word of God, and whose existence can in no sense be proved by the Scripture" ("The Biblical Covenants, Part III," 572).

[52] See John F. Walvoord, "The Theological Context of Premillennialism," *BibSac* 108 (July-September 1951): 271. Walvoord greatly expands this point in his book-length treatise, *The Millennial Kingdom* (Grand Rapids: Zondervan, 1959); in the chapter, "Amillennialism as a System of Interpretation," Walvoord gives this explanation for why the "spiritualization" hermeneutic of amillennialism is so popular: "It is not too difficult to account for the widespread approval of the spiritualizing method adopted by many conservative theologians as well as liberal and Roman Catholic expositors. Fundamentally its charm lies in its flexibility. The interpreter can change the literal and grammatical sense of Scripture to make it coincide with his own system of interpretation. The conservative and liberal and Roman Catholic can each claim that the Bible does not contradict his concept of theology. It is this very factor, however, which raises grave doubts concerning the legitimacy of a method which produces such diverse systems of interpretation" (60). See also Nickolas Kurtaneck, "Excellencies of Dispensationalism," *GTJ* 3 (January 1962): 3-11; Charles C. Ryrie, *The Basis of the Premillennial Faith* (Neptune, NJ: Loizeaux Brothers, 1953), 38-39. In a later article, Ryrie expands this point to embrace a more ambitious contention, viz., that conservative Christian belief makes dispensationalism *necessary* ("The Necessity of Dispensationalism," *BibSac* 114 [July-September 1957]: 243-54. Ryrie persisted in arguing this contention in *Dispensationalism Today*, which, for many, defined the issues in contention between dispensationalism and covenant theology. It is a position he still maintains today, not only against covenant amillennialism, but also against historic premillennialism and progressive dispensationalism (see Ryrie, *Dispensationalism*, 79-95, 161-95).

[53] Cf. Ryrie, *Dispensationalism Today*; and "The Report of the [1943] AIC" or "The Report of the [1944] AIC." Meanwhile, Chafer's successor as president, John Walvoord, has gone on record as affirming the unity of the covenant of grace ("The New Covenant," in *Integrity of Heart, Skillfulness of Hands: Biblical and Leadership Studies in Honor of Donald K. Campbell*, ed. Charles H. Dyer and Roy B. Zuck [Grand Rapids: Baker, 1994], 187-99), potentially satisfying what was covenant theologians' primary objection to "dispensationalism" in the late 1940s!

theologians, but it also distinguished them from earlier classical dispensationalists. Advocacy of this flatter, "literal" hermeneutic is also not identical to affirmation of grammatical-historical interpretation, which covenant theology also affirms.[54]

The misunderstandings provoked by these polemical hermeneutical charges and exchanges have taken years to sort through and clarify – and, even today, may not have been completely resolved. Furthermore, these misunderstandings, perhaps more than anything else, are to blame for the acrimonious level of discourse between dispensationalism and covenant theology that has characterized their relationship to the end of the twentieth century.[55]

6.2.2 By Covenant Theologians

Perhaps the greatest mistake of covenant theologians throughout the 1930s-1940s controversies was in their identifying the idiosyncrasies of C.I. Scofield's theology, which were replicated and expanded by Lewis Sperry Chafer, as an "-ism" (viz., "dispensationalism"). In truth, the distinctives of Scofield's and Chafer's theology may actually have been truly idiosyncratic. By forcing a showdown, covenant theologians may have provoked a controversy between "movements" that might have been avoided had they merely critiqued the views they found objectionable in Scofield's and Chafer's theology as a set of incorrect, but isolated, viewpoints.

What ignited the controversy seems to have been Oswald T. Allis' article, "Modern Dispensationalism and the Doctrine of the Unity of Scripture."[56] Being the first such critique to be written by so renowned a scholar, this article came to serve as something of a prototype for criticisms against "dispensationalism." Most of those who were influential in later critiques of "dispensationalism" quoted this article and employed much of its logic.[57]

One common pattern was the use of the Scofield Bible for defining what is "dispensationalism." The very title of Allis' article declares that "modern dispensationalism" is the focus of critique when, in fact, aside from one quotation,[58]

---

[54] This point is argued effectively by Vern Poythress, *Understanding Dispensationalists* (Grand Rapids: Zondervan, 1987), 19-38, 78-96.

[55] For helpful, candid analysis of the "deplorable" (his term) polemics involving "brash charges of 'allegorizing' or 'hyperliteralism'" (286) in the debate between dispensationalists and covenant theologians in the post-Chafer era, see David L. Turner, "The Continuity of Scripture and Eschatology: Key Hermeneutical Issues," *GTJ* 6 (fall 1985): 275-87.

[56] *EvQ* 8 (January 1936): 22-35; this article was followed later in the year by one like unto it, viz., "Modern Dispensationalism and the Law of God," *EvQ* 8 (September 1936): 272-89. This latter article, however, for some reason seems never to have gained the readership or influence that the first article did. The first article is quoted often in later discussions; the latter, almost never (see below).

[57] E.g., see the contribution of this article by Allis to the influential articles of John Murray, "The Reformed Faith and Modern Substitutes, Part VI: Modern Dispensationalism," *PrGuard* 2 (18 May 1936): 78, n. 3; and Bear, "Dispensationalism and the Covenant of Grace," 290, n. 12.

[58] This quotation was of Isaac M. Haldeman's *How to Study the Bible* (New York: Charles C. Cook, 1904), pp. 135, 140.

only the Scofield Reference Bible (with one cross reference to Scofield's book, *Rightly Dividing the Word of Truth*) is actually cited. No other dispensational authors are ever even mentioned in either of Allis' articles against "Modern Dispensationalism."[59]

A phenomenon seems to have begun here that would become more problematic as time went on. At first, covenantalist critics of dispensationalists seemed to recognize that, while the Scofield Bible represented *a* dispensational viewpoint, it did not represent exhaustively or consistently the views of *all* "dispensationalists."[60] Gradually, however, frustration seemed to grow with trying to distinguish where the views represented by Scofield were distinct and where they represented the standard, shared views of most all dispensationalists. Thus, more and more, covenant theologians seemed satisfied simply to shrug off exceptions and use the Scofield Bible as the *de facto* confessional standard of dispensationalists.

Doubtless, such covenant theologians saw the influence of the Scofield Bible and the degree of problematic implications as sufficient warrant to take such an approach. The great problem with this, though, is that, even among self-described "dispensationalists," those taking "exceptions" to Scofield's teachings may actually have outnumbered those who did not – recall Allan A. MacRae's remark, "Never have I met a man who said that he held the un-Biblical [Scofieldian] views which are attacked."[61]

In the end, no one really knows who was right about what "the majority of dispensationalists" believed in the late 1930s. We do know, however, that there were more exceptions than was allowed by critiques which simply equated dispensationalism with the Scofield notes.[62] A significant misunderstanding, therefore, was fostered by this common practice among covenant theologians.

One might ask what exactly is wrong with a committee such as the AIC using a term such as "dispensationalism" as short-hand for views under critique, so long as it is clearly defined. After all, the conclusion of the AIC's report clearly states, "It is the unanimous opinion of your Committee that Dispensationalism *as defined and*

---

[59] We should acknowledge that Allis' framing of issues was not as misleading as it could have been. Sprinkled throughout his article are clarifications such as the following: "Dispensationalists differ as to the number and extent of these dispensations" (Allis, "Modern Dispensationalism and the Doctrine of the Unity of Scripture," 24). "This will sound like a gross misrepresentation to many dispensationalists" (Ibid., 34). "In what has been said above the writer has been speaking of consistent Dispensationalism and its implications, and has appealed especially to the express statements of the *Scofield Bible*. Fortunately the Dispensationalists are not thoroughly consistent. Doubtless many of the Dispensationalists who read this article, if they do read it, will say that they do not draw these conclusions. The reason the *Scofield Bible* is such an extremely difficult book to understand is because the attempt to avoid the logical implications of a consistent dispensationalism makes it at many points a jumble of inconsistencies and contradictions" (Allis, "Modern Dispensationalism and the Doctrine of the Unity of Scripture," 35).

[60] Ibid.

[61] Allan A. MacRae, "Dr. Allan A. MacRae Resigns Seminary," 2.

[62] E.g., James Bear, "The Presbyterian Standards vs. The Scofield Bible, Parts I-VI" *PrSouth* 116 (1941) and *idem*, "Dispensationalism, Parts I-II," *PrOut* 118 (1944).

set forth above is out of accord with the system of the doctrine set forth in the Confession of Faith."[63]

The problem is not a lack of clarity, but the implied all-or-nothing nature of the terminology. Such terminology could even be perceived as an ultimatum by those who believed, like Wilbur Smith, "that the Scofield Bible is right more times than it is wrong."[64] Such persons as Smith were then very nearly limited to a choice between: 1) distancing themselves completely from a set of doctrines with which, despite minor disagreements here and there, they were in agreement overall; or 2) being placed, via guilt-by-association, into a "camp," with the assumption being that they held to specific views that they did not hold, but which nonetheless had been linked to them, by definition, given the label attached to their "camp."

We might wonder, too, exactly what James Bear meant, for instance, or how extensive had been his research, when he claimed that "many Premillenarians today refuse to be classified as Dispensationalists."[65] In truth, *no one* was willing to be "classified as a Dispensationalist" before 1936 – it was a derogatory term coined by Philip Mauro.[66] Rollin Chafer objected to usage of the term entirely early in 1936;[67] later that year, his brother Lewis agreed to "suffer" the term only "reluctantly," in order that the issue under "discussion may be identified in its relation to various articles others have written on this theme."[68] With this in mind, Rollin's response to Bear's claim seems appropriate:

> It seems to me to be significant that the vast majority of those who have repeated the very questionable statement that there are *many* Premillenarians who refuse to be classed as Dispensationalists, have been Amillennial writers. Where are these "many" persons? Where do they live and flourish? What literature have they produced? How does it come that they themselves are not more vocal and that Amillennial writers are their spokesmen?[69]

Rollin Chafer's point is made even sharper once it be recognized that some of the very premillennialists who did balk at the label "dispensationalist," and who

---

[63] "The Report of the [1944] AIC," 126 (emphasis added).
[64] Wilbur Smith, "Israel and the Church in Prophecy, Part I: A review of an important book written to refute some teachings of dispensationalism," *SSTimes* 87 (24 November 1945): 927.
[65] Bear, "Dispensationalism and the Covenant of Grace," 286. No sources are cited in substantiation of this claim.
[66] Philip Mauro, *The Gospel of the Kingdom with an Examination of Modern Dispensationalism* (Boston, MA: Hamilton Brothers, 1928).
[67] Rollin Thomas Chafer, "'Modern' Dispensationalism," *BibSac* 93 (Jan.-March 1936): 129-30.
[68] "Author's Note: (a) The title of this thesis has been chosen reluctantly. It is not intended by it to imply that those who hold what are here set forth as dispensational beliefs are abnormal or disproportionate in doctrine. This thesis purports to demonstrate that so-called Dispensationalists find the specific meaning of the Scriptures which God intended to impart and are, therefore, by the most exacting proofs found to be both reasonable and normal in their interpretations. This title is suffered only that this discussion may be identified in its relation to various articles others have written on this theme" (Chafer, "Dispensationalism," 390).
[69] Rollin Thomas Chafer, "'Dispensationally-Colored Premillennialism,'" *BibSac* 95 (1938): 257.

published their reservations,[70] were classified by Bear as "dispensationalists" anyway.[71]

Bear's unsubstantiated generalization is just one of many that we have observed were submitted by both sides, all along the way. As a counterpart to Bear on the dispensationalist side, we recall Lewis Chafer's claim that his dispensational view was held by the "great mass" of premillennialist Bible expositors "throughout the world."[72]

It is doubtful that anyone was being deliberately misleading. People naturally relate to their own circles of fellowship; in this case, all concerned seem to be simply assuming that their own experience is the "common," "normal" one – it is those outside of one's own experience that form the "exceptions." What this does for us, in historical hindsight, however, is make it difficult to discern where the lines of demarcation between exponents of various positions really were.

I suggest that misimpressions over "lines of demarcation" were exacerbated, if not actually caused, by misunderstandings that originated from covenantalists' insistence on defining "dispensationalism" in terms of the peculiar viewpoints of the Scofield Bible. Had covenantalist critics of the Scofield Bible simply limited the focus of their critiques to the individual viewpoints of certain dispensationalist writers or even to the popular Scofield Bible itself – which popularity seems to have made its "errors" fair game as a target of such criticisms – then perhaps premillennialists in disagreement with those same notes might not have been so insistent on qualifying their dissent with general defenses of Scofield's theology.

Instead, as it happened, covenant theologians seemed repeatedly to engage in bombastic criticism of the "movement" allegedly joined by those who found the Scofield Bible useful. Perhaps covenant theologians were actually projecting their own creedal mentality onto the much more doctrinally diverse affiliation of persons that would come to be known as "dispensationalist." Mistaking the Scofield notes as a *de facto* confessional statement of dispensationalist theology seemed to preclude the covenantalist critics from seeing the wide diversity of "dispensationalist" views. This meant that their critiques took on a "take-no-prisoners" sort of tone, which polarized parties in the debate and alienated those who affirmed mediating positions. Further, this tactic may have provoked a backlash among those who affirmed (Scofieldian) *premillennialism* or who were personally loyal to Chafer (even among those in this group who may actually have disagreed with his views).

Some of these "dispensationalists" would themselves eventually come to remove and renounce the very notes in the Scofield Bible that covenant theologians found so offensive.[73] Every single one of the points at issue against so-called

---

[70] We have in mind, particularly, J. Oliver Buswell, Jr., "A Premillennialist's View," and Allan A. MacRae, "Dr. Allan A. MacRae Resigns Seminary: Founder of Westminster Opposes Present Stand," *CBeac* 2 (29 April 1937): 1-2, 8.

[71] E.g., see Bear, "Dispensationalism and the Covenant of Grace," 285-307; *idem*, "Shall We Revise the Standards?," 3-4; *idem*, "Premillenarians and Our Church Standards," 4-6; *idem*, "Historic Premillennialism," 193-222.

[72] Chafer, "Dispensational Distinctions Challenged," 341.

[73] Cf. the changes in the notes on Gen. 15:18; Ex. 19:1, 5, 6, 9; John 1:17; and Gal. 3:19 from *The*

"dispensationalism" in the 1930s-1940s debate was quietly retracted by these "dispensationalists" in the 1950s-1960s.[74] This makes one wonder how differently things might have turned out if only the critics of dispensationalism had used a kinder, gentler means of engagement.

The sweeping attack on "dispensationalism" enabled both the PCUS and the OPC to eject anti-Confessional views from their respective denominations; however, because so little allowance was made for mediating positions, this removal was accomplished in a manner less like a surgical excision than as a bludgeoning gouge. True, "anti-Confessional," "heretical" "dispensationalist" views[75] were successfully removed, but completely innocuous, Reformed, Confessionally-consistent views and persons were also ripped out right along with them. In historical hindsight, we see that this did not have to be. We can see that mediating views did exist even at the time, but were marginalized or ignored by the way the issues were framed from the beginning.[76]

Scofield Reference Bible (1917) to *The New Scofield Reference Bible* (1967). See also the survey of differences between the "Old Scofield" Bible and the "New Scofield" Bible by Herbert W. Bateman IV, "Dispensationalism Yesterday and Today," in *Three Central Views in Contemporary Dispensationalism* (Grand Rapids: Kregel, 1999), 21-34. Cf. also English, "The New Scofield Reference Bible," 130.

[74] By 1964, even such an avid dispensationalist as W.W. Barndollar was willing to call some of Scofield's more stridently dispensationalist notes (e.g., the note on John 1:17) a "slip of the pen" (*The Validity of Dispensationalism* [Johnson City, NY: Baptist Bible Seminary Press, 1964], 6-7). In addition to the changes of notes from the "Old Scofield" Bible to the "New Scofield" Bible, see John Walvoord's 1974 revisions of Lewis Sperry Chafer, *Major Bible Themes* (Grand Rapids: Zondervan, 1926). Chafer's antinomian sounding explanations were greatly qualified, and sometimes completely reversed, by later dispensationalists. Roy L. Aldrich began a series of articles on the law in 1955, which apparently he wrote to set apart dispensationalism from covenant theology on the proper role of the law. He ended up, however, arguing that their dispute had been mostly a misunderstanding. See Roy L. Aldrich, "An Apologetic for Dispensationalism," *BibSac* 112 (January-March 1955): 46-54; idem, "Causes for Confusion of Law and Grace," *BibSac* 116 (April-June 1959): 221-29; idem, "Has the Mosaic Law Been Abolished?" *BibSac* 116 (July-September 1959): 322-35; idem, "An Outline Study on Dispensationalism," *BibSac* 118 (January-March 1961): 133-41; idem, "The Mosaic Ten Commandments Compared to Their Restatements in the New Testament," *BibSac* 118 (April-June 1961): 251-58; idem, "A New Look at Dispensationalism," *BibSac* 120 (January-March 1963): 42-49. Cf. also George Cowan, "The Prohibitions of Grace," *BibSac* 103 (April-June 1946): 223-26; idem, "The Prohibitions of Grace [Part II]," *BibSac* 103 (July-September 1946): 363-75; idem, "The Prohibitions of Grace [Part III]," *BibSac* 103 (October-December 1946): 464-76; Hoyt Chester Woodring, Jr., "Grace Under the Mosaic Covenant" (Th.D. diss., Dallas Theological Seminary, 1956); and J. Dwight Pentecost, "The Purpose of the Law," *BibSac* 128 (April-June 1971): 228-29. And, as we have already observed, above, dispensationalists also made some adjustments in the Chafer-Scofield theology on Old Testament salvation, particularly as concerns the efficacy of animal sacrifices in that dispensation (see Freeman, "The Problem of the Efficacy of the Old Testament Sacrifices," 21-28; Feinberg, "Salvation in the Old Testament,", 39-77; and Ross, "The Biblical Method of Salvation: A Case for Discontinuity," 161-78.

[75] We are here using the terminology employed by John Murray, in his three-part series of articles entitled, "The Reformed Faith and Modern Substitutes: Modern Dispensationalism."

[76] We still must be careful not to overstate how thoroughly is dispensationalism, even today,

We also might well wonder what might have happened if Chafer had been allowed to present his positions to the AIC, as he requested. The response of the PCUS generally seems to have been to note his complaint, but not to be convinced or moved by its contention.[77] Even Chafer was willing to admit of some variegation within "dispensationalism" and of some idiosyncrasy in the particular conclusions he reached.[78] His repeatedly being refused the opportunity to appear before the

---

characterized by such mediating positions. There are strands of dispensationalism that insist today, every bit as stridently as Chafer did, that New Testament grace must consistently be set in sharp, antinomian contrast to Old Testament law in order to do justice to Pauline language and to remain faithful to a proper, traditional dispensationalist conception of this teaching. The most prominent representatives of this position are Zane Hodges and the members of the "Free Grace Society," which Hodges founded; see Zane Hodges, *The Gospel Under Siege* (Dallas, TX: Rendencion Viva, 1981); idem, *Absolutely Free!: A Biblical Reply to Lordship Salvation* (Grand Rapids: Zondervan, 1989). *Idem*, "Calvinism Ex Cathedra: A Review of John H. Gerstner's *Wrongly Dividing the Word of Truth: A Critique of Dispensationalism,*" *Journal of the Grace Evangelical Society* 104 (autumn, 1991): 69. In the conclusion of this last article, Hodges laments what the book he is reviewing had applauded: "Gerstner is correct in perceiving a theological drift by some dispensationalists in the direction of Reformed thought. Dallas Seminary is his major illustration of this . . . " (69). The "Lordship salvation" debate, a debate that is largely an *intra-dispensationalist* debate, may be viewed as a disagreement between those dispensationalists who have come to affirm a more mediating position, and those dispensationalists who are thoroughly satisfied with classical dispensationalism's original, total separation of Old Testament and New Testament salvation.

[77] See "Dr. Chafer Protests '44 Assembly Action: Says Dispensationalism Biblical; Distinction from Pre's 'Fantastic'," *PrOut* 118 (4 October 1944): 3-4. E.C. Scott, stated clerk of the PCUS General Assembly, responded to Chafer's formal complaint of the Assembly's action, as follows: "Dear Dr. Chafer: Your communication to the General Assembly was presented to that body and referred to the Standing Committee on Bills and Overtures. I quote in full the action of the General Assembly in reply: 'Careful and prayerful consideration has been given to Dr. L.S. Chafer's protest against the statement found in the report of the Ad Interim Committee on "Dispensationalism and the Confession of Faith." The Assembly is unable to see that Dr. Chafer's teachings have been misrepresented. It therefore is unwilling to rescind the statement or suppress the literature containing the same.' Very cordially yours, E.C. Scott, Stated Clerk."; letter, E.C. Scott to Lewis Sperry Chafer, 5 June 1945, Lewis Sperry Chafer papers, ADTS. Cf. "Report of the [1944] AIC," 126, which stated, "As Dr. Chafer clearly recognizes, there are two schools of interpretation represented here, which he rightly designates as 'Covenantism' as over against 'Dispensationalism.' (*Bibliotheca Sacra*, Vol. 100, No. 399, [i.e., "Dispensational Distinctions Challenged," 1943], p. 338.) In fact, the divergence of Dispensationalism from the Covenant Theology of our Church is so obvious to Dr. Chafer that he suggests a revision of the Standards of the Church so as to make room for those who no longer hold to the Reformed tradition of a Covenant Theology. (*Ibid.*, p. 345)." Apparently the committee concluded that, since he had publicly conceded this point already, allowing Chafer to appear personally before either the AIC or the GA to defend his views would be unnecessary, unhelpful, and unwise.

[78] E.g., to Buswell he wrote, "Our graduates are not characterized by disproportions or errors in doctrine. No peculiar dispensational doctrines are taught in this Seminary [i.e., Dallas Theological Seminary]. When the question is a mooted one the student is given full liberty to decide the issues and follow the course which seems best to him. . . . There is evidently a difference of opinion as to what the human terms [of salvation] may have been in past ages, but this is certainly a very minor issue and does not justify statements which create the impression

committee not only miffed him, but gave Chafer legitimate grounds for claiming that he had been misrepresented.

Chafer did, after all, seem to vacillate at times on some of the questions at issue (e.g., at one point claiming that human merit was the real test for salvation in the dispensation of Law, at another point claiming that the human merit test was really a foil, designed to drive men to faith in God's mercy as represented typically in the animal sacrifices[79]). Privately, he was willing to concede that he had not fully drawn out the implications of his theology for salvation in the Old Testament.[80] Perhaps Chafer genuinely believed that personal dialogue on the issue would clarify the question at issue in the minds of all concerned.[81]

At any rate, Chafer was technically correct to point out that the PCUS Committee had quoted only a portion (even if it was the predominant portion) of what he had said on the issues in dispute. Chafer may have sensationalized how great was the Committee's level of misunderstanding; he may have exaggerated how extensive was their misconstrual of his position.[82] Nevertheless, it does seem that they left themselves open to such objections when they refused Chafer the opportunity to defend himself. Moreover, their report did leave out a portion of what Chafer had said on the issue in question – the very portion that might have allayed

---

that I am heretical if, after forty years of careful research, I have come to certain Biblical conclusions on these matters" (letter, Lewis Sperry Chafer to J. Oliver Buswell, 8 May 1937, Lewis Sperry Chafer Papers, ADTS).

[79] Cf. the following sections in Lewis Sperry Chafer, *Grace* (Grand Rapids: Zondervan, 1922), 25-26, 42-43, 113-14, 195, 215, 222-23, 232-43. Cf. also letter, Lewis Sperry Chafer to Charles Trumbull, 30 March 1937, Lewis Sperry Chafer Papers, ADTS.

[80] Letter, Lewis Sperry Chafer to Charles Trumbull, 30 March 1937, Lewis Sperry Chafer Papers, ADTS.

[81] Interesting in this regard is J. Dwight Pentecost's recollection of the investigation of Lewis Sperry Chafer's views by the Presbytery of Dallas in 1940. Pentecost, then a young student of Chafer's, accompanied him to the meeting where Chafer was brought before the Dallas Presbytery for questioning. According to Pentecost, the presbyters "asked Dr. Chafer a few 'doctrinalish' questions (they seemed [doctrinally] illiterate) and then gave him the floor. . . . Dr. Chafer developed the doctrine of grace and brought in his 'pet subjects,' propitiation and reconciliation and so on. By the end, they were in stunned silence. It seemed like they didn't want to make *any* decision [on the matter]. . . . So, they 'took it [Chafer's explanation] under advisement' and concluded that his views were within the broad bounds of the Westminster Confession" (J. Dwight Pentecost, interview by the author, 31 May 1995, Dallas, TX). Chafer, apparently, could be very compelling when allowed to define his own terms and frame the issues as he saw fit. He might well have believed that, were he given the chance to appear personally, he could render the PCUS General Assembly in "stunned silence," just as he had done with the presbytery who had investigated his views four years earlier. The PCUS Committee might also have feared such an eventuality.

[82] See Chafer, "Dispensational Distinctions Denounced," 258-59; *idem*, "Inventing Heretics Through Misunderstanding," *BibSac* 102 (January-March 1945): 1-5; "Dr. Chafer Protests '44 Assembly Action,'" 3-4; letter, Lewis Sperry Chafer to E.C. Scott, D. D., Stated Clerk, 11 June 1945; letter, E.C. Scott to Lewis Sperry Chafer, 5 June 1945; letter, E.C. Scott to Lewis Sperry Chafer, 23 May 1945; letter, Lewis Sperry Chafer to the General Assembly of the Presbyterian Church, U.S. c/o Rev. E.C. Scott, D.D., Clerk, 19 May 1945; all in Lewis Sperry Chafer papers, ADTS.

the most objectionable aspects of his teaching upon which their charges against him focused. Thus, on this point, Chafer's objection seems legitimate.[83]

Finally, we may observe a problem with how sweeping was the covenant theologians' attack on "dispensationalism" alongside their insistence that the legitimacy of "Reformed premillennialism" was unaffected. Specifically, it is unclear what exactly is in mind in Bear's objection to "the distinction the Dispensationalists make between the various dispensations" or "between Israel and the Church"[84] (which affected both the 1943 and the 1944 AIC reports). The impression was sometimes created that drawing *any* distinction between dispensations, or between the Old Testament people of God (i.e., what dispensationalist call "Israel") and the New Testament people of God (i.e., what dispensationalists call "the Church") is inherently dangerous, and potentially anti-confessional.

The 1943 AIC Report seems to have relied most heavily on Bear's framing of this point. The 1944 committee, which had three premillennialists on it, corrected some of the imprecision of Bear's framing, but, intriguingly, did not eliminate potential problems on this point entirely. While the 1944 report was emphatic that it was not objecting to premillennialism *per se*, its final objection to dispensationalism was as follows:

> Dispensationalism teaches a series of resurrections and judgments, spaced over more than a thousand years. It is the opinion of your Committee that the above statement of the Confession of Faith [i.e., "At the last day, such as are found alive shall not die, but be changed; and all the dead shall be raised up with the self-same bodies, . . . "; also quotes from the *Larger Catechism*, question 88] does not admit of a multiplicity of resurrections and judgments as taught by many Dispensationalists.[85]

We will not re-surface the discussion of whether the Westminster Confession precludes a premillennial eschatology. That was *not* a question entertained by the PCUS committee, who emphatically insisted that its report did not constitute "in any sense a criticism of Premillennialism as such."[86]

---

[83] We should point out, however, that, in the end, Chafer's supporters seemed reluctant, as well, to encourage further "personal dialogue." Having been denied the opportunity to appear personally before the 1944 General Assembly to give his rebuttal to the Committee Report, Chafer sent a letter to be read to the Assembly by representatives who supported him. "On the advice of other dispensationalists at the meeting, [Graham] Gilmer withheld Chafer's letter. He explained, 'I showed your letter to several of the brethren who agree with us, but they thought it best not to read it to the Assembly and felt that the whole matter would quiet down more quickly if it were let alone'" (Glass, "Northern Patterns of Fundamentalism in the South," 245-46, quoting a letter from Graham Gilmer to Lewis Sperry Chafer, 1 June 1944, in the Lewis Sperry Chafer papers, ADTS).

[84] Bear, "Dispensationalism and the Covenant of Grace," 286.

[85] "Report of the [1944] Ad Interim Committee," 126.

[86] We are quoting, actually, from the very last words of the 1944 Committee report (p. 127).

The concern here is how a premillennial view is allowed if "a multiplicity of resurrections" be disallowed. I know of no premillennial view that is not built in large part upon Revelation 20:4-5:

> And I saw souls of those who had been beheaded because of the testimony of Jesus and because of the Word of God, and those who had not worshiped the beast or his image, and had not received the mark upon their forehead and upon their hand; and they came to life and reigned with Christ for a thousand years. The rest of the dead did not come to life until the thousand years were completed. This is the first resurrection.

Put simply, "premillennialism as such" is intrinsically built on the idea that Rev. 20:4-5 teaches a "multiplicity of resurrections," two resurrections, at the very least. How could the PCUS report *deny* that its doctrinal standards preclude a premillennial view, but at the same time *insist* that these standards do preclude the view that affirms "a multiplicity of resurrections"? They could legitimately do one or the other, but not both. By trying to "have it both ways," the PCUS report seems to have conflated criticisms of Scofieldian anti-confessional anomalies with criticisms of confessionally-consistent (by its own judgment) premillennialism.

The implications of this point may be extended. If distinctions between dispensations be allowed, such as the distinction between Old Testament and New Testament (which the Confession itself specifies), and such as the distinction between the present age and the future millennial kingdom (which seems inherently allowed with the allowance of a premillennial eschatology), then further nuance is needed to distinguish confessionally-acceptable premillennialism from confessionally-unacceptable premillennialism – more than is gained merely by using an ambiguous term (viz., "dispensationalism") to denote the latter. As we have just observed, satisfaction with just such a strategy seemed to lure the PCUS into at least one significant misunderstanding. Are there others?

One might wonder, for instance, what is meant throughout the section entitled, "The Rejection of the Bible as God's one Revelation to His One People"; point 2 of this section says, "Dispensationalism rejects both the unity of God's revelation and the fact that God's purpose is 'held forth with more fullness' (*Confession of Faith*, Ch. VII, Sec. 6) in the New Testament than it is in the Old. Dispensationalism holds that large portions even of the New Testament are for the Jewish Nation, not for the Church."[87] What exactly is being objected to in this assessment is unclear.

The committee doubtless had classical, Scofieldian-Chaferian dispensationalism in mind, a "dispensationalism" that, as noted earlier, insisted upon greater dispensational discontinuity and more severe denial of the application of significant portions of Scripture to the present-day believer than most dispensationalists since the 1940s have. Perhaps it is only that form of dispensationalism that is the target of this objection. On the other hand, it does also seem possible that (at least some on) the committee intended to preclude any sort of recognition of dispensational

---

[87] "Report of the [1944] Ad Interim Committee," 125.

variegation in Scripture. We simply cannot know how extensive is the intended application; or even if there was a consensus as to the intention.

We do know that the line between these two possibilities was not always clear in covenantalist criticism either before or after this ruling. One example of this confusion is found in *The Church Faces the Isms*, a book edited by former committee member, Frank Caldwell. Among the objections to "dispensationalism" in this work, is the following:

> Its [i.e., dispensationalism's] distinguishing feature is its seven dispensations, . . . This system of seven dispensations differs radically from the teaching of the rest of Christendom – Eastern Orthodox, Roman Catholic, and Protestant – as it does also from the plain meaning of the Bible itself. Having been made aware of many criticisms leveled against their doctrines, the dispensationalists now find it useful to defend their name by saying that all Christians are dispensationalists: "Any person is a dispensationalist who observes the first day of the week rather than the seventh" [Chafer, "Dispensationalism," 391]. . . . To be sure, Christians do believe in the distinction between the Old and New Testaments; in that sense, they may be said to believe in two dispensations, but that does not put them in the category of those who identify seven or more dispensations. Since the word "dispensationalism" is in bad repute, it hardly clears the reputation to say, "You too are one, if you are a Christian." The Church has not taught seven dispensations because they are not in the Bible. As the main body of Protestants observe two sacraments rather than seven, with no concern about being incomplete Roman Catholics, just so they accept two dispensations rather than seven without concern about being incomplete dispensationalists. . . . Chafer implies that Christians who accept only two dispensations are "partial" dispensationalists, who can be completed only by coming over into the dispensational camp and observing the full quota of seven dispensations.[88]

The claim that "dispensationalism" affirms an inherent claim to *seven* dispensations is obviously in error; even the Dallas Seminary doctrinal statement insists only upon *three* dispensations.[89] Clearly, Chamberlain has mistaken

---

[88] William D. Chamberlain, "Dispensationalism," in *The Church Faces the Isms*," edited by Arnold Black Rhodes, Frank H. Caldwell, and L.C. Rudolph (Nashville, TN: Abingdon Press, 1958), 96-97.

[89] "We believe that the changes in the dispensational dealings of God with man depend on changed conditions or situations in which man is successively found with relation to God, and that these changes are the result of the failures of man and the judgments of God. We believe that different administrative responsibilities of this character are manifest in the biblical record, that they span the entire history of mankind, and that each ends in the failure of man under the respective test and in an ensuing judgment from God. We believe that three of these dispensations or rules of life are the subject of extended revelation in the Scriptures, viz., the dispensation of the Mosaic law, the present dispensation of grace, and the future dispensation of the millennial kingdom"; "Article V: The Dispensations," in "Doctrinal Statement," *Dallas*

Scofield's system for a confessional dictum of dispensationalism *per se*. Beyond that, one gets the impression that Chamberlain finds problematic the observation of dispensations, at all, save the observation of distinctions between Old Testament and New Testament.

This is what I mean when I say that the points at issue got blurred as the controversy between "dispensationalism" and "covenant theology" polarized the parties involved. Simply put: after the 1940s controversy, dispensationalists seem to have become more reluctant to observe (much less emphasize) areas of continuity between dispensations;[90] likewise, covenant theologians seemed to grow less willing to observe legitimate discontinuities or distinctive characteristics of various scriptural dispensations. This had not before then been the case;[91] and, we must wonder if the reluctance to moderate the tendencies toward the extremes, on either side, has not hurt both positions.

Today, we clearly see modifications on both sides. On no single point is this so clear as in the case of the "people(s) of God," Old Testament and New Testament (Israel and the Church). Covenantalists early on objected to the eternal and ontological separation of "Israel" and "the Church" as suggested by Scofield and Chafer; many dispensationalists since the 1940s have conceded that Scofield's and Chafer's dualistic separation of "the two peoples of God" was indeed overstated.[92]

The question remains, however, whether covenant theologians may not have overstated the *continuity* between the Old Testament and New Testament people of God, as an "equal and opposite (over)reaction" to classical dispensationalist overstatements. Vern Poythress' analysis of these points is helpful. Acknowledging, as we have, the presence of overstatements in the history of the debate between dispensationalists and covenant theologians, Poythress says:

> In the light of dispensationalist concern for diversity and discontinuity between historical epochs, it is particularly necessary

---

Theological Seminary 1997-98 Catalogue (Dallas, TX: Dallas Theological Seminary, 1997), 151.

[90] This is exactly the point of Ken Barker, "False Dichotomies Between the Testaments."

[91] E.g., see the dispensational distinctives suggested by Charles Hodge, *Systematic Theology*, II:354-77; or even Louis Berkhof, who, though he opposes "present day dispensationalists" at several points, nevertheless finds the dispensational divisions themselves useful; see Berkhof, *Systematic Theology*, 290-301. We find in Berkhof's treatise (1939) evidence that the controversy has not yet reached its peak, and that the polarization is not yet so intense (e.g., as is evident in Chamberlain's 1958 treatise). Berkhof is still able to critique the anomalies of "dispensationalism" without attempting to debunk the "system" of dispensations entirely. It seems as time went on, such a distinction would become too subtle for most to be able to articulate.

[92] For a survey of various dispensationalist modifications of Scofield's and Chafer's bifurcation of "the two peoples of God," see Blaising, "Dispensationalism: The Search for Definition," in *Dispensationalism, Israel and the Church: The Search for* Definition, ed. Craig Blaising and Darrell Bock (Grand Rapids: Zondervan, 1992), 13-34; and *idem*, "The Extent and Varieties of Dispensationalism," in *Progressive Dispensationalism: An Up-to-Date Handbook of Contemporary Dispensational Thought*, ed. Craig Blaising and Darrell Bock (Wheaton, IL: Bridgepoint, 1993), 31-46.

to reckon with the radical break in history that took place in the life of Christ, above all in his death, resurrection, and ascension. There is a dichotomy here, a dichotomy of "before" and "after." Christ's work made a real and lasting difference. God's relation to human beings can never be the same afterwards because now redemption has been accomplished. There is, then, a very great distinction between Israel and the church.[93]

Though Poythress is still critical of the eternal, ontological separation of classical dispensationalism,[94] he nevertheless acknowledges "Dispensationalists have rightly objected to th[e] kind of 'spiritualization'"[95] that results from overemphasizing a continuity between Old Testament and New Testament. Such an overemphasis, Poythress suggests, has sometimes brought a de-emphasis on the truly "physical," "earthly" nature of some prophetic predictions.[96]

I suggest that all this reveals an early misunderstanding on the part of covenant theologians. The misunderstanding provoked alarmist criticisms as to how "dangerous" were the implications of the suggested dispensationalist distinction between Old Testament Israel and the New Testament Church. The alarmist criticisms likewise provoked distortions in some covenantalist treatises.

The ramifications of this misunderstanding are still today being fleshed out. The dispensational "distinction between Israel and the Church" is a core issue allegedly

---

[93] Poythress, *Understanding Dispensationalists*, 43.

[94] E.g., immediately following the quotation, above, he says: "But the distinction is basically a historical one, not a metaphysical one. It is the distinction between before and after Christ's resurrection, not a distinction between heavenly and earthly" (ibid). Poythress also recognizes, nonetheless, that, once the eternal, ontological dualism of classical dispensationalism be removed, dispensationalism and covenant theology are really not far apart in terms of the relationship between "Israel and the Church." When he engages the "errors" of classical dispensationalism's "two peoples of God," he clarifies: "The central distinctive of classic dispensationalism is the principle of the parallel-but-separate destinies of Israel and the church. Israel and the church are two peoples of God, earthly and heavenly. As we now approach this principle from the standpoint of systematic theology, we need to remember that many present-day dispensationalists have modified the principle of parallel destinies. The criticism of this chapter may therefore not apply to them" (126). On the dispensationalist side, J. Lanier Burns seems to have grasped the implications of the resulting similarity more than anyone; see Burns, "The Future of Ethnic Israel in Romans 11," in *Dispensationalism, Israel and the Church*, 188-229; idem, "Israel and the Church of a Progressive Dispensationalist," in *Three Central Issues in Contemporary Dispensationalism: A Comparison of Traditional and Progressive Views*, ed. Herbert W. Bateman IV, (Grand Rapids: Kregel, 1999), 263-303.

[95] Poythress, *Understanding Dispensationalists*, 47.

[96] Poythress remains convinced of the correctness of an amillennial eschatology, but he credits dispensationalism for being partly responsible for the renewed discovery of the "physical, earthly" emphasis in, especially, Old Testament prophecy. This has caused even amillennialists to recognize, he says, the "literal," "physical" character of the "new earth"; Poythress, *Understanding Dispensationalists*, 47-51, 97-129. For a dispensational premillennial account of the "re-discovery" of the "literal" character of the new earth, see Blaising, "Premillennialism," in *Three Views on the Millennium and Beyond*, ed. Darrell Bock (Grand Rapids: Zondervan, 1999), 160-81.

A Concluding Analysis 209

in contention between dispensationalism and covenant theology still today.[97] If there were significant misunderstandings of both the biblical teaching[98] and one another on this point, the ramifications could be great.

It is still too early to tell what exactly will be the full ramifications of correcting this misunderstanding; consensus could yet form between dispensationalists and covenant theologians on even this "core," "central" issue concerning the proper relationship of the Old Testament people of God and the New Testament people of God. J. Lanier Burns' remarks on this point are insightful.

> If Christ is the true Israel, and surely His comprehensive fulfillment of biblical predictions and righteousness suggests that He exemplifies such a premise (cf. Luke 24:13045; Rev. 19:10), then covenant theologians go on to infer that Israel's rejection of the Messiah forfeited its distinctive privileges and promises and transferred them to the church, the people of faith in Christ. Thus, in Romans 11 the "engrafting" of Gentiles and "regrafting" of Jews are simultaneous processes until the return of the Lord.
>
> Covenant and dispensational theologians have long debated this issue and corollary themes like hermeneutics and kingdom. . . . These insights are important . . . because their questions about the text expose preunderstandings of dispensationalists that might otherwise be glossed. . . . [D]ispensational premillennialists have distinguished between Israel and the church in various ways. An older approach treated Old Testament covenantal texts as exclusively Israelite in reference and, accordingly, deflected their fulfillment to the Millennium. The underlying premise was that national Israel, as the physical seed of Abraham, was to be eternally bifurcated from the church, a heavenly mystery that could not have been known in a dispensation of earthly issues. . . . A more moderate dispensational position has arisen in recent years. On the basis of the New Testament's use of crucial Old Testament texts, progressive dispensationalists acknowledge degrees of Old Testament content in the church, though complete fulfillment of Israel's promises awaits the Millennium as an intermediate kingdom that exists with Israel's Messiah ruling in the midst of the nations [cites Blaising, Bock, and Saucy]. The progressives insist on distinguishing Israel and the church, but they see both continuity and discontinuity in Israel/church and Old/New testamental relationships. Thus, the fulfillments of messianic promises relate to both present and future ages and both advents of Messiah, an "already-not yet" mediating position. Accordingly, this position

---

[97] Robert Saucy, "The Crucial Issue Between Dispensational and Non-Dispensational Systems," *Criswell Theological Review* 1 (fall, 1986): 149-65; Bock, *Three Central Issues in Contemporary Dispensationalism*, 90-94, 172-73; idem, *Three Views on the Millennium and Beyond*, 290-99.

[98] We have observed (above) those *on both sides* who critique their own tradition on this point.

would see both continuity and discontinuity between Israel and the church.[99]

Interacting also with recent covenant amillennialist modifications,[100] Burns suggests continued dialogue between dispensationalists (of all varieties) and covenant theologians could be profitable for forging further agreement among all sides on traditionally contentious points.

We may wonder whether such dialogue (and such modifications on both sides) might not have taken place sooner had the discussion not been marred from the beginning with such misunderstandings as we have explored in this study. Our wonder only grows when we consider that there might have been a latent form of "progressive dispensationalism" always present in the dispensationalist constituency from the beginning.

6.3 Conclusion: Is It Safe Today to Build on the Old Fault Lines?

Our study has demonstrated that the old lines of demarcation between "dispensationalists" and "covenant theologians" are inadequate. What should now be done with such a recognition?

Certainly, simply parroting the older dispensationalist canard that the dispensationalist-covenant theology debate is between those who take the Bible "literally" and those who "allegorize" or "spiritualize" Scripture should come to an abrupt halt. Likewise, covenant theologians should avoid thinking that their "system" represents a monolithic stance that, being incontrovertibly correct, has now moved dispensationalism slowly but surely toward its embrace.

---

[99] Burns, "Israel and the Church of a Progressive Dispensationalist," 272-74. For other examples of such a "mediating position" among progressive dispensationalists on the relationship between the Old Testament people of God (Israel) and the New Testament people of God (the Church), see the following essays in *Dispensationalism, Israel and the Church*: Bruce Ware, "The New Covenant and the People(s) of God," 68-97; Carl B. Hoch, Jr., "The New Man of Ephesians 2," 98-126; David L. Turner, "The New Jerusalem in Revelation 21:1-22:5: Consummation of a Biblical Continuum," 264-92; Kenneth L. Barker, "The Scope of Old and New Testament Theology and Hope," 293-328.

[100] E.g., Anthony Hoekema, *The Bible and the Future* (Grand Rapids: Eerdmans, 1979), 145-46; William Hendriksen, *Israel in Prophecy* (Grand Rapids: Baker, 1968); and, especially, C.E.B. Cranfield, who offers this startling *mea culpa*: "It is only where the Church persists in refusing to learn this message, where it secretly – perhaps unconsciously! – believes that its own existence is based on human achievement, and so fails to understand God's mercy to itself, that it is unable to believe in God's mercy for still unbelieving Israel, and so entertains the ugly and unscriptural notion that God has cast off His people Israel and simply replaced it by the Christian Church. These three chapters [Rom. 9-11] emphatically forbid us to speak of the Church as having once and for all taken the place of the Jewish people. . . . And I confess with shame to having also myself used in print on more than one occasion this language of the replacement of Israel by the Church" (*A Critical and Exegetical Commentary on the Epistle to the Romans*, ICC [Edinburgh: T & T Clark, 1979], 2:448).

In truth, both sides today can claim some vindication from the progress of history in their traditional debate. Dispensationalists can point to the 1948 restoration of the nation of Israel to the Holy Land as a reason to give reconsideration to some elements of their approach, including perhaps some of their eschatological proposals. Many dispensationalists, on the other hand, have been forced by exegetical and theological evidence to give new consideration to covenant theology's emphasis on continuity between the testaments, and its "inaugurated kingdom" emphases, and to face squarely the New Testament's emphasis on the *oneness* of the Jewish-Gentile people of God.

Perhaps it is time to cease grasping for new *sine qua non*'s, on either side. Efforts to show where the "line of division" is, beyond which one cannot cross without "succumbing" to the "other system," seems to manifest an unhelpful, "us-vs.-them" mentality. I suspect that this sort of drawing of lines in the sand is done primarily to reassure the more hard-line in one or the other constituency. But, such hard-line attitudes are exactly what wreaked such havoc on twentieth-century evangelicalism, and contributed greatly to the misunderstandings that have vexed both sides.

It is still too early to tell whether a clearer analysis of the points traditionally thought to be at issue between dispensationalism and covenant theology will bring rapprochement, or simply a clearer delineation of their inherent differences. We do know that a good portion of the twentieth century saw evangelicals occupied with needless clamoring over misunderstandings and misrepresentations provoked by the falling out between dispensationalism and covenant theology. What advances in evangelicalism might have been achieved if only these misunderstandings had been clarified earlier? Evangelicals entering the twenty-first century have good reason to hope that clearer heads will now prevail.

APPENDIX 1

The Data Regarding the Denominational Affiliation of Students at Dallas Theological Seminary (1924-1995)

The year increments in the chart on page 168 are chosen in order to provide a comparison of a comparable *number* of graduates: from 1925-1930, there were 59 graduates; from 1931-1933, there were 69 graduates; from 1934-1936, there were 72 graduates; from 1937-1939, there were 69 graduates; from 1940-1941, there were 71 graduates; from 1942-1944, there were 77 graduates; from 1945-1946, there were 75 graduates; from 1947-1949, there were 87 graduates; and in 1950, there were 62 graduates. Hence, the differentiation between the actual *number* of graduates being compared in the chart never exceeds 28; the mean number of graduates being compared in each segment is 70. 1985 and 1995 are exceptions, of course, but these are included merely to demonstrate that the trends illustrated from 1945 to 1950 continued to the end of the twentieth century. Records after 2003 were not available at the time of this writing, but records from 1995 to 2003 were consistent with the previous findings; it therefore seemed best simply to close off data gathering at 1995.

For our purposes, the category labeled "independent missions organizations" may not seem particularly helpful, since this designation tells us little about denominational affiliation. However, since no other information is available to determine a more specific denominational affiliation of those serving in these organizations, it seemed best simply to list them in this category rather than leave them out altogether. We might reasonably assume that most (though certainly not all) of those working for independent missions organizations would likely be non-denominational in church affiliation, too.

The very best records of the time (i.e., the Alumni Directories that specifically poll for denominational affiliation) are incomplete, leaving an average of 22 percent of the graduates unaccounted for. Many of these may never have been placed. The hardest figures to attain were from 1934-1939; over 40 percent of the graduates are unaccounted for during this period. This is high, even given the possibility that a higher number of graduates may have had trouble finding placement during these late-Depression years. One survey of entering students taken during this period does show a higher percentage of independents than what we have found elsewhere. According to this survey, of the 29 entering students, 31 percent were independent, 20.5 percent were Baptists, 10.5 percent were Methodists, and 10.5 percent were Presbyterians. It is possible that this was an unusual year (with an entering class of only 29 students, percentages are dramatically affected by even one or two students); if this be the case, our other records indicate that the statistics must have resumed their normal pattern within the next year or two. It is also highly possible that there were more independents represented in the student body, generally, than among actual graduates of the school; this assumption correlates with Hannah's observation that of the 9 independents included in the 1938 survey, only 3 had been to college ("History of the Evangelical Theological College," 267-72). It seems that in these financially distressing years, many academically unqualified students were allowed to attend classes, despite the understood impossibility of their ever actually graduating.

In the final analysis, the percentages derived from even the sparsely documented late-1930s matches closely those of the years immediately before and after (when only 20-30 percent of the graduates are unaccounted for). And, the pattern established concurs with the memory of those living at the time.

J. Dwight Pentecost remembers that about three fourths of the student body were Presbyterian in the late 1930s (interview by the author, Dallas, Texas, 31 May 1995). This recollection is reinforced by John Walvoord, who remembers that many students were Presbyterian, but had trouble being placed upon graduation (interview by the author, Dallas, Texas, 19 June 1996). Despite the impossibility of a complete accounting, the overall impression of the numbers may be presumed accurate.

The specific sources used to construct the chart on page 168 were as follows: in 1931, Rollin Chafer, registrar of the Seminary, surveyed the graduates of 1925-1930 for their denominational affiliations ("Confusion of Ideas," *Bulletin of the Evangelical Theological College* 7 [June 1931]: 5). Numbers for the years 1931-1944 are derived from the commencement announcements of the *Bulletin of the Evangelical Theological College*, which included a section detailing the ministry plans of that year's graduates: 4 (June 1932), supplement, [1]; 9 (March 1933), [1-2]; 10 (October 1934): [2-4]; 11 (May 1935): [4-5]; 12 (April-June 1936): [2-3]; 13 (April-June 1937), [3]; 14 (April-June 1938): [3]; 15 (April-June 1939): [2-3]; 16 (April-June 1940): [5]; and "With Our Alumni," 16 (July-September 1940): [3]; 17 (July-September 1941): [5]; and "Alumni News," 17 (July-September 1941): [11-12]. These findings were supplemented by the Alumni Directories of the *Dallas Theological Seminary Catalogues* of 1942-1944. The alumni directories were discontinued in 1945, but an Alumni Directory began to be published separately around 1960 (1960 was the earliest available issue in the Archives of Dallas Theological Seminary) and was cumulative, including listings of the ministry placements of graduates from 1945-1950. The statistics for 1985 and 1995 are from the *Dallas Theological Seminary Catalogue*. While these figures are from a survey of

Appendix 1: Data on DTS Students (1924-95)

students *enrolled* rather than *graduates*, the measure is sufficient for our purposes and is actually an even more accurate gauge of the constituency of the school.

The raw data are as follows: of the 53 graduates on record from 1925-1930, 27 were Presbyterian, 9 were Baptist, 13 were from other denominations, and 4 were independent; of the 39 students on record from 1931-1933, 20 were Presbyterian, 2 were Baptist, 7 were from other denominations; 4 were from independent churches and 2 were working for independent missions organizations; of the 37 students on record from 1934-1936, 15 were Presbyterian, 4 were Baptist, 4 were from other denominations, 2 were from independent churches and 8 were working for independent missions organizations; of the 37 graduates on record from 1937-1939, 15 were Presbyterian, 2 were Baptist, 2 were from other denominations, 4 were from independent churches and 9 were working for independent missions organizations; of the 57 graduates on record from 1940-1941, 26 were Presbyterian, 4 were Baptist, 9 were from other denominations, 5 were from independent churches, and 5 were working for independent missions organizations; of the 51 graduates on record from 1942-1944, 15 were Presbyterian, 9 were Baptist, 4 were from other denominations, 6 were from independent churches, and 6 were working for independent missions organizations; of the 62 graduates on record from 1945-1946, 12 were Presbyterian, 10 were Baptist, 6 were from other denominations, 15 were from independent churches, and 13 were working for independent missions organizations; of the 54 students on record from 1947-1949, 3 were Presbyterian, 11 were Baptist, 2 were from other denominations, 19 were from independent churches, and 10 were working for independent missions organizations; of the 44 graduates on record in 1950, 2 were Presbyterian, 9 were Baptist, 2 were from other denominations, 16 were from independent churches, and 10 were working for independent missions organizations.

Of the 1,307 students enrolled at Dallas Seminary in 1985, 38 were Presbyterian, 401 were Baptist, 108 were from other denominations (excluded in this figure are another 163 students listed in the obtuse category "other"; they are probably "in transition" denominationally, since "independent" was a category available, but not taken; it seemed best just to leave out altogether those listed in this category rather than assume that all in this category were independent, though, doubtless, many of them will end up as independents); 597 were from independent churches. Of the 1,197 on-campus students enrolled at Dallas Seminary in 1995, 50 were Presbyterian, 436 were Baptist, 118 were from other denominations (again, excluded from this figure are the 229 students listed as "other"); 364 were from independent churches.

APPENDIX 2

The Data Regarding the Denominational Affiliation of Faculty at Dallas Theological Seminary (1924-1995)

Both John Hannah ("History of the Evangelical Theological College," 260-66) and Rudolf Renfer ("A History of Dallas Theological Seminary," 211-29) provide a historical survey of the faculty of the 1930s and 1940s that includes their denominational affiliations. These were supplemented, in a few cases, with biographical sketches of new faculty in the *Bulletin of the Evangelical Theological College.*

No official records exist that list the denominational affiliations of faculty members from 1945-75. The denominational affiliations of these men were obtained from John Walvoord (interview with author, Dallas, Texas, 19 June 1996), who was registrar and then president of the seminary during this time – he hired most of these persons and remembered the denominational affiliations of most of them. Those that he did not remember were obtained from John Witmer (interview with author, Dallas, Texas, 21 June 1996). The 1995 statistics were obtained from the office of the Academic Dean from the Self-Study Survey conducted as part of the accreditation process for the Association of Theological Schools.

The data behind the statistics for the chart on page 169 are as follows: from 1925-1930, the seminary employed fifteen faculty members; eight were PCUS (Lewis S. Chafer, William M. Anderson, Jr., Antonio H. Perpetuo, W. Irving Carroll, Frederick Z. Browne, Rollin T. Chafer, Merwin Stone, and Manford Gutzke); two were PCUSA (Everett Harrison and Roy L. Aldrich); two were Brethren (James T. Spangler, who was United Brethren and Fred H. Leach, Jr. who was Plymouth Brethren); and three were Baptists (Robert Dixon, Artur Zieten, and Paul Jackson; these last three were part-time). From 1930-1935, of twenty faculty, the PCUS members included the brothers Chafer, Stone, Carroll, Wick Broomall and George Guille; the PCUSA members included Harrison and two additions, Morris Roach and Bert Sutcliffe; other Presbyterians were Charles Feinberg (Cumberland Presbyterian) and A.B. Winchester (Canadian Presbyterian); the two Baptists were Henry Thiessen and Ellwood Schofield; the two independents were C. Fred Lincoln and Herbert Mackenzie. The 1935-1945 faculty consisted of sixteen members; the Presbyterians were Lewis Chafer

(Rollin, who died in 1940, is not included); Feinberg, E. Harrison, Norman Harrison, John Walvoord, Charles Nash, Roy Aldrich, and Cullen I.K. Story; there were no Baptists to replace Thiessen or Schofield, who both had resigned; the Brethren were Spangler, Carl Armerding, and Henry A. Ironside; there was one Lutheran, John Henry Bennetch, one member of the Christian and Missionary Alliance, Bert Blaine Siegel; and three independents, Lincoln, Arnold Ehlert, and John Mitchell. From 1945-1950, the Presbyterians were Chafer, Feinberg, E. Harrison, Walvoord, Nash, Aldrich, S. Lewis Johnson, Fred Z. Browne, and Rudolf A. Renfer (who was Cumberland Presbyterian); Rand was the sole Baptist, Siegel the sole Christian and Missionary Alliance representative, and Bennetch the sole Lutheran; the independents were Lincoln, Ehlert, Mitchell, John Witmer (who was ordained United Brethren, but who joined an independent church upon moving to Dallas – a not uncommon pattern), Merrill Unger, and J. Ellwood Evans. From 1950-1955, the Presbyterians were Johnson, Nash, Aldrich, and Renfer; two Baptists, Rand and Charles Caldwell Ryrie; Armerding was the lone Plymouth Brethren; Bennetch remained the one Lutheran; the independents were Donald K. Campbell, Evans, Lincoln, Unger, Witmer, Mitchell, J. Vernon McGee and Walvoord (who joined the IFCA upon being denied transfer from the Ft. Worth Presbytery to the Dallas Presbytery); in 1965, only Aldrich and Feinberg were left of the Presbyterians, three new Baptists joined Ryrie: George Dollar, Haddon Robinson and Bruce Waltke; Zane Hodges was the sole Plymouth Brethren representative; George William Peters was Mennonite; the rest were independents: Campbell, Evans, Pentecost, Unger, Walvoord, Witmer, McGee, Mitchell, joined by Howard Hendricks and Stanley D. Toussaint; S. Lewis Johnson had also left the Presbyterian Church and become independent by this time. In 1975, there were 45 faculty; all but 12 were independent. The non-independents were Edwin Blum (Presbyterian); Ken Barker, John Best, Fred Howe, John William Reed, Phillip Roland Williams, Robinson, Ryrie and Waltke (Baptists); Thomas Constable and Zane Hodges (Brethren); Warren Benson (Evangelical Free); and George Peters (Mennonite). The 1995 faculty denominational affiliations are recorded from biographical information kept in the academic office at Dallas Theological Seminary, from personal interviews and from publicly available biographical profiles published by Dallas Theological Seminary. Since the faculty has remained stable from 1995 until now, the 1995 figures listed on page 169 may be presumed to provide a generally reliable picture of faculty denominational affiliation at the present time, as well.

APPENDIX 3

Copy of Eugene W. McLaurin, *A Suggested Report of the Ad Interim Committee on Changes in the Confession of Faith and Catechisms with Regard to the "Question as to Whether the Type of Bible Interpretation Known as 'Dispensationalism' is in Harmony with the Confession of Faith"* (Austin, TX: Austin Presbyterian Theological Seminary, 1942)

This appendix (beginning on the next page) and the next two appendices consist of xeroxed copies of original documents. This appendix (appendix 3) is a copy of the original "suggested report" composed and submitted to the AIC by committee member, Eugene McLaurin; this document was obtained from Austin Presbyterian Theological Seminary, Austin, TX. Appendix 4 is a copy of the original 1943 AIC report; appendix 5 is a copy of the original 1944 AIC report, both obtained from the minutes of GA meetings, found at the Department of History of the PCUSA in Montreat, NC. Comparison of these three documents allows one to see the progression of the AIC's thought and rationale as it came to it final conclusions regarding dispensationalism and submitted its findings to the PCUS GA (which 1944 report was finally adopted).

Austin Presbyterian Theological Seminary

A SUGGESTED REPORT OF THE AD INTERIM COMMITTEE ON CHANGES IN THE CONFESSION OF FAITH AND CATECHISMS WITH REGARD TO THE "QUESTION AS TO WHETHER THE TYPE OF BIBLE INTERPRETATION KNOWN AS 'DISPENSATIONALISM' IS IN HARMONY WITH THE CONFESSION OF FAITH"

(The General Assembly of 1941 referred to its Ad Interim Committee on Changes in the Confession of Faith and the Catechisms, a Committee composed of one member from the faculty of each of our seminaries, the question of whether Dispensationalism is in harmony with the standards of our church. The chairman of the committee requested the faculty of each seminary to prepare and submit to the committee a suggested report for the committee, to be used by the committee in formulating its report to the General Assembly. The faculty of Austin Presbyterian Theological Seminary, through Rev. E.W. McLaurin, submitted the following paper. This paper, with some additions not included below, and with some minor changes, became the report of the committee.)

The Ad Interim Committee on Changes in the Confession of Faith and the Catechisms was charged with the responsibility of answering, in a report to be submitted to the General Assembly in 1942, "the question as to whether the type of Bible interpretation known as 'Dispensationalism' is in harmony with the Confession of Faith" (Minutes, 1941, p.80). A preliminary statement will set the problem in clearer light.

I. Preamble

1. The Point At Issue

The main point at issue is whether the type of Bible interpretation known as 'Dispensationalism' is in harmony with the Confession of Faith and the Catechisms. It is not primarily a view of the millennium.

2. The Data for Answering the Question.

The material from which an answer is to be formulated is the Confession of Faith, with, your committee assumes, such additional light as may be gained from the Catechisms and the Book of Church Order. On the other hand, it is difficult to determine exactly the principles of Dispensationalism accepted by most Dispensationalists, since there is no officially formulated system of this school of Bible interpretation. In this report only those beliefs held by all Dispensationalists as recorded in the writings of their leading authors, and in opposition to the teachings of our standards, are considered.

3. Only Important Doctrines are Considered

Finally, the committee has considered only important doctrines where disagreement is evidenced. Our church has always recognized and accepted in its membership differences of opinion in minor points of belief.

II. Brief Statement of Doctrines Held in Disagreement

Your committee finds, in the matters of belief named below, some important views of Dispensationalism not in harmony with the views

Appendix 3: E.W. McLaurin's suggested AIC report on dispensationalism (1942)

-2-

set forth in our standards:

1. Views of the Church

a. The Temporal Beginning of the Church

Our standards do not state the exact point in time at which the church began to exist, but frequently, directly and indirectly, assert its existence in Old Testament times.

Dispensationalists hold that the church began to exist only at Pentecost.

b. The Temporal End of the Church

The Confession of Faith asserts that the Church will continue to exist to the 'end of the world'.

Dispensationalism holds that the church will be removed from the earth at the rapture (I Thes.4:13-17), at a secret coming of Christ from His church before His visible, pre-millennial coming.

c. Kingship of Jesus Christ in the Church

Our standards assert that Jesus Christ now exercises kingly office and rule in His church.

Dispensationalism asserts that our Lord exercises no kingly functions in His relations to His Church.

d. Mission of the Church

According to our standards the mission of the church is the gathering and perfecting of the saints.

Dispensationalism holds that the church has no particular mission.

2. Number of Dispensations

Our standards hold that between the fall of man and the 'end of the world', there are only two dispensations.

Dispensationalism affirms there are six dispensations in this same period of time.

3. The Final Judgment

Our standards hold that there is one final judgment of "men and angels at the end of the world".

Dispensationalists deny a final universal judgment at the end of the world, but assert that there will be several judgments, embracing different groups or sections of mankind, at or accompanying various eschatological events.

-3-

4. The Destiny of the Righteous

Our standards teach that all the righteous shall live forever with the Lord in heaven, in the kingdom of glory.

The Dispensationalists assert that there will be, from the time of the rapture of the church, two peoples of God, one on earth, the other in heaven, continuing separate and distinct throughout all eternity.

III. Detailed Presentation of Evidence

1. The Church

a. The Temporal Beginning of the Church

i. The Evidence in the Standards

While the Confession of Faith is not clear as to the time when the church came into existence, it does affirm, clearly and unequivocally, its existence in Old Testament times. The Old Testament church was 'a church under age'(XIX,3); it was called specifically 'the Jewish church'(XX,1); and it was 'confined to one nation......under the law'(XXV,2).

The existence of the church in OT times is implied, as we must logically conclude from OT proof-texts embodied in the Confession, in our doctrines of the divine care of the church(V,7; Amos 9:8,9), and of divine revelation to the church(I,1; Deut.4:12,14).

Further proof in support of this statement of the existence of the church in OT times is contained in our Book of Church Order: "The Church which the Lord Jesus Christ has erected in this world for the gathering and perfecting of the saints is his visible kingdom of grace, and is one and the same in all ages."(Ch.I,parag. 2);"The visible church before the law, under the law, and now under the Gospel, is one and the same, and consists of all those who make profession of the true religion, together with their children"(Ch. III, parag. 12).

Thus, the Confession of Faith, strongly supported by the Book of Church Order, clearly teaches the existence of the church in OT times.

ii. The Evidence of Dispensationalism

Negatively, we know of no Dispensationalist who holds to the existence of the church in OT times. Positively, on the other hand, evidence that Dispensationalism considers the church to have come into existence at Pentecost is plentiful and voluminous. Only a few of widely influential Dispensationalist writers will be quoted. Scofield: "The Church, corporately, is not in the vision of the O.T. prophet"(Reference Bible,p.711). "Church (true), Summary: The true church, composed of the whole number of regenerate persons from Pentecost to the first resurrection (I Cor.15:52)"(Heb.12:23, note). "On the day of Pentecost the church came into existence" (Unsearchable Riches, 34).

Church doctrine was revealed only to and through Paul. Compare also,"It is evident that the really dangerous sect in Corinth was that which said,'and I of Christ'(I Cor. 1:12). They rejected the new revelation through Paul of the doctrines of grace; grounding themselves, probably, on the kingdom teachings of our Lord as a minister of the circumcision'(Rom.15:8); seemingly oblivious that a new dispensation had been introduced by Christ's death"(Ref.Bib., Introduction,II Cor.). On his views compare further Ref.Bib.,Acts 15:13ff,note;7:36,note;ch.2,note; Mt.16:18,note; Eph.3:6,note; I Tim.3:15,note; etc.).

Chafer: "An extensive body of Scripture declares directly or indirectly that the present age is unforeseen and parenthetical in its character and in it a new humanity appears on earth with an incomparable new headship in the resurrected Christ, which company is being formed by the regenerating power of the Spirit"(Lewis Sperry Chafer, Dispensationalism,407). "The theological term, The Old Testament Church, has no Scriptural warrant.....The true church began at Pentecost"(Grace,240f).

Riley: "The church grows up in the world, is growing up now, and has been since the days of Pentecost"(Wm.B.Riley, in Light on Prophecy, Report of the Philadelphia Prophetic Conference,1918; p.346).

Gregg: "We are not surprised to learn that the church is a 'mystery'; that is, not revealed to Moses and the prophets. It was foretold by Christ (Mt.16), but fully; developed by the Holy Ghost, after the day of Pentecost"(Light on Prophecy, 230).

Dispensationalists here are in fullest agreement among themselves, however much they may disagree about some other points. They emphatically affirm that there was no church in OT. times.

b. The Temporal End of the Church

i. The Evidence of the Confession

The Confession of Faith holds that the church will continue in the world 'to the end of the world'. This is asserted in several places.

"Christ hath given the ministry, oracles and ordinances of God, for the perfecting of the saints, in this life, to the end of the world"(XXV,3). Proof-texts: Eph.4:11-13; Is.59:21; Mt.28:19,20. "Which sacrament(i.e.baptism) is, by Christ's own appointment, to be continued in His church until the end of the world"(XXVIII,1). Proof-text: Mt.28:19,20.

"Our Lord Jesus instituted the sacrament of His body and blood...

-5-

to be observed in His church, unto the end of the world"(XXIX,1). Proof-texts: I Cor.11:23-26; Mt.26:27; Lk.22:19,20.

The meaning of the phrase 'the end of the world' in the Confession of Faith is determined beyond reasonable doubt. The first day of the week "is to be continued to the end of the world, as the Christian sabbath"(XXI,7). One passage seems to fix it clearly and unmistakably: The Lord Jesus "shall return to judge men and angels, at the end of the world"(VIII,4). Proof-texts: Acts 10:42; Mt.13:40-42; 16:27; 25:31-33; II Tim.4:1. This judgment is further described as "the judgment of the great day"(XXXII,1). Proof-texts: Lk.16:23,24; II Pet.2:9. "God hath appointed a day, wherein he will judge the world in righteousness by Jesus Christ.... In which day, not only the apostate angels shall be judged; but likewise all persons, that have lived upon earth, shall appear before the tribunal of Christ"(XXXIII,1). Proof-texts: Acts 17:31; Mt. 25:31-34; etc. Furthermore, "at the last day.....all the dead shall be raised up"(XXXII,2). Proof-texts: I Cor.15:51,52. The judgment occurs at the end of the world, at the last day. The resurrection of all the dead occurs at this same time. And the church visible, which has continued to exist from OT times to that day, ceases her earthly existence and becomes the church triumphant.

So, according to the teaching of the Confession, the church on earth with all her regulations, sacraments, her holy Lord's day, will continue to exist until the general resurrection and the final judgment.

ii. The Evidence of Dispensationalism

Dispensationalism sets the end of the existence of the church upon earth at the rapture of the church at the secret return of Christ preceding the great tribulation.

Schofield: See note on I Cor.15:24, which asserts that before the visible premillennial coming of Christ to restore the Davidic monarchy in His own person, the church will have "previously been caught up to meet Him in the air(I Thes.4:14-17)".

Gray: "It (i.e. the church) will have its earthly ending when He comes again, and it is caught up to meet Him in the air(I Thes. 4:13-18)" (James M. Gray, Synthetic Bible Studies,141).

Gregg: "The church's destiny is, to be caught up from among the dead and living nations, in resurrection bodies, to meet the Lord in the air (I Thes.4:13-18); and, in the 'age to come', to reign, from the heavenlies with Him over the earth (Rev.5)"(Light on Prophecy,230).

Chafer: "The scene (i.e. of the nations before 'the Messiah King', Mt.25:31-46) is at the close of the Great Tribulation (Mt. 24:21) after the removal of the church from the earth"(Dispensationalism, 390).

Dispensationalism, then, on the basis of its written records, asserts that the church will be removed from the earth before the visible return of Christ, and will not be in the world until the general resurrection and the great judgment.

c. Kingship of Jesus Christ in the Church

i. Evidence of the Westminster Standards

The Confession of Faith declares that "the visible church...... is the kingdom of our Lord Jesus Christ, the house and family of God" (XXV,2). Furthermore, Christ as our Mediator is "prophet, priest, and king; the head and Saviour of His Church"(VIII,1). Compare also S.C. 26: "Christ executeth the office of a king in subduing us to Himself, in ruling and defending us, and in restraining and conquering all His and our enemies"; and S.C. 23: "Christ, as our Redeemer, executeth the offices of a prophet, of a priest, and of a king, both in His estate of humiliation and exaltation." The Book of Church Order, ch.II, parag.8, under the caption "The King and Head of The Church", states "Jesus Christ sits upon the throne of David and upon His kingdom"; and in ch. ii, parag.10, "Christ, as King, has given to His church officers, oracles, and ordinances".

The doctrine of our church, then, is that Christ now exercises kingly rule over His people, especially in a corporate sense. The church is the visible kingdom of our Lord Jesus Christ. These statements are diametrically opposed to any doctrine of the church that denies the kingship of Jesus Christ in His church now, but asserts a subsequent kingdom-age in which He will exercise royal authority and power.

ii. The Evidence of Dispensationalism

Dispensationalists deny to Jesus Christ as Head of the church any prerogatives of kingly power or any throne.

Chafer: "The Christian possesses.....no king to whom he is subject (Matt.2:2); though Christians may speak of Christ as 'The King' (I Tim.1:17; 6:15)"(Dispensationalism, 408f). "He (i.e.Christ) is now serving as Priest and not as King"(Major Bible Themes,52).

Scofield: "Christ is never called 'King of the Church'. He is 'King of the Jews', and Lord and 'Head of the Church'(Eph.1:22,23)" (Ref. Bible, Mt.2:2,n.;cf also note on Rev.3:21).

Chafer says, with regard to Christians, that the "elect heavenly people.....are not now nor at any future time said to be subjects of the King"(Dispensationalism,406). The church, he further asserts, is Christ's Bride, His consort, not His subject, and will reign with Him on earth during the kingdom-age (idem,404).

Dispensationalists sometimes describe the relation of Christ to the church as its Head as being organic, never figurative, or as

-7-

exercising authority and kingship. Christ seems not to be exercising any kingly authority in this age, not even in His church.

According to the doctrine of our standards, Christ is now head and king of the church. Dispensationalism takes a position that absolutely denies any such kingship in the church. Kingship will be exercised by Him with the church as His bride only when this age comes to an end and the kingdom is set up with Christ ruling from Jerusalem.

d. The Mission of the Church

In one other important point Dispensationalists take different ground from that held by our standards. The church has a mission in the earth, according to our standards, and its work is for the fulfilment of that obligation. The Confession states, "Unto this catholic visible church, Christ hath given the ministry, oracles, and ordinances of God, for the gathering and perfecting of the saints, in this life, to the end of the world: and doth by His own presence and Spirit, according to His promise, make them effectual thereunto"(XXV,3). The Book of Church Order describes the church as follows: "The church which the Lord Jesus Christ has erected in this world for the gathering and perfecting of the saints, is His visible kingdom of grace, and is one and the same in all ages"(ch.I,2). The church has received from her divine Head gifts and endowments necessary for carrying out her mission: "Jesus Christ.....who sits upon the throne of David and upon his kingdom to order and establish it with judgment and with justice from henceforth and for ever; having all power given unto Him in heaven and in earth by the Father.....received gifts for His church, and gave all officers necessary for the edification of the church and for the perfecting of the saints" (ch.II,parag.8). Although "the purest churches under heaven are subject both to mixture and error.....nevertheless, there shall always be a church on earth, to worship God according to His will" (Conf.of Faith, XXV,5). These dogmatic statements of our beliefs are in strong opposition to any beliefs or views that consider the church merely a man-made fallible institution. Her Head and King has given her a definite responsibility, "the gathering and perfecting of the saints", and with the task has given her endowments of power, wisdom, and organization adequate for performing the task. There is no "ordinary possibility of salvation" outside of her (XXV,2), and throughout all the ages she has felt in varying degree the responsibility of carrying out her great commission.

ii. Evidence of Dispensationalism

Dispensationalists hold that the church has no particular mission.

Gray: "He(i.e. God) is not now converting the world, not setting up His kingdom" (Light on Prophecy, 136).

Chafer: "Strictly speaking, the church has no mission; for God

-8-

has never commissioned her as a corporate body to undertake any task whatsoever.....Another error to be avoided in connection with this subject (i.e. the mission of the church) is the supposition that the divine purpose in this age is the conversion of the world. It is true that the world will be converted and there is yet to be a kingdom of righteousness in the earth; but, according to the Bible, that day of a transformed earth, so far from being the result of Christian service, is said to follow rather than precede the return of Christ, and is said to be possible only by His personal presence and immediate power"(Major Bible Themes,212).

Dispensationalism thus holds to a view of the work and mission of the church that does not at all accord with the definite goals assigned to the church by her great Head, as these goals are set forth in our standards.

The Dispensationalist view of the church, as specified in the above points of doctrine, affirms that the church began at Pentecost, and did not exist in OT times; that the church will not be in the earth in the great conflict immediately issuing in the final and victorious overthrow of all evil and the beginning in of the glorious universal reign of Christ in His eternal Kingdom of glory; that Christ exercises no royal power as King of the church, whereas our standards assert He is now King; and, lastly, Dispensationalism denies that the church has any particular mission in the world, in contrast to the assertion by our standards that the work of the church is the gathering and perfecting of the saints.

2. Number of the Dispensations

a. The Evidence of the Confession of Faith

According to the Confession of Faith, between the fall of man and the final judgment of men and angels there are only two dispensations, the one covering the Old Testament, the other the New Testament to the judgment (VII,5,6). But in these two dispensations "there are not two covenants of grace differing in substance, but one and the same under various dispensations"(VII,5,6). Throughout all the ages since the fall of man, man's relation to God has been characterized by grace on the part of God. Salvation has been predicated on the same Redeemer, Jesus Christ; the same condition, faith; and to the same end, eternal life.

b. The Evidence of Dispensationalism

Dispensationalism receives its distinctive name from its emphasis upon the different methods of God's dealings with man which it assumes and which it considers fundamental in any correct understanding of the Bible. The word must be defined before prodeeding further. Schofield defines the term thus: "A dispensation is a period of time during which man is tested in respect of obedience to some specific (his italics) revelation of the will of God. Seven such dipsensations are distinguished in Scripture"

-9-

(Ref.Bible,5). Ironside defines it thus: "A dispensation is a period of time, long or short, in which God is dealing with men in a different way than He has ever dealt with them before"(The Lamp of Prophecy, 43). Dispensationalists distinguish seven dispensations in all in God's dealings with man, holding that, after the original state of innocence, from the fall to the final judgment as described in Rev.20:11-15, there are six dispensations. These are: Conscience, Human Government, Promise, Law, Grace, and Kingdom. For a description of these, see Schofield Reference Bible, notes on Gen.1:28; 3:23; 8:20; 12:1; Ex.19:8; Jn.1:17; and Eph.1:10.

It is important to note that the basis of God's dealings with man in any particular period is asserted to be different from that of any other period. This principle seems to cut directly across any principle of grace running across the ages in the relations of God with man. In regard to salvation by grace, dispensationalists, in their writings, seem to be inconsistent and at times even contradictory. But it is certainly true that under several of these assumed dispensations, the test of man's acceptance with God is legal obedience, and not at all faith in Jesus Christ. Faith is the test in only two dispensations; in all the others the test is works.

Whatever may be the exact relation of grace and works under the various dispensations of Dispensationalism, the interpretation of the Bible that divides God's dealings with man into several distinct dispensations, or unrelated periods, is in opposition to the view of the Confession of Faith which asserts that there is only one covenant of grace in the two dispensations of the Old and the New Testaments.

3. The Final Judgment

The Church universal has always held to a belief in a great day of judgment, when all mankind shall be gathered before the great white Throne to be judged according to their works. This found expression in the familiar sentence in the Apostles' Creed: "From thence He shall come to judge the quick and the dead". But the views of Dispensationalism are not in harmony with the statements of the Creed and of the Confession of Faith in regard to the final general judgment of man.

a. The Evidence of the Confession of Faith

The Confession is quite clear and unequivocal on this matter: Jesus Christ "shall return to judge men and angels, at the end of the world"(VIII,4); "God hath appointed a day, wherein He will judge the world in righteousness by Jesus Christ, to whom all power and judgment is given by the Father. In which day, not only the apostate angels shall be judged; but likewise all persons, that have lived upon earth, shall appear before the tribunal of Christ, to give an account of their thoughts, words, and deeds; and to receive according to what they have done in the body, whether good or evil"(XXXIII,1).

The belief of the great majority of Christians in all ages has been that all men, both righteous and unrighteous, must appear together before the judgment throne of Almighty God and Christ. The good are to be publicly awarded and the evil are to be publicly condemned.

b. The Evidence of Dispensationalism

Dispensationalism denies a great universal final judgment, and posits in its stead a varying number of judgments dealing with certain section of men.

Schofield: "Among the many judgments mentioned in Scripture, seven are invested with a special significance. These seven are:... believers' sins....(Jn.12:31,note);....believers' self-judgment (I Cor.11:31,note);....believers' works (II Cor. 5:10,note);..... nations at the return of Christ (Mt.25:32,note);....Israel at the return of Christ (Exek.20:37,note);....angels after the one thousand years (Jude 6,note); the judgment of the wicked dead with which the history of the present earth ends."(Ref.Bible,Rev.20: . 12,note).

Chafer calls special attention to three judgments: Believers' Works, the Nations, and the Wicked (Major Bible Themes,chs.XLVI, XLVII,XLVIII); he affirms, though, that "The Bible distinguishes seven in all, which fact is in marked disagreement with the almost universal conception that there is but one final and all-inclusive judgment"(idem,p.288).

Gray does away with a final universal judgment, asserting sectional judgments (Synthetic Bible Studies,110,136).

According to Dispensational doctrine of the appearing of man before the divine judgment seat to be formally acquitted and rewarded, or condemned and punished, men come before Him in groups determined by race or moral quality. These judgments extend over a period of a thousand years. "God hath appointed a day (which word in Scripture in reference to the last things represents a period of time of more than a thousand years, commencing with the visible, personal and premillennial return of Christ), wherein He will judge the world in righteousness by Jesus Christ"(Form of Government of the Bible Presbyterian Church; Changes in the Westminster Confession of Faith and Catechisms, p.21). Dispensationalists, therefore, in affirming several separate sectional judgments of men, extending over a period of more than a thousand years of time, are not in harmony with our standards and the general belief of the church universal as expressed in the Apostles' Creed, which affirm a final universal judgment of all mankind.

4. Final Destiny of God's People

In regard to the final destiny of God's people, Dispensationalism is not in harmony with our standards.

-11-

a. The Evidence of Westminster Standards

The Confession is not explicitly clear as to the place of the ultimate destiny of the righteous, although it is unambiguously clear as to their being in one place; in one group. "For then (i.e. the "day wherein He will judge the world in righteousness by Jesus Christ") shall the righteous go into everlasting life, and receive that fulness of joy and refreshing which shall come from the presence of the Lord"(XXXIII,2). The Larger Catechism (Answer 90) is very definite in its statement on this point of belief: "At the day of judgment, the righteous, being caught up to Christ in the clouds, shall be set on His right hand,...and shall be received into heaven, where they shall be fully and for ever freed from all sin and misery; filled with inconceivable joy; made perfectly holy and happy both in soul and body, in the company of innumerable saints and angels, but especially in the immediate vision and fruition of God the Father, of our Lord Jesus Christ, and of the Holy Spirit, to all eternity". Two affirmations here bear on the point under consideration: All the righteous are in heaven; and they continue there throughout all eternity.

The teachings of these statements are definite enough for the formulation of a coherent doctrine of the destiny of the righteous. After the resurrection and the final judgment, they are all in one group in one place with the triune God throughout all eternity. And the place or locality is heaven.

b. The Evidence of Dispensationalism

Dispensationalism contends that the righteous will be divided into two groups, based on a division growing out of two distinct divine purposes of the ages, one group a heavenly people of God, the other an earthly people of God.

Chafer: "The Dispensationalist believes that throughout the ages God is pursuing two distinct purposes: one related to the earth with earthly people and earthly objectives involved, while the other is related to heaven with heavenly objectives involved. Why should this belief be deemed so incredible in the light of the facts that there is a present distinction between earth and heaven which is preserved even after both are made new; when the Scriptures so designate an earthly people who go on as such into eternity; and an heavenly people who also abide in their heavenly calling forever?" "The important objective has been gained if it has been made clear that there is an eschatology of Judaism and an eschatology of Christianity and each, though wholly different as to details, reaches on into eternity. One of the great burdens of predictive prophecy is the anticipation of the glories of Israel in a transformed earth under the reign of David's Son, the Lord Jesus Christ the Son of God. There is likewise much prediction which anticipates the glories of the redeemed in heaven." "Israel's fundamental covenants are both earthly and eternal and their national entity is forever identified with the earth (Is.66:22)" (Dispensationalism,448,425f,426 n). For a fuller discussion and

-12-

eferences to other writers, see <u>Union Seminary Review</u>, vol.LII,1 (October,1940); also idem LII,2,3; articles By Pro. James E. Bear.

Thus, with regard to the eternal destiny of the righteous, Dispensationalism holds that this destiny is not one people in one place, but of two peoples, an earthly and an heavenly, going on with separate and distinct objectives, throughout all eternity. This is certainly out of harmony with the doctrine of the Westminster standards that the righteous people of God are together, in one place, that is heaven, throughout all eternity.

APPENDIX 4

Copy of the Original Report of the 1943 PCUS Ad Interim Committee on Changes in the Confession of Faith and Catechisms as to Whether the Type of Bible Interpretation Known as "Dispensationalism" is in Harmony with the Confession of Faith

II

THE QUESTION AS TO WHETHER THE TYPE OF BIBLE INTERPRETATION KNOWN AS DISPENSATIONALISM IS IN HARMONY WITH THE CONFESSION OF FAITH

(This section was recommitted and committee enlarged. See page 46.)

The Ad Interim Committee on Changes in the Confession of Faith and the Catechisms was charged with the responsibility of answering the "question as to whether the type of Bible Interpretation known as 'Dispensationalism' is in harmony with the Confession of Faith" (Minutes, 1941, p. 60). A preliminary statement will set the problem in clearer light.

I. Preamble:

1. Importance of the Question:

For several reasons, your Committee feels that this matter requires careful consideration by the Assembly. Overtures have been sent up to Aessmblies requesting deliverances on the subject. These overtures indicate that in various parts of the Church there exists considerable concern about the relation of Dispensationalism to the teachings of the Church. In other areas we find that many ministers and laymen are uninformed as to the characteristic teachings and emphases of Dispensationalism. Even more serious than the apparent logical divergence of Dispensational doctrines from the teaching in our Standards are the divisive practical effects of Dispensationalism in the Church. In many congregations which have become indoctrinated with its teachings, the Sunday School materials edited and published by our own Executive Committee are depreciated and are not used, so-called interdenominational Sunday School materials being substituted. Likewise our own Presbyterian institutions of Christian education, Young Peoples' Conferences, and other agencies of the Church are depreciated, and sometimes labelled as "modernistic" or "atheistic" because not "rightly dividing the word of truth" in accordance with Dispensationalist teachings and Dispensationalist methods of interpreting Scripture. Thus the loyalty of Presbyterians to their own agencies and institutions is undermined and funds which might otherwise be available for work carried on by our own Church are diverted to so-called "Faith Missions" and "Interdenominational Bible Institutes." In a number of instances the issue of Dispensationalism has become so acutely divisive in local congregations as to require drastic actions on the part of presbyteries, such actions usually being taken after it was too late to keep the congregations from being rent asunder.

Such practically disturbing and divisive effects in the Church imply significant doctrinal differences:

Appendix

2. The Point at Issue:

The main point at issue is whether the type of Bible interpretation known as "Dispensationalism" is in harmony with the Confession of Faith and the Catechisms. It is not primarily a matter of Biblical foundations for the two systems, since both claim to be based on the Bible alone. It is not a matter of a sound exegesis of Scripture, although ultimately the question of whether Dispensationalism is in harmony with the Standards of our Church will be answered by sound exegesis. It is not at all a controversy in regard to the millennium, since our denomination has always had, and still has, room for millennialists, a-millennialists, post-millennialists, and pre-millennialists in its ranks. The main point at issue, let it be emphasized, is whether the system of Bible interpretation known as Dispensationalism is in harmony with Presbyterian doctrines as set forth in the Westminster Standards.

3. The Data for Answering the Question:

On the one hand, the material from which an answer is to be formulated is the Standards of our Church—the Confession of Faith, the Catechisms, and the Book of Church Order.

On the other hand, your Committee has been compelled to seek to determine "the Type of Bible interpretation known as 'Dispensationalism'" from the writings of the generally-recognized exponents of these teachings.

4. Only Important Doctrines Are Considered:

Finally, the Committee has considered only important doctrines where disagreement is evidenced. Our Church has always recognized and accepted into its leadership men who hold differences of opinion on minor points of belief.

II. Some of the significant doctrinal differences between Dispensationalism and the Standards of the Presbyterian Church are now to be pointed out.

A. The root of the difference will be found in the Doctrine of Dispensations as contrasted with the Doctrine of the Covenant of Grace.

B. This difference in basic viewpoint manifests itself in radically divergent views of the Kingdom, its nature and subjects; the Kingly Work of Christ; and the Church, its nature and membership.[1] These divergent views and doctrines are integrated into two different "systems" each claiming to represent what has been revealed about God's dealings with the human race and His purposes for His own people. Both "systems" cannot be true.

A. *The Root of the Difference*

The Doctrine of Dispensations is the root out of which the peculiar Dispensational views take their rise. Dr. Scofield's definition of a dispensation is the one which is commonly accepted by them and constantly quoted in their literature. Dr. Scofield says, "A Dispensation is a period of time during which man is tested in respect of obedience to some *specific* revelation of the will of God. Seven such dispensations are distinguished in Scripture."[2] The basic features of this doctrine are, (1) God has dealt in various ways with various groups in the course of human history. (2) Each group had its own specific revelation of the will of God. (3) Man is tested as to his obedience to the specific revelation made to him in his dispensation.

---

[1] Dr. L. S. Chafer, President of Dallas Theological Seminary, Dallas, Texas, who is an outstanding advocate of Dispensationalism, recognizes this divergence. In his article on *Dispensationalism* published in the *Bibliotheca Sacra* (No. 372, Vol. 93) he says,

"When good men disagree as to doctrine it is usually due to a fundamental difference in premise. Perfect logic, when built on divergent premises, will usually result in irreconcilable conclusions.—The situation which necessitates the writing of this thesis serves to demonstrate the wide doctrinal differences that may exist between supposedly orthodox men.—At the beginning of this thesis it was stated that the doctrinal differences herein discussed are due to the fact that the two schools of interpretation involved stand on widely divergent premises." (pp. 396, 417, 448)

[2] *Scofield Reference Bible*, p. 5, note 4. In the excellent index to this Reference Bible one may find listed where these various dispensations are described. Practically all Dispensationalists follow this scheme of dispensations, and insist on the distinction between Israel and the Church with all the implications involved. Some, however, do not follow Dr. Scofield in his distinction between "law" and "grace," but hold that all are saved by grace.

124   APPENDIX

The way this doctrine affects our understanding of God and His purposes for men will be seen if we center our attention on just three of these dispensations: Law, Grace and the Kingdom. The Law Dispensation, they say, extended from Sinai to Calvary; Grace, from Calvary to the Second Coming; and the Kingdom, during Christ's postadvent reign upon the earth. The test of the Law Dispensation was obedience to the Mosaic law. In the Dispensation of Grace, "the point of testing is no longer legal obedience as the condition of salvation, but acceptance or rejection of Christ with good works as a fruit of salvation."[3] John 1.17

In the Kingdom Dispensation, the test is again obedience to the Law which had been intensified by the words of Christ.[4]

The Doctrine of Dispensationalism also involves a doctrine of various groups of the human race which must be clearly distinguished, — to wit, the Jew, the Gentile and the Church of God.[5] The distinction between the Jew and the Church is vital to their system, for they believe that to each God made specific, different and eternal promises. Thus arise their peculiar views of the Church and the Kingdom. These will become clearer in our further discussion.

To summarize: The Doctrine of Dispensations declares that God has not one purpose for the saved of the human race, but there are at least two parallel purposes of God, one revealed in His plans for the Jewish race and the other in His plans for the Church. Some Dispensationalists follow this distinction between Israel and the Church out to its logical end and teach that God has two kinds of *eternal* destiny for His two peoples.[6] Furthermore, it is taught by some Dispensationalists that for some groups *legal obedience* is the condition of salvation, while for others it is faith in Christ, so implying on *man's side* two different conditions by which men may be saved.[7]

The Doctrine of the Covenant of Grace is clearly set forth in Ch. VII. of our *Confession of Faith*. In it God "freely offered unto sinners life and salvation by Jesus Christ, requiring of them faith in him, that they may be saved."[8] "This covenant was differently administered in the time of the law, and in the time of the Gospel,"[9] yet there are not "two covenants of grace differing in substance, but one and the same under various dispensations."[10] The destiny set before those who are saved through faith in Christ is "an everlasting inheritance in the kingdom of heaven."[11]

---

[3]*Ibid.*, p. 1115, note 1, (2).

[4]Chafer, *Dispensationalism*, "When under the Mosaic Law, the individual Israelite, it will be seen, was on an unyielding meritorious basis." . . . "The rule governing the conduct of Israelites is in two principle divisions, namely, that which obtained from Moses to Christ, or the Mosaic Law, and that which determines entrance into and conditions life within the yet future kingdom on earth. The terms of admission into the Kingdom as set forth in Matthew 5:1 to 7:27, are, in reality, the Mosaic requirements intensified by Christ's own interpretation of them. The contrasts which He draws between the former interpretation of these laws and His own interpretation (Matt. 5:21-44) does not tend to soften anything in the interests of grace, but rather binds with greater legal demands than any unaided person in the present age can hope to achieve." (pp. 440, 443).

[5]1 Corinthians 10:32 is given as a "proof text" for this division. For a thorough discussion of these three groups, cf. Chafer, *Dispensationalism*, 397-409

[6]Chafer, *Dispensationalism*, p. 448. "The Dispensationalist believes that throughout the ages God is pursuing two distinct purposes: one related to the earth with earthly people and earthly objectives involved, while the other is related to heaven with heavenly people and heavenly objectives involved. . . ."

[7]Dispensationalists believe that on *God's side* the cross of Christ makes salvation possible, but that on man's side the "test" of obedience required varies. See Chafer, *Dispensationalism*, p. 430. The difference in the requirement is plainly stated by some in these words: Scofield is speaking of the dispensation of Grace, "The point of testing is no longer legal obedience as the condition of salvation, but acceptance or rejection of Christ." *(Reference Bible*, p. 1115, Note 1, (2)) William Evans, in contrasting the dispensation of Law with that of Grace, says, "Here we have the covenant of works as contrasted with the covenant of grace found in the New Testament. Then it was 'he that doeth,' now it is 'he that believeth' shall live." *(Outline of Bible Study*, p. 34)

[8]This chapter of the Confession should be read as a whole. This particular sentence is taken from sec. 3.

[9]*Confession of Faith*, Ch. VII. sec. 5.

[10]*Ibid.*, sec. 6. It may be noted that our Confession here uses the word "dispensation" but in a sense quite different from the Dispensational use. Dispensationalism uses the word to indicate distinct and contrasted periods of time. On the other hand the Church has long used the word to indicate stages or parts of a whole. In the patriarchal dispensation God dealt with the family; in the Mosaic, with the nation; in the Christian, with the Church; but these dispensations were all part of the one "plan of salvation."

[11]*Confession of Faith*, Ch. VIII. sec. 5.

Appendix

Thus, the Covenant of Grace regards the human race as a unit, — a race of sinners. It tells us that from the Fall on, God has made *one demand* on men, — faith, and it has set before God's people *one destiny*, — heaven.

B. This Divergence in basic viewpoint leads naturally to radically different views of the Kingdom Christ came to establish, the Kingly Work of Christ, and of the Church.

1. *The Kingdom*

a. According to the Dispensational view the Kingdom which Christ preached to the Jews as "at hand" and then "postponed"[12] till his Second Advent because of their nonacceptance, was the Davidic Kingdom foretold in the Old Testament. This kingdom is to be set up on earth with Jerusalem as its capital. It is established first over regathered, restored, converted Israel, and then it becomes universal. Righteousness and peace will characterize the kingdom. The enormous majority of the earth's inhabitants will be converted. The kingdom will be established by power not persuasion.[13]

Ezekiel 40-48, according to Dr. Scofield,[14] tells us about the rebuilt temple at Jerusalem, the restored priesthood, and the bloody sacrifices which will characterize the life of Israel in the land in the Kingdom Age. According to some, this earthly Messianic, Jewish Kingdom will last only a thousand years. But others, like Dr. Chafer, are more consistent and loyal to the Old Testament which declares that it will continue *forever*. So Dr. Chafer says that it is wrong to say that "there is nothing in eternity but heaven and hell", for he holds that the earthly kingdom also continues.[15]

This Dispensational view of Christ's Kingdom pictures a kingdom that is still *future*. It is imperfect, having among its subjects some men who are unconverted. It is also religiously unsatisfactory, for the priesthood and the temple and the sacrifices once again come between man and God. It is Jewish, for the Gentiles only "share, as a subordinate people, with Israel in her coming kingdom glory."[16]

The Church, says the Dispensationalist, is something quite different from the Kingdom. Their view of the Church will be explained shortly.

b. The Kingdom of Christ of which our *Confession* speaks is quite different from that of the Dispensationalists. It is a present kingdom which extends into the future, the present stage being spoken of as "the kingdom of grace", and the future and perfected form as "the kingdom of glory."[17] The visible Church is identified with this present Kingdom of Christ.[18] Of course it follows that racial privileges and distinctions are done away in Christ, and so our *Confession* knows nothing of a kingdom in which the Jewish race, because they are Jews, have the place of preeminence. On the other hand, our Standards declare that Christ now rules over the Church.[19]

The early Millenarians, (and others like them down through the ages), believed that the present kingdom of Christ would have a glorious *earthly* stage after His Advent, but they insisted that this earthly stage of the kingdom was to be enjoyed

---

[12] This curious and non-Biblical theory of the "postponement" of the kingdom you will find in Dr. Scofield's notes on Matthew, especially on Matt. 11:20, 28 and 16:20. It is also expounded in Chafer's "*The Kingdom in History and Prophecy*," Ch. V.

[13] These statements are drawn from Dr. Scofield's long note on pp. 976-977.

[14] Note Dr. Scofield's chapter and paragraph headings for this section.

[15] Chafer, *Dispensationalism*, p. 448.

[16] Chafer, *Dispensationalism*, p. 397.

[17] *Shorter Catechism*, Ques. 102. "In the second petition, which is 'Thy Kingdom come,' we pray that Satan's kingdom may be destroyed, and that the kingdom of grace may be advanced, ourselves and others brought into it, and kept in it, and that the kingdom of glory may be hastened."

[18] *Confession of Faith*, XXV. 2. "The visible church—is the kingdom of the Lord Jesus Christ".—*Form of Government*, Ch. I. par. 2, "The Church which the Lord Jesus Christ has erected in this world for the gathering and perfecting of the saints, is his visible kingdom of grace, and is one and the same in all ages."

[19] *Form of Government*, Ch. II. par. 9. "It belongs to his Majesty from his throne of glory, to rule and teach the Church, —".

Appendix 4: AIC report on dispensationalism (1943)   237

by the *Church*, and expressly reject the idea that the Jewish nation as such was to receive the blessings promised to God's people in the Old Testament.[20]

2. *The Kingly Work of Christ.*

With these contrasted views of the Kingdom naturally go contrasted views of the kingly work of Christ.

a. According to the Dispensational view, Christ is not *now* exercising kingly power, and will not do so till He comes at His Second Advent to set up His kingdom, and not even then are members of the Church subjects of His kingdom.[21] They contrast the statements, 'Jesus sitting on His Father's throne,' with 'Jesus sitting on his own throne', reserving the exercise of His kingly authority for the latter. For them, the sitting at the Father's right hand is practically a place of withdrawal, retirement, until the time comes for Him to begin His reign.[22]

b. Our Standards hold the opposite view. They declare that Jesus is *now* reigning, that He is reigning over the Church, that He is exercising His authority in the world, "ruling and defending us and restraining and conquering all his and our enemies."[23] In place of His being in retirement at the Father's right hand, the Confession teaches that He is sitting in the seat of power, fulfilling the promise made to David of one sitting upon his throne.[24] So we in faith sing, "Lead on, O King Eternal, We follow, not with fears." And since the day has not yet come when every knee shall bow and every tongue confess that Jesus is Lord, we recognize that his kingly conquest is not yet complete, so we sing, "The Son of God goes forth to war, A kingly crown to gain; His blood-red banner streams afar: Who follows in His train?" Jesus is now engaged in His kingly conquest, and when He comes and raises all the dead, then shall the last enemy be put down. Hence, the Standards put the kingly conquest of Christ now, culminating in His Advent, while the Dispensationalists put this conquest after His Advent.

3. *The Contrasted Views of the Church*

a. The Dispensational view of the Church is integrated with their view of the Kingdom and their view of the Kingly Work of Christ. They see a glorious, earthly kingdom promised to the Jewish people in the Old Testament, and they declare that these promises are to be literally fulfilled. Since this has not yet been done, they say the promised kingdom still lies in the future. The Old Testament promises are not fulfilled in the Church, for the Old Testament prophets did not foresee the Church, it was a mystery hidden from their gaze.[25] Thus, according to the Dispensa-

---
[20] For evidence for this see J. E. Bear, *Union Seminary Review*, July, 1941, "The People of God According to the Early Church Fathers."
[21] *Scofield Reference Bible*, p. 990. "The sphere and character of Christ's *Kingly* office are defined in the Davidic Covenant,—Christ is never called King of the Church. 'The King' is indeed one of the divine titles, and the Church in her worship joins Israel in exalting 'the king, eternal, immortal, invisible'.— But the Church is to reign with Him. The Holy Spirit is now calling out, *not the subjects*, but the co-heirs and co-rulers of the kingdom." (Italics ours.)
Ironside, *The Lamp of Prophecy*, pp. 61-62. "We recognize Him as King. Does that not mean that His kingdom is already set up? Not at all. It implies this: We believe that a usurper is dominating this world, that the rightful King is rejected. We acknowledge the authority of the rightful King. We own His authority, *but that kingdom is not being displayed in any sense*. When Christians try to exert the authority of the King over the world they always make a mistake. The kingdom is not set up yet.—After the church is taken out, the gospel of the kingdom will again be proclaimed, i.e., *the gospel that the King is coming to reign*." (Italics ours.)
[22] Gaebelein, *The Hope of the Ages*, p. 94. "Twice our Lord speaks of 'the throne of His glory.' At once we are told that He is upon the throne of His glory *now*, therefore when He spoke of the throne of His glory, He meant His exaltation to the right hand of God. This view is unscriptural."
[23] *Larger Catechism*, Ans. 45. "Christ executeth the office of a king, in calling out of the world a people for himself; and giving them officers, laws, and censures, by which he visibly governs them, —"
Shorter Catechism, Ans. 26. "Christ executeth the office of a king, in subduing us to himself, in ruling and defending us, and in restraining and conquering all his and our enemies."
[24] *Form of Government*, Ch. II., par. 8. "Jesus Christ, upon whose shoulders the government is,—who sits upon the throne of David, and upon his kingdom to order it and to establish it with judgment and justice from henceforth, even for ever; having all power given unto him in heaven and in earth by the Father, —". Cp. *Larger Catechism*, Ans. 54.
[25] *Scofield Reference Bible*, pp. 989-990. "The Old Testament is a divinely provided Introduction to the New; and whoever comes to the study of the four Gospels with a mind saturated with the Old Testament foreview of the Christ, His person, work and kingdom, will find them open books.—
"Therefore, in approaching the study of the Gospels, the mind should be freed, so far as possible, from mere theological concepts and presuppositions. Especially is it necessary to exclude the notion—a legacy

tionalists, the Church is something quite different from the Kingdom which the Old Testament led men to expect, and is not to be identified with it. The Kingdom, which is to be the fulfillment of the Old Testament expectation is to follow the Church age. The Kingdom was promised to the physical seed of Abraham, and his seed, the Jews, are to enjoy the kingdom glory. The Church is the Body of Christ, His Bride, and is made up of all who believe on Christ, both from the Jews and the Gentiles. They are the "called out" ones. As contrasted with the "earthly people" of the Kingdom, the Church is a "heavenly people" with a spiritual blessing.[26] The Church, according to the Dispensationalists, came into being only after the resurrection of Christ, and will remain on earth till the "rapture"[27] when it will be caught up with Christ, and so will avoid the "great tribulation" during the reign of the Antichrist.[28] Seven years (according to most Dispensationalists) after the Rapture the Church will return with Christ at His "Revelation" in glory when He comes to establish His millennial Kingdom. The Church will then reign with Christ *over* the Kingdom and is itself not a part of the Kingdom.[29] This Church, of course, is the "true Church". The Dispensationalist has a low view of the visible church, declaring that its predicted end is apostasy.[30]

Thus for the Dispensationalist, the Church is a unique body, — separate from all others who may receive God's blessing. There is a unique means of access into this Body, — faith in Christ. It has a unique destiny, — to reign with Christ over the men in the earthly Kingdom.

b. The term "Church" as used in our Standards. Whether wisely or not, our Standards use the term "church" as synonymous with God's people in every age. Of course the "Church" in its present form of organization began with Pentecost, and it might have been well to reserve the term "church" for that form of organization in which God's people are now organized. Be that as it may, it is important to note that our Standards by their use of the term "church" teach the *unity of God's people*, "Before the law, under the law, and now under the Gospel."[31] It makes no distinction between Israel and the Church, two peoples of God with different promises and different destinies, but just the reverse. In contrast to the Dispensational teaching that the Church shall be taken out of the world at the "rapture" seven years before the end of this age, our Confession twice states that the Church will be here till *the end of the world*.[32] To this Church is given a work, "the gathering and the

---

in Protestant thought from post-apostolic and Roman Catholic theology, — that the Church is the true Israel, and that *the Old Testament foreview of the Kingdom is fulfilled in the Church*.— (Italics ours) "The Gospels do not unfold the doctrine of the Church. The word occurs in Matthew only. After his rejection as King and Saviour by the Jews, our Lord, announcing a mystery until that moment 'hid in God', said, 'I will build my church'"—
Chafer, *Dispensationalism*, p. 407. "An extensive body of Scripture declares directly or indirectly that the present age is unforeseen and parenthetical in its character—"
Feinberg, *Premillennialism or Amillennialism?*, p. 111. In speaking of the seventy weeks prophecy of Daniel, he says, "The clock of God stopped at the end of the sixty-ninth week and the Jewish age has been interrupted. This interval is the Church age, not foreseen in the Old Testament."
[26]Feinberg, *Premillennialism vs. Amillennialism*, see pp. 184 ff. "Israel and the Church."
Chafer, *Dispensationalism*, pp. 406-426.
Scofield Reference Bible, cf. "Church" in the index.
[27]Feinberg, *op. cit.*, pp. 204-208 on "The Rapture and the Revelation." Wm. E. Blackstone, *Jesus is Coming*, Ch. IX. Rapture and Revelation.
[28]Ironside, *Lamp of Prophecy*, Ch. VIII. The Great Tribulation.
Feinberg, *op. cit.*, pp. 125-136. The Tribulation Period.
[29]Scofield Reference Bible, p. 990, "not the subjects, but the co-heirs and co-rulers of the kingdom."
[30]Scofield Reference Bible, p. 1276, note 1, "The predicted future of the visible Church is apostasy."
[31]*Confession of Faith*, Chap. XXV. sec. 1 and 2. "The catholic or universal church, which is invisible, consists of the whole number of the elect, that have been, are, or shall be gathered into one, under Christ the head thereof; and is the spouse, the body, the fulness of him that filleth all in all.
"The visible church, which is also catholic or universal under the gospel, (not confined to one nation as before under the law) consists of all those throughout the world, that profess the true religion, together with their children; and is the kingdom of the Lord Jesus Christ, —."
Form of Government, Ch. III., par. 12, "The visible church before the law, under the law, and now under the Gospel, is one and the same, and consists of all those who make profession of the true religion, together with their children."
[32]*Confession of Faith*, Ch. XXV., sec. 3, — "to the end of the world."
Ibid., sec. 5, —"there shall be always a church on earth."
Ibid., sec. 3, For a proof text on this Matt. 28:19-20 is given.
Cp. also *Form of Government*, Ch. 2, par. 9, "the edification and establishment of his kingdom."

APPENDIX

perfecting of the saints."[33] Contrary to Dr. Scofield,[34] Christ's kingdom (which is His Church) is *not* established by power, but by persuasion, — that of the Holy Spirit.[35] It is also the belief of the Reformed Theology that when Christ comes again, the opportunity to be saved is gone. If men are to be saved, they must be saved before the Second Advent.

Some Dispensationalists carry out to logical conclusions the implications of their doctrines of the "Postponed Kingdom" and the distinction between Law and Grace, and teach that all that Jesus said in the Synoptic Gospels[36] was addressed to the Jews and spoke of life in the *Kingdom*, and so was not intended for the Church. This means, for example, that the Sermon on the Mount is not for the Church, but is the law for the Kingdom,[37] and that the Lord's Prayer is not for the Church but for the Jews of the tribulation period.[38]

Conclusion. Thus we see that out of these divergent starting points divergent doctrines naturally sprang. Out of the Dispensational doctrine of "Dispensations" naturally comes their distinction between Israel and the Church, between Law and Grace. Their view of the Kingdom as another "dispensation" naturally leads them to reserve the kingly work of Christ for that Kingdom. With these dispensations there also naturally goes their doctrine multiple resurrections and judgments, some before and some after the Kingdom age.

Out of the doctrine of the Covenant of Grace which our Standards teach, there naturally flows the teaching that God's people are one, saved in one way and having one destiny. The identification in our Standards of the Church and the Kingdom

---

[34]*Scofield Reference Bible*, p. 977, (e).
[35]*Shorter Catechism*, Ans. 31.
[36]Haldeman, *How to Study the Bible*, p. 2 "We must recognize that the Bible was written to or about distinct classes. According to the general view everything from Genesis to Revelation is written to or about the Church and Christians. No greater mistake could be made. The truth is that the Church and Christians occupy a very restrained area of the Bible. If all that is said directly about the Church and Christians was printed by itself it would make a very small book. Not even all the New Testament is written to and about the Church. In his Epistle to the Corinthians (I Cor. 10:32) the Apostle speaks of Jew, Gentile and the Church of God. The Bible is written to or about one of these three classes." Chafer, *Dispensationalism*, pp. 406-407. "The Christians. — The Scriptures addressed specifically to this company are, the Gospel of John —, especially the upper room discourse, — the Acts and the Epistles. The Synoptic Gospels, though on the surface presenting a simple narrative are, nevertheless, a field for careful, discriminating study on the part of the true expositor. In these Gospels Christ is seen as loyal to and vindicating the Mosaic Law under which He lived; He also anticipates the Kingdom age in connection with the offer of Himself as Israel's King; —"
[37]*Dr. C. I. Scofield's Question Box*, p. 64. "The Sermon on the Mount is kingdom, not church, truth." Chafer, *Dispensationalism*, p. 423. "Matthew 7:13, 14, which passage is found in that portion of Scripture that defines the terms of admission into, and condition of life in, the earthly Messianic Kingdom; which kingdom occupies the supreme place in the eschatology of Judaism. The passage imposes the most drastic human effort as essential if one would enter the narrow way that leads to life."
Ibid., p. 443. "The rule governing the conduct of Israelites is in two principal divisions, namely, that which obtained from Moses to Christ, or the Mosaic Law, and that which determines entrance into and conditions life within the yet future kingdom on the earth. The terms of admission into the Kingdom as set forth in Matthew 5:1 to 7:27, are, in reality, the Mosaic requirements intensified by Christ's own interpretation of them. The contrasts which He draws between the former interpretation of these laws and His own interpretation (Matt. 5:21-44) does not tend to soften anything in the interests of grace, but rather binds with greater legal demands than any unaided person in the present age can hope to achieve."
[38]*Dr. C. I. Scofield's Question Box*, pp. 113-114. "It is undeniable that the Lord's Prayer so-called (Disciples' Prayer would be a more accurate designation), is a prayer upon kingdom rather than upon Church ground. (1) It is not in Christ's name. (2) It makes human forgiveness the ground for expecting divine forgiveness. This is righteousness, not grace."
I. M. Haldeman, *How to Study the Bible*, p. 21. "Dispensational classification explains the place of what is commonly known as the Lord's Prayer. That prayer belongs to the closing hours of this dispensation when the Church is gone and when the elect remnant among the Jews, suffering under the persecution of the Willful King, call on God to deliver them from the Great Tribulation, and the power of the Evil One, give them the daily bread which the Antichrist makes it impossible for them to touch without sin, and bring in the long promised Kingdom of the Messiah. The prayer belongs essentially to that part of the present dispensation because grace will be gone and law and righteousness will be in vogue.
Ibid., pp. 185-140. "This prayer is so wrought into the general service of the Christian Church, so made use of on public and private occasions and thought to be so preeminently an expression of the Christian faith and devotion that it is impossible to touch it or put it out of its accepted place without offending the common consensus of opinion concerning it; yet it does not belong to the church, it is not for the Christian at all; and the reason ought to be self evident. — Such is the full and prophetic meaning of this prayer. A prayer that has no more place in the Christian Church than the thunders of Sinai, or the offerings of Leviticus."
Gaebelein, *Gospel of Matthew*, p. 139. "All this practise, the use of this model for prayer, as the Lord's prayer given to the Church, to be used by the Church, is wrong, decidedly unchristian, nor can it be proven from the New Testament that it is intended for the Church."

APPENDIX

naturally leads to the teaching that Christ is now exercising His kingly power, subduing "his and our enemies," which conquest will culminate in His Second Advent when there shall be the general resurrection and final judgment.

Dr. Chafer was right when he said, "When good men disagree as to doctrine it is usually due to a fundamental difference in premise. Perfect logic when built on divergent premises, will usually result in irreconcilable conclusions. The controversy between the partial dispensationalists and the dispensationalists is due to a wide difference in premise."[39] It would seem that the logical mind must agree that the conclusions are irreconcilable, — that Dispensationalism and the teaching of the Confession on these great themes belong to two different systems of Bible interpretation.

Respectfully submitted,

B. R. LACY, JR., *Chairman,*
F. H. CALDWELL,
J. B. GREEN,
E. W. MCLAURIN.

NOTE: Judge S. H. Sibley declines to sign the second part of the report—on Dispensationalism.

---

[39] Chafer, *Dispensationalism,* p. 396.

Appendix 5

Copy of the Original Report of the 1944 PCUS Ad Interim Committee on Changes in the Confession of Faith and Catechisms as to Whether the Type of Bible Interpretation Known as "Dispensationalism" is in Harmony with the Confession of Faith

III. REPORTS OF AD INTERIM COMMITTEES

1. Report of the Ad Interim Committee on Changes in the Confession of Faith and Catechisms

THE QUESTION AS TO WHETHER THE TYPE OF BIBLE INTERPRETATION KNOWN AS DISPENSATIONALISM IS IN HARMONY WITH THE CONFESSION OF FAITH

The Ad Interim Committee appointed by the Assembly to consider this question (Minutes, 1941, p. 60; 1943, p. 46) presents the following report.

Before calling attention to certain doctrines which we believe to be out of accord with the Standards of our Church, we desire to define the terms DISPENSATION and DISPENSATIONALISM.

The word "Dispensation" is used by both the Confession of Faith and by Dispensationalism. Both systems use it in the sense of "an administration" of some purpose or plan of God, but they differ on the question of *what is administered.*

That which is "administered" is made very plain in the Confession of Faith (Ch. VII, Sec. 5-6), where, speaking of the Covenant of Grace, we read, "This covenant was differently administered in the time of the law, and in the time of the gospel: under the law it was administered by promises, prophecies, . . . Under the gospel, when Christ the substance, was exhibited, the ordinances in which this covenant is dispensed, are the preaching of the word, and the administration of the sacraments of baptism and the Lord's Supper; . . . There are not, therefore, two covenants of grace differing in substance, but one and the same under various dispensations."

Here it will be seen that the administration of God's purpose under the law (the O. T. dispensation) is stated to be different in *form*, as we know it was in organization and ceremony, from the administration under the gospel (our own dispensation); but the point which the Confession of Faith emphasizes is that these two dispensations do not *differ in substance,* but there is *only one and the same Covenant of Grace* to be administered under the various dispensations. Students of the Reformed Faith

124 APPENDIX

have differed as to the number of dispensations into which we may properly divide the dealing of God with man since the fall; but they have all agreed, in accordance with our Confession of Faith, that these various dispensations are all administrations of *one and the same Covenant of Grace.*

The opposing viewpoint, on the other hand, as presented by Dr. L. S. Chafer, is as follows: "Since there is so much in the Confession of Faith which is in no way related to this discussion and which is the common belief of all, the issue should yet be narrowed to the difference which obtains between Dispensationalism and Covenantism. The latter is that form of theological speculation which attempts to unify God's entire program from Genesis to Revelation under one supposed Covenant of Grace. That no such covenant is either named or exhibited in the Bible and that the covenants which are set forth in the Bible are so varied and diverse that they preclude a one-covenant idea, evidently does not deter many sincere men from adherence to the one-covenant theory." (Chafer, *Bibliotheca Sacra*, editorial on "Dispensational Distinctions Challenged," Vol. 100, No. 399, p. 338.)

Thus the "various and diverse" covenants are set over against the "one Covenant of Grace," i. e., one plan of salvation, which is central to our Church's view of the teaching of the Bible. All acquainted with dispensational thought know what Dispensationalists mean by their rejection of the Covenant of Grace; they do not hold that God has one plan of salvation for all men, but that He has had various and diverse plans for different groups. (Chafer, *Grace*, p. 135.) Some of the chief points of divergence will be pointed out below.

DISPENSATIONALISM, therefore, as shown above, rejects the doctrine that God has, since the fall, but one "plan of salvation" for all mankind and affirms that God has been through the ages "administering" various and diverse plans of salvation for various groups.

Such dispensational teaching is expounded by many in our day, but we shall limit our quotations to the writings of two outstanding exponents of Dispensationalism: Dr. C. I. Scofield (especially as found in certain notes in the *Scofield Reference Bible*) and Dr. L. S. Chafer, who has written extensively on this subject. They both teach a dispensational view of God's various and divergent plans of salvation for various groups in different ages, although they do not agree on all inferences which may be drawn from this fundamental starting point.

I

This Fundamental Divergence of Dispensationalism From the Covenant Theology of the Presbyterian Church Manifests Itself in Many Ways, Some of Which Are the Following:

A. The Rejection of the Unity of God's people.

1. The Confession of Faith clearly teaches that God has one people who were brought into saving relation with Him, some under the law, others under the gospel dispensation. The Confession of Faith calls this one people of God "The Church." (*Confession of Faith*, Ch. XXV, Sec. 2.) Whatever may be the national destiny of the Jewish people, according to the Confession of Faith their becoming a spiritual blessing to the world and to the Church will be contingent upon their acceptance of Jesus as the Messiah and thereby becoming a part of the Church.

2. Dispensationalism teaches that God has at least two distinct peoples, namely, the Jewish Nation and the Christian Church. He has distinctly different purposes for them, and each of these two peoples is united to Him by various and diverse covenants quite different in character. (*Dispensationalism* reprinted from *Bibliotheca Sacra*, No. 372, Vol. 93, p. 396 ff., esp. p. 448.)

Appendix 125

B. The Rejection of One Way of Salvation.

1. The Confession of Faith teaches that there is but one plan of salvation—that men are saved only in Christ, by grace through faith. (*Confession of Faith*, Ch. III, Sec. 5; VII, Sec. 3; VIII, Sec. 6; X, Sec. 1, 2, 4.)

2. Dispensationalism, magnifying the distinction which is made between law and grace (*which dispensationalists hold to be mutually exclusive*—Chafer, *Grace*, p. 231 ff.), agrees that men are NOW saved by grace through faith, but teaches that in other dispensations men have been saved by "legal obedience." "The point of testing is no longer legal obedience as the condition of salvation, but acceptance or rejection of Christ . . ." (*Scofield Reference Bible*, p. 1115; also see Chafer, *Dispensationalism*, pp. 415-16; *Grace*, pp. 123, 124-126.) It also holds that after the present age of grace, there will be a reversion in the kingdom age to an extreme system of meritorious obligation. (Chafer, *Dispensationalism*, pp. 416, 440, 441, 443; *Grace*, p. 223.)

C. The Rejection of One Destiny for All of God's People.

1. The Confession of Faith teaches that God's people, the righteous, go into "everlasting life" (*Confession of Faith*, Ch. XXXIII, Sec. 2) which is also spoken of as "an everlasting inheritance in the kingdom of heaven." (*Confession of Faith*, Ch. VIII, Sec. 5.) The wicked shall be cast into everlasting torment. Such is the final destiny of the saved and the lost, and the Confession of Faith nowhere suggests that the saved are divided into different and distinct groups which will enjoy different blessings according to the purpose of God.

2. Dispensationalism teaches that the two groups of God's people, the Jewish Nation and the Christian Church, are entirely distinct bodies, and in the millennial kingdom will enjoy different blessings, the Jews enjoying earthly and material blessings, and the Church spiritual and heavenly blessings. Some Dispensationalists, like Dr. Chafer, continue this distinction in destiny into eternity, holding that in eternity there are three groups: the lost in hell, the earthly people of God on earth forever, and the Church, the heavenly people of God in heaven forever. (*Dispensationalism*, p. 448.)

D. The Rejection of the Bible as God's one Revelation to His One People.

1. The writers of the Confession of Faith had not heard of the Dispensational method of "rightly dividing the word of truth" for it was not taught in their day. However, all acquainted with the view of the Reformed Church know that the Church has held that "God, who at sundry times and in divers manners spake unto the fathers by the prophets, hath in these last days spoken unto us by His Son." (Hebrews 1:12) The Confession of Faith states that God has given His people (which the Confession of Faith calls the Church) a unified and progressive revelation, culminating in the revelation in Christ, and most clearly expressed in the New Testament which was written under the guidance of the Holy Spirit who led the Apostles to see the purpose of God in Christ. (*Confession of Faith*, Ch. I, Sec. 1, 2; VII, Sec. 6.)

2. Dispensationalism rejects both the unity of God's revelation and the fact that God's purpose is "held forth with more fullness" (*Confession of Faith*, Ch. VII, Sec. 6) in the New Testament than it is in the Old. Dispensationalism holds that large portions even of the New Testament are for the Jewish Nation, not for the Church. In speaking of the Scriptures for the Church, Dr. Chafer says, "The Scriptures addressed specifically to this company are the Gospel by John—especially the upper room discourse,—the Acts and the Epistles." (*Dispensationalism*, pp. 406-07.) Dispensationalism declares that the Sermon on the Mount is for the Jews of the Kingdom period, and is "law not grace." *Scofield Reference Bible*, pp. 989, 1230; *Dispensationalism*, p. 443.) The Lord's Prayer and the Great Commission are assigned by some to the Jews of the "tribulation" period, and not to the Church. (*Grace*, pp. 174, 176, 179, 181.)

126 APPENDIX

II

THERE ARE ALSO DISPENSATIONAL DIVERGENCIES FROM THE CONFESSIONAL INTERPRETATION OF THE WORK OF THE EXALTED CHRIST

A. The Confession of Faith speaks of the kingly work of Christ and what is included in the exaltation of Christ. A study, for example, of answers 26 and 28 of the *Shorter Catechism* will show that Christ, "sitting on the right hand of God the Father," is now exercising His kingly function, "in subduing us to himself, in ruling and defending us, and in restraining and conquering all his and our enemies." (It should be noted that the *Larger Catechism*, in answer to question 45, devotes twice as much space to His kingly as to the prophetic and priestly work.)

The second function of the Exalted Christ taught by our Confession of Faith is His coming to judge the world at the last day. This "judgment" naturally is the climax of his victorious activity in "subduing all his and our enemies." All that then remains will be the pronouncement of the final verdict.

B. Dispensationalism rejects or minimizes the present kingly office of Christ, and deviates from the conception of the Resurrection and Judgment, as set forth in our Standards.

1. Dispensationalism teaches that Christ is not now exercising His kingly power, but is only Head of the Church. It reserves the kingly work of "subduing his and our enemies" exclusively to the kingdom dispensation which will follow his second advent. (*Scofield Reference Bible*, note on p. 990.)

2. The Confession of Faith speaks of the Resurrection as follows: "At the last day, such as are found alive shall not die, but be changed; and all the dead shall be raised up with the self-same bodies, . . ." (*Confession of Faith*, Ch. XXXII, paragraph II.) The *Larger Catechism*, in answer to question 88, states that "Immediately after the resurrection shall follow the general and final judgment of angels and men, . . ." In dealing with the Judgment, the Confession of Faith says, "God hath appointed a day, wherein he will judge the world in righteousness by Jesus Christ, to whom all power and judgment is given of the Father. In which day, not only the apostate angels shall be judged; but likewise all persons, that have lived upon the earth, shall appear before the tribunal of Christ, to give an account of their thoughts, words, and deeds; and to receive according to what they have done in the body, whether good or evil." (*Confession of Faith*, Ch. XXXIII, paragraph I. See answers to questions 85, 86, 87, 88 of *Larger Catechism*.)

Dispensationalism teaches a series of resurrections and judgments, spaced over more than a thousand years. It is the opinion of your Committee that the above statement of the Confession of Faith does not admit of a multiplicity of resurrections and judgments as taught by many Dispensationalists.

CONCLUSION:

It is the unanimous opinion of your Committee that Dispensationalism as defined and set forth above is out of accord with the system of the doctrine set forth in the Confession of Faith, not primarily or simply in the field of eschatology, but because it attacks the very heart of the Theology of our Church, which is unquestionably a Theology of one Covenant of Grace. As Dr. Chafer clearly recognizes, there are two schools of interpretation represented here, which he rightly designates as "Covenantism" as over against "Dispensationalism." (*Bibliotheca Sacra*, Vol. 100, No. 399, p. 338.)

In fact, the divergence of Dispensationalism from the Covenant Theology of our Church is so obvious to Dr. Chafer that he suggests a revision of the Standards of the Church so as to make room for those who no longer hold to the Reformed tradition of a Covenant Theology. (*Ibid.*, p. 345.)

Inasmuch as there is some difference of opinion concerning the status and use of such a report, your Committee desires to state that it does not understand that the Assembly instructed it to provide a statement of doctrine which shall be a substitute for, or an amendment to, any doctrinal statements contained in the Constitution of the Church or any part thereof. Nor does it understand that this report, if approved by the Assembly, is to be regarded as an amendment to ordination vows of ministers, ruling elders, or deacons. It is simply an interpretative statement which may be used by the Presbyteries as they deem wise.

Your Committee wishes also to make the following statement of clarification: Most, if not all, adherents to the type of Dispensationalism dealt with in this report hold the Premillennial view of our Lord's return; but not all Premillennialists accept this form of Dispensationalism. Therefore, the Committee wishes to make it clear that it has endeavored solely to consider the particular type of Biblical interpretation defined above, and known as Dispensationalism and that it understood the assignment of the Assembly to limit it to this task. In view of this fact, this report should not be considered as in any sense a criticism of Premillennialism as such.

Respectfully submitted;

F. B. GEAR, *Chairman*
J. E. BEAR
L. NELSON BELL.
J. B. GREEN
J. P. MCCALLIE
E. W. MCLAURIN
SAMUEL H. SIBLEY

Appendix 6

The Members of the 1943 and 1944 Ad Interim Committees on Changes in the Confession of Faith and Catechisms

The 1943 AIC

Benjamin R. Lacy, Jr. **(Chairman)**   Frank H. Caldwell   James B. Green   Eugene W. McLaurin   Samuel H. Sibley

The 1944 AIC

James E. Bear   Felix B. Gear **(Chairman)**   James B. Green   Eugene W. McLaurin   Samuel H. Sibley

L. Nelson Bell   J.P. McCallie

Bibliography

Books

Abraham, William J., *The Coming Great Revival: Recovering the Full Evangelical Tradition* (San Francisco, CA: Harper & Row, Publishers, 1984).
- *The Divine Inspiration of Holy Scripture* (New York, NY: Oxford University Press, 1981)).

Allan, Fredrick Lewis, *Only Yesterday: An Informal History of the 1920s* (New York, NY: Harper & Bros., 1931).

Allis, Oswald T., *The Five Books of Moses* (Philadelphia, PA: Presbyterian and Reformed Publishing Co., 1943).
- *God Spake By Moses* (Philadelphia, PA: Presbyterian and Reformed Publishing Co., 1951).
- *The Old Testament: Its Claims and Its Critics* (Nutley, NJ: Presbyterian and Reformed Publishing Co., 1972).
- *Prophecy and the Church* (Philadelphia, PA: Presbyterian and Reformed Publishing Co., 1945).
- *The Unity of Isaiah* (Philadelphia, PA: Presbyterian and Reformed Publishing Co., 1950).

Ammerman, Nancy Tatom, *Bible Believers: Fundamentalists in the Modern World* (New Brunswick, NJ: Rutgers University Press, 1987).

Anderson, Sir Robert, *The Coming Prince* (Grand Rapids, MI: Kregel Publications, 1957[10]).

Auger, Wes, *A Critique of the Scofield Bible* (Little Rock, AR: Challenge Press, 1972).

Averill, Lloyd J., *American Theology in the Liberal Tradition* (Philadelphia, PA: Westminster Press, 1967).

Bahnsen, Greg L., *Theonomy in Christian Ethics* (Nutley, NJ: Presbyterian and Reformed Publishing Co., 1991).

Bahnsen, Greg L., and Kenneth L. Gentry, Jr., *House Divided: The Break-Up of Dispensational Theology* (Tyler, TX: Institute for Christian Economics, 1989).

Balmer, Randall, *Mine Eyes Have Seen the Glory: A Journey into the Evangelical Subculture* (New York, NY: Oxford University Press, 1989).

Barker, Kenneth L., "The Scope of Old and New Testament Theology and Hope," in *Dispensationalism, Israel and the Church: The Search for Definition*, ed. Craig A. Blaising, and Darrell L. Bock, 293-328 (Grand Rapids, MI: Zondervan Publishing House, 1992).

Barker, William S., and W. Robert Godfrey (eds.), *Theonomy: A Reformed Critique* (Grand Rapids, MI: Academie Books, 1990).

Barndollar, W.W., *The Validity of Dispensationalism* (Johnson City, NY: Baptist Bible Seminary Press, 1964).

Barth, Karl, *Church Dogmatics*, vol. 1, *Doctrine of the Word of God*, ed. and tr. G.W. Bromiley and T.F. Torrance (Edinburgh: T. & T. Clarke, 1936).

Bass, Clarence B., *Backgrounds to Dispensationalism: Its Historical Genesis and Ecclesiastical Implications* (Grand Rapids, MI: William B. Eerdmans Publishing Co., 1960).

Bateman, Herbert W., IV (ed.), *Three Central Issues in Contemporary Dispensationalism: A Comparison of Traditional and Progressive Views* (Grand Rapids, MI: Kregel Publications, 1999).

Bavinck, Herman, *The Doctrine of God*, tr. and ed. William Hendricksen (Grand Rapids, MI: William B. Eerdmans Publishing Co., 1951).
- *Our Reasonable Faith*, tr. Henry Zylstra (Grand Rapids, MI: William B. Eerdmans Publishing Co., 1956).

- *The Philosophy of Revelation* (New York, NY: Longman Press, 1909).
Bear, James E., *A Literal vs. a Spiritual Interpretation of the Bible* (Richmond, VA: Presbyterian Committee of Publication, 1938).
- *Notes on the Text of the New Testament* (Richmond, VA: Union Theological Seminary, 1941).
Beattie, Francis R., Charles R. Hemphill, and Henry V. Escott (eds.), *Memorial Volume of the Westminster Assembly, 1647-1897* (Richmond, VA: The Presbyterian Committee of Publication, 1897).
Beecher, Willis J., *The Prophets and the Promise* (Grand Rapids, MI: Baker Book House, 1905).
Beeke, Joel, *Assurance of Faith: Calvin, English Puritanism, and the Dutch Second Reformation* (New York, NY: Peter Lang, 1991).
Bell, L. Nelson, *Convictions to Live By* (Grand Rapids, MI: William B. Eerdmans Publishing Co., 1966).
- *While Men Slept*. Garden City, NY: Doubleday & Co., 1970).
Benton, W. Wilson, Jr., "Federal Theology: Review for Revision," in *Through Christ's Word: A Festschrift for Dr. Philip E. Hughes*, ed. W. Robert Godfrey and Jesse L. Boyd, III, 180-204 (Phillipsburg, NJ: Presbyterian and Reformed Publishing Co., 1985).
Berger, Peter, *The Sacred Canopy*. Garden City, NY: Anchor Books, 1969).
Berkhof, Louis, *The History of Christian Doctrines*. 1937, reprint (London: Banner of Truth Trust, 1969).
- *The Kingdom of God* (Grand Rapids, MI: William B. Eerdmans Publishing Co., 1951).
- *Principles of Biblical Interpretation (Sacred Hermeneutics)* (Grand Rapids, MI: Baker Book House, 1950).
- *The Second Coming of Christ* (Grand Rapids, MI: William B. Eerdmans Publishing Co., 1953).
- *Systematic Theology* (Grand Rapids, MI: William B. Eerdmans Publishing Co., 1939).
Berry, George Richer, *Premillennialism and Old Testament Prediction* (Chicago, IL: University of Chicago Press, 1929).
Besier, Gerhard and Eduard Lohse (eds.), *Glaube -Bekenntnis - Kirchenrecht: Festschrift fur Vizeprasident i.R. D. theol. Hans Philipp Meyer zum 70. Geburtstag* (Hanover: Lutherisches Verlagshaus, 1989).
Blackstone, William E., *Jesus is Coming* (New York, NY: Fleming H. Revell Publishing Co., 1932^4).
- *The Millennium* (New York, NY: Fleming H. Revell Publishing Co., 1904).
Blaising, Craig A., "Lewis Sperry Chafer," in *Handbook of Evangelical Theologians*, ed. Walter A. Elwell, 83-96 (Grand Rapids, MI: Baker Book House, 1993).
Blaising, Craig A., and Darrell L. Bock (eds.), *Dispensationalism, Israel and the Church: The Search for Definition* (Grand Rapids, MI: Zondervan Publishing House, 1992).
- *Progressive Dispensationalism: An Up-to-Date Handbook of Contemporary Dispensational Thought* (Wheaton, IL: Bridgepoint Books, 1993).
Bloesch, Donald, *Holy Scripture: Revelation, Inspiration & Interpretation* (Downers Grove, IL: Inter-Varsity Press, 1994).
- *A Theology of Word & Spirit: Authority & Method in Theology* (Downers Grove, IL: Inter-Varsity Press, 1992).
- *Essentials of Evangelical Theology*. 2 vols. (San Francisco, CA: Harper & Row, Publishers, 1978).
- *The Future of Evangelical Christianity: A Call for Unity Amid Diversity* (Colorado Springs, CO: Helmers & Howard, Publishers, 1988).
The Book of Church Order of the Presbyterian Church in the United States (Richmond, VA: Presbyterian Committee of Publication, 1938).

Bock, Darrell L., "Covenants in Progressive Dispensationalism," in *Three Central Issues in Contemporary Dispensationalism: A Comparison of traditional and Progressive Views*, ed. Herbert W. Bateman IV, 169-223 (Grand Rapids, MI: Kregel Publications, 1999).
- *Proclamation from Prophecy and Pattern: Lucan Old Testament Christology*. Sheffield: JSOT Press, 1987.
- "Hermeneutics of Progressive Dispensationalism," in *Three Central Issues in Contemporary Dispensationalism: A Comparison of traditional and Progressive Views*, ed. Herbert W. Bateman IV, 85-118 (Grand Rapids, MI: Kregel Publications, 1999).
- (ed.), *Three Views on the Millennium and Beyond* (Grand Rapids, MI: Zondervan Publishing House, 1999).
Boyd, Blanche McCrary, *The Redneck Way of Knowledge: Down-Home Tales* (New York, NY: Alfred A. Knopf, 1982).
Boyer, Paul, *When Time Shall Be No More: Prophecy Belief in Modern American Culture* (Cambridge, MA: Harvard University Press, 1992).
Bozeman, Dwight Theodore, *Protestants in an Age of Science: The Baconian Ideal and Antebellum American Religious Thought* (Chapel Hill, NC: University of North Carolina Press, 1977).
Bray, Gerald, *Biblical Interpretation Past and Present* (Downers Grove, IL: Inter-Varsity Press, 1996).
Brookes, James Hall, *I Am Coming* (Glasgow: Pickering & Inglis, 1895).
- *Israel and the Church: The Terms Distinguished as Found in the Word of God* (Chicago, IL: Bible Institute Colportage Ass'n, 1900).
- *Maranatha, or The Lord Cometh*. 10th ed (New York, NY: Fleming H. Revell Publishing Co., 1889).
- *Till He Come* (Chicago, IL: Gospel Publishing House, 1891).
- *The Way Made Plain* (Philadelphia, PA: American Sunday School Union, n.d).
Brunner, Emil, *The Christian Doctrine of God* (Philadelphia, PA: Westminster Press, 1950).
Bullinger, E.W., *The Apocalypse: or, "The Day of the Lord"*, (London: Samuel Bagster & Sons, n.d).
- *The Foundations of Dispensational Truth* (London: Eyre & Spottiswoode, 1931^2).
- *How to Enjoy the Bible* (London: Eyre & Spottiswoode, 1910^2).
Burch, Maxie B., *The Evangelical Historians: The Historiography of George Marsden, Nathan Hatch, and Mark Noll* (New York, NY: University Press of America, 1996).
Burns, J. Lanier, "The Future of Ethnic Israel in Romans 11," in *Dispensationalism, Israel and the Church: The Search for Definition*, ed. Craig A. Blaising, and Darrell L. Bock, 188-229 (Grand Rapids, MI: Zondervan Publishing House, 1992).
- "Israel and the Church of a Progressive Dispensationalist," in *Three Central Issues in Contemporary Dispensationalism: A Comparison of Traditional and Progressive Views*, ed. Herbert W. Bateman IV, 263-303 (Grand Rapids, MI: Kregel Publications, 1999).
Buswell, J. Oliver, Jr., *The Christian Life* (Grand Rapids, MI: Zondervan Publishing House, 1937).
- *A Systematic Theology of the Christian Religion* (Grand Rapids, MI: Zondervan Publishing House, 1962).
- *Unfulfilled Prophecies* (Grand Rapids, MI: Zondervan Publishing House, 1937).
Caldwell, Frank H., *Preaching Angles* (Nashville, TN: Abingdon Press, 1954).
Caldwell, Frank H., Guy T. Gillespie, James A. Jones and John R. Richardson, *A Pamphlet Concerning the Matter of the Union of The United Presbyterian Church of North America, The Presbyterian Church in the United States of America, and The Presbyterian Church in the United States* (Richmond, VA: Presbyterian Committee of Publication, 1954).
Calhoun, David B., "Honest Subscription": Old Princeton Seminary and Subscription to the Westminster Standards," in *The Practice of Confessional Subscription*, ed. David W. Hall, 237-45 (Lanham, MD: University Press of America, 1995).

Calvin, John, *Institutes of the Christian Religion*, 2 vols., ed. John T. McNeill, tr. Ford Lewis Battles (Philadelphia, PA: Westminster Press, 1960).
– *Selected Works of John Calvin: Tracts and Letters*, 7 vols., ed. and tr. Henry Beveridge (Grand Rapids, MI: Baker Book House, 1983).
Cameron, Nigel M. de S., *The Challenge of Evangelical Theology: Essays in Approach and Method* (Edinburgh: Rutherford House Books, 1987).
– (ed.), *Dictionary of Scottish Church History & Theology* (Downers Grove, IL: Inter-Varsity Press, 1993).
Campbell, Donald K. (ed.), *Walvoord: A Tribute* (Chicago, IL: Moody Press, 1982).
Campbell, Donald K., and Jeffrey L. Townsend (eds.), *A Case for Premillennialism: A New Consensus* (Chicago, IL: Moody Press, 1992).
Campbell, Roderick, *Israel and the New Covenant* (Philadelphia, PA: Presbyterian Board of Christian Education, 1936).
Camping, Harold, *1994?* New York, NY: Vantage Press, 1992).
Canfield, Joseph M., *The Incredible Scofield and His Book* (Asheville, NC: by the author, 1984).
Carpenter, Joel, *Revive Us Again: The Reawakening of American Fundamentalism* (New York, NY: Oxford University Press, 1997).
Carruthers, S.W., *The Everyday Work of the Westminster Assembly* (Philadelphia, PA: The Presbyterian Historical Society (of America) and the Presbyterian Historical Society of England, 1943).
Carson, Donald A. (ed.), *Biblical Interpretation and the Church: The Problem of Contextualization* (Nashville, TN: Thomas Nelson, Publishers, 1985).
– (ed.), *From Sabbath to Lord's Day: A Biblical, Historical and Theological Perspective* (Grand Rapids, MI: Zondervan Publishing House, 1982).
Cash, Wilbur J., *The Mind of the South* (New York, NY: A.A. Knopf, 1941), reprint (New York, NY: Doubleday & Co., 1956).
Cauthen, Kenneth, *The Impact of American Religious Liberalism* (New York, NY: Harper & Row, Publishers, 1962).
Chafer, Lewis Sperry, *Grace* (Wheaton, IL: Van Kampen Press, 1922).
– *He That is Spiritual* (New York, NY: Our Hope Press, 1918).
– *The Kingdom in History and Prophecy* (Findlay, OH: Dunham Publishing Co., 1915).
– *Major Bible Themes* (Philadelphia, PA: Sunday School Times Co., 1926).
– *Must We Dismiss the Millennium?* (Crescent City, FL: Florida Testimony Association, 1921).
– *Salvation: A Clear Doctrinal Analysis* (Wheaton, IL: Van Kampen Press, 1917).
– *Systematic Theology*, 8 vols. (Dallas, TX: Dallas Seminary Press, 1947).
– *True Evangelism* (Grand Rapids, MI: Kregel Publications, 1911).
Chafer, Rollin Thomas, *The Science of Biblical Hermeneutics: An Outline Study of Its Laws* (Dallas, TX: Bibliotheca Sacra, 1939).
Chamberlain, William D., "Dispensationalism," in *The Church Faces the Isms*, ed. Arnold Black Rhodes, Frank H. Caldwell, and L.C. Rudolph, 95-110 (Nashville, TN: Abingdon Press, 1958).
Cheeseman, Lewis, *Differences Between Old and New School Presbyterians* (Rochester, NY: Erastus Darrow, 1848).
Churchill, Robert, *Lest We Forget: A Personal Reflection on the Formation of the Orthodox Presbyterian Church* (Philadelphia, PA: Committee for the History of the Orthodox Presbyterian Church, 1986).
Clouse, R.G. (ed.), *The Meaning of the Millennium: Four Views* (Downers Grove, IL: Inter-Varsity Press, 1977).
Clouser, G.B.M., *Dispensations and Ages of Scripture: A Study of the Divine Plan for the "End Times,"* New York, NY: Francis E. Fitch, 1903).
Cole, Stewart G., *The History of Fundamentalism* (New York, NY: Richard B. Smith, 1931).

Colyer, Elmer M. (ed.), *Evangelical Theology in Transition: theologians in Dialogue with Donald Bloesch* (Downers Grove, IL: Inter-Varsity Press, 1999).
Cox, William E., *Biblical Studies in Final Things* (Philadelphia, PA: Presbyterian and Reformed Publishing Co., 1967).
– *An Examination of Dispensationalism* (Phillipsburg, NJ: Presbyterian and Reformed Publishing Co., 1963).
– *Why I Left Scofieldism* (Nutley, NJ: Presbyterian and Reformed Publishing Co., 1977).
Cranfield, C.E.B., *A Critical and Exegetical Commentary on the Epistle to the Romans*, 2 vols., ICC, ed. J.A. Emerton and C.E.B. Cranfield, (Edinburgh: T.& T. Clark, 1979).
Crenshaw, Curtis I., and Grover Gunn, *Dispensationalism Today, Yesterday, and Tomorrow* (Memphis, TN: Footstool Publication, 1985).
Crutchfield, Larry V., *The Origins of Dispensationalism: The Darby Factor* (Lanham, MD: University Press of America, 1995).
Dabney, Robert L., *Syllabus and Notes of the Course of Systematic and Polemic Theology taught in Union Theological Seminary, Virginia* (Richmond, VA: Presbyterian Committee of Publication, 1890).
Daniel, Curt, *The History and Theology of Calvinism* (Dallas, TX: Scholarly Reprints, 1993).
Darby, John Nelson, *The Collected Writings of J N. Darby*, 32 vols., ed. William Kelly, (London: G. Morrish, [1867-1900]), reprint (Sunbury, PA: Believers Bookshelf, 1971-72).
– *Lectures on the Second Coming* (London: W.H. Broom, 1868).
Davis, John Jefferson, *Foundations of Evangelical Theology* (Grand Rapids, MI: Baker Book House, 1984).
Dayton, Donald W., and Robert K. Johnston (eds.), *The Variety of American Evangelicalism* (Downers Grove, IL: Inter-Varsity Press, 1991).
DeJong, Peter Y., *The Covenant Idea in New England Theology* (Grand Rapids, MI: William B. Eerdmans Publishing Co., 1945).
Dennison, Charles G., and Richard C. Gamble (eds.), *Pressing Toward the Mark: Essays Commemorating the Fifty Years of the Orthodox Presbyterian Church* (Philadelphia, PA: Committee for the Historian of the Orthodox Presbyterian Church, 1986).
The Distinctive Principles of the Presbyterian Church in the United States, Commonly Called the Southern Presbyterian Church, as Set Forth in the Formal Declarations, and Illustrated by the Extracts from the Proceedings of the General Assembly from 1861-1870; to which is added from the proceedings of the Old School Assembly from 1861-1866. 2d ed (Richmond, VA: Presbyterian Committee of Publication, 1871).
Dixon, Amzi C., Louis Meyer, and Reuben A. Torrey (eds.), *The Fundamentals: A Testimony to the Truth* (Chicago, IL: Testimony Press, 1910-1915).
Dockery, David S. (ed.), *The Challenge of Postmodernism: An Evangelical Engagement* (Grand Rapids, MI: Baker Books, 1995).
Dollar, George W., *A History of Fundamentalism in America* (Greenville, SC: Bob Jones University Press, 1973).
Douglas, Mary, *Purity and Danger* (Boston, MA: Routledge & Kegan Paul, 1966).
Duncan, J. Ligon, III, "Owning the Confession: Subscription in the Scottish Presbyterian Tradition," in *The Practice of Confessional Subscription*, ed. David W. Hall, 77-91 (Lanham, MD: University Press of America, 1995).
Ellingsen, Mark, *The Evangelical Movement: Growth, Impact, Controversy, Dialog* (Minneapolis, MN: Augsburg Press, 1988).
English, E. Schuyler, *Re-Thinking the Rapture* (Neptune, NJ: Loizeaux Brothers, 1954^2).
– *Studies in the Gospel According to Matthew* (New York, NY: Fleming H. Revell Publishing Co., 1935).
– (ed.), *The Holy Bible*, Pilgrim edition (New York, NY: Oxford University Press, 1948).

Ezell, John Samuel, *The South Since 1895* (New York, NY: Macmillan & Co., 1963).
Fairbairn, Patrick, *The Revelation of Law in Scripture* (Edinburgh: T. & T. Clark, 1869).
Faust, Drew Gilpin, *The Creation of Confederate Nationalism: Ideology and Identity in the Civil War South* (Baton Rouge, LA: Louisiana State University Press, 1988).
Feinberg, Charles Lee, *Premillennialism or Amillennialism?* (Grand Rapids, MI: Zondervan Publishing House, 1936).
Feinberg, John S., "Salvation in the Old Testament," in *Tradition and Testament: Essays in Honor of Charles Lee Feinberg*, ed. John S. Feinberg and Paul D. Feinberg, 39-77 (Chicago, IL: Moody Press, 1981).
– (ed.), *Continuity and Discontinuity: Perspectives on the Relationship Between the Old and New Testaments; Essays in Honor of S. Lewis Johnson, Jr.* (Westchester, IL: Crossway Books, 1988).
Feinberg, John S., and Paul D. Feinberg (eds.), *Tradition and Testament: Essays in Honor of Charles Lee Feinberg* (Chicago, IL: Moody Press, 1981).
Fischer, Paul B., *Ultra-Dispensationalism is Modernism: Exposing a heresy among us* (Chicago, IL: Weir Brothers, 1936).
F[isher], E[dward], *The Marrow of Modern Divinity: in two parts, with Notes by the Rev. Thomas Boston* (Edinburgh: s.n., 1726), reprinted, with notes added (Philadelphia, PA: Presbyterian Board of Publication, n.d).
Foreman, Kenneth J., Felix B. Gear, James I. McCord and John N. Thomas, *Our Theologians Speak for Presbyterian Reunion* (Charlottesville, VA: Friends of Presbyterian Union, [1964]).
Fosdick, Harry Emerson, *Christianity and Progress* (New York, NY: Fleming H. Revell Publishing Co., 1922).
– *The Living of the Days: An Autobiography* (New York, NY: Harper & Bros., 1956).
– *The Meaning of Faith* (New York, NY: Association Press, 1917).
– *The Modern Use of the Bible* (New York, NY: Association Press, 1926).
Foster, Frank Hugh, *The Modern Movement in American Theology: Sketches in the History of American Protestant Thought from the Civil War to the World War* (New York, NY: Fleming H. Revell Publishing Co., 1939).
Fowler, C. L., *Building the Dispensations*. Denver, CO: Maranatha Press, 1940).
Frame, John, "Cornelius Van Til," in *Handbook of Evangelical Theologians*, ed. Walter A. Elwell, 156-67 (Grand Rapids, MI: Baker Book House, 1993).
– *Cornelius Van Til: An Analysis of His Thought* (Phillipsburg, NJ: Presbyterian and Reformed Publishing Co., 1995).
– "Machen's Warrior Children," in *Alister E. McGrath and Evangelical Theology: A Dynamic Engagement*, ed. Sung Wook Chung, 113-46 (Carlistle, Cumbria, England: Paternoster Press, 2003).
Frank, Douglas, *Less Than Conquerors: How Evangelicals Entered the Twentieth Century* (Grand Rapids, MI: William B. Eerdmans Publishing Co., 1986).
Frost, Henry West, *The Second Coming of Christ: A Review of the Teaching of Scripture Concerning the Return of Christ* (Grand Rapids, MI: William B. Eerdmans Publishing Co., 1934).
Fuller, Daniel P., *Gospel and Law: Contrast or Continuum? The Hermeneutics of Dispensationalism and Covenant Theology* (Grand Rapids, MI: William B. Eerdmans Publishing Co., 1980).
Furniss, Norman F., *The Fundamentalist Controversy: 1918-1931* (New Haven, CT: Yale University Press, 1954).
Gaebelein, Arno C. (ed.), *The Annotated Bible* (Wheaton, IL: Van Kampen Press, 1913).
– *Gaebelein's Concise Commentary on the Whole Bible* (New York, NY: Our Hope Publishers, 1910).
– *Half a Century: The Autobiography of a Servant* (New York, NY: Our Hope Publishers, 1930).

- *The Harmony of the Prophetic Word: A Key to Old Testament Prophecy Concerning Things to Come* (New York, NY: Our Hope Publishers, 1907).
- *Hath God Cast Away His People?* (New York, NY: Gospel Publishing House, 1905).
- *The History of the Scofield Reference Bible* (New York, NY: Our Hope Publishers, 1943).
- *The Hope of the Ages* (New York, NY: Our Hope Publishers, 1938).
- *The Jewish Question* (New York, NY: Our Hope Publishers, 1925).
- *The Return of the Lord: What the New Testament Teaches about the Second Coming of Christ* (New York, NY: Our Hope Publishers, 1925).
- *Studies in Prophecy* (New York, NY: Our Hope Publishers, 1918).
- *World Prospects: How Is It All Going to End?* (New York, NY: Our Hope Publishers, 1934).

Gaebelein, Frank E., *The Story of the Scofield Reference Bible, 1909-1959* (New York, NY: Oxford University Press, 1959).

Gatewood, Willard B., Jr., *Controversy in the Twenties: Fundamentalism, Modernism and Evolution* (Nashville, TN: Vanderbilt University Press, 1969).

Gear, Felix B., *Basic Beliefs of the Reformed Faith: A Biblical Study of Presbyterian Doctrine* (Richmond, VA: John Knox Press, 1946).
- *Can Calvinism Live Again?* (Richmond, VA: Presbyterian Committee of Publication, 1964).
- *Our Presbyterian Belief: Class Study Book* (Atlanta, GA: Board of Women's Work, Presbyterian Church in the United States, n.d).

Gerstner, John H., *A Primer on Dispensationalism* (Phillipsburg, NJ: Presbyterian and Reformed Publishing Co., 1982).
- *Wrongly Dividing the Word of Truth: A Critique of Dispensationalism* (Brentwood, TN: Wolgemuth & Hyatt, 1991).

Getz, Gene A., *MBI: The Story of Moody Bible Institute* (Chicago, IL: Moody Press, 1969).

Godfrey, W. Robert, "Subscription in the Dutch Reformed Tradition," in *The Practice of Confessional Subscription*, ed. David W. Hall, 67-75 (Lanham, MD: University Press of America, 1995).

Graham, Billy, *Just As I Am: The Autobiography of Billy Graham* (Grand Rapids, MI: Zondervan Publishing House, 1997).

Graves, James Robinson, *The Dispensational Expositions of the Parables and Prophecies of Christ* (Memphis, TN: Graves & Mahaffy, 1887).
- *The Work of Christ in the Covenant of Redemption Consummated in Seven Dispensations* (Memphis, TN: Baptist Book House, 1883).

Gray, James (ed.), *The Coming and Kingdom of Christ* (Chicago, IL: Bible Institute Colportage Association, 1914).
- *Prophecy and the Lord's Return* (New York, NY: Fleming H. Revell Publishing Co., 1917).
- *Synthetic Bible Studies* (London: Fleming H. Revell Publishing Co., 1923^2).
- *A Textbook on Prophecy* (New York, NY: Fleming H. Revell Publishing Co., 1918).

Green, James B., *A Harmony of the Westminster Presbyterian Standards, with Explanatory Notes* (Richmond, VA: John Knox Press, 1951).
- *Studies in the Holy Spirit* (New York, NY: Fleming H. Revell Publishing Co., 1936).

Grenz, Stanley J., and John R. Franke, *Beyond Foundationalism: Shaping Theology in a Postmodern Context* (Louisville, KY: Westminster/John Knox Press, 2001).

Haldeman, I.M., *A Dispensational Key to the Scriptures* (New York, NY: Charles C. Cook, 1915).
- *How to Study the Bible* (New York, NY: Charles C. Cook, 1904).
- *The Kingdom of God. What is it? When is it? Where is it? An Answer to Mr. Philip Mauro's Book "The Gospel of the Kingdom,"* (New York, NY: Francis Emory Fitch, 1931).

Hall, David W. (ed.), *The Practice of Confessional Subscription* (Lanham, MD: University Press of America, 1995).

Hamilton, Floyd E., *The Basis of Millennial Faith* (Grand Rapids, MI: William B. Eerdmans Publishing Co., 1932).
Hamilton, Ian, *The Erosion of Calvinist Orthodoxy: Seceders and Subscription in Scottish Presbyterianism*. Rutherford Studies Series One: Historical Theology. 5th ed (Edinburgh: Rutherford House Books, 1990).
Harrell, David Edwin, Jr. (ed.), *Varieties of Southern Evangelicalism* (Macon, GA: Mercer University Press, 1981).
Hart, D.G., *Defending the Faith: J. Gresham Machen and the Crisis of Conservative Protestantism in Modern America* (Baltimore, MD: Johns Hopkins University Press, 1994).
– (ed.), *Reckoning With the Past: Historical Essays on American Evangelicalism from the Institute for the Study of American Evangelicals* (Grand Rapids, MI: Baker Books, 1995).
Hart, D.G., and John Muether, *Fighting the Good Fight: A Brief History of the Orthodox Presbyterian Church* (Philadelphia: The Committee on Christian Education and the Committee for the Historian of the Orthodox Presbyterian Church, 1995).
Hatch, Nathan O., and Mark A. Noll (eds.), *The Bible in America: Essays in Cultural History* (New York, NY: Oxford University Press, 1982).
Hendriksen, William, *The Covenant of Grace* (Grand Rapids, MI: William B. Eerdmans Publishing Co., 1932).
– *Israel in Prophecy* (Grand Rapids, MI: Baker Book House, 1968).
Henry, Carl F.H., *Christian Personal Ethics* (Grand Rapids, MI: William B. Eerdmans Publishing Co., 1957).
– (ed.), *Contemporary Evangelical Thought* (Great Neck, NY: Channel Press, 1957).
– (ed.), *The Protestant Dilemma: An Analysis of the Current Impasse in Theology* (Grand Rapids, MI: William B. Eerdmans Publishing Co., 1949).
– *The Uneasy Conscience of Modern Fundamentalism* (Grand Rapids, MI: William B. Eerdmans Publishing Co., 1947).
Heppe, Heinrich, *Reformed Dogmatics: Set Out and Illustrated from the Sources*, ed. Ernst Bizer, tr. G.T. Thompson (Grand Rapids, MI: Baker Book House, 1950).
Heron, Alasdair I.C. (ed.), *The Westminster Confession in the Church Today* (Edinburgh: St. Andrew Publishers, 1982).
Hetherington, W.M., *History of the Westminster Assembly of Divines* (New York, NY: Mark H. Newman, 1843).
Hill, Samuel S., Jr., *Religion and the Solid South* (Nashville, TN: Abingdon Press, 1972).
– *Southern Churches in Crisis* (New York, NY: Holt, Rinehart and Winston, 1967).
Hillers, Delbert R., *Covenant: The History of a Biblical Idea* (Baltimore, MD: Johns Hopkins University Press, 1982).
Hoch, Carl B., Jr., "The New Man of Ephesians 2," in *Dispensationalism, Israel and the Church: The Search for Definition*, ed. Craig A. Blaising, and Darrell L. Bock, 98-126 (Grand Rapids, MI: Zondervan Publishing House, 1992).
Hodge, A.A., *Outlines of Theology* (Philadelphia, PA, Presbyterian Board of Publication, 1860), reprint (Grand Rapids, MI: Zondervan Publishing House, 1979).
Hodge, Charles, *Justification By Faith Alone*, 1841, reprint, ed. John W. Robbins (Hobbs, NM: Trinity Foundation, 1995).
– *Systematic Theology*, 3 vols. (London and Edinburgh: T. Nelson and Sons, 1872-73), reprint (Grand Rapids, MI: William B. Eerdmans Publishing Co., 1993).
Hodges, Zane, *Absolutely Free!: A Biblical Reply to Lordship Salvation* (Grand Rapids, MI: Zondervan Publishing House, 1989).
– *The Gospel Under Siege* (Dallas, TX: Rendencion Viva, 1981).
Hoekema, Anthony A., *The Bible and the Future* (Grand Rapids, MI: William B. Eerdmans Publishing Co., 1979).

Hofstadter, Richard, *Anti-Intellectualism in American Life* (New York, NY: Alfred A. Knopf, 1963).
Holifield, E. Brooks, *The Gentleman Theologians: American Theology in Southern Culture, 1795-1860* (Durham, NC: Duke University Press, 1978).
Horton, Michael (ed.), *Confessing theology for Postmodern Times* (Wheaton, IL: Crossway Books, 2000).
Horton, T.C., *These Premillennialists – Who are they?* (Los Angeles, CA: BIOLA Press, 1921).
Hospers, G.H., *The Calvinistic Character of Premillennialism* (by the author, 1935).
– *The Principle of Spiritualization in Hermeneutics* (by the author, 1935).
Hoste, William, *Bullingerism, or, Ultra Dispensationalism Examined* (London: Pickering & Inglis, 1930).
House, H. Wayne, and Thomas Ice, *Dominion Theology: Blessing or Curse?* (Portland, OR: Multnomah Press, 1988).
Hoyt, Herman A., *The End Times* (Chicago, IL: Moody Press, 1969).
Hunter, James Davison, *American Evangelicalism: Conservative Religion and the Quandary of Modernity* (New Brunswick, NJ: Rutgers University Press, 1983).
Hutcheson, Richard G., Jr., and Peggy Shriver, *The Divided Church: Moving Liberals and Conservatives from Diatribe to Dialogue* (Downers Grove, IL: Inter-Varsity Press, 1999).
Hutchinson, George P., *The History Behind the Reformed Presbyterian Church Evangelical Synod*. Cherry Hill, NJ: Mack Publishing Co., 1974).
Hutchison, William R. (ed.), *American Protestant Thought: The Liberal Era* (New York, NY: Harper & Row, Publishers, 1968).
– *The Modernist Impulse in American Protestantism* (Durham, NC: Duke University Press, 1992).
Ironside, Harry A., *The Great Parenthesis* (Grand Rapids, MI: Zondervan Publishing House, 1943).
– *A Historical Sketch of the Brethren Movement* (Grand Rapids, MI: Zondervan Publishing House, 1942).
– *The Lamp of Prophecy* (Grand Rapids, MI: Zondervan Publishing House, 1940).
– *Lectures on the Book of Revelation* (New York, NY: Loizeaux Brothers, 1919).
– *Looking Back Over a Century of Prophecy Fulfillment* (New York, NY: Loizeaux Brothers, 1930).
– *The Mysteries of God* (New York, NY: Loizeaux Brothers, 1946).
– *Not Wrath, But Rapture* (Neptune, NJ: Loizeaux Brothers, n.d).
– *The Unchanging Christ, and Other Sermons* (Grand Rapids, MI: William B. Eerdmans Publishing Co., 1935).
– *Wrongly Dividing the Word of Truth: Ultra-Dispensationalism Examined in the Light of Holy Scripture*. [n.p., n.d.]).
Jacobsen, Douglas, and William Vance Trollinger, Jr., *Reforming the Center: American Protestantism, 1900 to the Present* (Grand Rapids, MI: William B. Eerdmans Publishing Co., 1998).
Johnson, Elliot E., *Expository Hermeneutics: An Introduction* (Grand Rapids, MI: Zondervan Publishing House, 1990).
Johnson, S. Lewis, Jr., *The Old Testament in the New: An Argument for Biblical Inspiration* (Grand Rapids, MI: Zondervan Publishing House, 1980).
Johnson, Thomas Carey, *A History of the Southern Presbyterian Church*, The American Church History Series, ed. Philip Schaff, no. 11 (New York, NY: The Christian Literature Co., 1894).
Johnson, William Stacy, and John H. Leith (eds.), *Reformed Reader, A Sourcebook in Christian Theology*, vol. 1, *Classical Beginnings, 1519-1799* (Louisville, KY: Westminster/John Knox Press, 1993).
Johnston, Robert K. (ed.), *The Use of the Bible in Theology: Evangelical Options* (Atlanta, GA: John Knox Press, 1985).

Kadushin, Max, *Organic Thinking* (New York, NY: Bloch Publishing Co., 1938).
- *The Rabbinic Mind* (New York, NY: Bloch Publishing Co., 1952).
Kantzer, Kenneth (ed.), *Evangelical Roots* (Nashville, TN: Thomas Nelson, Publishers, 1978).
Kantzer, Kenneth S., and Carl F.H. Henry (eds.), *Evangelical Affirmations*, Conference Papers of the National Association of Evangelicals and Trinity Evangelical Divinity School, May 1989 (Grand Rapids, MI: Zondervan Publishing House, 1990).
Kantzer, Kenneth S., and Stanley N. Gundrey (eds.), *Perspectives on Evangelical Theology* (Grand Rapids, MI: Baker Book House, 1979).
Karleen, Paul S., *The Pre-Wrath Rapture of the Church: Is it Biblical?* (Langhorne, PA: BF Press, 1991).
Kaufman, Gordon, *Systematic Theology* (New York, NY: Charles Scribner's Sons, 1968).
Kelly, J.N.D., *Early Christian Doctrines* (New York, NY: Harper & Row, Publishers, 1958).
Kelly, John, *The Divine Covenants* (London: Jackson, Walford, & Hodder, 1861).
Kelly, William, *Daniel's Seventy Weeks* (Los Angeles, CA: Berean Bookshelf, n.d).
- *Elements of Prophecy* (London: G. Morrish, 1876).
- *Lectures on the Second Coming and Kingdom of the Lord and Savior Jesus Christ* (London: W.H. Broom, 1865), reprint (Sunbury, PA: Believers Bookshelf, 1970).
- *The Rapture of the Saints: Who Suggested It, or Rather on What Scripture?* (London: T. Weston, 1903).
Kline, Meredith G., *By Oath Consigned: A Reinterpretation of the Covenant Signs of Circumcision and Baptism* (Grand Rapids, MI: William B. Eerdmans Publishing Co., 1968).
- *The Structure of Biblical Authority*. Revised ed (Grand Rapids, MI: William B. Eerdmans Publishing Co., 1975).
- *Treaty of the Great King* (Grand Rapids, MI: William B. Eerdmans Publishing Co., 1963).
Knight, George W., III, "Subscription to the Westminster Confession of Faith and Catechisms," in *The Practice of Confessional Subscription*, ed. David W. Hall, 119-48 (Lanham, MD: University Press of America, 1995).
Kraus, C. Norman, *Dispensationalism in America: Its Rise and Development* (Richmond, VA: John Knox Press, 1958).
Kromminga, D.H., *The Millennium* (Grand Rapids, MI: William B. Eerdmans Publishing Co., 1948).
- *The Millennium in the Church* (Grand Rapids, MI: William B. Eerdmans Publishing Co., 1945).
Kuiper, R.B., *As To Being Reformed* (Grand Rapids, MI: William B. Eerdmans Publishing Co., 1926).
Kuyper, Abraham, *Encyclopedia of Sacred Theology: Its Principles*, tr. J. Hendrik De Vries (New York, NY: Scribner's Sons, 1898).
- *Principles of Sacred Theology*, tr. J. Hendrik De Vries, 1854, reprint (Grand Rapids, MI: William B. Eerdmans Publishing Co., 1954).
- *The Work of the Holy Spirit*, tr. J. Hendrik De Vries (New York, NY: Funk & Wagnalls, 1900).
Lachman, David C., *The Marrow Controversy: 1718-1723; An Historical and Theological Analysis*, Rutherford Studies Series One: Historical Theology (Edinburgh: Rutherford House Books, 1988).
Lacy, Benjamin R., *Revivals in the Midst of the Years* (Richmond, VA: Presbyterian Committee of Publication, 1943).
Ladd, George Eldon, *The Blessed Hope* (Grand Rapids, MI: William B. Eerdmans Publishing Co., 1956).
- *Crucial Questions About the Kingdom of God* (Grand Rapids, MI: William B. Eerdmans Publishing Co., 1952).
- *Jesus and the Kingdom* (Waco, TX: Word Books:1964).
- *The Last Things* (Grand Rapids, MI: William B. Eerdmans Publishing Co., 1978).

- "Paul and the Law," in *Soli Deo Gloria: New Testament Studies in honor of William Childs Robinson*, ed. J. McDowell Richards, 50-67 (Richmond, VA: John Knox Press, 1968).
- *The Presence of the Future* (Grand Rapids, MI: William B. Eerdmans Publishing Co., 1974).
- *A Theology of the New Testament* (Grand Rapids, MI: William B. Eerdmans Publishing Co., 1974).

Larkin, Clarence, *The Book of Revelation* (by the author, 1919).
- *Rightly Dividing the Word of Truth* (Philadelphia, PA: Erwin W. Moyer, 1920).

LaRondelle, Hans K., *The Israel of God in Prophecy* (Berrien Springs, MI: Andrews University Press, 1983).

Leonard, Bill J. (ed.), *Dictionary of Baptists in America* (Downers Grove, IL: Inter-Varsity Press, 1994).

Lindbeck, George A., *The Nature of Doctrine: Religion and Theology in a Postliberal Age* (Philadelphia, PA: Westminster Press, 1984).

Lindsey, Hal, *The Late Great Planet Earth* (Grand Rapids, MI: Zondervan Publishing House, 1970).

Lingle, Walter L., *The Bible and Social Problems* (New York, NY: Fleming H. Revell, 1929).
- *Presbyterianism: A Heritage and a Challenge* (Richmond, VA: Presbyterian Committee of Publication, n.d).
- *Presbyterians, Their History and Beliefs* (Richmond, VA: Presbyterian Committee of Publication, 1928).
- *Why I Believe in the Deity of Jesus Christ* (Richmond, VA: Presbyterian Committee of Publication, 1936).

Loetscher, Lefferts A., *The Broadening Church: A Study of Theological Issues in the Presbyterian Church since 1869* (Philadelphia, PA: University of Pennsylvania Press, 1954).

Longfield, Bradley J., *The Presbyterian Controversy: Fundamentalists, Modernists, & Moderates* (New York, NY: Oxford University Press, 1991).

Loveland, Anne C., *Southern Evangelicals and the Social Order, 1800-1860* (Baton Rouge, LA: Louisiana State University Press, 1980).

Macartney, Clarence Edward, *The Making of a Minister*. Great Neck, NY: Channel Press, 1961).

Machen, J. Gresham, *Christianity and Liberalism* (Grand Rapids, MI: William B. Eerdmans Publishing Co., 1923).
- *The Origin of Paul's Religion* (New York, NY: Macmillan, 1929).
- "What Fundamentalism Stands For Now," *New York Times* (21 June 1925), republished in *What is Christianity?*, ed. Ned B. Stonehouse (Grand Rapids, MI: William B. Eerdmans Publishing Co., 1951).
- *What is Faith?* (New York, NY: The Macmillan Company, 1925), reprint (Grand Rapids, MI: William B. Eerdmans Publishing Co., 1979).

Macleod, John, *Scottish Theology: In Relation to Church History since the Reformation* (Edinburgh: The Banner of Truth Trust, 1973).

Marsden, George M. (ed.), *The Evangelical Mind and the New School Presbyterianism Experience: A Case Study of Thought and Theology in Nineteenth-Century America* (New Haven, CT: Yale University Press, 1970).
- *Evangelicalism and Modern America* (Grand Rapids, MI: William B. Eerdmans Publishing Co., 1984).
- *Fundamentalism and American Culture: The Shaping of Twentieth-Century Evangelicalism, 1870-1925* (New York, NY: Oxford University Press, 1980).
- *Reforming Fundamentalism: Fuller Seminary and the New Evangelicalism* (Grand Rapids, MI: William B. Eerdmans Publishing Co., 1987).
- *Understanding Fundamentalism and Evangelicalism* (Grand Rapids, MI: William B. Eerdmans Publishing Co., 1991).

Marty, Martin E., *A Short History of Christianity* (New York: World Publishing Co., 1959).
- *Modern American Religion*, vol. 1, *The Irony of It All, 1893-1919* (Chicago, IL: University of Chicago Press, 1986).
- *Modern American Religion*, vol. 2, *The Noise of Conflict, 1919-1941* (Chicago, IL: University of Chicago Press, 1986).
- *Pilgrims in Their Own Land: Five Hundred Years of Religion in America* (Boston, MA: Little, Brown & Co., 1984).
Mason, Clarence E., Jr., *Prophetic Problems with Alternative Solutions* (Chicago, IL: Moody Press, 1973).
Masselink, William, *Why Thousand Years?* (Grand Rapids, MI: William B. Eerdmans Publishing Co., 1930).
Mathison, Keith A., *Dispensationalism: Rightly Dividing the People of God?* (Phillipsburg, NJ: Presbyterian and Reformed Publishing Co., 1995).
Matthews, Shailer, *The Faith of Modernism* (New York, NY: Macmillan Company, 1924), reprint (New York, NY: AMS Press, 1969).
Mauro, Philip, *Baptism and the New Covenant* (Boston, MA: Hamilton Brothers, Scripture Truth Depot, n.d).
- *The Church, The Churches and the Kingdom* (Washington, DC: The Perry Studio, 1936).
- *Dispensationalism Justifies the Crucifixion* (Washington, DC: The Perry Studio, 1936).
- *Evolution at the Bar* (New York, NY: Doran Press, 1922).
- *God's Present Kingdom* (New York, NY: Fleming H. Revell, 1919).
- *The Gospel of the Kingdom with an Examination of Modern Dispensationalism* (Boston, MA: Hamilton Brothers, 1928).
- *The Hope of Israel: What is it?* (Boston, MA: Hamilton Bros., 1929).
- *The Inwardness of the Postponement Theory, as Revealed by S. D. Gordon in his Quiet Talks about Jesus* (Washington, DC: The Perry Studio, 1936).
- *The Kingdom of Heaven: What is it? And When? And Where?* (Boston, MA: Hamilton Brothers, 1920).
- *A Letter to a Dispensationalist* (Washington, DC: The Perry Studio, 1936).
- *The Number of Man: The Climax of Civilization* (New York, NY: Fleming H. Revell Publishing Co., 1909).
- *Of Things Which Soon Must Come to Pass: A Commentary on the Book of Revelation* (Grand Rapids, MI: William B. Eerdmans Publishing Co., 1933).
- *The Patmos Visions: A Study of the Apocalypse* (Boston, MA: Hamilton Bros., Scripture Truth Depot, 1925).
- *The Seventy Weeks and the Great Tribulation; A Study of the Last Two Visions of Daniel, and of the Olivet Discourse by Jesus Christ* (Boston, MA: Hamilton Bros., Scripture Truth Depot, 1923).
- *Which Version? Authorized or Revised?* (Boston, MA: Scripture Truth Depot, 1924).
- *The Wonders of Biblical Chronology* (London: S.E. Roberts, 1923).
McCarroll, Walter, *Why I Did Not Become a Premillennialist: An inquiry into the true meaning of the Scriptures* (Topeka, KS: The Service Print Shop, 1942).
McClain, Alva J., *Daniel's Prophecy of the Seventy Weeks* (Grand Rapids, MI: William B. Eerdmans Publishing Co., [1940]), reprint (Grand Rapids, MI: Zondervan Publishing House, 1969).
- *The Greatness of the Kingdom* (Grand Rapids, MI: Zondervan Publishing House, 1959).
- *Law and Grace*, (Winona Lake, IN: BMH Books, 1954).
McClendon, James Wm., Jr., *Convictions: Defusing Religious Relativism* (Valley Forge, PA: Trinity Press International, 1994).

McCoy, Charles Sherwood, and J. Wayne Baker, *Fountainhead of Federalism: Heinrich Bullinger and the Covenantal Tradition* (Louisville, KY: Westminster/John Knox Press, 1991).

McGrath, Alister E., *The Genesis of Doctrine* (Cambridge, MA: Blackwell Publishers, 1990).

McKee, Elsie Anne, and Brian G. Armstrong (eds.), *Probing the Reformed Tradition: Historical Studies in Honor of Edward A. Dowey, Jr.* (Louisville, KY: John Knox Press, 1989).

McLaurin, Eugene W., *A Suggested Report of the Ad Interim Committee on Changes in the Confession of Faith and Catechisms with Regard to the "Question as to Whether the Type of Bible Interpretation Known as 'Dispensationalism' is in Harmony with the Confession of Faith* (Austin, TX: Austin Presbyterian Theological Seminary, 1942).

McQuilkin, Robert, *Law and Grace* (Grand Rapids, MI: William B. Eerdmans Publishing Co., 1958).

Mead, Sydney E., *The Lively Experiment: The Shaping of Christianity in America* (New York, NY: Harper & Row, 1963).

Mead, Willis W., *The Apocalypse of Jesus Christ* (New York, NY: Francis Emory Fitch, 1909).

– *The Modern Outcry Against the Law* (London: Samuel E. Roberts, 1914).

Michaelsen, Robert S., and Wade Clark Roof (eds.), *Liberal Protestantism: Realities & Possibilities* (New York, NY: Pilgrim Press, 1986).

Moore, Russell D., *The Kingdom of Christ: The New Evangelical Perspective* (Wheaton, IL: Crossway Books, 2004).

Muether, John R., "Confidence in Our Brethren: Creedal Subscription in the Orthodox Presbyterian Church," in *The Practice of Confessional Subscription*, ed. David W. Hall, 301-10 (Lanham, MD: University Press of America, 1995).

Muller, Richard, *Christ and the Decree: Christology and Predestination in Reformed Theology from Calvin to Perkins*, Studies in Historical Theology, vol. 2, ed. David C. Steinmenz, Durham, NC: Labyrinth Press, 1986).

– *Dictionary of Latin and Greek Theological Terms: Drawn Principally from Protestant Scholastic Theology* (Grand Rapids, MI: Baker Books, 1985).

– *Post-Reformation Reformed Dogmatics*, vol. 1, *Prolegomena to Theology* (Grand Rapids, MI: Baker Book House, 1987).

– *Post-Reformation Reformed Dogmatics*, vol. 2, *Holy Scripture: The Cognitive Foundation of Theology* (Grand Rapids, MI: Baker Book House, 1993).

Murphy, Nancey, *Beyond Liberalism and Fundamentalism: How Modern and Postmodern Philosophy Set the Theological Agenda* (Valley Forge, PA: Trinity Press International, 1996).

Murray, Iain H., *The Life of John Murray* (Edinburgh: The Banner of Truth Trust, 1982).

Murray, John, *The Atonement* (Philadelphia, PA: Presbyterian and Reformed Publishing Co., 1962).

– *Calvin on Scripture and Divine Sovereignty* (Grand Rapids, MI: Baker Book House, 1960).

– *Christian Baptism* (Nutley, NJ: Presbyterian and Reformed, 1977).

– *Collected Writings of John Murray*, ed. Iain Murray, vol. 1, *The Claims of Truth* (Edinburgh: The Banner of Truth Trust, 1976).

– *Collected Writings of John Murray*, ed. Iain Murray, vol. 2, *Select Lectures in Systematic Theology* (Edinburgh: The Banner of Truth Trust, 1977).

– *Collected Writings of John Murray*, ed. Iain Murray, vol. 3, *Life of John Murray; Sermons & Reviews* (Edinburgh: The Banner of Truth Trust, 1982).

– *Collected Writings of John Murray*, ed. Iain Murray, vol. 4, *Studies in Theology; Reviews* (Edinburgh: The Banner of Truth Trust, 1982).

– *The Covenant of Grace: A Biblico-Theological Study* (London: Tyndale House Publishers, 1953).

– *Divorce* (Phillipsburg, NJ: Presbyterian and Reformed Publishing Co., 1978).

- *The Epistle to the Romans*, The New International Commentary on the New Testament, ed. Ned B. Stonehouse, 2 vols. (Grand Rapids, MI: William B. Eerdmans Publishing Co., 1959).
- *The Imputation of Adam's Sin* (Grand Rapids, MI: William B. Eerdmans Publishing Co., 1959).
- *Principles of Conduct: Aspects of Biblical Ethics* (Grand Rapids, MI: William B. Eerdmans Publishing Co., 1957).
- *Redemption Accomplished and Applied* (Grand Rapids, MI: William B. Eerdmans Publishing Co., 1955).
- *The Sovereignty of God* (Philadelphia, PA: Committee on Christian Education of the Orthodox Presbyterian Church, 1945).

Nash, Ronald H. (ed.), *Evangelical Renewal in the Mainline Churches* (Westchester, IL: Crossway Books, 1987).
- *Evangelicals in America* (Nashville, TN: Abingdon Press, 1987).

Neatby, W. Blair, *A History of the Plymouth Brethren* (London: Hodder and Stoughton, 1902).

Niebuhr, H. Richard, *The Social Sources of Denominationalism* (New York, NY: Henry Holt & Co., 1929).

Nielands, David L., *Studies in the Covenant of Grace* (Phillipsburg, NJ: Presbyterian and Reformed Publishing Co., 1980).

Noll, Mark A., *A History of Christianity in the United States and Canada* (Grand Rapids, MI: William B. Eerdmans Publishing Co., 1992).
- *Between Faith and Criticism: Evangelicals, Scholarship, and the Bible in America* (Grand Rapids, MI: Baker Book House, 1986).
- *The Princeton Theology, 1812-1921: Scripture, Science, and Theological Method from Archibald Alexander to Benjamin Breckinridge Warfield* (Grand Rapids, MI: Baker Book House, 1983).

Noll, Mark A., and Ronald F. Thiemann (eds.), *Where Shall My Wond'ring Soul Begin?: The Landscape of Evangelical Piety and Thought* (Grand Rapids, MI: William B. Eerdmans Publishing Co., 2000).

Oberman, Heiko, *The Dawn of the Reformation* (New York, NY: T. & T. Clark, 1986), reprint (Grand Rapids, MI: William B. Eerdmans Publishing Co., 1992).
- *Forerunners of the Reformation: The Shape of Late Medieval Thought Illustrated by Key Documents* (London: Lutterworth Press, 1966), reprint (Philadelphia, PA: Fortress Press, 1981).

Oden, Thomas C., *Requiem: A Lament in Three Movements* (Nashville, TN: Abingdon Press, 1995).

Payne, J. Barton, *Encyclopedia of Biblical Prophecy* (New York, NY: Harper & Row, Publishers, 1973).
- *The Imminent Appearing of Christ* (Grand Rapids, MI: William B. Eerdmans Publishing Co., 1962).
- *An Outline of Hebrew History* (Grand Rapids, MI: Baker Book House, 1954).
- *The Theology of the Older Testament* (Grand Rapids, MI: Zondervan Publishing House, 1962).

Pelikan, Jaroslav, *Reformation of Church and Dogma (1300-1700)*, vol. 4, *The Christian Tradition: A History of the Development of Doctrine* (Chicago, IL: University Press, 1984).
- *The Christian Tradition, A History of the Development of Doctrine*, 4 vols. (Chicago, IL: University of Chicago Press, 1984).

Pentecost, J. Dwight, *Things to Come: A Study in Biblical Eschatology*, 1958, reprint, (Grand Rapids, MI: Zondervan Publishing House, 1979).

Peters, George N.H., *The Theocratic Kingdom of Our Lord Jesus, the Christ, as Covenanted in the Old Testament and Presented in the New Testament*, 3 vols. (Grand Rapids, MI: Kregel Publications, 1957).

Pettingill, William L., *God's Prophecies for Plain People* (Wilmington, DE: Just A Word, 1923).

- *The Gospel of the Kingdom: Simple Studies in Matthew* (Findlay, OH: Dunham Publishing Co., 1934).
- *Nearing the End: Simple Studies Concerning the Second Coming of Christ and Related Events* (Chicago, IL: Van Kampen Press, 1948).

Pieters, Albertus, *A Candid Examination of the Scofield Bible* (Swengel, PA: Bible Truth Depot, [1938]).

- *The Facts and Mysteries of the Christian Faith* (Grand Rapids, MI: William B. Eerdmans Publishing Co., 1933).
- *The Lamb, the Woman and the Dragon* (Grand Rapids, MI: Zondervan Publishing House, 1937).
- *The Seed of Abraham: A Biblical Study of Israel, the Church and the Jew* (Grand Rapids, MI: Zondervan Publishing House, 1937).
- *The Ten Tribes in History and Prophecy* (Grand Rapids, MI: William B. Eerdmans Publishing Co., 1934).

Pollock, John Charles, *A Foreign Devil in China: The Story of Dr. L. Nelson Bell, an American Surgeon in China* (Minneapolis, MN: World Wide Publications, for the Billy Graham Evangelistic Association, 1971).

Poythress, Vern Sheridan, *Science and Hermeneutics: Implications of Scientific Method for Biblical Interpretation*, Foundations of Contemporary Interpretation, vol. 6, ed. Moisés Silva, (Grand Rapids, MI: Zondervan Publishing House, 1988).

- *The Shadow of Christ in the Law of Moses* (Brentwood, TN: Wolgemuth & Hyatt, 1991).
- *Symphonic Theology: The Validity of Multiple Perspectives in Theology* (Grand Rapids, MI: Zondervan Publishing House, 1987).
- *Understanding Dispensationalists* (Grand Rapids, MI: Zondervan Publishing House, 1987).

Presbyterian Church in the United States. "Appendix: Report of the Ad Interim Committee on Changes in the Confession of Faith and Catechisms: The Question as to Whether the Type of Bible Interpretation Known as Dispensationalism Is in Harmony with the Confession of Faith," in *Minutes of the Eighty-Third General Assembly of the Presbyterian Church in the United States, with an Appendix*, 122-29 (Austin, TX: Von Boeckmann-Jones, Co., 1943).

- *The Book of Church Order of the Presbyterian Church in the United States* (Richmond, VA: Presbyterian Committee of Publication, 1938).
- *A Digest of the Acts and Proceedings of the General Assembly of the Presbyterian Church in the United States, 1861-1944: Authorized by the General Assembly*, ed. E.C. Scott, Stated Clerk of the 1944 General Assembly (Richmond, VA: Presbyterian Committee of Publication, 1945).
- *Minutes of the Eighty-First General Assembly of the Presbyterian Church in the United States, with an Appendix* (Austin, TX: Von Boeckmann-Jones, Co., 1941).
- *Minutes of the Eighty-Fourth General Assembly of the Presbyterian Church in the United States, with an Appendix* (Austin, TX: Von Boeckmann-Jones, Co., 1944).
- *Minutes of the Eighty-Second General Assembly of the Presbyterian Church in the United States, with an Appendix* (Austin, TX: Von Boeckmann-Jones, Co., 1942).
- *Minutes of the Eighty-Second Session of the Synod of Texas of the Presbyterian Church in the United States*. Kingsville, TX, 1937).
- *Minutes of the Eighty-Third General Assembly of the Presbyterian Church in the United States, with an Appendix* (Austin, TX: Von Boeckmann-Jones, Co., 1943).
- *Minutes of the One Hundred and Fifth Stated Meeting of the Presbytery of Dallas*. Crandall, TX, 1932).
- *Minutes of the One Hundred and Fourteenth Stated Meeting of the Presbytery of Dallas*. Waxahachie, TX, 1936).
- *Minutes of the One Hundred and Fourth Stated Meeting of the Presbytery of Dallas* (Dallas, TX, 1931).

- *Minutes of the One Hundred and Sixth Stated Meeting of the Presbytery of Dallas.* Wichita Falls, TX, 1932).
- *Minutes of the One Hundred and Thirteenth Stated Meeting of the Presbytery of Dallas* (Dallas, TX, 1936).
- *Minutes of the One Hundred and Thirty-Fourth Stated Meeting of the Presbytery of Dallas.* McKinney, TX, 1946).
- *Minutes of the One Hundred and Twentieth Stated Meeting of the Presbytery of Dallas.* Happy, TX, 1939).
- *Minutes of the One Hundred and Twenty-Eighth Stated Meeting of the Presbytery of Dallas.* Ennis, TX, 1943).
- *Minutes of the One Hundred and Twenty-Fifth Stated Meeting of the Presbytery of Dallas* (Dallas, TX, 1942).
- *Minutes of the One Hundred and Twenty-Fourth Stated Meeting of the Presbytery of Dallas.* Amarillo, TX, 1941).
- *Minutes of the One Hundred and Twenty-Ninth Stated Meeting of the Presbytery of Dallas* (Dallas, TX, 1944).
- *Minutes of the One Hundred and Twenty-Second Stated Meeting of the Presbytery of Dallas.* Quanah, TX, 1940).
- *Minutes of the One Hundred and Twenty-Third Stated Meeting of the Presbytery of Dallas.* Wichita Falls, TX, 1941).
- *Minutes of the Stated Fall Meeting of the Presbytery of North Alabama.* Decatur, AL, 1938).
- *Minutes of the Stated Fall Meeting of the Presbytery of North Alabama.* Decatur, AL, 1948).
- *Minutes of the Stated Fall Meeting of the Presbytery of North Alabama.* Huntsville, AL, 1943).
- *Minutes of the Stated Fall Meeting of the Presbytery of North Alabama.* Piedmont, AL, 1939).
- *Minutes of the Stated Fall Meeting of the Presbytery of North Alabama.* Sheffield, AL, 1940).
- *Minutes of the Stated Fall Meeting of the Presbytery of North Alabama.* Sylacauga, AL, 1944).
- *Minutes of the Stated Fall Meeting of the Presbytery of North Alabama.* Tuscumbia, AL, 1941).
- *Minutes of the Stated Spring Meeting of the Presbytery of North Alabama.* Decatur, AL, 1944).
- *Minutes of the Stated Spring Meeting of the Presbytery of North Alabama.* Florence, AL, 1940).
- *Minutes of the Stated Spring Meeting of the Presbytery of North Alabama.* Gadsden, AL, 1942).
- *Minutes of the Stated Spring Meeting of the Presbytery of North Alabama.* Huntsville, AL, 1939).
- *Minutes of the Synod of Mississippi of the Presbyterian Church in the U.S., the One Hundred Thirty-Eighth Annual Session* (Jackson, MS, 1968).
- *Minutes of the Synod of Texas of the Presbyterian Church in the United States: Eighty-Sixth Session* (Dallas, TX, 1941).
- *Minutes of the Synod of Texas of the Presbyterian Church in the United States: Eighty-Third Session.* Kerrville, TX, 1938).
- *A Pamphlet Concerning the Matter of the Union of The United Presbyterian Church of North America, The Presbyterian Church in the United States of America, and The Presbyterian Church in the United States* (Richmond, VA: Presbyterian Committee of Publication, 1954).
- *Report of the Ad Interim Committee on Curricula of the Theological Seminaries, as amended and adopted by the General Assembly, May 25, 1936* (Richmond, VA: Presbyterian Committee of Publication, 1936).

Proceedings of a Special Session of the Court En Banc in Memory of the Honorable Samuel H. Sibley (Atlanta, GA: United States Court of Appeals for the Fifth Circuit, 1959).

Queen, Edward L., II, *In the South the Baptists are the Center of Gravity: Southern Baptists and Social Change, 1930-1980*, Chicago Studies of American Religion (Brooklyn, NY: Carlson Publishing House, 1991).

Rall, Harris F., *Modern Premillennialism and the Christian Hope* (New York, NY: Abingdon Press, 1920).
Ramm, Bernard, *After Fundamentalism: The Future of Evangelical Theology* (San Francisco, CA: Harper & Row, Publishers, 1983).
— *Protestant Biblical Interpretation: A Textbook of Hermeneutics* (Grand Rapids, MI: Baker Book House, 1970^4).
Rausch, David A., *Arno C. Gaebelein (1861-1945): Irenic Fundamentalist and Scholar* (New York, NY: Edwin Mellen, 1983).
— *Zionism within Early American Fundamentalism,1878-1918: A Convergence of Two Traditions* (New York, NY: Edwin Mellen, 1979).
Rauschenbusch, Walter, *A Theology for the Social Gospel* (New York, NY: The MacMillan Company, 1917).
Reed, John Shelton, and Dale, *1001 Things Everyone Should Know About the South* (New York, NY: Doubleday & Co., 1996).
Reese, Alexander, *The Approaching Advent of Christ: An Examination of the Teaching of J.N. Darby and His Followers* (Edinburgh: Marshall, Morgan & Scott, 1937).
Reid, R.J., *Amillennialism* (New York, NY: Loizeaux Brothers, 1943).
"Reports of Ad Interim Committees: 1. Report of the Ad Interim Committee on Changes in the Confession of Faith and Catechisms – The Question as to Whether the Type of Bible Interpretation Known as Dispensationalism is in Harmony with the Confession of Faith," in *Minutes of the Eighty-Fourth General Assembly of the Presbyterian Church in the United States with an Appendix*, 123-27, Anderson Auditorium, Montreat, NC, May 25-30, 1944.
Rhodes, Arnold Black, Frank H. Caldwell, and L.C. Rudolph, *The Church Faces the Isms: [Written by The Members of the Faculty of the Louisville Presbyterian Theological Seminary, Louisville, Kentucky]* (Nashville, TN: Abingdon Press, 1958).
Rian, Edwin H., *The Presbyterian Conflict* (Grand Rapids, MI: William B. Eerdmans Publishing Co., 1940).
Richards, Jeffrey Jon, *The Promise of the Dawn: The Eschatology of Lewis Sperry Chafer* (Lanham, MD: University Press of America, 1991).
Ridderbos, Herman, *The Coming of the Kingdom*. 1953, reprint, tr. H. de Jongste, ed. Raymond O. Zorn (Nutley, NJ: Presbyterian and Reformed Publishing Co., 1962).
Rogers, Jack B., and Donald K. McKim, *The Authority and Interpretation of the Bible: An Historical Approach* (New York, NY: Harper & Row, Publishers, 1979).
Rosell, Garth M. (ed.), *The Evangelical Landscape: Essays on the American Evangelical Tradition* (Grand Rapids, MI: Baker Books, 1996).
Ross, Allen P., "The Biblical Method of Salvation: A Case for Discontinuity," in *Continuity and Discontinuity: Perspectives on the Relationship Between the Old and New Testaments: Essays in Honor of S. Lewis Johnson, Jr.*, ed. John S. Feinberg, 161-78 (Westchester, IL: Crossway Books, 1988).
Runkle, Gerald, *Good Thinking: An Introduction to Logic* (Philadelphia, PA: Holt, Rinehart and Winstonk, 1981).
Russell, C. Allyn, *Voices of American Fundamentalism: Seven Biographical Studies* (Philadelphia, PA: Westminster Press, 1976).
Rutgers, William H., *Premillennialism in America* (Goes, Holland: Oosterbaan & Le Cointre, 1930).
Ryrie, Charles C., *Balancing the Christian Life* (Chicago, IL: Moody Press, 1969).
— *The Basis of the Premillennial Faith* (Neptune, NJ: Loizeaux Bros., 1953).
— *The Best is Yet to Come* (Chicago, IL: Moody Press, 1981).
— *Biblical Theology of the New Testament* (Chicago, IL: Moody Press, 1959).
— *Dispensationalism* (Chicago, IL: Moody Press, 1995).

- *Dispensationalism Today* (Chicago, IL: Moody Press, 1965).
- *The Final Countdown* (Wheaton, IL: Victor Books, 1982).
- *The Grace of God* (Chicago, IL: Moody Press, 1963).
- (ed.), *The Ryrie Study Bible* (Chicago, IL: Moody Press, 1976).
- "Update on Dispensationalism," in *Issues in Dispensationalism*, ed. Wesley R. Willis, and John R. Master, 15-27 (Chicago, IL: Moody Press, 1994).
- *What You Should Know About the Rapture* (Chicago, IL: Moody Press, 1981).

Salmon, T.H., *Why I Left the Futurist School* (Auckland, New Zealand: Anchor Printery, 1938).

Sandeen, Ernest R., *The Roots of Fundamentalism: British and American Millennarianism: 1800-1930* (Chicago, IL: University of Chicago Press, 1970).

Sanders, E.P., *Paul and Palestinian Judaism* (Philadelphia, PA: Fortress Press, 1977).
- *Paul, the Law, and the Jewish People* (Philadelphia, PA: Fortress Press, 1983).

Sandmel, Samuel, *We Jews and You Christians* (Philadelphia, PA: Lippencott Press, 1967).

Saucy, Robert, *The Case for Progressive Dispensationalism: The Interface Between Dispensational & Non-Dispensational Theology* (Grand Rapids, MI: Zondervan Publishing House, 1993).

Sauer, Erich, *The Dawn of World Redemption: A Survey of Historical Revelation in the Old Testament*, tr. G.H. Lang (Grand Rapids, MI: William B. Eerdmans Publishing Co., 1951).
- *From Eternity to Eternity: An Outline of Divine Purposes*, tr. G.H. Lang (Grand Rapids, MI: William B. Eerdmans Publishing Co., 1954).
- *The Triumph of the Crucified: A Survey of the Historical Revelation of the New Testament*, tr. G.H. Lang (Grand Rapids, MI: William B. Eerdmans Publishing Co., 1952).

Schaff, Philip, *The Creeds of Christendom*, vol. 2, *The Greek and Latin Creeds*, 1889, reprint (Grand Rapids, MI: Baker Book House, 1983).

Schmidt, Jean Miller, *Souls or the Social Order: The Two-Party System in American Protestantism*, Chicago Studies of American Religion (Brooklyn, NY: Carlson Publishing, 1991).

Schrenk, Gottlob, *Gottesreich und Bund im alteren Protestantismus: vornehmlich bei Johannes Cocceius* (Gutersloh: Druck und Verlog von C. Bertelsmann, 1923).

Scofield, Cyrus Ingerson, *Addresses on Prophecy* (New York, NY: A.C. Gaebelein, 1910).
- *Dr. Scofield's Question Box*. Compiled by Ella E. Pohle (Chicago, IL: Bible Institute Colportage Association, 1917).
- *In Many Pulpits with Dr. C. I. Scofield* (New York, NY: Oxford University Press, 1922).
- *Prophecy Made Plain* (Glasgow: Pickering & Inglis, n.d).
- *Rightly Dividing the Word of Truth* (Oakland, CA: Western Book and Tract Co., 1921).
- *Scofield Bible Correspondence Course* (Chicago, IL: Moody Bible Institute, 1934).
- *Ten Bible Readings on Important Subjects* (by the author, 1911).
- *Things New and Old* (New York, NY: Our Hope Publishers, 1920).
- *What Do the Prophets Say?* (Philadelphia, PA: Philadelphia School of the Bible, 1916).
- *Will the Church Pass through the Great Tribulation? Eighteen Reasons which Prove that It Will Not* (Philadelphia, PA: Philadelphia School of the Bible, n.d).
- *The World's Approaching Crisis* (Philadelphia, PA: Philadelphia School of the Bible, 1913).

Scofield Reference Bible (New York, NY: Oxford University Press, 1911).

The Scofield Reference Bible: 1917 Edition (New York, NY: Oxford University Press, 1992).

The Scofield Reference Bible: 1967 Edition (New York, NY: Oxford University Press, 1967).

Sheldon, Charles, *In His Steps*, 1897, reprint (Waco, TX: Word Books, 1988).

Showers, Renald E., *There Really is a Difference! A Comparison of Covenant and Dispensational Theology* (Bellmawr, NJ: Friends of Israel Gospel Ministry, 1990).

Silber, Irwin, *Songs of the Civil War* (New York, NY: Columbia University Press, 1960).

Simpson, William John Sparrow, *Dispensations* (London: Society for Promoting Christian Knowledge, 1935).

Smith, Christian, *American Evangelicalism: Embattled and Thriving* (Chicago, IL: University of Chicago Press, 1998).
Smith, Morton H., "The Case for Full Subscription," in *The Practice of Confessional Subscription*, ed. David W. Hall, 185-205 (Lanham, MD: University Press of America).
– *Studies in Southern Presbyterian Theology* (Phillipsburg, NJ: Presbyterian and Reformed Publishing Co., 1962).
Smith, Wilbur M., *Arno C. Gaebelein: A Memoir* (New York, NY: Our Hope Press, n.d).
– *The Atomic Age and the Word of God* (Boston, MA: W.A. Wilde Co., 1948).
– *Before I Forget* (Chicago, IL: Moody Press, 1971).
Smock, C. M., *God's Dispensations* (Chicago, IL: Bible Institute Colportage Association, 1918).
Soulen, R. Kendall, *The God of Israel and Christian Theology* (Minneapolis, MN: Fortress Press, 1996).
Spencer, Stephen R., "Francis Turretin's Concept of the Covenant of Nature," in *Later Calvinism: International Perspectives*, Sixteenth Century Essays & Studies, vol. 22, ed. W. Fred Graham 70-91 (Kirksville, MO: Northeast Missouri State University, 1994).
– "Reformed Theology, Covenant Theology, and Dispensationalism," in *Integrity of Heart, Skillfulness of Hands: Biblical and Leadership Studies in Honor of Donald K. Campbell*, ed. Charles H. Dyer and Roy B. Zuck, 238-54 (Grand Rapids, MI: Baker Books, 1994).
Stam, Cornelius R., *The Fundamentals of Dispensationalism* (Milwaukee, WI: Berean Searchlight, 1951).
– *Moses and Paul* (Chicago, IL: Berean Bible Society, 1956).
– *The Present Peril: The New Evangelicalism* (Chicago, IL: Berean Bible Society, 1973).
– *Things That Differ* (Chicago, IL: Berean Bible Society, 1959).
Stanton, Gerald B., *Kept From the Hour* (Grand Rapids, MI: Zondervan Publishing House, 1956).
Steer, Roger, *Guarding the Holy Fire: The Evangelicalism of John R. W. Stott, J. I. Packer, and Alister McGrath* (Grand Rapids, MI: Baker Books, 1999).
Stevenson, Wendell Holmes and E. Merton Coulter, *A History of the South* (Baton Rouge, LA: Louisiana State University Press and the Littlefield Fund for Southern History of the University of Texas, 1967).
Stoever, William B., *"A Faire and Easie Way to Heaven": Covenant Theology and Antinomianism in Early Massachusetts* (Middletown, CT: Wesleyan University Press, 1978).
Stone, Jon R., *On the Boundaries of American Evangelicalism: The Postwar Evangelical Coalition* (New York, NY: St. Martin's Press, 1999).
Stonehouse, Ned B., *J. Gresham Machen: A Biographical Memoir* (Grand Rapids, MI: William B. Eerdmans Publishing Co., 1954).
– (ed.), *"What is Christianity?", and Other Addresses* (Grand Rapids, MI: William B. Eerdmans Publishing Co., 1951).
Stroupe, George (ed.), *Reformed Reader, A Sourcebook in Christian Theology: Volume II, Contemporary Trajectories: 1799-Present* (Louisville, KY: Westminster/John Knox Press, 1994).
Sweet, Leonard I. (ed.), *The Evangelical Tradition in America*, (Macon, GA: Mercer University Press, 1984).
Szasz, Ferenc Morton, *The Divided Mind of Protestant America, 1880-1930* (Birmingham, AL: University of Alabama Press, 1982).
Talbot, L.T., *God's Plan of the Ages* (Los Angeles, CA: by the author, 1936).
Thiessen, Henry C., *Lectures in Systematic Theology* (Grand Rapids, MI: William B. Eerdmans Publishing Co., 1979).
– *Will the Church Pass Through the Tribulation?* (New York, NY: Loizeaux, 1941).
Thiselton, Anthony C., *New Horizons in Hermeneutics: The Theory and Practice of Transforming Biblical Reading* (Grand Rapids, MI: Zondervan Publishing House, 1992).

- *The Two Horizons: New Testament Hermeneutics and Philosophical Description with Special Reference to Heidegger, Bultmann, Gadamer, and Wittgenstein* (Grand Rapids, MI: William B. Eerdmans Publishing Co., 1980).
Thomas, W.H. Griffith, *Ministerial Life and Work* (Chicago, IL: Bible Institute Colportage Association, 1927).
- *The Principles of Theology: An Introduction to the Thirty-Nine Articles* (London: Longmans, Green and Co., 1930).
Thompson, Ernest Trice, *Presbyterians in the South, Volume One: 1607-1861* (Richmond, VA: John Knox Press, 1963).
- *Presbyterians in the South, Volume Two: 1861-1890* (Richmond, VA: John Knox Press, 1973).
- *Presbyterians in the South: Volume Three: 1890-1972* (Richmond, VA: John Knox Press, 1973).
- *The Spirituality of the Church: A Distinctive Doctrine of the Presbyterian Church in the United States* (Richmond, VA: John Knox Press, 1961).
Thornwell, James Henley, *The Collected Writings of James Henley Thornwell*, ed. John B. Adger and John L. Girardeau (Richmond, VA: Presbyterian Committee of Publication, 1873).
- *Election and Reprobation*, 1840, reprint (Philadelphia, PA: Presbyterian and Reformed Publishing Co., 1961).
Tillich, Paul, *Systematic Theology*, vol. 1 (Chicago, IL: University of Chicago Press, 1951).
Torrance, T.F., *Reality and Evangelical Theology: The Realism of Christian Revelation* (Downers Grove, IL: Inter-Varsity Press, 1999).
Torrey, Reuben A., *Difficulties and Alleged Errors and Contradictions in the Bible* (Chicago, IL: Bible Institute Colportage Assn., 1907).
- *The Return of the Lord Jesus* (Los Angeles, CA: BIOLA University Press, 1913).
Toussaint, Stanley D., *Behold the King* (Portland, OR: Multnomah Press, 1980).
Trumbull, Charles Gallaudet, *The Life Story of C.I .Scofield* (New York, NY: Oxford University Press, 1920).
Turner, David L., "The New Jerusalem in Revelation 21:1-22:5: Consummation of a Biblical Continuum," in *Dispensationalism, Israel and the Church: The Search for Definition*, ed. Craig A. Blaising, and Darrell L. Bock, 264-92 (Grand Rapids, MI: Zondervan Publishing House, 1992).
Turner, W.G., *John Nelson Darby* (London: C.A. Hammond, 1944).
Turretin, Francis, *Institutes of Elenctic Theology*, ed. James Dennison, Jr., tr. George Musgrave Giger (Phillipsburg, NJ: Presbyterian and Reformed Publishing Co., 1992/94).
Unger, Merrill F., *Great Neglected Bible Prophecies* (Chicago, IL: Scripture Press, 1955).
Vander Stelt, John C., *Philosophy and Scripture: A Study in Old Princeton and Westminster Theology* (Marlton, NJ: Mack Publishing Co., 1978).
Vander Velde, Lewis G., *The Presbyterian Churches and the Federal Union, 1861-69* (Cambridge, MA: Harvard University Press, 1932).
VanGemeren, Willem, Greg L. Bahnsen, Walter C. Kaiser, Jr., Wayne G. Strickland, and Douglas J. Moo, *The Law, The Gospel, and the Modern Christian: Five Views* (Grand Rapids, MI: Zondervan Publishing House, 1993).
Van Woodward, C., *Origins of the New South* (Baton Rouge, LA: Louisiana State University Press, 1951).
Vignaux, Paul, *Nominalisme au XIVe Siècle* (Paris: Librairie Armand Colin, 1948).
Vos, Geerhardus, *Biblical Theology: Old and New Testaments* (Grand Rapids, MI: William B. Eerdmans Publishing Co., 1948).
- *The Covenant in Reformed Theology*, tr. S. Voorwinde and W. VanGemeren (Philadelphia, PA: Privately published by K.M. Kampbell, 1971).

- *The Idea of Biblical Theology as a Science and as a Theological Discipline* (New York, NY: Anson D. F. Randolph, 1894).
- *The Kingdom of God and the Church*, reprint (Nutley, NJ: Presbyterian and Reformed Publishing Co., 1972).
- *The Pauline Eschatology* (Princeton, NJ: Princeton University Press, 1930).
- *Redemptive History and Biblical Interpretation: The Shorter Writings of Geerhardus Vos*, ed. Richard B. Gaffin (Phillipsburg, NJ: Presbyterian and Reformed Publishing Co., 1980).
- *The Teaching of Jesus Concerning the Kingdom of God and the Church* (New York, NY: American Tract Society, 1903).

Wagner, Don M., *The Expository Method of G. Campbell Morgan*. Westwood, NJ: Fleming H. Revell Publishing Co., 1957).

Walsh, Brian and Richard Middleton, *Truth is Stranger Than It Used to Be: Biblical Faith in a Postmodern Age* (Downers Grove, IL: Inter-Varsity Press, 1995).

Walvoord, John F., *The Blessed Hope and the Tribulation* (Grand Rapids, MI: Zondervan Publishing House, 1976).
- *The Church in Prophecy* (Grand Rapids, MI: William B. Eerdmans Publishing Co., 1964).
- *Daniel: The Key to Prophetic Revelation* (Chicago, IL: Moody Press, 1971).
- *Israel in Prophecy* (Grand Rapids, MI: Zondervan Publishing House, 1962).
- *Major Bible Prophecies* (Grand Rapids, MI: Zondervan Publishing House, 1991).
- *Matthew: Thy Kingdom Come* (Chicago, IL: Moody Press, 1974).
- *The Millennial Kingdom* (Grand Rapids, MI: Zondervan Publishing House, 1959).
- *The Nations in Prophecy* (Grand Rapids, MI: Zondervan Publishing House, 1967).
- *The Nations, Israel and the Church in Prophecy* (Grand Rapids, MI: Zondervan Publishing House, 1988).
- "The New Covenant," in *Integrity of Heart, Skillfulness of hands: Biblical and Leadership Studies in Honor of Donald K. Campbell*, ed. Charles H. Dyer and Roy B. Zuck, 186-200 (Grand Rapids, MI: Baker Book House, 1994).
- *The Prophecy Knowledge Handbook* (Wheaton, IL: Victor Books, 1990).
- *The Rapture Question* (Findlay, OH: Dunham Publishing Co., 1957).
- *The Return of the Lord* (Grand Rapids, MI: Zondervan Publishing House, 1955).
- *The Revelation of Jesus Christ* (Chicago, IL: Moody Press, 1966).

Walvoord, John F., and John E. Walvoord, *Armageddon, Oil and the Middle East Crisis* (Grand Rapids, MI: Zondervan Publishing House, 1976).

Ward, Henry Dana, *The Faith of Abraham and of Christ His Seed in the Coming Kingdom of God on Earth, with the Restitution of All Things Which God Hath Spoken: The Grand Cycle of Divine Dispensations Begins in Eden and Ends in the Kingdom of Heaven on Earth* (Philadelphia, PA: Claxton, Remson & Heffelfinger, 1872).
- *The Gospel of the Kingdom; A Kingdom Not of this World: Not in this World; but to Come in the Heavenly Country, of the Resurrection from the Dead, and of the Restitution of All Things* (Philadelphia, PA: Claxton, Remsen & Heffelfinger, 1870).

Ware, Bruce, "The New Covenant and the People(s) of God," in *Dispensationalism, Israel and the Church: The Search for Definition*, ed. Craig A. Blaising, and Darrell L. Bock, 68-97 (Grand Rapids, MI: Zondervan Publishing House, 1992).

Warfield, Benjamin Breckinridge, *Biblical Doctrines* (New York, NY: Oxford Press, 1929).
- *Calvin and Calvinism* (New York, NY: Oxford University Press, 1931).
- *Faith and Life* (Carlisle, PA: Banner of Truth Trust, 1916).
- *Perfectionism*, ed. Samuel G. Craig (Philadelphia, PA: Presbyterian and Reformed Publishing Co., 1958).
- *The Works of Benjamin B. Warfield*, 10 vols. (Grand Rapids, MI: Baker Book House, 1981).

Warnke, Georgia, *Gadamer: Hermeneutics, Tradition, and Reason* (Stanford, CA: Stanford University Press, 1987).
Watson, Sydney, *In the Twinkling of an Eye* (New York, NY: Fleming H. Revell Publishing Co., 1933).
– *The Mark of the Beast* (New York, NY: Fleming H. Revell, 1933).
Watt, David Harrington, *A Transforming Faith: Explorations of Twentieth-Century American Evangelicalism* (New Brunswick, NJ: Rutgers University Press, 1991).
Weaver, Richard Malcolm, *The Southern Tradition at Bay: A History of Postbellum Thought* (New Rochelle, NY: Arlington House, 1968).
Webber, Robert E., *Ancient-Future Faith: Rethinking Evangelicalism for a Postmodern World* (Grand Rapids, MI: Baker Books, 1999).
– *Evangelicals on the Canterbury Trail: Why Evangelicals are Attracted to the Liturgical Church.* Harrisburg, PA: Morehouse Publishing, 1985).
Weber, Timothy, *On the Road to Armageddon: How Evangelicals Became Israel's Best Friend* (Grand Rapids, MI: Baker Academic Press, 2004).
– *Living in the Shadow of the Second Coming: American Premillennialism, 1875-1925* (New York, NY: Oxford University Pres, 1979).
Weir, David A., *The Origins of the Federal Theology in Sixteenth-Century Reformation Thought.* Oxford: Clarendon, 1990).
Wells, David F., *No Place for Truth, or Whatever Happened to Evangelical Theology?* (Grand Rapids, MI: William B. Eerdmans Publishing Co., 1993).
– (ed.), *Reformed Theology in America: A History of Its Modern Development* (Grand Rapids, MI: William B. Eerdmans Publishing Co., 1985).
Wells, David F., and John D. Woodbridge (eds.), *The Evangelicals: What They Believe, Who They Are, and Where They are Changing* (Nashville, TN: Abingdon Press, 1975).
West, Nathaniel (ed.), *Premillennial Essays of the Prophetic Conference Held at the Church of the Holy Trinity, New York City* (Chicago, IL: Fleming H. Revell Publishing Co., 1879).
The Westminster Standards: The Westminster Confession of Faith, The Larger Catechism, The Shorter Catechism, 1647-48, reprint, The doctrinal standards of The Orthodox Presbyterian Church and The Presbyterian Church in America (Philadelphia, PA: Great Commission Publications, n.d.).
Wildinson, S.H., *The Israel Promises and Their Fulfillment* (London: John Bale, Sons & Danielsson, 1936).
Wilkinson, J., *Israel, My Glory* (London: Mildmay Mission to the Jews, 1921).
Williams, Michael D., *This World is Not My Home: The origins and development of dispensationalism.* Geanies House, Fearn, Ross-shire, Scotland: Mentor Press, 2003).
Williams, Stephen B., *Dispensational Truth* (Alexandria, LA: Good Tidings Press, n.d.).
Willis, Wesley R., John R. Master and Charles Ryrie (eds.), *Issues in Dispensationalism* (Chicago, IL: Moody Press, 1994).
Wilson, Charles Reagan (ed.), *Religion in the South* (Jackson, MS: University of Mississippi Press, 1985).
Wimberley, C.F., *Behold the Morning: The Imminent and Premillennial Coming of Jesus Christ* (New York, NY: Fleming H. Revell Publishing Co., 1916).
– *The Seven Seals of the Apocalypse* (New York, NY: Fleming H. Revell Publishing Co., 1922).
Witmer, S.A., *The Bible College Story: Education with Dimension* (Nanhasset, NY: Channel Press, 1962).
Witsius, Herman, *The Economy of the Covenants between God and Man*, 2 vols. (Phillipsburg, NJ: Presbyterian and Reformed Publishing Co., 1990).
Woodbridge, John D., Mark A. Noll, and Nathan O. Hatch, *The Gospel in America: Themes in the Story of America's Evangelicals* (Grand Rapids, MI: Zondervan Publishing House, 1979).

Woodbridge, John D., and Thomas Edward McComiskey (eds.), *Doing Theology in Today's World: Essays in Honor of Kenneth S. Kantzer* (Grand Rapid, MI: Zondervan Publishing House, 1991).

Woolley, Paul, *The Significance of J. Gresham Machen Today* (Nutley, NJ: Presbyterian and Reformed Publishing Co., 1977).

Works, George A., *Report of a Survey of the Colleges and Theological Seminaries of the Presbyterian Church in the U.S* (Louisville, KY: Board of Christian Education of the Presbyterian Church, U.S., 1942).

Wright, N.T., *Jesus and the Victory of God* (Minneapolis, MN: Fortress Press, 1996).

– *The New Testament and the People of God* (Minneapolis, MN: Fortress Press, 1992)).

Wuthnow, Robert, *Meaning and Moral Order: Explorations in Cultural Analysis* (Los Angeles, CA: University of California Press, 1987).

– *Rediscovering the Sacred: Perspectives on Religion in Contemporary Society* (Grand Rapids, MI: William B. Eerdmans Publishing Co., 1992).

– "Restructuring of American Presbyterianism," in *The Presbyterian Predicament: Six Perspectives*, ed. Milton J. Coalter, John M. Mulder, and Louis B. Weeks, 27-48 (Louisville, KY: Westminster/John Knox Press, 1990).

– *The Restructuring of American Religion: Society and Faith Since World War II* (Princeton, NJ: Princeton University Press, 1988).

Wyngaarden, Martin J., *The Future of the Kingdom: A Study of the Scope of Spiritualization in Scripture* (Grand Rapids, MI: Baker Book House, 1955).

Zens, Jon, *Dispensationalism: A Reformed Inquiry into its Leading Figures and Features* (Phillipsburg, NJ: Presbyterian and Reformed Publishing Co., 1980).

Zuck, Roy B., *Basic Bible Interpretation* (Wheaton, IL: Victor Books, 1991).

– (ed.), *A Biblical Theology of the Old Testament* (Chicago, IL: Moody Press, 1991).

Dictionaries, Encyclopedias, and Periodicals

"Actions by the Presbytery of California: The Overture," *Presbyterian Guardian* 3 (14 November 1936): 55.

Ahlstrom, Sydney E., "The Scottish Philosophy and American Theology," *Church History* 24 (September 1955): 257-72.

Aldrich, Roy L., "An Apologetic for Dispensationalism," *Bibliotheca Sacra* 112 (January-March 1955): 46-54.

– "Causes for Confusion of Law and Grace," *Bibliotheca Sacra* 116 (April-June 1959): 221-29.

– "Has the Mosaic Law Been Abolished?", *Bibliotheca Sacra* 116 (July-September 1959): 322-35.

– "The Mosaic Ten Commandments Compared to Their Restatements in the New Testament," *Bibliotheca Sacra* 118 (April-June 1961): 251-58.

– "A New Look at Dispensationalism," *Bibliotheca Sacra* 120(January-March 1963): 42-49.

– "An Outline Study on Dispensationalism," *Bibliotheca Sacra* 118 (January-March 1961): 133-41.

Alexander, Chalmers W., "Dr. Anderson Please Explain," *Southern Presbyterian Journal* 10 (18 July 1951): 5-8.

– "What the Northern Presbyterian Church Did to Dr. J. Gresham Machen," *Southern Presbyterian Journal* 8 (15 September 1949): 6-16.

– "What the Northern Presbyterian Church Did to Dr. J. Gresham Machen [Part 2]," *Southern Presbyterian Journal* 8 (15 October 1949): 8-12.

Alexander, John M., "Must a Theological Conservative Be a Social Conservative[?]", *Presbyterian of the South* 118 (3 November 1943): 6-7.
- "Must a Theological Conservative Be a Social Conservative? Part II," *Presbyterian of the South* 118 (10 November 1943): 5-6.
- "The Separation of Church and State," *Presbyterian of the South* 117 (8 July 1942): 3.
Allan, D. Maurice, "A Southern Presbyterian elder looks at movements operating with the church today and points out what seem to him to be: The Real Issues That Divide Us," *Presbyterian Outlook* 130 (23 February 1948): 5-7.
- "The Real Issues That Divide Us, Part II: Russia, race, labor and sectionalism, as well as some motives which seem to be operative," *Presbyterian Outlook* 130 (1 March 1948): 5-7.
Allis, Oswald T., "The Blessing of Abraham," *Princeton Theological Review* 25 (1927): 263-298.
- "Isaiah 7:14 According to the RSV Old Testament," *Southern Presbyterian Journal* 11 (29 October 1952): 5-6.
- "The Marginal Note to Mt. 1:16 in the RSV Bible," *Southern Presbyterian Journal* 11 (4 February 1953): 7.
- "Modern Dispensationalism and the Doctrine of the Unity of the Scriptures," *Evangelical Quarterly* 8 (January 1936): 22-35.
- "Modern Dispensationalism and the Law of God," *Evangelical Quarterly* 8 (September 1936): 272-89.
- "The New Presbyterian USA Curriculum for Sunday Schools: 'Christian Faith and Life – A Program for Church and Home,'" *Southern Presbyterian Journal* 7 (15 November 1948): 6-9.
- "The New Presbyterian USA Curriculum for Sunday Schools: 'Christian Faith and Life – A Program for Church and Home'; A Critique of the New Curriculum," *Southern Presbyterian Journal* 7 (1 December 1948): 5-10.
- "The New Presbyterian USA Curriculum for Sunday Schools: 'Christian Faith and Life – A Program for Church and Home'; A Critique of the New Curriculum," *Southern Presbyterian Journal* 7 (15 December 1948): 12-15.
"Alumni Banquet to Honor Professor Kuiper," *Presbyterian Guardian* 21 (15 April 1952): 77.
Anderson, Curtis, "The Postman, the Singing Seminarians, and a Surprise Encounter," *Kindred Spirit* 19 (Summer 1995): 8.
"An Announcement," *Presbyterian Guardian* 2 (12 September 1936): [1].
Appleby, James, "Science and Religion," *Presbyterian of the South* 111 (12 February 1936): 2-3.
- "What is Religion?", *Presbyterian of the South* 111 (19 February 1936): 2.
"The Assembly at a Glance," *Presbyterian Outlook* 118 (7 June 1944): [1].
Atwell, Robert L., "The Marrow of All Theology: A Study in Protestant Principles," *Presbyterian Guardian* 10 (25 September 1941): 65-66, 74.
"Auburn *Affirmation* Becomes Issue in South," *Presbyterian Guardian* 20 (15 October 1951): 200.
Baker, B.W., "Is There Modernism in the Teachings of Dr. C.I. Scofield?", *Presbyterian of the South* 109 (28 February 1934): 6-7.
- "Is There Modernism in the Teachings of Dr. C.I. Scofield?: II," *Presbyterian of the South* 109 (7 March 1934): 7-8.
- "Is There Modernism in the Scofield Bible? A Reply to Dr. L.S. Chafer," *Presbyterian of the South* 111 (18 March 1936): 2-4.
Balmer, Randall H., "The Princetonians and Scripture: A Reconsideration," *Westminster Theological Journal* 44 (Fall 1982): 352-65.
Barker, Kenneth. "False Dichotomies Between the Testaments," *Journal of the Evangelical Theological Society* 25 (March 1982): 3-16.
Barnhouse, Donald Grey, "An Open Letter to the Board of Foreign Missions of the Presbyterian Church in the U.S.A," *Presbyterian Guardian* 2 (20 April 1936): 24-27.

Barr, Thomas C., "How Does the Kingdom Come?", *Presbyterian of the South* 115 (12 June 1940): 4-6.
Bauman, Clarence, "The Theology of 'Two Kingdoms': A Comparison of Luther and the Anabaptists," *Mennonite Quarterly Review* 38 (January 1964): 37-49, 60.
Bean, W.S., "Pre-Millenarianism and the Standards," *Presbyterian Standard* 58 (25 April 1917): 8-9.
– "Pre-Millenarianism and the Standards (Continued from last week)," *Presbyterian Standard* 58 (2 May 1917): 9.
Bear, James E., "A Biblical Study of the Position of Women in the Church," *Southern Presbyterian Journal* 15 (26 September 1956): 10-13.
– "Dispensationalism: I. The Heart of this System," *Presbyterian Outlook* 118 (26 April 1944): 6.
– "Dispensationalism: II. Dispensationalism vs. The Reformed Faith," *Presbyterian Outlook* 118 (3 May 1944): 5-6.
– "Dispensationalism and the Covenant of Grace," *Union Seminary Review* 49 (July 1938): 285-307.
– "Distinguish the Ages," *Presbyterian of the South* 115 (17 July 1940): 5-6.
– "Historic Premillennialism," *Union Seminary Review* 55 (May 1944): 193-222.
– "The Kingdom of God or World Revolution," *Presbyterian Outlook* 127 (15 October 1945): 5-7.
– "The Kingdom of God or World Revolution (Part II)," *Presbyterian Outlook* 127 (27 October 1945): 5-7.
– "The People of God," *Union Seminary Review* 52 (October 1940): 33-63.
– "The People of God According to the Fathers of the Early Church," *Union Seminary Review* 52 (July 1941): 351-74.
– "The People of God in the Light of the Teaching of the New Testament," *Union Seminary Review* 52 (January 1941): 128-58.
– "Premillenarians and Our Church Standards," *Presbyterian of the South* 115 (24 July 1940): 4-6.
– "The Presbyterian Standards vs. The Scofield Bible," *Presbyterian of the South* 116 (19 March 1941): 6-7.
– "The Presbyterian Standards vs. The Scofield Bible: II. The Doctrine of the Covenant of Grace," *Presbyterian of the South* 116 (26 March 1941): 5-6.
– "The Presbyterian Standards vs. The Scofield Bible: The Doctrine of the 'Church,'" *Presbyterian of the South* 116 (2 April 1941): 7-8.
– "The Presbyterian Standards vs. The Scofield Bible: III. The Mediatorial King and His Kingdom," *Presbyterian of the South* 116 (9 April 1941): 5-6.
– "The Presbyterian Standards vs. The Scofield Bible: IV. Divergent Views of God's Revelation," *Presbyterian of the South* 116 (16 April 1941): 5-6.
– "The Presbyterian Standards vs. The Scofield Bible: V. The General Resurrection and Final Judgment," *Presbyterian of the South* 116 (23 April 1941): 5-6.
– "The Presbyterian Standards vs. The Scofield Bible: VI. Concluding Statement," *Presbyterian of the South* 116 (30 April 1941): 6-7.
– "The Scofield Bible Can't Be Quoted!" *Presbyterian of the South* 115 (21 August 1940): 4-5.
– "The Second Coming of Christ," *Presbyterian of the South* 115 (29 May 1940): 3-6.
– "Shall We Revise the Standards?", *Presbyterian of the South* 115 (12 June 1940): 3-4.
– "A Statement," *Union Seminary Review* 50 (January 1939): 112.
Beaton, D., "Review of *The Modern Outcry Against the Law*, by Willis M. Mead," *Evangelical Quarterly* 1 (1929): 29-30.
Bedinger, R.D., "Sabbath Observance," *Southern Presbyterian Journal* 3 (September 1944): 24-25.

Bell, Bob, Jr., "Church Youth Camps Are Urged for Race Mixing: Participation in 'Demonstrations' Proposed at Conference Here," Clipping from the *Nashville Banner* (10 January 1964), in Felix B. Gear Papers. Department of History, Presbyterian Church of the United States of America, Montreat, NC.
– "Destroy Southern 'System,'" Clipping from the *Nashville Banner* (7 January 1964), in Felix B. Gear Papers. Department of History, Presbyterian Church of the United States of America, Montreat, NC.
Bell, Eugene, "'Rejoiceth Not in Iniquity' [with an Editors' Reply]," *Presbyterian Standard* 62 (6 July 1921): 5.
– "Some Objections to Dr. Caldwell's 'Exegetical Study of Revelation,'" *Presbyterian Standard* 62 (16 February 1921): 5.
Bell, L. Nelson, "Against Something," *Southern Presbyterian Journal* 4 (August 1944): 4-5.
– "An Analysis of an Address: 'The Bible for Today' by Ernest Trice Thompson," *Southern Presbyterian Journal* 10 (23 January 1952): 4-22.
– "Attention!! What Have We Here?", *Southern Presbyterian Journal* 7 (1 April 1949): 16A-16D.
– "The Auburn Affirmation Is Actually Not an Affirmation of Faith But a . . . Dissent From Evangelical Truth," *Southern Presbyterian Journal* 10 (10 October 1951): 3-4.
– "Blowing Out Sparks at a Three-Alarm Fire," *Southern Presbyterian Journal* 3 (October 1944): 2.
– "'Economic Justice,'" *Southern Presbyterian Journal* 5 (15 April 1947): 2.
– "In God We Trust – Is It Legal?", *Southern Presbyterian Journal* 6 (1 April 1948): 3-4.
– "'Intellectually Static But Emotionally Dynamic,'" *Southern Presbyterian Journal* 6 (1 April 1948): 3.
– "Is Neutrality Christian?", *Mississippi Visitor* (March 1938): 6-7.
– "A Layman Looks at Liberalism," *Southern Presbyterian Journal* 4 (15 September 1945): 3-4.
– "One Elder Looks at the General Assembly," *Southern Presbyterian Journal* 2 (June 1943): 6-7.
– "The One Thing Which Counts," *Southern Presbyterian Journal* 3 (August 1944): 11.
– "Progress and Change," *Southern Presbyterian Journal* 6 (1 April 1948): 4-5.
– "A Question of Emphasis," *Southern Presbyterian Journal* 3 (January 1945): 3.
– "Race Relations – Whither?", *Southern Presbyterian Journal* 2 (March 1944): 4-5.
– "Rationalizing Unbelief," *Southern Presbyterian Journal* 6 (15 April 1948): 2-3.
– "An Unfortunate Incident," *Southern Presbyterian Journal* 7 (15 November 1948): 2.
– "Unthinkable," *Southern Presbyterian Journal* 7 (1 March 1948): 2-3.
– "What is Progress?", *Southern Presbyterian Journal* 1 (April 1943): 20-21.
– "Why? – Why the Journal at this time?", *Southern Presbyterian Journal* 1 (May 1942): 2-3.
Bennetch, John Henry, "Editorial: Capitalism," *Bibliotheca Sacra* 106 (April-June 1949): 258.
– "Editorial: Communism," *Bibliotheca Sacra* 106 (April-June 1949): 259.
– "Editorial: Racial Lines," *Bibliotheca Sacra* 106 (January-March 1949): 131-32.
Bennett, John Coleman, "The Christian Faith and the Communist Faith," *Presbyterian Outlook* 134 (4 February 1952): 5.
– "The Impact of Communism in Asia," *Presbyterian Outlook* 134 (21 January 1952): 5-6.
– "The Issues Raised by Communism for Christians," *Presbyterian Outlook* 134 (14 January 1952): 5-6.
Beyer, Lisa, "The Gulf War: What Kind of Peace?", *TIME*, 28 January 1991, 38-40.
"Bible Presbyterian Fellowship Formed," *Christian Beacon* 2 (10 June 1937): 1, 8.
"Bible Pres. Church Form of Government," *Christian Beacon* 3 (18 August 1938): 1-2, 4-5.
"Bible Presbyterian Synod Adopts Historic Westminster Confession; Form of Government Determined," *Christian Beacon* 3 (15 September 1938): 1-2, 5, 7.
"Bible Presbyterian Synod Constituted a Church of the Lord Jesus Christ," *Christian Beacon* 3 (8 September 1938): 1-2.

"'Bible Presbyterian Synod' Organized by Members Withdrawing from Presbyterian Church of America: New Organization Joined by Fourteen Members and Three Elders," *Presbyterian Guardian* 4 (26 June 1937): 99-100.

Bierma, Lyle Dean, "Covenant or Covenants in the Theology of Olevianus," *Calvin Theological Journal* 22 (November 1987): 228-50.

– "Federal Theology in the Sixteenth Century: Two Traditions?", *Westminster Theological Journal* 45 (Fall 1983): 304-21.

– "The Role of Covenant Theology in Early Reformed Orthodoxy," *Sixteenth Century Journal* 21 (1990): 458-62.

Bigger, E.E., "The Sabbath Permanent But Movable," *Southern Presbyterian Journal* 1 (July 1942): 12-13.

Birch, Thomas R., "The Concluding Days of the General Assembly," *Presbyterian Guardian* 14 (25 June 1945): 182-84, 186-91.

– "The Fourth General Assembly of the Presbyterian Church of America," *Presbyterian Guardian* 5 (July 1938): 123-29.

– "Editorial: Strange Bedfellows!" *Presbyterian Guardian* 12 (15 August 1943): 233-34.

– "The Eleventh General Assembly: A Report of This Year's Assembly of the Orthodox Presbyterian Church," *Presbyterian Guardian* 13 (10 June 1944): 165-80.

– "The Fifth General Assembly of the Presbyterian Church of America," *Presbyterian Guardian* 6 (March 1939): 56-7.

– "The First Three Days of the General Assembly," *Presbyterian Guardian* 14 (10 June 1945): 162, 169-76.

– "Glasgow vs. Thompson: Heresy Charges in the Presbyterian Church in the U.S," *Presbyterian Guardian* 9 (10 February 1941): 35-36.

– "More Deliberation on the Clark Case," *Presbyterian Guardian* 14 (25 April 1945): 115-16.

– "The Passing Parade: Philadelphia's Battle of the Air Waves," *Presbyterian Guardian* 14 (10 April 1945): 98, 112.

– "Philadelphia Presbytery Considers Clark Case," *Presbyterian Guardian* 14 (10 April 1945): 108-12.

– "The Presbyterian Guardian and the Southern Church," *Presbyterian Guardian* 7 (25 March 1940): 88.

– "The Second General Assembly of the Presbyterian Church of America," *Presbyterian Guardian* 3 (28 November 1936): 78-85.

– "The Third General Assembly of the Presbyterian Church of America," *Presbyterian Guardian* 4 (26 June 1937): 88-96.

Blaising, Craig A., "Contemporary Dispensationalism," *Southwestern Journal of Theology* (Spring 1993): 5-13.

– "Developing Dispensationalism; Part 1: Doctrinal Developments in Orthodoxy; Part 2: Developments by Contemporary Dispensationalists," *Bibliotheca Sacra* 145 (April-June 1988): 133-40; (July-September 1988): 254-80.

Bock, Darrell L., "Charting Dispensationalism," *Christianity Today* (12 September 1994): 26-9.

– "Current Messianic Activity and OT Davidic Promise: Dispensationalism, Hermeneutics, and NT Fulfillment," *Trinity Journal* 15 (Spring 1994): 55-87.

– "Evangelicals and the Use of the Old Testament in the New," *Bibliotheca Sacra* 142 (October-December 1985): 209-23.

– "Why I Am a Dispensationalist with a Small 'd'," *Journal of the Evangelical Theological Society* 41 (July 1998): 386-88.

Bowers, Russell H., "Dispensational Motifs in the Writings of Eric Sauer," *Bibliotheca Sacra* 148 (July-September 1991): 259-73.

Bowman, John Wick, "The Bible and Modern Religions: Part II. Dispensationalism," *Interpretation* 10 (April 1956): 170-87.
- "I Believe in the Gospel: I Do Not Believe in War," *Presbyterian* 110 (1 August 1940): 3, 6.
- "I Believe in the Gospel: I Do Not Believe in War (Conclusion)," *Presbyterian* 110 (5 September 1940): 6-7, 18-19.

Bozeman, Dwight Theodore, "Federal Theology and the National Covenant: An Elizabethan Presbyterian Case Study," *Church History* 61 (December 1992): 394-407.

Bradshaw, Hugh E., "The Presbyterian Church in the U.S.: Its Origin and History," *Presbyterian Guardian* 15 (25 February 1946): 53-54.
- "The Presbyterian Church in the U.S.: Its Present Position and Its Problems," *Presbyterian Guardian* 15 (10 March 1946): 71-72.

Bridges, J.R., "Book Notices: Union Seminary Review," *Presbyterian Standard* 57 (10 May 1916): 9.

Bridges, J.R., and R.C. Reed, "Editorial: The Abuse of Scripture," *Presbyterian Standard* 60 (17 September 1919): 2.
- "Editorial: The Benighted South," *Presbyterian Standard* 59 (18 December 1918): 3.
- "Editorial: The Cloud in the Sky," *Presbyterian Standard* 60 (27 August 1919): 3.
- "A Decrease in Lynching," *Presbyterian Standard* 61 (14 July 1920): 2-3.
- "Editorial: A Divided Team," *Presbyterian Standard* 60 (6 August 1919): 2.
- "Editorial: Dr. William M. Anderson at Columbia Seminary," *Presbyterian Standard* 60 (3 December 1919): 2.
- "Editorial: The Jews and Palestine," *Presbyterian Standard* 61 (22 December 1920): 3.
- "Editorial: The Kingdom of Heaven," *Presbyterian Standard* 62 (31 August 1921): 2.
- "Editorial: The Last Days at Montreat," *Presbyterian Standard* 62 (31 August 1921): 3, 7.
- "Editorial: Liberal Theology among the Missionaries," *Presbyterian Standard* 62 (7 September 1921): 3.
- "Editorial: Lo, the Poor Negro!" *Presbyterian Standard* 57 (8 November 1916): 3.
- "Editorial: Lo, the Poor Negro!" *Presbyterian Standard* 62 (22 June 1921): 3.
- "Editorial: Locating the Beast," *Presbyterian Standard* 59 (10 April 1918): 2.
- "Editorial: The Negro a Stumbling Block to Church Union," *Presbyterian Standard* 59 (3 April 1918): 3.
- "Editorial: The Old-Time Religion," *Presbyterian Standard* 59 (18 December 1918): 3.
- "Editorial: Paul to the Contrary Notwithstanding," *Presbyterian Standard* 61 (4 February 1920): 3.
- "Editorial: Premillennialism and Patriotism," *Presbyterian Standard* 59 (2 October 1918): 3.
- "Editorial: The Present and Future of the Negro," *Presbyterian Standard* 61 (27 October 1920): 2.
- "Editorial: Progressiveness in Doctrine," *Presbyterian Standard* 62 (14 September 1921): 3.
- "Editorial: Race Prejudice," *Presbyterian Standard* (7 July 1920): 2-3.
- "Editorial: The Race Problem," *Presbyterian Standard* 59 (4 September 1918): 3
- "Editorial: The Race Riots," *Presbyterian Standard* 60 (20 August 1919): 3.
- "Editorial: 'Rejoiceth Not in Iniquity,'" *Presbyterian Standard* 62 (22 June 1921): 3.
- "Editorial: The Scofield Bible Again," *Presbyterian Standard* 62 (6 April 1921): 2.
- "Editorial: The Second Coming of Christ," *Presbyterian Standard* 59 (2 October 1918): 3.
- "Editorial: The Second Coming – Pre? or Post?", *Presbyterian Standard* 60 (26 February 1919): 3.
- "Editorial: Sunday at Montreat," *Presbyterian Standard* 60 (20 August 1919): 3.
- "Editorial: Two Great Bible Teachers at Montreat," *Presbyterian Standard* 60 (27 August 1919): 3.
- "Editorial: The Union Seminary Review," *Presbyterian Standard* 61 (3 March 1920): 2-3.

- "Editorial: Up to Date Prophecy," *Presbyterian Standard* 58 (6October 1917): 2.
- "Editorial: The Victorious Life," *Presbyterian Standard* 61 (11 February 1920): 2.
- "Editorial: What is Politics?", *Presbyterian Standard* 60 (6 August 1919): 2.
- "Editorial: Woman's Suffrage – Its Fruits," *Presbyterian Standard* 61 (4 February 1920): 3.
- "Editorial: The Wreck of a Great Movement," *Presbyterian Standard* 61 (7 July 1920): 2.
- "Editorial: The Young People and Presbyterian Conservatism," *Presbyterian Standard* 60 (6 August 1919): 2.

Bronkema, Frederick, "Theological Notes on the Five Main Truths of Calvinism," *Southern Presbyterian Journal* 4 (1 February 1946): 6-9.

Brookes, James Hall, "What is a Premillennialist?", *Our Hope* 18 (November 1912): 289-91.

Brown, Colin, "Herman Samuel Reimarus," in *Historical Handbook of Major Biblical Interpreters*, ed. Donald K. McKim, 346-49 (Downers Grove, IL: Inter-Varsity Press, 1998).

Brown, Frank C., "The Immediacy of Evangelism," *Southern Presbyterian Journal* 2 (November 1943): 17.
- "Our Presbyterian Heritage: A Sermon, Delivered by the Moderator, Rev. Frank C. Brown, D.D., Before the General Assembly May 22, 1941," *Presbyterian of the South* 116 (28 May 1941): 4-7.
- "The Outlook Pulpit: Spared for What?", *Presbyterian Outlook* 127 (26 November 1945): 5-6.

Brown, Harold O.J., "Covenant and Dispensation," *Trinity Journal* 2 (Spring 1981): 69-70.

Brown, Robert E., "Ordination Vows: What Do They Mean in the Presbyterian Church in the U.S.A.?", *Presbyterian Guardian* 12 (25 July 1943): 213-14.
- "Presbyterian Orthodoxy," *Presbyterian Guardian* 12 (15 August 1943): 228-29.
- "What is Presbyterian Orthodoxy?", *Presbyterian Guardian* 12 (25 March 1943): 91.

Brown, W.A., "Covenant Theology," in *Encyclopedia of Religion and Ethics*, vol. 4, ed. James Hastings, (New York, NY: Charles Scribner's Sons, 1926), 216-24.

Bruce, F.F., "Paul and the Law of Moses," *Bulletin of the John Rylands University Library of Manchester*, 51 (1968): 292-310.

Bruggink, Donald, "Calvin and Federal Theology," *Reformed Review* 13 (1959): 15-22.

Buchanan, Walter McS., "Dogmatic Totalitarianism," *Presbyterian of the South* 118 (22 March 1944): [14].

Buck, Pearl S., "Can the Church Lead?", *Presbyterian Outlook* 118 (9 August 1944): 5-6.

Buswell, J. Oliver, Jr., "Buswell Speaks on Millennial Issue," *Christian Beacon* 1 (17 December 1936): 7.
- "Come Out and Be Ye Separate: Our Testimony to Christians in the Presbyterian Church in the U.S.A," *Presbyterian Guardian* (10 October 1936): 3-6.
- "Premillennialism and the Reformed Faith: Has the 'Pre' a good standing?", *Sunday School Times* 76 (5 May 1934): 289-91.
- "A Premillennialist's View," *Presbyterian Guardian* 3 (14 November 1936): 46-47.
- "Two Communications from Dr. Buswell," *Presbyterian Guardian* 4 (10 April 1937): 12-16.

"Buswell Trial Ends in Chicago," *Presbyterian Guardian* 2 (17 February 1936): 169-71.

Caldwell, C.T., "The Baptism of a Baby," *Southern Presbyterian Journal* 2 (November 1943): 17.

Caldwell, Frank H., "More on the Lordship of Christ," *Presbyterian Outlook* 129 (13 October 1947): 6-7.
- "The Outlook Pulpit: The Christian as a Lover," *Presbyterian Outlook* 128 (18 February 1946): 5-6

Campbell, R.F., "Grace and Works," *Southern Presbyterian Journal* 3 (October 1944): 5-7.

"Carl McIntire Convicted, Appeal Notice Given," *Presbyterian Guardian* (7 October 1935): 16-17.

Carpenter, Joel A., "Fundamentalist Institutions and the Rise of Evangelical Protestantism, 1929-1942," *Church History* 49 (March 1980): 62-75.

Carr, Archibald Fairly, "Theology of the Future," *Presbyterian Quarterly* 14 (April 1900): 165-72.

Carroll, B.H., "The Second Advent of Christ and the Millennium," *Baptist Standard* (February 18, 1904).
"Catholics Study South's Problems," *Presbyterian of the South* 118 (29 December 1943): [1].
Chafer, Lewis Sperry, "Are There Two Ways to be Saved?", *Bibliotheca Sacra* 105 (January-March 1948): 1-2.
- "Are Victorious Life Teachers 'Side Tracked'?", *Presbyterian Standard* 60 (7 April 1920): 4, 8.
- "An Attack upon a Book," *Bibliotheca Sacra* 104 (April-June 1947): 130-34.
- "Bullingerism," *Bibliotheca Sacra* 104 (July-September 1947): 257-58.
- "The Calvinistic Doctrine of Security," *Bibliotheca Sacra* 107 (January-March 1950): 9-41.
- "Careless Misstatements of Vital Truth," *Our Hope* 30 (1924): 540-51.
- "Dispensational Distinctions Challenged," *Bibliotheca Sacra* 100 (July-September 1943): 337-345.
- "Dispensational Distinctions Denounced," *Bibliotheca Sacra* 101 (April-June 1944): 257-60.
- "Dispensationalism," *Bibliotheca Sacra* 93 (October-December 1936): 390-449; also published as *Dispensationalism* (Dallas, TX: Dallas Seminary Press, [1936].
- "Dr. C.I. Scofield," *Bibliotheca Sacra* 100 (April-June 1943): 4-6.
- "Editorial: Things New and Old," *Bibliotheca Sacra* 97 (October-December 1940): 386-88.
- "Editorial: Why Substitutes?", *Bibliotheca Sacra* 97 (October-December 1940): 385-86.
- "Evils Resulting from an Abridged Systematic Theology," Parts 1, 2. *Bibliotheca Sacra* 91 (January-March 1934): 134-54, (July-September 1934): 261-85.
- "For Whom Did Christ Die?", *Bibliotheca Sacra* 105 (January-March 1948): 7-35.
- "In a Moment," *Our Hope* 22 (February 1916): 510.
- "Infinite Grace," *Bibliotheca Sacra* 98 (April-June 1941): 131-32.
- "Inventing Heretics Through Misunderstanding," *Bibliotheca Sacra* 102 (January-March 1945): 1-5.
- "Judaism. Part 1," *Bibliotheca Sacra* 104 (April-June 1947): 129-30.
- "Judaism. Part 2," *Bibliotheca Sacra* 106 (October-December 1949):385-86.
- "Our Assurance of Infant Salvation," *Sunday School Times* 70 (10 November 1928): 653-54.
- "Populating the Third Heaven, Part I," *Bibliotheca Sacra* 108 (April-June 1951): 138-52.
- "Populating the Third Heaven, Part II," *Bibliotheca Sacra* 108 (July-September 1951): 263-69.
- "Repentance," *Bibliotheca Sacra* 108 (April-June 1951): 131-32.
- "The Scofield Bible," *Bibliotheca Sacra* 109 (January-March 1952): 97-99.
- "Twenty Years of Experience," *Dallas Theological Seminary Bulletin* 19 (July-September 1943): [3].
- "Unabridged Systematic Theology," *Bibliotheca Sacra* 91 (January-March 1934): 8-23.
- "Was C.I. Scofield a Modernist?", *Our Hope* 41 (September 1934): 160-65; reprinted, with the same title, in *Presbyterian of the South* 111 (12 February 1936): 3-5.
- "When I Learned from Dr. Scofield," *Sunday School Times* 64 (4 March 1922): 120.
- "Why Was it Necessary for Christ to Die?", *Sunday School Times* 60 (27 April 1918): 241.
Chafer, Rollin Thomas, "The Boundaries of Greater Canaan," *Presbyterian Standard* 62 (2 February 1921): 4, 8.
- "Confusion of Ideas," *Evangelical Theological College Bulletin* 7 (June 1931): 5.
- "Dispensationally-Colored Premillennialism," *Bibliotheca Sacra* 95 (April-June 1938): 257-58.
- "Dr. C.I. Scofield Honored," *Presbyterian Standard* 60 (2 April 1919): 4.
- "Eschatological Freedom," *Bibliotheca Sacra* 93 (July-September 1936): 387-88.
- "'Modern' Dispensationalism," *Bibliotheca Sacra* 93 (January-March 1936): 129-30.
- "The Modernity of Dispensationalism," *Evangelical Theological College Bulletin* 6 (June 1930): 1-3.
- "Of the Same Opinion Still," *Bibliotheca Sacra* 94 (July-September 1937): 262-63.

- "Unfounded Charges Against the Patriotic Loyalty of Premillenarians," *Presbyterian Standard* 59 (13 November 1918): 9-10.
"Charles Gallaudet Trumbull," *Presbyterian Guardian* 9 (10 February 1941): 34.
"The Christian World: Negro Leader Charges Church with Racism," *Presbyterian of the South* 118 (6 January 1943): 10.
"Church of Open Door Observes Anniversary," *Christian Beacon* 2 (17 June 1937): 1.
"Churches Plan Post-War Buildings: Conover Reports Debts Being Paid; Reserves Accumulating," *Presbyterian of the South* 118 (29 December 1943): [1].
Clark, Gordon H., "An Appeal to Fundamentalists," *Presbyterian Guardian* 12 (10 March 1943): 65-67.
- "The Auburn Heresy," *Christian Beacon* 1 (20 August 1936): 3.
- "The Auburn Heresy," *Southern Presbyterian Journal* 5 (15 July 1946): 7-9.
"The Clark Protest," *Presbyterian Guardian* 14 (25 January 1945) 25-26.
Clelland, John P., "The Bible Doctrine of Salvation by Grace," *Presbyterian Guardian* 10 (25 July 1941): 17-18, 27-28.
Clutter, Ronald T., "Dispensational Study Group: An Introduction," *Grace Theological Journal* 10 (1989): 123-24.
Clowney, Edmund P., "The Thirteenth General Assembly of the Orthodox Presbyterian Church," *Presbyterian Guardian* 15 (10 June 1946): 169-72.
- "Toward the Future of the Presbyterian Church," *Presbyterian Guardian* 48 (October 1979): 3.
Cochran, W.A., "Save the Southern Presbyterian Church," *Southern Presbyterian Journal* 5 (15 February 1947): 4.
Coker, Joe L., "Exploring the Roots of the Dispensationalist/Princeton 'Alliance': Charles Hodge and John Nelson Darby on Eschatology and Interpretation of Scripture," *Fides et Historia* 30 (Winter-Spring 1998): 41-56.
Cousar, R. Wilbur, "A Word to 'the Moderates,'" *Southern Presbyterian Journal* 9 (15 May 1950): 4-5.
"Covenant Union Meeting at Home of Dr. Trumbull," *Presbyterian Guardian* 2 (20 April 1936): 38.
"The Covenant Union Convention and the First General Assembly of the Presbyterian Church of America," *Presbyterian Guardian* 2 (22 June 1936): 113-17.
Cowan, George, "The Prohibitions of Grace," *Bibliotheca Sacra* 103 (April-June 1946): 223-226.
- "The Prohibitions of Grace [Part II]," *Bibliotheca Sacra* 103 (July-September 1946): 363-75.
- "The Prohibitions of Grace [Part III]," *Bibliotheca Sacra* 103 (October-December 1946): 464-76.
Cragoe, Thomas H., "W.H. Griffith Thomas," in *Handbook of Evangelical Theologians*, ed. Walter A. Elwell, 67-81 (Grand Rapids, MI: Baker Book House, 1993.
Criswell, W.A. "The Curse of Modernism," *Southern Presbyterian Journal* 8 (1 December 1949): 8-13.
Crouch, B.W., "Dr. Palmer on Racial Barriers," *Southern Presbyterian Journal* 5 (2 December 1946): 5-6.
Crowe, William, Jr., "A Mild Reply to James McBride Dabbs In *The Presbyterian Outlook* on "*The Last Stronghold of Segregation*," *Southern Presbyterian Journal* 10 (8 August 1951): 4-5.
- "Letter from Dr. William Crowe," *Southern Presbyterian Journal* 3 (August 1944): 8.
- "Our Church and the Negro in the South," *Union Seminary Review* 51 (April 1940): 248-63.
- "Our Church and the Negro in the South (Part 2),"*Union Seminary Review* 51 (July 1940): 329-40.
- "The Southern Presbyterian Church," *Presbyterian Standard* 60 (6 August 1919): 5.
Cummings, Calvin K., "The Gospel of the Kingdom," *Presbyterian Guardian* 11 (25 December 1942): 353-54; 367-68.

- "The Kingdom of God," *Presbyterian Guardian* 12 (25 January 1943): 21-23.
Curnow, James C., "The Blessed Hope," *Christian Beacon* 2 (27May 1937): 3.
Currie, Thomas W., "Reasons for the Revision of the Presbyterian Standards," *Union Seminary Review* 50 (January 1939): 112-30.
Dallas Theological Seminary 1997-98 Catalog (Dallas, TX: Dallas Theological Seminary, 1997.
Daniels, M.F., "'Illustrious Heretics,'" *Presbyterian Standard* 62 (14 September 1921): 9.
Dendy, Henry B., "The Calvinistic Creed of Presbyterians," *Southern Presbyterian Journal* 3 (May 1944): 3.
- "Forces Disrupting the Churches," *Southern Presbyterian Journal* 4 (August 1944): 2-4.
- "Needed – A Clear Distinction," *Southern Presbyterian Journal* 2 (August 1943): 2-3.
- "Overture on Plan of Reunion," *Southern Presbyterian Journal* 3 (May 1944): 2-3.
- "The Presbyterian Outlook Editor Concerned About New Department at Bob Jones University," *Southern Presbyterian Journal* 7 (1 March 1949): 2.
- "President of Federal Council Assails Doctrine of Original Sin," *Southern Presbyterian Journal* 4 (1 April 1946): 2.
- "Report of Meeting of the General Assembly: The Question as to Whether the Type of Bible Interpretation Known as Dispensationalism is in Harmony with the Confession of Faith," *Southern Presbyterian Journal* 3 (July 1944): 6-7.
- "Safeguarding Our Church Property," *Southern Presbyterian Journal* 5 (15 August 1946): 3.
Dendy, Henry B. and John Temple Graves, "Editorial: Two Nationally Known Editors Expose Radical Teachings of Federal Council Leaders," *Southern Presbyterian Journal* 5 (15 January 1947): 2-3.
Dendy, Henry B. and L. Nelson Bell, "Meeting of the General Assembly," *Southern Presbyterian Journal* 3 (June 1944): 2-7.
Detweiler, Richard C., "The Concept of Law and Gospel in the Writings of Menno Simons, Viewed Against the Background of Martin Luther's Thought," *Mennonite Quarterly Review* 43 (July 1969): 191-212.
DeVries, Dawn, "Friedrich Daniel Ernst Schleiermacher," in *Historical Handbook of Major Biblical Interpreters*, ed. Donald K. McKim, 350-55 (Downers Grove, IL: Inter-Varsity Press, 1998).
Dewey, John, "Fundamentalism," *New Republic* 38 (6 February 1924): 275.
De Young, Adrian, "Review of *Notes on Genesis*, by Albertus Pieters," *Southern Presbyterian Journal* 3 (March 1945): 31.
- "Southern Presbyterians Face Union," *Presbyterian Guardian* 16 (10 May 1947): 139.
Dieffenbacher, Arthur J., "The Faith of a Dispensationalist," *Christian Beacon* 2 (9 September 1937): 1, 8.
"'Dispenaionalism'[sic] Report Recommitted," *Presbyterian of the South* 118 (2 June 1943): 3, 14.
Dockery, David, "Forum: Eschatology," *SBC Life* 2 (June/July 1994): 6.
"The Doctrinal Issue in Philadelphia: Statement of Philadelphia Group to Assembly's Commission," *Presbyterian Guardian* 1 (18 November 1935): 57-58.
"Doctrinal Statement," *Annual Catalogue of The Officers and Students of Dallas Theological Seminary and Graduate School of Theology* 28 (March-April 1952): 71-75.
"Dr. Allis Replies to Dr. Chafer," *Christianity Today* 8 (August 1937): 73-74.
"Dr. Buswell Chosen Moderator," *Presbyterian Guardian* 3 (28 November 1936): 78-79.
"Dr. Buswell Convicted, Ordered Admonished," *Presbyterian Guardian* 2 (16March 1936): 207-09.
"Dr. Chafer Protests '44 Assembly Action: Says Dispensationalism Biblical; Distinction from Pre's 'Fantastic,'" *Presbyterian Outlook* 118 (4 October 1944): 3-4.
"Dr. Clark Resigns from Wheaton College Faculty," *Presbyterian Guardian* 12 (25 March 1943): 86.

"Dr. James M. Gray Dead in Chicago," *Presbyterian Guardian* 1(7 October 1935): 7.
"Dr. Lingle Urges Abolition of Separate Synod for Negro Work," *Presbyterian Outlook* 132 (10 April 1950): 3-4.
"Dr. Machen," *Christian Beacon* 1 (7 January 1937): 4, 6.
"Dr. Machen is Taken, Pneumonia Fatal: Prominent Fundamentalist Stricken on Preaching Tour," *Christian Beacon* 1 (7 January 1937): 1, 4.
Dunlop, H.P., "What is the Kingdom of God?", *Presbyterian* 114 (13 July 1944): 3, 5.
Dunzweiler, Robert J., "A Crucial Transition: A Personal Account of the Beginnings of Biblical Theological Seminary," *Stepping Stones* 2 (18 September 1995): 1, 3-7.
"Early Indications Point to Assembly of Achievement; J.B. Green, Columbia Professor is Moderator," *Presbyterian Outlook* 128 (3 June 1946): [1].
"Editorial: Capitalism and Communism," *Presbyterian Outlook* 130 (13 September 1948): 8.
"Editorial: Dispensationalism," *Presbyterian Outlook* 118 (7 June 1944): 8.
"Editorial: Freedom of Speech," *Presbyterian Outlook* 130 (13 September 1948): 8.
"Editorial: Short Circuits," *Southern Presbyterian Journal* 4 (1 April 1946): 2-3.
"Editorial: So This is Called 'Informing the Laymen'!" *Presbyterian Outlook* 129 (25 August 1947): 8-9.
"Editorial: The Campaign Against the Colleges," *Presbyterian Outlook* 127 (10 September 1945): 8.
"Editorial: The South and Southern Leaders," *Presbyterian Outlook* 128 (5August 1946): 8.
"Editorial: To Clarify Page Six," *Presbyterian Outlook* 129 (13 October 1947): 8-9.
"Editorial: What Are They Doing to Our Bible?", *Presbyterian Outlook* 134 (28 April 1952): 8.
"Editorial: Wilful [sic] Breaking of the Sabbath is NOT Grace but Disgrace," *Southern Presbyterian Journal* 10 (30 May 1951): 3-4.
Edwards, C.E., "Calvin on Infant Salvation," *Bibliotheca Sacra* 88 (October-December 1931): 316-28.
Eenigenburg, Elton, "The Place of the Covenant in Calvin's Thinking," *Reformed Review* 10 (1957): 1-22.
"The 82nd General Assembly; Confession of Faith," *Presbyterian of the South* 117 (10 June 1942): 9.
Elliot, Edwards E., "The Rapture," *Presbyterian Guardian* 12 (15 August 1943): 230-31.
– "Rightly Dividing St. Augustine," *Presbyterian Guardian* 11 (25 December 1942): 355-56.
Emerson, Everett H., "Calvin and Covenant Theology," *Church History* 25 (June 1956): 136-44.
English, E. Schuyler, "E. Schuyler English Looks at Dispensationalism," *Christian Life* 18 (September 1956): 24-27.
– "The New Scofield Reference Bible," *Bibliotheca Sacra* 124 (April-June 1967): 125-132.
Erdman, Charles R., "The Coming of Christ," *Union Seminary Review* 27(January 1916): 106-17.
"Eschatological Freedom," *Our Hope* 43 (September 1936):194-95.
"Extracts from an Address by Hon. William Jennings Bryan," *Presbyterian Standard* 62 (3 August 1921): 7, 9-10.
"Fading Fundamentalism," *Christian Century* 44 (10 June1927): 742-43.
Fensham, F.C., "The Covenant as Giving Expression to the Relationship Between Old and New Testament," *Tyndale Bulletin* 22 (1971): 82-94.
Findlater, J., "The Propaganda of Futurism," *Evangelical Quarterly* 9 (1937): 169-79.
Finlayson, Rod. A., "Review of *Why Thousand Years?* by William Masselink," *Evangelical Quarterly* 3 (1931): 329-30.
Fischer, Dean, and James Wilde, "Facing a No-Win Scenario: An Interview with King Hussein of Jordan," *TIME*, 5 November 1990, 41-42.
Flow, J.E., "Is Segregation UnChristian?", *Southern Presbyterian Journal* 10 (29 August 1951): 4-5.

- "The Second Coming of Christ," *Southern Presbyterian Journal* 2 (March 1943): 17.
- "Some Doctrines of the Southern Presbyterian Church," *Southern Presbyterian Journal* 7 (2 August 1948): 15-16.

Foreman, Kenneth J., "Christ is the End of the Law," *Presbyterian Outlook* 134 (3 March 1952): 9.
- "Have the Ten Commandments Been Abolished?", *Presbyterian Outlook* 133 (2 April 1951): 9.
- "Rules for Understanding the Ten Commandments. *Presbyterian Outlook* 133 (16 April 1951): 9.
- "The Ten Commandments: Professor's Preface," *Presbyterian Outlook* 133 (25 March 1951): 9.
- "What is the Moral Law?", *Presbyterian Outlook* 133(9 April 1951): 9.

Fosdick, Harry Emerson "Six Pillars of Peace," *Presbyterian of the South* 118 (4 August 1943): 6.

Foster, W.G., Jr. "Scriptural Dispensationalism," *Southern Presbyterian Journal* 2 (May 1943): 12-15.

Frame, John, "Infralapsarianism," in *Encyclopedia of the Reformed Faith*, ed. Donald K. McKim, 193-94 (Louisville, KY: Westminster/John Knox Press, 1992).

"Frank C. Brown Accepts Seminary Post," *Southern Presbyterian Journal* 11 (2 July 1952): 13-14.

Fraser, A.M, "Dr. Ogden's Smile," *Presbyterian Standard* 60 (12 March 1919): 9.

Frazer, W.H., "Why I Favor Preserving the Southern Church," *Southern Presbyterian Journal* 11 (23 July 1952): 7-9.

"Free Space for Dialogue Outside of Our Circles, Interview with Darrell L. Bock: Does the New Testament Reshape Our Understanding of the Old Testament?", *Modern Reformation* 9 (July/August 2000) 48-50.

Freeman, Hobart E., "The Problem of the Efficacy of the Old Testament Sacrifices," *Grace Theological Journal* 4 (January 1963): 21-28.

Fuller, Daniel P., "Paul and the 'Works of the Law,'" *Westminster Theological Journal* 38 (Fall 1975): 28-42.

"Fundamentalism and Modernism: Two Religions," *Christian Century* 40 (2 January 1924): 5-6.

"Fundamentalism, Modernism, and Christ," *Christian Century* 41 (17 April 1924): 495-97.

"Fundamentalism, Modernism, and God," *Christian Century* 41 (20 March 1924): 358-61.

"Fundamentalism, Modernism, and God," *Christian Century* 41 (27 March 1924): 392-94.

"Fundamentalism, Modernism, and Humanity," *Christian Century* 41 (14 August 1924): 1038-40.

"Fundamentalism, Modernism, and the Bible," *Christian Century* 41 (3 April 1924): 424.

"Fundamentalists Adopt Pre-Mil. View," *Christian Beacon* 2 (11 February 1937): 1-2.

Furlow, Frances, "Special Report: The Truth About the National Council of Churches," *Presbyterian Survey* 54 (December 1964): 33, 39-40.

Gage, Daniel S., "The Mistakes of the General Assembly of 1941," *Southern Presbyterian Journal* 1 (January 1943): 18-20.

Galbraith, John P., "Choose Ye This Day! An Analysis of the Reasons Why Christians Should Separate from the Presbyterian Church in the U.S.A," *Presbyterian Guardian* 5 (November 1938): 203-06.

"General Assembly Reports," *Christian Observer* 118 (12 May 1943): 6.

Gilmer, George H., "The Covenant of Grace," *Southern Presbyterian Journal* 1 (June 1942): 17-18.
- "The Supreme Fundamental," *Southern Presbyterian Journal* 3 (March 1945): 26.

Glasgow, Tom, "What Does the Southern Presbyterian Church Mean by 'Inspiration of Scripture?'", *Southern Presbyterian Journal* 5 (15 February 1947): 5-6.

Gleason, Randall, "B.B. Warfield and Lewis S. Chafer on Sanctification," *Journal of the Evangelical Theological Society* 40 (June 1997): 241-56.

Goddard, Burton L., "The New Covenant," *Presbyterian Guardian* 11 (10 January 1942): 11-12.

Gordon, E.C., "Christ's Kingdom of Glory," *Union Seminary Review* 27(January 1916): 118-29.

Graham, James B., "Second Adventism the Final Citadel of the Faith," *Christian Beacon* 2 (22 April 1937): 1, 4.

Gray, Richard W., "How to Interpret the Bible, Part One: False Methods and the True One," *Presbyterian Guardian* 14 (10 March 1945): 75-76.
- "How to Interpret the Bible, Part Two: General Rules," *Presbyterian Guardian* 14 (10 April 1945): 104-05.
- "How to Interpret the Bible, Part Three: Figurative Language," *Presbyterian Guardian* 14 (18 May 1945): 139-40.
- "How to Interpret the Bible, Part Four: Figures of Speech," *Presbyterian Guardian* 14 (10 June 1945): 164-65.
- "How to Interpret the Bible, Part Five: Allegory," *Presbyterian Guardian* 14 (10 July 1945): 204-05.
- "How to Interpret the Bible, Part Six: Parable," *Presbyterian Guardian* 14 (25 September 1945): 264-65.
- "How to Interpret the Bible, Part Seven: Symbols and Types," *Presbyterian Guardian* 14 (10 November 1945): 312-13.
- "Is Arminianism Another Gospel?", *Presbyterian Guardian* 14 (25 January 1945): 21-22.
Green, James B., "The Distinctive Teachings of Presbyterianism," *Mississippi Visitor* (October 1936): 4-6.
- "The Distinctive Teachings of Presbyterianism," *Union Seminary Review* 47 (July 1936): 366-78.
- "The Fourth and Final Statement on Behalf of Committee on Revision of Standards," *Mississippi Visitor* (September 1938): 6.
- "Further Statement on Behalf of Committee on Revision of the Standards," *Christian Observer* (15 March 1939): 10, 15.
- "God Hath Sworn," *Southern Presbyterian Journal* 6 (16 June 1947): 10-12.
- "Revision of the Confession of Faith and Catechism. Statement from a Member of the Ad Interim Committee," *Christian Observer* (22 June 1938): 11.
- "A Second Statement for Committee on Revision of Standards," *Mississippi Visitor* (July 1938): 5-6.
- "A Third Statement on Behalf of Committee on Revision of the Standards," *Christian Observer* (27 July 1938): 11.
- "Theology in a Changing World," *Union Seminary Review* 53 (November 1941): 20-34.
Gribble, Robert F., "Calvinistic Complexion," *Southern Presbyterian Journal* 3 (August 1944): 15-17.
- "Pity the Heathen!" *Southern Presbyterian Journal* 6 (1 April 1948): 5.
- "Sovereignty and Freedom," *Southern Presbyterian Journal* 2 (November 1943): 15-16.
- "What's New in the Sunday School?", *Southern Presbyterian Journal* 7 (15 November 1948): 6.
Griffiths, H. McAllister, "Eschatological Freedom," *Presbyterian Guardian* 2 (4 May 1936): 44, 52.
- "Since the Syracuse General Assembly: Machine Politics in the Presbyterian Church of America," *Christian Beacon* 2 (September 1937): 1-2.
- "Syracuse Swan Song: The 148th General Assembly: A Description and an Interpretation," *Presbyterian Guardian* 2 (22 June 1936): 112, 118-39.
- "The Character and Leadership of Dr. Machen," *Christian Beacon* 2 (2 September 1937): 2.
Gromacki, Gary, "Progressive Dispensationalism," *Journal of Ministry and Theology* 3 (Fall 1999): 97-100.
"Guest Editorial: Worship and Work Before Union," *Presbyterian Outlook* 128 (22 July 1946): 9.
Gunn, C.G., "Those Women," *Presbyterian of the South* 116 (17 December 1941): 8-10.
Hafemann, Scott, J., "Ferdinand Christian Baur," in *Historical Handbook of Major Biblical Interpreters*, ed. Donald K. McKim, 285-89 (Downers Grove, IL: Inter-Varsity Press, 1998).

Hall, Joseph H., "James Hall Brookes – New School, Old School, or No School," *Presbyterion: Covenant Seminary Review* 14 (Spring 1988): 35-54.
Hall, W.T., "The Federal Principle in the Westminster Standards," *Presbyterian Quarterly* 12 (1898): 378-90.
– "Some Objections to the Federal Theory of Immediate Imputation," *Presbyterian Quarterly* 16 (April 1903): 453-60.
Hamilton, Floyd E., "An Interpretation of the Answer," *Presbyterian Guardian* 14 (25 April 1945): 119-20, 127.
Harbin, Michael A., "The Hermeneutics of Covenant Theology," *Bibliotheca Sacra* 143 (July-September 1986): 246-59.
Harris, R. Laird, "Sunday School Lesson," *Presbyterian Guardian* 3 (24 October 1936): 33.
Hart, Darryl G., "The Princeton Mind in the Modern World and the Common Sense of J. Gresham Machen," *Westminster Theological Journal* 46 (Spring 1984): 1-25.
– "Robert Dick Wilson," in *The Dictionary of the Presbyterian and Reformed Tradition*, ed. D.G. Hart and Mark A. Noll, 278 (Downers Grove, IL: Inter-Varsity Press, 1999).
Hatch, Nathan O., and Michael S. Hamilton, "Can Evangelicalism Survive Its Success?", *Christianity Today* 36 (5 October 1992): 20-31.
Helm, Paul, "Calvin and the Covenant: Unity and Continuity," *Evangelical Quarterly* 55 (April 1983): 273-303.
Hesselink, I. John, "Calvin's Understanding of the Relation of the Church and Israel Based Largely on His Interpretation of Romans 9-11," *Ex Auditu* 4 (1988): 59-69.
– "Luther and Calvin on Law and Gospel in their Galatians Commentaries," *Reformed Review* 37 (Winter 1984): 69-82.
Hills, John C., Jr. and William E. Welmers, "Rethinking Revivals," *Presbyterian Guardian* 10 (10 July 1941): 10-12.
Hill, Samuel S., Jr. (ed.), *Encyclopedia of Religion in the South* (Macon, GA: Mercer University Press, 1984).
Hittson, Paul A., "Is the Sermon on the Mount for This Age?", *Presbyterian Guardian* 7 (July 1940): 27-28.
Hoch, Carl, "The Significance of the SYN-Compounds for Jew-Gentile Relationships in the Body of Christ," *Journal of the Evangelical Theological Society* 25 (June 1982): 175-83.
Hodge, Caspar Wistar, "The Reformed Faith," *Evangelical Quarterly* 1 (1929):3-24.
Hodge, Charles, "Adoption of the Confession of Faith," *Princeton Review* (1858): 669; and "The General Assembly," *Princeton Review* (1867): 506; reprinted as "What is the 'System of Doctrine?'", *Presbyterian Guardian* 2 (3 August 1936): 192-96.
Hodges, Zane, "Calvinism Ex Cathedra: A Review of John H. Gerstner's *Wrongly Dividing the Word of Truth: A Critique of Dispensationalism*," *Journal of the Grace Evangelical Society* 104 (autumn, 1991): 69.
Hoekema, Anthony A., "Calvin's Doctrine of the Covenant of Grace," *Reformed Review* 15 (May 1962): 1-12.
– "The Covenant of Grace in Calvin's Teaching," *Calvin Theological Journal* 2 (November 1967): 133-61.
Hogue, Addison, "'Rejoiceth Not in Iniquity,'" *Presbyterian Standard* 62 (13 July 1921): 5.
"[Hon. Arthur W., brother of J. Gresham] Machen Complains to Southern Church," *Christian Beacon* 2 (22 April 1937): 1, 5.
"Hon. William J. Bryan to Lecture at Union Seminary," *Presbyterian Standard* 62 (27 April 1921): 6-7.
Houghton, George C., "Lewis Sperry Chafer: 1871-1952," *Bibliotheca Sacra* 128 (October-December 1971): 291-99.

Hu, Shiu-Ying, "A Call to Young American Christians: A young Chinese Christian teacher in her address at the Nashville convention poses some questions for young people and their elders to think about," *Presbyterian Outlook* 129 (10 February 1947): 6-7.

Hutchinson, Paul, "The Battle of Princeton – 1925," *Christian Century* 42 (28 May 1925): 699-701.

"Ind. Board Object of New Attack: Westminster Men Lead Attack and Move to Form New Board," *Christian Beacon* 2 (10 June 1937): 1, 4-5, 7.

"Independency," *Christian Beacon* 2 (3 June 1937): 4.

"The Independent Board Carries On Despite New Attacks," *Christian Beacon* 2 (24 June 1937): 2, 4, 7.

"In Passing, A Column of News and Opinion: Unanimous Report," *Presbyterian of the South* 118 (8 March 1944): 16.

"Iowa Church Votes to Leave Old Body: Will Affiliate with the Presbyterian Church of America," *Presbyterian Guardian* 2 (30 August 1936): 220.

"Ironside Dies," *Presbyterian Guardian* 20 (15 February 1951): 38.

Irving, W.M., "Opposition Scored by Famous Pastor," *Christian Beacon* 1 (13 February 1936): 1, 4.

"Is Evangelical Theology Changing?", *Christian Life* (March 1956): 16-19.

"Is the American Sabbath Worth Preserving? With Some Comments on "The Outlook" and the St. Louis Fair," *Sunday School Times* 46 (30 July 1904): 417-18.

"I Was an Hungered and Ye Gave Me No Meat," *Presbyterian Outlook* 128 (28 January 1946): 5-6.

Jackson, J.W., "Editorial: Against Something," *Presbyterian Outlook* 118 (5 July 1944): 8.

Jansma, Theodore, "The Westminster Confession and the Sovereignty of God," *Presbyterian Guardian* 11 (10 January 1942): 10-11.

Jewett, Paul K., "Is the Victorious Life Movement Scriptural?", *Presbyterian Guardian* 21 (10 September 1943): 257-58, 268-70.

"John Allan MacLean Fellowship Established by Ginter Park Church," *Presbyterian Outlook* 130 (2 February 1948): 1.

Johnson, Elliot E., "Dual Authorship and the Single Intended Meaning of Scripture," *Bibliotheca Sacra* 143 (July-September 1986): 218-23.1-12.

– "What I Mean by Historical-Grammatical Interpretation and How that Differs from Spiritual Interpretation," *Grace Theological Journal* 11 (Fall 1990): 157-69.

Johnson, S. Lewis, Jr., "The Paralysis of Legalism," *Bibliotheca Sacra* 120 (April-June 1963): 109-16.

"J.P. McCallie to Get Colgate Citation for Outstanding Service: International Council to Present Year's Award at Columbus Meeting," *Presbyterian Outlook* 131 (24 January 1949): [1].

"June 11, 1936: A Significant Day in American Presbyterian History," *Presbyterian Guardian* 20 (15 May 1951): 85-87.

Kantzer, Kenneth S., "The Doctrine Wars: Instead of feeling battle weary, evangelicals should gird themselves for new skirmishes ahead," *Christianity Today* 36 (5 October 1992): 32-34.

Karlberg, Mark W., "Justification in Redemptive History," *Westminster Theological Journal* 43 (Spring 1981): 213-46.

– "Legitimate Discontinuities Between the Testaments," *Journal of the Evangelical Theological Society* 28 (March 1985): 9-20.

– "Moses and Christ – The Place of Law in Seventeenth-Century Puritanism," *Trinity Journal* 10 (Spring 1989): 11-32.

– "The Original State of Adam: Tensions within Reformed Theology," *Evangelical Quarterly* 59 (October 1987): 291-309.

– "Reformed Interpretation of the Mosaic Covenant," *Westminster Theological Journal* 43 (Fall 1980): 1-57.

Karleen, Paul S., "Understanding Covenant Theologians: A Study in Presuppositions," *Grace Theological Journal* 10 (Fall 1989): 125-38.
Kelley, Alford, "'Stay in the Church' v. 'Be Ye Separate,'" *Presbyterian Guardian* 2 (1 June 1936): 92-94.
Kemeny, Paul, "Princeton and the Premillennialists: The Roots of the *marriage de convenance*," *American Presbyterians* 71, 1 (1993): 17.
Kennedy, James W., "Snake Handling and the New Testament," *Presbyterian Outlook* 128 (22 July 1946): 9.
Kennedy, John W., "Presbyterians: Reform-Minded Activists Retain Unmuzzled Voice," *Christianity Today* 39 (11 September 1995): 80-81.
Kevan, E.F., "The Covenants and the Interpretation of the Old Testament," *Evangelical Quarterly* 26 (1954): 19-28.
Klempa, William, "Supralapsarianism," in *Encyclopedia of the Reformed Faith*, ed. Donald K. McKim, 360-61 (Louisville, KY: Westminster/John Knox Press, 1992).
Kline, Meredith G., "Comments on an Old-New Error," *Westminster Theological Journal* 41 (Fall 1978): 172-189.
– "Law Covenant," *Westminster Theological Journal* 27 (November 1964): 1-20.
– "Oath and Ordeal Signs," *Westminster Theological Journal* 27 (November 1965): 115-139.
– "Of Works and Grace," *Presbyterion: Covenant Seminary Review* 9 (Spring-Fall 1983): 85-92.
Klooster, Fred H., "The Uniqueness of Reformed Theology: A Preliminary Attempt at Description," *Calvin Theological Journal* 14 (April 1979): 32-54.
Kucharsky, David E., "The Urgent Gentleman," *Christianity Today* 17 (31 August 1973): 6-7.
Kuiper, R.B., "The Glory of the Christian Church; Part I: Has Its Glory Departed?", *Presbyterian Guardian* 16 (10 October 1947): 283-84.
– "The Glory of the Christian Church; Part XLIII: Its Inclusiveness," *Presbyterian Guardian* 20 (15 April 1951): 70-71; 78.
– "The Glory of the Christian Church; Part XLIV: Its Exclusiveness," *Presbyterian Guardian* 20 (15 May 1951): 90-91; 98.
– "The Glory of the Christian Church; Part XLVI: The Keys of the Kingdom," *Presbyterian Guardian* 20 (16 July 1951): 130-31; 133.
– "Has the Presbyterian Guardian Attacked Premillennialism?: The Reply of Dr. Kuiper," *Presbyterian Guardian* 3 (14 November 1936): 54-55.
– "A Plea for Peace," *Presbyterian Guardian* 4 (24 April 1937): 21-24.
– "Presbyterianism versus Independentism," *Presbyterian Guardian* 6 (April 1939): 63-64.
– "The Reply of Professor Kuiper," *Presbyterian Guardian* 3 (14 November 1936): 54.
– "Two Features of the Reformed Faith," *Presbyterian Guardian* 4 (October 1937): 161-63.
– "What's Right with the Orthodox Presbyterian Church?", *Presbyterian Guardian* 15 (25 November 1946): 323-24; 333.
– "What's Right with the Orthodox Presbyterian Church?; Part Two: Broad in the Good Sense," *Presbyterian Guardian* 15 (10 November 1940): 341-43.
– "Why Separation Was Necessary," *Presbyterian Guardian* 2 (12 September 1936): 225-27.
Kurtaneck, Nickolas, "Excellencies of Dispensationalism," *Grace Theological Journal* 3 (January 1962): 3-11.
Kuschke, Arthur W., Jr., "Five Years for the South?", *Presbyterian Guardian* 17 (July 1948): 172.
– "The Incomprehensibility of God: A Review of a Committee Report," *Presbyterian Guardian* 17 (10 April 1948): 105-06.
Lacy, Benjamin R., Jr., "American Seminaries and Protestant Reconstruction: Seminary president says withdrawal from cooperation in face of world's present needs would be 'a sin calling for great repentance,'" *Presbyterian Outlook* 130 (2 February 1948): 6-7.

- "The First General Assembly of the Presbyterian Church in the United States," *Union Seminary Review* 47 (July 1936): 359-66.
- "Leading Men to Jesus Christ," *Presbyterian Outlook* 132 (23 October 1950): 4.
Lamkin, Bill., "Dr. L. Nelson Bell, prime mover in founding the Presbyterian Journal, has resigned as a director and associate editor . . .," *Presbyterian News Service* (23 August 1971): 1-5.
Lapsley, R.A., Jr., "Review of *Salvation*, by Lewis Sperry Chafer," *Union Seminary Review* 29 (July 1918): 377-78.
- "Has the Southern Presbyterian Church Any Distinctive Principles?", *Presbyterian Quarterly* 15 (July 1901): 414-30.
- "Side Tracked," *Presbyterian Standard* 60 (10 March 1920): 6-7.
- "What God Wants His Church to Be," *Southern Presbyterian Journal* 6 (16 June 1947): 13-16.
"The Law and the Gospel," *Southern Presbyterian Journal* 9 (24 January 1951): 4-5.
Law, P.R., "Editorial: Modernism," *Presbyterian Standard* 51 (19 July 1911): 2.
Lee, Randolph B., "An Open Letter to the Officers and Members of the Presbyterian Church in the United States," *Southern Presbyterian Journal* 5 (15 March 1947): 4, 21.
- "Comments Upon the Proposed Plan of Re-Union Between the Presbyterian Church in the United States of America and the Presbyterian Church in the United States," *Southern Presbyterian Journal* 5 (2 December 1946): 6-7.
Leith, John H., "John Calvin and Social Responsibility: On Reformation Day (October 31) it is well to be reminded that Calvin was concerned with politics, race, business practices, magistrates, etc., etc. [*sic*]" *Presbyterian Outlook* 130 (25 October 1948): 5-7.
Letham, Robert, "The *Foedus Operum*: Some Factors Accounting for Its Development," *Sixteenth Century Journal* 14 (Winter 1983): 457-68.
"Letters," *Presbyterian Outlook*. 118 (26 April 1944): 7
"Letters," *Presbyterian Outlook*. 118 (17 May 1944): 10.
"Letter from the Editor of the Presbyterian Outlook; Our Reply," *Southern Presbyterian Journal* 4 (1 March 1946): 5.
"Letters to the Editors: Negroes at Montreat Debated Pro and Con," *Presbyterian Outlook* 129 (13 January 1947): 2.
Lewis, Alan E, "Eschatology," in *Encyclopedia of the Reformed Faith*, ed. Donald K. McKim (Louisville, KY: Westminster/John Knox Press, 1992).
Lillback, Peter Alan, "Ursinus' Development of the Covenant of Creation: A Debt to Melanchthon or Calvin?", *Westminster Theological Journal* 43 (Spring 1981): 247-88.
Lincoln, C. Fred, "The Biblical Covenants," Parts 1-3. *Bibliotheca Sacra* 100 (April-June 1943): 309-23, (July-September 1943): 442-49, (October-December 1943): 565-73.
- "The Development of the Covenant Theory," *Bibliotheca Sacra* 100 (January-March 1943): 134-63.
- "Lewis Sperry Chafer," *Bibliotheca Sacra* 109 (October-December 1952): 332-37.
Lindsell, Harold, "L. Nelson Bell: In Memoriam," *Christianity Today* 17 (31 August 1973): 5-6.
Lingle, Walter L., "The Auburn Affirmation," *Presbyterian Outlook* 128 (8 April 1946): 6-7.
- "Changes I Have Seen . . . (1) In the Position and Work of Women in the Church," *Presbyterian Outlook* 133 (22 January 1951): [1], 4-6.
- "Changes I Have Seen . . . 2. Attitudes Toward the Bible, and Science, the Confession of Faith, Inspiration of the Scriptures," *Presbyterian Outlook* 133 (5 February 1951): 4-5.
- "Changes I Have Seen . . . 3. In Theological Education, Worship, the Minister, and Preaching," *Presbyterian Outlook* 133 (19 February 1951): 5-6.
- "The Church and the Kingdom – for the Presbyterian Standard," *Presbyterian Standard* 57 (17 May 1916): 9.
- "Dr. Green and Fundamental Principles," *Presbyterian Standard* 60 (24 September 1919): 4, 8.

- "Editorial Comment: The Second Coming of Our Lord," *Union Seminary Review* 27 (January 1916): 169-71.
- "The Last Fifty Years," *Union Seminary Magazine* 24 (1912): 48-75.
- "Some of Dr. Scofield's Interpretations," *Christian Observer* 124 (21 October 1936): 3,9.
- "The Story of the Westminster Assembly," *Union Seminary Review* 54 (August 1943): 321-32.
- "The Sunday Meetings in Richmond," *Presbyterian Standard* 60 (12 March 1919): 4, 8.
- "The Teachings of Jesus and Modern Social Problems," *Union Seminary Review* 27 (April 1916): 191-205.
- "What Does Presbyterianism Stand For?", *Christian Observer* 127 (10 May 1939): 3,7.

Link, Luther, "The Abrahamic Covenant," *Presbyterian Quarterly* 14 (October 1900): 520-31.
- "The Adamic Principle in Theology," *Presbyterian Quarterly* 16 (April 1903): 485-502.
- "Revelation XX and the Millennial Reign," *Presbyterian Quarterly* 14 (April 1900): 173-82.

"Listing Sound Bible Institutes," *Sunday School Times* 66 (26 January 1924): 50.

"L. Nelson Bell: 1894-1973," *Christianity Today* 17 (31 August 1973).

Longman, Tremper, III, "What I Mean By Historical-Grammatical Exegesis – Why I Am Not a Literalist," *Grace Theological Journal* 11 (Fall 1990): 137-55.

Lyons, J. Sprole, "The Problem of Relation of White and Colored Races," *Presbyterian Standard* 60 (8 October 1919): 4.

MacArthur, Douglas, "The Church and War," *Southern Presbyterian Journal* 1 (May 1942): 14-16.

Macartney, Clarence Edward, "Review of *Prophecy and the Church*, by Oswald T. Allis," *Presbyterian* 115 (24 May 1945): 9, 21.
- "The Causes and Conditions Leading to the Disruption of 1837 and 1838," *Presbyterian* 110 (23 May 1930): 6-7, 18.
- "The Crux of the Present Protestant Controversy," *Sunday School Times* 65 (21 April 1923): 247.
- "Shall Unbelief Win?: An Answer to Dr. Fosdick [Parts 1 and 2]," *Presbyterian* 102 (13 and 20 July 1922): 8-10, 26, and 8-10.

Machen, J. Gresham, "The 1903 Amendments," *Presbyterian Guardian* 3 (14 November 1936): 45.
- "The Changing Scene and the Unchanging Word: A True Presbyterian Church at Last," *Presbyterian Guardian* 2 (22 June 1936): 110.
- "Congregations and the Millennial Question," *Presbyterian Guardian* 3 (14 November 1936): 45.
- "The Dispensationalism of the Scofield Bible," *Presbyterian Guardian* 3 (14 November 1936): 42-43.
- "Editorial: Looking Backward and Ahead," *Presbyterian Guardian* 2 (22 June 1936): 111.
- "Editorial: Why a New Paper? – The Word of God and the Word of Man," *Presbyterian Guardian* 1 (7 October 1935): 3.
- "A Hard Church to Get Out Of," *Presbyterian Guardian* 3 (10 October 1936): 2.
- "The Man for the Hour," *Presbyterian Guardian* (12 September 1936): 221-22.
- "The Millennial Question," *Presbyterian Guardian* 3 (14 November 1936): 43-44.
- "Premillennialism," *Presbyterian Guardian* 3 (24 October 1936): 21.
- "The Presbytery of California and the 'Christian Beacon.'" *Presbyterian Guardian* 3 (28 November 1936): 71.
- "The Root of the Trouble," *Presbyterian Guardian* 3 (14 November 1936): 42.
- "The Second General Assembly of the Presbyterian Church," *Presbyterian Guardian* 3 (14 November 1936): 41-45.
- "The Second General Assembly of the Presbyterian Church of America," *Presbyterian Guardian* 3 (28 November 1936): 69-71.
- "A Step to Avoid," *Presbyterian Guardian* 3 (10 October 1936): [1].

- "What Should True Presbyterians Do at the 1936 General Assembly?", *Presbyterian Guardian* 2 (18 May 1936): 68-72.
MacInnis, John M., "Is Fundamentalism Being Redefined?", *King's Business* 19 (September 1928): 517-18.
MacLean, John Allan, "Liberalism in the Southern Presbyterian Church: First of Three Articles Seeking to Building [sic] a Bridge of Understanding Between Men of the Same Loyalties, but of Different Temperaments," *Presbyterian Outlook* 127 (13 August 1945): 4-6.
- "The Minister and the Modern World," *Union Seminary Review* 49 (January 1938): 116-28.
- "Needed-An Evangelistic Creed: Can We Overcome the Calvinistic Complex?", *Presbyterian of the South* 118 (29 March 1944): 5-7.
- "The Outlook Pulpit: Heresies of the Heart," *Presbyterian Outlook* 127 (31 December 1945): 5-7.
- "The Prayer of a Modern Pharisee: By One of Them," *Presbyterian Outlook* 118 (24 May 1944): 5.
- "Progressive Presbyterianism," *Presbyterian Outlook* 118 (19 April 1944): 5-7.
- "What Southern Presbyterian Liberals Are Driving At," *Presbyterian Outlook* 127 (27 August 1945): 6-7.
- "What Southern Presbyterian Liberals Believe," *Presbyterian Outlook* 127 (20 August 1945): 5-7.
- "Which Church Would Jesus Join?", *Presbyterian Outlook* 129 (8September 1947): 5-7.
MacLeod, David J., "Walter Scott, A Link in Dispensationalism Between Darby and Scofield?", *Bibliotheca Sacra* 153 (April-June 1996): 155-78.
MacLeod, John, "Review of *Dispensationalism*, [A Review of Two Pamphlets by Philip Mauro]," *Evangelical Quarterly* 8 (1936): 439-40.
- "Review of *The Church, the Churches and the Kingdom*, by Philip Mauro," *Evangelical Quarterly* 9 (1937): 93-97.
- "Review of *The Inwardness of the Postponement Theory*, by Philip Mauro," *Evangelical Quarterly* 8 (1936): 323-24.
- "Review of *The Unchanging Christ, and Other Sermons*, (by Pastor H. A. Ironside, Litt. D, Moody Memorial Church, Chicago)," *Evangelical Quarterly* 7 (1935): 220-21.
- "New Light and Moral Right," *Southern Presbyterian Journal* 3 (August 1944): 10-11.
MacPherson, Merrill T., "Why I Am Pastor of an Independent Church," *Christian Beacon* 2 (12 August 1937): 3-4, 7.
MacRae, Allan A., "Dr. Allan A. MacRae Resigns Seminary: Founder of Westminster Seminary Opposes Its Present Stand," *Christian Beacon* 2 (29 April 1937): 1-2, 8.
- "The Millennial Kingdom of Christ," *Christian Beacon* 2 (11 March 1937): 3-4.
- "The Millennial Kingdom of Christ [Part 2],"*Christian Beacon* 2 (16 March 1937): 3-4, 7.
- "Scholarship Needful in Minister Training," *Christian Beacon* 3 (21 July 1938): 1-2.
Maddex, Jack P., Jr., "Old School/New School," in *Encyclopedia of Religion in the South*, ed. Samuel S. Hill, Jr., 570-72 (Macon, GA: Mercer University Press, 1984).
"The Major Issue at Princeton," *Presbyterian* 97 (19 May 1927): 1-5.
Male, W. Benson, "The New Testament Commands Infant Baptism," *Presbyterian Guardian* 17 (July 1948): 173-74.
Marion, John H., "Our Present Social Obligation," *Presbyterian of the South* 116 (31 December 1941): 4-5.
Marsden, George M., "American Culture and Fundamentalism as a Belief System," *Presbyterian Journal* 43 (21 November 1984): 6-8.
- "Defining Fundamentalism," *Christian Scholar's Review* 1 (Winter 1971): 141-51.
- "Fundamentalism as an American Phenomenon: A Comparison with English Evangelicalism," *Church History* 46 (June 1977): 215-32.

- "Kingdom and Nation: New School Presbyterian Millennialism in the Civil War Era," *Journal of Presbyterian history* 46 (December 1968): 254-73.
- "The New School Heritage and Presbyterian Fundamentalism," *Westminster Theological Journal* 32 (May 1970): 129-47.

Marsden, Robert S., "The Fundamentals," *Presbyterian Guardian* 18 (July 1949): 123-24.
- "Perhaps I Should, But – [Part I]," *Presbyterian Guardian* 5 (December 1938): 242.
- "Perhaps I Should, But – [Part II]," *Presbyterian Guardian* 6 (January 1939): 4.
- "Twelve Facts About Westminster," *Presbyterian Guardian* 17 (November 1948): 254.

Martin, Hugh, "My Ordination Vow Binds My Church," *Southern Presbyterian Journal* 3 (August 1944): 11.

Martindale, C. O'N., "The Coming of the Lord, Our Hope," *Union Seminary Review* 32 (October 1920): 55-70.
- "What Do Presbyterians Believe?", *Presbyterian Standard* 58 (31 January 1917): 4-5, 23.

Marty, Martin E., "Reformed America and America Reformed," *Reformed Journal* (March 1989): 8, 10.

Matthews, Donald G., "'We have left undone those things which we ought to have done': Southern Religious History in Retrospect and Prospect," *Church History* 67 (June 1998): 305-25.

Matthews, Shailer, "Fundamentalism and Modernism: An Interpretation," *American Review* 2 (January-February 1924): 1-9.

McCallie, J.P., "Earth's Golden Age," *Southern Presbyterian Journal* 1 (December1942): 22-24.
- "I Went to Cleveland," *Southern Presbyterian Journal* 1 (February 1943): 10-11.
- "Our Church and World Missions," *Southern Presbyterian Journal* 2 (February 1944): 16-18.
- "Why I Want to Co-operate with the National Association of Evangelicals Rather Than with the Federal Council," *Southern Presbyterian Journal* 6 (15 December 1947): 7-8.

McClain, Alva J., "A Premillennial Philosophy of History," *Bibliotheca Sacra* 113 (April-May 1956): 111-16.

McClelland, Joseph C., "Covenant Theology: A Re-Evaluation," *Canadian Journal of Theology* 3 (1957): 182-88.

McCoy, Charles Sherwood, "Johannes Cocceius: Federal Theologian," *Scottish Journal of Theology* 16 (December 1963): 352-70.

McCoy, W.K., "The Continent and Mr. Bryan," *Presbyterian Standard* 62 (7December 1921): 5.

McDougall, Worth, "Moderator Candidates Interviewed," *Presbyterian Survey* 62 (June 1972): 3, 15.

McGeachy, D.P., "Dr. Bell on the Question of Neutrality," *Mississippi Visitor* (April 1938): 6.

McGee, J. Vernon, "The Ten Commandments in the Age of Grace," *Bibliotheca Sacra* 115 (October-December 1958): 348-56.

McGiffert, Michael, "From Moses to Adam: The Making of the Covenant of Works," *Sixteenth Century Journal* 19 (Summer 1988): 131-55.
- "Grace and Works: The Rise and Division of Covenant Divinity in Elizabethan Puritanism," *Harvard Theological Review* 75 (October 1982): 463-502.

McIntire, Carl, "Abstinence," *Christian Beacon* 2 (17 June 1937): 4.
- "Announcing Faith Theological Seminary: A Standard, Three-Year Theological Seminary. Fundamental! Evangelical! Scholarly! Premillennial! Opening Date First Week in October to be Located Somewhere in the Philadelphia, PA Area," Advertisement in *Christian Beacon* [Beginning] 2 (15 July 1937): (8.
- "Are Babies Who Die Lost?", *Christian Beacon* 3 (20 October 1938): 3-4.
- "Are World Events Today Fulfilling Bible Prophecy?", *Christian Beacon* 1 (7 January 1937): 2, 8.
- "'Auburn Affirmation,'" *Christian Beacon* 1 (20 August 1936): 1-2, 7-8.

- "Barnhouse in Protest: Modernist Attacked – Scores the Election of George E. Barnes as Moderator," *Christian Beacon* 1 (16 April 1936): 1.
- "Barnhouse Not 'Silenced'; Says Church Action 'Utter Iniquity': Commission's Report to Assembly Concerning Him Moves Him to Fresh Attack on Church; Minister Ordained 'a Self-Confessed Apostate,'" *Christian Beacon* 2 (17 June 1937): 1-2.
- "Bible Synod Adopts Historic Westminster Confession; Form of Government Determined," *Christian Beacon* 3 (15 September 1938): 1-2, 5, 7.
- "Brumbaugh Leaves Seminary Board," *Christian Beacon* 2 (29 April 1937): 1, 7.
- "Charter of Faith Seminary Adopted: Institution Established to Train Fundamental Ministers," *Christian Beacon* 2 (9 December 1937): 1-2, 8.
- "Chicago Deposes President Buswell: Jesus Christ Never Called Him to Preach Gospel, They Say," *Christian Beacon* 1 (24 September 1936): 1, 5.
- "Chicago Overtures 'Total Abstinence': Abstinence Only Sure Protection Against Drunkenness," *Christian Beacon* 2 (20 May 1937): 1, 8.
- "Church Session Refuses Member Right to Resign," *Christian Beacon* 1 (15 October 1936): 1.
- "Constitut'l Covenant Union Dissolved," *Christian Beacon* 1 (18 June 1936): 2.
- "Covering Letter on Constitution: Committee on Constitution of Bible Pres. Synod Gives Report," *Christian Beacon* 3 (18 August 1938): 1, 7.
- "Doctrine," *Christian Beacon* 2 (17 June 1937): 4.
- "Famous Five Points," *Christian Beacon* 1 (20 August 1936): 1.
- "Flock Follows Ousted Minister: MacPherson Draws Vast Gathering at Lulu Temple," *Christian Beacon* 1 (18 June 1936): 1-2.
- "Founder's Week at Moody Institute," *Christian Beacon* 2 (6 January 1938): 2.
- "Fundamental Baptists Quit Church Machine," *Christian Beacon* 2 (18 November 1937): 1, 7.
- "Fundamentalists Hold Big Banquet: Bennet and Buswell Guest Speakers at Annual Dinner," *Christian Beacon* 2 (22 April 1937): 1-2.
- "Give Thanks," *Christian Beacon* 2 (10 June 1937): 4.
- "'Guilty' for Obeying God: What is the Issue?", *Christian Beacon* 1 (14 May 1936): 1, 7.
- "Important Actions of Southern Church: Assembly Sends Federal Council Matter to Presbyters," *Christian Beacon* 2 (24 June 1937): 1-2, 8.
- "The Independent Board Challenged the Great Apostasy of the 20th Century and Drew the Line Between Belief and Unbelief in Christian Ministries and Made Church History," *Biblical Missions* (August 1993): 5-7.
- "Introduction," *Christian Beacon* 1 (13 February 1936): 1.
- "Irresistible Grace," *Christian Beacon* 1 (19 November 1936): 3-4, 8.
- "Jesus Christ Dethroned: Fundamentalists Ousted – Church to Split," *Christian Beacon* 1 (4 June 1936): 1-2, 7.
- "Laird Makes Statement for Board," *Christian Beacon* 2 (24 June 1937):1, 5.
- "Limited Atonement," *Christian Beacon* 1 (12 November 1936): 3-4, 6.
- "Machen Complains to Southern Church," *Christian Beacon* 2 (22 April 1937): 1, 5.
- "Machen's Reasons for 'Disobedience,'" *Christian Beacon* 1 (7 January1937): 1-2.
- "Maine Pastor Deposed After Resignations: Receives Deposition after Renouncing Old Body," *Christian Beacon* 1 (15 October 1936): 1-2.
- "Making History; Machen Elected," *Christian Beacon* 1 (18 June 1936): 2, 4.
- "Moderator Disrupts Prayer Meeting: Attempt by Presbytery to Take Over Church Foiled," *Christian Beacon* 2 (25 March 1937): 1-2.
- "Moody Championed Lay Preaching," *Christian Beacon* 1 (7 January 1937): 1.
- "N.A.E. Holds Second Annual Convention in Columbus, Ohio," *Christian Beacon* 9 (20 April 1944): 1, 4-5.

- "New Book On Fulfilled Prophecy: George T.B. Davis Gives New Data on Palestine Development," *Christian Beacon* 2 (25 November 1937): 1-2, 7.
- "Notice Removed from Church Door: Presbytery Places Notice on Church; People Remove It," *Christian Beacon* 1 (8 October 1936): 1.
- "Pentecostal Group Overwhelms N.A.E. Denominations: An Editorial," *Christian Beacon* 9 (20 April 1944): 1, 4-5.
- "The Perseverance of the Saints," *Christian Beacon* 1 (26 November 1936): 3.
- "Phila. Rally for Independent Board: Rev. James R. Graham, Jr. Speaks on Crisis in Far East," *Christian Beacon* 2 (25 November 1937): 1, 7.
- "Premillenarian Request of Duryea," *Christian Beacon* 1 (20 August 1936): 2.
- "Premillennialism," *Christian Beacon* 1 (1 October 1936): 4.
- "Premillennial Protest of California Leaders," *Christian Beacon* 1 (26 November 1936): 1-2.
- "Presbyterian," *Christian Beacon* 2 (6 May 1937): 4.
- "'Presbyterian Church of America' Formed: Assembly Organized; Philadelphia Presbytery Tries to Block Meeting of Covenant-Union," *Christian Beacon* 1 (18 June 1936): 1, 4, 7.
- "Presbyterian Church, U.S.A. Fights for Injunction on Church Name: Would Have Name 'Presbyterian Church of America' Taken Away From New Body Formed After Split Over Modernism in Old Church," *Christian Beacon* 2 (6 May 1937): 1-3.
- "Prophecy," *Christian Beacon* 2 (19 August 1937): 4.
- "Proposed Changes to Confession of Faith," *Christian Beacon* 3 (18 August 1938): 1-2, 4-5.
- "Rev. H.S. Laird Brought to Trial: Three Charges Filed Against Him as Rebel," *Christian Beacon* 1 (13 February 1936): 1, 5.
- "Seminary Makes Rian President," *Christian Beacon* 1 (4 February 1937): 7.
- "Smith Explains Board Withdrawal: Full Correspondence Printed; Long Letter By Smith Given," *Christian Beacon* 2 (6 May 1937): 1-2, 4, 8.
- "Smith Leaves Independent Board: Revelation Announces Move; Mandate of Assembly Obeyed," *Christian Beacon* 2 (22 April 1937): 1-2.
- "'Total Abstinence' Presby. Tradition," *Christian Beacon* 2 (6 May 1937): 1, 7.
- "Total Inability," *Christian Beacon* 1 (29 October 1936): 3-5.
- "The True Facts in the Machen and McIntire Cases," *Christian Beacon* 1 (8 October 1936): 1-8.
- "The True Facts in the Machen and McIntire Cases (Continued from Last Week)," *Christian Beacon* 1 (15 October 1936): 1-8.
- "The True Facts in the Machen and McIntire Cases (Continued from Last Week)," *Christian Beacon* 1 (22 October 1936): 2, 4, 6.
- "The True Presbyterian Church: Sermon Delivered Sunday Evening, June 7, 1936," *Christian Beacon* 1 (11 June 1936): 3-5.
- "Unconditional Election," *Christian Beacon* 1 (5 November 1936): 3-4.
- "The United Presbyterian Church Since 1936," *Biblical Missions* (August 1993): 7-10.
- "Victorious Life Spring Conference," *Christian Beacon* 2 (25 March 1937): 8.
- "'Wet' and 'Dry' Resolution Made," *Christian Beacon* 2 (24 June 1937): 2, 7.
- "W.W. Rugh is Called Home: Philadelphia Bible Teacher Founded Great Bible Institute," *Christian Beacon* 1 (7 January 1937): 1-2.

McLaurin, Eugene W., "The Outlook Pulpit: One Man's Christ," *Presbyterian Outlook* 134 (21 April 1952): 5.
- "What is the Church?", *Presbyterian Outlook* 128 (11 March 1946): 5-6.

McPheeters, W.M., "The Issue Raised by Dr. Lingle," *Presbyterian Standard* 60 (19 November 1919): 6-7.

McWilliams, David B., "The Covenant Theology of the Westminster Confession of Faith and Recent Criticism," *Westminster Theological Journal* 53 (Spring 1991): 109-24.

"Meeting of the General Assembly," *Southern Presbyterian Journal* 2 (June 1943): 2-6.

Meldau, Fred John, "'Apostasy': The Coming Crisis and Chaos – and Then the Millennium," *Christian Beacon* 3 (13 October 1938): 4-5.
Mills, W.H., "Our Church's Duty to the Negro," *Presbyterian of the South* 116 (19 February 1941): 5-6.
"Ministerial Mention: Degree [second Ph.D. awarded to] Eugene W. McLaurin," *Presbyterian Outlook* 134 (21 April 1952): 16.
"Miss Stewart, Mr. Thompson Convicted by Holland Session: Vote Six to Three," *Presbyterian Guardian* 2 (20 January 1936): 133.
"Moderator Candidate Interviews: L Nelson Bell, Worth McDougald, Joseph A. Norton, and David L. Stitt," *Presbyterian Survey* 62 (June 1972): 2-3, 11-15.
"The Moderators on the Federal Council," *Presbyterian Outlook* 129 (29 September 1947): 1, 12-13.
"The Moderators Speak: We Support Protestant Cooperation! (Continued from last week)," *Presbyterian Outlook* 129 (6 October 1947): 7.
Monro, Hugh R., "The Dispensations," *Presbyterian* 111 (21 August 1941): 6-7.
Moore, LeRoy, Jr., "Another Look at Fundamentalism: A Response to Ernest R. Sandeen," *Church History* 37 (June 1968): 195-202.
Moore, W.W., "Mr. Bryan of Union Seminary," *Presbyterian Standard* 62 (23 November 1921): 4-5.
Moorehead, James H., "Between Progress and Apocalypse: A Reassessment of Millennialism in American Religious Thought: 1800-1880," *Journal of American Religion* 71 (December 1984): 524-42.
– "The Erosion of Postmillennialism in American Religious Thought, 1865-1925," *Church History* 53 (March 1984): 61-77.
"A More Christian Economic System," *Presbyterian Outlook* 130 (25 October 1948): [1].
Morgan, Robert C., "David Friedrich Strauss," in *Historical Handbook of Major Biblical Interpreters*, ed. Donald K. McKim, 364-68 (Downers Grove, IL: Inter-Varsity Press, 1998).
Morrow, Lance, "Saddam and the Arabs: the Devil in the Hero," *TIME* (28 January 1991), 64-66.
"Mr. Laird Files Appeal Notice, States Position to Congregation," *Presbyterian Guardian* 2 (20 April 1936): 38-40.
Muller, Richard, "Covenant and Conscience in English Reformed Theology: Three Variations on a Sixteenth Century Theme," *Westminster Theological Journal* 42 (Spring 1980): 308-34.
– *Dictionary of Latin and Greek Theological Terms: Drawn Principally from Protestant Scholastic Theology* (Grand Rapids, MI: Baker Books, 1985).
– "The Spirit and the Covenant: John Gill's Critique of the *Pactum Salutis*," *Foundations* 24 (January-March 1981): 4-14.
Murray, John, "Arminianism in the Pilgrimage of the Soul," *Presbyterian Guardian* 7 (25 March 1940): 83-84.
– "Covenant Theology," in *Encyclopedia of Christianity*, vol. 3, ed. Philip E. Hughes, 199-216 (Marshallton, DE: The National Foundation for Christian Education, 1972).
– "Dr. Buswell's Premillennialism: A Review by John Murray," *Presbyterian Guardian* 3 (27 February 1937): 206-09.
– "The 'Kingdom of Heaven' and the 'Kingdom of God,'" *Presbyterian Guardian* 3 (9 January 1937): 139-41.
– "Proposed Confessional Revision in the Presbyterian Church in the United States," *Presbyterian Guardian* 4 (November, 1938): 207-10.
– "The Reformed Faith and Modern Substitutes, Part I," *Presbyterian Guardian* 1 (16 December 1935): 87-89.
– "The Reformed Faith and Modern Substitutes, Part II," *Presbyterian Guardian* 2 (3 February 1936): 142-43.

- "The Reformed Faith and Modern Substitutes, Part III," *Presbyterian Guardian* 2 (17 February 1936): 163-64.
- "The Reformed Faith and Modern Substitutes, Part IV: Limited Atonement," *Presbyterian Guardian* 2 (16 March 1936): 200-01, 211.
- "The Reformed Faith and Modern Substitutes, Part V," *Presbyterian Guardian* 2 (20 April 1936): 27-29.
- "The Reformed Faith and Modern Substitutes, Part VI: Modern Dispensationalism," *Presbyterian Guardian* 2 (18 May 1936): 77-79.
- "The Reformed Faith and Modern Substitutes, Part VII – Modern Dispensationalism: The 'Kingdom of Heaven' and the 'Kingdom of God,'" *Presbyterian Guardian* 2 (17 August 1936): 210-12.
- "Shall We Include the Revision of 1903 in Our Creed? A consideration of the theological character of certain amendments to the doctrinal standards of the Presbyterian Church in the U.S.A," *Presbyterian Guardian* 2 (26 September 1936): 249-51.
- "What is Amillennialism?", *Presbyterian Guardian* 3 (27 March 1937): 242-44.

"NAE Convention in Chicago," *Presbyterian Guardian* 17 (10 February 1948): 47.

"Name of Dr. J.B. Thwing Erased from Presbytery Roll," *Presbyterian Guardian* 2 (9 January 1936): 116-17.

"A Negro Looks at Racial Issues," *Southern Presbyterian Journal* 7 (15 October 1948): 5.

Needham, N.R., "Sabbatarianism," in *Dictionary of Scottish Church History and Theology*, ed. Nigel M. de S. Cameron, David F. Wright, David C. Lachman, and Donald E. Meek, 737-38 (Downers Grove, IL: Inter-Varsity Press, 1993).

Nelan, Bruce W., "They Don't Need to Fight," *TIME* (12 November 1990): 34.

"New Books Concerning Jesus Christ: Review of *The Lord of Glory: A Study in the Designations of Our Lord in the New Testament, with Especial Reference to His Deity* by Professor B.B. Warfield," *Sunday School Times* 50 (18 April 1908): 196.

"New Jersey Synod Commission Affirms McIntire Conviction," *Presbyterian Guardian* 2 (16 March 1936): 209.

"A New Name," *Presbyterian of the South/Presbyterian Outlook* 118 (29 March 1944): [1].

"News of the Church: Death of Rev. Thomas W. Currie," *Christian Observer* 131 (5 May 1943): 8.

Noll, Mark A., "Common Sense Traditions and Evangelical Thought," *American Quarterly* 37 (Summer 1985): 216-38.
- "The Founding of Princeton Seminary," *Westminster Theological Journal* 42 (Fall 1980): 72-110.
- "Misreading the Signs of the Times," *Christianity Today* 31 (6 February 1987): 10-11.

Noll, Mark A., Alister E. McGrath, Richard Mouw, and Darrell L. Bock, "Scandal? A Forum on the Evangelical Mind," *Christianity Today* 39 (14 August 1995): 20-27.

"Notables of the Year: John Allan MacLean," *Presbyterian Outlook* 129 (20 January 1947): 8-9.

"Notes on Open Letters: A Common Error on Infant Damnation," *Sunday School Times* 46 (17 September 1904): 517.

"Notes on Open Letters: Marring God's Plans, and God's Foreknowledge," *Sunday School Times* 46 (5 November 1904): 640

Oberman, Heiko, "Some Notes on the Theology of Nominalism, with Attention to its Relation to the Renaissance," *Harvard Theological Review* 53 (1960): 47-76.

"Ockenga Leaves U.S.A. Church," *Presbyterian Guardian* 17 (25 May 1948): 144-45.

Ogden, D.H., "Dr. Green and Union," *Presbyterian Standard* 60 (2 April 1919): 5.

"An Open Letter to the Commissioners of the Next Assembly Regarding the Special Report on Princeton," *Presbyterian* 97 (12 May 1927): 25.

Osterhaven, M. Eugene, "Calvin on the Covenant," *Reformed Review* 33 (Spring 1980): 136-49.

"The Outlook Pulpit [Biographical Sketch]," *Presbyterian Outlook* 128 (18 February 1946): 1, 5.

"Pastor Holds Service Despite Locked Doors and Presbyterial Ban: The Rev. H.G. Welbon Ignores Surprise Move of Former Presbytery," *Presbyterian Guardian* 2 (30 August 1936): 220.
Patterson, Paige, David Dockery and Millard J. Erickson, "Forum: Eschatology," *SBC Life* (June/July 1994): 6-10.
Peale, Norman Vincent, "What I Saw from the Pew," *Presbyterian of the South* 117 (4 March 1942): 5-6.
Pentecost, J. Dwight, "The Purpose of the Law," *Bibliotheca Sacra* 128(April-June 1971): 227-33.
– "The Purpose of the Sermon on the Mount," *Bibliotheca Sacra* 140 (April-June 1958): 317.
– "Review of *The New Scofield Reference Bible*," *Bibliotheca Sacra* 124 (January-March 1967): 170.
– "Salvation in the Tribulation," *Bibliotheca Sacra* 115 (January-March 1958): 50-61.
"Philadelphia Fundamentalists Express Sympathy with Mr. MacPherson," *Presbyterian Guardian* 2 (17 February 1936): 172.
Pieters, Albertus, "Israel and the Church," *Presbyterian* 27 (1 July 1937): 9-11.
– "The Millennial Problem," *Intelligencer Leader* (5 March 1943): 17.
– "The Millennial Problem, Part II," *Intelligencer Leader* (19 March 1943): 20.
Poythress, Vern Sheridan, "Divine Meaning of Scripture," *Westminster Theological Journal* 48 (Fall 1986): 241-79.
– "Response to Paul S. Karleen's Paper," *Grace Theological Journal* 10 (Fall 1989): 147-56.
– "Response to Robert L. Saucy's Paper," *Grace Theological Journal* 10 (Fall 1989): 157-60.
Pratt, H. Waddell, "Breach of Contract by U.S.A. Church: Sets forth Issue Involved in Property Seizing Civil Suits," *Christian Beacon* 3 (18 August 1938): 1, 8.
"Premillenarian Request of Duryea," *Christian Beacon* 1 (20 August 1936): 2, 8.
"Premillennialism Adopted Constitutionally by Philadelphia Fundamentalist Group," *Presbyterian Guardian* 3 (27 September 1937): 214.
"Presbyterians Fill Vacancies on Board for Foreign Missions: Small Group Resigns, and Declares Board Would Not Adopt Resolution Approving Its Charter and Denouncing Independency," *Christian Beacon* 2 (3 June 1937): 1-2, 4.
"Presbytery of Greenbrier and Closer Relations," *Southwestern Presbyterian* (7 September 1904): 7.
"Protestant, Catholic and Jewish Leaders Unite in a Declaration of Economic Justice," *Presbyterian Outlook* 128 (4 November 1946): 5-6.
Pruden, Edward H., "Brethren, Let's Be Fair," *Presbyterian Outlook* 133 (13 August 1951): 5-6.
Pyne, Robert A., "Antinomianism and Dispensationalism," *Bibliotheca Sacra* 153 (April-June 1996): 141-54.
Quarles, James, "Predestination and Election: Does the Confession of Faith Present a Sound View of Them?", *Union Seminary Review* 55 (February 1944): 139-46.
– "Review of *Studies in the Confession of Faith: The Five Points of Calvinism Examined*, by Rev. Robert Ware Jopling," *Union Seminary Review* 55 (February 1944): 139-46.
"Questions and Answers [:Two salvations, one for the Jews and another for the Church?]" *Christian Beacon* 2 (8 April 1937): 4.
Racke, G., "Gesetz und Evangelium bei Calvin," *Theologische Literatuzeitung* 80 (1955): 179.
Rand, James F., "Problems in Literal Interpretation of the Sermon on the Mount," *Bibliotheca Sacra* 112 (January-March 1955): 28-29.
Reed, R.C., "Dr. Lingle and the Kingdom," *Presbyterian Standard* 57 (24 May 1916): 9, 23.
– "Editorial: The Church and the Kingdom," *Presbyterian Standard* 57 (3 May 1916): 2.
Reid, J. Calvin, "Is Hitler the Anti-Christ?", *Presbyterian of the South* 115 (16 October 1940): 3-5.
– "Today's Anti-Christs," *Presbyterian of the South* 115 (23 October 1940): 4-5.
Reid, W. Stanford, "Dispensationalism and History," *Presbyterian Guardian* 12 (25 March 1943): 83-86.

- "The Meaning of History," *Presbyterian Guardian* 6 (April 1939): 61-62, 79-80.
- "The New Testament Belief in an Old Testament Church," *Evangelical Quarterly* 24 (October 1952): 194-205..

"Reports to the General Assembly," *Presbyterian Outlook* 118 (26 April 1944): 4.

"Reports to the General Assembly; Report on Dispensationalism: The Question as to whether the Type of Bible Interpretation known as Dispensationalism is in Harmony with the Confession of Faith," *Presbyterian Outlook* 118 (10 May 1944): 5.

"Reunion Opponents Organize: Want Plan Submitted Soon; Wells Named in Montreat Meeting to Lead Church-Wide Campaign," *Presbyterian Outlook* 127 (3 September 1945): [3].

"Rev. Harold S. Laird Leaves Westminster: Secretary to the Board of Trustees Since Organization," *Christian Beacon* 2 (29 April 1937): 1-2.

Rian, Edwin H., "Editorial: Dr. Machen and a True Presbyterian Church," *Presbyterian Guardian* 13 (10 January 1944): 9-10.
- "Editorial: The National Association and the American Council," *Presbyterian Guardian* 13 (25 March 1944): 95-96.
- "Editorial: Organic Union," *Presbyterian Guardian* 7 (18 May 1940): 137.
- "Editorial: 'The Southern Presbyterian Journal' and Union," *Presbyterian Guardian* 13 (10 September 1944): 251-52.
- "Why the Constitutional Covenant Union?", *Presbyterian Guardian* 1 (7 October 1935): 6-7.

Richard, Ramesh P., "Premillennialism as a Philosophy of History, Part 1: Non-Christian Interpretations of History," *Bibliotheca Sacra* 138 (January-March 1981): 13-21.
- "Premillennialism as a Philosophy of History, Part 2: Elements of a Biblical Philosophy of History," *Bibliotheca Sacra* 138 (April-June 1981): 108-18.
- "Premillennialism as a Philosophy of History, Part 3: The Premillennial Interpretation of History," *Bibliotheca Sacra* 138 (July-September 1981): 203-12.

Richards, J. McDowell, "Brothers in Black," *Presbyterian of the South* 116 (5 November 1941): 4-6.

Richardson, Donald W., "The Moderators Speak: The Presbyterian Church and Evangelism," *Presbyterian Outlook* 118 (24 May 1944): 5.

Richardson, John R., "Straining Out a Gnat and Swallowing a Coffin," *Southern Presbyterian Journal* 4 (1 April 1946): 2.
- "Stronger Theological Education," *Southern Presbyterian Journal* 3 (January 1945): 3-4.
- "The Unity of Modernism," *Southern Presbyterian Journal* 5 (1 November 1946): 2.
- "Who is Right?", *Southern Presbyterian Journal* 6 (1 May 1947): 4.
- "Our Distinctive Presbyterian Emphasis," *Southern Presbyterian Journal* 3 (August 1944): 12-15.
- "Verbal Inspiration," *Southern Presbyterian Journal* 3 (October 1944): 3-4.
- "What it Means to be Sound in the Christian Faith," *Southern Presbyterian Journal* 2 (August 1943): 8-11.

Robertson, O. Palmer, "Current Reformed Thinking on the Nature of the Divine Covenants," *Westminster Theological Journal* 40 (Fall 1977): 63-76.
- "Genesis 15:6: New Covenant Expositions of an Old Covenant Text," *Westminster Theological Journal* 42 (Spring 1980): 259-81.
- "Tongues: Sign of Covenantal Curse and Blessing," *Westminster Theological Journal* 38 (Fall 1975): 43-53.

Robertson, R.P., "A Fundamental Difference," *Southern Presbyterian Journal* 9 (15 July 1950): 10-11.

Robinson, William Childs, "The Authority of the Lord Jesus Christ as Exercised in the Presbyterian Church U.S," *Southern Presbyterian Journal* 1 (November 1942): 11-14.
- "Distinguishing Things That Differ," *Southern Presbyterian Journal* 5 (15 January 1947): 3-4.

- "Facing Fire," *Southern Presbyterian Journal* 3 (October 1944): 3.
- "Is Southern Presbyterianism Ready to Receive a Theological Liberalism Which Does Not Accept the Deity of Christ?", *Southern Presbyterian Journal* 3 (August 1944): 9-10.
- "'The Real Issues that Divide Us': What is Truth?", *Southern Presbyterian Journal* 6 (1 April 1948): 2-3.
- "Saul and the Gibeonites: Georgia and the Slain Negroes," *Southern Presbyterian Journal* 5 (15 August 1946): 2-3.
- "Theological Liberalism," *Southern Presbyterian Journal* 4 (15 September 1945): 5-6.
- "The Theology of Jesus and the Theology of Paul," *Evangelical Quarterly* 8 (1936): 373-97.

Rollman, Hans, "William Wrede," *Historical Handbook of Major Biblical Interpreters*, ed. Donald K. McKim, 394-98 (Downers Grove, IL: Inter-Varsity Press, 1998).

Rolston, Holmes, "Editorial: I'm Against It," *Presbyterian Outlook* 131 (31 January 1949): 8.
- "Editorial: Report of a Survey," *Presbyterian of the South* 118 (6 January 1943): 2.
- "Editorial: What Shall the Friends of Union Do?", *Presbyterian Outlook* 127 (31 December 1945): 8.

Rolston, Holmes, III, "Responsible Man in Reformed Theology: Calvin versus the Westminster Confession," *Scottish Journal of Theology* 23 (May 1970): 129-56.

Ross, Alexander, "Review of *The Future of the Kingdom*, by Martin J. Wyngarden," *Evangelical Quarterly* 6 (1934): 446-47.
- "Review of *Of Things Which Soon Must Come to Pass*, by Philip Mauro," *Evangelical Quarterly* 5 (1933): 325-26.
- "Review of *A Thousand Wonderful Things About the Bible*, by Henry Pickering," *Evangelical Quarterly* 6 (1934): 448.

Rowan, Jesse C., "Another View of the Washington Riots," *Presbyterian Standard* 60 (8 October 1919): 6.

"RPC/ES Statement on Dispensationalism," *Presbyterian Guardian* (August-September, 1974): 239-47.

Rumscheidt, H. Martin, "Adolf von Harnack," *Historical Handbook of Major Biblical Interpreters*, ed. Donald K. McKim, 491-94 (Downers Grove, IL: Inter-Varsity Press, 1998).

Russell, James, "A Rejected Bible," *Presbyterian Standard* 63 (22 February 1922): 5.

Ryrie, Charles C., "The End of the Law," *Bibliotheca Sacra* 124 (July-September 1967): 239-47.
- "The Mystery in Ephesians 3," *Bibliotheca Sacra* 123 (January-March 1966): 24-31.
- "The Necessity of Dispensationalism," *Bibliotheca Sacra* 114 (July-September 1957): 243-54.

Saint, Phil, "Still Waving the Cross" [a cartoon], *Presbyterian Guardian* 1 (16 March 1936): 204.

"Samuel H. Sibley: When competency is recognized . . .", *Presbyterian Outlook* 130 (24 May 1948): 16.

Sandeen, Ernest R., "Defining Fundamentalism: A Reply to Prof. Marsden," *Christian Scholar's Review* 1 (Spring 1971): 227-32.
- "The Princeton Theology," *Church History* 31 (September 1962): 307-21.
- "Toward a Historical Interpretation of the Origins of Fundamentalism," *Church History* 36 (March 1967): 66-83.

Sanderson, John W., Jr., "Buswell as Churchman," *Presbyterion: Covenant Seminary Review* 2 (Spring-Fall 1976): 118-19.

Saucy, Robert, "A Rationale for the Future of Israel," *Journal of the Evangelical Theological Society* 28 (December 1985): 433-42.
- "Contemporary Dispensational Thought," *Tyndale Student Fellowship Bulletin* 7, (March-April 1984): 10-11.
- "The Crucial Issue Between Dispensational and Nondispensational Systems," *Criswell Theological Review* 1 (Fall 1986): 149-165.

- "Dispensationalism and the Salvation of the Kingdom," *Tyndale Student Fellowship Bulletin* 7 (May-June 1984): 6-7.
- "The Presence of the Kingdom and the Life of the Church," *Bibliotheca Sacra* 145 (January-March 1988): 30-46.
- "Response to *Understanding Dispensationalists*, by Vern S. Poythress," *Grace Theological Journal* 10 (Fall 1989): 138-146.

"Schauffler Hall," *Presbyterian Standard* 60 (6 August 1919): 5.

Scofield, Cyrus Ingerson, "The Course and End of the Age," (Reprint.) *Bibliotheca Sacra* 108 (January-March 1951): 105-16.
- "God's Purpose in This Age," *Our Hope* (March 1902): 465-66.
- "In Memoriam: James Brookes," *Truth* 23 (June 1897): 312.
- "The Last World Empire and Armageddon," (Reprint.) *Bibliotheca Sacra* 108 (October-December 1951): 355-62.
- "The Return of Christ in Relation to the Church," (Reprint.) *Bibliotheca Sacra* 109 (January-March 1952): 77-89.
- "The Return of Christ is Relation to the Jews and the Earth," (Reprint.) *Bibliotheca Sacra* 108 (October-December 1951): 477-87.
- "Tested by Grace," (Reprint.) *Bibliotheca Sacra* 107 (October-December 1950): 488-96.
- "The Times of the Gentiles," (Reprint.) *Bibliotheca Sacra* 107 (October-December 1950): 343-55.

"The Second General Assembly of the [OPC]," *Presbyterian Guardian* 3 (28 November 1936): 70, 83.

See, C.S.M., "Christ's Second Coming Cannot Be Before the Millennium," *Presbyterian Quarterly* 15 (July 1901): 342-63.

Shaw, J. Lyle, "How to Determine Fellowships," *Christian Beacon* 2 (8 July 1937): 1-2.

Shedd, "Liberal Methods," *Southern Presbyterian Journal* 6 (1 March 1948): 5.

Shields, Charles, "Historical and Critical Notes: The Doctrine of Calvin Concerning Infant Salvation," *Presbyterian and Reformed Review* 1 (1890): 634-51.

Siler, John C., "Review of : *The God that Jesus Saw* by W. Garrett Horder and *Grace* by Lewis Sperry Chafer," *Union Seminary Review* 35 (January 1924): 178-79.

Silva, Moisés, "Old Princeton, Westminster and Inerrancy," *Westminster Theological Journal* 50 (Spring 1988): 65-80.

Sloat, Leslie W., "About the *Guardian*," *Presbyterian Guardian* 17 (December 1948): 267-68.
- "Calvinists Can and Do Cooperate!" *Presbyterian Guardian* 19 (March 1950): 43.
- "Fifteenth General Assembly of the Orthodox Presbyterian Church," *Presbyterian Guardian* 17 (June 1948): 153-55, 159-65.
- "General Assembly Report; Part 1: The First Three Days," *Presbyterian Guardian* 16 (10 June 1947): 163-67.
- "General Assembly Report; Part 2: Concluding Sessions," *Presbyterian Guardian* 16 (25 June 1947): 179-82, 184.
- "Pilgrim on the Wrong Road: New Bible Edition Promotes Dispensational Teachings," *Presbyterian Guardian* 17 (September 1948): 220-22.
- "Pilgrim on the Wrong Road (2): Ancient and Modern Errors Among Teachings of New Bible," *Presbyterian Guardian* 17 (October 1948): 239-41.
- "Should Conservatives Co-operate?", *Presbyterian Guardian* 19 (February 1950): 23.
- "Taking Documents Seriously," *Presbyterian Guardian* 20 (15 May 1951): 84.
- "What is Orthodox Presbyterianism?", *Presbyterian Guardian* 6 (July 1939): 127-28.

Smith, Edward Everett, "Millennialism," *Presbyterian Standard* 62 (28 September 1921): 6-7.

Smith, Elwyn A., "Presbyterianism in America," in *Encyclopedia of the Reformed Faith*, ed. Donald K. McKim, 293-99 (Louisville, KY: Westminster/John Knox Press, 1992).

Smith, H.H., "Lee: The Christian Soldier," *Presbyterian of the South* 116 (31 December 1941): 5.
Smith, Lillian, "The White Christian and His Conscience," *Presbyterian Outlook* 127 (23 July 1945): 4-6.
Smith, Morton H., "The Church and Covenant Theology," *Journal of the Evangelical Theological Society* 21 (March 1978): 47-65.
Smith, Wilbur M., "Dispensations and the Scofield Reference Bible: Light from Church History on both," *Sunday School Times* 71 (15 June 1929): 335-38.
- "Is Evangelical Theology Changing?", *Christian Life* 17 (March 1956): 16-19.
- "Israel and the Church in Prophecy. Parts I and II: A review of an important book written to refute some teachings of dispensationalism," *Sunday School Times* 87 (24 November 1945 and 1 December 1945): 927, 940-41, 957-58.
Smoot, Dan, "Churches and Politics," *Dan Smoot Report* 10(23 November 1964): 369-76.
"Southern Church," *Christian Beacon* 2 (24 June 1937): 4.
"Southern Church Division Similar," *Christian Beacon* 1 (23 July 1936): 1, 7.
"Southern Church Girds for F. C. Battle," *Presbyterian Guardian* 16 (10 September 1947): 251.
"Southern Presbyterians Enjoy Visit of Dr. Young," *Presbyterian Guardian* 14 (15 August 1945): 236-37.
"Southern Presbyterian Notables: John Allan MacLean," *Presbyterian Outlook* 129 (20 January 1947): 8-9.
"Southern Presbyterian Property," *Presbyterian Guardian* 19 (July 1950): 124.
Spangler, James T., "The Philosophy of Dallas Seminary," *Bibliotheca Sacra* 100 (April-June 1943): 199-207.
Spectator [nom de plume], "Premillennialism and Patriotism," *Presbyterian Standard* 59 (28 August 1918): 5.
Steele, Edward, A., III, "Buswell, The Man," in the "J. Oliver Buswell Commemorative Issue," *Presbyterion: Covenant Seminary Review* 2 (Spring-Fall 1976): 9-10.
"Sprunt Lectures," *Southern Presbyterian Journal* 11 (4 February 1953): 16-17.
"S.S. Times Speaks on 'Pre-Mil.' Question," *Christian Beacon* 2 (25 February 1937): 2, 4-5.
Stackhouse, John G., "Perpetual Adolescence: The Emerging Culture of North American Evangelicalism," *Crux* 29 (September 1993): 32-37.
Stafford, J. Marion, "Review of *Dispensational Truth*, by Clarence Larkin," *Union Seminary Review* 32 (January 1921): 179-80.
Steele, Edward A., III, "Buswell the Man," *Presbyterion: Covenant Seminary Review* 2 (Spring-Fall 1976): 9.
Stonehouse, Ned B., "Amillennialism and Westminster Seminary," *Presbyterian Guardian* 3 (13 March 1937): 219-20.
- "The Assembly in Retrospect," *Presbyterian Guardian* 17 (June 1948): 151.
- "A Clarification of Some Issues," *Presbyterian Guardian* 3 (13 March 1937): 217-20.
- "The Creed of Our Fathers," *Presbyterian Guardian* 4 (10 April 1937): 1-2.
- "Editorial: Doctrine and the Clark Case," *Presbyterian Guardian* 14 (25 April 1945): 121-23.
- "Editorial: Issues and Convictions," *Presbyterian Guardian* 13 (10 December 1944): 349-51.
- "Modernism and the Board of Christian Education of the Presbyterian Church in the U.S.A," *Presbyterian Guardian* 2 (6 January 1936): 108-09.
- "The Presbyterian Church of America," *Presbyterian Guardian* 4 (26 June 1937): 85-87.
- "Some Lessons from *The Presbyterian*," *Presbyterian Guardian* 17 (July 1948): 171-72.
- "Taking Inventory," *Presbyterian Guardian* 17 (10 January 1948): 3-4.
- "The Thirteenth General Assembly," *Presbyterian Guardian* 15 (25 June 1946): 183.
- "Westminster Seminary Today," *Presbyterian Guardian* 4 (15 May 1937): 37-40.

– "What was Back of the Revision of 1903? An historical survey of the movement of 1890-1903 for revision of the Confession in the Presbyterian Church in the U.S.A," *Presbyterian Guardian* 2 (26 September 1936): 247-49.

Stonehouse, Ned B. and Paul Woolley, "The Assembly," *Presbyterian Guardian* 16 (25 June 1947): 183-84.

– "Fundamentalist Progress," *Presbyterian Guardian* 16 (15 August 1947): 331.

– "Grist for the Modernist Mill," *Presbyterian Guardian* 16 (25 July 1947): 215-16.

– "Stars or a Team?", *Presbyterian Guardian* 16 (10 June 1947): 199.

Strombeck, J.F., "Grace and Truth," *Bibliotheca Sacra* 96 (1939): 88-116; 205-223.

Strong, Robert, "Amillennialism in the New Testament," *Presbyterian Guardian* 11 (10 January 1942): 1-2, 14.

– "The Day of the Lord Jesus Christ; Amillennialism in the New Testament: Part V," *Presbyterian Guardian* 11 (10 March 1942): 67-69.

– "The Final Conquest of Death; Amillennialism in the New Testament: Part IX," *Presbyterian Guardian* 11 (10 May 1942): 131-34.

– "Interpreting the Book of Revelation; Amillennialism in the New Testament: Part XII," *Presbyterian Guardian* 11 (25 June 1942): 180-82.

– "Interpreting the Book of Revelation (Continued); Amillennialism in the New Testament: Part XIII," *Presbyterian Guardian* 11 (10 July 1942): 203-05.

– "The Millennial Discussion Continues; Amillennialism in the New Testament: Part III," *Presbyterian Guardian* 11 (10 February 1942): 40-43.

– "New Testament Interpretation of Old Testament Prophecy; Amillennialism in the New Testament: Part VIII," *Presbyterian Guardian* 11 (25 April 1942): 121-23.

– "The Olivet Discourse and the Lord's Return; Amillennialism in the New Testament: Part VII," *Presbyterian Guardian* 11 (10 April 1942): 99-102.

– "The Parables and the Second Coming; Amillennialism in the New Testament: Part VI," *Presbyterian Guardian* 11 (25 March 1942): 89-91.

– "Peter on the Second Coming of the Lord.; Amillennialism in the New Testament: Part XI," *Presbyterian Guardian* 11 (10 June 1942): 170-73.

– "Satan a Defeated and Doomed Foe; The Fifteenth and Concluding Article on Amillennialism in the New Testament," *Presbyterian Guardian* 11 (15 August 1942): 235-38.

– "The Second Coming and the Second Century; Amillennialism in the New Testament: Part II," *Presbyterian Guardian* 11 (25 January 1942): 20-22.

– "The Second Coming in the Thessalonian Epistles; Amillennialism in the New Testament: Part X," *Presbyterian Guardian* 11 (25 May 1942): 154-56.

– "The Structure and Terms of New Testament Eschatology: Amillennialism in the New Testament: Part IV," *Presbyterian Guardian* 11 (25 February 1942): 54-56.

– "Three Interpretations of Revelation Twenty; Amillennialism in the New Testament: Part XIV," *Presbyterian Guardian* 11 (25 July 1942): 219-21.

"A Summary of the Argument in Defense of Premillennialism," Parts 1-3. *Our Hope* 42 (April, May, June 1936): 687-95, 779-84, 826-33.

Taylor, Charlotte A., "Presbyterian Church and the Negro Woman," *Presbyterian of the South* 117 (18 March 1942): 8, 16.

Tenney, S.F., "The Millennium and Second Coming of Christ," *Presbyterian Standard* 59 (25 September 1918): 4.

"A Testimony: Prepared at Quarryville, Pa., Sept. 3 and 4, 1947," *Presbyterian Guardian* 17 (10 January 1948): 14.

Thiessen, Henry C., "Will the Church Pass Through the Tribulation?", *Bibliotheca Sacra* 42 (April-June 1935): 187-205.

Thomas, W.H. Griffith., "Modernism in China," *Princeton Theological Review* 19 (October 1921): 630-71.
- "Mr. Mauro and Daniel IX and XI," *Our Hope* 30 (August 1923): 95-108.
- "The Return of the Lord," *Our Hope* 25 (July 1918): 26-29.
- "The Victorious Life. Part I," *Bibliotheca Sacra* 76 (1919): 267-88.
- "The Victorious Life. Part II," *Bibliotheca Sacra* 76 (1919): 455-67.

Thompson, Ernest Trice, "The Alcohol Problem: Past and Present," *Presbyterian of the South* 117 (26 August 1942): 11-13.
- "Apocalyptic Literature of the Bible," *Presbyterian Outlook* 130 (20 December 1948): 13-14.
- "The Bible for Today," *Presbyterian Outlook* 134 (11 February 1952): 4-9.
- "Bible Study: Victorious Daily Living," *Presbyterian Outlook* 132 (4 December 1950): 13-14.
- "The Campaign Against the Colleges," *Presbyterian Outlook* 127 (10 September 1945): 8.
- "The Christian and His Economic Relations," *Presbyterian Outlook* 127 (26 November 1945): 13-14.
- "The Color Line in the Pacific War," *Presbyterian of the South* 117 (18 February 1942): 2.
- "A Committee Draws a Line," *Presbyterian Outlook* 118 (17 May 1944): 12.
- "Editorial: A Matter of Paper," *Presbyterian Outlook* 127 (31 December 1945): 8.
- "Editorial: The Presbyterian Outlook," *Presbyterian Outlook* 118 (5 April 1944): 8.
- "Editorial: 'The Southerner' Missed Its Chance," *Presbyterian Outlook* 127 (10 September 1945): 8-9.
- "The Laws of the People," *Presbyterian Outlook* 128 (14 January 1946): 13-14.
- "Negroes of the General Assembly," *Presbyterian of the South* 117 (19 June 1942): 3, 14.
- "Prophecy in the Bible," *Presbyterian Outlook* 130 (8 November 1948): 13-14.
- "Reunion of Presbyterians," *Presbyterian Outlook* 118 (5 April 1944): 8.
- "Scofield Bible's Heresy; *Prophecy and the Church* by Oswald T. Allis," *Presbyterian Outlook* 127 (13 August 1945): 15.
- "Summons to Evangelism," *Presbyterian Outlook* 118 (5 April 1944): 8.
"The South and Sectionalism," *Presbyterian Outlook* 131 (17 January 1949): 5-6.
- "This Is My Story: An account of the trials and the triumphs of 'The Paper Printed in the South Longer than Any Other Presbyterian Publication," *Presbyterian of the South* 118 (22 March 1944): [14].
- "Union Theological Seminary," *Commonwealth* 19 (February 1952): 15-18.

Thompson, Murray Forst, "The Auburn Betrayal: Part I," *Presbyterian Guardian* 10 (10 November 1941): 113-14, 125-27.
- "The Auburn Betrayal: Part II," *Presbyterian Guardian* 10 (25 November 1941): 133-34.
- "The Auburn Betrayal: Part III," *Presbyterian Guardian* 10 (10 December 1941): 154-55.
- "The Auburn Betrayal: Part IV," *Presbyterian Guardian* 10 (25 December 1941): 165-67.
- "The Auburn Betrayal: Conclusion," *Presbyterian Guardian* 11 (25 January 1942): 24-25.

Thompson, William O., "Report of Princeton Committee," *Presbyterian* 97 (12 May 1927): 16-17.

Thompson, Willis, "The Assembly's Committee on Church Union," *Presbyterian Standard* 60 (8 October 1919): 5-6.

Toon, Peter, "Hyper-Calvinism," in *Encyclopedia of the Reformed Faith*,. ed. Donald K. McKim, 190 (Louisville, KY: Westminster/John Knox Press, 1992).

Torrance, James B., "Covenant or Contract? A Study of the Theological Background of Worship in Seventeenth-Century Scotland," *Scottish Journal of Theology* 23 (Fall 1970): 51-76.
- "The Covenant Concept in Scottish Theology and Politics and Its Legacy," *Scottish Journal of Theology* 34 (Fall 1981): 225-43.
- "The Doctrine of Grace in the Old Testament," *Scottish Journal of Theology* 1 (Fall 1948): 55-65.

- "The Modern Eschatological Debate," *Evangelical Quarterly* 25 (January-October 1953): 101-06.
- Torrey, R.A., "Dr. Torrey's Reply," *Presbyterian Standard* 62 (6 July 1921): 5.
- Trumbull, Charles Gallaudet, "Dispensationalism and the Scofield Bible – Are They Heresies?", *Sunday School Times* 79 (20 February 1937): 130-33.
- "Fundamentalists Expose Modernism in the South," *Sunday School Times* 65 (26 May 1923): 1-2.
- "Mauro's Strange New Book: Review of *The Gospel of the Kingdom: With an Examination of Modern Dispensationalism*, by Philip Mauro," *Sunday School Times* 71 (2 March 1929): 135-36.
- "Notes on Open Letters: Dispensationalism and the Scofield Reference Bible – Are They Heresies?", *Sunday School Times* 79 (20 February 1937): 130, 132-33.
- "Taking Men Alive, Parts 1-5," *Sunday School Times* 49 (December 1907): 615-16; 631; 648-49; 664, 676.
- Turner, David L., "The Continuity of Scripture and Eschatology: Key Hermeneutical Issues," *Grace Theological Journal* 6 (Fall 1985): 275-87.
- Turner, Herbert S., "Literal or Real Meaning? Review of *Christ the Hope of Glory: Christological Eschatology* by Wm. Childs Robinson," *Presbyterian Outlook* 128 (14 January 1946): 15.
- "Two Communications from Dr. Buswell," *Presbyterian Guardian* 4 (10 April 1937): 12-16.
- Vance, James I., "The Northfield Conference," *Presbyterian Standard* 61 (1 September 1920): 5-6.
- Vance, Joseph A., "Presbyterianism in America Prior to 1861," *Union Seminary Review* 47 (July 1936): 349-59.
- VanGemeren, Willem, "Israel as the Hermeneutical Crux in the Interpretation of Prophecy, Part I," *Westminster Theological Journal* 46 (Spring 1984): 132-44.
- "Israel as the Hermeneutical Crux in the Interpretation of Prophecy, Part II," *Westminster Theological Journal* 46 (Fall 1984): 254-97.
- Vining, Robert L., "The Federal Council: Foe of Capitalism," *Southern Presbyterian Journal* 2 (August 1943): 5-7.
- "The Federal Council's 'Bible,'" *Southern Presbyterian Journal* 3 (August 1944): 17-19.
- Visser, Derk, "The Covenant in Zecharius Ursinus," *Sixteenth Century Journal* 18 (1987): 531-44.
- Walsh, Chad, "Last Things, First Things: The Eschatology of C.S. Lewis," *Theology Today* 6 (April 1949): 25-26.
- Waltke, Bruce K., "Is it Right to Read the New Testament into the Old?", *Christianity Today* 27 (2 September 1983): 77.
- Walvoord, John F., "The Abrahamic Covenant and Premillennialism," *Bibliotheca Sacra* 108 (October-December 1951): 414-22.
- "The Abrahamic Covenant and Premillennialism (continued)," *Bibliotheca Sacra* 109 (January-March 1952): 37-46.
- "Dispensational Premillennialism," *Christianity Today* 2 (15 September 1958): 11.
- "The Doctrine of Grace in the Interpretation of Prophecy," *Bibliotheca Sacra* 140 (April-June 1983): 99-107.
- "Does the Church Fulfill Israel's Program?", *Bibliotheca Sacra* 137 (January-March 1980): 212-22.
- "The Fulfillment of the Davidic Covenant," *Bibliotheca Sacra* 102 (January-March 1945): 154-55.
- "Law in the Book of Romans," *Bibliotheca Sacra* 94 (April-June 1937): 15-30; 281-95.
- "Lewis Sperry Chafer," *Sunday School Times* 94 (October 1952): 855, 868-70.
- "The New Testament Doctrine of the Kingdom," *Bibliotheca Sacra* 139 (July-September 1982): 205-15.

- "Our Future Hope: Eschatology and Its Role in the Church," *Christianity Today* 31 (6 February 1987): 12.
- "Posttribulationism Today," Parts I-IV. *Bibliotheca Sacra* 132 (1975): 16-24; 114-22; 208-15; 304-15.
- "Premillennialism and the Church as Mystery," *Bibliotheca Sacra* 111 (January-March 1954): 6-7.
- "Premillennialism and the Tribulation," *Bibliotheca Sacra* 111 (October-December 1954): 298-99.
- "Review of *Crucial Questions about the Kingdom of God*, by George Eldon Ladd," *Bibliotheca Sacra* 110 (January-March 1953): 6.
- "Review of *The Uneasy Conscience of Modern Fundamentalism*, by Carl F. Henry," *Bibliotheca Sacra* 104 (July-September 1947): 364.
- "The Theological Context of Premillennialism," *Bibliotheca Sacra* 108 (July-September 1951): 271.

Warfield, Benjamin Breckinridge, "How Princeton Seminary Got to Work," *Journal of the Presbyterian Historical Society* 9 (June 1918): 256-66.
- "Predestination in the Reformed Confessions," *Presbyterian and Reformed Review* 12 (1901): 49-128.
- "Systematical Theology: Review of *He That is Spiritual*, by Lewis Sperry Chafer," *Princeton Theological Review* 17 (April 1919): 322-27.

Webb, R.A., "The Adamic Principle in Theology," *Presbyterian Quarterly* 16 (July 1902): 1-29.
- "The Second Coming of Christ (A Postmillennarian View)," *Union Seminary Review* 27 (January 1916): 97-105.

Weinfeld, Moshe, "The Covenant of Grace in the Old Testament and in the Ancient Near East," *Journal of the American Oriental Society* 90 (1970): 184-203.

Weisiger, Cary N., III, "The National Association of Evangelicals," *Southern Presbyterian Journal* 2 (September 1943): 14-15.
- "Who Distrusts Whom?", *Southern Presbyterian Journal* 5 (15 April 1947): 2-3.

Wells, Jno. M, "Dr. Lingle on Fundamental Principles," *Presbyterian Standard* 60 (15 October 1919): 5, 8.

Wells, Paul, "Covenant, Humanity, and Scripture: Some Theological Reflections," *Westminster Theological Journal* 48 (Spring 1986): 17-45.

"Westminster Board Reorganized, Original Policies to Continue," *Presbyterian Guardian* 2 (20 January 1936): 132.

"Westminster Faculty Adopts Statement on Liquor Question," *Presbyterian Guardian* 4 (26 June 1937): 100.

Whaling, Thornton, "Federal Union," *Presbyterian Standard* 60 (12 March 1919): 9.

"What is the Moody/Dallas Agenda?", *Eternity* 32 (December 1981): 26-29.

Whitcomb, John C., "Christ's Atonement and Animal Sacrifices in Israel," *Grace Theological Journal* 6 (Fall 1985): 201-17.

Whiteley, Charles D., "Brunner, Lacy and Union Seminary," *Christian Beacon* 3 (2 March 1939): 1, 5.

"[Wilbur] Smith Leaves Independent Board: Revelation Announces Move; Mandate of Assembly Obeyed," *Christian Beacon* 2 (22 April 1937): 1-2.

Wilson, Charles Reagan and William Ferris (eds.), *Encyclopedia of Southern Culture* (Chapel Hill, NC: University of North Carolina Press, 1989).
- "The Lost Cause," in *Encyclopedia of Religion in the South*, ed. Samuel S. Hill, Jr., 412-13 (Macon, GA: Mercer University Press, 1984).

Wilson, W.J., "God's Sovereignty," *Presbyterian* 112 (15 October 1942): 3, 5-6.

Wirecoff, J.E.L., "Is the Kaiser 'That Man of Sin' or 'The Anti-Christ?'", *Presbyterian Standard* 59 (31 July 1918): 4.
"With the New Books: Our King's Program for the Present Age – Review of *The Parables of the Kingdom* by G. Campbell Morgan," *Sunday School Times* 49 (14 December 1907): 620.
"With the New Books: The Scofield Reference Bible," *Sunday School Times* 51 (20 June 1909): 293.
Witmer, John A., "What Hath God Wrought? – Fifty Years of Dallas Theological Seminary, Part I: God's Man and His Dream," *Bibliotheca Sacra* 130 (October 1973): 291-304.
– "What Hath God Wrought? – Fifty Years of Dallas Theological Seminary, Part II: Building Upon the Foundation," *Bibliotheca Sacra* 131 (January 1974): 3-13.
Woodbridge, Charles J., "The Independent Board," *Christian Beacon* 1 (14 May 1936): 8.
– "Why I Have Resigned as General Secretary of the Independent Board," *Presbyterian Guardian* 4 (12 June 1937): 69-71.
Woodworth, R.B., "Organic Union: Presbyterian Churches U.S. and U.S.A," *Presbyterian* 109 (21 September 1939): 23-24.
Woolley, Paul, "Assemblies North and South," *Presbyterian Guardian* 17 (July 1948): 178-79.
– "What Have We Learned?", *Presbyterian Guardian* 2 (4 May 1936): 45-46.
"Woolley Protests Seminary Story," *Christian Beacon* 2 (1 July 1937): 2.
Young, Edward J., "A Calvinist Looks at Prophecy: Review of *Prophecy and the Church* by Oswald T. Allis," *Presbyterian Guardian* 14 (10 June 1945): 165-66.
– "A Difficult Verse," *Southern Presbyterian Journal* 11 (6 August 1952): 6.
– "Gog and Magog: Does the Bible Predict the Russo-German Alliance?", *Presbyterian Guardian* 7 (25 February 1940): 49-49-50, 60-62.
– "Is Arminianism the Gospel?", *Presbyterian Guardian* 13 (25 September 1944): 264-65.
– "Literal or Spiritual?", *Presbyterian Guardian* 10 (10 July 1941): 4-5.
Zens, Jon, "The Believer's Rule of Life: A Study of Two Extremes: Postponed Ethics: Dr. Lewis Sperry Chafer; Retrogressive Ethics: Dr. Greg Bahnsen," *Baptist Reformation Review* 8 (1979): 5-19.
– "Dispensationalism: A Reformed Inquiry into Its Leading Figures and Features," *Baptist Reformation Review* 2 (1973): 25-56.
– "Dispensationalism in Conflict," *The Researcher* 4 (1974): 8-14.
Zoba, Wendy Murray, "Future Tense," *Christianity Today* 39 (2 October 1995): 19-23.

Unpublished Materials

Ahn, Keumyoung, "The Sinaitic Covenant and Law in the Theology of Dispensationalism," Ph.D. diss., Andrews University, 1989.
Ariel, Yaakov Shalom, "American Premillennialism and its Attitudes Towards the Jewish People, Judaism and Zionism, 1875-1925," Ph.D. diss., University of Chicago, 1986.
Bear, James E., "Analysis of the Book of Romans," unpublished course notes, archives of Union Theological Seminary, Richmond, VA, 1941.
– "How may you know that you are saved?", mimeographed notes from Ginter Park Presbyterian Church men's Bible study class, archives of Union Theological Seminary, Richmond, VA, 1958.
– "The Kingdom of Christ, the Second Coming, and Judgment," an outline for a U.T.S. faculty discussion, mimeographed notes, Richmond, VA: Union Theological Seminary, 1950.
– "Our Assumptions and the Interpretation of the Bible," lecture notes in papers, archives of Union Theological Seminary, Richmond, VA, 1938.

Bibliography 303

- James E. Bear Papers, Department of History, Presbyterian Church of the United States of America, Montreat, NC.
- "Studying the Bible Through Its Historical Background," for the Leadership Training School, typescript, archives of Union Theological Seminary, Richmond, VA, 1938.

Beeke, Joel, "Personal Assurance of Faith: English Puritanism and the Dutch 'nadere reformatie,'" Ph.D. diss., Westminster Theological Seminary, 1988.

Bell, L. Nelson, Biographical File, Department of History, Presbyterian Church of the United States of America, Montreat, NC.
- "Humanism: Counterfeit Christianity," cassette tape (Stahlstown, PA: Thompson Media, 1973).
- "Why I Am Against Church Union," phonotape, Richmond, VA: Union Theological Seminary, 1953.
- *A Physician Looks at the Virgin Birth*, pamphlet, in Biographical File, Department of History, Presbyterian Church of the United States of America. Montreat, NC.

BeVier, William A., "A Biographical Sketch of C.I. Scofield," M.A. thesis, Southern Methodist University, 1960.

Bierma, Lyle Dean, "The Covenant Theology of Caspar Olevian," Ph.D. diss., Duke University, 1980.

Blaising, Craig A., "Dispensationalism at the End of the Twentieth Century," unpublished paper presented to the Evangelical Theology Group of the American Academy of Religion, 1990.

Boles, Joe R., "The Theology of Lewis Sperry Chafer in the Light of His Theological Method," Th.D. diss., Southwestern Baptist Theological Seminary, 1963.

Boon, Harold W., "The Development of the Bible College or Institute in the United States and Canada since 1880 and Its Relationship to the Field of Theological Education," Ph.D. diss., New York University, 1950.

Caldwell, Frank H., Frank H. Caldwell Papers, Department of History, Presbyterian Church of the United States of America, Montreat, NC.

Campbell, Donald K., "Interpretation and Exposition of the Sermon on the Mount," Th.D. diss., Dallas Theological Seminary, 1956.
- Interview by author, 2 May 1995, Dallas, TX.

Carpenter, Joel A., "The Renewal of American Fundamentalism, 1930-1945," Ph.D. diss., Johns Hopkins University, 1984.

Cawood, John W., "A Definitive Study of Dispensational Interpretation," Th.D. diss., Dallas Seminary, 1959.

Cobb, John W., "The Origin, Development and Meaning of Dispensational Premillennialism," Ph.D. diss., Southwestern Baptist Theological Seminary, 1949.

Colbenson, Pamela Elwyn Thomas, "Millennial Thought Among Southern Evangelicals: 1830-1885," Ph.D. diss., Georgia State University, 1980.

Culver, Robert D., "The Strange Irrelevance of the Dispensational-Covenantal [Federalist] Debate Over Hermeneutics," unpublished paper presented to the Evangelical Theological Society, 1994.

Elmore, Floyd, "A Critical Examination of the Doctrine of the Two Peoples of God in John Nelson Darby," Th.D. diss., Dallas Theological Seminary, 1990.

Feinberg, Charles Lee, "The Premillennial and Amillennial Systems of Biblical Interpretation Analyzed and Compared," Th.D. diss., The Evangelical Theological College, Dallas, TX 1935.

Gannett, Alden Arthur, "Law in the New Testament," Th.D. diss., Dallas Theological Seminary, 1956.

Gear, Felix B., "Lectures on Prophecy: Dispensationalism," in Felix B. Gear Papers, Department of History, Presbyterian Church of the United States of America. Montreat, NC.
- Felix B. Gear Papers, Department of History, Presbyterian Church of the United States of America, Montreat, NC.

Glass, William R., "The Development of Northern Patterns of Fundamentalism in the South, 1900-1950," Ph.D. diss., Emory University, 1991.

Green, James B., James B. Green Papers, Department of History, Presbyterian Church of the United States of America, Montreat, NC.

Gullon, David Pio, "An Evaluation of Dispensational Premillennialism: An Analysis and Evaluation of the Eschatology of John F. Walvoord," Ph.D. diss., St. Andrews University, 1992.

Hannah, John David, "The Social and Intellectual History of the Origins of the Evangelical Theological College," Ph.D. diss. University of Texas at Dallas, 1988.

Herman, Douglas Edward, "Flooding the Kingdom: The Intellectual Development of Fundamentalism, 1930-1941," Ph.D. diss., Ohio University, 1980.

Hester, Malcolm O'Neal, "Millennialism in Southern Baptist Thought since 1900," Ph.D. diss., Southern Baptist Seminary, 1981.

Hilgenberg, Robert J., "The Law of Moses: Its Character and Function in the Old Testament," Th.D. diss., Dallas Theological Seminary, 1972.

Howe, Danny E., "An Analysis of Dispensationalism and its Implications for the Theologies of James Robinson Graves, John Franklyn Norris, and Wallie Amos Criswell," Ph.D. diss., Southwestern Baptist Theological Seminary, 1988.

Hutchison, John Charles, "The Relationship of theAbrahamic, Mosaic, and Palestinian Covenants in Deuteronomy 29-30," Th.D. diss., Dallas Theological Seminary, 1981.

Johnson, S. Lewis, Jr., Interview by author, 7 and 14 April 1995, Dallas, TX.

Karlberg, Mark W., "The Mosaic Covenant and the Concept of Works in Reformed Hermeneutics: A Historical-Critical Analysis with Particular Attention to Early Covenant Eschatology," Th.D. diss., Westminster Theological Seminary, 1980.

Kilgore, C.W., "William Henry Griffith Thomas," Th.M. thesis, Dallas Theological Seminary, 1974.

Lacy, Benjamin R., Benjamin R. Lacy Papers, Archives of Union Theological Seminary, Richmond, VA.

Letham, Robert, "Saving Faith and Assurance in Reformed Theology: Zwingli to the Synod of Dort," Ph.D. diss, Aberdeen University, 1979.

Lillback, Peter Alan, "The Binding of God: Calvin's Role in the Development of Covenant Theology," Ph.D. diss., Westminster Theological Seminary, 1985.

Lincoln, C. Fred, "The Covenants," Th.D. diss., Dallas Theological Seminary, 1942.

Lowery, Paul DeWitt, "Covenant Implications for Old Testament Exposition: An Overview of Some Pertinent Themes," Th.D. diss., Dallas Theological Seminary, 1979.

Ludwigson, Carl R., "The Apocalyptic Interpretation of History of American Premillennial Groups," Ph.D. diss., University of Iowa, 1945.

Lum, Richard A., "W.H. Griffith Thomas and Emergent American Fundamentalism," Ph.D. diss., Dallas Theological Seminary, 1994.

MacCorkle, Douglas B., "A Study of Amillennial Eschatology," Th.M. thesis, Dallas Theological Seminary, 1947.

MacRae, Allan A., Interview by author, 22 July and 3 August 1993, Quarryville, PA.

McCallie, J.P., J.P. McCallie Papers, Department of History, Presbyterian Church of the United States of America, Montreat, NC.

McCoy, Charles Sherwood, "The Covenant Theology of Johannes Cocceius," Ph.D. diss., Yale University, 1956.

McGahey, John F., "An Exposition of the New Covenant," Th.D. diss., Dallas Theological Seminary, 1957.

McKinney, Larry J., "An Historical Analysis of the Bible College Movement during Its Formative Years," Ed.D. diss., Temple University, 1985.

Mink, Timothy G., "John F. Walvoord at Dallas Theological Seminary," Ph.D. diss., North Texas State University, 1987.
Murray, John, "Creedal Subscription in the Presbyterian Church in the U.S.A.," an essay (photocopy), Westminster Theological Seminary, [n.d.]
Nevin, Paul D., "Some Major Problems in Dispensational Interpretation," Th.D. diss., Dallas Theological Seminary, 1965.
Payne, Homer Lemuel, "Amillennial Theology as a System," Th.D. diss., Dallas Theological Seminary, 1948.
Pentecost, J. Dwight, Interview by author, 31 May 1995, Dallas, TX.
Pettegrew, Larry Dean, "The Historical and Theological Contributions of the Niagara Bible Conference to American Fundamentalism," Th.D. diss., Dallas Theological Seminary, 1976.
Quirk, Charles E., "The Auburn *Affirmation*: A Critical Narrative of the Document Designed to Safeguard the Unity and Liberty of the Presbyterian Church in the United States of America in 1924," Ph.D. Diss., University of Iowa, 1967.
Renfer, Rudolf A., "A History of Dallas Theological Seminary," Ph.D. diss., University of Texas at Austin, 1959.
Richards, Jeffrey Jon, "The Eschatology of Lewis Sperry Chafer: His Contribution to a Systematization of Dispensational Premillennialism," Ph.D. diss., Drew University, 1985.
Robbins, Jerry Robert, "R.L. Dabney, Old Princeton and Fundamentalism," Ph.D. diss., Florida State University, 1991.
Sanders, Carl E., II, "The Myth of Normative Dispensationalism," unpublished paper presented to the Evangelical Theological Society, 17 November 1999.
– "The Premillennial Faith of James Brookes," Ph.D. diss., Dallas Theological Seminary, 1995.
Sebestyen, Paul, "The Object of Faith in the Theology of Calvin," Ph.D. diss., University of Chicago, 1963.
Sibley, Samuel H., Samuel H. Sibley Papers, Department of History, Presbyterian Church of the United States of America, Montreat, NC.
Spencer, Stephen R., "Reformed Scholasticism in Medieval Perspective: Thomas Aquinas and Francis Turrettini on the Incarnation," Ph.D. diss., Michigan State University, 1988.
Stoute, Douglas Andrew, "The Origins and Early Development of the Reformed Idea of the Covenant," Ph.D. diss., Cambridge University, 1979.
Strehle, Stephen A., "The Extent of the Atonement Within the Theological Systems of the Sixteenth and Seventeenth Centuries," Th.D. diss., Dallas Theological Seminary, 1980.
Tipson, Lynn Baird, Jr., "The Development of a Puritan Understanding of Conversion," Ph.D. diss., Yale University, 1972.
Toft, Daniel John, "Zacharius Ursinus: A Study in the Development of Calvinism," M.S. thesis, University of Wisconsin, 1962.
Turner, Helen Lee, "Fundamentalism in the Southern Baptist Convention: The Crystallization of a Millennialist Vision," Ph.D. diss., University of Virginia, 1990.
Veninga, James Frank, "Covenant Theology and Ethics in the Thought of John Calvin and John Preston," Ph.D. diss, Rice University, 1974.
Walvoord, John F., Interview by author, 11, 18, and 20 April, 2 and 30 May 1995; 19 June 1996, Dallas, TX.
Wenger, Robert Elwood, "Social Thought in American Fundamentalism, 1918-1933," Ph.D. diss., University of Nebraska, Lincoln, 1974.
Wiley, David Neeld, "Calvin's Doctrine of Predestination: His Principal Soteriological and Polemical Doctrine," Ph.D. diss., Duke University, 1971.
Wilson, Talmage, "A History of Dispensationalism in the United States of America: The Nineteenth Century," Th.M. thesis, Pittsburgh-Xenia Theological Seminary, 1956.
Witmer, John A., Interview by author, 18 May 1995, Dallas, TX.

Woodring, Hoyt Chester, Jr., "Grace Under the Mosaic Covenant," Th.D. diss., Dallas Theological Seminary, 1956.

Index

Abraham, W.J. 3n, 100n
Abstinence, see Alcoholic beverages (also see Prohibition; also Fundamentalism, Personal lifestyle issues)
Adventism, see Seventh-Day Adventism
AIC (PCUS Ad Interim Committee on Changes in the Confession of Faith and Catechisms) xii, 5-6, 11-16, 24, 80n, 95, 96n, 97, 110n, 118, 122-24, 125-73, 178-80, 184, 185n, 187, 190n, 196n, 198-99, 202, 204-05, 219-46
Alcoholic beverages (see also Prohibition) 40-42, 50, 55, 66
Aldrich, R.L. 201n, 217-18
Alexander, J.M. 98n
Allan, F.L. 26n
Allegorizing (see also Hermeneutics) 67, 68n, 195, 197n, 210
Allis, O.T. 6n, 10-11, 33n, 35, 40n, 53, 64, 68, 75, 77-78, 80-82, 110n, 134, 139n, 141, 165n, 197-98
American Anti-Saloon League 41n
American Tract Society 154n
Ames, W. 180n
Amillennialism 21n, 23, 39, 88, 141-42, 150, 152n, 176, 195, 196n, 199, 208n, 210, 234
Ammerman, N.T. 26n
Anti-denominationalism, see Independent or Independent Bible churches; also see Dispensationalism, and Plymouth Brethrenism
Anderson, W.M., Jr. 218
Anti-intellectualism 20, 26
Anglican Church 9
Apostles' Creed 127
Armerding, C. 218
Arminian/Arminianism 31, 32, 33, 52, 61, 66, 105, 125n, 171n
"Assembly of God" teachings (i.e., charismatic teachings) 163
Assembly's Training School (Richmond, VA) 98n, 120
Atonement, see Substitutionary atonement
Auburn *Affirmation* 28n, 108, 114, 148, 160

Auger, W. 165n
Augustine 189n
Austin Presbyterian Theological Seminary (PCUS) 15n, 115n, 116, 131, 132, 219-20
Averill, L.J. 100n

Bahnsen, G.L. 19n
Baker, B.W. 110-12
Balmer, R. 26n
Baptist Bible Seminary 201n
Baptists, see Southern Baptists; also see Dispensationalism and Southern Baptist Convention
Barker, K.L. 17n, 186n, 192n, 207n, 210n, 218
Barndollar, W.W. 201n
Barnhouse, D.G. 56n
Barrows, Cliff 147n
Barth, K./Barthianism 100, 159
Bass, C.B. 5n
Bateman, H.W., IV 201n, 208n
Battles, F.L. 90n, 181n, 189n
Bauer, F.C. 67n
Bear, J.E. 12, 15n, 85n, 95-97, 115n, 131, 133n, 135n, 140, 141-46, 151, 155n, 156n, 160n, 165n, 171n, 176, 178n, 181n, 188n, 190n, 197-98n, 199-200, 204, 237n, 245-46
Belgian Gospel Mission 154n
Bell, L.N. 28n, 104, 108n, 109n, 117n, 123n, 129n, 130-31, 137, 138, 140n, 146-53, 161, 245-46
Bennetch, J.H. 109n, 218
Bennett, J. 42n
Bennett, J.C. 105n
Benson, W. 218
Berkhof, L. 8n, 68n, 69, 207n
Best, J. 218
Beyer, L. 77n
Bible Conference movement (see also Niagara Bible Conference) 4n, 79
Bible Institute of Los Angeles 145n, 155n
Bible Presbyterian Church 5, 47n, 43, 45, 46n, 47n, 60n, 61n, 62n, 71-72, 81-82, 95-96, 115n, 116, 141n, 142, 144, 229
Bibliotheca Sacra 134, 171

Billy Graham Evangelistic Association (see also Graham, B.) 147n, 148
Birch, T.R. 52n, 110n, 120-21n
Black-white issues, see Racial issues
Blaising, C.A. 11n, 15-16, 18n, 28n, 86, 172n, 180n, 184n, 207n, 208n, 209
Bloesch, D.E. 2n, 3n, 100n
Blum, E.A. 218
Bob Jones University 117n
Bock, D.L. 4n, 15-16, 17n, 18n, 86, 90n, 207-08n, 209
Boles, J.R. 5n
Boon, H.W. 116n
Bowman, J.W. 165n
Boyd, B.M. 26n, 97n
Boyer, P. 5n
Boyle, G. 161
Bray, G. 67n
Bridges, J.R. 103n, 105n, 154n
Brookes, J.H. 8-9, 28n, 128n
Broomall, W. 217
Brown, C. 67n
Brown, R.E. 148n
Browne, F.Z. 217-18
Brumbaugh, R.T. 54n
Brunner, E. 100
Bulletin of the Evangelical Theological College 214, 217-18
Bullinger, E.W. 84
Bullingerism ("Hyper-Dispensationalism") 83-84, 89
Burch, M.B. 2n
Burns, J.L. xi-xii, 90-91n, 152n, 208n, 209-10
Buswell, J.O., Jr. xi-xii, 36-38, 41n, 42, 45, 49n, 50n, 54, 58, 59n, 60n, 63n, 64, 66n, 78n, 79-93, 115n, 141, 176n, 187n, 200n, 202-03n

Caldwell, F.H. 14n, 15n, 128-29, 130n, 137-40, 206, 240, 246
   resignation from AIC 129, 137-38
Calvin, J. 100, 139n, 140, 180-81n, 189n
Calvinism 7, 30, 32n, 44n, 52, 53, 57, 66, 72n, 74, 101-02, 105-06, 109, 114, 118n, 125, 140
Campbell, D.K. xiv, 7n, 11n, 87n, 92n, 124n, 172n, 183n, 187n, 196n, 218
Capitalism 104-05, 109n
Cards, Card-playing, see Fundamentalism, Personal lifestyle issues
Carpenter, J.A. 25n, 26n

Carroll, W.I. 217
Carson, D.A. 3n
Cash, W.A. 26n, 97n
Causes of salvation, as factor in the dispensational-covenantal debate:
   instrumental cause 180-82, 187, 189, 193
   meritorious cause 180-82, 189
Cauthen, K. 100
Central-North Presbyterian Church, Philadelphia, PA 40
Chafer, L.S. 5n, 6, 8n, 9n, 10-12, 13, 14, 58-59n, 64, 68, 69n, 70-71, 72n, 73, 74, 78-85, 87n, 88, 90-91, 92n, 109, 111-12, 114, 119n, 123, 132, 133n, 134-35, 136n, 141, 143-46, 148-49, 151-55, 157, 158n, 159, 161, 164, 166-67n, 170n, 171-72, 175, 176n, 177-84, 185-86n, 187, 188n, 195-96n, 197, 199-200, 201n, 202-04, 206-07, 217-18, 223-27, 229-30, 234-35n, 236, 238-39n, 240, 242-44
Chafer, R.T. 6n, 70-71, 176n, 199, 214, 217-18
Chamberlain, W.D. 129n, 206-07
Cheeseman, L. 46n
Christian, G.S. 62n
Christian Beacon, The 33, 73-74, 95, 141n, 142, 176n, 179n
Christian Church (i.e., Disciples of Christ) 163
Christian Fundamentalist, The 27n
Christian Fundamentals in School and Church 27n
Christian Observer 107n, 127
Christian Reformed Church 33, 53, 55
Christianity Today 40n, 147n, 148
Church of the Open Door 39, 40n
Churchill, R.K. 5n, 25n, 27n, 29n, 30n, 43n, 45n, 47n, 56, 57, 58, 60n, 66, 67n
Civil Rights, see Racial issues
Civil War, The (U.S.) 107, 110
Clark, G.H. 28n, 108n
Clement of Alexandria 68n
Cocceius 68n
Cochran, W.A. 108n
Coker, J.L. 20n, 67n
Cole, S.G. 4n, 26n, 28n, 29n
Colgate (i.e., Russell Colgate) Citation for distinguished service in education 152n
Columbia Bible College 79n, 123n, 145-46n, 154, 155n
Columbia Presbyterian Theological Seminary (PCUS) 15n, 116, 117n, 118n, 120, 127, 129, 139n

Index 309

Colyer, E.M. 3n
Communism 104-05, 109n
Confessional revision, see AIC
Confessional subscription (see also Westminster Confession of Faith) 4, 10, 11, 12, 24, 28, 30-31, 34, 35, 36, 37n, 43, 45-46, 48n, 49, 50n, 51n, 52, 53n, 57, 58, 63, 65, 66, 69-72, 79, 80n, 89, 95-96, 108n, 109, 113-15, 118n, 120-21, 131-138, 142-46, 148, 150-51, 153, 155, 158-60, 164, 176n, 178n, 179, 181n, 198-99, 200-01, 203n, 220, 234-45
Congregational Church 111
Conservatism vs. Liberalism in the PCUS 97-117, 119, 121, 123, 126-31, 147-49, 151-53, 158-60, 164, 182-83
  Theological 98-101
  Confessional 101-03, 113-14, 148
  Socio-Political 103-06
Constable, T. 218
Continuity and Discontinuity: Perspectives on the Relationship Between the Old and New Testaments (*Festschrift* for S. Lewis Johnson, ed. John S. Feinberg) 17n, 193-95
Council of Trent 189n
"Covenant of faith" 172n
Covenant of Grace 7-8n, 11-12, 34n, 73, 74-75, 76n, 78, 83, 84, 85n, 86-89, 131n, 134, 142n, 143, 145, 151, 155n, 157n, 158, 172, 176n, 181, 188n, 196n, 200n, 234-36, 239, 241-42, 244
Covenant of Redemption 7, 8n, 11, 67n, 172n
Covenant of Works 7, 8n, 11, 172n
Covenant Theology (see also Covenant of Grace; also Covenant of Redemption; also Covenant of Works; also Reformed Theology; also Premillennialism, "covenant premillennialism")
  and federalism 6n, 8-9n
  and Reformed theology 8n, 9, 16n, 31, 74-75, 86-87, 89, 91, 143, 157, 164-65, 171, 176n, 201, 202n, 239, 241-44
  and Westminster Confession of Faith 10, 12, 134-35, 142-43, 145-46, 151, 156-59, 171n, 176n, 201, 202n, 234-45
  origins of debate with dispensationalism 6-12, 19-24, 32-43, 55-64, 65-91, 109-24, 128, 130-46, 148-58, 160-72, 176-207, 233-40, 242-45
  origins of the term 6n
Covenant Union, The 154n

"Covenantism" (Chafer's terminology) 11-12
Cowan, G.201n
Cox, W.E. 14n, 165n
Cragoe, T.H. 9n
Craig, S.D. 40n
Cranfield, C.E.B. 210n
Creedalism, see Confessional subscription
Crenshaw, C.I. 14n, 165n
Criswell, W.A. 7n
Crowe, W. 104n
Crutchfield, L.V. 9n
Cumberland Presbyterians 102, 125n
Currie, T.W. 125n, 126n

Dabney, R.L. 8n, 103n, 106, 140-41
Dallas Theological Seminary (originally, the Evangelical Theological College) xi, 5, 9n, 10, 28n, 58-59n, 70, 79, 87n, 88, 92n, 115n, 116-17, 123, 145-46n, 152n, 155n, 164, 165-72, 195n, 201-02n, 206, 213-18, 234n
  impact of AIC ruling re: dispensationalism on the school's (formerly predominant) Presbyterian constituency 165-72 (charts: 168-69), 213-18
  revision of DTS doctrinal statement (1952) 172
Dancing, see Fundamentalism, Personal lifestyle issues
Daniel, C. 193n
Darby, J.N. (see also Dispensationalism, and Plymouth Brethrenism) 7n, 8n, 9, 20n, 67n, 70
Davidic throne 68
Davidson College xi, 108, 115n
Davis, J.J. 2n
Dayton, D.W. 3n
Deity of Christ 29, 30, 98, 99, 108n, 111n
Dendy, H.B. 101n, 105n, 109n, 114, 129n, 138, 147, 148n, 156n, 158n, 161n
DeVries, D. 67n
Dieffenbacher, A.J. 73, 74n
Disciples of Christ, see the Christian Church
Dispensationalism
  and fundamentalism 4, 9n, 33, 56-57, 109-10, 115, 117, 134, 149-51, 153-55, 164n, 195-96, 233
  and PCUS 10, 109-17, 128-73, 177-83, 187, 201-05, 217-18, 219-45
  and Plymouth Brethrenism 9, 70, 141, 169, 217-18

and premillennialism 4, 9, 12, 15, 16, 32-43, 54-59, 61, 63-64, 67-68, 71, 74-93, 96-97, 112, 115, 130-31, 133, 136n, 137, 139-45, 150-55, 160-61, 165n, 175-76, 195-96, 199-200, 202n, 204-05, 209-10, 220, 229, 234, 236-39, 243-45
and Southern Baptist Convention 7-8
Classical dispensationalism, see Scofieldism
conflicting understandings of 18-19, 33-36, 63-64, 65, 70-71, 72-93, 131, 137n, 141-42, 145-46n, 153, 154n, 161, 177-83, 184n, 201-02n, 205, 220-21, 234n, 239, 241-42, 245
Dispensationalist-Princetonian alliance 19-21, 67n
distinguished (as heterodox) from (acceptable) premillennialism (e.g., by Northern Presbyterians and by AIC) 15, 34-36, 59, 63-64, 67-68, 82-91, 96-97, 115, 133, 142-43, 145, 150-51, 158, 160-61, 165n, 175-80, 199, 202-07, 220, 234, 236-37, 245
Essentialist dispensationalism 16, 17n, 86, 88-90, 183-97 (agreements and disagreements between essentialist dispensationalism, classical dispensationalism and covenant theology 187-94),
"Extreme Dispensationalism," see Scofieldism
Four phases of 15-16, 86, 90
"Hyper-dispensationalism," see Bullingerism
Israel-Church distinction 8n, 17, 18n, 73, 78n, 80, 142, 150, 155n, 182, 195n, 197-200, 204-11, 221-22, 224, 230-31, 234-40, 242-44
Normative dispensationalism, see Essentialist dispensationalism
Old Testament-New Testament distinction (see also Mosaic Law) 11, 69, 73, 79n, 175-88, 193-98, 201-02n, 203-10, 221-23, 234-39, 242-44
origins, origins of the term 6, 9n, 73-78, 82, 199-200
origins of debate with covenant theology 6-12, 19-24, 32-43, 55-64, 65-92, 95-97, 109-12, 115-24, 132-73, 195-96, 207
Progressive dispensationalism 16, 18n, 86, 88-90, 184n, 187-89, 196n, 209-10

role of animal sacrifices in the Old Testament 189-94, 201n, 203
two ways of salvation 11, 34n, 73-74, 80-81, 85n, 150, 155n, 175-95, 202n, 203, 234-36, 242-43
view of grace (or Law-Grace distinction; see also Keswickian view of sanctification) 8n, 10, 17-18n, 34n, 73-74, 79n, 80, 81, 83, 87n, 133-34, 150, 155n, 172n, 175-97, 201-02n, 203, 234-36, 239, 242-44
view of the kingdom 8, 18n, 33n, 72n, 73, 86n, 87n, 89, 109, 111n, 142-43, 150, 153, 156, 157n, 160-61, 175, 209-11, 221, 225-27, 234-40, 243-44
Dispensationalism Today (by Charles C. Ryrie) 186-93, 196n
Dixon, R. 217
Dockery, D.S. 3n, 7n, 8n
Dodd, C.H. 67n
Dollar, G.W. 8n, 27n, 218
Donatists 189n
Douglas, M. 23n
Dubuque Theological Seminary 100n
Duncan, J.L. III 53n
Dutch Reformed theology, see Reformed, Dutch Reformed theology
Dyer, C.H. 172n, 196n

Earthly people-heavenly people distinction (see also Dispensationalism, Israel-Church distinction) 10, 208n, 222, 224, 230-31, 238, 243
Economic issues as factor in controversies 103-05, 116-17, 122, 123n, 136
Edinburgh University 139n
Edwards, D.L. xiv
Edwards, J. 139n
Ehlert, A. 218
Ellingsen, M. 3n
Elmore, F. 8n
English, E.S. 42, 77n, 87n, 92n, 184-85, 201n
Erdman, C.E. 31n
Erickson, M.J. 8n
"eschatological freedom" (within Presbyterian churches) 32n, 35, 54n, 76, 80, 97, 142n, 176n
Eschatology, see Amillennialism; also see Postmillennialism; also Premillennialism

Index 311

Essentialist Dispensationalism, see Dispensationalism, Essentialist dispensationalism
Evangelical Quarterly 141n
Evangelical Theological College, see Dallas Theological Seminary
Evangelical Theological Society 17n
Evangelicalism 1-4, 17, 19, 21-24, 25n, 26, 32, 41n, 43, 57, 63, 65-66, 70, 87n, 100, 112, 152, 165n, 166n, 173, 210-11
Evans, J.E. 218
Evans, W. 178n
Evolution, theory of (see also Scopes Trial) 152, 159
ex opere operato 189-90, 191n, 193
"Extreme Dispensationalism," see Scofieldism

Fackre, G. 26n
Faith Theological Seminary 116
Fallacies contributing to misunderstandings in the dispensational-covenantal debate:
guilt-by-association 110-12, 195-96, 199
ignoratio elenchi 178, 188, 190n, 194
overgeneralization 197-201
quibbling 179-80
reductio ad absurdum 195-96n
Faust, D.G. 103n
Federal Council of Churches 105, 148n, 152-53
Feinberg, C.L. 72n, 134, 183n, 185n, 217-18, 238n
Feinberg, J.S. 17n, 189n, 193n, 194-95, 201n
Fence Rail, The 27n
First and Central Presbyterian Church of Wilmington, DE 39
First Presbyterian Church of Birmingham, AL 118n
First Presbyterian Church of Dallas, TX 167
Flow, J.E. 101n, 104n
Fosdick, H.E. 27n, 29n
Frame, J.M. 45n, 52n, 55n, 58n
Frank, D.W. 5n
Franke, J.R. 2n
Frazer, W.H. 107n
Free Grace Society 202n
Free Presbyterian Church of Scotland 50, 51n, 53
Freeman, H.E. 193n, 201n
Fuller, D.P. 87n, 146n, 162n, 165n
Fuller Theological Seminary 100n
Fundamentalist, The 27n

Fundamentalism 3, 4, 8-9, 19, 21-24, 25-32, 39-43, 47, 56, 59, 60, 61n, 62, 63, 66-70, 79, 97n, 98-99, 109n, 110n, 112-14, 117, 148, 154
confusion over lists of "five fundamentals" 29-30, 66-67, 166n
Niagara Fundamentalism 16, 29-32, 60, 61, 62, 63, 65-72, 78, 79, 81, 82n, 195
Personal lifestyle issues 40-42, 50n, 51n, 55, 66
Presbyterian Fundamentalism 29-32, 45, 47, 48-55, 59, 61, 62, 63, 65-72, 78, 79, 81, 82n, 112-14, 148
term "fundamentalism" narrowing in its meaning among conservatives to refer exclusively to Niagara Fundamentalism or to independent fundamentalists 33, 63n, 66-68
Fundamentalist-modernist controversy, 1, 5n, 15, 22, 25n, 40, 43, 44, 52n, 56, 57, 61, 63, 65, 66-70, 72, 98, 106-08, 110-13, 119, 233
in the South 8n, 97-117, 119, 136, 148, 152, 233
Furniss, N.F. 4n, 8n, 26n, 27n, 97n, 106n

Gadamer, H.G. 2n
Gaebelein, A.C. 72n, 111, 134, 237n, 239n
Gage, D.S. 121n
Gear, F.B. 139-41, 160n, 190n, 245-46
Gentry, K.L. 19n
Gerstner, J.H. 14n, 18n, 75n, 146n, 165n, 193n, 202n
Gillespie, G.T. 128n
Gilmer, G. 167n, 204n
Ginter Park Presbyterian Church (Richmond, VA) 98, 99n
Glasgow, T. 120-21n
Glass, W.R. 5n, 8n, 42n, 79n, 97-98n, 100-01n, 112, 113n, 115-16n, 117, 123n, 130n, 145n, 154, 155n, 164n, 166-67, 183n, 204n
Gleason, R. 9n
Godfrey, W.R. 53n
Gould, E.C. 10n
Graham, B. (see also Billy Graham Evangelistic Association) 147
Graham, Ruth (Bell) 147
Grammatical-historical interpretation, see Hermeneutics
Graves, J.R. 7-8, 10, 67n
Graves, J.T. 105n

Gray, J.M. 132, 134, 224, 226, 229
Great Depression 92, 116
Green, J.B. 14-15n, 126-30, 139n, 240, 245-46
Gregg, H.H. 132, 134, 223-24
Grenz, S.J. 2n
Gribble, R.F. 101n
Griffiths, H.M. 34n, 49, 54n, 71n, 74n, 75n, 76, 77n, 82n, 85n
Gromacki, G. 90n
Gulf War as illustration/analogy of sociological dynamics 77
Guille, G. 217
Gunn, G.E. III 14n, 165n
Gutzke, M. 217

Hafemann, S.J. 67n
Hagner, D.A. 67n
Haldeman, I.M. 197n, 239n
Hall, D.W. 53n
Hall, J.H. 9n
Hamilton, I. 51n
Hannah, J.D. xiii, 5n, 9n, 10n, 28n, 58n, 71n, 79n, 92n, 112n, 123n, 135n, 145n, 162n, 164n, 165n, 166n, 214, 217-18
Harnack, A., von 67n
Harris, R.L. 41n
Harrison, E. 217-18
Harrison, N. 218
Hart, D.G. xiii, 2n, 5n, 26n, 27n, 31n, 32n, 39n, 40-44n, 46-47n, 49-50n, 53n, 55n, 56-58, 59n, 61n, 63n, 70n
Harvard University 139n
Hatch, N.O. 2n
Hauerwas, S. 2n
Hause, J. xiii
Hemingway, E. 48n
Hendricks, H.G. 218
Hendriksen, W. 210n
Henry, C.F.H. 2n, 109n
Herman, D.E. 30n
Hermeneutics 67-69, 71, 87n, 175-76, 195-97, 208-10
Hill, S.S., Jr. 106n
Hoch, C.B., Jr. 210n
Hodge, C. 20n, 67n, 180-81n, 188n, 193n, 194-95, 207n
Hodges, Z.C. 202n, 218
Hoekema, A.A. 210n
Hofstadter, R. 26n
Holifield, E.B. 106n

Horton, M. 3n
Howe, D.E. 7n
Howe, F.R. 218
Hunter, J.D. 25n
Hutcheson, R.G., Jr. 3n
Hutchinson, G.P. 5n, 25n, 41n, 43-44n, 46n, 47n, 49n, 50n, 54n, 59n, 60n, 82n
Hutchinson, W.R. 20n, 39n, 40n, 41n, 100n
Hyper-dispensationalism, see Bullingerism
Ibach, R.D. xiii
Independent, Independent theological institutions or Independent (Bible) churches 8, 30n, 39-40, 42, 46-47n, 54n, 67n, 70-71, 72n, 79, 82, 111, 115, 117, 122, 136, 149, 154-55, 166, 168-69, 171, 175, 213-18, 233
Independent Board for Presbyterian Foreign Missions 27, 39-40, 42n, 47n, 50, 54n, 60n, 63n, 71n, 76n
Independent Fundamental Churches of America 170, 218
Independentism, see Independent, Independent theological institutions, or Independent Bible churches
Inerrancy (or infallibility) of Scripture 29, 30, 98, 99-100, 111, 113, 120
Infralapsarianism 45
In His Steps 41n
International Council of Religious Education 152n
Intoxicating liquors, see Alcoholic beverages
Ironside, H.A. 132, 218, 228, 237n

Jackson, P. 217
Jacobsen, D. 25n
Jamison, M. 46n
Jehovah's Witnesses, see Russellism
Johnson, E.E. 17-18n
Johnson, S.L. xiv, 17n, 118n, 124n, 164n, 167, 183n, 192n, 193, 218
Johnston, R.K. 3n
Jones, J.A. 128n
Jopling, R.W. 102n
jure divino Presbyterianism 106, 163n

Kadushin, M. 21n, 44n
Kantzer, K.S. 2n
Kaufman, G.D. 100n
Kemeny, P. 20n
Kennedy, D.S. 166n
Keswickian view of sanctification 9, 145n, 154n

Index 313

Klooster, F.H. 194-95
Konscics, M. xiv
Kraus, C.N. 5n
Kuiper, R.B. 31n, 32n, 33, 34, 35, 45n, 49-51n, 53, 54, 58, 61n, 64, 71-72n, 75, 176n
Kurtaneck, N. 92n, 196n
Kuschke, A.W., Jr. 106n

Lachman, D.C. 51n, 83n
Lacy, B.R. 14n, 15n, 128-29, 130n, 137-39, 141, 240, 246
  resignation from AIC 129, 137-38, 141
Lacy, D. 128n
Ladd, G.E. 165n
Laird, H.S. 39, 40, 50, 54n
Landmarkism 7
Lapsley, R.A. 154n
Larkin, C. 9-10
Leach, F.H., Jr. 217
Lewis, A.E. 31n
Liberalism, definition and taxonomy of (also see Conservatism vs. Liberalism in the PCUS) 67-69, 100-06, 114, 119-21, 128, 152-53, 158-60, 183n, 195-96
Lincoln, C.F. 88, 92n, 171-72, 186-88n, 195-96n, 217-18
Lindbeck, G.A. 2n, 91n
Lindsell, H. 147n
Lingle, W.L. 108, 115n
"Literal" hermeneutic, see Hermeneutics
Loetscher, L.A. 46-47n, 62n
Longfield, B.J. 5n, 27n, 31n, 40n, 46n, 60n
Longman, T. III 17-18n
Lordship salvation debate 202n
"Lost Cause, The" (in Southern sociology) 103n, 106-07
Louisville Presbyterian Theological Seminary 15, 118n, 120, 128, 129n, 139n
Loveland, A.C. 106n
Lum, R.A. 9n
Luther, M. 100
Lyons, J.S. 103n

Macartney, C.E. 27n, 40n, 60
Machen, A.W. 110n
Machen, H.W. 42n
Machen, J.G. 5n, 26-27, 28n, 31-32n, 34-35, 36, 37n, 40, 41n, 42, 45, 47, 48n, 49-61n, 63n, 67, 68n, 75, 82n, 97n, 110n, 142n, 154n, 176n

  death of, as factor in exacerbating intra-conservative tensions 42, 55, 60-61, 63n, 67
Mack Publishing Company 47n
Mackenzie, H. 217
MacLean, J.A. 98-102, 104n, 105n, 114, 126
MacLeod, D.J. 7n
MacPherson, M.T. 30n, 39-40, 42, 49n, 54n, 63n, 72n
MacRae, A.A. xiv, 20n, 36, 39n, 40n, 42n, 45, 49n, 50n, 51n, 52n, 53, 54, 55, 57, 58, 64, 69, 71n, 75, 77n, 84, 89, 92n, 124n, 183n, 185n, 198, 200n
MacRae, G. 52n
Maddex, J.P., Jr. 46n, 97n
Mangum, G.D. xiv
Marrow Controversy 51n, 83n
Marsden, G.M. xii, 2-3n, 4-5n, 20, 26n, 27n, 28n, 29, 30, 41n, 43, 44, 45n, 46n, 47, 48n, 49n, 50n, 62, 63, 67n, 71n, 76, 112n, 154n
Martin, H. 148n
Marty, M.E. 25n
Mason, C.E., Jr. 185n
Master, J.R. 18n
Mathison, K.A. 14n, 18n, 165n
Matthews, D.G. 98n
Mauro, P. 6n, 10n, 199
McBeth, H.L. 7n
McCallie, J.P. 15n, 123-24n, 130, 137, 152-55, 161, 245-46
McCallie, S.J. 152
McCallie School for Boys (Chattanooga, TN) xi, 15n, 137, 152
McClain, A.J. 92n, 185n, 192n
McClendon, J.W., Jr. 3n
McDougald, W. 149n
McGee, J.V. 218
McGrath, A.E. 2n, 3n, 4n, 58n, 91n
McGregor, J.R. 118n
McIntire, C. 28n, 32n, 33, 34n, 35, 37n, 40n, 45, 46n, 47, 49n, 50n, 52, 54, 55, 58, 60, 61n, 63n, 64, 71n, 75n, 92n, 108n, 176n
McKim, D.K. 67n, 100n
McKinney, L.J. 116n
McLaurin, E.W. 14-15n, 130n, 131-34, 146, 156n, 160n, 181n, 219-31, 240, 245-46
McQuilkin, R.C. 79n, 123-24n, 145-46n, 154-55
Mead, W.W. 10n
Medical College of Virginia (Richmond, VA) 147n

Mercer, C.R. 67n
Methodists 61, 111, 214
Michaelsen, R.S. 100n
Middleton, R. 2n
Millerite movement, see Seventh Day Adventism
Mills, W.H. 104n
Mississippi Visitor 127
Mitchell, J. 218
Modern dispensationalism, see Dispensationalism
Modernist-fundamentalist controversy, see Fundamentalist-modernist controversy
Montreat, NC (see also Presbyterian Historical Society, Montreat, NC; also Montreat Presbyterian Church) 140n
Montreat Presbyterian Church (PCUS) 147n
Moody Bible Institute 134, 145n, 155n
Mooney, J. 166-67n
Moore, L., Jr. 5n
Moore, R.D. 8n, 18n
Moral influence theory of the atonement 99-100
Morgan, R.C. 67n
Morrow, L. 77n
Mosaic Law (see also Dispensationalism, view of grace; and Old Testament-New Testament distinction) 10, 18n, 73-74, 83, 87n, 176-77, 178n, 182-86, 187n, 189-190, 191n, 192, 201n, 203, 206n, 235
Mouw, R.J. 4n
Movie attendance, see Fundamentalism, Personal lifestyle issues
Muether, J.R. 5n, 27n, 32, 40n, 41n, 43n, 46n, 47n, 49n, 50n, 53n, 55n, 56-59
Muller, R.A. 180n, 189n
Murphy, N. 2n, 3n
Murray, I.H. 5n, 51n, 53n
Murray, J. 5n, 6n, 10-11, 20n, 33n, 35, 36-38, 48n, 49n, 50-51, 53, 54, 58, 61n, 64, 72n, 75, 76, 80, 81, 82, 83, 110n, 125n, 134, 139n, 141, 142n, 181n, 183n, 197n, 201n

Nash, C.A. 172n, 218
Nash, R.H. 3n
Nation, M. 2n
National Association of Evangelicals 152
National Council of Churches, see Federal Council of Churches
Needham, N.R. 51n
Nelan, B.W. 77n

Neo-orthodoxy 100, 123
New School Presbyterianism 44, 45, 46, 47, 62
New York Times 31n
Niagara Bible Conference 5n, 8, 28, 29n
Niagara fundamentalism, see Fundamentalism, Niagara fundamentalism
Noll, M.A. 2n, 3n, 4n, 41n
Normative dispensationalism, see Dispensationalism, Essentialist dispensationalism
Norris, J.F. 7n, 27n
Northern Presbyterian Church, see Presbyterian Church in the U.S.A.; see also Orthodox Presbyterian Church

Oberman, H. 190n
Oden, T.C. 26n
Old School Presbyterianism 44, 45, 46, 56, 62, 97, 112, 129n
Organic complex 21-24, 44
 and basic beliefs and aims 22, 44
 and worldview 21
Origen 68n
Orthodox Presbyterian Church (OPC) 5, 27, 29n, 32-34, 36, 37n, 39-50, 52-54, 56-61, 63, 64, 65, 66, 67n, 69, 71, 75-76, 77n, 78, 79, 81-82, 91, 92, 116, 141, 201
Our Hope 111
Oxford University 9

Packer, J.I. 3n
Patterson, P. 8n
Payne, J.B. 193n
Pelikan, J. 189n
Pentecost, J.D. xiv, 124n, 183-84n, 201n, 203n, 214,
Perkins School of Theology (at Southern Methodist University) 100n
Perpetuo, A.H. 217
Peters, D. xiv
Peters, G.N.H. 195n
Peters, G.W. 218
Pettegrew, L.D. 5n, 28n
Philadelphia College of Bible (aka Philadelphia Bible Institute, Philadelphia Biblical University) 170n
Philadelphia Fundamentalists 39, 40n, 42, 53n
Philo 68n
Pieters, A. 10n
Pietism 20, 43

Index 315

Pilgrim Bible 92n
Pioneer Mission Agency 154n
Plan of Reunion, see Reunification of PCUS and PCUSA
Plymouth Brethren, see Dispensationalism and Plymouth Brethrenism)
Pollock, J.C. 147n
Postmillennialism (or, "Postmillenarianism") 32n, 67, 69, 133, 138, 141n, 150
Postmodernism 2-3
Potts, A.H. xiv
Poythress, V.S. 2n, 14n, 18n, 69n, 197n, 207-08
Pratt, H.W. 119n, 145n
Premillennialism (see also Dispensationalism, and premillennialism; also see Dispensationalism, distinguished [as heterodox] from [acceptable] premillennialism *per se* by Northern Presbyterians and/or by AIC) 9, 12, 15, 30-31, 32-43, 45, 46, 49, 50n, 53, 54, 55, 56, 58-61, 63-64, 65-93, 95-97, 112, 115, 123n, 130-31, 133, 137-45, 150-55, 160-61, 165n, 175-76, 195-96, 199-200, 204-05, 209-10, 220, 229, 234, 236-39, 243-45
    confusion of premillennial return and bodily return of Christ 30, 66-70, 99, 195
    "covenant premillennialism" (or "Reformed premillennialism") 165n, 187n, 204
    "Historic Premillennialism" 85n, 142-44, 176n, 196n, 236-37
Presbyterian, The 166n
Presbyterian Church in the Confederate States of America 105n
Presbyterian Church in the U.S. (aka PCUS, "Southern Presbyterian Church"; see also Reunification of PCUS and PCUSA) xi, 13, 24, 95-96, 97-173, 201-05, 217-18
    ecclesiology, ecclesiastical (judicial) structure 8, 13, 101, 105-06, 107n, 110n, 113-14, 117-24, 125-64, 202n, 219-46
    PCUS Ad Interim Committee on Changes in the Confession of Faith and Catechisms, see AIC
    PCUS Ad Interim Committee on Curricula of the Theological Seminaries 119
    PCUS Advisory Committee on Christian Education 129n
    PCUS Board of World Missions 147
    PCUS Book of Church Order 13n
    PCUS Standing Committee on Bills and Overtures 202n
    PCUS Standing Committee on Theological Seminaries 118, 119n, 122-24, 132
Presbyterian Church in the U.S.A. (aka PCUSA, "Northern Presbyterian Church"; see also Reunification of PCUS and PCUSA) 6, 25-28, 29n, 31n, 32n, 39-40, 46, 48, 49, 50, 52-56, 59n, 60, 63, 65, 67n, 82n, 98, 106-08, 114, 125, 148n, 154n, 160, 217-18
    Mission Board of the PCUSA 40
Presbyterian Constitutional Covenantal Union 76n
Presbyterian fundamentalism, see Fundamentalism, Presbyterian fundamentalism
Presbyterian Guardian 34n, 37, 38n, 39, 49, 54n, 76, 81, 106n, 108, 110n, 141
Presbyterian Historical Society (Montreat, NC) xiii, 127n, 139n, 140n, 147-48n, 190n, 219
Presbyterian Ministers' Association of Atlanta, GA 122n
Presbyterian Outlook (before 1944, *Presbyterian of the South*) 98-99n, 104, 153
Presbyterian School of Christian Education, see Assembly's Training School
Presbyterian of the South (after 1944, *Presbyterian Outlook*) 95, 99n, 101, 111, 135n, 138, 156n
Presbyterian Standard 115n
Presbytery of Birmingham, AL 118n
Presbytery of California (OPC) 35-36n, 49
Presbytery of Concord, NC 121n
Presbytery of Dallas, TX 112n, 170, 203n, 218
Presbytery of East Hanover, VA 121n, 125
Presbytery of Ft. Worth, TX 170, 218
Presbytery of Harmony, SC 120n
Presbytery of Knoxville, TN 120n
Presbytery of Louisiana 163n
Presbytery of Memphis, TN 126, 140n
Presbytery of North Alabama 117-24
Presbytery of West Hanover, VA 148n
Presuppositionalist apologetics 53
Princeton Theological Seminary (see also Dispensationalism, Dispensationalist-Princetonian alliance) xii, 19, 20n, 21, 26-27, 31n, 40n, 46, 51, 53, 55, 56, 58n, 139n
Progressive Dispensationalism, see Dispensationalism, Progressive Dispensationalism

Prohibition (see also Alcoholic beverages) 41-42, 55
Prophecy Conferences, see Bible Conference Movement
Putnam, F.C. xiv

Quarles, J. 102n
Queen, E.L. II 8n
Quirk, C.E. 28n, 108n

Racial issues 46n, 103-04, 109n, 140n
Radmacher, E.D. 17n
Rapture (i.e., pretribulational) 153, 155, 222, 224, 238
Rauschenbusch, W. 100
Reed, D. 97n
Reed, J.S. 97n
Reed, J.W. 218
Reed, R.C. 103n, 105n, 115n, 154n
Reformed confessionalism, see Confessional subscription
Reformed Presbyterian Church Evangelical Synod (aka RPC/ES) 5n, 25n, 39n, 40n, 41n, 43n, 44n, 46n, 47n, 49n, 50n, 54n, 59n, 60n, 82n, 165n
Reformed theology (see also Calvinism; also Covenant theology) 9, 30n, 31, 33, 35, 49, 54-57, 59-61, 65, 66, 68, 69, 71, 73-76, 79, 82, 86, 88-89, 91, 105-06, 139n, 140, 142n, 143-44, 164-66, 171-72, 176n, 201, 202n, 239, 241-44
    Dutch Reformed theology (see also Christian Reformed Church) 21n, 45, 51, 52, 53, 55, 60, 61n, 62, 68
    Scottish Reformed theology (see also Free Presbyterian Church of Scotland) 51, 53, 61n, 62
Reid, J.C. 138
Reimarus, H.S. 67n
Renfer, R.A. 5n, 9n, 123n, 217-18
Reunification of PCUS and PCUSA 102-03, 106-08, 114, 118n, 126, 128
Revivalism 20, 25n, 43, 63
Rhodes College, see Southwestern Presbyterian University
Rian, E.H. 5n, 25n, 26n, 27n, 40n, 43n, 46n, 49n, 52n, 108n
Richards, J.J. 5n
Richards, J.M. 104n
Richardson, D.W. 102, 158

Richardson, J.R. 101n, 105, 117n, 119-20, 122, 123n, 128n, 149n
Richmond, Virginia (see also Ginter Park Presbyterian Church; also Union Theological Seminary) 98, 121, 128
Riley, W.B. 27n, 132, 134, 223
Roach, M. 217
Roberts, J.K. 137n
Robinson, H.W. 218
Robinson, W.C. 101n, 104n, 113, 114n, 121-22n, 127, 148, 158, 159n
Rockefeller Foundation 147n
Rogers, J.B. 100n
Rollman, H. 67n
Rolston, H. 105n
Roof, W.C. 100n
Rosell, G.M. 3n
Rosen Heights Presbyterian Church (Ft. Worth, TX) 167
Ross, A.P. 192n, 201n
Ross, K.J. xiii
Rumscheidt, H.M. 67n
Runkle, G. 179n
Russellism (as in, theology and movement of Charles Taze Russell) 12, 96
Ryrie, C.C. 7n, 16n, 17n, 18n, 87, 90n, 92n, 170n, 172n, 183-84n, 186-196, 218

Sabbatarianism 50, 51n
Sacramentalism 9
Sandeen, E.R. xii, 4-5n, 20, 29n
Sanders, C.E. II 8-9n, 89-90n
Sanders, E.P. 21n, 44n
Sanderson, D.R. xiii
Sanderson, J.W., Jr. 59n
Saucy, R.L. 18n, 90n, 209
Schauffler Hall 99n
Schleiermacher, F.D.E. 67n
Schofield, E. 217-18
Schweitzer, A. 67n
Scofield, C.I. 7n, 8, 14-15, 28n, 35, 73, 74-75, 85, 90, 110n, 111, 128n, 130n, 134, 136n, 154n, 157, 170n, 183, 196-97, 207, 222-25, 227-29, 234, 235n, 236, 237-38n, 239, 242
Scofieldism/theology and notes of Scofield Reference Bible 7n, 8n, 10n, 15-16, 33, 34-35, 36n, 37, 54, 59, 63, 64, 72, 74-78, 81, 83-87, 89-91, 110-11, 115, 128n, 132, 133-34, 136n, 138, 140, 142n, 143, 157, 159,

Index 317

165n, 170-71, 175-200, 201n, 205-08, 222-30, 234-40, 242-44
New Scofield Reference Bible (1967) 77n, 84, 89, 92n, 184-86, 200-01
Scopes Trial 152
Scott, E.C. 107n, 157-58n, 202-03n
Scott, W. 7n
Scottish Presbyterianism, see Reformed Theology, Scottish Reformed Theology; also see Free Presbyterian Church of Scotland
Searchlight, The 27n
Senior Harvard, see Ward, H.D.
Separation of church and state 105
Seventh-Day Adventism 10n, 12, 96, 163
Shea, G.B. 147n
Sheldon, C.M. 41n
Showers, R.E. 170n, 172n
Shriver, P.L. 3n
Sibley, S.H. 14n, 123n, 130-31, 133, 137, 155, 161, 240, 245-46
Siegel, B.B. 218
Slavery 46n, 103n
Sloat, L.W. 32n, 72n, 92n
Smith, B. 128n
Smith, C. 26n
Smith, E.A. 44n
Smith, M.H. 129n
Smith, W.M. 71n, 77n, 87n, 185n, 199
Smoking, see Fundamentalism, Personal lifestyle issues
Social Gospel, see Rauschenbusch, W.
Socialism 159
Sociology as a significant element in historical-theological development xii, 1-5, 13, 16-25, 44n, 53, 63, 65, 66, 77, 88, 89, 91, 103-10, 112, 116, 136, 143-45, 166-73, 175, 182, 195-96, 211, 233
sola fide 181, 190-92
Soulen, R.K. 150n
South Highland Presbyterian Church (Birmingham, AL) 118n
Southeastern Bible College 118n, 166
Southern Baptists 7-8
Southern culture, effect on the context and dynamics of the theological conflict 97-117
Southern Methodist University, see Perkins School of Theology
Southern Presbyterian Church, see Presbyterian Church in the U.S.

Southern Presbyterian Journal 108n, 110n, 117n, 131, 138, 147-48
Southwestern Presbyterian University (PCUS; aka Southwestern College; Stewart College; and Rhodes College) 120, 139n
Spangler, J.T. 217-18
Spencer, S.R. xiii, 7n, 16, 87n, 172
Spiritual nature of the church 8, 103, 106
"Spiritualizing" hermeneutic, see Hermeneutics
Stackhouse, J.G. 4n
Steele, E.A. III 37n, 79n
Steer, R. 3n
Stewart College, see Southwestern Presbyterian University
Stone, M. 217
Stone, J.R. 3n
Stonehouse, N.B. 5n, 31-32n, 39n, 48n, 50n, 51n, 53, 55n, 71n, 75, 125n, 176n
Story, C.I.K. 218
Stott, J.R.W. 3n
Strauss, D.F. 67n
Subscriptionism, see Confessional subscription
Substitutionary atonement 29, 30, 99, 100, 108n, 111n, 113, 180
Sunday School Times 79, 154
Supersessionism 150
Supralapsarianism 45
Sutcliffe, B. 217
Sweets, H.H. 126
Synod of Appalachia 121n
Synod of Kentucky 14n
Synod of Louisiana 163n
Synod of Mississippi 129-30n
Synod of North Carolina 14n, 121n, 128n
Synod of South Carolina 119n
Synod of Texas 14n
Synod of Virginia 121n
Synod of West Virginia 121n

Tacoma Independent Bible Church (Tacoma, Washington) 67n
Temperance Party 41n
Thiemann, R.F. 3n
Thiessen, H.C. 217-18
Thiselton, A.C. 2n
Thomas, M.L. 37n, 50n
Thomas, W.H.G. 9-10, 154n
Thompson, E.T. 13-14, 46n, 98n, 103n, 104n, 105n, 106n, 107n, 110n, 116n, 117, 119-

23n, 126, 129n, 159, 162n, 163n, 164n, 166, 167n
Thompson, M.F. 28n, 108n
Thornwell, J.H. 8, 103n, 105-06
Tillich, P. 100
Todd, H.R. 58n
Toon, P. 52n
Torrance, T.F. 3n
Toussaint, S.D. 218
Trollinger, W.V., Jr. 25n
Trotti, J.B. xiv
"Truly Reformed," see Reformed theology
Trumbull, C.G. 36n, 38-39, 79-80, 154-55, 181n, 203n
Turner, D.L. 197n, 210n
Turretin, F. 180n
Typology/Typologizing (see also Hermeneutics) 68n, 69, 195n, 196
Tsingkiangup General Hospital (China) 147

Undenominationalism, see Independent or Independent Bible Church; also see Dispensationalism, and Plymouth Brethrenism
Unger, M.F. 218
Union Presbyterian Theological Seminary (Richmond, VA) xiv, 15, 95, 98-99n, 120n, 121, 126, 128, 139n, 141
Union Seminary Review 98n, 146n, 155n
United Brethren Church 170, 218-19
University of Chicago 97n, 131n
University of Texas (Austin, TX) 131
University of Virginia (Charlottesville, VA) 152

Van Til, C. 37n, 51n, 52, 53
Victorious life teaching, see Keswickian view of sanctification
Vietnam War 152n
Vignaux, P. 190n
Virgin birth of Christ 29, 30, 68-69, 98, 108n, 113
Viser, J.R. 164n
Vos, G. 38n

Walker, J. xiii
Walsh, B.J. 2n
Waltke, B.K. 218
Walvoord, J.F. xiv, 11n, 84, 86-89, 90n, 92n, 109n, 124n, 165n, 167, 170, 171-72n, 183-185n, 190n, 196n, 201n, 214, 217-18

Ward, H.D. (aka "Senior Harvard") 10n
Ware, B.A. 210n
Warfield, B.B. 9n, 38n, 154n
Warnke, G. 2n
Washington and Lee University (Lexington, VA) 147n
Watch Tower Bible and Tract Society, see Russellism
Watt, D.H. 25n
Weaver, R.M. 97n
Weber, T.P. 5n
Webber, R.E. 2n, 3n
Wells, D.F. 3n
Wenger, R.E. 5n
Westminster Confession of Faith/Westminster Standards/Westminster Divines (see also Confessional subscription; also Covenant Theology, and Westminster Confession of Faith) 7n, 10-12, 15, 24, 34, 35, 36, 39, 45, 46, 48, 49, 52n, 72n, 81, 82, 96, 101-02, 108n, 110n, 113-15, 117, 118n, 120, 125-28, 131-36, 138, 141-46, 148, 150, 153, 155-64, 166n, 171-72n, 181n, 190n, 199, 203n, 204-05, 220-31, 233-45
"Westminster Group," or "Westminster Men," see Westminster Theological Seminary
Westminster Standards, see Westminster Confession of Faith
Westminster Theological Seminary 5, 20n, 27, 32, 36, 39, 40n, 45, 47n, 50n, 51, 52, 53, 54n, 55n, 56, 57, 58n, 59, 60n, 61, 71, 76, 116, 154, 200n
Wheaton College 37, 79, 81, 92n
Williams, M.D. 14n, 18n
Williams, P.R. 218
Williams, S.B. 163n, 164
Willis, W.R. 18n
Wilson, C.R. 103n, 106n
Wilson, R.D. 53
Winchester, A.B. 217
Witmer, J.A. xiv, 123n, 170, 217-18
Witmer, S.A. 116n
Women's Christian Temperance Union 41n
Woodbridge, C.J. 154n
Woodbridge, J.D. 3n
Woodring, H.C. 183n, 201n
Woodward, C.V. 106n
Woolley, P. 53, 55n, 110n
Works Report (i.e., *The Report of a Survey of the Colleges and Theological Seminaries of*

Index

the Presbyterian Church in the U.S., by George A. Works [1942]) 116-17, 119n, 122, 129n
World Council of Churches 128n
World War I 131
World War II 92, 116, 122, 170
World's Christian Fundamentals Association 27n, 42, 56n, 154n
Wrede, W. 67n

Wright, N.T. 21-22n, 44n, 47n
Wuthnow, R. 23n, 25n, 26n, 116n

Young, E.J. 110n

Zens, J. 14n, 165n
Zieten, A. 217
Zuck, R.B. 87n, 172n, 196n

Studies in Evangelical History and Thought
(All titles uniform with this volume)
Dates in bold are of projected publication

Andrew Atherstone
Oxford's Protestant Spy
The Controversial Career of Charles Golightly
Charles Golightly (1807–85) was a notorious Protestant polemicist. His life was dedicated to resisting the spread of ritualism and liberalism within the Church of England and the University of Oxford. For half a century he led many memorable campaigns, such as building a martyr's memorial and attempting to close a theological college. John Henry Newman, Samuel Wilberforce and Benjamin Jowett were among his adversaries. This is the first study of Golightly's controversial career.
***2006** / 1-84227-364-7 / approx. 324pp*

Clyde Binfield
Victorian Nonconformity in Eastern England
Studies of Victorian religion and society often concentrate on cities, suburbs, and industrialisation. This study provides a contrast. Victorian Eastern England—Essex, Suffolk, Norfolk, Cambridgeshire, and Huntingdonshire—was rural, traditional, relatively unchanging. That is nonetheless a caricature which discounts the industry in Norwich and Ipswich (as well as in Haverhill, Stowmarket and Leiston) and ignores the impact of London on Essex, of railways throughout the region, and of an ancient but changing university (Cambridge) on the county town which housed it. It also entirely ignores the political implications of such changes in a region noted for the variety of its religious Dissent since the seventeenth century. This book explores Victorian Eastern England and its Nonconformity. It brings to a wider readership a pioneering thesis which has made a major contribution to a fresh evolution of English religion and society.
***2006** / 1-84227-216-0 / approx. 274pp*

John Brencher
Martyn Lloyd-Jones (1899–1981) and Twentieth-Century Evangelicalism
This study critically demonstrates the significance of the life and ministry of Martyn Lloyd-Jones for post-war British evangelicalism and demonstrates that his preaching was his greatest influence on twentieth-century Christianity. The factors which shaped his view of the church are examined, as is the way his reformed evangelicalism led to a separatist ecclesiology which divided evangelicals.
2002 / 1-84227-051-6 / xvi + 268pp

Jonathan D. Burnham
A Story of Conflict
The Controversial Relationship between Benjamin Wills Newton and John Nelson Darby
Burnham explores the controversial relationship between the two principal leaders of the early Brethren movement. In many ways Newton and Darby were products of their times, and this study of their relationship provides insight not only into the dynamics of early Brethrenism, but also into the progress of nineteenth-century English and Irish evangelicalism.
2004 / 1-84227-191-1 / xxiv + 268pp

Grayson Carter
Anglican Evangelicals
Protestant Secessions from the Via Media, c.1800–1850
This study examines, within a chronological framework, the major themes and personalities which influenced the outbreak of a number of Evangelical clerical and lay secessions from the Church of England and Ireland during the first half of the nineteenth century. Though the number of secessions was relatively small—between a hundred and two hundred of the 'Gospel' clergy abandoned the Church during this period—their influence was considerable, especially in highlighting in embarrassing fashion the tensions between the evangelical conversionist imperative and the principles of a national religious establishment. Moreover, through much of this period there remained, just beneath the surface, the potential threat of a large Evangelical disruption similar to that which occurred in Scotland in 1843. Consequently, these secessions provoked great consternation within the Church and within Evangelicalism itself, they contributed to the outbreak of millennial speculation following the 'constitutional revolution' of 1828–32, they led to the formation of several new denominations, and they sparked off a major Church–State crisis over the legal right of a clergyman to secede and begin a new ministry within Protestant Dissent.
2007 / 1-84227-401-5 / xvi + 470pp

J.N. Ian Dickson
Beyond Religious Discourse
Sermons, Preaching and Evangelical Protestants in Nineteenth-Century Irish Society

Drawing extensively on primary sources, this pioneer work in modern religious history explores the training of preachers, the construction of sermons and how Irish evangelicalism and the wider movement in Great Britain and the United States shaped the preaching event. Evangelical preaching and politics, sectarianism, denominations, education, class, social reform, gender, and revival are examined to advance the argument that evangelical sermons and preaching went significantly beyond religious discourse. The result is a book for those with interests in Irish history, culture and belief, popular religion and society, evangelicalism, preaching and communication.

2005 / 1-84227-217-9 / approx. 324pp

Neil T.R. Dickson
Brethren in Scotland 1838–2000
A Social Study of an Evangelical Movement

The Brethren were remarkably pervasive throughout Scottish society. This study of the Open Brethren in Scotland places them in their social context and examines their growth, development and relationship to society.

2003 / 1-84227-113-X / xxviii + 510pp

Crawford Gribben and Timothy C.F. Stunt (eds)
Prisoners of Hope?
Aspects of Evangelical Millennialism in Britain and Ireland, 1800–1880

This volume of essays offers a comprehensive account of the impact of evangelical millennialism in nineteenth-century Britain and Ireland.

2004 / 1-84227-224-1 / xiv + 208pp

Khim Harris
Evangelicals and Education
Evangelical Anglicans and Middle-Class Education in Nineteenth-Century England

This ground breaking study investigates the history of English public schools founded by nineteenth-century Evangelicals. It documents the rise of middle-class education and Evangelical societies such as the influential Church Association, and includes a useful biographical survey of prominent Evangelicals of the period.

2004 / 1-84227-250-0 / xviii + 422pp

Mark Hopkins
Nonconformity's Romantic Generation
Evangelical and Liberal Theologies in Victorian England

A study of the theological development of key leaders of the Baptist and Congregational denominations at their period of greatest influence, including C.H. Spurgeon and R.W. Dale, and of the controversies in which those among them who embraced and rejected the liberal transformation of their evangelical heritage opposed each other.

2004 / 1-84227-150-4 / xvi + 284pp

Don Horrocks
Laws of the Spiritual Order
Innovation and Reconstruction in the Soteriology of Thomas Erskine of Linlathen

Don Horrocks argues that Thomas Erskine's unique historical and theological significance as a soteriological innovator has been neglected. This timely reassessment reveals Erskine as a creative, radical theologian of central and enduring importance in Scottish nineteenth-century theology, perhaps equivalent in significance to that of S.T. Coleridge in England.

2004 / 1-84227-192-X / xx + 362pp

Kenneth S. Jeffrey
When the Lord Walked the Land
The 1858–62 Revival in the North East of Scotland

Previous studies of revivals have tended to approach religious movements from either a broad, national or a strictly local level. This study of the multifaceted nature of the 1859 revival as it appeared in three distinct social contexts within a single region reveals the heterogeneous nature of simultaneous religious movements in the same vicinity.

2002 / 1-84227-057-5 / xxiv + 304pp

John Kenneth Lander
Itinerant Temples
Tent Methodism, 1814–1832

Tent preaching began in 1814 and the Tent Methodist sect resulted from disputes with Bristol Wesleyan Methodists in 1820. The movement spread to parts of Gloucestershire, Wiltshire, London and Liverpool, among other places. Its demise started in 1826 after which one leader returned to the Wesleyans and others became ministers in the Congregational and Baptist denominations.

2003 / 1-84227-151-2 / xx + 268pp

Donald M. Lewis
Lighten Their Darkness
The Evangelical Mission to Working-Class London, 1828–1860

This is a comprehensive and compelling study of the Church and the complexities of nineteenth-century London. Challenging our understanding of the culture in working London at this time, Lewis presents a well-structured and illustrated work that contributes substantially to the study of evangelicalism and mission in nineteenth-century Britain.

2001 / 1-84227-074-5 / xviii + 372pp

Herbert McGonigle
'Sufficient Saving Grace'
John Wesley's Evangelical Arminianism

A thorough investigation of the theological roots of John Wesley's evangelical Arminianism and how these convictions were hammered out in controversies on predestination, limited atonement and the perseverance of the saints.

2001 / 1-84227-045-1 / xvi + 350pp

Lisa S. Nolland
A Victorian Feminist Christian
Josephine Butler, the Prostitutes and God

Josephine Butler was an unlikely candidate for taking up the cause of prostitutes, as she did, with a fierce and self-disregarding passion. This book explores the particular mix of perspectives and experiences that came together to envision and empower her remarkable achievements. It highlights the vital role of her spirituality and the tragic loss of her daughter.

2004 / 1-84227-225-X / xxiv + 328pp

Don J. Payne
The Theology of the Christian Life in J.I. Packer's Thought
Theological Anthropology, Theological Method, and the Doctrine of Sanctification

J.I. Packer has wielded widespread influence on evangelicalism for more than three decades. This study pursues a nuanced understanding of Packer's theology of sanctification by tracing the development of his thought, showing how he reflects a particular version of Reformed theology, and examining the unique influence of theological anthropology and theological method on this area of his theology.

2005 / 1-84227-397-3 / approx. 374pp

Ian M. Randall
Evangelical Experiences
A Study in the Spirituality of English Evangelicalism 1918–1939
This book makes a detailed historical examination of evangelical spirituality between the First and Second World Wars. It shows how patterns of devotion led to tensions and divisions. In a wide-ranging study, Anglican, Wesleyan, Reformed and Pentecostal-charismatic spiritualities are analysed.
1999 / 0-85364-919-7 / xii + 310pp

Ian M. Randall
Spirituality and Social Change
The Contribution of F.B. Meyer (1847–1929)
This is a fresh appraisal of F.B. Meyer (1847–1929), a leading Free Church minister. Having been deeply affected by holiness spirituality, Meyer became the Keswick Convention's foremost international speaker. He combined spirituality with effective evangelism and socio-political activity. This study shows Meyer's significant contribution to spiritual renewal and social change.
2003 / 1-84227-195-4 / xx + 184pp

James Robinson
Pentecostal Origins
Early Pentecostalism in Ireland in the Context of the British Isles
Harvey Cox describes Pentecostalism as 'the fascinating spiritual child of our time' that has the potential, at the global scale, to contribute to the 'reshaping of religion in the twenty-first century'. This study grounds such sentiments by examining at the local scale the origin, development and nature of Pentecostalism in Ireland in its first twenty years. Illustrative, in a paradigmatic way, of how Pentecostalism became established within one region of the British Isles, it sets the story within the wider context of formative influences emanating from America, Europe and, in particular, other parts of the British Isles. As a synoptic regional study in Pentecostal history it is the first survey of its kind.
2005 / 1-84227-329-1 / xxviii + 378pp

Geoffrey Robson
Dark Satanic Mills?
Religion and Irreligion in Birmingham and the Black Country
This book analyses and interprets the nature and extent of popular Christian belief and practice in Birmingham and the Black Country during the first half of the nineteenth century, with particular reference to the impact of cholera epidemics and evangelism on church extension programmes.
2002 / 1-84227-102-4 / xiv + 294pp

Roger Shuff
Searching for the True Church
Brethren and Evangelicals in Mid-Twentieth-Century England
Roger Shuff holds that the influence of the Brethren movement on wider evangelical life in England in the twentieth century is often underrated. This book records and accounts for the fact that Brethren reached the peak of their strength at the time when evangelicalism was at it lowest ebb, immediately before World War II. However, the movement then moved into persistent decline as evangelicalism regained ground in the post war period. Accompanying this downward trend has been a sharp accentuation of the contrast between Brethren congregations who engage constructively with the non-Brethren scene and, at the other end of the spectrum, the isolationist group commonly referred to as 'Exclusive Brethren'.
2005 / 1-84227-254-3 / xviii+ 296pp

James H.S. Steven
Worship in the Spirit
Charismatic Worship in the Church of England
This book explores the nature and function of worship in six Church of England churches influenced by the Charismatic Movement, focusing on congregational singing and public prayer ministry. The theological adequacy of such ritual is discussed in relation to pneumatological and christological understandings in Christian worship.
2002 / 1-84227-103-2 / xvi + 238pp

Peter K. Stevenson
God in Our Nature
The Incarnational Theology of John McLeod Campbell
This radical reassessment of Campbell's thought arises from a comprehensive study of his preaching and theology. Previous accounts have overlooked both his sermons and his Christology. This study examines the distinctive Christology evident in his sermons and shows that it sheds new light on Campbell's much debated views about atonement.
2004 / 1-84227-218-7 / xxiv + 458pp

Kenneth J. Stewart
Restoring the Reformation
British Evangelicalism and the Réveil at Geneva 1816–1849
Restoring the Reformation traces British missionary initiative in post-Revolutionary Francophone Europe from the genesis of the London Missionary Society, the visits of Robert Haldane and Henry Drummond, and the founding of the Continental Society. While British Evangelicals aimed at the reviving of a foreign Protestant cause of momentous legend, they received unforeseen reciprocating emphases from the Continent which forced self-reflection on Evangelicalism's own relationship to the Reformation.
2006 / 1-84227-392-2 / approx. 190pp

Martin Wellings
Evangelicals Embattled
Responses of Evangelicals in the Church of England to Ritualism, Darwinism and Theological Liberalism 1890–1930
In the closing years of the nineteenth century and the first decades of the twentieth century Anglican Evangelicals faced a series of challenges. In responding to Anglo-Catholicism, liberal theology, Darwinism and biblical criticism, the unity and identity of the Evangelical school were severely tested.
2003 / 1-84227-049-4 / xviii + 352pp

James Whisenant
A Fragile Unity
Anti-Ritualism and the Division of Anglican Evangelicalism in the Nineteenth Century
This book deals with the ritualist controversy (approximately 1850–1900) from the perspective of its evangelical participants and considers the divisive effects it had on the party.
2003 / 1-84227-105-9 / xvi + 530pp

Haddon Willmer
Evangelicalism 1785–1835: An Essay (1962) and Reflections (2004)
Awarded the Hulsean Prize in the University of Cambridge in 1962, this interpretation of a classic period of English Evangelicalism, by a young church historian, is now supplemented by reflections on Evangelicalism from the vantage point of a retired Professor of Theology.
2006 / 1-84227-219-5 / approx. 350pp

Linda Wilson
Constrained by Zeal
Female Spirituality amongst Nonconformists 1825–1875

Constrained by Zeal investigates the neglected area of Nonconformist female spirituality. Against the background of separate spheres, it analyses the experience of women from four denominations, and argues that the churches provided a 'third sphere' in which they could find opportunities for participation.

2000 / 0-85364-972-3 / xvi + 294pp

Paternoster
9 Holdom Avenue,
Bletchley,
Milton Keynes MK1 1QR,
United Kingdom
Web: www.authenticmedia.co.uk/paternoster

July 2005

www.ingramcontent.com/pod-product-compliance
Lightning Source LLC
Chambersburg PA
CBHW071152300426
44113CB00009B/1182